# SRA Read-Aloud
## Vocabulary, Comprehension and Writing

MW01200607

## Teacher Edition
aligned with *Reading Mastery*

# Grade 1

**Terry Dodds**
**Fay Goodfellow**
**Jennifer Weinstein**

SRA

*Columbus, OH*

**SRAonline.com**

 **SRA**

Copyright © 2008 by SRA/McGraw-Hill.

Printed in the United States of America.

Send all inquiries to this address:
SRA/McGraw-Hill
4400 Easton Commons
Columbus, OH 43219

ISBN: 978-0-07-612491-6
MHID: 0-07-612491-6

1 2 3 4 5 6 7 8 9 10 MAZ 13 12 11 10 09 08 07

*The McGraw-Hill Companies*

# Table of Contents

# Introduction

## Rationale for the Program

Long before children are able to speak using higher level vocabulary, they are able to understand and respond to sophisticated words. An extensive vocabulary is vital to a child's success in all aspects of language arts. It is important for beginning readers to develop higher level vocabulary on a verbal level long before they are able to read more difficult words. Higher level vocabulary is crucial to helping a beginning reader develop his or her reading comprehension skills.

In their book *Bringing Words to Life*, Beck, McKeown, and Kucan define three levels of vocabulary instruction by placing words into three tiers. Words in the first tier are words that do not require direct instruction. They are basic words that young children learn in their everyday lives. These are words like *house, tree,* and *car.* The second tier of words are those words that require explicit direct instruction. They are words that will allow children to expand their vocabulary into the world of mature speakers. Tier Two words enable children to become more precise and descriptive with their language. They are higher level words that are easy to explain in simple terms to young children. These are words like *curious, amazing,* and *starving.* Tier Three words are words that are best taught within a content area such as science, social studies, or literature. These are words like *metamorphosis, community,* and *plot.*

*The SRA Read-Aloud Library: Vocabulary, Comprehension and Writing Teacher Edition* combines two research-validated instructional approaches: Direct Instruction as designed by Siegfried Engelmann and robust vocabulary instruction as designed by Beck, McKeown, and Kucan. Vocabulary instruction in this program is explicit and developmental. It follows a tight instructional sequence that offers children an opportunity to interact with each word in a number of contexts, both literature-based and expository. Simple, easy to understand definitions are offered to the children. The conceptual framework for parts of speech are provided to children as words are categorized as naming, action, or describing words. The focus of this program is to provide children with instruction in Tier Two words and Tier Three words as related to literary analysis.

*The SRA Read-Aloud Library: Vocabulary, Comprehension and Writing Teacher Edition* provides you and your students a vocabulary development program that is trade book based. An important goal of this program is to provide children lessons that will instill a joy and enthusiasm for learning new words.

This multidimensional program offers the students literary works including folk tales, fairy tales, legends, and poetry, as well as social studies and science expository works.

A special feature of this program is ten blackline master independent reading selections that accompany the expository lessons. These books can be copied for children to read independently and provide an easy to follow fluency building routine that is integrated into each day's lesson. This routine allows you to model prosody and provides children the opportunity to silent read independently and to read with a peer. The process followed in this part of each week's lesson enables you to give important feedback to children as they develop their fluency. Each book provides children with a reading comprehension test.

In most lessons the children are presented with six Tier Two words each week. Four of the target words are words directly from the story. Two words each week are concept words. These concept words represent an abstract concept that can be applied to what is happening in the story. For example, children can understand the concept behind the word *confident* as applied to *Suki's Kimono* as "you strongly believe in yourself and what you can do."

## Program Components

A library of read-aloud trade books

A teacher edition that includes

- Explicit direct instruction lessons
- Activity Blackline Masters (BLMs)
- BLM folding expository books for independent reading (Lessons 16–25)
- Vocabulary Tally Sheet BLM
- Picture Vocabulary Card BLMs
- Quiz Answer Sheet BLM
- Weekly classroom center instructions
- A BLM homework program
- A glossary of all of the words taught in this program

## Teaching the Lessons

The lessons for each trade book should take five days to teach. Lessons will take 30–45 minutes each day, depending on the length of the trade book. The preparation box provides an easy reference of the materials required for each day's lesson.

Lessons are designed to provide a thorough instructional sequence that uses the following conventions:

- What you say is printed in blue.
- (What you do is in parenthesis.)
- *Responses that are expected from children are written in black italics.*

For example:
(Show the illustration on pages 1 and 2.)
Where do you think the girls are? (Ideas: *In the jungle; in Africa*.) What makes you think so? (Idea: *There are lots of trees and large plants*.) What do you think the girls are doing in this illustration?

A variety of formats for children's responses are offered:

- The question requires an answer that calls for the same response from all children. A hand or verbal signal can be used to get children to respond in unison. This provides children with an opportunity to become more actively involved in the lesson and to respond

to more questions. For example: John Steptoe also made the pictures for this book. Who is the illustrator of *Mufaro's Beautiful Daughters*? *John Steptoe.* Who made the illustrations for this book? *John Steptoe.*

- If there are a number of possible responses to a question, the expected responses from children will be preceded by the word *Idea* or *Ideas.* These open-ended responses will produce a variety of answers. For example: Why did the woman shout at the animals? (Idea: *Because they made a mess in her house.*)
- Some questions require a response based on the personal experiences of children. For these items the question is asked with no expected response listed. For example: Tell about a time when you were compassionate.

Lessons follow a consistent pattern throughout the program that provides explicit direct instruction as well as cumulative practice and review. Numerous encounters over time with the words enable children to incorporate them into their speaking vocabulary. Children participate in a number of activities that enable them to interact with the words in a variety of situations.

A typical week's sequence may be as follows:

**Day 1:** On the first day children are introduced to the book and learn the key elements of a book such as title, author, and illustrator. They participate in making predictions about what will happen in the story and share those predictions with their classmates. Children are invited to take a picture walk as they explore the possibilities of what is happening in the story. Children are offered the opportunity to formulate questions they may have about the story or the book. The story is read aloud to children with minimal interruptions. The four target vocabulary words and their meanings are introduced for the first time within the context of how they are used in the story. Words for the week are placed on the Vocabulary Tally Sheet. Finally, a Homework Sheet is given to the children to take home.

**Day 2:** The second day's lesson begins with the story being read aloud and then discussed. The questioning sequence in the story encourages children to become actively involved in responding to the story and to use higher level thinking skills. Children are encouraged throughout this discussion to use the target words in their discussion. Target vocabulary that was introduced on Day 1 is reviewed. One word each week is extended by teaching the children an alternate meaning for the word. The two concept or expanded target vocabulary words and their meanings are also taught to the children.

**Day 3:** Children are taught various literary analysis skills as they learn about various literary elements. Children play the first round of a word game that allows them to practice using the new target vocabulary words. Children complete an activity sheet that reinforces skills taught in the lesson.

**Day 4:** Further literary analysis and cumulative review are provided in the fourth day of instruction. Children play a second round of the word game. In this round of the game they use all of the new words in addition to some words that have been taught in earlier lessons.

**Day 5:** On the last day children retell the story. An assessment is administered to measure for mastery of the new vocabulary as well as review items.

Children are allowed to choose a book that they would like you to read as a reward. Each week children are taught the routine for the learning center that they will work in the following week. The Super Words Center provides children with an opportunity to practice using the new vocabulary and to review vocabulary that has been taught in previous lessons. Words that are taught each week should be placed on a word wall and added to each week.

(Note: This sequence is different during the lessons with the expository books.)

## Using the Picture Vocabulary Cards

The Picture Vocabulary Cards for the week can be found at the top of the BLM for the homework program. These word cards should be copied and used in each day's lesson as well as in the Super Words Center at the end of each week.

You may wish to enlarge and laminate the cards for classroom use. The smaller size cards work well in the Super Words Center and may also be laminated for greater durability. You may find it useful to have a small pocket chart for displaying the words during the lessons.

Children are not expected to read the words on the Picture Vocabulary Cards. The words are for your information only. However, as children use the cards, some children will begin to read the words.

## Using the Vocabulary Tally Sheet

The Vocabulary Tally Sheet (BLM A) provides you with a place to record the number of times each of the target words is used within a week. Each time you or children use the word, a tally mark should be placed on the Vocabulary Tally Sheet. It is important to model the use of the words in your everyday interactions with the children. This modeling is important for helping children incorporate the higher level words into their speaking vocabulary.

## Using the Homework Program

Homework helpers can provide valuable practice and reinforcement that is important to the success of this vocabulary program. Each lesson provides you with a BLM Homework Sheet. The sheet gives the homework helper a simple weekly homework routine that can be used to reinforce the vocabulary words taught each week. The homework routine is consistent from week to week. Once the homework helper and the child know the routine, it remains the same throughout the program.

Copies of the Picture Vocabulary Cards are on the sheet as well as the word game that was played in class with those words that week.

You may wish to send a letter at the beginning of the program to introduce the homework helper to the homework routine. Another option is to have an information session to explain and demonstrate the homework routine.

It is important to explain to the homework helper that when the expected answer is preceded by the word *idea*, the child may not use the exact wording given. The homework helper should encourage the child to give an answer that is as close as possible to the idea. If the child makes a mistake, the homework helper should be instructed to tell the child the answer and to repeat the item at the end of the game.

Encourage the homework helper to make the homework routine fun and interactive. Remind him or her that children are not expected to read the words on the Picture Vocabulary Cards. The words are for homework helper information only. However, as children use the cards, some children will begin to read the words.

The homework program can also be used at school as an intervention component if homework cannot be completed outside of the school day.

## Playing the Word Games

The word games in this program offer children an opportunity to interact with the new vocabulary words and their meanings in a number of fun contexts. The games challenge children to use higher level thinking skills as they try to beat you at "word play."

The correction procedure for most of the games is the same. If children make an error, simply tell them or demonstrate the correct answer and then repeat the item at the end of the game.

The same game that is played in class that week is on the Homework Sheet for the homework helper to use. This provides further reinforcement of the vocabulary words and their meanings that were taught in that day's lesson.

## The Show Me, Tell Me Game

In the Show Me, Tell Me Game, children are asked to show, through actions or facial expressions, what a vocabulary word means. They are then asked what the word is that they are "showing."

Today you will play the Show Me, Tell Me Game. I'll ask you to show me how to do something. If you show me, you will win one point. If you can't show me, I get the point.

Next I'll ask you to tell me. If you tell me, you will win one point. If you can't tell me, I get the point.

## Whoopsy!

In the game *Whoopsy!* children are asked to discriminate between sentences that use the vocabulary word correctly or incorrectly. When they catch you making an error, they must provide a corrected version of the sentence to earn a point.

Today you will play *Whoopsy!* I'll say sentences using words we have learned. If the word doesn't fit in the sentence, you say "Whoopsy!" Then I'll ask you to say a sentence where the word fits. If you can do it, you get a point. If you can't do it, I get the point. If the word I use fits the sentence, don't say anything.

## Chew the Fat

*Chew the Fat* develops children's listening and discrimination skills as they try to catch you using a vocabulary word incorrectly. They are then asked to finish the sentence starter with correct usage of the word.

Today you will play *Chew the Fat.* Remember that a long time ago, when people wanted to just sit and talk about things that were happening in their lives, they would say that they would sit and "chew the fat."

In this game, I will say some sentences with our vocabulary words in them. If I use the vocabulary word correctly, say "well done." If I use the word incorrectly, say "Chew the fat." That means that you want to talk about how I used the word. I'll say the beginning of the sentence again. If you can make the sentence end so that it makes sense, you'll get a point. If you can't, I get the point.

## Tom Foolery

*Tom Foolery* develops children's listening and discrimination skills as they try to catch you making up a false meaning for words that have more than one meaning. They are then asked to finish the sentence starter with correct usage of the word.

Today I will teach you a new game called *Tom Foolery*. I will pretend to be Tom. Tom Foolery tries to trick students. Tom knows that some words have more than one meaning. He will tell you one meaning that will be correct. Then he will tell you another meaning that might be correct or it might be incorrect.

If you think the meaning is correct, don't say anything. If you think the meaning is incorrect, sing, "Tom Foolery." Then Tom will have to tell the truth and tell the correct meaning. Tom is sly enough that he may include some words that do not have two meanings. Be careful! He's tricky!

## Hear, Say

*Hear, Say* is another game that develops children's listening and discrimination skills as they try to catch you making up "untruths" about how to use the vocabulary words. They are then asked to finish the sentence starter with correct usage of the word.

In *Hear, Say*, I will say some sentences with our vocabulary words in them. Some of the sentences I say will include hearsay—there might be some untruths and extra bits in them. If you think what I am saying is not true, say "Hear, Say!" That means you want to suggest a way to make the sentence truthful and not just hearsay. I'll say the beginning of the sentence again. If you can make the sentence end so that it makes sense, you'll get a point. If you can't, I get the point.

If I use the vocabulary word correctly and there are no untruths in what I say, say "That's the honest truth!" Be careful, though—if you say "That's the honest truth!" when there is hearsay in the sentence, I will get a point!

## The Choosing Game

The Choosing Game challenges children to make choices by choosing the correct word from the two choices that are given. In the easier version of the game, children are shown the two Picture Vocabulary Cards and must make the correct choice.

Today you will play the Choosing Game. Let's think about the four words we have learned: **decided, shouted, squeaked, and muttered.** (Display the word cards.) I will say a sentence that has two of our words in it. You will have to choose which word is the correct word for that sentence.

## What's My Word?

In this riddle game the children are given clues. It is their job to guess which word is being described.

Today you will play *What's My Word?* I'll give you three clues. After I give each clue, if you are sure you know my word you may make a guess. If you guess correctly, you will win one point. If you make a mistake, I get the point.

## Using the Activity Sheet

A BLM Activity Sheet is provided each week. These sheets can be copied for individual children to use. Activity sheets give children practice with skills introduced in the program such as sequencing, matching, and beginning written expression.

## Assessing Progress

Each week you should assess children's progress by giving them a True or False Quiz. True or False Quiz is a weekly assessment tool that tests the children's understanding of that week's words and provides some cumulative review. BLM B, the Quiz Answer Sheet, recording sheet for children can be found in the Appendix .

A child must score 9 out of 10 to be at the mastery level. If a child does not achieve mastery, insert the missed words as additional items in the games for next week's lessons. Retest those children individually for the missed items before they take the next mastery test.

## Using the Super Words Classroom Center

At the end of each week children should be introduced to the Super Words Center activity. Children's participation in the Super Words Center will provide them with important hands-on practice as they interact conversationally with their peers using the new vocabulary.

Instructions for preparing each week's center are provided in the preparation box. The centers are designed to require a minimal amount of additional materials. Picture Vocabulary Cards for the games should be copied and placed in plastic bags or containers. One set of materials will be needed for each pair of children who will be working at any given time in a center. For example, if four children will be working in the center, you will need two sets of cards.

A procedure for demonstrating the game is provided each week. It is important to demonstrate the use of the center before children are expected to use it independently.

# Chart Graphics

**Week 1**

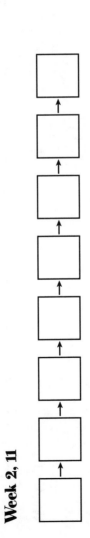

**Week 2, 11**

**Week 7**

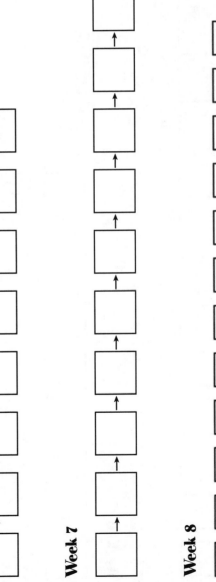

**Week 8**

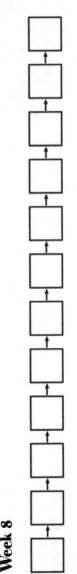

# Chart Graphics

**Week 9**

**Week 10**

**Week 12**

**Week 13**

# Word List

**accepting** taking someone for who they are, in spite of any disabilities or problems they might have

**active** busy and full of energy

**admit** 1. to tell the truth even though you may not really want to 2. to let in

**advice** a suggestion about what you should do

**amazed** very, very surprised by something.

**ambitious** you have big plans to get a lot done

**amuse** to entertain someone or hold their interest

**astonishing** amazing and hard to believe

**bird** an animal that has a skeleton, is warm blooded, lays eggs, has wings, and is covered with feathers

**bolted** 1. ran away very quickly 2. closed or attached something with a bolt or something like a bolt

**both** one thing and the other thing

**braggart** a person who is always bragging and telling everyone how good he is

**brave** not afraid to do something even though it is very hard

**calm** 1. become less angry, upset, or excited 2. not moving, or still

**Canada** the country to the north of the United States

**captive** a prisoner

**capture** to catch by force

**challenging** very difficult and takes lots of extra work and effort to do

**chaos** complete confusion or disorder

**characteristics** the things that make a person or thing different from others

**clever** understands things quickly and is good at making plans

**cold-blooded** an animal whose body temperature changes to match the temperature around it

**colossal** extremely large; huge; or enormous

**commotion** a lot of noise and confusion, a hullabaloo

**companions** those who spend time together, enjoying each other's company

**compassionate** feels sorry for another person's suffering and wants to help that person

**compete** take part in a contest or game

**complained** told someone you were unhappy about something

**concentrated** 1. thought only about one thing 2. a liquid that is thicker and stronger because most of the water has been removed from it

**concentrating** focusing attention on something

**confident** you strongly believe in yourself and in what you can do

**considerate** pay attention to what someone else needs, or wants, or wishes for

**contented** satisfied with things just the way they are

**contest** 1. a competition to win something 2. to fight or argue for something

**cooperate** work together

**coordinated** the different parts of your body all work together to do something

**cranky** grouchy or in a bad mood

**creative** able to make or do something with imagination

**curious** 1. interested in something and want to know more about it 2. unusual, or hard to understand.

**custom** a tradition or way of acting among a group of people

**customers** the people who buy things in a store

**decision** result of thinking about something and making up your mind

**delighted** very pleased and excited

**desert** 1. a dry, sandy place where few plants grow 2. to leave someone or something behind even though it is your duty to stay

**determined** made up your mind about something and won't let anything stop you

**different** not the same

**disappointed** feeling let down because you failed to do something

**disgrace** shameful thing

**disgusting** very unpleasant and sickening

**doubt** 1. not sure about something 2. a feeling of not being sure

**dream** something a person thinks about often and really wants to have happen

**election** 1. the process of choosing someone for office by voting 2. a choice made by a group

**elevator** a machine that carries people up and down between floors of buildings

**endless** having no end

**enemies** animals or people that want to hurt or harm each other

**equipment** things made for a particular use

**escalator** a moving staircase

**eventually** finally; at last

**exaggerated** said something was larger, more important, or more valuable than it really was

**exhausted** so tired you can hardly move

**faithful** never forget you; you can always depend on them if you need help

**fascinated** interested in something and you think about it a lot

**feast** 1. a big meal where everyone can eat as much as they want 2. to eat a lot of food at a large, special meal

**festival** a special party that has lots of activities like music, dancing, and good things to eat

**fish** an animal that has a skeleton, is cold-blooded, has fins and gills, and lives in water

**flock** 1. gather or travel in a group 2. a group of one kind of animals that live, travel, or feed together

**fool** 1. a person who can easily be tricked or made to look silly 2. to trick someone

**forgiving** you don't blame people for the bad things they've done to you or want to get back at them

**frazzled** very tired and stressed out

**frustrated** feeling angry about not being able to do something after you have tried and tried

**gathering** 1. picking things up and putting them together in a pile so you can use them later 2. a group of people who have come together for a purpose

**gaze** look at something for quite a long time before looking away

**generous** happy to share what you have with others

**grateful** appreciate what someone has done for you and are thankful

**grief** a deep, deep sadness

**grumpy** grouchy or in a bad mood

**gullible** believe anything anybody tells him or her; easily fooled

**hatch** break the shell and comes out

**heroic** doing brave things and acting as a role model for others

**hibernate** spend the winter in a deep sleep

**honest** always truthful and would never lie, steal, or cheat someone

**horrible** really, really bad

**hullabaloo** a lot of noise and confusion

**humorous** funny or amusing

**imagination** the part of your mind that lets you make pictures of things that haven't happened yet, or of things that aren't real

**incredible** amazing or astonishing

**ingredients** the things you need to make something

**injured** have been hurt or have been harmed by someone else

**insect** an animal that has a skeleton on the outside of its body, has six legs, and has three body parts

**interest** 1. a wish to learn more about something 2. persuade you to do something or tempt you

**introduce** tell people your name

**invisible** cannot be seen

**jealous** want what someone else has

**journey** a long trip to a place that is far away

**literate** able to read and write

**magnificent** grand in size or very beautiful to look at

**mammal** an animal that:has a skeleton, is warm-blooded, makes milk for its babies, and has hair for at least part of its life

**market** 1. a place where people buy food and other goods 2. to go shopping in a market or store

**marsh** a low, wet area of land that often has lots of grasses

**Mexico** the country to the south of the United States

**migrate** fly away to spend the winter somewhere else

**mischievous** troublesome or annoying

**miserable** 1. cold, gloomy, and makes you feel bad. 2. very unhappy

**mistake** a thought or action that is not correct

**mournful** filled with grief

**muck** anything that is dirty, wet, sticky, or slimy

**notice** 1. see or are aware of something 2. the same letter sent to a lot of people giving them information or asking them to do something

**nourishment** the food needed to keep a plant or animal strong and healthy

**opinion** what a person thinks or believes about something or someone

**optimistic** believe everything will turn out right

**ornaments** decorations that are added to make something more beautiful to look at

**orphan** a child or a young animal whose parents have died

**overcame** won against or got past a problem

**paralyzed** unable to move

**peaceful** quiet and calm

**perseverance** the characteristic of keeping on trying and never giving up, even though it is difficult

**pests** 1. insects that destroy or damage plants and bite people. 2. persistent, annoying people

**physician** a doctor

**pleasure** a feeling of happiness, delight, or joy

**plod** walk in a slow and heavy way

**plot** 1. a small piece of land 2. make secret plans to do something bad

**polite** you do the right thing and act with your best manners and actions

**positive** going through life with a good attitude

**precious** very special and important

**predator** an animal that hunts other animals for food

**prey** 1. an animal that is hunted by another animal for food 2. hunt and eat

**promise** 1. something you say that will happen for sure

**protect** keep safe from danger or injury

**proud** feel pleased and important

**quarrel** 1. argue and disagree 2. an angry argument or disagreement

**rascal** 1. someone who would lie and trick to get their own way 2. a young child who does things he or she knows is wrong

**recipe** the instructions for mixing and cooking food

**reluctant** don't want to do something

**remarkable** unusual or very special

**reptile** an animal that has a skeleton, is cold-blooded, lays eggs, and has dry scales or hard plates on its skin

**rescued** got someone or something away from danger and saved them

**ridiculous** extremely silly or foolish

**routine** 1. a series of movements used in a performance. 2. a usual way or pattern of doing things

**rude** showed bad manners, not polite

**scarce** there is very little of something

**schools** 1. groups of fish or other sea creatures 2. places where people go to learn things

**situation** how things are going for you

**skeleton** bones that support and protect an animal

**slave** 1. a person who is owned by another and forced to work with no pay or rights 2. to work very hard

**slimy** wet, soft, and slippery

**sly** very good at tricking others

**some** an amount of something, but not an exact number

**sound** 1. (sound asleep) in a deep sleep. 2. something you hear

**souvenir** a small item you keep to help you remember a special person, place, or time

**sparkling** shining with many flashing points of light; glittering

**special** 1. not ordinary; better than usual 2. a sale of certain things for lower prices

**species** a group of plants or animals that all share similar characteristics

**steep** 1. has a sharp slope or slant 2. to soak in a liquid

**stubborn** not willing to do something

**suggestion** an idea or plan for someone to think about

**suspicious** a feeling that something is wrong or bad, even though you can't be sure

**sweaty** covered with moisture because you are hot or nervous

**tease** make fun of someone by saying unkind or hurtful things

**temper** get irritated and angry very quickly

**terrified** very, very afraid

**thoughtful** considers the feelings and needs of others

**tourist** a person who travels and visits places to enjoy themselves

**tropical** located near the equator and very hot

**unbelievable** very hard to believe

**unjust** not fair or right

**untidy** not tidy or neat; messy

**venom** poison made by some snakes, spiders, and insects

**victory** a win in a game or contest

**vote** to make a choice in an election or other poll

**voyage** a long journey by air, land, sea, or outer space

**wakes** 1. the waves that are left behind when something moves through the water 2. comes out of a sleep

**warm-blooded** an animal whose body temperature stays the same no matter what the temperature around it is

**warning** something that tells that something bad could happen

**waterproof** does not let water in

**wheel** 1. to push something on wheels 2. a round object that helps a vehicle move smoothly or any object that is shaped like a wheel

**wilderness** a place where no people live

**woods** a place with many trees

**Preparation:** You will need a copy of *Suki's Kimono* for each day's lesson.

Post a copy of the Vocabulary Tally Sheet, BLM A, with this week's Picture Vocabulary Cards attached.

Each child will need one copy of the Homework Sheet, BLM 1a.

## *Suki's Kimono*
author: Chieri Uegaki • illustrator: Stephanie Jorisch

### Target Vocabulary

| Tier II | Tier III |
|---|---|
| festival | title |
| souvenir | author |
| concentrated | illustrator |
| introduce | circle story |
| *confident | |
| *different | |

*Expanded Target Vocabulary Word

---

### DAY 1

### Introduce Program

Today we are going start a program that will help you learn to use hard words. We will work together to learn about books and the things that make up a story. We will have lots of fun reading books and playing games together. Let's get started!

### Introduce Book

The name of this week's book is *Suki's Kimono*. The name of a book or story is called the title. What is a title? *The name of a book or story.* What's another way of saying "the name of a book or story"? *Title.*

The title of this week's book is *Suki's Kimono*. What's the title of this week's book? *Suki's Kimono.*

This book was written by Chieri Uegaki [she-ar-ee u-ih-gah-kee]. The person who writes a book or story is called the author. What's another word for the person who writes a book or story? *Author.* What is an author? *The person who writes a book or story.* Who's the author of *Suki's Kimono*? *Chieri Uegaki.*

Stephanie Jorisch [jor-ish] made the pictures for this book. The person who makes the pictures for a book or story is called the illustrator. What's another word for the person who makes the pictures for a book or a story? *Illustrator.* What is an illustrator? *The person who makes the pictures for a book or story.* Who's the illustrator of *Suki's Kimono*? *Stephanie Jorisch.*

The cover of a book usually gives us some hints of what the book is about. Let's look at the front cover of *Suki's Kimono*. What do you see in the picture? (Ideas*: There is a girl in a kind of robe; she looks like she's dancing.*)

(Assign each child a partner.) Get ready to tell your partner what you think this story will be about. Use the information from the cover to help you.

(Ask the following questions, allowing sufficient time for children to share their predictions with their partners.)

- Whom do you think this story is about?
- What do you think the girl will do?
- Where do you think this story happens?
- When do you think this story happens?
- Why do you think the girl is dancing?
- How do you think the girl is feeling?
- Do you think this story is about a real person? Tell why or why not.

(Call on several children to share their predictions with the class.)

### Take a Picture Walk

We're going to take a picture walk through this book. When we take a picture walk, we look at the pictures and tell what we think will happen in the story.

**Pages 1–2.** Where is this happening? (Idea: *In the girl's bedroom.*) Why do you think so? (Idea: *There is a bed and toy shelf.*) Who do you think the girls are? (Ideas: *Sisters; friends; cousins.*)

(Point to the little girl in the kimono.) This is Suki. What is this little girl's name? *Suki.* How does Suki look different from the other two girls? (Idea: *Suki is wearing a robe; the other two girls are wearing regular clothes.*) The robe that Suki is wearing is called a **kimono.** What do we call the robe that Suki is wearing? *A kimono.* People in Japan often wear kimonos on special days.

**Page 3.** Where do you think the girls are going? (Idea: *To school.*) Why do you think so? (Idea: *The first two girls have book bags.*) What time of day do you think it is? (Idea: *Morning.*)

**Page 4.** Where is Suki in this picture? (Idea: *At a restaurant; at a party.*)

**Pages 5–6.** What do you think the people are doing in this illustration? (Ideas: *Celebrating; having a party.*) How do you think Suki feels here? (Ideas: *Happy, excited.*)

**Pages 7–8.** What is happening in this illustration? (Ideas: *A band is playing drums; people are watching.*) What is Suki looking at here? (Ideas: *A piece of material; a scarf.*)

**Page 9.** What is happening here? (Idea: *The mother is taking a picture of the sisters.*)

**Page 10.** What is Suki doing in this illustration? (Idea: *Waving to her mother.*) How do you think the two older girls are feeling? (Ideas: *Angry; mad; upset; embarrassed.*) Why do you think they feel that way?

**Pages 11–12.** What is Suki doing here? (Ideas: *Pretending to fly; dancing.*) How are the other children reacting to her? (Ideas: *They are laughing at her; making fun of her.*) Does Suki notice the other kids laughing at her? *No.*

**Page 13.** Where do you think this part of the story happens? (Idea: *On the school playground.*) When do you think this part of the story happens? (Idea: *Before school starts.*) What clues tell you that this might be the first day of school? (Ideas: *There are balloons; children are running to talk to each other; parents are waiting with their children.*)

**Page 14.** What is Suki doing? (Idea: *Swinging.*)

**Page 15.** Do you think these two girls have met each other before? (Idea: *Probably not.*) Tell why you think so. (Ideas: *They're just looking at each other; they're not talking.*)

**Page 16.** How do you think Suki feels in this illustration? (Idea: *Happy.*)

**Page 17.** Where is Suki here? (Idea: *In class.*)

**Page 18.** What is happening here? (Idea: *One boy is laughing while another is teasing Suki.*)

**Page 19.** How do you think Suki feels? (Idea: *Angry; mad; embarrassed.*)

**Page 20.** What do you think is happening here? (Idea: *The teacher is talking to Suki; Suki is showing the teacher her shoes.*)

**Pages 21–22.** What is Suki doing in this illustration? (Ideas: *Talking to the class; telling the class about her kimono and shoes; "Show and Tell."*)

**Pages 23–24.** What is Suki doing in this illustration? (Idea: *Dancing.*)

**Pages 25–26.** What do you think the children think of Suki's dance? How do you think Suki feels? (Ideas: *Embarrassed; uncomfortable.*)

**Pages 27–28.** What are the teacher and the other children doing in this illustration? (Ideas: *Clapping; telling Suki they liked her dance.*)

**Page 29.** When do you think this part of the story is happening? (Idea: *After school.*) Where do you think the girls are walking? *Home.* Do you think Suki enjoyed her first day of school? *Yes.*

It's your turn to ask me some questions. What would you like to know about the story? (Accept questions. If children tell about the pictures or the story instead of ask questions, prompt them to ask a question.) Ask me a who question. Ask me a why question.

**Read the Story Aloud**
(Read the story to children with minimal interruptions.)

Tomorrow we will read the story again, and I will ask you some questions. (If children have difficulty attending for an extended period of time, you may wish to present the next part of this day's lesson at another time of day.)

# Present Target Vocabulary

 **Festival**

In the story, Suki's obāchan, or grandmother, had taken her to a street festival. That means her grandmother had taken her to a special party that was held on a street in her neighborhood. There was music, dancing, and special food at this festival. **Festival.** Say the word. *Festival.*

**Festival** is a naming word. It names a thing. What kind of word is **festival?** *A naming word.*

**A festival is a special party that has lots of activities like music, dancing, and good things to eat.** Say the word that means "a special party that has lots of activities like music, dancing, and good things to eat." *Festival.*

**(Correct any incorrect responses, and repeat the item at the end of the sequence.)**

Let's think about things that might be a festival. I'll tell about something. If I tell you about a festival, say "festival." If not, don't say anything.

- We went to a jazz party where there was lots of music, singing, and dancing. *Festival.* What kind of festival? *A jazz festival.*
- Greek people had a summer party and invited everyone to come hear the music, sing and dance, and try Greek food. *Festival.* What kind of festival? *A Greek summer festival.*
- We had a bonfire on the beach.
- It was my birthday and all my friends came over.
- Hundreds of people came to the beach to enjoy the music, water activities, and good food. *Festival.* What kind of festival? *A beach festival.*
- Everyone in town came to the special party put on by Chinese people. The guests made Chinese lanterns and fans, heard Chinese music and learned to do a Chinese dance. *Festival.* What kind of festival? *A Chinese festival.*

What word means "a special party that has lots of activities like music, dancing, and good things to eat"? *Festival.*

 **Souvenir**

In the story, Suki's obāchan bought her a pretty pink handkerchief decorated with tiny maple leaves and cherry blossoms as a souvenir. Suki's grandmother bought the handkerchief to help her remember the special day they had at the festival. **Souvenir.** Say the word. *Souvenir.*

**Souvenir** is a naming word. It names a thing. What kind of word is **souvenir?** *A naming word.*

**A souvenir is a small item you keep to help you remember a special person, place, or time.** Say the word that means "a small item you keep to help you remember a special person, place, or time." *Souvenir.*

Let's think about some things you might keep as souvenirs. I'll name some things. If you might keep that thing to help you remember a special person, place, or time, say "souvenir." If not, don't say anything.

- Joni kept a special rock to remind her of her trip to the mountains. *Souvenir.*
- Munroe's father bought him a cap to help him remember their trip to the big league ball game. *Souvenir.*
- Bill and Ted had lots of good memories of their trip to Oregon.
- Mrs. Peterson always buys a special pair of salt and pepper shakers whenever she visits a new city. *Souvenir.*
- Salvatore visits his grandparents in Italy every summer.
- When the Reid family went to France, Naomi bought a small model of the Eiffel Tower. *Souvenir.*

What word means "a small item you keep to help you remember a special person, place, or time"? *Souvenir.*

 **Concentrated**

In the story, when the boys sitting in front of Suki were bothering her, Suki just concentrated on sitting up straight and tall. That means she thought only about sitting up straight and tall. She didn't think about anything else. **Concentrated.** Say the word. *Concentrated.*

**Concentrated** is an action word. It tells what someone did. What kind of word is **concentrated?** *An action word.*

**If you concentrated on something, you thought only about that thing. You didn't think**

**about anything else.** Say the word that means "thought only about one thing." *Concentrated.*

Let's think about times when someone might have concentrated on something. I'll tell about a time. If someone concentrated, say "concentrated." If not, don't say anything.

- Raven thought only about how to steer her bike. *Concentrated.*
- Elias thought only about how to make his printing perfect. *Concentrated.*
- Uncle Antonio thought about playing golf while he did the dishes.
- The giant thought only about catching Jack. *Concentrated.*
- The teacher thought about getting the art supplies ready while she wrote on the board.
- The wolf thought about eating the third little pig while climbing on the roof.

What word means "thought only about one thing"? *Concentrated.*

◎—◄ Introduce

In the story, Mrs. Paggio told the children she wanted them to introduce themselves. That means Mrs. Paggio wanted the children to tell each other their names. **Introduce.** Say the word. *Introduce.*

**Introduce** is an action word. It tells what people do. What kind of word is **introduce?** *An action word.*

**If you introduce yourself to someone, you tell him or her your name.** Say the word that means "tell people your name." *Introduce.*

Let's think about when people might introduce people. If I say a time when someone might introduce someone, say "introduce." If not, don't say anything.

- We told our new neighbors our names. *Introduce.*
- Our new neighbors told us their names. *Introduce.*
- I told my teacher my parents' names and my parents my teacher's name. *Introduce.*
- I didn't know the names of everyone in my class.

- I said, "This is my principal, Mrs. Romirez. Mrs. Romirez, please meet my parents, Mr. and Mrs. Lai." *Introduce.*
- Everyone on the baseball team was friends.

What word means "tell people your name"? *Introduce.*

### Introduce Vocabulary Tally Sheet
(Display the Vocabulary Tally Sheet, BLM A. Explain to children that each time you or they use a new vocabulary word you will put a mark by that word. Use the new vocabulary words throughout the week whenever an opportunity presents itself. Encourage children to do the same.)

### Assign Homework
(Homework Sheet, BLM 1a. See the Introduction for homework instructions.)

---

| DAY 2 |
| --- |

**Preparation:** Picture Vocabulary Cards for *festival, souvenir, concentrated, introduce.*

---

### Read and Discuss Story

(Read story to children. Ask the following questions at the specified points. Encourage children to use target words in their answers.)

**Page 2.** What did Suki want to wear on the first day of school? *Her kimono.* Why did her sisters say she couldn't wear it? (Ideas: *People would think she was weird; no one would play with her; the other kids would laugh at her.*)

**Page 4.** Why did Suki want to wear her kimono? (Idea: *It was her favorite thing.*) Who gave Suki her kimono? *Her obāchan.* Obāchan is the Japanese word for grandmother. What does obāchan mean? *Grandmother.* Sōmen are thin, white noodles. What are sōmen? *Thin, white noodles.* Why was the kimono Suki's favorite thing? (Ideas: *Her grandmother had given it to her; the first time she wore it, her grandmother took her to a street festival.*)

**Page 6.** What did Suki and her obāchan do at the festival? (Idea: *They danced a circle dance.*)

**Page 8.** What made Suki feel like she'd swallowed a ball of thunder? (Idea: *The sound of the drums.*) Taiko drums are great big drums. What are great big drums called in Japanese? *Taiko drums.* What did Suki's obāchan buy her to help her remember this day? (Idea: *A beautiful silk handkerchief; a souvenir.*) A handkerchief is like a tissue; only it's made of cloth. Handkerchiefs can be used again and again, because you can wash them.

**Page 9.** An obi is a sash that helps keep the kimono closed and in place. What is the Japanese word for the sash that helps keep a kimono closed and in place? *Obi.* Why did Suki's sisters pretend they didn't know her? (Idea: *They were embarrassed by the way she was dressed; they thought that she was being weird.*)

**Page 10.** How do you think Suki felt about her clothes? (Idea: *Proud, excited.*) Geta are wooden shoes. What is the Japanese word for wooden shoes? *Geta.*

**Page 11.** Do you think the sleeves of Suki's kimono are big or small? *Big.* What clues tell you that the sleeves are big? (Ideas: *They are described as "butterfly sleeves"; they make her feel like she has wings.*)

**Page 14.** Why did some of the other children stare and giggle at Suki? (Ideas: *They thought her kimono looked funny; it wasn't new or "cool."*) Does Suki have clothes like the rest of the children? *Yes.* Why didn't she wear clothes like the rest of the children were wearing? (Idea: *She wanted to wear her favorite thing for the first day of school.*)

**Page 16.** What did Penny think of Suki's clothes? (Idea: *They were funny.*) Did Suki think her clothes were funny? *No.*

**Page 18.** Did Suki's clothes make Penny not want to be her friend? *No.* How do you know? (Idea: *Penny chose a seat next to Suki.*) Why did one of the boys call Suki a bat? (Idea: *The sleeves of Suki's kimono were very big and looked like wings.*)

**Page 19.** (Read to the end of the first sentence.) How do people feel when they feel their cheeks burn? (Ideas: *Embarrassed; picked-on; angry.*) (Read the rest of the page.) Who did Suki try to be like? *Her grandmother.* Why do you think Suki wants to be like her grandmother?

**Page 20.** When Suki shows Mrs. Paggio her kimono, what part of her clothing is she showing? (Idea: *Her robe.*) When Suki shows Mrs. Paggio her geta, what part of her clothing is she showing? (Idea: *Her wooden shoes.*)

**Page 21.** How do you think Suki felt about talking in front of the class? (Idea: *Nervous.*)

**Page 23.** How did Suki feel when she was dancing? (Ideas: *Happy; like she was back at the festival.*)

**Page 24.** How did Suki try to remember the dance steps? (Idea: *She pictured the other dancers in her mind.*) What did Suki do when she forgot a step? (Idea: *She made it up.*) Why did she do that? (Idea: *So that she could keep dancing.*)

**Page 25.** Why would Suki think she might be in trouble?

**Page 27.** What did Mrs. Paggio think of Suki's dance? (Idea: *She thought it was wonderful.*)

**Page 29.** Why were Suki's sisters upset about their day? (Idea: *Nobody had noticed their new, cool clothes.*) Why did Suki just smile? (Idea: *Everybody had noticed Suki's clothes.*) Who had a better first day of school, Suki or her sisters? *Suki.*

## Review Vocabulary

(Display the Picture Vocabulary Cards. Point to each card as you say the word. Ask children to repeat each word after you.) These pictures show **festival, souvenir, concentrated,** and **introduce.**

- What word means "tell people your name"? *Introduce.*
- What word means "a special party that has lots of activities like music, dancing, and good things to eat"? *Festival.*
- What word means "thought only about one thing"? *Concentrated.*
- What word means "a small item you keep to help you remember a special person, place, or time"? *Souvenir.*

## Extend Vocabulary

 Concentrated

In the story *Suki's Kimono*, we learned that **concentrated** is an action word that means "thought only about one thing." Say the word that means "thought only about one thing." *Concentrated.*

Raise your hand if you can tell us a sentence that uses **concentrated** as an action word meaning "thought only about one thing." (Call on several children. If they don't use complete sentences, restate their examples as sentences. Have the class repeat the sentences.)

Here's a new way to use the word **concentrated.**

- She mixed the **concentrated** orange juice with water so they could have orange juice for breakfast. Say the sentence.
- Her mom needed to use only a little bit of the soap because it was **concentrated.** Say the sentence.
- The vanilla was so **concentrated** the cook used only two drops in her recipe. Say the sentence.

**In these sentences, concentrated is a describing word that tells about a liquid that is thicker and stronger because most of the water has been removed from it.** What word describes "a liquid that is thicker and stronger because most of the water has been removed from it"? *Concentrated.*

Raise your hand if you can tell us a sentence that uses **concentrated** as a describing word meaning "a liquid that is thicker and stronger because most of the water has been removed from it." (Call on several children. If they don't use complete sentences, restate their examples as sentences. Have the class repeat the sentences.)

## Present Expanded Target Vocabulary

 Confident

In the story, Suki didn't care about new or cool clothes. She wanted to wear her kimono. Suki strongly believed in herself and what she wanted. Another way of saying that Suki strongly believed in herself is to say that Suki was confident. **Confident.** Say the word. *Confident.*

**Confident** is a describing word. It tells more about someone. What kind of word is **confident**? *A describing word.*

**If you are confident, you strongly believe in yourself and what you can do.** Say the word that means "strongly believe in yourself and what you can do." *Confident.*

Let's think about when people might feel confident. If I say a time when someone would feel confident, say "confident." If not, don't say anything.

- How you would feel if you knew you could read the story to the children in your class all by yourself. *Confident.*
- How your friend would feel if she didn't want to read out loud in front of the other children.
- How you would feel if you were sure you could swim to the end of the pool. *Confident.*
- How you would feel if you knew you could count to 100 without making a mistake. *Confident.*
- How you would feel if you were afraid to run in a race.
- How you would feel if you knew you could jump rope twenty times without stepping on the rope. *Confident.*

What word means "strongly believe in yourself and what you can do"? *Confident.*

 Different

In the story, Penny asked Suki why she was dressed so funny. Penny wanted to know why Suki wore different clothes and shoes from Penny. **Different.** Say the word. *Different.*

**Different** is a describing word. It tells more about something or someone. What kind of word is **different**? *A describing word.*

**Another way of saying Suki's clothes were different from Penny's is to say that Suki's clothes were not the same.** Say the word that means "not the same." *Different.*

**Different** and the same are opposites. What is the opposite of **different**? *The same.* What is the opposite of the same? *Different.*

Let's think about things that might be different. I'll name two things. If they are different, say "different." If they are the same, say "the same."

- A penny and a quarter. *Different.*
- Two brand new yellow crayons. *The same.*
- The socks in a pair of socks. *The same.*
- Two copies of the story *Jack and the Bean Stalk*. *The same.*
- A book titled *Suki's Kimono* and a book titled *Cinderella*. *Different.*
- A stapler and a paper clip. *Different.*

What word means "not the same"? *Different.*

<br>

---

### DAY 3

**Preparation:** Activity Sheet, BLM 1b.

---

## Literary Analysis
## (Beginning, Middle, End, Problem)

Let's think about what we already know about how books are made.

- What do we call the name of a book? *Title.*
- What do we call the person who writes a story? *Author.*
- What do we call the person who draws the pictures? *Illustrator.*

Today we will learn about how stories are made. Stories have a beginning, a middle, and an end. What do stories have? *A beginning, a middle, and an end.*

The beginning of a story introduces the people or animals in the story. The people or animals in a story are called the characters. What do you call the people or animals in a story? *The characters.* Who are some of the characters in *Suki's Kimono*? (Ideas: *Suki; her sisters; her mother; her obāchan; Mrs. Paggio; the children in her class.*)
(**Note:** You may wish to show the illustrations from pages 1, 2, 16, 18, 20, and 26 to assist children in recalling the characters in the story.)

The most important characters are called the main characters. What do we call the most important characters? *The main characters.* Who do you think is the most important character in *Suki's Kimono*? *Suki.*

The beginning of the story also tells where and when the story happens. What else does the beginning of a story tell? *Where and when the story happens.* Where does *Suki's Kimono* begin?
(**Note:** You may wish to show the illustrations on pages 1 and 2.) (Ideas: *At Suki's house; in Suki's bedroom.*) When does Suki's story begin? (Idea: *On the first day of school.*)
(**Note:** If the children cannot recall when the story begins, read the first sentence of the story.)

The beginning of a story often has a problem. Listen while I read the first page of the story again. (Page 1.) What is the problem? (Ideas: *Suki wore clothes to school that were very different from what the other children wore.*)

The middle of a story tells what the main character did to solve the problem. What did Suki do? (Ideas: *She wore her kimono; she made a new friend; she ignored the boys who were making fun of her; she danced for the class.*)
(**Note:** You may wish to show the illustrations from pages 11–28 to assist children in recalling the story events.)

The end of a story tells what finally happened. (Read page 29.) What happened at the end of the story? (Idea: *Suki's sisters were upset that no one noticed their new clothes; Suki had had a great day.*)

You did a great job of thinking about the beginning, the middle, the end, and the problem in *Suki's Kimono.* Now it's time to play a game.

### Introduce the Choosing Game

Today you will play the Choosing Game. Let's think about the six words we have learned: **festival, souvenir, concentrated, introduce, confident,** and **different.** (Display the Picture Vocabulary Cards.) I will say a sentence that has two target words in it. You will have to choose the correct word for that sentence. Let's practice. (Display the word cards for the two words in each sentence as you say the sentence.)

- If you thought only about doing a somersault, would you have **concentrated** or **confident?** *Concentrated.*

- When you tell someone your name, do you **introduce** yourself or **concentrate**? *Introduce.*
- If you buy something small to help you remember your trip to New York City, do you buy a **souvenir** or a **festival**? *A souvenir.*

If you tell me the correct answer, you will win one point. If you can't tell me the correct answer, I get the point.

T Now you're ready to play the game. (Draw a T-chart on the board for keeping score. Children earn one point for each correct answer. If they make an error, correct them as you normally would, and record one point for yourself. Repeat missed words at the end of the game. Display the word cards for the two words in each sentence as you say the sentence.)

- If you had to mix water with a can of orange juice to be able to drink it, was the orange juice **concentrated** or **confident**? *Concentrated.*
- When you put on one black shoe and one running shoe, were your shoes **concentrated** or **different**? *Different.*
- When Tia stood on the diving board and knew she could do a forward dive, was she **confident** or **festival**? *Confident.*
- If you went to a special party and ate great Japanese food, listened to the Japanese drums, and watched the ladies do a Bon dance, were you at a **souvenir** or a **festival**? *A festival.*
- When you first meet someone, do you **confident** or **introduce** yourself? *Introduce.*

(Count the points and declare a winner.)
You did a great job of playing the Choosing Game.

### Complete the Activity Sheet

(Give each child a copy of the Activity Sheet, BLM 1b. Review with children the order they will place the pictures to put them in sequence to show beginning, middle, and end. Instruct children to complete the sentences, color the pictures, cut them out, and assemble them in sequential order. These pictures can be fastened together to produce a little booklet. This booklet may be sent home with the children so they can retell the story at home.)

(You may wish to create a word bank on the board by writing the words children will use in the sentence completion part of this activity. Word Bank: *mean, danced, clapped, Suki, kimono, friend.*)

(The completed sequence should be similar to this:
Suki wanted to wear her kimono.
Suki made a new friend.
The boys were mean to her.
Suki danced for the class.
Everyone clapped for Suki.
Suki danced all the way home.)

---

### DAY 4

**Preparation:** Prepare a sheet of chart paper, portrait direction, titled *Suki's Kimono*. Underneath the title make a circle of 6 circles connected by arrows.

See the Introduction for Week 1's chart.

Record children's responses by writing the underlined words in the circles.

---

### Introduce Circle Story Pattern

When authors write stories, they sometimes write in patterns. Let's see if we can figure out the pattern for this story. You tell me what happened in the story and I'll write it down.

**Pages 1–2.** Where is Suki when the story begins? (Idea: *At home.*)

**Page 13.** Then what happens? (Idea: *Suki and her sisters go to school.*)

**Page 16.** Then what happens? (Idea: *Suki makes a new friend.*)

**Page 18.** Then what happens? (Idea: *The boys are mean to Suki.*)

**Pages 23–24.** Then what happens? (Idea: *She dances for the class.*)

**Page 28.** Then what happens? (Idea: *The class claps for Suki.*)

**Page 29.** Where are Suki and her sisters when the story ends? (Idea: *At home.*)

(Point to the story map that is on the chart paper.) Look at the shape of this story. It's a circle. This story starts and ends at the same place so this story has a **circle** pattern. What kind of a story has a pattern that starts and ends at the same place? *A circle pattern.*

## Play the Choosing Game (Cumulative Review)

Let's play the Choosing Game. I will say a sentence that has two target words in it. You will have to choose the correct word for that sentence.

(Display the Picture Vocabulary Cards for *festival, souvenir, concentrated, introduce, confident,* and *different* for the two words in each sentence as you say the sentence.)

Now you're ready to play the Choosing Game. (Draw a T-chart on the board for keeping score. Children earn one point for each correct answer. If they make an error, correct them as you normally would, and record one point for yourself. Repeat missed words at the end of the game.)

- If it was the first day of school and you didn't know any of the other children, would you **introduce** or **different** yourself? *Introduce.*
- If your mom had to use only two drops of dish soap when she did the dishes, was the soap **confident** or **concentrated?** *Concentrated.*
- If Jane's eyes are brown and her brother's eyes are green, are their eyes **concentrated** or **different?** *Different.*
- If you went to a Mexican street party, would you be at a **souvenir** or a **festival?** *A festival.*
- If the teacher asked you to stand up in front of the class and read your story and you were sure you could do it, would you be **different** or **confident?** *Confident.*
- If you brought home a pretty shell from the beach to help you remember your trip, would the shell be a **souvenir** or a **concentrated?** *A souvenir.*
- If everyone worked in the garden and didn't think about anything else, would you say the people **different** or **concentrated?** *Concentrated.*
- If I said, "Hello, my name is _____," did I **introduce** or **confident** myself? *Introduce.*

Now you will have to listen very carefully, because I'm not going to show you the word cards.

- If you bought a shell necklace on your trip to Hawaii, would the necklace be **concentrated** or a **souvenir?** *Souvenir.*
- If you strongly believe in yourself and what you can do, are you **confident** or **concentrated?** *Confident.*
- If you are building sand castles and your friend is collecting shells, are you doing **introduced** things or **different** things? *Different.*
- If you danced, listened to the music, and tried out different foods, would you be at a **festival** or a **souvenir?** *A festival.*
- If it took only a few drops of shampoo to wash your hair, was the shampoo **confident** or **concentrated?** *Concentrated.*
- Do people shake hands and say, "How do you do?" when you **introduce** them or **confident** them? *Introduce.*
- Would you be **confident** or **concentrated** if you liked to try new things because you believed you would be able to do them? *Confident.*
- If I like squash and you like spinach, do we like the **souvenir** or **different** things? *Different.*

(Tally the points and declare a winner.)
You did a great job of playing the Choosing Game.

---

### DAY 5

**Preparation:** Quiz Answer Sheet, BLM B.

### Retell Story

Today I'll show you the pictures Stephanie Jorisch made for *Suki's Kimono.* As I show you the pictures, I'll call on one of you to tell the class that part of the story.

Tell me what happens at the **beginning** of the story. (Show the pictures on pages 1 and 2. Call on a child to tell what's happening.)

Tell me what happens in the **middle** of the story. (Show the pictures on pages 3–28. Call on a child to tell what's happening. Encourage use of target words when appropriate. Model use as necessary.)

Tell me what happens at the **end** of the story. (Show the picture on page 29. Call on a child to tell what's happening.)

Do you think Suki will wear her kimono to school the next day? (Idea: *Probably not.*) Tell why you think so. (Idea: *Tomorrow isn't a special day.*)

When might Suki wear her kimono to school again? (Ideas: *On another special day; on her birthday.*) Tell why you think so. (Ideas: *She only wears her kimono on special days; she'll want to wear the same things as the other kids most of the time.*)

### Assess Vocabulary

 (Give each child a copy of the Quiz Answer Sheet, BLM B.)

Today you're going to have a True or False quiz. When you do the True or False quiz, it shows me how well you know the hard words you are learning.

Before you can do the True or False quiz, you have to know about true and false.

If something is true, it's right or correct. What word means "right" or "correct"? *True.* What does **true** mean? *Right or correct.*

I'll say some things. If I say something that is true, say "true." If not, don't say anything.

- You wear a shoe on your foot. *True.*
- You wear a hat on your hand.
- A dog has ears. *True.*
- A boy has ears. *True.*
- A table has ears.
- A table has legs. *True.*

What word means "right" or "correct"? *True.*

If something is false it's wrong. What word means "wrong"? *False.* What does **false** mean? *Wrong.*

I'll say some things. If I say something that is false, say "false." If not, don't say anything.

- You wear a shoe on your head. *False.*
- A dog can sit.

- A dog can fly. *False.*
- A fish can swim.
- An elephant can fly. *False.*
- Girls have wings. *False.*

What word means "wrong"? *False.*

If I say something that is true, circle the word **true.** What will you do if I say something that is true? *Circle the word true.*

If I say something that is false, circle the word **false.** What will you do if I say something that is false? *Circle the word false.*

Listen carefully to each item that I say. Don't let me trick you!

Item 1: If you are **confident,** you would probably enjoy trying new things. (*True.*)

Item 2: If two things are **not** the same, they are **different.** (*True.*)

Item 3: A **festival** is a small item you keep to help you remember a special person, place, or time. (*False.*)

Item 4: If you thought really, really hard about reading your story and you didn't think about anything else, you **concentrated** on reading your story. (*True.*)

Item 5: If you were at a party where lots of different people played African music, sang African songs, and ate African food, you were at an African **souvenir.** (*False.*)

Item 6: An **author** is the person who draws the pictures for a book. (*False.*)

Item 7: If you buy orange juice that has most of the water taken out of it, you buy **concentrated** orange juice. (*True.*)

Item 8: Things that are the same are **different.** (*False.*)

Item 9: The **title** of a book is the person who wrote the words. (*False.*)

Item 10: If you told your teacher your name and she told you her name, you **introduced** yourselves. (*True.*)

You did a great job completing your quiz!

(Score children's work. A child must score 9 out of 10 to be at the mastery level. If a child does not achieve mastery, insert the missed words as additional items in the games in next week's lessons. Retest those children individually for the missed items before they take the next mastery test.)

## Extensions

### Read a Story as a Reward

(Display the copy of *Suki's Kimono* or other books that celebrate children of different cultures. Allow children to choose which book they would like you to read to them as a reward for their hard work.)

(Read the story aloud for enjoyment with minimal interruptions.)

**Preparation:** Word containers for the Super Words Center.

### Introduce the Super Words Center

(Place the Picture Vocabulary Cards in the center. Show children one of the word containers. If children need more guidance in how to work in the Super Words Center, role-play with two to three children as a demonstration.)

Let's think about how we work with our words in the Super Words Center.

This week's activity is called *Draw a Card.* What's the name of this week's activity? *Draw a card.*

You will work with a partner in the Super Words Center. Whom will you work with? *A partner.*

First you will draw a word out of the container. What do you do first? (Idea: *Draw a word out of the container.*)

Next you will show your partner the picture and ask what word the picture shows. What do you do next? (Idea: *I show my partner the picture and ask what word the picture shows.*)

If your partner tells the correct word for the picture, he or she gets to keep the card. What happens if your partner tells the correct word? *He or she gets to keep the card.*

If your partner doesn't know the correct word, you tell your partner the word. What do you do if your partner doesn't know the word? *Tell my partner the word.* Then you get to keep the card.

Next you give your partner a turn. What do you do next? *Give my partner a turn.*

The person who has the most cards at the end of the game is the winner.

## *Jalapeño Bagels*
author: Natasha Wing • illustrator: Robert Casilla

**Preparation:** You will need a copy of *Jalapeño Bagels* for each day's lesson.

Familiarize yourself with the pronunciation of the Spanish and Yiddish words found in the Glossary.

Post a copy of the Vocabulary Tally Sheet, BLM A, with this week's Picture Vocabulary Cards attached.

Each child will need one copy of the Homework Sheet, BLM 2a.

### Target Vocabulary

| Tier II | Tier III |
|---|---|
| ingredients | title |
| recipe | author |
| special | illustrator |
| customers | prediction |
| *decision | linear story |
| *proud | |

*Expanded Target Vocabulary Word

### DAY 1

#### Introduce Book

The name of this week's book is *Jalapeño Bagels.* The name of a book or story is called the title. What's a title? *The name of a book or story.* What's another way of saying "the name of a book or story"? *The title of a book.*

The title of this week's book is *Jalapeño Bagels.* What's the title of this week's book? *Jalapeño Bagels.*

This book was written by Natasha Wing. The person who writes a book or story is called the author. What's another word for the person who writes a book or story? *An author.* What is an author? *The person who writes a book or story.* Who's the author of *Jalapeño Bagels*? *Natasha Wing.*

Robert Casilla [cass-ee-yah] made the pictures for this book. Who made the pictures for *Jalapeño Bagels*? *Robert Casilla.* The person who makes the pictures for a book or story is called the illustrator. What's another word for the person who makes the pictures for a book or a story? *An illustrator.* What is an illustrator? *The person who makes the pictures for a book or story.* Who's the illustrator of *Jalapeño Bagels*? *Robert Casilla.*

The cover of a book usually gives us some hints of what the book is about. Let's look at the front cover of *Jalapeño Bagels.* What do you see in the picture? (Idea: *There is a little boy putting an "open" sign in the door of a bakery.*)

We have looked carefully at the picture on the cover of *Jalapeño Bagels.* Now we can make guesses as to what the book is about. Our guesses are called predictions. What are our guesses called? *Predictions.*

(Assign each child a partner.) Get ready to tell your partner your predictions about *Jalapeño Bagels.* That means you tell your partner your guesses about what this story will be about. Use the information from the cover to help you.

(Ask the following questions, allowing sufficient time for children to share their predictions with their partners.)

• Whom do you think this story is about?
• What do you think the boy will do in the bakery?
• Where do you think the story happens?
• When do you think this story happens?
• Why do you think the boy is smiling?
• How many bagels do you think are in the baskets?
• Do you think this story is about a real person? Tell why or why not.

(Call on several children to share their predictions with the class.)

## Take a Picture Walk

(Encourage children to use target words in their answers.) We're going to take a picture walk through this book. When we take a picture walk, we look at the pictures and tell what we think will happen in the story.

**Page 1.** Who do you think these people are? (Ideas: *A family; mother; father; son.*) What do you think they are talking about?

**Page 2.** What kind of store does this look like? (Idea: *A bakery.*) A shop or store that sells bread and other baked goods is called a **bakery.** What do we call a shop that sells baked goods? *A bakery.*

**Page 3.** What time of day do you think it is in this illustration? (Ideas: *Morning; night.*) What clues tell you that it could be morning? (Idea: *It looks like the little boy is asleep and the mother is waking him up.*)

**Page 4.** Where do you think this part of the story happens? (Ideas: *In the bakery; in a kitchen.*) What do you think the mother and the little boy are making?

**Page 5.** What is the mother doing? (Idea: *Putting something in the oven.*) Those things she is putting in the oven are called turnovers. They are like little pies that don't need a pie pan. How can you tell that the oven is probably hot? (Ideas: *She is using a long board to put the turnovers in; the oven must be hot to bake the turnovers.*) What do you think the boy is doing while his mother puts the turnovers in the oven? *Making more turnovers.*

**Page 6.** What do we call these little pies that don't need a pan? *Turnovers.*

**Page 7.** What do you think the boy is making now?

**Page 8.** Mmmm. It looks like the boy made a type of cake or cookie bar.

**Page 9.** What do you see on this page? (Ideas: *A recipe card; dough in different shapes.*)

**Page 10.** Who is the little boy working with now? (Idea: *His father.*) What are they doing? (Idea: *Rolling out dough.*) What do you think they are making?

**Page 11.** What do you think the little boy is making? (Ideas: *A knotted bread; a pretzel.*) What do you think they are saying?

**Page 12.** The father is eating something in this illustration. Do you think it's something the boy likes to eat? *No.* How can you tell? (Ideas: *He's got an unpleasant look on his face; his arms are crossed.*)

**Pages 13–14.** It looks like the family is working together in this illustration. What do you think they are making?

**Pages 15–16.** What time of day do you think it is in this part of the story? (Idea: *Morning.*) What clues tell you that it could be morning? (Ideas: *The family is getting their bakery ready to open.*) What do you think the boy is thinking here?

**Page 17.** Who are those people behind the boy? (Idea: *Customers; people who want to buy something in the store.*) What is the little boy doing? (Idea: *Putting bagels into a bag.*)

**Page 18.** Do you think this family had a good time together? *Yes.* What clues tell you that? (Idea: *They all look happy.*)

**Pages 19–20.** These are instructions for making some of the baked goods the little boy in the story made.

**Page 22.** Where do you think the little boy is in this illustration? (Idea: *At school.*) That banner says "International Day." **International** is a word that means things come from different countries all over the world. What word means that things come from different countries all over the world? *International.* It looks like it's International Day at the boy's school. What do you think children do on International Day? (Idea: *Share food and other things from different countries.*)

It's your turn to ask me some questions. What would you like to know about the story? (Accept questions. If children tell about the pictures or the story instead of ask questions, prompt them to ask a question.) Ask me a who question. Ask me a why question.

## Read the Story Aloud
(Read the story to children with minimal interruptions.)

Tomorrow we will read the story again, and I will ask you some questions. **(If children have difficulty attending for an extended period of time, you may wish to present the next part of this day's lesson at another time of day.)**

## Present Target Vocabulary

 Recipe

In the story, Pablo's father uses Pablo's bubbe's recipe to make the bagels. That means he follows the instructions Pablo's bubbe gave him for mixing and cooking the bagels. **Recipe.** Say the word. *Recipe.*

Recipe is a naming word. It names a thing. What kind of word is **recipe?** *A naming word.*

**A recipe is the instructions for mixing and cooking food.** A recipe tells what things you need to make the food and how to cook it. Say the word that means "the instructions for mixing and cooking food." *Recipe.*

(Correct any incorrect responses, and repeat the item at the end of the sequence.)

Let's think about things that might be recipes. I'll tell about something. If that thing could be a recipe, say "recipe." If not, don't say anything.

- This paper tells you how to make "Oh-So-Delicious Oatmeal." *Recipe.*
- Here are the instructions for making a strawberry smoothie. *Recipe.*
- This paper tells you how to fix your bike.
- These are the instructions for traveling from Los Angeles to San Francisco.
- These are the instructions for making southern-style cornbread. *Recipe.*
- This is the letter I wrote to my grandma.

What word means "the instructions for mixing and cooking food"? *Recipe.*

 Ingredients

In the story, Pablo's mother "gets out the pans and ingredients for pan dulce." That means she gets out the things she needs to make pan dulce. She would need flour, water, sugar, salt, eggs, butter, and cinnamon. **Ingredients.** Say the word. *Ingredients.*

**Ingredients** is a naming word. It names things. What kind of word is **ingredients?** *A naming word.*

**Ingredients are the things you need to make something.** There is always a list of ingredients in a recipe when you are making a special food. What word means "the things you need to make something"? *Ingredients.*

Let's think about some of the things you would need to make different foods. I'll name something. If the thing I name would be an ingredient in that food, say "ingredient." If not, don't say anything.

- I'm making chicken soup—chicken. *Ingredient.*
- I'm making mud pies—oranges.
- I'm making a salad—lettuce. *Ingredient.*
- I'm making a peach pie—peaches. *Ingredient.*
- I'm making a sandwich—chocolate chips.
- I'm making beef stew—**beef.**

What word means "the things you need to make something"? *Ingredients.*

 Special

In the story, Pablo's parents used their own special recipe to make jalapeño bagels. That means they used a recipe that was not an ordinary recipe. The recipe they used was better than the usual recipe. **Special.** Say the word. *Special.*

**Special** is a describing word. It tells more about someone or something. What kind of word is **special?** *A describing word.*

**If something is special it is not ordinary; it is better than usual.** Say the word that means "not ordinary; better than usual." *Special.*

Let's think about some things that might be special. I'll tell about something. If you think that thing is special, say "special." If not, don't say anything.

- We went to a fancy restaurant to celebrate my birthday. *Special.*
- Your painting won a prize in the art show. *Special.*
- It's just an ordinary day.
- Joanna has felt pens that are sparkly. *Special.*
- Martin uses an ordinary pencil to do his work.
- It's the day of the big school concert. *Special.*

What word means "not ordinary; better than usual"? *Special.*

 Customers

In the story, Pablo's mother says, "You should decide before we open, or else our customers will buy everything up." That means there were many people who wanted to buy things from their bakery. If Pablo didn't make a decision, the customers would buy everything and he would have nothing to take to school. **Customers.** Say the word. *Customers.*

**Customers** is a naming word. It names people. What kind of word is **customers?** *A naming word.*

**Customers are the people who buy things in a store.** Say the word that means "the people who buy things in a store." *Customers.*

Let's think about some people who might be customers. I'll tell about someone. If you think that person is a customer, say "customer." If not, don't say anything.

- Al went into The Game Store to buy a checkers game. *Customer.*
- Mrs. Burnham went into the Sunrise Hair Salon to get her hair cut. *Customer.*
- The Ragland family went camping in the wilderness.
- We bought seven pounds of oranges and four pounds of apples from Mr. Kang. *Customer.*
- My Uncle Dale bought gas at the gas station. *Customer.*
- LaToya shoveled the gravel in the back yard for her dad.

What word means "the people who buy things in a store"? *Customers.*

### Present Vocabulary Tally Sheet

(See Lesson 1, page 4, for instructions.)

### Assign Homework

(Homework Sheet, BLM 2a. See the Introduction for homework instructions.)

**Preparation:** Picture Vocabulary Cards for *ingredients, recipe, special, customers.*

### Read and Discuss Story

(Read story to children. Ask the following questions at the specified points. Encourage children to use target words in their answers.)

**Page 2.** What is Mama talking about when she says, "the panderia"? *The bakery.* What problem is the boy trying to solve in this story? (Idea: *What he should bring to school for International Day.*)

**Page 3.** Why is Mama waking Pablo up so early? (Idea: *He is going to work in the bakery today.*) What is one thing Pablo thinks he could bring to school? (Idea: *Pan dulce; Mexican sweet bread.*) Pablo is supposed to bring something from his culture. What culture does pan dulce come from? (Idea: *Mexican.*)

**Page 6.** What do Pablo and his mother bake next? (Ideas: *Empanadas de calabaza; pumpkin turnovers.*)

**Page 8.** What is Pablo's favorite dessert? (Idea: *Chango bars; monkey man bars.*) What is going to make this batch especially good? (Idea: *Pablo and Mama both added extra chocolate chips.*) So far, Pablo has suggested bringing three treats to school. Let's see if he can make up his mind.

**Page 9.** What does Pablo's father want him to do? (Idea: *Help make the bagels.*) What languages does Pablo's father speak? (Idea: *English and Yiddish.*) Yiddish is a language spoken by people from the Jewish culture. What language do some people from the Jewish culture speak? *Yiddish.* Where did Pablo's father learn to make bagels? (Idea: *From his bubbe; from Pablo's grandmother.*)

**Page 11.** What does Pablo think he might bring to school in this part of the story? (Idea: *Challah bread.*)

**Page 12.** What does Pablo like to eat on his bagels? *Jam.*

**Page 13.** What does the family make together? (Idea: *Jalapeño bagels.*) Why can't Pablo wait until the bagels are ready? (Ideas: *He's hungry; they are one of his favorites.*)

**Page 16.** Has Pablo solved his problem yet? *No.* Why not? (Idea: *He still can't decide what to bring to school.*) Why should he decide before the bakery opens? (Idea: *The customers will buy everything and he won't have anything to bring to school.*)

**Page 17.** What did Pablo finally decide to bring to school? *Jalapeño bagels.*

**Page 18.** Why did Pablo decide to bring jalapeño bagels? (Idea: *Because they are a mixture of the cultures of both his parents.*) What does that mean? (Ideas: *Jalapeño bagels are a combination of Mexican and Jewish cultures; they take Jewish bread and add a Mexican flavor.*)

Do you think you would like to try jalapeño bagels? Tell why or why not. (Call on several children. Encourage them to use this frame to state their answers: *I would/not like to try jalapeño bagels because____.*)

### Review Vocabulary

(Display the Picture Vocabulary Cards. Point to each card as you say the word. Ask children to repeat each word after you.) These pictures show **recipe, ingredients, special,** and **customers.**

- What word means "the things you need to make something"? *Ingredients.*
- What word means "the instructions for mixing and cooking food"? *Recipe.*
- What word means "people who buy things in a store"? *Customers.*
- What word means "not ordinary; better than usual"? *Special.*

### Extend Vocabulary
◎—⊏ Special

In *Jalapeño Bagels,* we learned that **special** is a describing word that means "not ordinary; better than usual." Say the word that means "not ordinary; better than usual." *Special.*

Raise your hand if you can tell us a sentence that uses **special** as a describing word meaning "not ordinary; better than usual." (Call on several children. If they don't use complete sentences, restate their examples as sentences. Have the class repeat the sentences.)

Here's a new way to use the word **special.**

- Los Bagels Bakery and Café had a **special** on jalapeño bagels. Say the sentence.
- The **special** at Rosie's diner was roast chicken. Say the sentence.
- The sporting goods store had a **special** on two-person tents. Say the sentence.

**In these sentences, special is a naming word that means a sale of certain things for lower prices.** What naming word means "a sale of certain things for lower prices"? *Special.*

Raise your hand if you can tell us a sentence that uses **special** as a naming word meaning "a sale of certain things for lower prices." (Call on several children. If they don't use complete sentences, restate their examples as sentences. Have the class repeat the sentences.)

### Present Expanded Target Vocabulary
◎—⊏ Decision

In the story, Pablo finally decided to bring jalapeño bagels to International Day at school. Another way of saying "Pablo thought about it and made up his mind to bring jalapeño bagels" is to say "Pablo made a decision to bring jalapeño bagels." When Pablo decided what to do, he made a decision. **Decision.** Say the word. *Decision.*

**Decision** is a naming word. It names an idea. What kind of word is **decision**? *A naming word.*

**A decision is the result of thinking about something and making up your mind.** Say the word that means "the result of thinking about something and making up your mind." *Decision.*

Let's think about things that people might make a decision about. If someone made a decision about something, say "decision." If not, don't say anything.

- The family made up their minds to move to Seattle. *Decision.*
- You thought about it and made up your mind to buy flowers for Mother's Day. *Decision.*
- Jerry couldn't decide what to wear to school.

- It is hot outside.
- Dad thought about it and made up his mind to buy a new lawn mower. *Decision.*
- You thought about it and made up your mind to have fish for dinner. *Decision.*

What word means "the result of thinking about something and making up your mind"? *Decision.*

◎─ Proud

In *Jalapeño Bagels,* Pablo was having trouble making a decision about what to bring to school for International Day. Sometimes he wanted to bring something from his mother's culture. Sometimes he wanted to bring something from his father's culture. When Pablo finally made the decision, he brought something that was a mixture of both cultures, just like he was. When Pablo made this decision, he showed that he was proud that his mother was Mexican and his father was Jewish. **Proud.** Say the word. *Proud.*

**Proud** is a describing word. It tells more about how someone feels. What kind of word is **proud?** *A describing word.*

**If you feel proud, you feel pleased and important.** Say the word that means "pleased and important." *Proud.* The opposite of **proud** is ashamed. What is the opposite of **proud?** *Ashamed.* What is the opposite of ashamed? *Proud.*

Let's think about some times when people might feel proud. If I say a time when someone would feel proud, say "proud." If not, don't say anything.

- Ben felt pleased and important when he could read the book by himself. *Proud.*
- You like playing with your favorite toy.
- You got all the words on your spelling test correct. *Proud.*
- Daniel finally learned to swim the length of the swimming pool. *Proud.*
- You made your own lunch for the very first time. *Proud.*
- You didn't tell the truth when your mom asked you how your coat got torn.

What word means "pleased and important"? *Proud.*

## Literary Analysis
### (Beginning, Middle, End, Problem)

Let's think about what we already know about how books are made.

- What do we call the name of a book? *Title.*
- What do we call the person who writes a story? *Author.*
- What do we call the person who draws the pictures? *Illustrator.*

Today we will learn more about how stories are made. Stories have a beginning, a middle, and an end. What do stories have? *A beginning, a middle, and an end.*

The beginning of a story introduces the people or animals in the story. The people or animals in a story are called the characters. What do you call the people or animals in a story? *The characters.*

Who are some of the characters in *Jalapeño Bagels?* (Ideas: *Pablo, Pablo's father; Pablo's mother; the customers; the children in Pablo's class.*)
(**Note:** You may wish to show the illustrations from page 1, 17, and 22 to assist children in recalling the characters in the story.)

The most important characters are called the main characters. What do we call the most important characters? *The main characters.* Who do you think are the most important characters in *Jalapeño Bagels*? (Ideas: *Pablo, his father; his mother.*)

The beginning of the story also tells where and when the story happens. What else does the beginning of a story tell? *Where and when the story happens.* Where does *Jalapeño Bagels* begin?
(**Note:** You may wish to show the illustrations on pages 1 and 2.) (Ideas: *At Pablo's house; in the kitchen.*)

We'll have to be detectives to figure out when Pablo's story begins. (Show page 1.) What time of day do you think this is? (Ideas: *Evening; after supper.*)

Now I'll read you a sentence from the next page of the story. (Show page 3.) "Early Sunday morning, when it is still dark, my mother wakes me up." When does this part of the story happen? *Early Sunday morning.*

(Show page 1.) If the next morning was Sunday morning, what day do you think the story started? *Saturday.* When on Saturday did the story start? (Idea: *After supper.*) So, now we know the story started Saturday after supper. You were great detectives to figure that out!

The beginning of a story often has a problem. Listen while I read the first page of the story again. (Read first two sentences on page 2.) What is the problem? (Idea: *Pablo doesn't know what he should bring to school on Monday for International Day.*)

The middle of a story tells what the main character did to solve the problem. What did Pablo do? (Ideas: *He went to the bakery; he thought maybe he'd bring pan dulce; maybe he'd bring empanadas de calabaza; maybe he'd bring chango bars; maybe he'd bring challah; maybe he'd bring sesame-seed bagels with cream cheese.*)
(**Note:** You may wish to show the illustrations from pages 4–12 to assist children in recalling the story events.)

The end of a story tells what finally happened. (Show pages 17 and 18.) What happened at the end of the story? (Idea: *Pablo decided to bring jalapeño bagels.*)

You did a great job of thinking about the beginning, the middle, the end, and the problem in the story *Jalapeño Bagels*. Now it's time to play a game.

### Play the Choosing Game

Today you will play the Choosing Game. Let's think about the six words we have learned: **ingredients, recipe, special, customers, decision,** and **proud.** (Display the Picture Vocabulary Cards.) I will say a sentence that has two target words in it. You will have to choose the correct word for that sentence.

Let's practice. (Display the word cards for the two words in each sentence as you say the sentence.)

- If you read the instructions to make Swedish flatbread, do you read the **recipe** or the **customers?** *The recipe.*
- If you wear your best shoes to school, do you wear your **special** shoes or your **proud** shoes? *Special.*
- If you need onions, ground beef, an egg, and breadcrumbs to make a meatloaf, are those items the **recipes** or the **ingredients?** *The ingredients.*

If you tell me the correct answer, you will win one point. If you can't tell me the correct answer, I get the point.

Now you're ready to play the game. (Draw a T-chart on the board for keeping score. Children earn one point for each correct answer. If they make an error, correct them as you normally would, and record one point for yourself. Repeat missed words at the end of the game. Display the word cards for the two words in each sentence as you say the sentence.)

- If you went to the store and the price of bananas was less than it was yesterday, are the bananas **proud** or on **special?** *On special.*
- Is the first day of school a **special** day or a **customer?** *Special.*
- If your mom asks you to go to the corner store to buy milk, are you an **ingredient** or a **customer?** *A customer.*
- If you made up your mind to learn to play soccer, did you make a **decision** or a **recipe?** *A decision.*
- When you score a goal for your team, do you feel **proud** or **ingredients?** *Proud.*

(Count the points and declare a winner.)
You did a great job of playing the Choosing Game.

### Complete the Activity Sheet

(Give each child a copy of the Activity Sheet, BLM 2b. Review with children the order they will place the pictures to put them in the sequence to show beginning, middle, and end. Instruct children to complete the sentences, color the pictures, cut them out, and assemble them in sequential order. These pictures can be fastened together to produce a little booklet. This booklet may be sent home with children so they can retell the story at home.)

(You may wish to create a word bank on the board by writing the words children will use in the sentence completion part of this activity. Word Bank: *school, pan dulce, empanadas de calabaza, chango bars, sesame-seed bagels, jalapeño bagels.*)

(The completed sequence should be similar to this:

Pablo asked, "What should I bring to school?"

"Maybe I'll bring pan dulce."

"Maybe I'll bring empanadas de calabaza."

"Maybe I'll bring chango bars."

"Maybe I'll bring sesame-seed bagels."

"I know, I'll bring jalapeño bagels.")

## DAY 4

**Preparation:** Prepare a sheet of chart paper, landscape direction, titled *Jalapeño Bagels.* Underneath the title draw a row of 8 boxes connected by arrows.

See the Introduction for Week 2's Chart.

Record children's responses by writing the underlined words in the boxes.

### Introduce Linear Story Pattern

When authors write stories, they sometimes write in patterns.

Let's see if we can figure out the pattern for this story. You tell me what happened in the story, and I'll write it down.

**Pages 1–2.** What are Pablo and his mother talking about? (Idea: *What Pablo should bring to school for International Day.*)

**Pages 3–4.** (And read the last 2 paragraphs.) Then what happened? (Ideas: *Pablo helped his mother make pan dulce; he said maybe he should bring pan dulce.*)

**Pages 5–6.** (And read the first sentence on page 6 and the first sentence on page 8.) Then what happened? (Ideas: *Pablo helped his mother make empanadas de calabaza; he said maybe he should bring empanadas de calabaza.*)

**Page 8.** (Read "Ready to make chango bars?" "I could bring chango bars. They're my favorite dessert.") Then what happened? (Ideas: *Pablo helped his mother make chango bars; he said maybe he should bring chango bars.*)

**Pages 11–12.** (And read page 11.) Then what happened? (Ideas: *Pablo helped his father make challah; he said maybe he should bring challah.*)

**Pages 9–10.** (And read the first paragraph on page 12.) Then what happened? (Ideas: *Pablo helped his father make sesame-seed bagels; he said maybe he should bring sesame-seed bagels.*)

**Pages 13, 14, 18, and 22.** Then what happened? (Ideas: *Pablo helped his mother and father make jalapeño bagels; he brought jalapeño bagels to school.*)

(Point to the story map on the chart paper. Draw a line under the story map.) Look at the shape of this story. It's a line. This story starts and ends at different places, so this story has a **linear** pattern. What kind of a story has a pattern that starts and ends at a different place? *A linear pattern.*

### Play the Choosing Game (Cumulative Review)

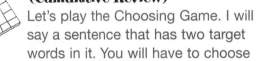

Let's play the Choosing Game. I will say a sentence that has two target words in it. You will have to choose the correct word for that sentence. (Display the Picture Vocabulary Cards for *ingredients, recipe, special, customers, decision,* and *proud* for the two words in each sentence as you say the sentence.)

Now you're ready to play the Choosing Game. (Draw a T-chart on the board for keeping score. Children earn one point for each correct answer. If they make an error, correct them as you normally would, and record one point for yourself. Repeat missed words at the end of the game.)

- If you made up your mind to go to the movies, did you make a **decision** or a **customer**? *A decision.*
- If I read a paper to find out how to make a banana smoothie, would I read a **recipe** or a **special**? *A recipe.*
- If I bought lettuce at a lower price than usual, was the lettuce on **special** or **proud**? *On special.*
- If the teacher held up your picture and showed it to the rest of the children, would you feel **proud** or **decision**? *Proud.*
- If you went to the Happy Feet Shoe store and bought a new pair of running shoes, would you be a **recipe** or a **customer**? *A customer.*
- If you looked on the cereal box and found out there were oats, cinnamon, honey, and nuts in the cereal, would those things be **ingredients** or **customers**? *Ingredients.*
- If you save your best clothes to wear on Sunday, are those clothes **ingredients** or **special**? *Special.*

Now you will have to listen very carefully, because I'm not going to show you the word cards. Think carefully; some of the sentences will have words you learned when we read *Suki's Kimono*.

- If it takes only a few drops of shampoo to wash your hair, is the shampoo **concentrated** or **proud**? *Concentrated.*
- If you go to a street party where there is Caribbean food, music, and dancing, are you at a **festival** or a **recipe**? *A festival.*
- If you make up your mind to learn to jump rope backwards, did you make a **decision** or a **souvenir**? *A decision.*
- If you put water, sugar, yeast, eggs, and flour out on the table, would you have the **recipe** or the **ingredients** to make challah? *The ingredients.*
- If your mother told you to wear your best sweater, would you wear your **special** sweater or your **confident** sweater? *Special.*
- If you feel pleased and important, do you feel **proud** or **concentrated**? *Proud.*
- Would you be a **customer** or a **recipe** if you went to the store to buy two apples? *A customer.*

- If those apples you bought were priced less than yesterday, were the apples on **special** or **confident**? *On special.*

(Tally the points and declare a winner.) You did a great job of playing the Choosing Game.

---

## DAY 5

**Preparation:** Quiz Answer Sheet, BLM B.

---

## Retell Story

Today I'll show you the pictures Robert Casilla made for *Jalapeño Bagels*. As I show you the pictures, I'll call on one of you to tell the class that part of the story.

Tell me what happens at the **beginning** of the story. (Show the pictures on pages 1 and 2. Call on a child to tell what's happening.)

Tell me what happens in the **middle** of the story. (Show the pictures on pages 3–16. Call on a child to tell what's happening. Encourage use of target words when appropriate. Model use as necessary.)

Tell me what happens at the **end** of the story. (Show the pictures on pages 17, 18, and 22. Call on a child to tell what's happening.)

If we were having International Day at our school, what would you bring from your culture?

## Assess Vocabulary

 (Give each child a copy of the Quiz Answer Sheet, BLM B.)

Today you're going to have a True or False quiz. When you do the True or False quiz, it shows me how well you know the hard words you are learning.

Before you can do the True or False quiz, you have to remember about true and false.

If something is true it's right or correct. What word means "right" or "correct"? *True.* What does **true** mean? *Right or correct.* If something is false it's wrong. What word means "wrong"? *False.* What does **false** mean? *Wrong.*

I'll say some things. If I say something that is true, say "true." If I say something that is false, say "false."

- You have hair on your head. *True.*
- Dogs say, "Meow!" *False.*
- Airplanes fly. *True.*
- A room has a door. *True.*
- You walk on the ceiling. *False.*
- You blow your nose and wipe your feet. *True.*
- Books are good to eat. *False.*

If I say something that is true, circle the word **true.** What will you do if I say something that is true? *Circle the word true.*

If I say something that is false, circle the word **false.** What will you do if I say something that is false? *Circle the word false.*

Listen carefully to each item that I say. Don't let me trick you!

Item 1: If you read a page in a book that tells you how to make macaroni and cheese, you read a **recipe.** (*True.*)

Item 2: If you think about what book you want to read and you make up your mind to read *The Big Book of Airplanes*, you made a **customer.** (*False.*)

Item 3: If your sweater has red, green, and yellow stripes, the stripes are **different** colors. (*True.*)

Item 4: The **ingredients** you need to make something are listed in a **recipe.** (*True.*)

Item 5: You're **proud** of yourself if you feel pleased and important. (*True.*)

Item 6: If something is **special,** it is ordinary. (*False.*)

Item 7: If the **special** at Maria's restaurant were catfish, you wouldn't have to pay as much for it as you usually would. (*True.*)

Item 8: If you read the menu, and thought about it, and then made up your mind to have the catfish, you would have made a **decision.** (*True.*)

Item 9: If you're **confident,** you think you're not very good at doing things. (*False.*)

Item 10: If you told your new neighbor your name and he told you his name, you **introduced** yourselves. (*True.*)

You did a great job completing your quiz!

(Score children's work. A child must score 9 out of 10 to be at the mastery level. If a child does not achieve mastery, insert the missed words as additional items in the games in next week's lessons. Retest those children individually for the missed items before they take the next mastery test.)

## Extensions

### Read a Story as a Reward

(Display *Suki's Kimono* and *Jalapeño Bagels,* as well as other books that celebrate children of different cultures. Allow children to choose which book they would like you to read to them as a reward for their hard work.)

(Read the story aloud for enjoyment with minimal interruptions.)

**Preparation:** Word containers for the Super Words Center.

### Introduce the Super Words Center

(Add the new Picture Vocabulary Cards to the words from the previous week. Show children one of the word containers. If children need more guidance in how to work in the Super Words Center, role-play with two to three children as a demonstration.)

Let's review how we work with our words in the Super Words Center.

This week's activity is called *Draw a Card.* What's the name of this week's activity? *Draw a card.*

You will work with a partner in the Super Words Center. Whom will you work with? *A partner.*

First you will draw a word out of the container. What do you do first? (Idea: *Draw a word out of the container.*)

Next you will show your partner the picture and ask what word the picture shows. What do you do next? (Idea: *I show my partner the picture and ask what word the picture shows.*)

If your partner tells the correct word for the picture, he or she gets to keep the card. What happens if your partner tells the correct word? *He or she gets to keep the card.*

If your partner doesn't know the correct word, you tell your partner the word. What do you do if your partner doesn't know the word? *Tell my partner the word.* Then you get to keep the card.

Next you give your partner a turn. What do you do next? *Give my partner a turn.*

The person who has the most cards at the end of the game is the winner.

Christopher, please clean up your room!

## Week 3

# Christopher, Please Clean Up Your Room!

author: Itah Sadu • illustrator: Roy Condy

## 🎯 Target Vocabulary

| Tier II | Tier III |
| --- | --- |
| complained | title |
| untidy | author |
| sound | illustrator |
| amazed | prediction |
| *uncooperative | repeating story |
| *disgusting | |

*Expanded Target Vocabulary Word

### DAY 1

### Introduce Book

This week's book is called *Christopher, Please Clean Up Your Room!* Remember that the name of a book is called the title. What's the title of this week's book? *Christopher, Please Clean Up Your Room!*

This book was written by Itah Sadu [ee-tah sah-du]. Remember that an author is the person who writes a book or story. Who's the author of *Christopher, Please Clean Up Your Room! Itah Sadu.*

Roy Condy made the pictures for this book. Remember that an illustrator is the person who makes the pictures for a book or story. Who is the illustrator of *Christopher, Please Clean Up Your Room! Roy Condy.*

The cover of a book usually gives us some hints of what the book is about. Let's look at the front cover of *Christopher, Please Clean Up Your Room!* What do you see in the picture? (Ideas: *There is a little boy who looks angry; he is sitting in a messy room.*)

(Assign each child a partner.) Remember that when you make a prediction about something, you say what you think will happen. What do you do when you make a prediction? *You say what you think will happen.*

Get ready to make some predictions to your partner about this book. Use the information from the cover to help you.

(Ask the following questions, allowing sufficient time for children to share their predictions with their partners.)

- Whom do you think this story is about?
- What do you think the boy in the story will do?
- Where do you think the story happens?
- When do you think this story happens?
- Why do you think the boy is sitting there?
- How do you think the boy is feeling?
- Do you think this story is about a real boy? Tell why or why not.

(Call on several children to share their predictions with the class.)

### Take a Picture Walk

(Encourage children to use target words in their answers.) We're going to take a picture walk through this book. Remember that when we take a picture walk, we look at the pictures and tell what we think will happen in the story.

**Page 1.** Where do you think this story happens, in the city or in the country? *In the city.* Why do you think so? (Idea: *There are lots of buildings.*) What time of year do you think it is? (Ideas: *Spring, early/late summer.*) Tell me why you think so. (Ideas: *It is sunny out and the boy is wearing sunglasses, but he is also wearing a sweatshirt and long pants.*)

**Pages 2–3.** What is this? (Idea: *A very messy bedroom.*) Do you think the little boy cleans his room very often? *No.* What kinds of things do you see in this room?

**Pages 4–5.** Who do you think these people are? (Ideas: *His brothers; mom; dad; grandma.*)

What seems to be coming out of the little boy's bedroom? (Idea: *Snakes and rats.*) Do you think those are real? *No.* What has happened to Grandma? (Idea: *She fainted.*)

**Page 7.** How do you think the little boy feels? (Ideas: *Mad; angry.*) What clues tell us that he's angry? (Ideas: *Crossed arms; pouting mouth; lowered eyelids.*) Why do you think the little boy is angry?

**Pages 8–9.** What do you see in this illustration? (Ideas: *A dirty fish bowl; escaping snails; bugs; toys; crayons; a bit of food.*)

**Pages 10–11.** What do you think the fish are doing here? (Ideas: *Trying to escape; talking to the bug.*)

**Pages 12–13.** How do you think the fish are feeling? (Ideas: *Sick; sad.*) What do you think the bug is thinking about?

**Pages 14–15.** What do you think the bug is telling the fish?

**Pages 16–17.** What do you think is going on here? (Idea: *The big bug is calling a meeting with all the other bugs.*)

**Pages 18–19.** What do you think the bugs are going to do?

**Pages 20–21.** What has happened? (Ideas: *The bugs are bothering the boy; a bug crawled into the boy's mouth and he spat it out.*)

**Pages 22–23.** How do you think the boy feels? (Ideas: *Scared; afraid; disgusted.*) What do you think the bug is saying to him? (Idea: *Clean up your room!*)

**Pages 24–25.** What is the boy doing? (Idea: *Sweeping stuff out from under his bed.*)

**Pages 26–27.** What has happened to the fish bowl? (Idea: *It has been cleaned.*) How do the fish feel now? (Ideas: *Happy; healthy.*)

**Pages 28–29.** What is the boy doing in his room? *Dancing.* Do you think the boy is happy about having a clean room? *Yes.*

**Page 30.** The bug is winking like he has a secret. What do you think its secret is? (Idea: *He was the one to get the boy to finally clean his room.*)

It's your turn to ask me some questions. What would you like to know about the story? (Accept questions. If children tell about the pictures or the story instead of ask questions, prompt them to ask a question.) Ask me a who question. Ask me a why question.

### Read the Story Aloud
(Read the story to children with minimal interruptions.)

Tomorrow we will read the story again, and I will ask you some questions. (If children have difficulty attending for an extended period of time, you may wish to present the next part of this day's lesson at another time of day.)

### Present Target Vocabulary
◎— *Complained*

In the story, when Christopher's family and friends complained, Christopher just told them that he liked his room the way it was. When the family complained, they told Christopher they were unhappy with the way he kept his room. **Complained.** Say the word. *Complained.*

**Complained** is an action word. It tells what someone did. What kind of word is **complained?** *An action word.*

**If you complained about something, you told someone that you were unhappy about something.** Say the word that means "told someone that you were unhappy about something." *Complained.*

(Correct any incorrect responses, and repeat the item at the end of the sequence.)

Let's think about some times when someone might have complained. I'll tell about a time. If you would have heard someone complain, say "complained." If not, don't say anything. (Whenever children respond with the word *complained,* ask them, "Who would have complained? What might they have said?")

- You didn't put away your toys before you went to bed. *Complained.*
- Rebecca's mom served meatloaf for dinner and Rebecca hated meatloaf. *Complained.*
- Your parents took you to your favorite place, the zoo.

- Mr. Harcher said you had done a beautiful job painting your picture.
- You helped your father by setting the table.
- You told the doctor you had a sore throat. *Complained.*

What word means "told someone that you were unhappy about something"? *Complained.*

 **Untidy**

In the story, Christopher's room was untidy. That means his room was not tidy or neat; it was messy. **Untidy.** Say the word. *Untidy.*

**Untidy** is a describing word. It tells more about a person or a place. What kind of word is **untidy**? *A describing word.*

**If something is untidy, it is not tidy or neat; it is messy.** A person can be untidy. A place can be untidy. Say the word that means "not tidy or neat; messy." *Untidy.* Untidy is the opposite of tidy. What word is the opposite of tidy? *Untidy.* What word is the opposite of **untidy**? *Tidy.*

Let's think about some people or places that might be untidy. I'll tell about something or someone. If that person or place is untidy, say "untidy." If not, don't say anything.

- Papers were all crumpled up at the back of the desk. There were crayon wrappings, peanut shells, and bits of old sandwiches stuffed inside it. *Untidy.*
- Arlene washed and dried the dishes and put them away in the cupboard.
- Lego blocks were scattered all over the floor. The game pieces were mixed in the building blocks. The cushions were off the sofa and lying in a heap on the floor. *Untidy.*
- Michael's shirt was buttoned unevenly. It hung out over his pants. His shoelaces were untied. His hands and face were dirty and his hair needed to be combed. *Untidy.*
- Kente wore his best clothes. He tucked in his shirt. He polished his shoes and tied them carefully. He washed his face and combed his hair. He was getting ready to go see his grandpa.
- Nothing was put away in the teenager's bedroom. The bedcovers were on the floor. There were three lunch bags with bits falling out. Clothes and shoes were everywhere. *Untidy.*

What word means "not tidy or neat; messy"? *Untidy.*

 **Sound**

In the story, Christopher was sound asleep when the cockroaches came. That means he was in a deep sleep. **Sound.** Say the word. *Sound.*

When you say **sound** asleep, **sound** is a describing word. It tells more about how someone was sleeping. What kind of word is **sound**? *A describing word.*

**If someone was sound asleep, they were in a deep sleep.** Say the words that mean "in a deep sleep." *Sound asleep.*

Let's think about times when a person or animal might be in a deep sleep. I'll tell about a time. If the person or animal might be in a deep sleep, say "sound asleep." If not, don't say anything.

- The bear slept in its cave for the whole winter. *Sound asleep.*
- The reindeer were traveling across the northern plains.
- The baby slept through the night. *Sound asleep.*
- I called my dad's name and touched his shoulder, but he didn't wake up. *Sound asleep.*
- My grandma had a little nap in her chair.
- The little boy didn't even wake up when his father carried him into the house. *Sound asleep.*

What words means "in a deep sleep"? *Sound asleep.*

 **Amazed**

In the story, the morning after the cockroaches came, Christopher's family was amazed to see his room. That means they were very, very surprised by how clean and tidy his room was. **Amazed.** Say the word. *Amazed.*

**Amazed** is a describing word. It tells how someone is feeling. What kind of word is **amazed**? *A describing word.*

**When someone is amazed they are very, very surprised by something.** Say the word that means "very, very surprised by something." *Amazed.*

I'll tell about some times. If someone would feel amazed, say "amazed." If not, don't say anything.

- When the teacher came in the room, all the children were sitting still and being quiet. *Amazed.*
- The boy won the very first race he ever ran in. *Amazed.*
- You read a long chapter book all by yourself for the very first time. *Amazed.*
- A friend came over and you played hide and seek.
- Mom made dinner.
- It snowed in the middle of the summer. *Amazed.*

What word means "very, very surprised by something"? *Amazed.*

Show me how your face would look if you were **amazed** by something you saw. Tell me how you were feeling. *Amazed.*

### Present Vocabulary Tally Sheet
(See Lesson 1, page 4, for instructions.)

### Assign Homework
(Homework Sheet, BLM 3a. See the Introduction for homework instructions.)

## DAY 2

**Preparation:** Picture Vocabulary Cards for *complained, untidy, sound, amazed.*

### Read and Discuss Story
(Read story to children. Ask the following questions at the specified points. Encourage children to use target words in their answers.)

**Page 1.** Who is this story about? *Christopher.* What kind of young man is Christopher? (Ideas: *A fine young man.*) What did Christopher do that made him a fine young man? (Ideas: *Helped his neighbors run errands; did his chores.*) What kind of student was Christopher? (Idea: *He was a good student; got good grades.*)

**Page 2.** What was the one thing Christopher wouldn't do? *Clean his room.*

**Page 3.** What made Christopher's room stink? (Ideas: *He had cheesy socks under the bed; he had a rotten sandwich behind the door; his shoes smelled funky; the fish bowl stank.*) What do you think cheesy socks are? (Idea: *Socks that smell like stinky cheese.*)

**Page 5.** Why wouldn't Christopher's mother go in his room? (Idea: *She thought there might be snakes in there.*) What happened to Grandma when she visited and saw Christopher's room? (Idea: *She fainted.*) What happened when Christopher's friends slept over? (Idea: *They had nightmares about rats.*) Did Christopher like his room messy? *Yes.*

**Page 6.** What did Christopher's parents do to try to get him to clean his room? (Ideas: *They punished him; they didn't let him have dessert; they took away TV; they wouldn't let his friends come over.*)

**Page 9.** Why were the goldfish concerned about their health? (Ideas: *Christopher hadn't changed their water in weeks and it was green and murky; they felt like they were choking.*) What did the fish want to do? (Idea: *Find a way to make Christopher clean his room.*)

**Page 11.** Who did the fish ask for help? *A cockroach.* Why doesn't the cockroach like to be in Christopher's room? (Idea: *It's too dirty.*)

**Page 13.** What does it mean that the fish were **doomed?** (Idea: *They were going to die.*)

**Page 14.** Is the cockroach going to help the fish? *Yes.*

**Page 15.** What made the fish happy? (Idea: *Knowing that the cockroaches were going to help them.*)

**Page 16.** Why did the cockroaches need gas masks? (Idea: *Because Christopher's room smelled so bad.*)

**Page 18.** Did Christopher plan to clean his room any time soon? *No.* Why did he like his room this way? (Idea: *He thought it was comfortable.*)

**Page 20.** How did the cockroaches finally wake Christopher up? (Idea: *One cockroach landed in his mouth.*) How did the cockroaches tell

Christopher to clean up his room? (Idea: *They spelled it out on the wall with their bodies.*)

**Page 22.** What did Christopher tell the cockroaches at first? *I'll do it tomorrow.* Did the cockroaches like Christopher's answer? *No.*

**Page 24.** Why was Christopher terrified? (Idea: *He was afraid of the cockroaches attacking him.*) What decision did Christopher make? (Idea: *He started cleaning his room.*) What did the cockroaches do as Christopher cleaned? (Idea: *They started leaving.*)

**Page 26.** What did Christopher do after he cleaned his room? (Ideas: *He cleaned the fish bowl; he opened the window; he went to sleep.*) How did Christopher feel now that he had a nice, clean room? (Ideas: *Better; proud.*)

**Page 28.** Why did everyone come to see Christopher's room? (Idea: *They were amazed that he had cleaned it.*)

**Page 29.** Who made Christopher clean his room? *The cockroaches.* Why won't Christopher tell anyone? (Ideas: *He doesn't want anyone to know the cockroaches had made him clean up his room; he didn't want anyone to know his room was too dirty even for cockroaches.*) Why does Christopher keep his room very clean now? (Idea: *He's afraid the cockroaches will come back.*)

**Page 30.** What was the night of the cockroaches? (Idea: *The night thousands of cockroaches came into Christopher's room and told him to clean it.*)

## Review Vocabulary

(Display the Picture Vocabulary Cards. Point to each card as you say the word. Ask children to repeat each word after you.) These pictures show **complained, untidy, sound,** and **amazed.**

- What words mean "in a deep sleep"? *Sound asleep.*
- What word means "very, very surprised by something"? *Amazed.*
- What word means "told someone that you were unhappy about something"? *Complained.*
- What word means "not tidy or neat; messy"? *Untidy.*

## Extend Vocabulary

 Sound

In *Christopher, Please Clean Up Your Room!* we learned that **sound** is a describing word. If you use the word **sound** to tell about a sleep it means "in a deep sleep." Say the words that mean "in a deep sleep." *Sound asleep.*

Raise your hand if you can tell us a sentence that uses **sound asleep,** meaning "in a deep sleep." (Call on several children. If they don't use complete sentences, restate their examples as sentences. Have the class repeat the sentences.)

Here's a new way to use the word **sound.**

- I could hear the **sound** of the dog barking. Say the sentence.
- Mom said the **sound** of the dripping tap was bothering her. Say the sentence.
- We heard the **sound** of the jet taking off. Say the sentence.

**In these sentences, sound is a naming word that means something you hear.** What word means "something you hear"? *Sound.*

Raise your hand if you can tell us a sentence that uses **sound** as naming word meaning "something you hear." (Call on several children. If they don't use complete sentences, restate their examples as sentences. Have the class repeat the sentences.)

## Present Expanded Target Vocabulary

Uncooperative

In the story, Christopher refused to clean his room even though his family and friends complained. Even when he was punished, he refused to clean his room. Christopher was being uncooperative. **Uncooperative.** Say the word. *Uncooperative.*

**Uncooperative** is a describing word. It tells more about someone. What kind of word is **uncooperative?** *A describing word.*

**If someone is uncooperative, he or she refuses to help people or do what he or she is asked.** Say the word that means "refusing to help people or do what is asked." *Uncooperative.*

Let's think about times when someone might be uncooperative. If I tell about a time when someone is being uncooperative, say "uncooperative." If not, don't say anything.

- You drop all of your crayons on the floor and everyone refuses to help you pick them up. *Uncooperative.*
- It's clean-up time but no one will help you put things away. *Uncooperative.*
- Your friend helps you fix your bike.
- You are trying to move a bench but no one will pick up the other end. *Uncooperative.*
- Your mom asks you to turn off the TV, but you refuse. *Uncooperative.*
- Everyone plays well together.

What word means "refusing to help people or do what is asked"? *Uncooperative.*

Tell about a time when you were uncooperative. **(Call on several children. Encourage them to start their answers with *I was uncooperative when*.)**

**(After each response, ask the child:)** What might you have done to be more cooperative?

◎= Disgusting

In the story, Christopher's room had stinky socks under the bed, a rotten sandwich by the door, smelly shoes on the floor, and a filthy fish bowl. Christopher's room was disgusting. When something is disgusting, it is very unpleasant and sickening. **Disgusting.** Say the word. *Disgusting.*

**Disgusting** is a describing word. It tells more about someone or something. What kind of word is **disgusting?** *A describing word.*

**If something is disgusting, it is very unpleasant and sickening.** Say the word that means "very unpleasant and sickening." *Disgusting.*

Let's think about things that might be disgusting. If I tell about something that would be disgusting, say "disgusting." If not, don't say anything.

- The smell of rotten fish. *Disgusting.*
- Eating bugs. *Disgusting.*
- A sunrise.

- A worm in your apple. *Disgusting.*
- Rotten garbage. *Disgusting.*
- Ripe, juicy strawberries.

What word means "very unpleasant and sickening"? *Disgusting.*

## DAY 3

**Preparation:** Activity Sheet, BLM 3b.

### Literary Analysis
### (Beginning, Middle, End, Problem)

Let's think about what we already know about how books are made.

- What do we call the name of a book? *Title.*
- What do we call the person who writes a story? *Author.*
- What do we call the person who draws the pictures? *Illustrator.*

Today we will learn more about how stories are made. Stories have a beginning, a middle, and an end. What do stories have? *A beginning, a middle, and an end.*

The beginning of a story introduces the people or animals in the story. The people or animals in a story are called the characters. What do you call the people or animals in a story? *The characters.*

Who are some of the characters in *Christopher, Please Clean Up Your Room!* **(Ideas: *Christopher; his mom; his dad; his brothers; his grandmother; the goldfish; the cockroaches.*)**
**(Note:** You may wish to show the illustrations from pages 1, 5, 11, and 22 to assist children in recalling the characters in the story.)

The most important characters are called the main characters. What do we call the most important characters? *The main characters.* Who do you think are the main characters in *Christopher, Please Clean Up Your Room!* **(Ideas:** *Christopher; the goldfish; the cockroach.*)

The beginning of the story also tells where and when the story happens. What else does the beginning of a story tell? *Where and when*

*the story happens.* Where does *Christopher, Please Clean Up Your Room!* happen? (Idea: *In Christopher's room.*)
(**Note:** You may wish to show the illustration on pages 2–3.)

It's going to be tricky to figure out when Christopher's story begins. (Show pages 2–3.) Do we know what day this part of the story happened? *No.* Do we know what month this part of the story happened? *No.* Do we know what year this part of the story happened? *No.* So, we'll have to think about what time in Christopher's life this part of the story happened.

We can use the words **before** and **after** to tell when something happened. What words can we use to tell when a story happened? *Before and after.* Did this part of the story happen before or after Christopher cleaned up his room? *Before.* What words could we use to tell when in Christopher's life this part of the story happened? (Idea: *Before Christopher cleaned up his room.*) Good thinking; we can see the beginning of the story happened before Christopher cleaned up his room. You were great detectives to figure that out!

The beginning of a story often has a problem. What was the problem? (Idea: *Christopher wouldn't clean his messy room.*)

The middle of a story tells what the main characters did to solve the problem. What did the goldfish do? (Idea: *They asked the cockroach to help them get Christopher to clean up his room.*) What did the cockroach do? (Ideas: *He got all the other cockroaches to come to Christopher's room; one cockroach dropped into Christopher's mouth and woke him up; the cockroaches spelled "Christopher, Tidy up your room now!" on his wall.*)
(**Note:** You may wish to show the illustrations from pages 16–23 to assist children in recalling the story events.)

The end of a story tells what finally happened. (Show pages 28 and 29.) What happened at the end of the story? (Idea: *Christopher cleaned up his room.*)

You did a great job of thinking about the beginning, the middle, the end, and the problem

in the story *Christopher, Please Clean Up Your Room!* Now it's time to play a game.

## Play the Choosing Game

Today you will play the Choosing Game. Let's think about the six words we have learned: **complained, untidy, sound, amazed, messy,** and **disgusting.** (Display the Picture Vocabulary Cards.) I will say a sentence that has two target words in it. You will have to choose the correct word for that sentence. Let's practice. (Display the word cards for the two words in each sentence as you say the sentence.)

- If your printing is messy and hard to read, is it **untidy** or **sound?** *Untidy.*
- If you are sleeping so deeply that it is hard to wake up, are you **uncooperative** or **sound** asleep? *Sound asleep.*
- Anything you can hear is **disgusting** or a **sound?** *A sound.*

If you tell me the correct answer, you will win one point. If you can't tell me the correct answer, I get the point.

Now you're ready to play the game. (Draw a T-chart on the board for keeping score. Children earn one point for each correct answer. If they make an error, correct them as you normally would and record one point for yourself. Repeat missed words at the end of the game. Display the word cards for the two words in each sentence as you say the sentence.)

- If you went to the doctor and told her you were unhappy about your sore arm, would you have **complained** or **amazed?** *Complained.*
- If your puppy was lying on the mat sleeping and he didn't wake up when you called him, would he be **untidy** or **sound** asleep? *Sound asleep.*
- If you saw an ant that could jump ten times its body length, would you be **sound** asleep or **amazed?** *Amazed.*
- If your room looked like Christopher's, would your room be **sound** or **untidy?** *Untidy.*
- If you heard the rain on the roof, would you have heard a **sound** or an **untidy?** *A sound.*

(Count the points and declare a winner.)
You did a great job of playing the Choosing Game.

## Complete the Activity Sheet

(Give each child a copy of the Activity Sheet, BLM 3b. Review with children the order they will place the pictures to put them in sequence to show beginning, middle, and end. Instruct children to complete the sentences, color the pictures, cut them out, and assemble them in sequential order. These pictures can be fastened together to produce a little booklet. This booklet may be sent home with children so they can retell the story at home.)

(You may wish to create a word bank on the board by writing the words the children will use in the sentence completion part of this activity. Word Bank: *the goldfish; the cockroach; clean his room; Christopher, tidy up your room now; the goldfish bowl was clean.*)

(The completed sequence should be similar to this:
Christopher would not clean his room.
The goldfish thought they would die.
The cockroach said he would get his people to help.
The cockroaches spelled, Christopher, tidy up your room now!
Christopher decided to clean his room.
The last cockroach went away when the goldfish bowl was clean.)

> ### DAY 4
>
> **Preparation:** Prepare a sheet of chart paper, titled *Christopher, Please Clean Up Your Room!* and the verse from page 6, with these key words missing: *cheesy, grew fungi, untidy, funky, fish bowl stank.*

## Introduce Repeating Story Pattern

When authors write stories, they sometimes write in patterns.

Let's see if we can figure out the pattern for this story. Listen while I read what Itah Sadu wrote on page 6. (Read page 6, emphasizing the words

at the end of each line in the verse and pointing to the blanks on the chart.)

Listen while I read what Itah Sadu wrote on page 11. (Read page 11 aloud, beginning with the paragraph *"What about your friends? Would they help?" asked the fish.* When you read the verse, emphasize the words at the end of each line while pointing to the blanks on the chart.)

Listen while I read what Itah Sadu wrote on page 18. (Read page 18, emphasizing the words at the end of each line and pointing to the blanks on the chart.)

What pattern did Itah Sadu use for *Christopher, Please Clean Up Your Room!* (Idea: *She used the same verse over and over.*) That's right. She repeated the verse over and over so this story has a **repeating** pattern. What kind of pattern repeats the same words over and over? *A repeating pattern.*

Let's read the verse she repeated together, and you tell me what words to write in the blanks. (Read the chart with children, having them fill in the blanks. Write the missing words on the chart.)

Now it's your turn to read the verse. (Have children read the verse by themselves.)

I hope your room never looks like Christopher's!

## Play the Choosing Game (Cumulative Review)

Let's play the Choosing Game. I will say a sentence that has two target words in it. You will have to choose the correct word for that sentence. (Display the Picture Vocabulary Cards for *complained, untidy, sound, amazed, uncooperative,* and *disgusting* for the two words in each sentence as you say the sentence.)

Now you're ready to play the Choosing Game. (Draw a T-chart on the board for keeping score. Children earn one point for each correct answer. If they make an error, correct them as you normally would and record one point for yourself. Repeat missed words at the end of the game.)

- If you told your mother you were unhappy because your shoes were too small, did you **complain** or **amaze**? *Complain.*

- If you like to hear a waterfall, do you like the **sound** or the **untidy**? *The sound.*
- If you refuse to do the dishes for your dad, are you **complained** or **uncooperative**? *Uncooperative.*
- If the smell of rotten vegetables makes you sick, do you find the smell **untidy** or **disgusting**? *Disgusting.*
- If you found the bones of a tyrannosaurus rex on the playground, would you be **amazed** or **disgusting**? *Amazed.*
- If your hair was messy and your shoes were untied, would you be **sound** or **untidy**? *Untidy.*
- If you didn't wake up when your mom called you in the morning, were you **untidy** or **sound** asleep? *Sound asleep.*

Now you will have to listen very carefully, because I'm not going to show you the word cards. Think carefully; some of the sentences will have words you learned from other stories we have read.

- If your family goes to Nick's Restaurant for dinner, are you **introduced** or **customers**? *Customers.*
- If you don't listen to the babysitter and do what she asks you to do, are you **uncooperative** or **confident**? *Uncooperative.*
- If the taste of liver makes you feel sick, do you find the taste **concentrated** or **disgusting**? *Disgusting.*
- If you buy lettuce, tomatoes, green onions, and carrots, do you have the **ingredients** for a salad or a **souvenir**? *Ingredients.*
- Do you like the **special** or the **sound** of music? *Sound.*
- If you found a chest full of treasure, would you be **complained** or **amazed**? *Amazed.*
- Is the opposite of neat **untidy** or **sound**? *Untidy.*
- If loud noises didn't wake up your cat, was your cat **proud** or **sound** asleep? *Sound asleep.*

(Tally the points and declare a winner.) You did a great job of playing the Choosing Game.

## Retell Story

Today I'll show you the pictures Roy Condy made for *Christopher, Please Clean Up Your Room!* As I show you the pictures, I'll call on one of you to tell the class that part of the story.

Tell me what happens at the **beginning** of the story. (Show the pictures on pages 1–5. Call on a child to tell what's happening.)

Tell me what happens in the **middle** of the story. (Show the pictures on pages 6–26. Call on a child to tell what's happening. Encourage use of target words when appropriate. Model use as necessary.)

Tell me what happens at the **end** of the story. (Show the pictures on pages 28–30. Call on a child to tell what's happening.)

Do you think the cockroaches will ever have to come back to have another talk with Christopher?

## Assess Vocabulary

 (Give each child a copy of the Quiz Answer Sheet, BLM B.)

Today you're going to have a True or False quiz. When you do the True or False quiz, it shows me how well you know the hard words you are learning.

Before you can do the True or False quiz, you have to remember about true and false.

If something is true, it's right or correct. What word means "right" or "correct"? *True.* What does **true** mean? *Right or correct.* If something is false, it's wrong. What word means "wrong"? *False.* What does **false** mean? *Wrong.*

If I say something that is true, circle the word **true.** What will you do if I say something that is true? *Circle the word true.*

If I say something that is false, circle the word **false.** What will you do if I say something that is false? *Circle the word false.*

Listen carefully to each item that I say. Don't let me trick you!

Item 1: If you're **sound** asleep, it is easy to wake you up. (*False.*)

Item 2: If someone did something that made you feel sick, they did something **disgusting.** (*True.*)

Item 3: A bee, a boy, and a bugle can all make a **sound.** (*True.*)

Item 4: **Untidy** means the opposite of tidy. (*True.*)

Item 5: If someone stole your uncle's car, he might **complain** to the police. (*True.*)

Item 6: If you saw an airplane doing somersaults, you might be **amazed.** (*True.*)

Item 7: If your dad went on a vacation to a cooking school, he might bring home a **recipe** as a **souvenir.** (*True.*)

Item 8: Teddy was **uncooperative** when he worked hard to tidy up the classroom. (*False.*)

Item 9: If you have a **special** day, your day was very ordinary. (*False.*)

Item 10: You would feel **proud** of yourself if you had been **uncooperative** all day. (*False.*)

You did a great job completing your quiz!

(Score children's work. A child must score 9 out of 10 to be at the mastery level. If a child does not achieve mastery, insert the missed words as additional items in the games in next week's lessons. Retest those children individually for the missed items before they take the next mastery test.)

## Extensions

### Read a Story as a Reward

(Display copies of the books that you have read since the beginning of the program or display two or three contemporary fiction books whose main characters are children. Allow children to choose which book they would like you to read to them as a reward for their hard work.)

(Read the story aloud for enjoyment with minimal interruptions.)

---

**Preparation:** Word containers for the Super Words Center.

### Introduce the Super Words Center

(Add the new Picture Vocabulary Cards to the words from the previous weeks. Show children one of the word containers. If children need more guidance in how to work in the Super Words Center, role-play with two to three children as a demonstration.)

Let's review how we work with our words in the Super Words Center.

This week's activity is called *Draw a Card.* What's the name of this week's activity? *Draw a card.*

You will work with a partner in the Super Words Center. Whom will you work with? *A partner.*

First you will draw a word out of the container. What do you do first? (Idea: *Draw a word out of the container.*)

Next you will show your partner the picture and ask what word the picture shows. What do you do next? (Idea: *I show my partner the picture and ask what word the picture shows.*)

If your partner tells the correct word for the picture, he or she gets to keep the card. What happens if your partner tells the correct word? *He or she gets to keep the card.*

If your partner doesn't know the correct word, you tell your partner the word. What do you do if your partner doesn't know the word? *Tell my partner the word.* Then you get to keep the card.

Next you give your partner a turn. What do you do next? *Give my partner a turn.*

The person who has the most cards at the end of the game is the winner.

**Preparation:** You will need a copy of *Flossie & the Fox* for each day's lesson.

Number the pages of the story to assist you in asking comprehension questions at appropriate points.

Post a copy of the Vocabulary Tally Sheet, BLM A, with this week's Picture Vocabulary Cards attached. Each child will need one copy of the Homework Sheet, BLM 4a.

## *Flossie & the Fox*
author: Patricia C. McKissack • illustrator: Rachel Isadora

### Target Vocabulary

| Tier II | Tier III |
|---|---|
| sly | character |
| rascal | folk tale |
| terrified | illustration |
| horrible | |
| *clever | |
| *frustrated | |

*Expanded Target Vocabulary Word

---

## DAY 1

### Introduce Book

This week's book is called *Flossie & the Fox*. What's the title of this week's book? *Flossie & the Fox.*

This book was written by Patricia C. McKissack [mick-kiss-ick]. Who's the author of *Flossie & the Fox*? *Patricia C. McKissack.*

Rachel Isadora [iz-a-dor-ah] made the pictures for this book. Who's the illustrator of *Flossie & the Fox*? *Rachel Isadora.* The pictures an illustrator makes for a book are called the illustrations. What do you call the pictures an illustrator makes for a book? *Illustrations.* What are illustrations? *The pictures an illustrator makes for a book.* Who made the illustrations for *Flossie & the Fox*? *Rachel Isadora.*

The cover of a book usually gives us some hints of what the book is about. Let's look at the front cover of *Flossie & the Fox*. What do you see in the illustration? (Ideas: *A girl carrying a basket of eggs; a fox; they look like they are smiling at each other.*)

(Assign each child a partner.) Remember that when you make a prediction about something, you say what you think will happen. Get ready to make some predictions to your partner about this book. Use the information from the cover to help you.

(Ask the following questions, allowing sufficient time for children to share their predictions with their partners.)

• Whom do you think this story is about?
• What do you think the fox will do?
• What do you think the girl will do?
• Where do you think the story happens?
• When do you think this story happens?
• Why do you think the girl and the fox are smiling at each other?
• How do you think the girl and the fox met each other?
• Do you think this story is about a real fox and a real girl? Tell why or why not.

(Call on several children to share their predictions with the class.)

### Take a Picture Walk

(Encourage children to use target words in their answers.) We're going to take a picture walk through this book. Remember that when we take a picture walk, we look at the pictures and tell what we think will happen in the story.

**Page 2.** What do you think is happening here? (Ideas: *The little girl is putting her doll into the cut-off tree; she is taking her doll out of the cut-off tree.*)

**Page 3.** What do you think is in the big tubs? (Ideas: *Peaches; fruit; oranges.*) Who do you think the woman is who's with the little girl?

**Pages 5–6.** When did this story happen? (Ideas: *A long time ago; on a sunny day.*) Why do you think so? (Ideas: *The woman is wearing a long dress; I can see the sun shining on the road; everything looks yellow.*) Where do you think the little girl is going?

**Page 7.** What do you think is happening here? (Ideas: *The girl is looking at the fox; the fox is looking at the girl.*)

**Page 10.** Why do you think the fox is standing on his back legs like that?

**Page 12.** Why do you think the fox is watching the little girl?

**Page 13.** What do you think is happening here? (Ideas: *The girl is touching the fox's fur; the girl is petting the fox.*)

**Pages 15–16.** Where are they now? (Ideas: *By a creek; near a pool; near some water.*) Why do you think the fox followed the girl?

**Page 18.** What is the girl looking at? *A cat.* Who is the cat looking at? *The girl.* Why do you think the fox is hiding in the bushes?

**Page 20.** What is the fox doing? (Idea: *Howling.*) How do you think the fox is feeling? (Ideas: *Angry; mad.*) What do you think the cat is thinking?

**Page 21.** What do you think is happening here? (Ideas: *The girl and the fox are watching the squirrel.*) Where is the squirrel? (Idea: *Up in a tree.*)

**Pages 23–24.** What is the girl looking at? (Idea: *The farm.*) How do you think the fox is feeling? (Idea: *Very angry; furious.*)

**Page 26.** What is the girl looking at? *The fox.* What do you think the fox is looking at? (Idea: *A dog; a wolf.*) Why do you think that? (Idea: *I can see the shadow on the road.*)

**Pages 27–28.** What do you think is happening here? (Ideas: *The fox is running away; the dog is chasing the fox.*)

**Page 29.** How do you think the girl is feeling? (Idea: *Happy.*) What is she carrying over her shoulder? (Idea: *A basket full of eggs.*)

It's your turn to ask me some questions. What would you like to know about the story? (Accept questions. If children tell about the pictures or the story instead of ask questions, prompt them to ask a question.) Ask me a who question. Ask me a why question.

### Read the Story Aloud
(Read the story to children with minimal interruptions.)

Tomorrow we will read the story again, and I will ask you some questions. (If children have difficulty attending for an extended period of time, you may wish to present the next part of this day's lesson at another time of day.)

### Present Target Vocabulary
 Sly

In the story, Big Mama says "I tell you, that fox is one sly critter." She is using the word sly to tell about the fox. Big Mama means the fox is very good at tricking others. She is warning Flossie to be careful around the fox, because he might try to trick her. **Sly.** Say the word. *Sly.*

**Sly** is a describing word. It tells more about someone. What kind of word is **sly**? *A describing word.*

**If you say someone is sly, it means that person is very good at tricking others.** You have to be careful around sly people, because they might try to trick you. Say the word that means "very good at tricking others." *Sly.*

(Correct any incorrect responses, and repeat the item at the end of the sequence.)

Let's think about some things that people or animals might do. I'll tell about someone or something. If you think that person or thing is being sly, say "sly." If not, don't say anything.

- The fox tried to trick the girl into giving him her ice cream cone. *Sly.*
- The mountain lion made the squirrel think that she was sleeping. *Sly.*
- The dog barked.
- Desiree's grandfather drove the car.
- Derrick hid the candy behind his back so no one could see it. *Sly.*
- The sunset was bright yellow, orange, and red.

What word means "very good at tricking others"? *Sly.*

## ⊙ ⊸ Rascal

In the story, Big Mama called the fox a rascal. That means she thought he wasn't honest. He would lie and trick to get his own way. **Rascal.** Say the word. *Rascal.*

**Rascal** is a naming word. It names a person or an animal. What kind of word is **rascal?** *A naming word.*

**When you call someone a rascal, you think he or she is someone who would lie and trick to get his or her own way.** Say the word that means "someone who would lie and trick to get his or her own way." *Rascal.*

Let's think about people or animals who would be a rascal. I'll tell about someone. If you think that person or animal was a rascal, say "rascal." If not, don't say anything.

- The wolf in *The Three Little Pigs. Rascal.*
- The little boy who lied and tricked people so he could win the game. *Rascal.*
- A girl with pigtails.
- A person who lies to you and tricks you. *Rascal.*
- A duck waddling down the street.
- Four puppies in a box.

What word means "someone who would lie and trick to get his or her own way"? *Rascal.*

Sometimes we put the words **sly** and **rascal** together to tell about someone. If I said the fox was a sly rascal, what would you know about the fox? **(Idea:** *The fox was very good at lying and tricking others to get his own way.***)**

## ⊙ ⊸ Terrified

In the story, the fox told Flossie, "A little girl like you should be simply terrified of me." That means he thought Flossie should be very, very afraid of the fox. **Terrified.** Say the word. *Terrified.*

**Terrified** is a describing word. It tells more about someone. What kind of word is **terrified?** *A describing word.*

**When you are terrified, you are very, very afraid.** Say the word that means "very, very afraid." *Terrified.*

Let's think about some things that might cause people to feel terrified. I'll name something. If you would be terrified, say "terrified." If not, don't say anything.

- The thunder and lightning are very loud. *Terrified.*
- The forest fire was coming near the city. *Terrified.*
- Grandma comes to visit.
- The car is going very fast and it has no brakes. *Terrified.*
- A bluebird flies across the sky.
- There is lots of tasty food on the table.

What word means "very, very afraid"? *Terrified.*

What kinds of things terrify you? **(Call on several children. Encourage them to start their answers with** *I am terrified of (by) _____.***)**

## ⊙ ⊸ Horrible

In the story, when Flossie said she didn't believe the fox was really a fox, he said it was a horrible situation. The fox was using the word horrible to tell how bad it was that Flossie didn't believe him. **Horrible.** Say the word. *Horrible.*

**Horrible** is a describing word. It tells more about someone or something. What kind of word is **horrible?** *A describing word.*

**When you say something is horrible, you mean it is really, really bad.** Say the word that means "really, really bad." *Horrible.*

Let's think about some horrible things. I'll name something or someone. If you think it is horrible, say "horrible." If not, don't say anything.

- The taste of cooked bugs. *Horrible.*
- A friend who pushes you down in the mud. *Horrible.*
- From now on, you have to come to school on Saturday and Sunday too. *Horrible.*
- It rained so much that there was a flood. *Horrible.*
- Your best friend.
- The most beautiful place in the world to live.

What word describes something or someone that is "really, really bad"? *Horrible.*

What are some things that are **horrible** to you? **(Call on several children. Encourage them to start their answers with** *Something that I think is horrible is _____.***)**

## Present Vocabulary Tally Sheet

(See Lesson 1, page 4, for instructions.)

## Assign Homework

(Homework Sheet, BLM 4a. See the Introduction for homework instructions.)

### DAY 2

**Preparation:** Picture Vocabulary
Cards for *sly, rascal, terrified, horrible.*

### Read and Discuss Story

(Read story to children. Ask the following questions at the specified points. Encourage children to use target words in their answers.)

**Page 1.** A smokehouse is a small shack where people used to smoke meat like ham. A chicken coop is a small building where chickens are kept. A smokehouse and a chicken coop are found in a farmyard. Where are a smokehouse and a chicken coop found? *In a farmyard.* What was the little girl's name? *Flossie Finley.* Who was calling her? *Her grandmother.*

**Page 4.** What did Flossie call her grandmother? *Big Mama.* Where does this story happen? *In Tennessee.* When does this story happen? *In August.* What did Big Mama ask Flossie to do? *Take a basket of eggs to Miz Viola.*

**Page 6.** Big Mama told Flossie, "Don't tarry now, and be particular 'bout those eggs." That means she wants Flossie to hurry to Miz Viola's, and to be careful not to break the eggs. Why did Flossie go through the woods to get to Miz Viola's house? (Ideas: *It was shorter and cooler than walking along the road.*) Has Flossie ever seen a fox? *No.* Do you think Flossie is worried about the fox? *No.* Why not?

**Page 8.** What do you think the fox wants? *The eggs.*

**Page 9.** How did the fox feel when Flossie said she didn't believe he was a fox? (Idea: *At first he was angry.*)

**Page 11.** Why wasn't Flossie afraid of the fox? (Ideas: *She wasn't sure he was a fox.*) What did

the fox have to do before Flossie would be afraid of him? (Idea: *He had to prove he was a fox.*)

**Page 14.** What did the fox do first to try to prove he was a fox? (Idea: *He let her feel his fur.*) What did Flossie say after she had touched his fur? (Idea: *She thought his fur felt like rabbit fur, so he must be a rabbit.*) How did the fox feel when Flossie said he was a rabbit? (Idea: *Angry.*) Was Flossie afraid of him? *No.* How do you know? (Ideas: *She tapped her foot; she put her hands on her hips; she told the fox she wouldn't accord him anything, and she skipped away.*)

**Page 16.** What did the fox do next to try to prove he was a fox? (Idea: *He told her he had a long pointed nose.*) What did Flossie say about that? (Idea: *Rats have long pointed noses, so he must be a rat.*) How did the fox feel when Flossie said he was a rat? (Idea: *Even angrier.*) Was Flossie afraid of him? *No.* How do you know? (Ideas: *She skipped on down the road.*)

**Page 19.** What did the fox do next to try to prove he was a fox? (Idea: *He told the cat to tell Flossie he was a fox.*) What did the cat say? *"This is a fox because he has sharp claws and yellow eyes."* What did Flossie say about that? (Idea: *Cats have sharp claws and yellow eyes, so he must be a cat.*) How did the fox feel when Flossie said he was a cat? (Idea: *Even angrier; furious.*) Was Flossie afraid of him? *No.* How do you know? (Ideas: *She told him not to use that kind of language, and she skipped away.*)

**Page 22.** What did the fox do next to try to prove he was a fox? (Idea: *He told her he had a bushy tail.*) What did Flossie say about that? (Idea: *Squirrels have bushy tails.*) How did the fox feel? (Idea: *So mad that he started to cry.*)

**Page 24.** What did the fox ask for? (Idea: *One last chance.*)

**Page 25.** What did the fox do next to try to prove he was a fox? (Idea: *He told her he had sharp teeth and he could run fast.*) What did Flossie say about that? (Idea: *She said Mr. McCutchin's hounds had sharp teeth and could run fast.*)

**Page 28.** Why wasn't the fox afraid of Mr. McCutchin's dogs? (Idea: *He could outsmart and outrun them, because he was a fox.*)

**Page 29.** Do you think Flossie knew the fox was really a fox? *Yes.* Why do you think so? (Idea: *She said, "I know, I know."*) Who was really the sly one in this story? (Idea: *Flossie.*)

## Review Vocabulary

(Display the Picture Vocabulary Cards. Point to each card as you say the word. Ask children to repeat each word after you.) These pictures show **sly, rascal, terrified,** and **horrible.**

- What word means "very good at tricking others"? *Sly.*
- What word means "very, very afraid"? *Terrified.*
- What word means "really, really bad"? *Horrible.*
- What word means "someone who would lie and trick to get his or her own way"? *Rascal.*

## Extend Vocabulary

 Rascal

In *Flossie & the Fox,* we learned that **rascal** is a naming word that means "someone who would lie and trick to get their own way."

Raise your hand if you can tell us a sentence that uses **rascal** as a naming word meaning "someone who would lie and trick to get his or her own way." (Call on several children. If they don't use complete sentences, restate their examples as sentences. Have the class repeat the sentences.)

Here's a new way to use the word **rascal.**

- My little brother is such a **rascal.** Say the sentence.
- The child who took the last of the grapes was a **rascal.** Say the sentence.
- That little **rascal** ate three cookies! Say the sentence.

**In these sentences, rascal is a naming word that means a young child who is poorly behaved.** What word means "a young child who is poorly behaved"? *Rascal.*

Raise your hand if you can tell us a sentence that uses **rascal** as naming word meaning "a young child who is poorly behaved." (Call on several children. If they don't use complete sentences, restate their examples as sentences. Have the class repeat the sentences.)

## Present Expanded Target Vocabulary

Clever

I think Flossie knew the fox was after her eggs. She quickly figured out a plan to stop the fox from getting the eggs. Someone who can understand things quickly and is good at making plans is clever. **Clever.** Say the word. *Clever.*

**Clever** is a describing word. It tells more about someone. What kind of word is **clever?** *A describing word.*

**If you are clever, you understand things quickly and you are good at making plans.** Say the word that means "understands things quickly and is good at making plans." *Clever.*

Let's think about when people might be clever. If I say a time when someone would be clever, say "clever." If not, don't say anything.

- Kerri figured out how to fix the brakes on her bike with a piece of tape. *Clever.*
- Deborah figured out how to stop the boys' fighting in just a second. *Clever.*
- The cat figured out how to get food from the cupboard before I could even turn around. *Clever.*
- The boys stood around while the water fountain overflowed onto the floor.
- The cookie jar was right where we could reach it.
- It didn't take long before David thought of a way to get the kitten out of the tree. *Clever.*

What word means "understands things quickly and is good at making plans"? *Clever.*

Name someone you know who is clever. Explain why that person is clever.

Frustrated

In the story, each time the fox made a new plan to prove he was a fox, his plan didn't work. The fox became more and more upset and angry. The fox was frustrated. **Frustrated.** Say the word. *Frustrated.*

**Frustrated** is a describing word. It tells more about someone. What kind of word is **frustrated?** *A describing word.*

**If someone is frustrated, they become upset and angry because, no matter how hard they try, they can't do something.** Say the word that means "upset and angry because, no matter how hard you try, you can't do something." *Frustrated.*

Let's think about times when someone might be frustrated. If I tell about a time when someone could be frustrated, say "frustrated." If not, don't say anything.

- I couldn't figure out how to do my homework no matter how hard I tried. *Frustrated.*
- Karen couldn't find her snack even though she knew she'd brought it to school. *Frustrated.*
- Jason finished all of his work and went to play with the others.
- Paige put her glasses down somewhere and was having trouble finding them. *Frustrated.*
- There wasn't any cereal in the cupboard like Grandma said there was. Barbie looked and looked over and over again. *Frustrated.*
- Everything was going just perfectly.

What word means "upset and angry because, no matter how hard you try, you can't do something"? *Frustrated.*

Tell about a time when you were frustrated. (Call on several children. Encourage children to start their answers with *I was frustrated when …*)

---

### DAY 3

**Preparation:** Prepare two sheets of chart paper, each with a circle drawn in the middle. Fold the sheets of paper in half vertically to divide the circle in half. When you record children's responses, physical descriptors should be recorded on the left-hand side of each chart. Personality characteristics or actions should be recorded on the right-hand side of each chart.

Each child will need a copy of the Activity Sheet, BLM 4b.

---

### Analyze Characters (Literary Analysis)

Today we will learn about the characters in a story. The characters in a story are the people or animals the story is about. What do we call the people or animals a story is about? *The*

*characters.* Who are the characters in a story? *The people or animals the story is about.*

In *Flossie & the Fox,* are the characters people or animals? (Ideas: *Flossie is a person; the fox is an animal.*)

Who are the characters in the story? (Ideas: *Flossie; the fox; Big Mama; the cat; the squirrel; the dog.*)

The most important characters in *Flossie & the Fox* are Flossie and the fox. Who are the most important characters in the story? *Flossie and the fox.* (Write *Flossie* in the circle on one of the sheets of chart paper; write *fox* in the circle on the other sheet.)

Let's remember what we know about Flossie. (Show page 3.) What does Flossie look like? (Call on several children. Record each child's response on the left-hand side of the *Flossie* chart. Ideas: *Girl; dark skin; black hair; yellow dress; white apron; black stockings; black boots.*)

(Show page 3.) Call on several children. Record each child's response on the right-hand side of the chart.) Do you think Flossie is happy or sad? (Idea: *Happy.*) Tell why you think that. (Idea: *She's smiling.*)

(Show pages 5–6.) Flossie paid attention to what her grandmother needed or wanted. People who pay attention to what other people need or want are called considerate. Say the word that means Flossie paid attention to what her grandmother needed or wanted. *Considerate.*

(Show page 29.) Flossie was able to make a plan to stop the fox from getting the eggs. We learned a new word that means someone can understand things quickly and is good at making plans. What word could we use to tell about Flossie? *Clever.*

(Follow a similar process to describe the fox. Record responses on the second piece of chart paper.)

Today you have learned about Flossie and the fox. They are the most important characters in *Flossie & the Fox.*

## Play Whoopsy!

Today you'll play a new game called *Whoopsy!* I'll say sentences using words we have learned. If the word doesn't fit in the sentence, say *Whoopsy!* Then I'll ask you to say a sentence where the word fits. If you can do it, you get a point. If you can't do it, I get the point. If the word I use fits the sentence, don't say anything.

Let's practice.

I was **frustrated** when … I could easily do my homework. *Whoopsy!*

Listen to the beginning of the sentence again. I was **frustrated** when. Say the beginning of the sentence. *I was frustrated when.*

Can you finish the sentence so the word fits? (Idea: *I was frustrated when I had trouble doing my homework.*)

Let's try another one. The wolf was **sly** when … he couldn't think of a way to trick the three little pigs. *Whoopsy!*

Listen to the beginning of the sentence again. The wolf was **sly** when. Say the beginning of the sentence. *The wolf was sly when.* Can you finish the sentence so the word fits? (Idea: *The wolf was sly when he thought of a way to trick the three little pigs.*)

Now you're ready to play the game. (Draw a T-chart on the board for keeping score. Children earn one point for each correct answer. If they make an error, correct them as you normally would, and record one point for yourself. Repeat missed words at the end of the game. Display the word cards for the two words in each sentence as you say the sentence.)

- Mrs. Winston was **terrified** by … the beautiful, sunny day. *Whoopsy!* Say the beginning of the sentence again. *Mrs. Winston was terrified by.* Can you finish the sentence? (Idea: *Mrs. Winston was terrified by the thunder and lightning.*
- It was **horrible** when … all my friends could come to my party. *Whoopsy!* Say the beginning of the sentence again. *It was horrible when.* Can you finish the sentence? (Idea: *It was horrible when none of my friends could come to my party.*)

- You are a **rascal** if … you lie and trick to get your own way.
- The **clever** boy … took a long time to understand things. *Whoopsy!* Say the beginning of the sentence again. *The clever boy.* Can you finish the sentence? (Idea: *The clever boy understood things quickly.*)
- My brother is a **rascal** because … he never lies and tricks to get his own way. *Whoopsy!* Say the beginning of the sentence again. *My brother is rascal because.* Can you finish the sentence? (Idea: *My brother is a rascal because he lies and tricks to get his own way.*)

(Count the points and declare a winner.) You did a great job of playing *Whoopsy!*

## Complete the Activity Sheet

(Give each child a copy of the Activity Sheet, BLM 4b. Review with children the facts the fox gave to try to prove he was a fox.) What did the fox do first to try to prove he was a fox? (Idea: *He let Flossie feel his fur.*) What did Flossie say after she had touched his fur? (Ideas: *She thought his fur felt like rabbit fur; she thought he was a rabbit.* Repeat procedure for remaining ideas: *pointed nose; sharp claws and yellow eyes; bushy tail; sharp teeth.*)

(Have children complete the sentences, and color the illustration of Flossie and the fox.)

### DAY 4

## Learn About Folk Tales

Today you will learn about folk tales. What will you learn about? *Folk tales.*

A tale is another word for a story. What is a tale? *A story.* Folk are people who come from the same country and live the same kind of life. What are people who come from the same country and live the same kind of life? *Folk.* So a folk tale is a story told by people who come from the same country and live the same kind of life. What do you call a story told by people who come from the same country and live the same kind of life? *A folk tale.*

Long, long ago, most ordinary people in the world didn't know how to read. Could most ordinary people read? *No.* When people gathered together, they told stories to entertain themselves. How did people entertain themselves? *They told stories.*

Sometimes when parents told these stories to their children, they were trying to teach their children important things they needed to know. When parents told these stories to their children, what were they trying to teach them? (Idea: *Important things they needed to know.*)

*Flossie & the Fox* is a folk tale. What kind of story is *Flossie & the Fox*? *A folk tale.*

What group of people do you think told this story? (Idea: *African-Americans; African-Americans from the southern United States.*) What did you notice about the way Flossie and Big Mama speak to each other? (Ideas: *They have accents; they use slang.*)

(**Note:** You may wish to identify some examples of the rich regional dialect included in this story.)

Raise your hand if you enjoyed *Flossie & the Fox.* (Pause.) Most of you enjoyed the story. That means you were entertained by the story.

When parents told this tale to their children, what do you think they were trying to teach them? (Ideas: *If you're in trouble, use your brains to help you; you might not be able to outrun your enemy, but you might be able to outsmart them.*)

### Play Whoopsy!
### (Cumulative Review)

Let's play *Whoopsy!* I'll say sentences using words we have learned. If the word doesn't fit in the sentence, say "Whoopsy!" Then I'll ask you to say a sentence where the word fits. If you can do it, you get a point. If you can't do it, I get the point. If the word I use fits the sentence, don't say anything.

Now you're ready to play the game. (Draw a T-chart on the board for keeping score. Children earn one point for each correct answer. If they make an error, correct them as you normally would, and record one point for yourself. Repeat missed words at the end of the game.)

- Your mother was **clever** when … she couldn't figure out how to fix her car. *Whoopsy!* Say the beginning of the sentence again. *Your mother was clever when.* Can you finish the sentence? (Idea: *Your mother was clever when she quickly figured out how to fix her car.*)
- I was **frustrated** when … I couldn't get my jacket zipper to work no matter how hard I tried.
- Eric was **terrified** when … he slept peacefully through the night. *Whoopsy!* Say the beginning of the sentence again. *Eric was terrified when.* Can you finish the sentence? (Idea: *Eric was terrified when he had nightmares.*)
- Arlene was **sly** when … she held out her chocolate bar so everyone could see it. *Whoopsy!* Say the beginning of the sentence again. *Arlene was sly when.* Can you finish the sentence? (Idea: *Arlene was sly when she hid her chocolate bar behind her back so no one could see it.*)
- Pete was a **rascal** when … he kept running up and snatching the book David was reading.
- The **horrible** smell made Keema … want to come closer. *Whoopsy!* Say the beginning of the sentence again. *The horrible smell made Keema.* Can you finish the sentence? (Idea: *The horrible smell made Keema want to run away.*)
- J.D. **complained** when … his toe felt just fine. *Whoopsy!* Say the beginning of the sentence again. *J.D. complained when.* Can you finish the sentence? (Idea: *J.D. complained when he stubbed his toe.*)
- Stacey made a **decision** when … she thought about it and couldn't make up her mind about what to do. *Whoopsy!* Say the beginning of the sentence again. *Stacey made a decision when.* Can you finish the sentence? (Idea: *Stacey made a decision when she thought about it and made up her mind about what to do.*)
- Lori's mother called her a **rascal** when … she lied and cheated to get her own way.

(Count the points and declare a winner.)
You did a great job of playing *Whoopsy!*

## Retell Story

Today I'll show you the pictures Rachel Isadora made for *Flossie & the Fox.* As I show you the pictures, I'll call on one of you to tell the class that part of the story.

Tell me what happens at the **beginning** of the story. (Show the pictures on pages 1–6. Call on a child to tell what's happening.)

Tell me what happens in the **middle** of the story. (Show the pictures on pages 7–26. Call on a child to tell what's happening. Encourage use of target words when appropriate. Model use as necessary.)

Tell me what happens at the **end** of the story. (Show the pictures on pages 27–29. Call on a child to tell what's happening.)

How do you think Flossie felt at the end of the story?

How do you think the fox felt at the end of the story?

## Assess Vocabulary

 (Give each child a copy of the Quiz Answer Sheet, BLM B.)

Today you're going to have a True or False quiz. When you do the True or False quiz, it shows me how well you know the hard words you are learning.

If I say something that is true, circle the word **true.** What will you do if I say something that is true? *Circle the word true.*

If I say something that is false, circle the word **false.** What will you do if I say something that is false? *Circle the word false.*

Listen carefully to each item that I say. Don't let me trick you!

Item 1: Characters in stories who lie and trick other characters are called **rascals.** (*True.*)

Item 2: If you couldn't get your dog to come, even though you tried and tried, you would feel **clever.** (*False.*)

Item 3: A child who tried and tried to learn to ride a bicycle but couldn't do it would not feel **frustrated.** (*False.*)

Item 4: If you are not scared of something, you are feeling **terrified.** (*False.*)

Item 5: Something that happens that is really, really bad is **horrible.** (*True.*)

Item 6: A **sly** fox is one who is very good at tricking others. (*True.*)

Item 7: If you **concentrated** on the TV show you were watching, you probably didn't notice your dad come home from work. (*True.*)

Item 8: A young child who is poorly behaved might be called a **rascal.** (*True.*)

Item 9: If you are **amazed** by something, you are not very surprised by that thing. (*False.*)

Item 10: **Untidy** and messy mean the same thing. (*True.*)

You did a great job completing your quiz!

(Score children's work. A child must score 9 out of 10 to be at the mastery level. If a child does not achieve mastery, insert the missed words as additional items in the games in next week's lessons. Retest those children individually for the missed items before they take the next mastery test.)

## Extensions

### Read a Story as a Reward

(Display copies of the books that you have read since the beginning of the program, as well as a variety of folk tales. Allow children to choose which book they would like you to read to them as a reward for their hard work.)

(Read the story aloud for enjoyment with minimal interruptions.)

### Introduce the Super Words Center

(Put the Picture Vocabulary Cards from weeks 1 and 4 into the word cans. Make duplicates of each card to create a "Concentration" game. You may make as many sets of duplicates as you wish to suit your class. Show children one of the word containers. Demonstrate how the game is played by role-playing with a child. Repeat the demonstration process until children can play the game with confidence.)

Let's think about how we work with our words in the Super Words Center.

This week's activity is called *Concentration.* What's the name of this week's activity? *Concentration.*

You will work with a partner in the Super Words Center. Whom will you work with? *A partner.*

There are two cards for each word in the Super Words Center. When you play *Concentration,* you try to find two cards that match. Match means that both cards show the same picture and word. What does match mean? *Both cards show the same picture and word.*

First you will take all of the cards out of the container and place them facedown on the table. What do you do first? (Idea: *Take all of the words out and place them facedown on the table.*)

Next you will pick one card, place it faceup where you found it, and ask your partner what word the picture shows. What do you do next? (Idea: *I pick a card, place it faceup where I found it, and ask what word the picture shows.*)

What do you do if your partner doesn't know the word? *Tell my partner the word.*

Next you will give your partner a turn. What do you do next? *Give my partner a turn.*

If your partner chooses a card that is the same as your first card, he or she can take those two cards. What can your partner do? (Idea: *He or she can take both cards if he or she chooses one that is the same as my first card.*)

If your partner doesn't find one that is the same, he or she leaves his or her card faceup in the same place where they picked it up. Then it is your turn again. Whoever has the most pairs of cards when all of the cards have been taken is the winner.

(There are many ways to play *Concentration.* This is one that is fast to play. You may choose to modify the game depending on children's skill level.)

## It Couldn't Be Worse!

author: Vlasta van Kampen • illustrator: Vlasta van Kampen

**Preparation:** You will need a copy of *It Couldn't Be Worse!* for each day's lesson.

Number the pages of the story to assist you in asking comprehension questions at appropriate points.

Post a copy of the Vocabulary Tally Sheet, BLM A, with this week's Picture Vocabulary Cards attached.

Each child will need one copy of the Homework Sheet, BLM 5a.

### Target Vocabulary

| Tier II | Tier III |
|---------|----------|
| frazzled | character |
| advice | folk tale |
| quarrel | illustration |
| situation | |
| *gullible | |
| *ridiculous | |

*Expanded Target Vocabulary Word

### DAY 1

#### Introduce Book

This week's book is called *It Couldn't Be Worse!* What's the title of this week's book? *It Couldn't Be Worse!*

This book was written by Vlasta van Kampen. Who's the author of *It Couldn't Be Worse! Vlasta van Kampen.*

Vlasta van Kampen also made the pictures for this book. Who's the illustrator of *It Couldn't Be Worse! Vlasta van Kampen.* The pictures an illustrator makes for a book are called the illustrations. What do you call the pictures an illustrator makes for a book? *Illustrations.* What are illustrations? *The pictures an illustrator makes for a book.* Who made the illustrations for this book? *Vlasta van Kampen.*

The cover of a book usually gives us some hints of what the book is about. Let's look at the front cover of *It Couldn't Be Worse!* What do you see in the illustration? **(Ideas:** *Children inside a house with a sheep and a goat; adults outside the house with a pig; the adults seem to be trying to push the pig into the house; chickens and roosters are watching.***)**

When things are so bad they couldn't possibly get any worse, we say "it couldn't be worse!" What do we say when things are so bad they couldn't possibly get worse? *It couldn't be worse!*

Remember that when you make a prediction about something, you say what you think will happen.

Now get ready to make some predictions to your partner about this book. Use the information from the cover to help you.

(Assign each child a partner. Ask the following questions, allowing sufficient time for children to share their predictions with their partners.)

- Who are the characters in this story? (Who do you think this story is about?)
- What are the adults doing?
- Where do you think the story happens?
- When do you think the story happens?
- Why do you think the adults are pushing that pig?
- Do you think the pig wants to go into the house?
- Why do you think these people have animals in their house?
- Do you think this story is about real people and animals? Tell why or why not.

(Call on several children to share their predictions with the class.)

#### Take a Picture Walk

(Encourage children to use target words in their answers.) We're going to take a picture walk through this book. Remember that when we take a picture walk, we look at the pictures and tell what we think will happen in the story.

**Page 1.** Where does this part of the story happen? (Idea: *On a farm.*)

**Pages 2–3.** What is the woman doing in this illustration? (Idea: *Buying fish.*) A person who catches and sells fish is called a **fishmonger**. This man catches and sells fish. What do we call him? *A fishmonger.*

**Page 4.** What animals will we see in this story? (Ideas: *A goat; a sheep; a pig; a rooster; chickens; a cow.*) Whom do you think these animals belong to?

**Page 5, top.** Who do you think sails on this ship? (Idea: *The fishmonger; the fish seller.*)

**Page 5, bottom.** What do you think the woman is saying to the man in this illustration? Does he like what she is saying? *No.*

**Pages 6–7.** What are the man and his wife doing in this illustration? (Idea: *Pushing the goat into the house.*) Why do you think they want the goat in the house?

**Pages 8–9.** What are the people doing to the goat? (Idea: *Giving it a bath.*) This seems to be a pretty large family. How do you think the family will feel about having a goat living in the house?

**Pages 10–11.** What are the man and his wife bringing into the house now? (Idea: *The sheep.*) What else is happening in this illustration? (Ideas: *The pig and a rooster are rolling down the hill after a chicken in a cart; the other animals and family members are watching the man and his wife push the sheep into the house.*)

**Pages 12–13.** Do you think the goat and the sheep are enjoying living in the house with the family? *Yes.*

**Pages 14–15.** What are the man and his wife doing here? (Idea: *Trying to get the pig into the house.*) Why do you think the man and his wife are putting the animals in their house?

**Pages 16–17.** (Point to each character as you ask the questions.) There is a lot going on in the house now. What is the woman doing? (Idea: *Cooking.*) What is the pig doing? (Idea: *Walking on the fireplace.*) What is the goat doing? (Idea: *Juggling pots and pans.*) What is the man

doing? (Idea: *Giving his son a haircut.*) What is the sheep doing? (Idea: *Knitting.*) How do you think everyone in the house is feeling?

**Pages 18–19.** What is the family doing here? (Idea: *Trying to get the chickens into the house.*)

**Pages 20–21.** Have the chickens made things better or worse? *Worse.*

**Pages 22–23.** What are the man and his family doing here? (Idea: *Trying to get the cow into the house.*)

**Pages 24–25.** What is happening here?

**Pages 26–27.** What are the man and his wife doing in this illustration? (Idea: *Getting all of the animals out of the house.*)

**Pages 28–29.** The woman is talking to the fishmonger again. What do you think she is telling him?

**Page 30.** How do the children feel here? *Happy.* Why do you think they are so happy now? (Idea: *All of the animals are out of the house.*)

It's your turn to ask me some questions. What would you like to know about the story? (Accept questions. If children tell about the pictures or the story instead of ask questions, prompt them to ask a question.) Ask me a who question. Ask me a why question.

### Read the Story Aloud
(Read the story to children with minimal interruptions.)

Tomorrow we will read the story again, and I will ask you some questions.

(If children have difficulty attending for an extended period of time, you may wish to present the next part of this day's lesson at another time of day.)

### Present Target Vocabulary
 Frazzled

In the story, "the noise, the quarreling, and the fighting" frazzled the farmer's wife. That means she was very tired and stressed out. **Frazzled.** Say the word. *Frazzled.*

**Frazzled** is a describing word. It tells more about how someone feels. What kind of word is **frazzled?** *A describing word.*

**If you are frazzled, you are very tired and stressed out.** Say the word that means "very tired and stressed out." *Frazzled.*

(Correct any incorrect responses, and repeat the item at the end of the sequence.)

Let's think about some times when someone might be frazzled. I'll tell about a time. If you think someone would be frazzled, say "frazzled." If not, don't say anything.

- Your mom planned an outside party for twenty of your friends, but it rained so the party had to be in the house. *Frazzled.*
- Everyone was enjoying building a snowman on the first day it snowed.
- You've been looking for your shoes and your books for half an hour, you haven't had your breakfast yet, and the school bus is honking its horn outside your house. *Frazzled.*
- It's the end of an "inside day" at school and your teacher hasn't even had time for her lunch. *Frazzled.*
- It's been a perfect day at school; everybody worked hard and had a lot of fun.
- You are cuddling on the sofa with your dad while he reads you a story.

What word means "very tired and stressed out"? *Frazzled.*

## ◎━ Advice

In the story, the woman and her husband decided to follow the fishmonger's advice. That means they decided to follow the fishmonger's suggestion about what they should do. **Advice.** Say the word. *Advice.*

**Advice** is a naming word. It names an idea. What kind of word is **advice?** *A naming word.*

**If someone gives you advice, it means they make a suggestion about what you should do.** Say the word that means "a suggestion about what you should do." *Advice.*

Let's think about some times that you might give or get advice. I'll name a time. If you would get or give advice, say "advice." If not, don't say anything. *Advice.*

- You can't decide if you should go to your friend's house or play with your little brother. *Advice.*
- Your friend has asked you which pants she should wear with her yellow shirt. *Advice.*
- You have already decided to play at the park.
- You asked your parents if you should take music lessons or dancing lessons. *Advice.*
- Your father can't make a decision about if he should cook spaghetti or lasagna for dinner. *Advice.*
- Your mom has already decided to paint the living room yellow.

What word means "a suggestion about what you should do"? *Advice.*

## ◎━ Quarrel

In the story, "the poor farmer, his wife, their six children and the grandparents quarreled and fought and got in each other's way." That means they always argued and disagreed about what they should do. **Quarrel.** Say the word. *Quarrel.*

**Quarrel** is an action word. It tells what someone is doing. What kind of word is **quarrel?** *An action word.*

**If someone quarrels, they argue and disagree.** Say the word that means "argue and disagree." *Quarrel.*

Let's think about when people might quarrel. I'll say something. If what I say is quarreling, say "quarrel." If not, don't say anything.

- The two boys argued and disagreed about who was the best player on their baseball team. *Quarrel.*
- Lenore wanted to go to her friend's house after school, but her mother wanted her to come straight home after school. *Quarrel.*
- The twins always agreed on what they should do.
- John and Kelly figured out a way that they could both get what they wanted.
- My sister and I always argue and disagree about whose turn it is to do the dishes. *Quarrel.*
- Gloria and Pearl couldn't agree about who should sleep in the top bunk. *Quarrel.*

What word means "argue and disagree"? *Quarrel.*

 **Situation**

In the story, the farmer's wife told the old fishmonger about their unhappy situation. That means she told him about how things were going for her. **Situation.** Say the word. *Situation.*

**Situation** is a naming word. It names a thing. What kind of word is **situation?** *A naming word.*

**Your situation is how things are going for you.** Say the word that means "how things are going for you." *Situation.* When things are going well for you, you are in a **good situation.** What kind of situation are you in when things are going well for you? *A good situation.* When things are not going well for you, you are in a **bad situation.** What kind of situation are you in when things are not going well for you? *A bad situation.*

Let's think about some different kinds of situations. I'll tell about a situation. You tell me if the situation the person is in is a good situation or a bad situation.

- Ramon was ready for school before the bus came. *Good situation.*
- Brittany was rushing around trying to find her books and her coat when the bus came. *Bad situation.*
- Dominic knew all the words for his spelling test the day before the test. *Good situation.*
- Everyone was happy and content. *Good situation.*
- The whole family quarreled and disagreed about where they should go for their vacation. *Bad situation.*
- The children in our class all have their own desks and books. *Good situation.*

What word means "how things are going for you"? *Situation.*

### Present Vocabulary Tally Sheet
(See Lesson 1, page 4, for instructions.)

### Assign Homework
(Homework Sheet, BLM 5a. See the Introduction for homework instructions.)

**Preparation:** Picture Vocabulary Cards for *frazzled, advice, quarrel, situation.*

### Read and Discuss Story

 (Read story to children. Ask the following questions at the specified points. Encourage children to use target words in their answers.)

**Page 1.** Who lived in this one-room house? (Idea: *A farmer; his wife; their six children; and the grandparents.*) What problems did the family have? (Idea: *They quarreled and fought and got in each other's way.*)

**Page 2.** Why did the farmer's wife tell the fishmonger about her problems? (Idea: *He asked about her family.*) The farmer's wife said, "It couldn't be worse!" What couldn't be worse? (Idea: *Her family's situation.*)

**Page 4.** What did the fishmonger tell the farmer's wife to do to make things better? (Idea: *Bring the goat into the house.*)

**Page 5.** (Read to the end of the first paragraph.) How did the woman feel about the fishmonger's advice? *Dumbfounded.* The woman was **dumbfounded.** That means she thought the advice the fishmonger gave her was strange and confusing. What word shows that the woman thought the advice was strange and confusing? *Dumbfounded.* (Read to the end of the page.) What did the farmer think of the fishmonger's advice? (Ideas: *He couldn't believe it; he was dumbfounded too.*)

**Page 7.** Did the farmer and his wife follow the fishmonger's advice? *Yes.* Why? (Ideas: *They thought he was a wise man; they thought he was more clever than they were.*)

**Page 8.** Did bringing the goat into the house make things better? *No.*

**Page 10.** What was the fishmonger's advice this time? (Idea: *They should bring the sheep into the house.*) How did the woman feel after bringing the sheep into the house? (Idea: *Frazzled.*)

**Page 12.** Why did the farmer and his wife make the decision to follow the fishmonger's advice? (Idea: *They thought he was a wise man.*) What do you think the woman will tell the fishmonger?

**Page 12.** What did the woman tell the fishmonger? (Idea: *Things couldn't be worse.*)

**Page 14.** What did the fishmonger tell the woman to do to make things better? (Idea: *Bring the pig into the house.*) Why did the farmer and his wife follow the fishmonger's advice? (Ideas: *They thought he was a wise man; they thought that he was clever.*) What do you think the woman will tell the fishmonger? (Idea: *Things couldn't be worse!*)

**Page 16.** Did bringing the pig into the house make things better? *No.*

**Page 18.** What did the fishmonger tell the woman to do this time? (Idea: *Bring the rooster and chickens into the house.*) What do you think the woman will tell the fishmonger? (Idea: *Things couldn't be worse!*)

**Page 20.** The woman keeps telling the fishmonger that things couldn't be worse, yet they get worse each time she brings another animal into the house. How do you think things could get worse this time?

**Page 22.** What advice did the fishmonger give the woman this time? (Idea: *Bring the cow into the house.*) Why do you think the woman burst into tears when she went back to see the fishmonger?

**Page 24.** Did bringing the cow into the house make things better? *No.*

**Page 26.** What advice did the fishmonger give the woman this time? (Idea: *Get all of the animals out of the house.*) Do you think things will get better now?

**Page 28.** What did the woman tell the fishmonger? (Idea: *Things couldn't be better.*) Why were things so much better with the animals out of the house? (Idea: *There was no quarreling, no fighting, and room for everyone.*)

**Page 29.** Were things better or worse than before? *Better.*

**Page 30.** What do you think the fishmonger knew that made him so wise? (Ideas: *Things*

could always be worse; if he made things worse and then went back to where they had started, things wouldn't look so bad.*)

## Review Vocabulary

(Display the Picture Vocabulary Cards. Point to each card as you say the word. Ask children to repeat each word after you.) These pictures show **frazzled, advice, quarrel,** and **situation.**

- What word means "very tired and stressed out"? *Frazzled.*
- What word means "how things are going for you"? *Situation.*
- What word means "argue and disagree"? *Quarrel.*
- What word means "a suggestion about what you should do"? *Advice.*

## Extend Vocabulary

◎ Quarrel

In *It Couldn't Be Worse!* we learned that **quarrel** is an action word that means "argue and disagree." Say the word that means "argue and disagree." *Quarrel.*

Raise your hand if you can tell us a sentence that uses **quarrel** as an action word meaning "argue and disagree." (Call on several children. If they don't use complete sentences, restate their examples as sentences. Have the class repeat the sentences.)

Here's a new way to use the word **quarrel.**

- They had a **quarrel** about whose turn it was to walk the puppy. Say the sentence.
- After their **quarrel,** Bly and Tala wouldn't speak to each other. Say the sentence.
- The **quarrel** between Jason and Ahmed went on for two days. Say the sentence.

**In these sentences, quarrel is a naming word that means an angry argument or disagreement.** What word means "an angry argument or disagreement"? *Quarrel.*

Raise your hand if you can tell us a sentence that uses **quarrel** as a naming word meaning "an angry argument or disagreement." (Call on several children. If they don't use complete sentences, restate their examples as sentences. Have the class repeat the sentences.)

## Present Expanded Target Vocabulary

### ⊙← Gullible

In the story, the family kept taking more and more animals into their house so things would get better, even though their house was already full of people. They should have known things would only get worse, but they did it because the fishmonger told them to do it. They were gullible. **Gullible.** Say the word. *Gullible.*

**Gullible** is a describing word. It tells more about a person. What kind of word is **gullible?** *A describing word.*

**When someone is gullible, they believe anything anybody tells him or her. He or she is easily fooled.** Say the word that means "believe anything anybody tells you; easily fooled." *Gullible.*

I'll tell about some people. If these people believe anything anybody tells them and are easily fooled, say "gullible." If not, don't say anything.

- Mr. Jones always got fooled by the children's April Fool's jokes. *Gullible.*
- I told my friend I could jump higher than the school and he believed me. *Gullible.*
- When I told my brother I had a hundred dollars in my pocket, he just laughed.
- We couldn't fool the principal no matter how hard we tried.
- I told my dad there was a 20-foot tall green elephant behind him and he turned around to see it. *Gullible.*
- We liked to play tricks on our next-door neighbor because it was easy to trick him. *Gullible.*

What word means "believe anything anybody tells you; easily fooled"? *Gullible.*

### ⊙← Ridiculous

In the story, the farmer and his wife kept putting more and more animals in their house, even though the house was already full and far too noisy. That was a ridiculous thing to do. **Ridiculous.** Say the word. *Ridiculous.*

**Ridiculous** is a describing word. It tells more about something or someone. What kind of word is **ridiculous?** *A describing word.*

**Ridiculous means extremely silly or foolish.** Say the word that means "extremely silly or foolish." *Ridiculous.*

I'll tell about some people and some things. If what I tell about is ridiculous, say "ridiculous." If not, don't say anything.

- A hat with a ten-foot long feather. *Ridiculous.*
- A person who makes really silly faces and noises. *Ridiculous.*
- A person who always tries to do things the right way.
- A brown pair of pants.
- A coat that has bells, stars, and seaweed sewn on it. *Ridiculous.*
- A teacher who comes to school with her clothes on backwards and inside out. *Ridiculous.*

What word means "extremely silly or foolish"? *Ridiculous.*

---

### DAY 3

**Preparation:** Prepare two sheets of chart paper, each with a circle drawn in the middle. Fold the sheets of paper in half vertically to divide the circle in half. When you record the children's responses, physical descriptors should be recorded on the left-hand side of each chart. Personality characteristics or actions should be recorded on the right-hand side of each chart. Each child will need a copy of the Activity Sheet, BLM 5b.

## Analyze Characters (Literary Analysis)

Today we will learn more about the characters in a story. The characters in a story are the people or animals the story is about. What do we call the people or animals a story is about? *The characters.* Who are the characters in a story? *The people or animals the story is about.*

In *It Couldn't Be Worse!* are the characters people or animals? (Idea: *People.*)

(**Note:** If the children suggest the characters are both people and animals, remind them of the definition of characters, and explain that although there are animals in the story, the story is about the people.)

Who are the characters in the story? (Ideas: *The farmer's wife; the farmer; the fishmonger; the children; the grandparents.*)

The most important characters in *It Couldn't Be Worse!* are the farmer's wife and the fishmonger. Who are the most important characters in the story? *The farmer's wife and the fishmonger.* (Write the words *farmer's wife* in the circle on one of the sheets of chart paper; write *fishmonger* in the circle on the other sheet.)

Let's remember what we know about the farmer's wife. (Show page 3.) What does the farmer's wife look like? (Call on several children. Record each child's response on the left-hand side of the *farmer's wife* chart. Ideas: *Woman; dark brown hair; orange dress; there are patches on her dress; red kerchief; black and red striped under-dress; black boots; gray stockings.*)

Now let's think about what kind of person the farmer's wife is. I'll read you parts of the story; you tell me what kind of person she is. (Read page 2. "She told him of their unhappy situation; the noise, the quarreling, the fighting!") How was the farmer's wife feeling? (Idea: *Unhappy.* Record *unhappy* on the right-hand side of the chart.)

What made her feel unhappy? (Ideas: *The noise, the quarreling, the fighting.*) Does she like noise? *No.* (Record *doesn't like noise* on the right-hand side of the chart.) Does she like quarreling? *No.* (Record *doesn't like quarreling* on the right-hand side of the chart.) Does she like fighting? *No.* (Record *doesn't like fighting* on the right-hand side of the chart.)

(Show page 4.) ("The next day the frazzled woman hurried back to the fishmonger.") What word tells about the farmer's wife? *Frazzled.* (Record *frazzled* on the right-hand side of the chart.)

(Read page 14.) ("The next day the frustrated woman was back at the fishmonger's stall.") What word tells about the farmer's wife? *Frustrated.* (Record *frustrated* on the right-hand side of the chart.)

(Read page 18.) ("The next day the agitated woman arrived at the fishmonger's stall.") What word tells about the farmer's wife? *Agitated.* **Agitated** means "very nervous and upset." What does **agitated** mean? *Very nervous and upset.* What word means "very nervous and upset"? *Agitated.* (Record *agitated* on the right-hand side of the chart.)

(Read page 22.) ("The next day the desperate woman returned to the fishmonger.") What word tells about the farmer's wife? *Desperate.* If you are desperate, you are in such a bad situation you are willing to do anything to change it. How is the farmer's wife feeling? *Desperate.* (Record *desperate* on the right-hand side of the chart.)

The farmer's wife kept adding more and more animals to her house, even though it was making things worse. She believed what the fishmonger told her, and did what he said, even though it was ridiculous advice. What new word did we learn that would tell about the farmer's wife? *Gullible.* (Record *gullible* on the right-hand side of the chart.)

(Follow a similar process to describe the fishmonger. Record responses on the second piece of chart paper.)

Today you have learned about the farmer's wife and the fishmonger. They are the most important characters in *It Couldn't Be Worse!*

### Play Whoopsy!

Today, you'll play the game *Whoopsy!* I'll say sentences using words we have learned. If the word doesn't fit in the sentence, say "Whoopsy!" Then I'll ask you to say a sentence where the word fits. If you can do it, you get a point. If you can't do it, I get the point. If the word I use fits the sentence, don't say anything. Let's practice.

I was **frazzled** when … everything was quiet and calm. *Whoopsy!*

Listen to the beginning of the sentence again. I was frazzled when. Say the beginning of the sentence. *I was frazzled when.*

Can you finish the sentence so the word fits? (Idea: *I was frazzled when everything was noisy and confused.*)

Let's try another one. I followed my dad's advice when … I didn't do what he suggested. *Whoopsy!*

Listen to the beginning of the sentence again. I followed my dad's advice when. Say the beginning of the sentence. *I followed my dad's advice when.*

Can you finish the sentence so the word fits? (Idea: *I followed by dad's advice when I did what he suggested.*)

Now you're ready to play the game. (Draw a T-chart on the board for keeping score. Children earn one point for each correct answer. If they make an error, correct them as you normally would, and record one point for yourself. Repeat missed words at the end of the game.)

- Leah and Tomás quarreled when … they agreed to do the dishes together. *Whoopsy!* Say the beginning of the sentence again. *Leah and Tomás quarreled when.* Can you finish the sentence? (Idea: *Leah and Tomas quarreled when they couldn't decide who would wash and who would dry the dishes.*)
- It was a good situation when … Grandpa lost his car keys. *Whoopsy!* Say the beginning of the sentence again. *It was a good situation when.* Can you finish the sentence? (Idea: *It was a good situation when Grandpa found his car keys.*)
- You are gullible if … you believe everything anyone tells you.
- My big brother looked ridiculous when … he wore a shirt and tie. *Whoopsy!* Say the beginning of the sentence again. *My brother looked ridiculous when.* Can you finish the sentence? (Idea: *My big brother looked ridiculous when he wore a silly hat.*)
- There was a big quarrel when … everyone wanted to play the same game. *Whoopsy!* Say the beginning of the sentence again. *There was a big quarrel when.* Can you finish the sentence? (Idea: *There was a big quarrel when everyone wanted to play a different game.*)

(Count the points and declare a winner.) You did a great job of playing Whoopsy!

## Complete the Activity Sheet

(Give each child a copy of the Activity Sheet, BLM 5b. Review with children the different pieces of advice the fishmonger gave to the farmer's wife.) What did the fishmonger tell her to do first? (Idea: *Bring in the goat.*) What did the farmer's wife say after she did that? (Idea: *It couldn't be worse.* Repeat procedure for remaining pieces of advice: *bring in the sheep, the pig, the rooster, the chickens, and the cow; take all the animals out of the house.*)

(Have children complete the sentences, and draw and color their favorite character or animal from the story on the back of the paper.)

## DAY 4

## Learn About Folk Tales

Today you will learn more about folk tales. What will you learn about? *Folk tales.*

A tale is another word for a story. What is a tale? *A story.* Folk are people who come from the same country and live the same kind of life. What are people who come from the same country and live the same kind of life? *Folk.* So a folk tale is a story told by people who come from the same country and live the same kind of life. What is a story told by people who come from the same country and live the same kind of life? *A folk tale.*

Long, long ago, most ordinary people in the world didn't know how to read. Could most ordinary people read? *No.* When people gathered together, they told stories to entertain themselves. How did people entertain themselves? *They told stories.*

Sometimes when parents told these stories to their children, they were trying to teach their children important things they needed to know. When parents told these stories to their children, what were they trying to teach their children? (Idea: *Important things they needed to know.*)

*It Couldn't Be Worse!* is a folk tale. What kind of story is *It Couldn't Be Worse! A folk tale.*

The first group of people to tell this story were Jewish. What group of people first told this story? *Jewish people.* Sometimes when this story is written in Yiddish, the title is *It Could Always Be Worse!*

Raise your hand if you enjoyed *It Couldn't Be Worse!* (Pause.) Most of you enjoyed the story. That means you were entertained by the story.

When parents told this folk tale to their children, what do you think they were they trying to teach them? (Ideas: *Sometimes your situation isn't as bad as it seems; be thankful for what you have; don't follow ridiculous advice.*)

## Play Whoopsy! (Cumulative Review)

 Let's play *Whoopsy!* I'll say sentences using words we have learned. If the word doesn't fit in the sentence, say "Whoopsy!" Then I'll ask you to say a sentence where the word fits. If you can do it, you get a point. If you can't do it, I get the point. If the word I use fits the sentence, don't say anything.

Now you're ready to play the game. (Draw a T-chart on the board for keeping score. Children earn one point for each correct answer. If they make an error, correct them as you normally would, and record one point for yourself. Repeat missed words at the end of the game.)

- You **quarrel** with your friends when … you agree with them. *Whoopsy!* Say the beginning of the sentence again. *You quarrel with your friends when.* Can you finish the sentence? (Idea: *You quarrel with your friends when you don't agree with them.*)
- Emil felt **ridiculous** when … he went to the party on the right day. *Whoopsy!* Say the beginning of the sentence again. *Emil felt ridiculous when.* Can you finish the sentence? (Idea: *Emil felt ridiculous when he went to the party on the wrong day.*)
- It was a bad **situation** when … the highway was closed because the road was flooded.
- Sharon was **gullible** when … she believed Ryan had a dog for a pet. *Whoopsy!* Say the beginning of the sentence again. *Sharon was gullible when.* Can you finish the sentence? (Idea: *Sharon was gullible when she believed Ryan had a dinosaur for a pet.*)

- Mrs. Williams was **frazzled** when … the oven timer, the telephone, and the doorbell all rang at the same time.
- Mr. Yu gave Peter some **advice** when … he wouldn't tell him how to fix his TV. *Whoopsy!* Say the beginning of the sentence again. *Mr. Yu gave Peter some advice when.* Can you finish the sentence? (Idea: *Mr. Yu gave Peter some advice when he told him how to fix his TV.*)
- Samantha felt **proud** when … she didn't know any of her spelling words. *Whoopsy!* Say the beginning of the sentence again. *Samantha felt proud when.* Can you finish the sentence? (Idea: *Samantha felt proud when she knew all her spelling words.*)
- The children heard lots of **sounds** when … it was quiet. *Whoopsy!* Say the beginning of the sentence again. *The children heard lots of sounds when.* Can you finish the sentence? (Idea: *The children heard lots of sounds when it was noisy.*)
- Faiza followed the **recipe** when … she made her grandmother's baklava.

(Count the points and declare a winner.) You did a great job of playing *Whoopsy!*

---

### DAY 5

**Preparation:** Quiz Answer Sheet, BLM B.

## Retell Story

Today I'll show you the pictures Vlasta van Kampen made for *It Couldn't Be Worse!* As I show you the pictures, I'll call on one of you to tell the class that part of the story.

Tell me what happens at the **beginning** of the story. (Show the pictures on pages 1–3. Call on a child to tell what's happening.)

Tell me what happens in the **middle** of the story. (Show the pictures on pages 4–27. Call on a child to tell what's happening. Encourage use of target words when appropriate. Model use when necessary.)

Tell me what happens at the **end** of the story. (Show the pictures on pages 28–30. Call on a child to tell what's happening.)

Do you think the fishmonger really was wise? Tell why you think that. (Encourage children to use this frame for their answers: *I think the fishmonger was/was not wise because _____.*)

### Assess Vocabulary

 (Give each child a copy of the Quiz Answer Sheet, BLM B.)

Today you're going to have a True and False quiz. When you do the True and False quiz, it shows me how well you know the hard words you are learning.

If I say something that is true, circle the word **true**. What will you do if I say something that is true? *Circle the word true.*

If I say something that is false, circle the word **false.** What will you do if I say something that is false? *Circle the word false.*

Listen carefully to each item that I say. Don't let me trick you!

Item 1: If two people **quarreled,** they argued and disagreed with each other. (*True.*)

Item 2: If your homework wasn't done, you were late for school, and everything seemed to be going wrong for you, you might have felt **frazzled.** (*True.*)

Item 3: Your teacher is a person who you might go to if you needed **advice** on how to do your worksheet. (*True.*)

Item 4: Being **frustrated** is lots and lots of fun. (*False.*)

Item 5: If you are outside in the cold without a coat, gloves, or a hat, you are in a good **situation.** (*False.*)

Item 6: **Sly** people are good at tricking others. (*True.*)

Item 7: A **horrible** taste is a taste that is very, very bad. (*True.*)

Item 8: A **gullible** person is a person who is easy to fool. (*True.*)

Item 9: An idea that is **ridiculous** is a good one and should be tried. (*False.*)

Item 10: If two children are having a **quarrel** over who won the game, they both agree. (*False.*)

You did a great job completing your quiz!

(Score children's work. A child must score 9 out of 10 to be at the mastery level. If a child does not achieve mastery, insert the missed words as additional items in the games in next week's lessons. Retest those children individually for the missed items before they take the next mastery test.)

## Extensions

### Read a Story as a Reward

(Display copies of the books that you have read since the beginning of the program, as well as a variety of folk tales. Allow children to choose which book they would like you to read to them as a reward for their hard work.)

(Read the story aloud for enjoyment with minimal interruptions.)

---

**Preparation:** Word containers for the Super Words Center.

**Note:** You will need to keep the cards that are removed from the center. They will be used again later in the program.

---

### Introduce the Super Words Center

 (Put the Picture Vocabulary Cards from weeks 1 and 4 into the word cans. Make duplicates of each card to create a "Concentration" game. You may make as many sets of duplicates as you wish to suit your class. Show children one of the word containers. Demonstrate how the game is played by role-playing with a child. Repeat the demonstration process until children can play the game with confidence.)

Let's think about how we work with our words in the Super Words Center.

This week's activity is called *Concentration.* What's the name of this week's activity? *Concentration.*

You will work with a partner in the Super Words Center. Whom will you work with? *A partner.*

There are two cards for each word in the Super Words Center. When you play *Concentration,* you try to find two cards that match. Match means that both cards show the same picture and word. What does match mean? *Both cards show the same picture and word.*

First you will take all of the cards out of the container and place them facedown on the table. What do you do first? (Idea: *Take all of the words out and place them facedown on the table.*)

Next you will pick one card, place it faceup where you found it, and ask your partner what word the picture shows. What do you do next? (Idea: *I pick a card, place it faceup where I found it, and ask what word the picture shows.*)

What do you do if your partner doesn't know the word? *Tell my partner the word.*

Next you will give your partner a turn. What do you do next? *Give my partner a turn.*

If your partner chooses a card that is the same as your first card, he or she can take those two cards. What can your partner do? (Idea: *He or she can take both cards if he or she chooses one that is the same as my first card.*)

If your partner doesn't find one that is the same, he or she leaves his or her card faceup in the same place where they picked it up. Then it is your turn again. Whoever has the most pairs of cards when all of the cards have been taken is the winner.

(There are many ways to play *Concentration.* This is one that is fast to play. You may choose to modify the game depending on children's skill level.)

# Week 6

**Preparation:** You will need a copy of *The Tortoise and the Hare* for each day's lesson.

Number the pages of the story to assist you in asking comprehension questions at appropriate points.

Post a copy of the Vocabulary Tally Sheet, BLM A, with this week's Picture Vocabulary Cards attached.

Each child will need one copy of the Homework Sheet, BLM 6a.

## DAY 1

### Introduce Book

This week's book is called *The Tortoise and the Hare.* What's the title of this week's book? *The Tortoise and the Hare.*

This book was written by Janet Stevens. Who's the author of *The Tortoise and the Hare*? *Janet Stevens.*

Janet Stevens also made the pictures for this book. Who's the illustrator of *The Tortoise and the Hare*? *Janet Stevens.* What do you call the pictures an illustrator makes for a book? *Illustrations.* What are illustrations? *The pictures an illustrator makes for a book.* Who made the illustrations for this book? *Janet Stevens.*

The cover of a book usually gives us some hints of what the book is about. Let's look at the front cover of *The Tortoise and the Hare.* What do you see in the illustration? (Ideas: *A rabbit (hare) hopping ahead of a turtle (tortoise); they are each wearing a sign; there is a flag on the path; they seem to be in a race.*)

Get ready to make some predictions to your partner about this book. Use the information from the cover to help you.

(Assign each child a partner. Ask the following questions, allowing sufficient time for children to share their predictions with their partners.)

## The Tortoise and the Hare
author: Janet Stevens • illustrator: Janet Stevens

### Target Vocabulary

| Tier II | Tier III |
|---|---|
| rude | character |
| tease | folk tale |
| bolted | fable |
| perseverance | illustration |
| *reluctant | |
| *braggart | |

*Expanded Target Vocabulary Word

- Who are the characters in this story? (Who do you think this story is about?)
- What is the hare doing?
- What is the tortoise doing?
- Where do you think the story happens?
- When do you think the story happens?
- Why do you think the tortoise and the hare are racing?
- How fast do you think the hare is going? How fast do you think the tortoise is going?
- Do you think the characters in this story are real? Tell why or why not.

(Call on several children to share their predictions with the class.)

### Take a Picture Walk

(Encourage children to use target words in their answers.) We're going to take a picture walk through this book. Remember that when we take a picture walk, we look at the pictures and tell what we think will happen in the story.

**Pages 1–2.** Where are the tortoise and the hare? (Idea: *In the kitchen.*) What is the tortoise doing? (Ideas: *Eating breakfast; reading the paper.*) What do you think the hare is saying to the tortoise? Is this story about real animals or make-believe animals? *Make-believe animals.* How do you know?

**Page 3.** What is happening here? (Idea: *The hare is watching as the tortoise works in his garden.*)

**Page 4.** What do you think the hare is saying to the tortoise here?

**Page 5.** Do you think the tortoise is happy about what the hare said? *No.*

**Page 6.** What do you think Tortoise's friends are saying to him?

**Pages 7–8.** What is happening here? (Idea: *Tortoise is getting ready for something.*) It looks like Tortoise is training for some sort of sport. What is he doing to get ready? (Ideas: *Lifting weights; eating healthy foods; jogging.*) Look at the last picture. Do you think Tortoise feels ready? *Yes.*

**Pages 9–10.** What are Tortoise and Hare doing? (Idea: *Getting ready to race.*) How do you think Hare feels? (Ideas: *Confident; like he is going to win.*) How do you think Tortoise feels? (Ideas: *Worried; like he is going to lose.*)

**Pages 11–12.** At the start of the race, who is running faster? *Hare.*

**Pages 13–14.** Who is winning the race in this illustration? *Hare.* Do you think Tortoise is running very fast? *No.*

**Pages 15–16.** What is Hare doing in this illustration? (Idea: *Visiting with Bear.*) Why do you think Hare stopped to visit with Bear in the middle of his race? (Idea: *He was so far ahead of Tortoise he thought he had lots of time to stop for a visit.*) What do Hare and Bear see outside the window? *Tortoise.* How do you think Hare feels?

**Pages 17–18.** (Point to Tortoise at the top of page 17.) Here's Tortoise. Who's winning the race in this illustration? *Hare.* How do you think Hare feels? Hare is near Mouse's house now. What do you think he will do?

**Pages 19–20.** Where is Hare in this part of the story? (Idea: *In Mouse's house.*) Does he look worried about the race? *No.* What is Mouse looking at out the window? *Tortoise.*

**Pages 21–22.** What is Hare looking at? (Ideas: *Tortoise far behind him.*) What do you think Hare will do next?

**Pages 23–24.** What is happening here? (Idea: *Hare is taking a nap.*)

**Pages 25–26.** What has happened while Hare was napping? (Idea: *Tortoise has passed him.*) How do you think Hare feels?

**Pages 27–28.** Who has won the race? *Tortoise.* How do you think Tortoise feels about winning? (Ideas: *Happy; proud.*) How do you think Hare feels about Tortoise winning? (Ideas: *Angry; upset; disappointed.*)

**Page 29.** Why is everyone celebrating? (Idea: *Tortoise won the race.*)

It's your turn to ask me some questions. What would you like to know about the story? (Accept questions. If children tell about the pictures or story instead of ask questions, prompt them to ask a question.) Ask me a why question. Ask me a how question.

## Read the Story Aloud
(Read the story to children with minimal interruptions.)

Tomorrow we will read the story again, and I will ask you some questions.

## Present Target Vocabulary

= Rude

In the story, "Hare was flashy and rude." That means he did things that showed bad manners. He did things that were not polite. **Rude.** Say the word. *Rude.*

**Rude** is a describing word. It tells about a way of acting or talking. What kind of word is **rude?** *A describing word.*

**If you are rude, you do or say things that show bad manners. You do or say things that are not polite.** Say the word that means "do or say things that show bad manners; are not polite." *Rude.*

(Correct any incorrect responses, and repeat the item at the end of the sequence.)

Let's think about some times when someone might be rude. I'll tell about a time. If you think the person I'm telling about is rude, say "rude." If not, don't say anything.

- Zach kept interrupting the teacher when she was talking to the class. *Rude.*
- When it was Colleen's turn to listen, she talked instead. *Rude.*
- Vinnie stuck out his tongue and made a noise. *Rude.*
- Fern walked quietly so she wouldn't be heard.

- Faith forgot to say thank you when she got a present. *Rude.*
- Greg and his brother waited until the speaker finished his speech to ask a question.

What word means "do or say things that show bad manners; are not polite"? *Rude.*

## ⊙◄ Tease

In the story, "Hare liked to tease Tortoise about being so slow." That means Hare liked to make fun of Tortoise by saying unkind and hurtful things. When Tortoise ate breakfast, Hare said things like, "By the time you finish your last bite, it will be dinnertime." When Tortoise worked in his garden, Hare said things like "By the time you pick those spring flowers, it will be winter." **Tease.** Say the word. *Tease.*

**Tease** is an action word. It tells what someone does. What kind of word is **tease**? *An action word.*

**If you tease, it means you make fun of someone by saying unkind or hurtful things.** Say the word that means "make fun of someone by saying unkind or hurtful things." *Tease.*

Let's think about some times when someone might tease someone else. I'll tell about a time. If someone is teasing, say "tease." If not, don't say anything.

- The little boy cried when his brother called him a sissy. *Tease.*
- "You're just a 'fraidy cat," she said. *Tease.*
- The children were laughing and playing together on the swings.
- "C'mon, slowpoke, we can't wait all day for you." *Tease.*
- "Let me help you find your boots."
- "What's the matter with you? Even a kindergartner can tie his own shoes." *Tease.*

What word means "make fun of someone by saying unkind or hurtful things"? *Tease.*

## ⊙◄ Bolted

In the story, when the Raccoon sounded the gong, "Hare bolted out of sight before Tortoise had taken his first step." That means Hare ran away very quickly. **Bolted.** Say the word. *Bolted.*

**Bolted** is an action word. It tells what a person or animal did. What kind of word is **bolted**? *An action word.*

**If someone bolted, they ran away very quickly.** Say the word that means "ran away very quickly." *Bolted.*

Let's think about when a person or an animal might have bolted. I'll tell about a time. If someone might have bolted, say "bolted." If not, don't say anything.

- The scared rabbit ran away from the garden very quickly. *Bolted.*
- The cat moved slowly across the room.
- The dog ran after the cat very quickly. *Bolted.*
- When the lightning flashed, the horse ran away very quickly. *Bolted.*
- The tiger hid in the grass waiting for a deer to come by.
- The man ran across the sidewalk very quickly. *Bolted.*

What word means "ran away very quickly"? *Bolted.*

## ⊙◄ Perseverance

*The Tortoise and the Hare* ends with the words "Hard work and perseverance bring reward." That means if you work hard and never give up, you'll succeed. **Perseverance.** Say the word. *Perseverance.*

**Perseverance** is a naming word. It names an idea. What kind of word is **perseverance**? *A naming word.*

**Perseverance means keeping on trying and never giving up, even though it is very difficult.** Say the word that means "keeping on trying and never giving up, even though it is very difficult." *Perseverance.*

Let's think about some times when a person might show perseverance. I'll tell about a time. If someone is showing perseverance, say "perseverance." If not, don't say anything.

- It was very difficult for Ally to learn to ride her bike, but she kept on trying and never gave up. *Perseverance.*
- It took two weeks for Milo to learn his +3 facts, but he kept on trying and never gave up. *Perseverance.*

- Leeza thought the words on the spelling test were too hard, so she never even tried to learn them.
- Tomiko practiced the piano every day until she could play her piece perfectly. *Perseverance.*
- Mark learned to read very easily.
- Everyone kept practicing and practicing their lines for the school play. *Perseverance.*

What word means "keeping on trying and never giving up, even though it is very difficult"? *Perseverance.*

### Present Vocabulary Tally Sheet

(See Lesson 1, page 4, for instructions.)

### Assign Homework

(Homework Sheet, BLM 6a. See the Introduction for homework instructions.)

---

## DAY 2

**Preparation:** Picture Vocabulary Cards for *rude, tease, bolted, perseverance.*

### Read and Discuss Story

(Read story to children. Ask the following questions at the specified points. Encourage children to use target words in their answers.)

**Page 2.** How were Tortoise and Hare different? (Ideas: *Tortoise was friendly and quiet and did everything slowly; Hare was loud and rude and did everything quickly.*) Why did Hare tease Tortoise? (Idea: *Because Tortoise was so slow.*)

**Page 3.** How long did Hare say it would take Tortoise to pick his spring flowers? (Idea: *Until winter.*)

**Page 4.** What did Hare say about Tortoise going to the store? (Idea: *By the time he got there the store would be closed.*) How do you think Hare's teasing makes Tortoise feel?

**Page 5.** What does Hare want Tortoise to do? (Idea: *Race him.*) Does Tortoise think he could beat Hare in a race? *No.* What do Tortoise's friends think? (Idea: *He could beat Hare with a little help.*)

**Page 6.** Why did Tortoise finally agree to race Hare? (Idea: *He didn't want to disappoint his friends.*)

**Page 7.** How long did Tortoise have to get ready for the race? (Idea: *Two-and-a-half weeks.*) Who helped him at the gym? *Rooster.* Who cooked him healthy meals? *Raccoon.*

**Page 8.** Who jogged with Tortoise every morning? *Frog.* Was Tortoise ready for the race? *Yes.*

**Page 9.** How far were Tortoise and Hare racing? (Idea: *Six miles.*)

**Page 11.** Who was the crowd cheering for? (Idea: *Tortoise.*)

**Page 14.** Why did Hare decide to stop for a drink at Bear's house? (Idea: *Because he was so far ahead of Tortoise.*)

**Page 16.** What was Hare doing when Bear noticed Tortoise go past? (Idea: *Sipping lemonade.*) Do you think Hare expected Tortoise to catch up with him?

**Page 18.** What did Hare want to get at Mouse's house? (Idea: *A snack.*)

**Page 20.** Was Hare worried about Tortoise beating him in the race? *No.*

**Page 21.** How many times has Hare passed Tortoise? (Idea: *Three times.*) What does Hare want to do now? (Idea: *Have a rest.*)

**Page 23.** It says that as he closed his eyes, Hare dreamed of victory. What do you think that means? (Idea: *He dreamed of winning the race.*) When you have a victory that means that you win. What happens when you have a victory? *You win.*

**Page 26.** What woke Hare from his nap? (Idea: *The cheering of the crowd.*) How far from the finish line was Tortoise? (Idea: *Two steps.*) How do you think Hare felt when he saw Tortoise winning the race?

**Page 28.** Who won the race? *Tortoise.* How did Hare feel about that? (Ideas: *Angry; upset; he couldn't believe it; amazed.*)

**Page 29.** Tortoise learned a lesson: Hard work and perseverance bring reward. What do you think that means? (Idea: *If you work hard and keep working hard you will be successful.*)

## Review Vocabulary

(Display the Picture Vocabulary Cards. Point to each card as you say the word. Ask children to repeat each word after you.) These pictures show **rude, tease, bolted,** and **perseverance.**

- What word means "do or say things that show bad manners; are not polite"? *Rude.*
- What word means "make fun of someone by saying unkind or hurtful things"? *Tease.*
- What word means "keeping on trying and never giving up, even though it is very difficult"? *Perseverance.*
- What word means "ran away very quickly"? *Bolted.*

## Extend Vocabulary

 Bolted

In *The Tortoise and the Hare,* we learned that **bolted** is an action word that means "ran away very quickly." Say the word that means "ran away very quickly." *Bolted.*

Raise your hand if you can tell us a sentence that uses **bolted** as an action word meaning "ran away very quickly." (Call on several children. If they don't use complete sentences, restate their examples as sentences. Have the class repeat the sentences.)

Here's a new way to use the word **bolted.**

- They **bolted** their door before they went to bed. Say the sentence.
- He **bolted** his bicycle to the bicycle stand. Say the sentence.
- The mechanic **bolted** the new bumper to the frame of my dad's car. Say the sentence.

**In these sentences, bolted is an action word that means to close or attach with a bolt or something like a bolt.** What word means "to close or attach with a bolt or something like a bolt"? *Bolted.*

Raise your hand if you can tell us a sentence that uses **bolted** as an action word meaning "to close or attach with a bolt or something like a bolt." (Call on several children. If they don't use

complete sentences, restate their examples as sentences. Have the class repeat the sentences.)

## Present Expanded Target Vocabulary

Reluctant

In the story, Tortoise didn't want to race against Hare. He was sure that Hare would beat him and then would tease him even more. Another way of saying Tortoise didn't want to race against Hare is to say Tortoise was reluctant to race against Hare. **Reluctant.** Say the word. *Reluctant.*

**Reluctant** is a describing word. It tells more about a person. What kind of word is **reluctant**? *A describing word.*

**When someone is reluctant they don't want to do something.** Say the word that means "don't want to do something." *Reluctant.*

I'll tell about some people. If these people are reluctant, say "reluctant." If not, don't say anything.

- Amy didn't want to go into the dark house. *Reluctant.*
- David didn't want to sleep over at his aunt's house. *Reluctant.*
- Graham really wanted to go camping.
- Peter really didn't want to try the smoked salmon. *Reluctant.*
- Russell didn't want to go to bed. *Reluctant.*
- Suki really wanted to wear her kimono the first day of school.

What word means "don't want to do something"? *Reluctant.*

Braggart

In the story, Hare was always bragging about what a fast runner he was. Hare was a braggart. **Braggart.** Say the word. *Braggart.*

**Braggart** is a naming word. It names a person. What kind of word is **braggart**? *A naming word.*

**A braggart is a person who is always bragging and telling everyone how good he or she is.** Say the word that means "a person who is always bragging and telling everyone how good he or she is." *Braggart.*

I'll tell what some people might say. If this person is a braggart, say "braggart." If not, don't say anything.

- I'm the best swimmer in the world. *Braggart.*
- I can run faster than anyone in this school. *Braggart.*
- I won the three-legged race.
- I like to play sports.
- I'm as good a painter as Picasso. *Braggart.*
- My favorite sport is gymnastics.

What word means "a person who is always bragging and telling everyone how good he or she is"? *Braggart.*

## DAY 3

**Preparation:** Prepare two sheets of chart paper, each with a circle drawn in the middle. Fold the sheets of paper in half vertically to divide the circle in half. When you record children's responses, physical descriptors should be recorded on the left-hand side of each chart. Personality characteristics or actions should be recorded on the right-hand side. Each child will need a copy of the Activity Sheet, BLM 6b.

### Analyze Characters (Literary Analysis)

Today we will learn more about the characters in a story. What do we call the people or animals a story is about? *The characters.* Who are the characters in a story? *The people or animals the story is about.*

In *The Tortoise and the Hare,* are the characters people or animals? (Idea: *Animals.*)

Who are the characters in the story? (Ideas: *Tortoise; Hare; Rooster; Raccoon; Frog; Bear; Mouse.*)

The most important characters in *The Tortoise and the Hare* are Tortoise and Hare. Who are the most important characters in the story? *Tortoise and Hare.* (Write the word *Tortoise* in the circle on one of the sheets of chart paper; write *Hare* in the circle on the other sheet.)

Let's remember what we know about Tortoise. (Show page 1.) What does Tortoise look like? (Record each child's response on the left-hand

side of the Tortoise chart. Ideas: *Green; looks like a turtle; has a shell; his neck is orange; his underside is orange; his arms and legs look scaly; he has claws; he wears pink mouse slippers.*)

(**Note:** As you show pictures to help children identify what Tortoise is like, they may add other details to Tortoise's appearance. Ideas: *He wears a garden hat; garden gloves; he has red sandals; he has a wristwatch; he has blue and white running shoes.*)

(Show page 1.) (Record each child's response on the right-hand side of the chart.) What does this illustration tell you about Tortoise? (Ideas: *He eats healthy food; he likes cereal; he reads the newspaper.*)

Do you think Tortoise is feeling happy or sad? *Sad.* What has made Tortoise sad? (Idea: *Hare was teasing him.*) So what does that tell you about Tortoise? (Idea: *He doesn't like to be teased.*)

(Show page 3.) What does this illustration tell us about Tortoise? (Idea: *He likes to garden.*)

(Show page 6.) Tortoise didn't really want to race Hare. What word could we use to tell about Tortoise? *Reluctant.*

(Show pages 7–8.) Tortoise worked hard every day to get ready for the race. He went to the gym; he ate healthy meals; he went jogging every morning. Tortoise kept on trying and he never gave up. What word could we use to tell about Tortoise? *Perseverance.*

(Follow a similar process to describe Hare. Record responses on the second piece of chart paper.)

Today you have learned about Tortoise and Hare. They are the most important characters in *The Tortoise and the Hare.*

### Play Whoopsy!

Today, you'll play the game *Whoopsy!* I'll say sentences using words we have learned. If the word doesn't fit in the sentence, say "Whoopsy!" Then I'll ask you to say a sentence where the word fits. If you can do it, you get a point. If you can't do it, I get the point. If the word I use fits the sentence, don't say anything.

Let's practice.

Taylor was **reluctant** when … he wanted to go in the water at the lake. *Whoopsy!*
Listen to the beginning of the sentence again. Taylor was **reluctant** when. Say the beginning of the sentence. *Taylor was reluctant when.*
Can you finish the sentence so the word fits?
(Idea: *Taylor was reluctant when he didn't want to go in the water at the lake.*)

Let's try another one. The clerk in the store was **rude** when … she asked if she could help us. *Whoopsy!*
Listen to the beginning of the sentence again. The clerk in the store was **rude** when. Say the beginning of the sentence. *The clerk in the store was rude when.*
Can you finish the sentence so the word fits?
(Idea: *The clerk in the store was rude when talked to her friends instead of helping us.*)

Now you're ready to play the game.
(Draw a T-chart on the board for keeping score. Children earn one point for each correct answer. If they make an error, correct them as you normally would, and record one point for yourself. Repeat missed words at the end of the game.)

- People **tease** you when … they say nice things to you. *Whoopsy!* Say the beginning of the sentence again. *People tease you when.* Can you finish the sentence? (Idea: *People tease you when they say mean things to you.*)
- The dog **bolted** after the cat when … it never moved from the porch. *Whoopsy!* Say the beginning of the sentence again. *The dog bolted after the cat when.* Can you finish the sentence? (Idea: *The dog bolted after the cat when it chased it off the porch.*)
- Jerome was a **braggart** when … he said he was the fastest runner in the world.
- My sister **bolted** the door when … she left the door unlocked. *Whoopsy!* Say the beginning of the sentence again. *My sister bolted the door when.* Can you finish the sentence? (Idea: *My sister bolted the door when she put on the lock.*)

- Teresa showed **perseverance** when … she gave up after she got one wrong answer. *Whoopsy!* Say the beginning of the sentence again. *Teresa showed perseverance when.* Can you finish the sentence? (Idea: *Teresa showed perseverance when she refused to give up.*)

(Count the points and declare a winner.) You did a great job of playing *Whoopsy!*

### Complete the Activity Sheet

(Give each child a copy of the Activity Sheet, BLM 6b. Have children cut apart the words in the word bank. If children are unfamiliar with Venn diagrams, do this as a guided activity.)

Hare and Tortoise are different in some ways and the same in some ways. (Point to the circle under the word *Tortoise*.) This circle is where we'll put things that tell **only** about Tortoise.

(Point to the circle under the word *Hare*.) This circle is where we'll put things that tell **only** about Hare. (Point to the place where the two circles overlap.) This is where we'll put things that tell about **both** Tortoise and Hare.

(Either read for children or have them read the words in the word bank one at a time. After each word is read ask:) Does this tell about Tortoise or Hare, or both Tortoise and Hare?

(If children identify the character trait or activity as belonging to only Tortoise, have them paste or glue the word in the large circle under the word *Tortoise*.)

(If children identify the character trait or activity as belonging to only Hare, have them paste or glue the word in the large circle under the word *Hare*.)

(If children identify the character trait or activity as belonging to both Tortoise and Hare, have them paste or glue the word in the area where the two circles overlap. Repeat procedure for each item in the word bank.)

(Tortoise: friendly; quiet; did things slowly; won the race; trained for the race; reluctant. Hare: rude; flashy; braggart; did things quickly; stopped to visit Bear; lost the race. Both: talked; animal; went in a race; learned a lesson.)

## Learn About Folk Tales

Today you will learn more about folk tales. What will you learn about? *Folk tales.*

A tale is another word for a story. What is a tale? *A story.* Folk are people who come from the same country and live the same kind of life. What are people who come from the same country and live the same kind of life? *Folk.*

So a folk tale is a story told by people who come from the same country and live the same kind of life. What is a story told by people who come from the same country and live the same kind of life? *A folk tale.*

Long, long ago, most ordinary people in the world didn't know how to read. Could most ordinary people read? *No.* When people gathered together, they told stories to entertain themselves. How did people entertain themselves? *They told stories.*

Sometimes when parents told these stories to their children, they were trying to teach their children important things they needed to know. When parents told these stories to their children, what were they trying to teach them? **(Idea:** *Important things they needed to know.)*

*The Tortoise and the Hare* is a special kind of folk tale called a fable. What kind of story is *The Tortoise and the Hare? A fable.* A fable is a story that is told especially to teach children important lessons they need to learn. What do you call a story that is told especially to teach children important lessons they need to learn? *A fable.*

Many people think a man named Aesop told fables to the people in Greece more than 2,500 years ago. When do we think fables such as *The Tortoise and the Hare* were first told? *2,500 years ago.* Where do we think fables such as *The Tortoise and the Hare* were first told? *In the country of Greece.* (You may wish to show children where Greece is located on a world map or globe in relationship to the school.)

When parents told this tale to their children, what do you think they were trying to teach them? **(Ideas:** *Work hard and never give up; keep on trying, even if you think you can't do something.)*

## Play Whoopsy! (Cumulative Review)

Let's play *Whoopsy!* I'll say sentences using words we have learned. If the word doesn't fit in the sentence, say "Whoopsy!" Then I'll ask you to say a sentence where the word fits. If you can do it, you get a point. If you can't do it, I get the point. If the word I use fits the sentence, don't say anything.

Now you're ready to play the game. (Draw a T-chart on the board for keeping score. Children earn one point for each correct answer. If they make an error, correct them as you normally would, and record one point for yourself. Repeat missed words at the end of the game.)

- Zoe was **rude** when ... she said "please" and "thank you." *Whoopsy!* Say the beginning of the sentence again. *Zoe was rude when.* Can you finish the sentence? (Idea: *Zoe was rude when she didn't say "please" and "thank you."*)
- Sean was a **braggart** when ... he told everyone he didn't know how to do his school work. *Whoopsy!* Say the beginning of the sentence again. *Sean was a braggart when.* Can you finish the sentence? (Idea: *Sean was a braggart when he told everyone he was the smartest person in the class.*)
- Audrey showed **perseverance** when ... she kept on trying and never gave up.
- Lucas heard a **sound** when ... nobody moved. *Whoopsy!* Say the beginning of the sentence again. *Lucas heard a sound when.* Can you finish the sentence? (Idea: *Lucas heard a sound when somebody moved.*)
- Bryan was **reluctant** to play the piano when ... he said he wanted to perform in front of the class. *Whoopsy!* Say the beginning of the sentence again. *Bryan was reluctant to play the piano when.* Can you finish the sentence? (Idea: *Bryan was reluctant to play the piano when he said he didn't want to perform in front of the class.*)
- The fox **bolted** across the field when ... it saw the rabbit.
- Madeline **teased** Evelyn when ... she told her she liked her new haircut. *Whoopsy!* Say the

beginning of the sentence again. *Madeline teased Evelyn when.* Can you finish the sentence? (Idea: *Madeline teased Evelyn when she said her new haircut made her look like a boy.*)

- The children were **terrified** when ... Tia brought her tiny puppy in for show and tell. *Whoopsy!* Say the beginning of the sentence again. *The children were terrified when.* Can you finish the sentence? (Idea: *The children were terrified when Tia brought in a boa constrictor for show and tell.*

- Mr. Page **bolted** the shed when ... he turned the key in the lock.

(Count the points and declare a winner.) You did a great job of playing *Whoopsy!*

---

## DAY 5

•••••••••••••••••••••••••••••••••
**Preparation:** Each child will need a copy of the Quiz Answer Sheet, BLM B.
•••••••••••••••••••••••••••••••••

### Retell Story

Today, I'll show you the pictures Janet Stevens made for *The Tortoise and the Hare.* As I show you the pictures, I'll call on one of you to tell the class that part of the story.

Tell me what happens at the **beginning** of the story. (Show the pictures on pages 1–4. Call on a child to tell what's happening.)

Tell me what happens in the **middle** of the story. (Show the pictures on pages 5–26. Call on a child to tell what's happening. Encourage use of target words when appropriate. Model use when necessary.)

Tell me what happens at the **end** of the story. (Show the pictures on pages 27–29. Call on a child to tell what's happening.)

If Tortoise and Hare race again, do you think Hare will behave the same way? Tell why or why not.

The lesson that is taught in a fable is called the moral of the story. What is the lesson that is taught in a fable called? *The moral.* What is the moral of the story *The Tortoise and the Hare*? *Hard work and perseverance bring reward.*

And what does that mean? (Idea: *If you work hard and never give up, you will be able to do whatever you want to do.*)

### Assess Vocabulary

 (Give each child a copy of the Quiz Answer Sheet, BLM B.)

Today you're going to have a True or False quiz. When you do the True or False Quiz, it shows me how well you know the hard words you are learning.

If I say something that is true, circle the word **true.** What will you do if I say something that is true? *Circle the word true.*

If I say something that is false, circle the word **false.** What will you do if I say something that is false? *Circle the word false.*

Listen carefully to each item that I say. Don't let me trick you!

Item 1: If you say thank you when your grandma takes you to the movies, you are **rude.** (*False.*)

Item 2: If someone **teases** you, they hurt your feelings. (*True.*)

Item 3: If you kept falling off your bike when you were learning to ride it, but you kept getting back on and trying again, you showed **perseverance.** (*True.*)

Item 4: If you really want to try something new you are **reluctant.** (*False.*)

Item 5: A **braggart** says good things about everyone else, but not about herself. (*False.*)

Item 6: If you **bolted** the door, it would be easy for someone to open it. (*False.*)

Item 7: It is easy to wake up someone who is **sound** asleep. (*False.*)

Item 8: If the garbage was **disgusting,** it was so **horrible** that it made you sick. (*True.*)

Item 9: If you **bolted** into the school, you ran as fast as you could through the door. (*True.*)

Item 10: If your aunt were making apple pie, apples would be one of the **ingredients.** (*True.*)

You did a great job completing your quiz!

(Score children's work. A child must score 9 out of 10 to be at the mastery level. If a child does not achieve mastery, insert the missed words as additional items in the games in next week's lessons. Retest those children individually for the missed items before they take the next mastery test.)

# Extensions

## Read a Story as a Reward

(Display copies of the books that you have read since the beginning of the program, as well as a variety of fables. Allow children to choose which book they would like you to read to them as a reward for their hard work.)

(**Note:** If children are unfamiliar with the traditional folk tale *The Three Little Pigs,* you may wish to read this story to them in preparation for next week's lesson.)

(Read the story aloud for enjoyment with minimal interruptions.)

**Preparation:** Word containers for the Super Words Center.

**Note:** You will need to keep the cards that are removed from the center. They will be used again later in the program.

## Introduce the Super Words Center

(Put the Picture Vocabulary Cards from weeks 1 and 4 into the word cans. Make duplicates of each card to create a "Concentration" game. You may make as many sets of duplicates as you wish to suit your class. Show children one of the word containers. Demonstrate how the game is played by role-playing with a child. Repeat the demonstration process until children can play the game with confidence.)

Let's think about how we work with our words in the Super Words Center.

This week's activity is called *Concentration.* What's the name of this week's activity? *Concentration.*

You will work with a partner in the Super Words Center. Whom will you work with? *A partner.*

There are two cards for each word in the Super Words Center. When you play *Concentration,* you try to find two cards that match. Match means that both cards show the same picture and word. What does match mean? *Both cards show the same picture and word.*

First you will take all of the cards out of the container and place them facedown on the table. What do you do first? (Idea: *Take all of the words out and place them facedown on the table.*)

Next you will pick one card, place it faceup where you found it, and ask your partner what word the picture shows. What do you do next? (Idea: *I pick a card, place it faceup where I found it, and ask what word the picture shows.*)

What do you do if your partner doesn't know the word? *Tell my partner the word.*

Next you will give your partner a turn. What do you do next? *Give my partner a turn.*

If your partner chooses a card that is the same as your first card, he or she can take those two cards. What can your partner do? (Idea: *He or she can take both cards if he or she chooses one that is the same as my first card.*)

If your partner doesn't find one that is the same, he or she leaves his or her card faceup in the same place where they picked it up. Then it is your turn again. Whoever has the most pairs of cards when all of the cards have been taken is the winner.

(There are many ways to play *Concentration.* This is one that is fast to play. You may choose to modify the game depending on children's skill level.)

**Preparation:** You will need a copy of *The Three Little Javelinas* for each day's lesson.

Number the pages of the story to assist you in asking comprehension questions at appropriate points.

Post a copy of the Vocabulary Tally Sheet, BLM A, with this week's Picture Vocabulary Cards attached.

Each child will need one copy of the Homework Sheet, BLM 7a.

## DAY 1

### Introduce Book

This week's book is called *The Three Little Javelinas* [ha-vay-LEE-nas]. What's the title of this week's book? *The Three Little Javelinas.*

Javelinas are pig-like animals that live in the deserts of southwestern Texas, New Mexico, and Arizona. Their name means "spear" in Spanish. They were given that name because they have razor-sharp tusks that are just like spears.

This book was written by Susan Lowell. Who's the author of *The Three Little Javelinas*? *Susan Lowell.*

Jim Harris made the pictures for this book. Who's the illustrator of *The Three Little Javelinas*? *Jim Harris.* Who made the illustrations for this book? *Jim Harris.*

The cover of a book usually gives us some hints of what the book is about. Let's look at the front cover of *The Three Little Javelinas*. What do you see in the illustration? (Ideas: *Three javelinas; one is dressed like a musician, one like a cowboy, and one like a cowgirl; they are walking in the desert.*)

(Assign each child a partner.) What do you do when you make a prediction about something? *You say what you think will happen.*

# The Three Little Javelinas
author: Susan Lowell • illustrator: Jim Harris

### ◎ Target Vocabulary

| Tier II | Tier III |
|---|---|
| hullabaloo | setting (where) |
| suspicious | folk tale |
| invisible | version |
| steep | |
| *determined | |
| *contented | |

*Expanded Target Vocabulary Word

Get ready to make some predictions to your partner about this book. Use the information from the cover to help you.

(Ask the following questions, allowing sufficient time for children to share their predictions with their partners.)

- Who do you think are the characters in this story?
- What do you think the javelinas in the story will do?
- Where do you think the story happens?
- When do you think this story happens?
- Why do you think the javelinas are walking through the desert?
- How do you think the javelinas are feeling?
- Do you think this story is about real javelinas? Tell why or why not.

(Call on several children to share their predictions with the class.)

### Take a Picture Walk

(Encourage children to use target words in their answers.) We're going to take a picture walk through this book. Remember that when we take a picture walk, we look at the pictures and tell what we think will happen in the story.

**Pages 1–2.** Here is the same illustration that is on the cover of this book. What helps us know that the story happens in the desert? (Ideas: *There is sand; rocks; cacti.*) Look at the javelina with the guitar. What does it look like he is doing? *Singing.* Do the javelinas look like they are in a hurry to get someplace? *No.*

**Page 3.** What is happening here? (Ideas: *A tornado is picking up things and people.*)

**Page 4.** What is this javelina doing? (Idea: *Painting something on his mailbox.*) The javelina painted *#1 Tumbleweed Ave.* on his mailbox. What is that? *His address.* What does it look like this javelina's house is made of? (Idea: *Tumbleweeds.*)

**Page 5.** (Point to the coyote.) This animal is called a coyote. What kind of animal is this? *A coyote.* What do you think the coyote is doing?

**Page 6.** What do we see in this illustration? (Idea: *The house of the first little javelina.*) Predict what you think is going to happen next.

**Pages 7–8.** What is the coyote doing? (Idea: *Blowing down the javelina's house.*)

**Page 9.** What is the woman in this illustration doing? (Idea: *Gathering sticks.*)

**Page 10.** How do you think this little javelina is feeling? (Ideas: *Hot; tired; thirsty.*)

**Pages 11–12.** The second little javelina has built his house. What does it look like he used? (Idea: *Sticks.*) The sign here says *Do Not Disturb.* Why do you think the little javelina put up that sign? (Ideas: *He wants to sleep; he is tired and doesn't want anyone to bother him.*)

**Pages 13–14.** What are the two javelinas running from? *The coyote.* The coyote is hiding behind a cactus and the javelinas are running from him. How do you think they feel? (Ideas: *Terrified; scared; frightened.*)

**Pages 15–16.** The third little javelina has met someone. What does this person have? *Bricks.* What do you think the third little javelina is going to do?

**Page 17.** Whose house do you think this is? (Idea: *The third little javelina's.*)

**Page 18.** Who is at the third little javelina's door? (Idea: *The other two little javelinas.*) Why do you think they are there?

**Page 19.** What is different about the coyote? (Idea: *He is using a cane; his arm is in a sling; he is wearing glasses.*) Why do you think the coyote looks like this?

**Page 20.** What are the three little javelinas doing in this illustration? (Idea: *They are hiding in the house.*) Why do you think they are hiding? (Idea: *The coyote is outside.*) How do you think the little javelinas feel? (Ideas: *Terrified; scared; afraid.*)

**Pages 21–22.** Where is the coyote going? (Idea: *Down the chimney.*) Where does that chimney pipe lead? (Idea: *Into the stove.*)

**Page 23.** What are the three little javelinas doing in this illustration? (Idea: *Looking out the window.*) Why do you think they are looking out the window? (Idea: *They are watching the coyote.*) Are the little javelinas still terrified? *No.*

**Page 24.** Who is that running through the desert? *The coyote.* How does the coyote look different now? (Idea: *He is made of smoke.*) What do you think happened to turn the coyote into smoke?

**Pages 25–26.** What time of day is it in this part of the story? *Nighttime.* What is the coyote doing? (Idea: *Howling at the moon.*) How do you think the coyote feels in this illustration?

It's your turn to ask me some questions. What would you like to know about the story? (Accept questions. If children tell about the story instead of ask questions, prompt them to ask a question.) Ask me a why question. Ask me a how question.

### Read the Story Aloud
(Read the story to children with minimal interruptions.)

Tomorrow we will read the story again, and I will ask you some questions.

### Present Target Vocabulary
◎═ Hullabaloo

In the story, when Coyote blew down the little tumbleweed house, the first little javelina got away in all the hullabaloo. The tumbleweeds were rolling away, the javelina was tumbling like a tumbleweed, the coyote was huffing and puffing, the javelina's things were crashing all around. In all the noise and confusion of the house falling down, the first little javelina got away. **Hullabaloo.** Say the word. *Hullabaloo.*

**Hullabaloo** is a naming word. It names a thing. What kind of word is **hullabaloo?** *A naming word.*

**A hullabaloo is a lot of noise and confusion.** Say the word that means "a lot of noise and confusion." *Hullabaloo.*

(Correct any incorrect responses, and repeat the item at the end of the sequence.)

Let's think about some times when there might be a hullabaloo. I'll tell about a time. If you think there would be a hullabaloo, say "hullabaloo." If not, don't say anything.

- The passengers from three different airplanes all arrived in the baggage area at the same time. *Hullabaloo.*
- The people waited patiently in line to get tickets for the movie.
- Noisy fans surrounded the rock star's car, trying to catch a glimpse of her. *Hullabaloo.*
- The children were all sitting at their desks working quietly on their drawings.
- The farmer and his wife, their six children, the grandparents, the goat, the sheep, the pig, the rooster and the hens were all inside the tiny little house. *Hullabaloo.*
- Everyone spoke in whispers in the library.

What word means "a lot of noise and confusion"? *Hullabaloo.*

### ◎⤙ Suspicious

In the story, Coyote made his voice sound like another javelina when he tried to convince each javelina to let him in. But the little javelinas were suspicious. That means the javelinas had a feeling that the voice wasn't that of a javelina, even though they couldn't be sure. They didn't think the visitor could be believed or trusted. **Suspicious.** Say the word. *Suspicious.*

**Suspicious** is a describing word. It tells more about how the javelinas felt. What kind of word is **suspicious?** *A describing word.*

**If you are suspicious, it means you have a feeling that something is wrong or bad, even though you can't be sure.** Say the word that means "a feeling that something is wrong or bad, even though you can't be sure." *Suspicious.*

Let's think about some times when someone might be suspicious. I'll tell about a time. If someone is suspicious, say "suspicious." If not, don't say anything.

- The family had a feeling that the person lurking around their house was trying to steal their bicycles. *Suspicious.*
- The children had a feeling the animal in the bushes was a skunk. *Suspicious.*
- Hansel and Gretel had a feeling something was wrong when their father left them in the woods with only a few crumbs to eat. *Suspicious.*
- Pablo liked working in his parents' bakery.
- Elena always believed what everyone told her.
- The bear sniffed around at the bait in the trap, but he had a feeling something was wrong. *Suspicious.*

What word means "a feeling that something is wrong or bad, even though you can't be sure"? *Suspicious.*

### ◎⤙ Invisible

In the story, Coyote ran so quickly that he was almost invisible. That means you could hardly see him he was so quick and so quiet. **Invisible.** Say the word. *Invisible.*

**Invisible** is a describing word. It tells more about a person or a thing. What kind of word is **invisible?** *A describing word.*

**Invisible means cannot be seen.** Say the word that means "cannot be seen." *Invisible.* **Invisible** is the opposite of **visible.** What word is the opposite of **visible?** *Invisible.* What word means "the opposite of **invisible?**" *Visible.*

Let's think about when a person or thing might be invisible. I'll tell about a time. If someone or something might be invisible, say "invisible." If not, don't say anything.

- When the deer stood still in the grass, it could not be seen. *Invisible.*
- I saw my brother riding his bike down the driveway.
- The rocky shore could not be seen through the heavy fog. *Invisible.*
- I couldn't see the car in the dark. *Invisible.*

- Looking out the window, she could see the cows in the field.
- When the lizard changed its color, it couldn't be seen. *Invisible.*

What word means "cannot be seen"? *Invisible.*

 Steep

*The Three Little Javelinas* takes place where steep purple mountains looked down on the desert where the cactus forests grew. That means the mountains had a sharp slope. They went almost straight up and down. **Steep.** Say the word. *Steep.*

**Steep** is a describing word. It tells more about a thing. What kind of word is **steep?** *A describing word.*

**If something is steep, it means it has a sharp slope or slant.** (Draw a horizontal line on the board.) This line shows land that is flat. What kind of land does this line show? *Flat.* (Draw a gently sloping hill.) This line shows a hill that has a gentle slope. What kind of land does this line show? *A hill that has a gentle slope.* (Draw a steep hill.) This line shows a hill that is **steep.** What kind of land does this line show? *A hill that is steep.*

Now it's your turn. Hold out your hand so it is flat. Hold out your hand so it has a gentle slant. Now hold out your hand so it has a steep slant. Good following directions. Say the word that means "has a sharp slope or slant." *Steep.*

Let's think about some things that might be steep. I'll tell about a thing. If you think it is steep, say "steep." If not, don't say anything.

- The hikers climbed straight up the side of the mountain. *Steep.*
- They wandered along the flat path to the river.
- The waterfall crashed over the cliff and fell straight down into the valley below. *Steep.*
- Although people couldn't go there, the mountain goat scampered easily down the sharp slope. *Steep.*
- No trees grew on the top of the sharp rocky slope. *Steep.*
- The gently sloping hill was covered in daisies.

What word means "has a sharp slope or slant"? *Steep.*

(See Lesson 1, page 4, for instructions.)

**Assign Homework**

(Homework Sheet, BLM 7a. See the Introduction for homework instructions.)

## DAY 2

**Preparation:** Picture Vocabulary Cards for *hullabaloo, suspicious, invisible, steep.*

### Read and Discuss Story

 (Read story to children. Ask the following questions at the specified points. Encourage children to use target words in their answers.)

**Page 1.** (Read to the end of the first paragraph.) What does a javelina look like? (Idea: *Like a hairy pig.*) Where do javelinas live? (Ideas: *In the desert; in the southwest.*)

(Read to the end of the second paragraph.) Where were the three javelinas going? (Idea: *To seek their fortunes.*) The javelinas were going to seek their fortunes. That means they were looking for a way to be successful.

(Read to the end of the page.) What happened when the javelinas came to a place where the road divided? (Idea: *They each went their own way.*)

**Page 3.** (Read to the end of the first paragraph.) What came whirling across the desert? (Idea: *A dust storm.*)

(Read to the end of the page.) Hmmm, I'm not sure I know what a **whirlwind** is. Earlier, the story said that a **dust storm** came whirling across the desert. Then it says, "The **whirlwind** blew away." So a **whirlwind** must be another name for a **dust storm.** What's another word for a dust storm? *A whirlwind.* What's another word for a whirlwind? *A dust storm.* What did the first little javelina decide to build his house with? (Idea: *Tumbleweeds.*)

**Page 6.** What did the coyote want to do to the javelina? *Eat him.*

**Page 7.** What did the coyote want the little javelina to do? (Idea: *Let the coyote in his house.*) Would the javelina let him in? *No.*

**Page 8.** What happened to the little javelina's house? (Idea: *It got blown away.*) Why was it easy for the coyote to blow the house down? (Ideas: *It was made out of tumbleweeds; it wasn't very strong.*) Where did the little javelina go? (Idea: *To find his brother and sister.*) Where did the coyote go? (Idea: *After the javelina.*)

**Page 9.** (Read to the end of the first paragraph.) Why was the second little javelina so hot? (Ideas: *He walked for miles in the desert; the saguaros gave no shade.*)

(Read to the end of the second paragraph.) Where did the Native American woman get the sticks? (Idea: *From inside a dried-up cactus.*) How was she going to use the sticks? (Idea: *She was going to use them to knock the fruit off the cactus.*)

(Read to the end of the page.) What did the second little javelina want to do with the sticks? (Idea: *Build a house.*)

**Page 12.** What did the little javelina do when he finished building his house? (Idea: *He lay down to rest.*) Who came to the second little javelina's house? (Ideas: *The first little javelina; his brother.*)

**Page 13.** (Read to the end of the first paragraph.) Who came to the second little javelina's house this time? *The coyote.* Why do you think the coyote is making his voice sound like a javelina's voice? (Idea: *To trick the javelinas.*) What do you think the coyote will say to the javelinas?

(Read to the end of the page.) What did the coyote do to the javelina's little house? (Idea: *He blew it down.*)

**Page 14.** What happened to the two little javelinas? (Idea: *They escaped.*) What does the coyote do when his trick fails? (Idea: *He comes up with another trick.*) What do you think his next trick might be?

**Page 16.** (Read to the end of the first paragraph.) What are some things the third little javelina saw on her journey? (Ideas: *Trees; flowers; a snake; a hawk; a man making adobe bricks.*) What are adobe bricks made of? (Idea: *Mud and straw.*)

(Read to the end of the page.) What did the third little javelina decide to build her house out of? (Idea: *Adobe bricks.*)

**Page 17.** Why are the adobe bricks good for building the javelina's house? (Ideas: *They are strong; they keep the house cool in the summer and warm in the winter.*) Who came to the third little javelina's house? *Her brothers.* Who else? *The coyote.*

**Page 19.** (Read to the end of the second paragraph.) What trick did the coyote try this time? (Ideas: *He acted like he was old and weak; he pretended he had no teeth and a sore paw.*) Were the javelinas fooled? *No.*

(Read to the end of the page.) Why couldn't the coyote blow the house down? (Idea: *It was made of strong adobe bricks.*)

**Page 22.** (Read to the end of the second paragraph.) Why do you think the little javelina wants to build a fire? (Idea: *The wolf is coming down the stovepipe and a fire in the stove will stop him.*)

(Read to the end of the page.) What sizzled at the end of this part? *The coyote.*

**Page 24.** What was the sound the javelinas heard? (Idea: *The coyote screaming in pain.*) What happened to the coyote? (Idea: *He became a puff of smoke and ran away.*)

**Page 26.** How did the story end? (Idea: *The three little javelinas lived happily ever after in the brick house.*) What is the coyote remembering when he howls? (Idea: *How the three little javelinas tricked and burned him.*)

### Review Vocabulary

(Display the Picture Vocabulary Cards. Point to each card as you say the word. Ask children to repeat each word after you.) These pictures show **hullabaloo, suspicious, invisible,** and **steep.**

- What word means "a lot of noise and confusion"? *Hullabaloo.*
- What word means "has a sharp slope or slant"? *Steep.*

- What word means "cannot be seen"? *Invisible.*
- What word means "a feeling that something is wrong or bad, even though you can't be sure"? *Suspicious.*

## Extend Vocabulary

 Steep

In *The Three Little Javelinas,* we learned that **steep** is a describing word that means "has a sharp slope or slant." Say the word that means "has a sharp slope or slant." *Steep.*

Raise your hand if you can tell us a sentence that uses **steep** as a describing word meaning "has a sharp slope or slant." (Call on several children. If they don't use complete sentences, restate their examples as sentences. Have the class repeat the sentences.)

Here's a new way to use the word **steep.**

- My grandma says tea tastes best if you **steep** it for five minutes before you pour it. Say the sentence.
- We always use boiling water to **steep** our tea. Say the sentence.
- The Chinese doctor **steeped** different plants in boiling water to make his medicines. Say the sentence.

**In these sentences, steep is an action word that means to soak in a liquid.** What word means "to soak in a liquid"? *Steep.*

Raise your hand if you can tell us a sentence that uses **steep** as an action word meaning "to soak in a liquid." (Call on several children. If they don't use complete sentences, restate their examples as sentences. Have the class repeat the sentences.)

## Present Expanded Target Vocabulary

Determined

In the story, Coyote never gave up trying to catch the javelinas. He just kept thinking of new ways to trick them. He really wanted to eat those javelinas. He wouldn't let anything stop him.

Another way of saying he had made up his mind and wouldn't let anything stop him is to say he was determined. When you are determined, you know what you want to do, and you won't let anything stop you. **Determined.** Say the word. *Determined.*

**Determined** is a describing word. It tells more about someone. What kind of word is **determined?** *A describing word.*

**If you are determined, you have made up your mind about something, and you won't let anything stop you.** Say the word that means "you made up your mind about something and won't let anything stop you." *Determined.*

Let's think about when people might feel determined. If I say a time when someone would feel determined, say "determined." If not, don't say anything.

- How you would feel if you wanted to finish all of your work before going home. *Determined.*
- How you would feel at the beach on a warm Saturday.
- How you would feel if you wanted to save enough money for a new bike. *Determined.*
- How you and your mom would feel watching a video together.
- How you would feel if you wanted to be first in a race. *Determined.*
- How you would feel if everyone said you couldn't do something, but you knew you could. *Determined.*

What word means "you made up your mind about something and won't let anything stop you"? *Determined.*

Contented

**Pages 11–12.** In this illustration we can see that the two javelinas are satisfied with their lives just the way they are. The javelinas are contented. **Contented.** Say the word. *Contented.*

**Contented** is a describing word. It tells more about how the javelinas were feeling. What kind of word is **contented?** *A describing word.*

**Contented means you are happy with things just the way they are.** Say the word that means "happy with things just the way they are." *Contented.*

I'll tell about some people. If those people are contented, say "contented." If not, don't say anything.

- Grandma Alma likes her house just the way it is. *Contented.*
- Grandpa Jim wished he had a bigger car.

- Nina wanted to have two more fish and an octopus in her aquarium.
- I had a baked potato, a steak, and some salad. It was just right. *Contented.*
- Gracie said that she had everything that she needed. *Contented.*
- I really want to get a new skateboard that goes faster than my old one.

What word means "happy with things just the way they are"? *Contented.*

---

## DAY 3

**Preparation:** Prepare a sheet of chart paper, landscape direction, titled *The Three Little Javelinas.* Underneath the title, draw 10 boxes connected by arrows.

See the Introduction for Week 7's chart.

You will record children's responses by writing the underlined words in the boxes.

---

### Analyze Setting—Where (Literary Analysis)

Today we will learn more about how stories are made.

The setting of a story tells two things. One thing the setting tells is where the story happens. What is one thing the setting tells? *Where the story happens.*

Let's look at the pictures and talk about the story to figure out where *The Three Little Javelinas* happened.

**Pages 1–2.** (Read the first sentence of the story.) Where did the story begin? *Way out in the <u>desert</u>.*

**Pages 3–8.** Where did the next part of the story happen? *At the <u>first little javelina's house</u>.*

**Pages 9–10.** Where did the next part of the story happen? *<u>Near a saguaro</u>.*

**Pages 11–12.** Where did the next part of the story happen? *At the <u>second little javelina's house</u>.*

**Pages 13–14.** Where did the next part of the story happen? *In the <u>desert</u>.*

**Pages 15–16.** Where did the next part of the story happen? *<u>Where the man was making adobe bricks</u>.*

**Pages 17–20.** Where did the next part of the story happen? Ideas: *At the <u>third little javelina's house</u>.*

**Page 21.** Where did the next part of the story happen? *On the <u>roof</u>.*

**Page 22.** (Read the words *Whoosh. S-s-sizzle.*) Where did the next part of the story happen? *In the <u>stove</u>.*

**Pages 24–26.** Where did the last part of the story happen? *In the <u>desert</u>.*

The desert, the first little javelina's house, near a saguaro, the second little javelina's house, the desert, where the man was making adobe bricks, the third little javelina's house, the roof, the stove, and the desert are all in the desert. So, if we could only use one word to tell the setting of the story, we would use the word **desert**. Where is the setting of *The Three Little Javelinas*? *The desert.*

Today you learned about one part of the setting of *The Three Little Javelinas*. You learned about where the story happened.

### Play Whoopsy!

Today, you'll play the game *Whoopsy!* I'll say sentences using words we have learned. If the word doesn't fit in the sentence, say "Whoopsy!" Then I'll ask you to say a sentence where the word fits. If you can do it, you get a point. If you can't do it, I get the point. If the word I use fits the sentence, don't say anything. Let's practice.

Air is **invisible** because … you can see it. *Whoopsy!*
Listen to the beginning of the sentence again. Air is **invisible** because. Say the beginning of the sentence. *Air is invisible because.*
Can you finish the sentence so the word fits? (Idea: *Air is invisible because you can't see it.*)

Let's try another one. There was a **hullabaloo** in the gym when … everyone was standing still listening to the teacher. *Whoopsy!*

Listen to the beginning of the sentence again. There was a **hullabaloo** in the gym when. Say the beginning of the sentence. *There was a hullabaloo in the gym when.*
Can you finish the sentence so the word fits? (Idea: *There was a hullabaloo in the gym when the children were shouting and running around.*)

Now you're ready to play the game. (Draw a T-chart on the board for keeping score. Children earn one point for each correct answer. If they make an error, correct them as you normally would, and record one point for yourself. Repeat missed words at the end of the game.)

- Gabriel was **suspicious** when … his best friend talked to him after school. *Whoopsy!* Say the beginning of the sentence again. *Gabriel was suspicious when.* Can you finish the sentence? (Idea: *Gabriel was suspicious when a stranger talked to him after school.*)
- When we climbed the **steep** hill … we had lots of energy left. *Whoopsy!* Say the beginning of the sentence again. *When we climbed the steep hill.* Can you finish the sentence? (Idea: *When we climbed the steep hill we were tired and out of breath.*)
- My grandma is **contented** when … her cat sits on her lap.
- I **steeped** the tea when … I put the teabag in the cupboard. *Whoopsy!* Say the beginning of the sentence again. *I steeped the tea when.* Can you finish the sentence? (Idea: *I steeped the tea when I put the teabag in the boiling water.*)
- You are **determined** when … you give up very easily. *Whoopsy!* Say the beginning of the sentence again. *You are determined when.* Can you finish the sentence? (Idea: *You are determined when you make up your mind and you won't give up.*)

(Count the points and declare a winner.) You did a great job of playing *Whoopsy!*

## Complete the Activity Sheet

(Give each child a copy of the Activity Sheet, BLM 7b. Have children cut apart the words in the word bank. If children are unfamiliar with Venn diagrams, do this as a guided activity.)

The third little javelina and the coyote are different in some ways and the same in some ways. (Point to the circle under the words *Third Little Javelina.*) This circle is where we'll put things that tell **only** about the third little javelina.

(Point to the circle under the word *Coyote.*) This circle is where we'll put things that tell **only** about Coyote.

(Point to the place where the two circles overlap.) This is where we'll put things that tell about **both** the third little javelina and Coyote.

(Either read for children or have them read the words in the word bank one at a time. After each word is read ask:) Does this tell about the third little javelina or Coyote, or both the third little javelina and Coyote?

(If children identify the character trait or activity as belonging to only the third little javelina, have them paste or glue the word in the large circle under the words *Third Little Javelina.*)

(If children identify the character trait or activity as belonging to only Coyote, have them paste or glue the word in the large circle under the word *Coyote.*)

(If children identify the character trait or activity as belonging to both the third little javelina and Coyote, paste or glue the word in the area where the two circles overlap.)

(Repeat procedure for each item in the word bank.)

(Third Little Javelina: girl (female); polite; clever; has two brothers; lived happily ever after; built an adobe house; has a sun umbrella.
Coyote: boy (male); sly; used tricks; got burned; howls at night.
Both: neckerchief; lived in the desert; determined.)

**Preparation:** You'll need a copy of *The Three Little Pigs* for today's lesson. We recommend the version written and illustrated by Margot Zemach.

Prepare a T-chart with *The Three Little Pigs* at the top of the first column and *The Three Little Javelinas* at the top of the second column.

## Learn About Folk Tales

Today you will learn more about folk tales. What will you learn about? *Folk tales.*

What is a tale? *A story.* What are people who come from the same country and live the same kind of life? *Folk.* So what is a story told by people who come from the same country and live the same kind of life? *A folk tale.*

Long, long ago, could most ordinary people read? *No.* How did people entertain themselves? *They told stories.* When parents told some of these stories to their children, what were they trying to teach their children? (Idea: *Important things they needed to know.*)

Many of you already know *The Three Little Pigs.* Listen while I read it to you once again. (Read the story with minimal interruptions.)

When Susan Lowell heard *The Three Little Pigs,* it gave her an idea for a story that was the same in some ways and different in some ways. Let's think about these two stories.

(As children respond to your questions, record the underlined information in the appropriate columns on the T-chart. Information that is the same should be recorded in both columns or recorded in one column and arrowed over to the second column to show that they are the same.)

Who were the main characters in *The Three Little Pigs*? (Ideas: *The three little pigs; the wolf.*) Who were the main characters in *The Three Little Javelinas*? (Ideas: *The three little javelinas; the coyote.*)

How were the stories' characters the same? (Ideas: *They both came in threes; someone was trying to eat them.*)

What was the first little pig's house made of? *Straw.* What was the first little javelina's house made of? *Tumbleweeds.*

How were their houses the same? (Ideas: *They were easy to build; they were easy to blow down.*)

What did the wolf say when he came to blow the house down? *"Little pig, little pig, Let me come in."* What did the coyote say when he came to blow the house down? *"Little pig, little pig, Let me come in."*

What did the first little pig say to the wolf? *"No, no, I won't let you in—not by the hair of my chinny-chin-chin."* What did the first little javelina say to the coyote? *"Not by the hair of my chinny-chin-chin."*

(Continue with this procedure identifying the similarities and differences between the two stories.)

(Ideas: Wolf: I"'ll huff and I'll puff and I'll blow your house down."
Coyote: "I'll huff and I'll puff and I'll blow your house in."
Both houses were blown down.

- The first little pig was eaten.
  The first little javelina escaped to his brothers.
- Second pig's house built of sticks.
  Second javelina's house built of sticks.
  Both houses were blown down.
- Second little pig was eaten.
  Second little javelina escaped to sister's.
- Third little pig's house built of bricks.
  Third little javelina's house built of adobe bricks.
  Wolf went down chimney.
  Coyote went down chimney.
- Wolf fell into pot of soup and was cooked.
  Coyote fell into stove and turned into smoke.
- The little pig ate the wolf soup.
  Three little javelinas lived happily ever after.)

When someone takes a story and changes parts of it and keeps parts of it the same, we say the person has written their own **version** of the story. Susan Lowell wrote her own version of *The Three Little Pigs.* She called her story *The Three Little Javelinas.* What kind of story did

Susan Lowell write? (Idea: *Her own version of The Three Little Pigs.*)

## Play Whoopsy! (Cumulative Review)

Let's play *Whoopsy!* I'll say sentences using words we have learned. If the word doesn't fit in the sentence, say "Whoopsy!" Then I'll ask you to say a sentence where the word fits. If you can do it, you get a point. If you can't do it, I get the point. If the word I use fits the sentence, don't say anything.

Now you're ready to play the game. (Draw a T-chart on the board for keeping score. Children earn one point for each correct answer. If they make an error, correct them as you normally would, and record one point for yourself. Repeat missed words at the end of the game.)

- A **hullabaloo** happens when … everyone is quiet and well behaved. *Whoopsy!* Say the beginning of the sentence again. *A hullabaloo happens when.* Can you finish the sentence? (Idea: *A hullabaloo happens when everyone is noisy and badly behaved.*)
- You are **suspicious** when … you are positive everything is going well. *Whoopsy!* Say the beginning of the sentence again. *You are suspicious when.* Can you finish the sentence? (Idea: *You are suspicious when you feel that something is wrong, even though you can't be sure.*)
- You **steep** tea when … you pour boiling water on the tea leaves.
- You are **invisible** when … you are standing where everyone can see you. *Whoopsy!* Say the beginning of the sentence again. *You are invisible when.* Can you finish the sentence? (Idea: *You are invisible when you are standing where no one can see you.*)
- You climb a **steep** path when … you walk where it is quite flat *Whoopsy!* Say the beginning of the sentence again. *You climb a steep path when.* Can you finish the sentence? (Idea: *You climb a steep path when you walk where the path goes up quickly.*)

- Joseph felt **contented** when … everything was going just the way he wanted it to.
- Al showed he was **determined** when … he gave up after the first try. *Whoopsy!* Say the beginning of the sentence again. *Al showed he was determined when.* Can you finish the sentence? (Idea: *Al showed he was determined when he tried again and again.*)
- Abigail's room was **untidy** when … she put everything away where it belonged. *Whoopsy!* Say the beginning of the sentence again. *Abigail's room was untidy when.* Can you finish the sentence? (Idea: *Abigail's room was untidy when nothing was put away where it belonged.*)

(Count the points and declare a winner.) You did a great job of playing *Whoopsy!*

## DAY 5

**Preparation:** Each child will need a copy of the Quiz Answer Sheet, BLM B.

### Retell Story

Today I'll show you the pictures Jim Harris made for *The Three Little Javelinas.* As I show you the pictures, I'll call on one of you to tell the class that part of the story.

Tell me what happens at the **beginning** of the story. (Show the picture on page 1. Call on a child to tell what's happening.)

Tell me what happens in the **middle** of the story. (Show the pictures on pages 3–22. Call on a child to tell what's happening. Encourage use of target words when appropriate. Model use when necessary.)

Tell me what happens at the **end** of the story. (Show the pictures on pages 23–26. Call on a child to tell what's happening.)

If you were going to write your own version of *The Three Little Pigs,* what parts of the story would you change? (Call on several children. Encourage them to use this frame to start their answers: *If I wrote a version of The Three Little Pigs I would _____.*)

## Assess Vocabulary

(Give each child a copy of the Quiz Answer Sheet, BLM B.)

Today you're going to have a True or False quiz. When you do the True or False quiz, it shows me how well you know the hard words you are learning.

If I say something that is true, circle the word **true.** What will you do if I say something that is true? *Circle the word true.*

If I say something that is false, circle the word **false.** What will you do if I say something that is false? *Circle the word false.*

Listen carefully to each item that I say. Don't let me trick you!

Item 1: Someone who is **contented** is unhappy with things the way they are. (*False.*)

Item 2: A **steep** hill is easy to climb. (*False.*)

Item 3: You can't see something that is **invisible.** (*True.*)

Item 4: If you are **determined** to learn to swim, you'll probably practice swimming nearly every day. (*True.*)

Item 5: If you **steep** something, you lay it out on a rock to dry. (*False.*)

Item 6: A **suspicious** person would probably want to check that what you said was true. (*True.*)

Item 7: It would be easy to sleep through a **hullabaloo.** (*False.*)

Item 8: An **uncooperative** child is one who refuses to do what is asked. (*True.*)

Item 9: A **sly** person never tricks anyone. (*False.*)

Item 10: If your baby brother poured his cereal on the floor, your mom might call him a little **rascal.** (*True.*)

You did a great job completing your quiz!

(Score children's work. A child must score 9 out of 10 to be at the mastery level. If a child does not achieve mastery, insert the missed words as additional items in the games in next week's lessons. Retest those children individually for the missed items before they take the next mastery test.)

## Extensions

### Read a Story as a Reward

(Display copies of the books that you have read since the beginning of the program, as well as a variety of modern versions of folk tales. Allow children to choose which book they would like you to read to them as a reward for their hard work.)

(Read the story aloud for enjoyment with minimal interruptions.)

> **Preparation:** Word containers for the Super Words Center.
>
> **Note:** You will need to keep the cards that are removed from the center. They will be used again later in the program.

### Introduce the Super Words Center

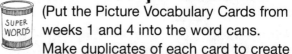

(Put the Picture Vocabulary Cards from weeks 1 and 4 into the word cans. Make duplicates of each card to create a "Concentration" game. You may make as many sets of duplicates as you wish to suit your class. Show children one of the word containers. Demonstrate how the game is played by role-playing with a child. Repeat the demonstration process until children can play the game with confidence.)

Let's think about how we work with our words in the Super Words Center.

This week's activity is called *Concentration.* What's the name of this week's activity? *Concentration.*

You will work with a partner in the Super Words Center. Whom will you work with? *A partner.*

There are two cards for each word in the Super Words Center. When you play *Concentration,* you try to find two cards that match. Match means that both cards show the same picture and word. What does match mean? *Both cards show the same picture and word.*

First you will take all of the cards out of the container and place them facedown on the table. What do you do first? (Idea: *Take all of the words out and place them facedown on the table.*)

Next you will pick one card, place it faceup where you found it, and ask your partner what word the picture shows. What do you do next? (Idea: *I pick a card, place it faceup where I found it, and ask what word the picture shows.*)

What do you do if your partner doesn't know the word? *Tell my partner the word.*

Next you will give your partner a turn. What do you do next? *Give my partner a turn.*

If your partner chooses a card that is the same as your first card, he or she can take those two cards. What can your partner do? (Idea: *He or she can take both cards if he or she chooses one that is the same as my first card.*)

If your partner doesn't find one that is the same, he or she leaves his or her card faceup in the same place where they picked it up. Then it is your turn again. Whoever has the most pairs of cards when all of the cards have been taken is the winner.

(There are many ways to play *Concentration*. This is one that is fast to play. You may choose to modify the game depending on children's skill level.)

## Week 8

**Preparation:** You will need a copy of *Cinderella* for each day's lesson.

Number the pages of the story to assist you in asking comprehension questions at appropriate points.

Post a copy of the Vocabulary Tally Sheet, BLM A, with this week's Picture Vocabulary Cards attached.

Each child will need one copy of the Homework Sheet, BLM 8a.

### Target Vocabulary

| Tier II | Tier III |
|---------|----------|
| temper | setting (when) |
| miserable | fairy tale |
| delighted | noun |
| magnificent | translated |
| *forgiving | |
| *generous | |

*Expanded Target Vocabulary Word

### DAY 1

#### Introduce Book

This week's book is called *Cinderella*. What's the title of this week's book? *Cinderella*.

This book was written by Marcia Brown. Who's the author of *Cinderella*? *Marcia Brown*.

Marcia Brown also made the pictures for this book. Who's the illustrator of *Cinderella*? *Marcia Brown*. Who made the illustrations for this book? *Marcia Brown*.

The cover of a book usually gives us some hints of what the book is about. Let's look at the front cover of *Cinderella*. What do you see in the illustration? (Ideas: *A girl riding in a carriage; a girl riding in a coach; a horse is pulling the carriage; there are four men with her.*)
(**Note:** If the children do not use the word coach, say:) Another name for a carriage is a coach. What's another name for a carriage? *A coach.* What is another name for a coach? *A carriage.*

(Assign each child a partner.) Get ready to make some predictions to your partner about this book. Use the information from the cover to help you.

(Ask the following questions, allowing sufficient time for children to share their predictions with their partners.)

- Who do you think are the characters in this story?

- What do you think the girl will do?
- Where do you think the girl is going?
- Why do you think the girl is riding in a coach?
- When do you think this story happens?
- How many men are riding on the back of the carriage?
- Do you think this story is about a real girl? Tell why or why not.

(Call on several children to share their predictions with the class.)

#### Take a Picture Walk

(Encourage children to use target words in their answers.) We're going to take a picture walk through this book. Remember that when we take a picture walk, we look at the pictures and tell what we think will happen in the story.

**Page 2.** What is the girl doing in this illustration? (Idea: *Washing a pot.*)

**Page 3.** Where does this part of the story happen? (Idea: *In a bedroom.*) Whose bedroom do you think this is?

**Page 4.** What do you think the girl is thinking?

**Page 5.** What do you think is happening here? (Ideas: *The girl is washing clothes; doing laundry.*)

**Page 6.** Who do you think these two girls are? What does it look like they are doing? (Ideas: *Looking at themselves; getting ready to go somewhere.*)

**Page 8.** What do you think is happening in this illustration? (Ideas: *The girl is helping another girl get dressed; a third girl is putting on makeup.*)

**Page 9.** Who is this with the girl? (Idea: *A fancy lady.*) What do you think she is saying to the girl?

**Page 10.** What is the girl carrying? *A pumpkin.* What do you think she will do with the pumpkin?

**Page 11.** What is the girl doing in this illustration? (Idea: *Letting mice out of the cage.*) What is the lady doing? (Idea: *Touching the mice with her wand; turning the mice into horses.*) How many mice has she turned into horses so far? *Two.* How many more mice does she have? *Four.* So how many horses do you think she wants? *Six.*

**Page 12.** What do you see in this illustration? (Idea: *A watering can with lizards crawling around it.*)

**Pages 13–14.** What do you think is happening here? (Ideas: *The fairy is turning the girl's clothes into a beautiful dress; the coach is waiting to take her somewhere.*) Where do you think the girl is going to go all dressed up and in a horse-drawn carriage?

**Page 15.** How do you think the girl is feeling as she is getting out of the coach? (Ideas: *Happy; beautiful; amazed; proud; special.*)

**Page 16.** Where do you think this part of the story happens? (Ideas: *In a palace; somewhere fancy.*) Who do you think the person is talking to the girl? (Idea: *A prince.*) What do you think he's saying to her?

**Page 17.** Who do you think these people are? (Idea: *The king and queen.*) What do you think they are smiling at? (Idea: *The girl and the prince.*)

**Page 18.** What is the girl doing in this illustration? (Idea: *Giving fruit to the girls she helped get dressed.*)

**Page 19.** Where does this part of the story happen? (Idea: *Back at the girls' house.*) What is happening in this part of the story? (Idea: *The sisters are returning home; the girl lets them in.*) How does the girl look like she feels here? *Tired.*

**Pages 21–22.** What is the girl in this illustration doing? (Idea: *Running away.*) Why do you think

the prince is down on one knee? (Idea: *He is picking something up.*)

**Page 23.** What is the prince looking at in this illustration? (Idea: *A shoe.*)

**Page 24.** What is the prince doing in this illustration? (Idea: *Trying to see who the shoe fits.*) Why do you think he is doing that? (Idea: *To find the girl who lost the shoe.*) Why would the prince go through all that trouble to return a lost shoe? (Idea: *Because he is in love with the girl who lost it.*) Why do you think all these girls are trying on the shoe? (Idea: *They want to be the one the prince is in love with.*) Did they all lose a shoe? *No.*

**Page 25.** Who is trying on the shoe here? (Idea: *The sisters.*) Do you think the shoe will fit them? *No.*

**Page 26.** Who does the shoe fit? (Idea: *The girl.*) How do you think the sisters feel about the shoe fitting her? (Ideas: *Surprised; shocked; amazed.*)

**Pages 27 and 28.** What has happened to the girl? (Idea: *The fairy has changed her clothes into a beautiful dress.*) What do you think the sisters are doing here?

**Page 29.** What do you think happens at the end of this story? (Idea: *The girl and the prince get married.*)

It's your turn to ask me some questions. What would you like to know about the story? (Accept questions. If children tell about the story instead of asking questions, prompt them to ask a question.) Ask me a who question. Ask me a why question.)

### Read the Story Aloud
(Read the story to children with minimal interruptions.)

Tomorrow we will read the story again, and I will ask you some questions.

### Present Target Vocabulary
◎⟜ Temper

In the story, "The marriage ceremony was hardly over when the stepmother's temper flared up." That means the stepmother often got irritated and angry very quickly. **Temper.** Say the word. *Temper.*

**Temper** is a naming word. Another word for a naming word is a noun. What is another word for a naming word? *A noun.* A noun names a person, place, thing, or idea. What does a noun name? *A person, place, thing, or idea.* What kind of word names a person, place, thing, or idea? *A noun.* **Temper** names a thing, so what kind of word is **temper**? *A noun.*

**If you have a temper you get irritated and angry very quickly.** Say the word that means "get irritated and angry very quickly." *Temper.*

(Correct any incorrect responses, and repeat the item at the end of the sequence.)

Let's think about some times when someone might show a temper. I'll tell about a time. If you think someone is showing a temper, say "temper." If not, don't say anything.

- The toddler threw himself on the floor, screaming, yelling, and kicking. *Temper.*
- Coyote got very angry when he couldn't catch the three javelinas. *Temper.*
- Flossie was always calm and in control of her feelings.
- The mechanic threw down his wrench and stomped off when he couldn't get the bolt loose. *Temper.*
- The fox got very angry and irritated with Flossie when she wouldn't believe he was a fox. *Temper.*
- Suki didn't get upset or irritated when she couldn't remember all the steps of the dance; she just made up new ones.

What noun means "get irritated and angry very quickly"? *Temper.*

⌖⚊ Miserable

In the story, Cinderella slept on an awful straw mattress in a miserable room away up in the top of the house. That means the room was cold, gloomy, and made her feel bad. **Miserable.** Say the word. *Miserable.*

**Miserable** is a describing word. It tells more about a thing. What kind of word is **miserable**? *A describing word.*

**If something is miserable, it means it is cold, gloomy, and makes you feel bad.** Say the word that means "cold, gloomy, and makes you feel bad." *Miserable.*

Let's think about some times when something might be miserable. I'll tell about a time. If something is miserable, say "miserable." If not, don't say anything.

- Nobody ever went in the basement because it was cold, gloomy, and made everyone feel bad. *Miserable.*
- It was a gray, wet, gloomy day. *Miserable.*
- The falling snow made the world seem like a white wonderland.
- She painted her bedroom a cheery yellow color.
- The javelinas' adobe house was cheery and warm.
- The empty room was dark and dreary. There were no pictures on the walls. It always made Joni sad when she went into it. *Miserable.*

What word means "cold, gloomy, and makes you feel bad"? *Miserable.*

⌖⚊ Delighted

In the story, Cinderella was delighted when the stepsisters told her about the beautiful, mysterious princess who came to the ball. That means she was very pleased and excited to hear them tell about the princess and the ball. **Delighted.** Say the word. *Delighted.*

**Delighted** is a describing word. It tells more about a person. What kind of word is **delighted**? *A describing word.*

**Delighted means very pleased and excited.** Say the word that means "very pleased and excited." *Delighted.*

Let's think about some times when a person might feel delighted. I'll tell about a time. If the person would feel delighted, say "delighted." If not, don't say anything.

- Carlos was very pleased and excited to see the fireworks on the Fourth of July. *Delighted.*
- Karli's grandpa was very pleased and excited when she came to visit him. *Delighted.*
- Sammy's aunt was pleased and excited to be invited to go hiking with Sammy. *Delighted.*
- The light was turned off in the room.

- The triplets didn't like it when people said how much alike they looked.
- The lazy dog snoozed in the bright sunlight.

What word means "very pleased and excited"? *Delighted.*

◎ Magnificent

In the story, Cinderella's godmother changed Cinderella's rags into a costume still more magnificent than any she had worn before. That means she turned the rags into a very beautiful gown. **Magnificent.** Say the word. *Magnificent.*

**Magnificent** is a describing word. It tells more about a thing. What kind of word is **magnificent?** *A describing word.*

**If something is magnificent, it is grand in size or very beautiful to look at.** Say the word that means "grand in size or very beautiful to look at." *Magnificent.*

Let's think about some things that might be magnificent. I'll tell about a thing. If you think it might be magnificent, say "magnificent." If not, don't say anything.

- The Rocky Mountains are very grand in size and very beautiful to look at. *Magnificent.*
- Their house was small but cozy.
- The king lived in a very grand and beautiful castle. *Magnificent.*
- The queen wore a beautiful gold crown decorated with diamonds and rubles. *Magnificent.*
- The sunset was the most beautiful she had ever seen. *Magnificent.*
- It was a cloudy, dreary day.

What word means "grand in size or very beautiful to look at"? *Magnificent.*

### Present Vocabulary Tally Sheet
(See Lesson 1, page 4, for instructions.)

### Assign Homework
(Homework Sheet, BLM 8a. See the Introduction for homework instructions.)

**Preparation:** Picture Vocabulary Cards for *temper, miserable, delighted, magnificent.*

### Read and Discuss Story
(Read story to children. Ask the following questions at specified points. Encourage them to use target words in their answers.)

**Page 1.** (Read to the end of the first paragraph.) How is the man's daughter different from her new stepmother and stepsisters? (Idea: *She is good and sweet, but they are mean.*)

(Read to the end of the page.) What was the man's daughter's name? *Cinderella.* What did the stepmother make Cinderella do? (*Ideas: Chores; scour the pots; scrub the stairs; clean the stepmother's and stepsisters' bedrooms.*)

**Page 4.** (Read to the end of the first paragraph.) When we compare two things we tell how they are the same and how they are different. What do we do when we compare two things? *We tell how they are the same and how they are different.*

Compare how Cinderella was treated differently from the stepsisters. (Ideas: *She slept on a straw mattress in a small room in the attic; the sisters slept in big, beautiful beds in beautiful bedrooms with large mirrors.*)

Tell how Cinderella was the same as her sisters. (Ideas: *They all are girls or women; they live in the same house; they live in the same town.*)

(Read to the end of the page.) Did Cinderella complain about the way she was treated? *No.* What did she do instead? (Idea: *She would creep up to the chimney corner and sit in the ashes.*) Another word for **ashes** is **cinders.** How do you think Cinderella got her name? (Idea: *Her stepsisters called her that because she sat in the cinders.*)

**Page 5.** What were the stepsisters so excited about? (Idea: *The king's son was throwing a ball and they were invited.*) Had Cinderella been invited to the ball? *No.*

**Page 6.** What was the older daughter talking about? (Idea: *Which dress she would wear to the ball.*)

**Page 7.** How did the stepsisters treat Cinderella? (Ideas*: They were mean to her; they teased her because she was not going to the ball.*) How did Cinderella react to the sisters' meanness? (Idea: *She ignored it and helped them get ready for the ball.*)

**Page 9.** (Read to the end of the first paragraph.) Why do you think Cinderella was crying? (Idea*: She wanted to go to the ball.*)

(Read to the end of the page.) Who found Cinderella crying? (Idea: *Her godmother.*) What was special about Cinderella's godmother? (Idea: *She was a fairy godmother.*)

**Page 10.** What did Cinderella's godmother tell her to go get? *A pumpkin.* What did the godmother do with the pumpkin? (Idea: *She scooped out the insides and used her wand to turn it into a coach.*) How do you think Cinderella will use the coach? (Idea: *She will ride in it to the ball.*)

**Page 11.** What did the fairy godmother do to the mice? (Idea: *She used her wand to turn them into horses.*) What do you think the horses are for? (Idea: *They will pull the carriage.*)

**Page 12.** (Read to the end of the first paragraph.) A coachman is the man who drives a coach. What do we call the man who drives a coach? *A coachman.* What did Cinderella suggest using to make a coachman? *A rat.*

(Read to the end of the sentence "Bring them to me.") What do you think the fairy godmother is going to turn the lizards into?

(Read to the end of the page.) A footman is a man who works as a servant, usually opening doors and serving food. His special uniform is called his livery. What did the fairy godmother use to make Cinderella's footmen? *Six lizards.*

**Page 13.** Why did the fairy godmother give Cinderella a gown and glass slippers? (Idea: *Cinderella's clothes were rags, she couldn't wear them to a ball.*)

**Page 14.** What time did the fairy godmother tell Cinderella to leave the ball? *Midnight.* What

would happen at midnight? (Ideas: *Her carriage would turn back into a pumpkin; the coachman would turn back into a rat; the horses would turn back into mice; her footmen would turn back into lizards; her gown would turn back into rags.*)

**Page 15.** Why did everyone become silent when Cinderella entered the ballroom? (Idea: *She was so beautiful people just stared at her.*)

**Page 17.** (Read to the end of the second paragraph.) Why did all the ladies stare at Cinderella's gown and headdress? (Idea: *They wanted to remember what they looked like so they could have the same made for themselves.*)

(Read to the end of the page.) What do you think people were wondering about Cinderella? (Ideas: *Who is she? Where did she come from?*)

**Page 18.** Did Cinderella treat her stepsisters kindly at the ball? *Yes.* Did they know who she was? *No.* Why not? (Ideas: *She was dressed like a beautiful princess; they only knew her in rags.*)

**Page 19.** Cinderella heard the clock chime eleven hours and three-quarters. Why did she leave the ball so quickly? (Idea: *It was almost midnight and she had to leave before everything turned back to what it had been.*) What did the prince beg Cinderella to do? (Idea: *To return to the ball the next night.*) Do you think she'll go?

**Page 20.** (Read to the end of the second paragraph.) Had Cinderella really been asleep? *No.*

(Read to the end of the sentence "What was the name of this princess?") Why was Cinderella delighted to hear the stepsisters talk about the princess? (Idea: *She was the princess and she was happy to hear that everyone thought she was so beautiful.*)

(Read to the end of the page.) Why was Cinderella secretly glad that her stepsister had refused to let her borrow a dress for the ball? (Idea: *If she went to the ball in her stepsister's dress, she wouldn't be able to go in the beautiful gown her fairy godmother made for her.*)

**Page 21.** Why did Cinderella lose track of the time? (Ideas: *The prince spent the evening with her; she was enjoying herself so much she lost track of the time.*) What happened as the clock started to strike midnight? (Idea: *Cinderella ran out of the ball.*) What did the prince find on the steps? (Idea: *Cinderella's glass slipper.*)

**Page 22.** (Read to the end of the first paragraph.) Why did Cinderella run all the way home instead of riding in her carriage? (Idea: *The carriage had turned back into a pumpkin.*)

(Read to the end of the page.) Who did the guards see leaving the palace? (Idea: *Cinderella in her rags.*)

**Page 23.** (Read to the end of the first paragraph.) Why did the prince spend the rest of the ball staring at the glass slipper? (Idea: *He had fallen in love with the girl who was wearing it.*)

(Continue reading to the end of page 24.)

What was the prince going to do when he found the girl whose foot fit in the glass slipper? (Idea: *Marry her.*)

**Page 25.** Why did the sisters try to squeeze their feet into the slipper? (Idea: *They wanted to marry the prince.*) What happened when Cinderella asked to try on the shoe? (Idea: *The sisters laughed and made fun of her.*) What do you think will happen next?

**Page 26.** Did the glass slipper fit Cinderella? *Yes.* What did Cinderella do that made the sisters even more astonished? (Idea: *She pulled the other slipper out of her pocket and put it on.*)

**Page 27.** Why did the sisters beg for Cinderella's forgiveness? (Idea: *Because they had been so mean to her and now she was going to marry the prince.*) Did Cinderella forgive them? *Yes.*

**Page 29.** What happened at the end of this story? (Ideas: *Cinderella married the prince; she brought her stepsisters to live at the palace; she got them married.*) Do you think this story has a happy ending? *Yes.*

## Review Vocabulary

(Display the Picture Vocabulary Cards. Point to each card as you say the word. Ask children to repeat each word after you.) These pictures show **temper, miserable, delighted, magnificent.**

- What word means "grand in size or very beautiful to look at"? *Magnificent.*

- What word means "cold, gloomy, and makes you feel bad"? *Miserable.*
- What word means "very pleased and excited"? *Delighted.*
- What word means "get irritated and angry very quickly"? *Temper.*

## Extend Vocabulary
 Miserable

In *Cinderella,* we learned that **miserable** is a describing word that means "cold, gloomy, and makes you feel bad." Say the word that means "cold, gloomy, and makes you feel bad." *Miserable.*

Raise your hand if you can tell us a sentence that uses **miserable** as a describing word meaning "cold, gloomy, and makes you feel bad." (Call on several children. If they don't use complete sentences, restate their examples as sentences. Have the class repeat the sentences.)

Here's a new way to use the word **miserable.**

- My mom felt miserable when she lost her purse. Say the sentence.
- My cold made me feel **miserable.** Say the sentence.
- The itchy mosquito bites made me **miserable.** Say the sentence.

**In these sentences, miserable is a describing word that means very unhappy.** What word means "very unhappy"? *Miserable.*

Raise your hand if you can tell us a sentence that uses **miserable** as a describing word meaning "very unhappy." (Call on several children. If they don't use complete sentences, restate their examples as sentences. Have the class repeat the sentences.)

## Present Expanded Target Vocabulary
Forgiving

In the story, even though Cinderella's stepsisters were mean to her, when she became queen she gave them "a home at the palace and on the same day married them to two great lords of the court." Cinderella's actions show that she was very forgiving. **Forgiving.** Say the word. *Forgiving.*

**Forgiving** is a describing word. It tells more about a person. What kind of word is **forgiving**? *A describing word.*

**When you are forgiving, you don't blame people for the bad things they've done to you or want to get back at them.** Say the word that means "you don't blame people for the bad things they've done to you or want to get back at them." *Forgiving.*

Let's think about some people who might be forgiving. If I tell about someone who is forgiving, say "forgiving." If not, don't say anything.

- My mom never mentioned her favorite cup that I broke. *Forgiving.*
- Even though Tomás knocked over Federico's bike and broke the handlebar, Federico never blamed him or tried to get even. *Forgiving.*
- I always get grounded when I come home late from school.
- I have trouble remembering things.
- No matter how much I misbehave, my grandma never blames me for the bad things I do. *Forgiving.*
- When my baby sister tore up my best drawing, I didn't get angry or blame her for doing it. *Forgiving.*

What word means "you don't blame people for the bad things they've done to you or want to get back at them"? *Forgiving.*

◎⚷ *Generous*

In the story, Cinderella shared with her stepsisters some oranges and lemons which the young prince had given her. That shows that Cinderella was generous. She was happy to share what she had with other people. **Generous.** Say the word. *Generous.*

**Generous** is a describing word. It tells more about a person. What kind of word is **generous**? *A describing word.*

**If you are generous, you are happy to share what you have with others.** Say the word that means "happy to share what you have with others." *Generous.*

Let's think about some people who might be generous. I'll tell about someone. If you think

that person is generous, say "generous." If not, don't say anything.

- Alesha shared her lunch with Mel. *Generous.*
- Saavas wouldn't let his little brother play with his toy cars, even though he wasn't playing with them.
- Mrs. Goodfellow shared what she knows with her students. *Generous.*
- Every time someone got a compliment, Brittany wanted one too.
- Jordan only had twenty-five cents but he gave it to someone who had nothing at all. *Generous.*
- Mrs. Rice gets a ride to work from Mrs. Thompson, even though it's a long way for her to drive. *Generous.*

What word means "happy to share what you have with others"? *Generous.*

---

### DAY 3

**Preparation:** Prepare a sheet of chart paper, landscape direction, titled *Cinderella*. Underneath the title, draw 12 boxes, connected by arrows.

See the Introduction for Week 8's chart.

You will record children's responses by writing the underlined words in the boxes.

### Analyze Setting–Where (Literary Analysis)

Today we will learn more about how stories are made.

The setting of a story tells two things. One thing the setting tells is where the story happens. What is one thing the setting tells? *Where the story happens.*

Let's look at the pictures and talk about the story, to figure out where *Cinderella* happened.

**Page 2.** Where did the story begin? *At Cinderella's house.*

**Page 3.** Where did the next part of the story happen? *In the stepsister's bedroom.*

**Page 4.** Where did the next part of the story happen? *By the <u>chimney</u>; in the <u>ashes</u>.*

**Pages 6–8.** Where did the next part of the story happen? *In the <u>stepsister's bedroom</u>.*

**Pages 10–14.** Where did the next part of the story happen? *In <u>Cinderella's garden</u>.*

**Page 15.** Where did the next part of the story happen? *<u>Outside the palace</u>.*

**Pages 16–18.** Where did the next part of the story happen? *<u>In the palace</u>.*

**Page 19.** Where did the next part of the story happen? *At <u>Cinderella's house</u>.*

**Pages 21–22.** Where did the next part of the story happen? *<u>Outside the palace</u>.*

**Pages 23–24.** Where did the next part of the story happen? *<u>In the palace</u>.*

**Pages 25–28.** Where did the next part of the story happen? *At <u>Cinderella's house</u>.*

**Page 29.** Where did the last part of the story happen? *<u>In the palace</u>.*

Cinderella's house, the stepsisters' bedroom, in the ashes by the chimney, Cinderella's garden, outside the palace, and in the palace are all in the land ruled by the king. So, if we could only use one group of words to tell the setting of the story we would use the words *in the land ruled by the king*. Where is the setting of *Cinderella*? *In the land ruled by the king.*

Today you learned about one part of the setting of *Cinderella*. You learned about where the story happened.

### Play Chew the Fat

Today you will play a game called *Chew the Fat*. A long time ago, when people wanted to just sit and talk about things that were happening in their lives, they would say that they would sit and "chew the fat."

In this game, I will say some sentences with our vocabulary words in them. If I use the vocabulary word correctly, say "Well done!"

If I use the word incorrectly, say "Chew the fat." That means that you want to talk about how I used the word. I'll say the beginning of the sentence again. If you can make the sentence

end so that it makes sense, you'll get a point. If you can't, I get the point.

Let's practice. I know Wyatt has a bad **temper** because … he is always calm and contented. *Chew the fat.* Let's chew the fat. The first part of the sentence stays the same. I'll say the first part. I know Wyatt has a bad **temper** because. How can we finish the sentence so it makes sense? (Idea: *He gets irritated and angry very quickly.*) Let's say the whole sentence together now. *I know Wyatt has a bad temper because he gets irritated and angry very quickly.* Well done! I'm glad we chewed the fat!

Let's do another one together. It was a **miserable** day because … the sun was shining and the air was warm. *Chew the fat.* The first part of the sentence stays the same. I'll say the first part. It was a **miserable** day because. How can we finish the sentence so that it makes sense? (Idea: *It was dark and cold.*) Let's say the whole sentence now. *It was a miserable day because it was dark and cold.* Well done! I'm glad we chewed the fat!

Let's try one more. Rick was **delighted** because … everyone enjoyed his poem. *Well done!* I used the word **delighted** correctly so you said, "Well done!"

Now you're ready to play the game. (Draw a T-chart on the board for keeping score. Children earn one point for each correct answer. If they make an error, correct them as you normally would, and record one point for yourself. Repeat missed words at the end of the game.)

- Her clothes were **magnificent** because … they were plain and ordinary. *Chew the fat.* I'll say the first part of the sentence again. Her clothes were **magnificent** because. How can we finish the sentence so it makes sense? (Idea: *They were very beautiful to look at.*) Let's say the whole sentence together. *Her clothes were magnificent because they were very beautiful to look at.* Well done! I'm glad we chewed the fat!
- Marissa's mom felt **miserable** because … she was healthy and full of energy. *Chew the fat.* I'll say the first part of the sentence again. Marissa's mom felt **miserable** because. How

can we finish the sentence so it makes sense? (Idea: *She was sick and had no energy.*) Let's say the whole sentence together. *Marissa's mom felt miserable because she was sick and had no energy.* Well done! I'm glad we chewed the fat!

- Dwight was **forgiving** because … he never blamed people for the bad things they did to him. *Well done!*

- Shaquille is generous because … he never shares with anyone else. *Chew the fat.* I'll say the first part of the sentence again. Shaquille is **generous** because. How can we finish the sentence so it makes sense? (Idea: *He always shares with everyone.*) Let's say the whole sentence together. *Shaquille is generous because he always shares with everyone.* Well done! I'm glad we chewed the fat!

- My big sister was **forgiving** because … she got angry and blamed me when I spilled juice on her art project. *Chew the fat.* I'll say the first part of the sentence again. My big sister was **forgiving** because. How can we finish the sentence so it makes sense? (Idea: *She didn't get angry or blame me when I spilled juice on her art project.*) Let's say the whole sentence together. *My big sister was forgiving because she didn't get angry or blame me when I spilled juice on her art project.* Well done! I'm glad we chewed the fat!

(Count the points and declare a winner.) You did a great job of playing *Chew the Fat.*

### Complete the Activity Sheet

(Give each child a copy of the Activity Sheet, BLM 8b. Have children cut apart the words in the word bank. If children are unfamiliar with Venn diagrams, do this as a guided activity.)

Let's compare Cinderella and her stepsisters. Cinderella and her stepsisters were different in some ways and the same in some ways.

(Point to the circle under the word *Cinderella.*) This circle is where we'll put things that tell about **only** Cinderella.

(Point to the circle under the words *The Stepsisters.*) This circle is where we'll put things that tell about **only** the stepsisters.

(Point to the place where the two circles overlap.) This is where we'll put things that tell about **both** Cinderella and the stepsisters.

(Either read for children or have them read the words in the word bank one at a time. After each word is read ask:) Does this tell about Cinderella or the stepsisters, or both Cinderella and the stepsisters?

(If children identify the character trait or activity as belonging to only Cinderella, have them paste or glue the word in the large circle under the word *Cinderella.*)

(If children identify the character trait or activity as belonging to only the stepsisters, have them paste or glue the word in the large circle under the words *The Stepsisters.*)

(If children identify the character trait or activity as belonging to both Cinderella and the stepsisters, have them paste or glue the word in area where the two circles overlap.)

(Repeat procedure for each item in the word bank.)

(Cinderella: good; sweet; beautiful; had a fairy godmother; married the prince

The Stepsisters: mean; rude; selfish; made fun of someone

Both: got married; girl; went to the balls; lived at the palace; had a beautiful gown.)

---

## DAY 4

**Preparation:** Map or globe of the world.

### Learn About Fairy Tales

Today you will learn about a special kind of folk tale called a fairy tale. What will you learn about? *A fairy tale.*

Folk tales and fairy tales are both stories that were once told out loud. How are folk tales and fairy tales the same? (Idea: *They are both stories that were once told out loud.*)

But a fairy tale is a story that someone decided to write down in a book a long time ago. How is a fairy tale different from a folk tale? (Idea: *Someone decided to write it down in a book a long time ago.*)

The first person to write down *Cinderella* was a man from France named Charles Perrault [per-oh].

(Locate France on the map or globe.) What country does *Cinderella* come from? *France.* Charles Perrault first wrote down this story almost 200 years ago. When did he write down this story? (Idea: *Almost 200 years ago.*) That's a very, very long time ago!

After Charles Perrault wrote the story down, many other people from other countries told the story. (Point to the word *Translated* on the cover of the book.) Marcia Brown translated the story. That means she changed the words of the story from French to English. Because Marcia Brown wrote the story in English, she is known as the author of this version of the story. Who is the author of this version of the story? *Marcia Brown.*

Fairy tales often begin with the same words. Listen while I read the first sentence of *Cinderella.* "Once upon a time there was a gentleman who took for his second wife the proudest and haughtiest woman that was ever seen." How does this fairy tale begin? *Once upon a time.*

Fairy tales often have good characters and evil characters. Who are the good characters in *Cinderella?* (Idea: *Cinderella; the prince.*) Who are the evil characters in *Cinderella?* (Idea: *The two stepsisters; the stepmother.*)

Fairy tales often have things that happen in threes. Tell about the things that happened in threes. (Ideas: *The fairy godmother used her wand three times to give Cinderella three different gowns; there were three pairs of horses; there were three pairs of footmen; there were three rats in the rat trap; three sisters got married on the same day.*)

Fairy tales often have royal people and places in them. Tell about the royal people in *Cinderella.* (Ideas: *King, queen, prince.*) Tell about the royal places in *Cinderella.* (Idea: *The palace.*)

Let's remember some important things about fairy tales. How do fairy tales often begin? *Once upon a time.* What kinds of characters are often in fairy tales? *Good characters and evil*

characters. What is the special number that is often in fairy tales? *Three.* What special people and places are often in fairy tales? *Royal people and places.* Good remembering about fairy tales.

### Play Chew the Fat (Cumulative Review)

Today, you will play the game called *Chew the Fat.* Remember that a long time ago, when people wanted to just sit and talk about things that were happening in their lives, they would say that they would sit and "chew the fat." In this game, I will say some sentences with our vocabulary words in them. If I use the vocabulary word correctly, say "Well done!"

If I use the word incorrectly, say "Chew the fat." That means that you want to talk about how I used the word. I'll say the beginning of the sentence again. If you can make the sentence end so that it makes sense, you'll get a point. If you can't, I get the point.

Let's practice. Mr. Gates is **generous** because … he never gives anyone anything. *Chew the fat.* Let's chew the fat. The first part of the sentence stays the same. I'll say the first part. Mr. Gates is **generous** because. How can we finish the sentence so it makes sense? (Idea: *He shares what he has with others.*) Let's say the whole sentence together now. *Mr. Gates is generous because he shares what he has with others.* Well done! I'm glad we chewed the fat!

Let's do another one together. My Auntie Mae is a **forgiving** person because … she always blames me for the bad things I do. *Chew the fat.* The first part of the sentence stays the same. I'll say the first part. My Auntie Mae is a **forgiving** person because. How can we finish the sentence so it makes sense? (Idea: *She never blames me for the bad things I do.*) Let's say the whole sentence now. *My Auntie Mae is a forgiving person because she never blames me for the bad things I do. Well done!* I'm glad we chewed the fat!

Now you're ready to play the game. (Draw a T-chart on the board for keeping score. Children earn one point for each correct answer. If they make an error, correct them as you normally would, and record one point for yourself. Repeat missed words at the end of the game.)

- Talia felt **miserable** when ... all of her friends came over to play. *Chew the fat.* I'll say the first part of the sentence again. Talia felt **miserable** when. How can we finish the sentence so it makes sense? (Idea: *None of her friends came over to play.*) Let's say the whole sentence together. *Talia was miserable when none of her friends came over to play.* Well done! I'm glad we chewed the fat!

- The painting was **magnificent** because ... it was so beautiful to look at. *Well done!*

- I was **delighted** when . . . I got a new puppy from my grandpa. *Well done!*

- She hated her **miserable** room because ... it was so beautiful and cheery. *Chew the fat.* I'll say the first part of the sentence again. She hated her **miserable** room because. (Idea: *It was cold, gloomy and made her feel bad.*) Let's say the whole sentence together. *She hated her miserable room because it was cold, gloomy, and made her feel bad.* Well done! I'm glad we chewed the fat!

- I know I have a **temper** because ... nothing ever upsets me. *Chew the fat.* I'll say the first part of the sentence again. I know I have a **temper** because. How can we finish the sentence so it makes sense? (Idea: *I get irritated and angry very quickly.*) Let's say the whole sentence together. *I know I have a temper because I get irritated and angry very quickly.* Well done! I'm glad we chewed the fat!

- The teacher got **frazzled** when ... the children were quiet and well behaved. *Chew the fat.* I'll say the first part of the sentence again. The teacher got **frazzled** when. How can we finish the sentence so it makes sense? (Idea: *The children were noisy and rude.*) Let's say the whole sentence together. *The teacher got frazzled when the children were noisy and rude.* Well done! I'm glad we chewed the fat!

- Alejandro followed his brother's **advice** when ... he did what his brother said he should do. *Well done!*

- Kelvin and Brock **quarreled** because ... they agreed to play the same game. *Chew the fat.* I'll say the first part of the sentence again. Kelvin and Brock **quarreled** because. How can we finish the sentence so it makes sense? (Idea: *they disagreed about what game to play.*) Let's say the whole sentence together. *Kelvin and Brock quarreled because they disagreed about what game to play.* Well done! I'm glad we chewed the fat!

- The little boy was **gullible** because ... it wasn't easy to trick him. *Chew the fat.* I'll say the first part of the sentence again. The little boy was **gullible** because. How can we finish the sentence so it makes sense? (Idea: *It was easy to trick him.*) Let's say the whole sentence together. *The little boy was gullible because it was easy to trick him.* Well done! I'm glad we chewed the fat!

(Count the points and declare a winner.) You did a great job of playing *Chew the Fat.*

## DAY 5

**Preparation:** Each child will need a copy of the Quiz Answer Sheet, BLM B.

### Retell Story

Today, I'll show you the pictures Marcia Brown made for *Cinderella.* As I show you the pictures, I'll call on one of you to tell the class that part of the story.

Tell me what happens at the **beginning** of the story. (Show the pictures on pages 1–4. Call on a child to tell what's happening.)

Tell me what happens in the **middle** of the story. (Show the pictures on pages 5–28. Call on a child to tell what's happening. Encourage use of target words when appropriate. Model use when necessary.)

Tell me what happens at the **end** of the story. (Show the pictures on page 29. Call on a child to tell what's happening.)

## Assess Vocabulary

(Give each child a copy of the Quiz Answer Sheet, BLM B.)

Today, you're going to have a True or False quiz. When you do the True or False quiz, it shows me how well you know the hard words you are learning.

If I say something that is true, circle the word **true.** What will you do if I say something that is true? *Circle the word true.*

If I say something that is false, circle the word **false.** What will you do if I say something that is false? *Circle the word false.*

Listen carefully to each item that I say. Don't let me trick you!

Item 1: Someone who has a **temper** is always calm and in control of themselves. (*False.*)

Item 2: If you are **miserable,** you feel **delighted.** (*False.*)

Item 3: A **generous** person shares with others. (*True.*)

Item 4: If you are a **forgiving** person you wouldn't blame your little brother if he accidentally broke your favorite toy. (*True.*)

Item 5: A **magnificent** house is plain and ordinary. (*False.*)

Item 6: A cellar could be a **miserable** place if it was cold, gloomy, and damp. (*True.*)

Item 7: Your **situation** could be good or bad. (*True.*)

Item 8: If you thought your supper tasted **disgusting,** you would eat lots of it. (*False.*)

Item 9: An **uncooperative** person is helpful and fun to be around. (*False.*)

Item 10: If your teacher **complains** about your printing, she thinks you're a really good printer. (*False.*)

You did a great job completing your quiz!

(Score children's work. A child must score 9 out of 10 to be at the mastery level. If a child does not achieve mastery, insert the missed words as additional items in the games in next week's lessons. Retest those children individually for the missed items before they take the next mastery test.)

## Extensions

### Read a Story as a Reward

(Display copies of the books that you have read since the beginning of the program, as well as some traditional retellings of fairy tales. Allow children to choose which book they would like you to read to them as a reward for their hard work.)

(Read the story aloud for enjoyment with minimal interruptions.)

---

**Preparation:** Word containers for the Super Words Center. You may wish to remove some of the words from earlier lessons the children have mastered. You will need 2 copies of each card that remains in the word containers.

---

### Introduce the Super Words Center

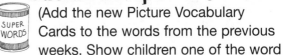(Add the new Picture Vocabulary Cards to the words from the previous weeks. Show children one of the word containers. If children need more guidance in how to work in the Super Words Center, role-play with two to three children as a demonstration.)

I will teach you how to play a new game today called *Go Fish.*

Let's think about how we work with our words in the Super Words Center.

You will work with a partner in the Super Words Center. Whom will you work with? *A partner.*

First you and your partner will each draw six word cards out of the container and hold them so your partner cannot see them. What do you do first? (Idea: *Draw six cards out of the container and hold them so my partner cannot see them.*)

Next you will look at the cards in your hand and lay down any cards that you have two of. You will tell your partner the word the pictures show. What do you do next? (Idea: *Lay down any cards that I have two of, and tell my partner the word the pictures show.*)

Then your partner has a chance to lay down any cards he or she has two of, and tell the word the pictures show. What does your partner do? (Idea: *Lay down any cards that he or she has two of, and tell the word the pictures show.*)

Next you will ask your partner for a card that you have only one of by saying the word the picture shows. If your partner has that card, he or she will give it to you. If your partner gives you the card, you will lay down the two cards. What does your partner do if they have the card you ask for? (Idea: *Give you the card.*) What will you do if your partner gives you a card? (Idea: *Lay down the two cards that are the same.*)

If your partner does not have the card you ask for, your partner will say, "Go Fish." What will your partner do if he or she doesn't have the card you ask for? (Idea: *Say "Go Fish."*) If your partner says "Go Fish," you must choose another card from the word container. What will you do if your partner says "Go Fish"? (Idea: *Choose a card from the word container.*)

Then it's your partner's turn.

Watch while I show you what I mean.

**(Demonstrate this process with one child as your partner.)**

When one partner has no cards left in his or her hand, the game is over. Each person gets one point for each pair of cards they have laid down. The winner is the person with the most points. Who wins the game? (Idea: *The person with the most points.*)

Have fun playing *Go Fish!*

## The Nightingale

author: Hans Christian Andersen • illustrator: Jerry Pinkney

**Preparation:** You will need a copy of *The Nightingale* for each day's lesson.

Number the pages of the story to assist you in asking comprehension questions at appropriate points.

Post a copy of the Vocabulary Tally Sheet, BLM A, with this week's Picture Vocabulary Cards attached.

Each child will need one copy of the Homework Sheet, BLM 9a.

### Target Vocabulary

| Tier II | Tier III |
|---|---|
| remarkable | setting (where) |
| precious | fairy tale |
| notice | noun |
| physician | translated |
| *grateful | |
| *captive | |

*Expanded Target Vocabulary Word

---

### DAY 1

### Introduce Book

This week's book is called *The Nightingale*. What's the title of this week's book? *The Nightingale.*

This book was written by Hans Christian Andersen. Who's the author of *The Nightingale*? *Hans Christian Andersen.*

Jerry Pinkney made the pictures for this book. Who's the illustrator of *The Nightingale*? *Jerry Pinkney.* Who made the illustrations for this book? *Jerry Pinkney.*

The cover of a book usually gives us some hints of what the book is about. Let's look at the front cover of *The Nightingale.* What do you see in the picture? (Ideas: *A man with a white beard; a monkey, a little girl; they are wearing clothes different from the clothes we wear; they are looking at a bird flying towards the man.*)

(Assign each child a partner.) Get ready to make some predictions to your partner about this book. Use the information from the cover to help you.

(Ask the following questions, allowing sufficient time for children to share their predictions with their partners.)

- Who do you think are the characters in this story?
- What do you think they will do?
- Where do you think the story happens?

- When do you think the story happens?
- Why do you think they are looking at the bird?
- How do you think the monkey got the piece of fruit?
- Do you think this story is about real people? Tell why or why not.

(Call on several children to share their predictions with the class.)

### Take a Picture Walk

(Encourage children to use target words in their answers.) We're going to take a picture walk through this book. Remember that when we take a picture walk, we look at the pictures and tell what we think will happen in the story.

**Page 2.** What do you think these men are doing? (Idea: *Catching fish.*) What do you think they are looking at?

**Pages 3–4.** What do you think the man is telling these people?

**Page 6.** Who do you think the man sitting down is? (Idea: *A king.*) What do you think the man is saying to the king?

**Pages 7–8.** (Point to the man in the flowered robes.) This is the same man that was talking to the king in the last illustration. What do you think he is saying to this young girl?

**Pages 9–10.** Where does this part of the story take place? (Ideas: *In a garden; in the woods.*) What is everyone looking at? *The bird.* This bird is called a nightingale. Nightingales sing very beautifully.

(**Note:** You may wish to play a recording for the children. Use the search words *nightingale song* on the Internet. The Freesound Project has some excellent recordings.)

**Pages 11–12.** (Point to the man in the flowered robe.) Here's the man who was talking to the king again. It looks like he is trying to get the nightingale to go somewhere. Where do you think he wants it to go? (Idea: *To the palace.*)

**Page 14.** Where does this part of the story happen? (Idea: *In the palace.*) What is the nightingale doing? *Singing.* What is the king doing? (Idea: *Crying.*) Why do you think the king is crying?

**Pages 15–16.** What is happening in this illustration? (Idea: *the bird is flying, but people are holding on to it with strings so it can't fly away.*) Why do you think the bird is not allowed to fly away? (Idea: *The king wants to keep it.*)

**Pages 17–18.** (Point to the man in the bottom right of the illustration.) What is this man holding? (Ideas: *A statue of a nightingale; a wind-up nightingale; a bird made out of gold and jewels.*)

**Pages 19–20.** Where does this part of the story happen? (Idea: *In the woods; in the jungle.*) What are the fishermen looking at? (Idea: *The nightingale.* If children have trouble answering this question, point to the nightingale among the trees on page 20, near the top.) Why do you think the nightingale has returned to the woods?

**Pages 21–22.** What is everyone looking at in this illustration? (Idea: *The gold nightingale.*) Why do you think they are all looking at it?

**Page 24.** The king looks upset. What do you think has happened? (Idea: *The gold nightingale broke.*)

**Pages 25–26.** What do you think is happening here? (Idea: *A man is trying to fix the king's gold nightingale.*)

**Page 28.** What do you think has happened to the king? (Idea: *He is sick.*) Do you think there's anything that might make the king feel better? (Idea: *The nightingale.*)

**Pages 29–30.** What time of day is it in this illustration? (Idea: *Nighttime.*) Who do you think that is that the nightingale is flying toward? (Idea: *A skeleton; a dead person.*)

**Page 32.** What has happened to the king? (Idea: *He has gotten better.*) Why do you think the king got better? (Idea: *The nightingale came to sing to him.*)

**Page 33.** What do you think the king is saying to the people?

It's your turn to ask me some questions. What would you like to know about the story? (Accept questions. If children tell about the pictures or the story instead of asking questions, prompt them to ask a question.) Ask me a what question. Ask me a when question.

 **Read the Story Aloud**
(Read the story to children with minimal interruptions.)

Tomorrow we will read the story again and I will ask you some questions.

## Present Target Vocabulary
◎—◁ Remarkable

In the story, "everything in the king's garden was remarkable." That means everything in the garden was unusual or very special. **Remarkable.** Say the word. *Remarkable.*

**Remarkable** is a describing word. It tells more about a thing. What kind of word is **remarkable?** *A describing word.*

**If something is remarkable it is unusual or very special.** Say the word that means "unusual or special." *Remarkable.*

(Correct any incorrect responses, and repeat the item at the end of the sequence.)

Let's think about some things that might be remarkable. I'll tell you about something. If you think that thing is remarkable, say "remarkable." If not, don't say anything.

- He is the very best tennis player in our state. *Remarkable.*
- This summer was unusual because we only had rain one day. *Remarkable.*
- Louis is an ordinary person who does ordinary things.

- That house is unusual because it is the only one on the street that is painted purple with blue flowers. *Remarkable.*
- Cinderella was unusual and very special because she was both beautiful and generous. *Remarkable.*
- We grow peas and carrots in our vegetable garden.

What word means "unusual or very special"? *Remarkable.*

## Precious

In the story, the king called the artificial bird a "little precious golden bird." That means the bird was very special and important to him. **Precious.** Say the word. *Precious.*

**Precious** is a describing word. It tells more about a thing. What kind of word is **precious?** *A describing word.*

**If something is precious, it is very special and important to the person who owns it.** Say the word that means "very special and important." *Precious.*

Let's think some things that might be precious to different people. I'll tell about something. If you think that thing is precious to the person, say "precious." If not, don't say anything.

- His violin was the most special thing he owned. *Precious.*
- Mom's wedding ring was very important to her. *Precious.*
- It was just an old piece of wood.
- That book isn't special—I have seven others just like it.
- The picture of her very first car was very special to her. *Precious.*
- He knew he could have fresh vegetables again tomorrow if he wanted them.

What word means "very special and important"? *Precious.*

What is most **precious** to you? Why is that **precious?** (Call on several children. Encourage children to use this frame for their answers: *The thing that is most precious to me is _____, because _____.)*

## Notice

In the story, "No one noticed the living nightingale when she flew out the open window back to her own green woods." That means no one saw her or was aware of her when she flew away. **Notice.** Say the word. *Notice.*

**Notice** is an action word. It tells what someone does. What kind of word is **notice?** *An action word.*

**If you notice something you see it or are aware of it.** Say the word that means "see something or are aware of something." *Notice.*

Let's think about some times when a person might notice something. I'll tell about a time. If the person would notice something, say "notice." If not, don't say anything.

- Jeremy was aware there was something wrong with his brakes when he pushed the pedal down. *Notice.*
- I wonder if Grandma will see I have a new haircut. *Notice.*
- I wrote a short letter to my dad.
- Do you think Auntie Jen will see how tall I've grown? *Notice.*
- The tree fell in the forest, but no one was there to see it.
- Were you aware of the song playing on the radio? *Notice.*

What word means "see something or are aware of it"? *Notice.*

## Physician

In the story, "The king immediately jumped out of bed and called for his physician" to try and heal the gold bird. That means the king called for his doctor. **Physician.** Say the word. *Physician.*

**Physician** is a naming word. Another word for a naming word is a noun. What is another word for a naming word? *A noun.* A noun names a person, place, thing, or idea. What does a noun name? *A person, place, thing, or idea.* What kind of word names a person, place, thing, or idea? *A noun.* **Physician** names a person, so what kind of word is **physician?** *A noun.*

**A physician is a doctor.** Say the word that means "a doctor." *Physician.*

Let's think about some people who might be physicians. I'll tell about what a person does. If you think that person might be a physician, say "physician." If not, don't say anything.

- The woman looked down the little girl's throat. *Physician.*
- The man listened to his patient's heart. *Physician*
- The man fixed the hockey player's broken tooth.
- The woman sent the sick baby to the hospital after examining her in her office. *Physician.*
- The woman fixed our car.
- The man wrote stories.

What noun means "a doctor"? *Physician.*

### Present Vocabulary Tally Sheet
(See Lesson 1, page 4, for instructions.)

### Assign Homework
(Homework Sheet, BLM 9a. See the Introduction for homework instructions.)

## DAY 2

**Preparation:** Picture Vocabulary Cards for *remarkable, precious, notice, physician.*

### Read and Discuss Story
(Read story to children. Ask the following questions at specified points. Encourage them to use target words in their answers.)

**Page 1.** When did this story happen? (Idea: *A great many years ago.*) Who lived in the forest beyond the palace? *A nightingale.* What was special about this nightingale? (Idea: *Her beautiful singing.*)

**Page 3.** What did people think was the greatest part of a visit to the palace? (Idea: *The nightingale's song.*) Did the king know about the nightingale? *No.*

**Page 5.** Why do you think the king and his court had not heard of the nightingale? (Idea: *They did not leave the palace and go into the forest.*) What did the king want his court to do? (Idea: *Find the nightingale and bring her to him so he could hear her sing.*)

**Pages 7–8.** (Read to the end of the sentence "And it is just as if my mother kissed me.") Who had heard the nightingale sing? (Idea: *A poor kitchen girl.*) What do you think will happen next? (Idea: *The people will ask the kitchen girl to take them to the nightingale.*) Do you think she'll take them to the nightingale? *Yes.*

**Page 9.** (Read to the end of the first paragraph.) Had the court ever been in the forest before? *No.*

(Read to the end of the page.) What was surprising about the nightingale? (Idea: *She looked very dull and plain.*)

**Page 11.** What did the nightingale's voice sound like? (Idea: *Tiny silver bells.*)

**Page 12.** Where did the nightingale think her song sounded the best? (Idea: *In the green woods.*)

**Page 13.** How did the king and the others react to the nightingale's song? (Ideas: *They cried; tears ran down their faces.*) Why did the nightingale's song make the king and the others cry? (*Idea: Because it was so beautiful.*) What was the nightingale's reward? (Idea: *Seeing tears in the king's eyes.*)

**Page 15.** What did the nightingale get for staying in the king's palace? (Idea: *A golden cage and a chance to go out twice a day.*)

**Page 16.** When two people in the kingdom met each other, what did the first person say? *Nightin.* What did the second person say? *Gale.*

**Page 17.** What special gift did the king receive? (Idea: *An artificial bird.*) **Artificial** means "not real." What does **artificial** mean? *Not real.* What word means "not real"? *Artificial.* What did the artificial bird look like? (Ideas: *It was made of silver and gold; it was covered with diamonds, shells, and rubies.*) What did the artificial nightingale do? (Ideas: *Sing like the real nightingale; move its tail up and down.*) How was the artificial nightingale different from the real nightingale? (Idea: *The real nightingale sang in its own natural way; the artificial nightingale sang the same song over and over.*)

**Page 19.** Why was the artificial nightingale better than the real nightingale? (Ideas: *The artificial nightingale was much prettier than the* real nightingale; the artificial nightingale could continue singing without getting tired.) The king wanted the real nightingale to sing, but she was gone. Where did she go? (Idea: *Back to the forest.*)

**Page 21.** What did the king's people say about the nightingale? (Idea: *They said that she was an ungrateful creature.*) What made the artificial nightingale better than the real one according to the king's people? (Ideas: *It was more beautiful; its singing was better because people always knew what was coming; the tune stayed the same.*)

**Page 23.** Which bird was more important to the king, the real nightingale or the artificial nightingale? *The artificial nightingale.* What happened to the artificial nightingale one evening? (Idea: *It broke and stopped singing.*)

**Page 26.** (Read to the end of the first paragraph.) Was the Great-Fixer-of-All-Things able to fix the artificial nightingale? *Yes.* Yes, he was able to fix the artificial nightingale, but what was the problem? (Idea: *The bird was only allowed to sing on special occasions.*)

(Read to the end of the page.) What happened to the king? (Idea: *He got very sick and was dying.*)

**Page 27.** (Read to the end of the first paragraph.) Who surrounded the king? (Idea: *Old Man Death and heads of the king's good and bad deeds.*)

(Read to the end of the page.) What did the king want? *Music.* Why did he want to hear music? (Idea: *He didn't want to hear what the heads around him were saying.*)

**Page 29.** Who saved the king from Old Man Death and the heads of his good and bad deeds? *The nightingale.* How did she save him? (Idea: *She sang so sweetly that Death wanted to go back to his garden, and he left.*)

**Page 31.** (Read to the end of the fourth paragraph.) What did the king want the nightingale to do? (Idea: *Come live in the palace.*)

(Read to the end of the fifth paragraph.) What did the nightingale agree to do? (Idea: *Come to*

the king's window when she likes and sing to him.)

(Read to the end of the page.) What did the nightingale want the king to promise her? (Idea: *That he will listen to his heart and always live in peace.*)

**Page 34.** Why were the king's servants amazed when they returned to the palace? (Ideas: *They expected him to be dead; he was standing on the balcony, healthy.*) Why did the poor kitchen girl receive the ribbon of honor? (Idea: *She was the one who first brought the nightingale to the king.*)

## Review Vocabulary

(Display the Picture Vocabulary Cards. Point to each card as you say the word. Ask children to repeat each word after you.) These pictures show **remarkable, precious, notice,** and **physician.**

- What noun means "a doctor"? *Physician.*
- What word means "very special and important"? *Precious.*
- What word means "see something or are aware of it"? *Notice.*
- What word means "unusual or exceptional"? *Remarkable.*

## Extend Vocabulary

◎ Notice

In *The Nightingale,* we learned that **notice** is an action word that means "see something or be aware of it." Say the word that means "see something or be aware of it." *Notice.*

Raise your hand if you can tell us a sentence that uses **notice** as an action word meaning "see something or be aware of it." (Call on several children. If they don't use complete sentences, restate their examples as sentences. Have the class repeat the sentences.)

Here's a new way to use the word **notice.**

- The school sent home a **notice** asking for volunteers to make costumes for the play. Say the sentence.
- The coach sent home a **notice** telling everyone the practice times. Say the sentence.

- I received a **notice** telling me the water would be shut off on Monday, from 9 to 10 A.M. Say the sentence.

In these sentences, **notice** is a naming word. Another word for a naming word is a noun. What is another word for a naming word? *A noun.* A noun names a person, place, thing, or idea. What does a noun name? *A person, place, thing, or idea.* What kind of word names a person, place, thing, or idea? *A noun.* **Notice** names a thing, so what kind of word is **notice?** *A noun.*

**Notice is a noun that means the same letter sent to a lot of people, giving them information or asking them to do something.** What noun means "the same letter sent to a lot of people, giving them information or asking them to do something"? *Notice.*

Raise your hand if you can tell us a sentence that uses **notice** as a noun meaning "the same letter sent to a lot of people giving them information or asking them to do something." (Call on several children. If they don't use complete sentences, restate their examples as sentences. Have the class repeat the sentences.)

## Present Expanded Target Vocabulary
◎ = Grateful

In the story, the king said, "Thanks, thanks, you heavenly little bird. How can I reward you?" The King wanted to show the little bird how much he appreciated the little bird and was thankful for it. Another way to say the king appreciated and was thankful to the little bird is to say the king was grateful. **Grateful.** Say the word. *Grateful.*

**Grateful** is a describing word. It tells more about a person. What kind of word is **grateful?** *A describing word.*

**When you are grateful, you appreciate what someone has done for you and are thankful.** Say the word that means "appreciate what someone has done for you and are thankful." *Grateful.*

Let's think about some times when you might be grateful. If I tell about a time when you would be grateful, say "grateful." If not, don't say anything.

- You appreciate it when your aunt and uncle take you to the park. *Grateful.*

- You are thankful you live in the United States of America. *Grateful.*
- You wish you could go to the beach.
- You don't like to eat spinach.
- You appreciate and are thankful that fire fighters are there to protect your community from fires. *Grateful.*
- You appreciate how far Johnny Appleseed had to walk in order to plant apple trees all across America. *Grateful.*

What word means "you appreciate what someone has done for you and are thankful"? *Grateful.*

◎ = Captive

In the story, when the little nightingale was let out of her cage, the servants held her by silken strings so she could not get away. Another way of saying they held her so she could not get away is to say she was a captive. **Captive.** Say the word. *Captive.*

**Captive** is a naming word. Another word for a naming word is a noun. What is another word for a naming word? *A noun.* A noun names a person, place, thing, or idea. What does a noun name? *A person, place, thing, or idea.* What kind of word names a person, place, thing, or idea? *A noun.* **Captive** names a person or a thing so what kind of word is **captive?** *A noun.*

**If you are a captive, you are a prisoner.** Say the word that means "a prisoner." *Captive.*

Let's think about some times when a person or an animal might be a captive. I'll tell about a time. If you think that person or animal is a captive, say "captive." If not, don't say anything.

- The hunters' ropes captured the lion and wouldn't let him go. *Captive.*
- The deer could go anywhere in the forest they wanted.
- The tigers were kept in cages. *Captive.*
- America is the land of the free.
- The Alonzo family traveled all over the United States.
- The prisoner was kept in jail for two years. *Captive.*

What noun means "a prisoner"? *Captive.*

**Preparation:** Prepare a sheet of chart paper, landscape direction, titled *The Nightingale.* Underneath the title, draw 15 boxes, connected by arrows.

See the Introduction for Week 9's chart.

You will record children's responses by writing the underlined words in the boxes.

Map or globe of the world.

Two sheets of chart paper or sufficient board space to record a brainstormed list of words and phrases for the Activity Sheet.

## Analyze Setting–Where (Literary Analysis)

Today we will learn more about how stories are made.

The setting of a story tells two things. One thing the setting tells is where the story happens. What is one thing the setting tells? *Where the story happens.*

Let's look at the pictures and talk about the story, to figure out where *The Nightingale* happens.

**Page 2.** Where did the story begin? *In the river.*

**Pages 4–8.** Where did the next part of the story happen? *In the palace.*

**Page 10** (And read the first sentence on page 9.) "So the girl went into the woods where the nightingale sang, and half the court followed her." Where did the next part of the story happen? *In the woods.*

**Page 12.** Where did the next part of the story happen? *Between the woods and the king's palace.*

**Page 14.** Where did the next part of the story happen? *In the palace.*

**Pages 15–16.** Where did the next part of the story happen? *In the king's garden.*

**Pages 17–18.** Where did the next part of the story happen? *In the palace.*

**Pages 19–20.** Where did the next part of the story happen? *In the woods near the river.*

**Pages 21–22.** Where did the next part of the story happen? *Outside the palace.*

**Page 24.** Where did the next part of the story happen? *In the king's bedroom.*

**Pages 25–26.** Where did the next part of the story happen? *In the workshop of the Great-Fixer-of-All-Things.*

**Pages 28–30.** Where did the next part of the story happen? *In the king's bedroom.*

**Page 32.** Where did the next part of the story happen? *At the window.*

**Page 33.** Where did the last part of the story happen? *Outside the palace.*

The river, the palace, the woods, between the woods and the palace, the garden, outside the palace, the king's bedroom, and the window all are in the country ruled by the king. The king in this story lived in the country of Morocco. Morocco is in Northwest Africa. So, if we could only use one word to tell the setting of the story, we would use the word *Morocco.* Where is the setting of *The Nightingale*? *Morocco.* (Locate Morocco on the map or globe.)

(Inside title page.) Let's think of some words and groups of words that could tell about the King of Morocco's palace. (Brainstorm with children a list of words and phrases that could describe the building. Record responses on the first sheet of chart paper.)

(Dedication page.) Let's think of some words and groups of words that could tell about the gardens around King of Morocco's palace. (Brainstorm with children a list of words and phrases that could describe the gardens. Record responses on the second sheet of chart paper.)

Today you learned about one part of the setting of *The Nightingale.* You learned about where the story happens.

## Play Chew the Fat

Now you will play a game called *Chew the Fat.* A long time ago, when people wanted to just sit and talk about things that were happening in their lives, they would say that they would sit and "chew the fat."

In this game, I will say some sentences with our vocabulary words in them. If I use the vocabulary word correctly, say "Well done!"

If I use the word incorrectly, say "Chew the fat." That means that you want to talk about how I used the word. I'll say the beginning of the sentence again. If you can make the sentence end so that it makes sense, you'll get a point. If you can't, I get the point.

Let's practice. Although Gloria is blind, she is **remarkable** because … she can't read. *Chew the fat.* Let's chew the fat. The first part of the sentence stays the same. I'll say the first part. Although Gloria is blind, she is **remarkable** because. How can we finish the sentence so it makes sense? (Idea: *She can read with her fingers.*) Let's say the whole sentence together now. *Although Gloria is blind, she is remarkable because she can read with her fingers.* Well done! I'm glad we chewed the fat!

Let's do another one together. Shynella **noticed** the black clouds when … she didn't see them. *Chew the fat.* The first part of the sentence stays the same. I'll say the first part. Shynella **noticed** the black clouds when. How can we finish the sentence so that it makes sense? (Idea: *She saw them coming closer.*) Let's say the whole sentence now. *Shynella noticed the black clouds when she saw them coming closer.* Well done! I'm glad we chewed the fat!

Let's try one more. Jermon's model of a Spitfire airplane was **precious** because … it was the first one he'd ever made. *Well done!* I used the word **precious** correctly so you said, "Well done!"

Now you're ready to play the game. (Draw a T-chart on the board for keeping score. Children earn one point for each correct answer. If they make an error, correct them as you normally would, and record one point for yourself. Repeat missed words at the end of the game.)

- Derrick's mom is a **physician** because … she sells things in a store. *Chew the fat.* I'll say the first part of the sentence again. Derrick's mom is a **physician** so. How can we finish

the sentence so it makes sense? (Idea: *She helps sick people get well.*) Let's say the whole sentence together. *Derrick's mom is a physician so she helps sick people get well.* Well done! I'm glad we chewed the fat!

- Enrique brought home a **notice** when … he told his dad about the school fair. *Chew the fat.* I'll say the first part of the sentence again. Enrique brought home a **notice** when. How can we finish the sentence so it makes sense? (Idea: *He gave the letter to his dad.*) Let's say the whole sentence together. *Enrique brought home a notice when he gave the letter to his dad.* Well done! I'm glad we chewed the fat!

- Savannah was **grateful** when … her cousin didn't invite her to go to the beach. *Chew the fat.* I'll say the first part of the sentence again. Savannah was **grateful** when. How can we finish the sentence so it makes sense? (Idea: *Her cousin invited her to go to the beach.*) Let's say the whole sentence together. *Savannah was grateful when her cousin invited her to go to the beach.* Well done! I'm glad we chewed the fat!

- The tiger was a **captive** when … it went hunting in the jungle. *Chew the fat.* I'll say the first part of the sentence again. The tiger was a **captive** when. How can we finish the sentence so it makes sense? (Idea: *It was kept in a cage.*) Let's say the whole sentence together. *The tiger was a captive when it was kept in a cage.* Well done! I'm glad we chewed the fat!

- Juanita's house is **remarkable** because … there is a rainbow painted on the front walls. *Well done!*

(Count the points and declare a winner.) You did a great job of playing *Chew the Fat.*

### Complete the Activity Sheet

(Give each child a copy of the Activity Sheet, BLM 9b. Read the writing frame to children, saying *blank* as you come to each blank space. Review with children the brainstormed lists of words and phrases telling about the King's palace and gardens. Children should complete the writing frame to produce a descriptive paragraph.)

**Preparation:** Map or globe of the world.

## Learn About Fairy Tales

Today you will learn more about a special kind of folk tale called a fairy tale. What will you learn about? *A fairy tale.*

Most fairy tales are stories that were first told out loud. Someone later decided to write down the story in a book.

After reading lots and lots of fairy tales, some authors decide to write new fairy tales of their own. One of the authors who wrote new fairy tales was a man from Denmark named Hans Christian Andersen. **(Locate Denmark on the map or globe.)** Where did Hans Christian Andersen live? *In Denmark.*

Hans Christian Andersen wrote many new fairy tales. One of the fairy tales he wrote was *The Nightingale*. When Hans Christian Andersen wrote his story, he made his story happen in China. **(Locate China on the map or globe.)** Where was the setting for Hans Christian Anderson's story *The Nightingale*? *China.*

When Jerry Pinkney made the illustrations for his version of *The Nightingale,* he made his story happen in Morocco. **(Locate Morocco on the map or globe.)** Where was the setting for Jerry Pinkney's version of *The Nightingale*? *Morocco.*

Fairy tales often begin with the words, "Once upon a time." Listen while I read the first sentence of *The Nightingale*. "The story I am about to tell happened a great many years ago, so it is well to hear it now before it is forgotten." How does this fairy tale begin? *The story I am about to tell happened a great many years ago.* Does this fairy tale begin with the words "Once upon a time"? *No.* You're right; but the words "happened a great many years ago" mean almost the same thing.

Fairy tales often have good characters and evil characters. Are there good characters and evil characters in *The Nightingale*? *No.*

Fairy tales often have things that happen in threes. Tell about the things that happened in threes. (Ideas: *Three and thirty times the artificial nightingale sang the same tune without getting tired; Old Man Death took three things from the king—the king's crown, his sword of state and his banner; the nightingale sang of three things from Death's garden—the white roses, the junipers; the fresh sweet grass.*)

Fairy tales often have royal people and places in them. Tell about the royal people in *The Nightingale*. (Ideas: *The king.*) Tell about the royal places in *The Nightingale*. (Idea: *The palace.*)

## Play Chew the Fat (Cumulative Review)

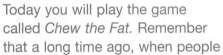

Today you will play the game called *Chew the Fat.* Remember that a long time ago, when people wanted to just sit and talk about things that were happening in their lives, they would say that they would sit and "chew the fat." In this game, I will say some sentences with our vocabulary words in them. If I use the vocabulary word correctly, say "Well done!"

If I use the word incorrectly, say "Chew the fat." That means that you want to talk about how I used the word. I'll say the beginning of the sentence again. If you can make the sentence end so that it makes sense, you'll get a point. If you can't, I get the point.

Let's practice. The elephant was a **captive** of the zoo when … they let it loose in Africa. *Chew the fat.* Let's chew the fat. The first part of the sentence stays the same. I'll say the first part. The elephant was a **captive** of the zoo when. How can we finish the sentence so it makes sense? (Idea: *They kept it in a pen.*) Let's say the whole sentence together now. *The elephant was a captive of the zoo when they kept it in a pen.* Well done! I'm glad we chewed the fat!

Let's do another one together. Tanya's mom was **grateful** when … their house burned down. *Chew the fat.* The first part of the sentence stays the same. I'll say the first part. Tanya's mom was **grateful** when. How can we finish the sentence so it makes sense? (Idea: *The firefighters saved their house.*) Let's say the whole sentence now. *Tanya's mom was grateful when the firefighters* *saved their house.* Well done! I'm glad we chewed the fat!

☐T Now you're ready to play the game. (Draw a T-chart on the board for keeping score. Children earn one point for each correct answer. If they make an error, correct them as you normally would, and record one point for yourself. Repeat missed words at the end of the game.)

- Mr. Johnson's ring was **precious** because … it was made of plastic. *Chew the fat.* I'll say the first part of the sentence again. Mr. Johnson's ring was **precious** because. How can we finish the sentence so it makes sense? (Idea: *It was made of gold.*) Let's say the whole sentence together. *Mr. Johnson's ring was precious because it was made of gold.* Well done! I'm glad we chewed the fat!
- The soccer coach sent home a **notice** with … all the dates of all the soccer games written on it. *Well done!*
- I **noticed** the crack on the wall when … I moved the sofa. *Well done!*
- A **physician** is a person who … is a mechanic. *Chew the fat.* I'll say the first part of the sentence again. A **physician** is a person who. How can we finish the sentence so it makes sense? (Idea: *Is a doctor.*) Let's say the whole sentence together. *A physician is a person who is a doctor.* Well done! I'm glad we chewed the fat!
- Something is **invisible** when … you can see it. *Chew the fat.* I'll say the first part of the sentence again. Something is **invisible** when. How can we finish the sentence so it makes sense? (Idea: *You can't see it.*) Let's say the whole sentence together. *Something is invisible when you can't see it.* Well done! I'm glad we chewed the fat!
- It would be **remarkable** if … you went swimming at the lake when it was sunny. *Chew the fat.* I'll say the first part of the sentence again. It would be **remarkable** if. How can we finish the sentence so it makes sense? (Idea: *You went swimming at the lake when it was snowing.*) Let's say the whole sentence together. *It would be remarkable if you went swimming at the lake when it was*

*snowing.* Well done! I'm glad we chewed the fat!

- Akeem showed **perseverance** when … he kept trying and trying and never gave up. *Well done!*
- Luke looked **ridiculous** when … he put his shoes on his feet and his gloves on his hands. *Chew the fat.* I'll say the first part of the sentence again. Luke looked **ridiculous** when. How can we finish the sentence so it makes sense? (Idea: *He put his shoes on his hands and his gloves on his feet.*) Let's say the whole sentence together. *Luke looked ridiculous when he put his shoes on his hands and his gloves on his feet.* Well done! I'm glad we chewed the fat!
- Makayla was a **braggart** when … she didn't tell everyone that she was the best speller in the state. *Chew the fat.* I'll say the first part of the sentence again. Makayla was a **braggart** when. How can we finish the sentence so it makes sense? (Idea: *She told everyone that she was the best speller in the state.*) Let's say the whole sentence together. *Makayla was a braggart when she told everyone that she was the best speller in the state.* Well done! I'm glad we chewed the fat!

(Count the points and declare a winner.) You did a great job of playing *Chew the Fat.*

---

## DAY 5

**Preparation:** Each child will need a copy of the Quiz Answer Sheet, BLM B.

### Retell Story

Today, I'll show you the pictures Jerry Pinkney made for *The Nightingale.* As I show you the pictures, I'll call on one of you to tell the class that part of the story.

Tell me what happens at the **beginning** of the story. (Show the pictures on pages 1 and 2. Call on a child to tell what's happening.)

Tell me what happens in the **middle** of the story. (Show the pictures on pages 3–32. Call on a child to tell what's happening. Encourage use of target words when appropriate. Model use when necessary.)

Tell me what happens at the **end** of the story. (Show the pictures on pages 33 and 34. Call on a child to tell what's happening.)

### Assess Vocabulary

 (Give each child a copy of the Quiz Answer Sheet, BLM B.)

Today, you're going to have a True or False quiz. When you do the True or False quiz, it shows me how well you know the hard words you are learning.

If I say something that is true, circle the word **true.** What will you do if I say something that is true? *Circle the word true.*

If I say something that is false, circle the word **false.** What will you do if I say something that is false? *Circle the word false.*

Listen carefully to each item that I say. Don't let me trick you!

Item 1: If you are a **captive,** you can go anywhere you want to. (*False.*)

Item 2: It would be **remarkable** if you could run up a **steep** mountain and not get tired. (*True.*)

Item 3: Diamonds, rubies, and sapphires are not **precious.** (*False.*)

Item 4: A **notice** can be a piece of paper that you take home from school. (*True.*)

Item 5: If you **notice** something, you might see it or hear it or smell it. (*True.*)

Item 6: Your dad might take you to see a **physician** if you needed new shoes. (*False.*)

Item 7: You would probably be **grateful** if someone found your stolen bike and returned it to you. (*True.*)

Item 8: If the rabbit **bolted** when it saw the dog, it sat really still and hid in the grass. (*False.*)

Item 9: It's a bad idea to **bolt** your door before you go to bed. (*False.*)

Item 10: If you always **tease** your friend about her freckles, she might get **frustrated** with you. (*True.*)

You did a great job completing your quiz!

(Score children's work. A child must score 9 out of 10 to be at the mastery level. If a child does not achieve mastery, insert the missed words

as additional items in the games in next week's lessons. Retest those children individually for the missed items before they take the next mastery test.)

## Extensions

### Read a Story as a Reward

(Display copies of the books that you have read since the beginning of the program, as well as a traditional retelling of *The Nightingale* that is set in China. Allow children to choose which book they would like you to read to them as a reward for their hard work.)

(Read the story aloud for enjoyment with minimal interruptions.)

---

**Preparation:** Word containers for the Super Words Center. You may wish to remove some of the words from earlier lessons the children have mastered.
You will need 2 copies of each card that remains in the word containers.

---

### Introduce the Super Words Center

 (Add the new Picture Vocabulary Cards to the words from the previous weeks. Show children one of the word containers. If children need more guidance in how to work in the Super Words Center, role-play with two to three children as a demonstration.)

Let's think about how we work with our words in the Super Words Center.

This week's activity is called *Go Fish.* What's the name of this week's activity? *Go Fish.*

You will work with a partner in the Super Words Center. Whom will you work with? *A partner.*

First you and your partner will each draw six word cards out of the container and hold them so your partner cannot see them. What do you do first? (Idea: *Draw six cards out of the container and hold them so my partner cannot see them.*)

Next you will look at the cards in your hand and lay down any cards that you have two of. You will tell your partner the word the pictures show. What do you do next? (Idea: *Lay down any cards that I have two of, and tell my partner the word the pictures show.*)

Then your partner has a chance to lay down any cards he or she has two of, and tell the word the pictures show. What does your partner do? (Idea: *Lay down any cards that he or she has two of, and tell the word the pictures show.*)

Next you will ask your partner for a card that you have only one of by saying the word the picture shows. If your partner has that card, he or she will give it to you. If your partner gives you the card, you will lay down the two cards. What does your partner do if they have the card you ask for? (Idea: *Give you the card.*) What will you do if your partner gives you a card? (Idea: *Lay down the two cards that are the same.*)

If your partner does not have the card you ask for, your partner will say, "Go Fish." What will your partner do if he or she doesn't have the card you ask for? (Idea: *Say "Go Fish."*)

If your partner says "Go Fish," you must choose another card from the word container. What will you do if your partner says "Go Fish"? (Idea: *Choose a card from the word container.*)

Then it's your partner's turn.

Watch while I show you what I mean. **(Demonstrate this process with one child as your partner.)**

When one partner has no cards left in his or her hand, the game is over. Each person gets one point for each pair of cards they have laid down. The winner is the person with the most points. Who wins the game? (Idea: *The person with the most points.*)

Have fun playing *Go Fish!*

## Preparation: You will
need a copy of *Mufaro's Beautiful Daughters* for each day's lesson.

Number the pages of the story to assist you in asking comprehension questions at appropriate points.

Post a copy of the Vocabulary Tally Sheet, BLM A, with this week's Picture Vocabulary Cards attached.

Each child will need one copy of the Homework Sheet, BLM 10a.

---

### DAY 1

### Introduce Book

This week's book is called *Mufaro's Beautiful Daughters*. What's the title of this week's book? *Mufaro's Beautiful Daughters.*

This book was written by John Steptoe. Who's the author of *Mufaro's Beautiful Daughters*? *John Steptoe.*

John Steptoe also made the pictures for this book. Who is the illustrator of *Mufaro's Beautiful Daughters*? *John Steptoe.* Who made the illustrations for this book? *John Steptoe.*

The cover of a book usually gives us some hints of what the book is about. Let's look at the front cover of *Mufaro's Beautiful Daughters*. What do you see in the illustration? (Idea: *A girl looking at herself in a mirror.*) Let's look at the back cover of *Mufaro's Beautiful Daughters*. What do you see in the illustration? (Ideas: *A girl working; a girl collecting plants; two animals that look like deer; four flamingoes.*)

Get ready to make some predictions to your partner about this book. Use the information from the cover to help you.

(Assign each child a partner. Ask the following questions, allowing sufficient time for children to share their predictions with their partners.)

- Who do you think are the characters in this story?

## *Mufaro's Beautiful Daughters*
### author: John Steptoe • illustrator: John Steptoe

### Target Vocabulary

| Tier II | Tier III |
|---------|----------|
| polite | setting (where) |
| considerate | fairy tale |
| calm | noun |
| commotion | |
| *jealous | |
| *ambitious | |

*Expanded Target Vocabulary Word

- What is each girl doing?
- Where do you think the story happens?
- When do you think the story happens?
- Why do you think only one girl is working?
- How long do you think it took the girl to collect three baskets full of plants?
- Do you think this story is about real people? Tell why or why not.

(Call on several children to share their predictions with the class.)

### Take a Picture Walk

(Encourage children to use target words in their answers.) We're going to take a picture walk through this book. Remember that when we take a picture walk, we look at the pictures and tell what we think will happen in the story.

**Pages 1–2.** Where do you think the girls are? (Ideas: *In the jungle; in Africa.*) What makes you think so? (Idea: *There are lots of trees and large plants.*) What do you think the girls are doing in this illustration?

**Pages 3–4.** What do you think is happening here? (Idea: *One of the girls is saying something mean to the other.*) How do you think the girls feel? (Ideas: *The first girl looks angry; the second girl looks miserable or hurt.*)

**Pages 5–6.** What is the girl doing in this illustration? (Ideas: *Pouring water; watering the flowers.*)

**Pages 7–8.** What is the girl doing here? (Idea: *Looking at a snake.*)

**Page 10.** Who do you think the man is? (Idea: *The girls' father.*)

**Pages 11–12.** When do you think this part of the story happens? (Idea: *Nighttime.*) What do you think the little boy asked the girl? Why do you think the girl is shouting at the boy?

**Pages 13–14.** Who do you think the old woman in the jungle is? What do you think the girl is running from? How do you think she feels? (Ideas: *Terrified; afraid; scared.*)

**Pages 15–16.** When is this part of the story happening? (Ideas: *In the morning; in the daytime.*) Where do you think the people are taking the girl?

**Pages 17–18.** What is the girl looking at? (Idea: *A city.*)

**Pages 19–20.** (Point to the girl on the right.) How do you think she is feeling here? (Ideas: *Scared; upset.*) What do you think she is saying to the other girl?

**Pages 21–22.** What does the girl see here? *A snake.* Do you think she is afraid of it? *No.* What do you think the girl is saying?

**Pages 23–24.** Who do you think this might be?

**Page 25.** What is happening in this illustration? (Idea: *An older woman is hugging one of the girls.*) Does the woman look happy? *Yes.* Why do you think she is happy?

**Pages 27–28.** What do you think is happening here? How do you think the girl is feeling now? (Ideas: *Happy; excited.*)

It's your turn to ask me some questions. What would you like to know about the story? (Accept questions. If children tell about the pictures or the story instead of ask questions, prompt them to ask a question.) Ask me a what question. Ask me a who question.

### Read the Story Aloud
(Read the story to children with minimal interruptions.)

Tomorrow we will read the story again, and I will ask you some questions.

## Present Target Vocabulary

 **Polite**

In the story, the old woman warned Manyara that she should be polite to the man with his head under his arm. That means that she must do the right thing and act with her best manners and actions. **Polite.** Say the word. *Polite.*

**Polite** is a describing word. It tells more about a person. What kind of word is **polite?** *A describing word.*

**If you are polite, you do the right thing and act with your best manners and actions.** Say the word that means "you do the right thing and act with your best manners and actions." *Polite.*

(Correct any incorrect responses, and repeat the item at the end of the sequence.)

Let's think about some situations where people might be polite. I'll tell about some situations. If the person or animal is polite in the situation, say "polite." If the person or animal is not polite say "rude." **Rude** is the opposite of **polite.** What word is the opposite of **polite?** *Rude.*

- The boy held the door open for the elderly lady to walk through. *Polite.*
- Gerald let Harold go ahead of him to see the whales. *Polite.*
- Bonnie and Maureen yelled at each other in the restaurant. *Rude.*
- Jill teased her little sister. *Rude.*
- Mr. Williams spoke nicely even when he was very frustrated. *Polite.*
- The spider hugged the baby bug too tightly. *Rude.*

What word means "to do the right thing and act with your best manners and actions"? *Polite.*

 **Considerate**

In the story, Nyasha was too considerate of her father's feelings to complain. That means Nyasha paid attention to what her father needed, wanted, or wished for, and didn't say anything. **Considerate.** Say the word. *Considerate.*

**Considerate** is a describing word. It tells more about a person. What kind of word is **considerate?** *A describing word.*

**If someone is considerate, they pay attention to what someone else needs, or wants, or**

**wishes for.** Say the word that means "pays attention to what someone else needs, or wants, or wishes for." *Considerate.*

Let's think about things that someone might do that would be considerate. If I say something that would be considerate, say "considerate." If not, don't say anything.

- Stands quietly in line. *Considerate.*
- Uses a quiet voice in the library. *Considerate.*
- Grabs the crayons.
- Shares a book with a partner. *Considerate.*
- Colors on the table.
- Sets the table for supper. *Considerate.*

What word means "pays attention to what someone else needs, or wants, or wishes for"? *Considerate.*

Tell about a time when you were considerate. (Call on several children. Encourage children to start their answers with the words *I was considerate when _____.*)

 Calm

In the story, Manyara told herself that she must be calm and not frightened. That means Manyara was going to become less angry, upset, or excited. **Calm.** Say the word. *Calm.*

**Calm** is an action word. It tells what someone is doing. What kind of word is **calm?** *An action word.*

**Calm means become less angry, upset, or excited.** Say the word that means "become less angry, upset, or excited." *Calm.*

Let's think about some time when someone might tell themselves to be calm. I'll tell about a time. If you think someone would tell themselves to be calm, say "be calm." If not, don't say anything.

- The babysitter hears the children jumping on their beds. *Be calm.*
- You are sitting peacefully at the table playing a game of checkers with your brother.
- You think you hear a scary noise in your closet. *Be calm.*
- You found your model airplane broken into hundreds of pieces. *Be calm.*

- Your family is at a restaurant and you are laughing and shouting with your friends. *Be calm.*
- You are sitting at your desk at school quietly drawing a picture.

What word means "become less angry, upset, or excited"? *Calm.*

 Commotion

In the story, Nyasha heard a commotion outside. That means there was a lot of noise and confusion. **Commotion.** Say the word. *Commotion.*

**Commotion** is a naming word. It names a thing. What do we call a naming word that names a person, place, thing, or idea? *A noun.* What kind of word is **commotion?** *A noun.*

**A commotion is a lot of noise and confusion.** Say the word that means "a lot of noise and confusion." *Commotion.*

Let's think about some times when there might be a commotion. I'll tell about a time. If you think there would be a commotion, say "commotion." If not, don't say anything.

- There was a lot of noise and confusion when someone yelled, "Fire!" *Commotion.*
- Everybody at our house was shouting and hunting for their things as we tried to get ready for the school bus. *Commotion.*
- During the fire drill, the children left the school in a calm and orderly way.
- The farmer, his wife, their six children, the grandparents, the goat, the sheep, the pig, the rooster and the hens were all inside the tiny little house. *Commotion.*
- The children were politely eating their lunches.
- Everyone pushed, shoved, and shouted as they tried to catch a glimpse of the movie star. *Commotion.*

What noun means "a lot of noise and confusion"? *Commotion.*

When we read *The Three Javelinas,* you learned another noun that means the same thing as commotion. What word was that? (Idea: *Hullabaloo.*) That's right, **commotion** and **hullabaloo** both mean "a lot of noise and confusion." What noun means the same thing as **commotion?** *Hullabaloo.* What noun means the same thing as **hullabaloo?** *Commotion.*

## Present Vocabulary Tally Sheet
(See Lesson 1, page 4, for instructions.)

## Assign Homework
(Homework Sheet, BLM 10a. See the Introduction for homework instructions.)

### DAY 2

**Preparation:** Globe or map of the world.

Picture Vocabulary Cards for *polite, considerate, calm, commotion.*

## Read and Discuss Story
(Read story to children. Ask the following questions at specified points. Encourage them to use target words in their answers.)

**Page 2.** Who were the characters in this story? (Ideas: *Mufaro, Manyara, and Nyasha.*) Where was the setting for this story? (Idea: *In a village in Africa.*) What was special about Mufaro's daughters? (Idea: *They were very beautiful.* Show the children where Africa is located on the globe or on a map of the world.)

**Page 3.** What was Manyara like? (Ideas: *She was mean and had a bad temper; she said mean things to her sister; she was clever, strong, and beautiful; she was unhappy.*)

**Page 4.** What kind of person was Nyasha? (Idea: *Kind.*) Why did Manyara behave so badly? (Ideas: *She was angry that everyone thought Nyasha was so kind; she believed their father loved Nyasha more.*)

**Page 5.** How did Manyara's words make Nyasha feel? *Sad.* Why did people think Nyasha's crops grew so well? (Idea: *Because she sang while she worked with them and she had a beautiful singing voice.*)

**Page 8.** Who was Nyoka? (Idea: *A garden snake.*) Do you think Nyasha liked animals? *Yes.* How do you know? (Idea: *She was kind even to a snake.*)

**Page 9.** (Read to the end of the first paragraph.) Why didn't Mufaro know how Manyara behaved? (Idea: *Nyasha never told him and Manyara always behaved well around him.*)

(Read to the end of the third paragraph.) Where was Mufaro going to take his daughters? (Idea: *To the city.*) Why were they going to the city? (Idea: *The king was looking for a wife and Mufaro hoped he would choose one of his daughters.*)

(Read to the end of the page.) Why do you think Manyara wanted her father to only send her to the city and not her sister? (Idea: *She wanted to marry the king; she didn't want the king to see Nyasha; she was afraid the king would choose Nyasha.*)

**Page 11.** (Read to the end of the first paragraph.) Why did Manyara sneak out of the village? (Idea: *She wanted to get to the king first so he would pick her to be his wife.*)

(Read to the end of the page.) Who did Manyara meet on the path? *A young boy.* What did the boy want from Manyara? *Food.* Was Manyara kind to the boy or mean to him? *Mean.*

**Page 13.** Who did Manyara meet in the clearing? (Idea: *An old woman.*) What advice did the old woman give to Manyara? (Idea: *She told her not to laugh at the trees and to be polite to the man with his head under his arm.*) Do you think Manyara will follow the old woman's advice?

**Page 14.** (Read to the end of the second paragraph.) What had the old woman told Manyara about the trees? (Idea: *She told her not to laugh back at them.*) Did Manyara follow the woman's advice? *No.*

(Read to the end of the page.) What had the old woman told Manyara about the man with his head under his arm? (Idea: *To be polite to him.*) Did Manyara follow the woman's advice? *No.*

**Page 15.** (Read to the end of the first paragraph.) Was Nyasha excited about possibly becoming the queen? *No.*

(Read to the end of the page.) Why were there shouts and commotion from the wedding party? (Idea: *They discovered that Manyara was missing.*) Why did they decide to go on to the city? (Idea: *They saw Manyara's footprints and decided she must have already gone to the city.*)

**Page 16.** (Read to the end of the second paragraph.) Who did Nyasha meet on the path? *The young boy.* What did Nyasha do when she saw the boy? (Idea: *She said, "You must be hungry." and gave him a yam to eat.*)

(Read to the end of the third paragraph.) Why do you think the old woman only pointed the way for Nyasha and didn't give her the same advice she gave Manyara? (Idea: *She knew that Nyasha would be kind and polite without her advice.*)

(Read to the end of the page.) What did the trees do when Nyasha passed? (Idea: *They bowed to her.*) What had they done when Manyara passed them? (Idea: *They had laughed at her.*)

**Page 17.** What is Nyasha looking at? (Idea: *The city where the king lives.*) How does Nyasha feel about the city? (Idea: *She thinks it is beautiful.*)

**Page 19.** What had scared Manyara? (Idea: *A monster; a snake with five heads.*) Do you think Nyasha believed that there is a monster in the chamber?

**Page 21.** What did Nyasha find on the chief's stool? (Idea: *Her little garden snake, Nyoka.*) Who did Nyoka turn into? *The king.*

**Page 23.** Why did the king decide that Nyasha was the most worthy and the most beautiful girl in the land? (Ideas: *She had been kind to him when he was a snake; she had given him food when he was a hungry boy; she had given him sunflower seeds when he was an old woman; she was kind and generous.*)

**Page 26.** What happened to Nyasha at the end of the story? (Idea: *She became the queen.*) What happened to Manyara at the end of the story? (Idea: *She became a servant in the king's household.*) Why is it interesting that Manyara should become a servant in the king's household? (Idea: *Manyara used to tell her sister that one day she would be queen and Nyasha would be one of her servants.*)

### Review Vocabulary

(Display the Picture Vocabulary Cards. Point to each card as you say the word. Ask children to repeat each word after you.) These pictures show **polite, considerate, calm,** and **commotion.**

- What word means "a lot of noise and confusion"? *Commotion.*
- What word means "pays attention to what someone else needs, or wants, or wishes for"? *Considerate.*
- What word means "become less angry, upset, or excited"? *Calm.*
- What word means "to do the right thing and act with your best manners and actions"? *Polite.*

### Extend Vocabulary

 Calm

In *Mufaro's Beautiful Daughters*, we learned that **calm** means "become less angry, upset, or excited."

Raise your hand if you can tell us a sentence that uses **calm** as a describing word meaning "become less angry, upset, or excited." (Call on several children. If they don't use complete sentences, restate their examples as sentences. Have the class repeat the sentences.)

Here's a new way to use the word **calm.**

- The water was **calm.** Say the sentence.
- We sailed into the **calm** waters of Roche Harbor. Say the sentence.
- Sunday was a clear and **calm** day. Say the sentence.

**In these sentences, calm is a describing word that means not moving or still.** What word means "not moving or still"? *Calm.*

Raise your hand if you can tell us a sentence that uses **calm** as a describing word meaning "not moving or still." (Call on several children. If they don't use complete sentences, restate their examples as sentences. Have the class repeat the sentences.)

### Present Expanded Target Vocabulary
Jealous

In *Mufaro's Beautiful Daughters,* Manyara didn't like it when everyone talked about how kind Nyasha was, and praised everything she did. She thought their father liked Nyasha the best. Manyara was feeling jealous of Nyasha. **Jealous.** Say the word. *Jealous.*

**Jealous** is a describing word. It tells more about the emotion Manyara was feeling. What kind of word is **jealous**? *A describing word.*

**When someone is feeling jealous, they want what someone else has.** Say the word that means "want what someone else has." *Jealous.*

I'll tell about some people. If you think those people are feeling jealous say, "jealous." If not, don't say anything.

- Billy wanted a new bike just like his brother's. *Jealous.*
- Sandy was happy her family was going camping.
- Joni wanted the teacher to like her picture as much as she liked Alex's. *Jealous.*
- Colleen asked, "Is my picture nice, too?" *Jealous.*
- It was okay that Bob got the new bike instead of me. I got the new tent last week.
- Miss Cahan whined, "When am I going to get a turn?" *Jealous.*

What word means "want what someone else has"? *Jealous.*

◎← Ambitious

In *Mufaro's Beautiful Daughters,* we met Manyara, a girl who wanted to be queen. Manyara had big plans. **Ambitious.** Say the word. *Ambitious.*

**Ambitious** is a describing word. It tells more about someone. What kind of word is **ambitious**? *A describing word.*

**Ambitious means that you have big plans to get a lot done.** Say the word that means "you have big plans to get a lot done." *Ambitious.*

I'll tell about some people or animals. If those people or animals are ambitious, say "ambitious." If not, don't say anything.

- The spider didn't want just flies or mosquitoes—he wanted big animals like humans and crocodiles. *Ambitious.*
- Fred had big plans. He wanted to build a huge model of a house using only toothpicks and glue. *Ambitious.*
- The cat was satisfied with cat food. She didn't need to catch an elephant or a rhinoceros to eat.

- Justin didn't have any big plans to travel far away. He was happy at home.
- The Egyptian king had big plans to build huge stone mountains without any big machines. *Ambitious.*
- My dad has big plans to be the president of the company he works for. *Ambitious.* What word means "you have big plans"? *Ambitious.*

## DAY 3

**Preparation:** Prepare a sheet of chart paper, landscape direction, titled *Mufaro's Beautiful Daughters.* Underneath the title, draw 7 boxes, connected by arrows.

See the Introduction for Week 10's chart.

You will record children's responses by writing the underlined words in the boxes.

### Analyze Setting–When (Literary Analysis)

Today we will learn more about how stories are made.

The setting of a story tells two things. One thing the setting tells is where the story happens. What is one thing the setting tells? *Where the story happens.* The second thing the setting tells is when the story happens. What is the second thing the setting tells? *When the story happens.*

Let's look at the pictures and talk about the story, to figure out **when** *Mufaro's Beautiful Daughters* happens.

**Page 1.** (Show the illustration and read the first sentence.) When did the story begin? (Idea: <u>A long time ago.</u>)

**Page 7.** (Show the illustration and read the first paragraph on page 8.) When did this part of the story happen? <u>One day</u> when Nyasha was working in her garden.

**Page 8.** (Read the first sentence in the second paragraph.) When did this part of the story happen? *Early one morning.*

**Pages 10–11.** (Show the illustration and read the first sentence.) When did this part of the story happen? *That night.*

**Page 14.** (Show the illustration and read the first sentence.) When did this part of the story happen? At *dawn.*

**Page 15.** (Show the illustration and read the second-to-last paragraph.) When did this part of the story happen? (Idea: *When the sun was high in the sky.*) The sun is high in the sky around noon. When is the sun high in the sky? (Idea: *Around noon.*) So when did this part of the story happen? *Around noon.*

**Page 25.** (Read the first sentence.) When did the end of the story happen? *A long time ago.*

(Point to the words as you say each time.) A long time ago, one day, early one morning, that night, at dawn, around noon, a long time ago (Draw a line underneath these 7 boxes.) These things all happened a long time ago. When does the story happen? *A long time ago.* (Write the words *a long time ago* underneath the line.)

When is the setting of *Mufaro's Beautiful Daughters*? (Idea: *A long time ago.*) Fairy tales often happen "once upon a time" or "a long time ago." When do fairy tales often happen? (Ideas: *Once upon a time; a long time ago.*)

### Play Chew the Fat

Now you will play the game called *Chew the Fat.* A long time ago, when people wanted to just sit and talk about things that were happening in their lives, they would say that they would sit and "chew the fat."

In this game, I will say some sentences with our vocabulary words in them. If I use the vocabulary word correctly, say "Well done!"

If I use the word incorrectly, say "Chew the fat." That means that you want to talk about how I used the word. I'll say the beginning of the sentence again. If you can make the sentence end so that it makes sense, you'll get a point. If you can't, I get the point.

Let's practice. There was a **commotion** when … the dog was asleep in its dog house. *Chew the fat.* Let's chew the fat. The first part of the sentence stays the same. I'll say the first part. There was a **commotion** when. How can we finish the sentence so it makes sense? (Idea: *The dog chased the cat around the back yard.*) Let's say the whole sentence together now. *There was a commotion when the dog chased the cat around the back yard.* Well done! I'm glad we chewed the fat!

Let's do another one together. Mason was **polite** when … he didn't write his uncle a thank you letter for his birthday gift. *Chew the fat.* The first part of the sentence stays the same. I'll say the first part. Mason was **polite** when. How can we finish the sentence so that it makes sense? (Idea: *He wrote his uncle a thank you letter for his birthday gift.*) Let's say the whole sentence now. *Mason was polite when he wrote his uncle a thank you letter for his birthday gift.* Well done! I'm glad we chewed the fat!

Let's try one more. Eva was **considerate** when … she used her quiet voice in the library. *Well done!* I used the word **considerate** correctly, so you said, "Well done!"

Now you're ready to play the game. (Draw a T-chart on the board for keeping score. Children earn one point for each correct answer. If they make an error, correct them as you normally would, and record one point for yourself. Repeat missed words at the end of the game.)

- Mrs. Winston told us to **calm** down when … we were quietly watching TV. *Chew the fat.* I'll say the first part of the sentence again. Mrs. Winston told us to **calm** down when. How can we finish the sentence so it makes sense? (Idea: *We were running around the house, shouting and laughing.*) Let's say the whole sentence together. *Mrs. Winston told us to* *calm down when we were running around the house, shouting and laughing.* Well done! I'm glad we chewed the fat!

- There was a **commotion** when … the wind blew a tree down on their house. *Well done!*
- Carlos felt **jealous** when … he got all the attention. *Chew the fat.* I'll say the first part of the sentence again. Carlos felt **jealous** when. How can we finish the sentence so it makes sense? (Idea: *His new baby brother got all the attention.*) Let's say the whole sentence together. *Carlos felt jealous when his new baby brother got all the attention.* Well done! I'm glad we chewed the fat!
- The lake is **calm** when … the wind is blowing really hard. *Chew the fat.* I'll say the first part of the sentence again. The lake is **calm** when. How can we finish the sentence so it makes sense? (Idea: *There is no wind.*) Let's say the whole sentence together. *The lake is calm when there is no wind.* Well done! I'm glad we chewed the fat!
- Jamaal's mom said he was **ambitious** when … he told her he didn't want to run any races. *Chew the fat.* I'll say the first part of the sentence again. Jamal's mom said he was **ambitious** when. How can we finish the sentence so it makes sense? (Idea: *He told her he was going to run in the Olympics.*) Let's say the whole sentence together. *Jamaal's mom said he was ambitious when he told her he was going to run in the Olympics.* Well done! I'm glad we chewed the fat!

(Count the points and declare a winner.) You did a great job of playing *Chew the Fat.*

### Complete the Activity Sheet

 (Give each child a copy of the Activity Sheet BLM 10b. Have children cut apart the words in the word bank. If children are unfamiliar with Venn diagrams, do this as a guided activity.)

What other fairy tale did we read where a girl from an ordinary family married the king? (Idea: *Cinderella.*)

We are going to compare Cinderella and Nyasha. Cinderella and Nyasha were the same in some ways and different in some ways.

(Point to the circle under the word *Cinderella.*) This circle is where we'll put things that tell about **only** Cinderella.

(Point to the circle under the word *Nyasha.*) This circle is where we'll put things that tell about **only** Nyasha.

(Point to the place where the two circles overlap.) This is where we'll put things that tell about **both** Cinderella and Nyasha.

(Either read for children or have them read the words in the word bank one at a time. After each word is read ask:) Does this tell about Cinderella or Nyasha, or both the Cinderella and Nyasha?

(If children identify the character trait or activity as belonging to only Cinderella, have them paste or glue the word in the large circle under the word *Cinderella.*)

(If children identify the character trait or activity as belonging to only Nyasha, have them paste or glue the word in the large circle under the word *Nyasha.*)

(If children identify the character trait or activity as belonging to both Cinderella and Nyasha, have them paste or glue the word in the area where the two circles overlap.) (Repeat procedure for each item in the word bank.)

(Cinderella: rode in a coach, married the prince, worked in the house, went to the balls, had a fairy godmother, had two stepsisters
Nyasha: worked in the garden, brave, lived in Africa, had one sister, married the king, talked to snakes
Both: treated badly, kind, polite, beautiful, got married, good, lived at the palace, had a beautiful gown, sweet.)

---

| DAY 4 |
|---|

**Preparation:** Map or globe of the world.

### Learn About Fairy Tales

Today you will learn about a special kind of folk tale called a fairy tale. What will you learn about? *A fairy tale.*

How are folk tales and fairy tales the same? (Idea: *They are both stories that were once told out loud.*) How is a fairy tale different from a folk tale? (Idea: *Someone decided to write it down in a book a long time ago.*)

The story of *Mufaro's Beautiful Daughters* comes from Africa. **(Locate Africa on the map or globe.)** The first person to write down the story of *Mufaro's Beautiful Daughters* was a man named G. M Theal, who wrote the story down more than a hundred years ago.

When John Steptoe illustrated his version of *Mufaro's Beautiful Daughters,* he used the ruins and the flowers of an ancient city from Zimbabwe. Zimbabwe is in southern Africa. **(Locate Zimbabwe on the map or globe.)**

Fairy tales often begin with the same words. Listen while I read the first sentence of *Mufaro's Beautiful Daughters.* **(Read the first sentence on page 1.)** How does this fairy tale begin? *A long time ago.*

Does this fairy tale begin with the words "Once upon a time"? *No.* You're right; but the words "A long time ago" mean almost the same thing.

Fairy tales often have good characters and evil characters. Who are the good characters in *Mufaro's Beautiful Daughters*? **(Idea:** *Nyasha, the king; Nyasha's father.*) Who is the evil character in *Mufaro's Beautiful Daughter*? **(Idea:** *Manyara; Nyasha's sister.*)

Fairy tales often have things that happen in threes. Tell about the things that happened in threes. **(Idea:** *Manyara and Nyasha both had to pass three tests on the way to the city; the boy who was hungry; not to laugh when the trees laughed; to be polite to the man with his head under his arm.*)

Fairy tales often have royal people and places in them. Tell about the royal people in *Mufaro's Beautiful Daughters*. **(Ideas:** *King, queen.*) Tell about the royal places in *Mufaro's Beautiful Daughters*. **(Idea:** *The palace.*)

Let's remember some important things about fairy tales. How do fairy tales often begin? **(Ideas:** *Once upon a time; long ago.*) What kinds of characters are often in fairy tales?

*Good characters and evil characters.* What is the special number that is often in fairy tales? *Three.* What special people and places are often in fairy tales? *Royal people and places.* Good remembering about fairy tales.

### Play Chew the Fat (Cumulative Review)

 Today, you will play the game called *Chew the Fat.* Remember that a long time ago, when people wanted to just sit and talk about things that were happening in their lives, they would say that they would sit and "chew the fat." In this game, I will say some sentences with our vocabulary words in them. If I use the vocabulary word correctly, say "Well done!"

If I use the word incorrectly, say "Chew the fat." That means that you want to talk about how I used the word. I'll say the beginning of the sentence again. If you can make the sentence end so it makes sense, you'll get a point. If you can't, I get the point.

Let's practice. Emilio showed he was **ambitious** when … he never made any plans for himself. *Chew the fat.* Let's chew the fat. The first part of the sentence stays the same. I'll say the first part. Emilio showed he was **ambitious** when. How can we finish the sentence so it makes sense? (Idea: *He made big plans for himself.*) Let's say the whole sentence together now. *Emilio showed he was ambitious when he made big plans for himself.* Well done! I'm glad we chewed the fat!

Let's do another one together. There was a huge **commotion** when … no one went to see them film the movie. *Chew the fat.* The first part of the sentence stays the same. I'll say the first part. There was a huge **commotion** when. How can we finish the sentence so that it makes sense? (Idea: *Everyone went to see them film the movie.*) Let's say the whole sentence now. *There was a huge commotion when everyone went to see them film the movie.* Well done! I'm glad we chewed the fat!

Now you're ready to play the game. **(Draw a T-chart on the board for keeping score. Children earn one point for each correct** answer. If they make an error, correct them as you normally would, and record one point for yourself. Repeat missed words at the end of the game.)

- I **calm** down when … I get angry, upset, or excited. *Chew the fat.* I'll say the first part of the sentence again. I **calm** down when. How can we finish the sentence so it makes sense? (Idea: *I become less angry, upset, or excited.*) Let's say the whole sentence together. *I calm down when I become less angry, upset, or excited.* Well done! I'm glad we chewed the fat!

- Irma was **considerate** when … she offered to carry the heavy grocery bags for her mom. *Well done!*

- On a **calm** day … the trees shake and bend in the wind. *Chew the fat.* I'll say the first part of the sentence again. On a calm day. How can we finish the sentence so it makes sense? (Idea: *The trees are still.*) Let's say the whole sentence together. *On a calm day the trees are still.* Well done! I'm glad we chewed the fat!

- You are **reluctant** … if you don't want to do something. *Well done!*

- You are being **polite** when … you don't bother to say "please" or "thank you." *Chew the fat.* I'll say the first part of the sentence again. You are being **polite** when. How can we finish the sentence so it makes sense? (Idea: *You remember to say "please" and "thank you."*) Let's say the whole sentence together. *You are being polite when you remember to say "please" and "thank you."* Well done! I'm glad we chewed the fat!

- Clinton was being a **braggart** when … he said Jamie was the best swimmer in the class. *Chew the fat.* I'll say the first part of the sentence again. Clinton was being a **braggart** when. (Idea: *He said he was the best swimmer in the class.*) Let's say the whole sentence together. *Clinton was being a braggart when he said he was the best swimmer in the class.* Well done! I'm glad we chewed the fat!

- There was quite a **hullabaloo** when … all the triplets started to cry at the same time. *Well done!*

- The detective was **suspicious** when … he saw the man pay for a new watch. *Chew the fat.* I'll say the first part of the sentence again. The detective was **suspicious** when. How can we finish the sentence so it makes sense? (Idea: *He saw the man put the new watch in his pocket without paying for it.*) Let's say the whole sentence together. *The detective was suspicious when he saw the man put the new watch in his pocket without paying for it.* Well done! I'm glad we chewed the fat!

- A deer is nearly **invisible** when … it stands in the middle of a field. *Chew the fat.* I'll say the first part of the sentence again. A deer is nearly **invisible** when. How can we finish the sentence so it makes sense? (Idea: *It lays down in the tall grass.*) Let's say the whole sentence together. *A deer is nearly invisible when it lays down in the tall grass.* Well done! I'm glad we chewed the fat!

(Count the points and declare a winner.) You did a great job of playing *Chew the Fat.*

## DAY 5

**Preparation:** Each child will need a copy of the Quiz Answer Sheet, BLM B.

### Retell Story

Today, I'll show you the pictures John Steptoe made for *Mufaro's Beautiful Daughters.* As I show you the pictures, I'll call on one of you to tell the class that part of the story.

Tell me what happens at the **beginning** of the story. (Show the pictures on pages 1 and 2. Call on a child to tell what's happening.)

Tell me what happens in the **middle** of the story. (Show the pictures on pages 3–24. Call on a child to tell what's happening. Encourage use of target words when appropriate. Model use when necessary.)

Tell me what happens at the **end** of the story. (Show the pictures on pages 25–29. Call on a child to tell what's happening.)

## Assess Vocabulary

(Give each child a copy of the Quiz Answer Sheet, BLM B.)

Today, you're going to have a True or False quiz. When you do the True or False quiz, it shows me how well you know the hard words you are learning.

If I say something that is true, circle the word **true.** What will you do if I say something that is true? *Circle the word true.*

If I say something that is false, circle the word **false.** What will you do if I say something that is false? *Circle the word false.*

Listen carefully to each item that I say. Don't let me trick you!

Item 1: A **festival** is a special party that has lots of activities like music, dancing, and good things to eat. (*True.*)

Item 2: A person who is **polite** is **rude**. (*False.*)

Item 3: A person who is **considerate** pays attention to what other people want or need. (*True.*)

Item 4: A **calm** day is a day with a lot of wind. (*False.*)

Item 5: A **commotion** and a **hullabaloo** are the same thing. (*True.*)

Item 6: You might feel **jealous** if your sister got a new bike and you didn't. (*True.*)

Item 7: If you are **ambitious,** you don't make any plans for yourself. (*False.*)

Item 8: Someone who is **clever** would probably never be able to figure out the answer to a riddle. (*False.*)

Item 9: People who buy things in stores are called **customers.** (*True.*)

Item 10: If your dad tells you to **calm** down, he wants you to become less angry, upset, or excited. (*True.*)

You did a great job completing your quiz!

(Score children's work. A child must score 9 out of 10 to be at the mastery level. If a child does not achieve mastery, insert the missed words as additional items in the games in next week's lessons. Retest those children individually for the missed items before they take the next mastery test.)

## Extensions

### Read a Story as a Reward

(Display copies of the books that you have read since the beginning of the program, as well as a variety of other *Cinderella* stories. There are over 1500 different *Cinderella* stories; here are a few that may reflect the ethnic diversity of your class: *Adelita: A Mexican Cinderella Story, The Persian Cinderella, Naya: The Inuit Cinderella: The Golden Sandal: A Middle Eastern Cinderella, Cendrillon: A Caribbean Cinderella, Smoky Mountain Rose: An Appalachian Cinderella: The Turkey Girl: A Zuni Cinderella Story, Sootface: An Ojibwa Cinderella, The Korean Cinderella, The Egyptian Cinderella, Yeh-Shen: A Cinderella Story from China.* Allow children to choose which book they would like you to read to them as a reward for their hard work.)

(Read the story aloud for enjoyment with minimal interruptions.)

---

**Preparation:** Word containers for the Super Words Center. You may wish to remove some of the words from earlier lessons the children have mastered.
You will need 2 copies of each card that remains in the word containers.

---

### Introduce the Super Words Center

(Add the new Picture Vocabulary Cards to the words from the previous weeks. Show children one of the word containers. If children need more guidance in how to work in the Super Words Center, role-play with two to three children as a demonstration.)

Let's think about how we work with our words in the Super Words Center.

This week's activity is called *Go Fish.* What's the name of this week's activity? *Go Fish.*

You will work with a partner in the Super Words Center. Whom will you work with? *A partner.*

First you and your partner will each draw six word cards out of the container and hold them so your partner cannot see them. What do you do first? (Idea: *Draw six cards out of the container and hold them so my partner cannot see them.*)

Next you will look at the cards in your hand and lay down any cards that you have two of. You will tell your partner the word the pictures show. What do you do next? (Idea: *Lay down any cards that I have two of, and tell my partner the word the pictures show.*)

Then your partner has a chance to lay down any cards he or she has two of, and tell the word the pictures show. What does your partner do? (Idea: *Lay down any cards that he or she has two of, and tell the word the pictures show.*)

Next you will ask your partner for a card that you have only one of by saying the word the picture shows. If your partner has that card, he or she will give it to you. If your partner gives you the card, you will lay down the two cards. What does your partner do if they have the card you ask for? (Idea: *Give you the card.*) What will you do if your partner gives you a card? (Idea: *Lay down the two cards that are the same.*)

If your partner does not have the card you ask for, your partner will say, "Go Fish." What will your partner do if he or she doesn't have the card you ask for? (Idea: *Say "Go Fish."*) If your partner says "Go Fish," you must choose another card from the word container. What will you do if your partner says "Go Fish"? (Idea: *Choose a card from the word container.*)

Then it's your partner's turn.

Watch while I show you what I mean. (Demonstrate this process with one child as your partner.)

When one partner has no cards left in his or her hand, the game is over. Each person gets one point for each pair of cards they have laid down. The winner is the person with the most points. Who wins the game? (Idea: *The person with the most points.*)

Have fun playing *Go Fish!*

THE POLAR BEAR SON
AN INUIT TALE

RETOLD AND ILLUSTRATED BY LYDIA DABCOVICH

**Preparation:** You will need a copy of *The Polar Bear Son* for each day's lesson.

Post a copy of the Vocabulary Tally Sheet, BLM A, with this week's Picture Vocabulary Cards attached.

Each child will need one copy of the Homework Sheet, BLM 11a.

## DAY 1

### Introduce Book

This week's book is called *The Polar Bear Son*. What's the title of this week's book? *The Polar Bear Son.*

This book was written by Lydia Dabcovich [dab-coh-vik]. Who's the author of *The Polar Bear Son*? *Lydia Dabcovich.*

Lydia Dabcovich also made the pictures for this book. Who is the illustrator of *The Polar Bear Son*? *Lydia Dabcovich.* Who made the illustrations for this book? *Lydia Dabcovich.*

The cover of a book usually gives us some hints of what the book is about. Let's look at the front cover of *The Polar Bear Son*. What do you see in the illustration? (Ideas: *A woman dressed in warm clothing; a polar bear cub; lots of ice and snow; mountains; the woman is talking to the polar bear cub.*)

(Assign each child a partner.) Get ready to make some predictions to your partner about this book. Use the information from the cover to help you.

(Ask the following questions, allowing sufficient time for children to share their predictions with their partners.)

- Who do you think are the characters in this story?
- What do you think the woman is saying to the polar bear cub?
- Where do you think the story happens?
- Where do you think the polar bear cub's mother is?

### The Polar Bear Son
author: Lydia Dabcovich • illustrator: Lydia Dabcovich

### ◎ Target Vocabulary

| Tier II | Tier III |
|---|---|
| injured | setting (when) |
| faithful | legend |
| feast | verb |
| custom | |
| *companions | |
| *orphan | |

*Expanded Target Vocabulary Word

- When do you think the story happens?
- Do you think this story is about real people and animals? Tell why or why not.

(Call on several children to share their predictions with the class.)

### Take a Picture Walk

(Encourage children to use target words in their answers.) We're going to take a picture walk through this book. Remember that when we take a picture walk, we look at the pictures and tell what we think will happen in the story.

**Pages 6–7.** Where does the story happen? (Ideas: *Alaska; the North Pole; someplace similarly cold.*) When does this story happen? (Ideas: *In winter; during the day.*) What do you think the woman is going to put in her bucket? What are the other people in this illustration doing? (Idea: *Packing their dogsled for a trip.*)

**Pages 8–9.** What does the woman see? (Idea: *A polar bear cub.*) What do you think she's saying to the cub?

**Pages 10–11.** Where do you think the woman is taking the cub?

**Pages 12–13.** Where does this part of the story happen? (Idea: *In the woman's house.*) What has the woman done? (Idea: *She brought the cub home to feed it.*)

**Pages 14–15.** What's happening in this illustration? (Idea: *Some children are playing with* *the cub.*) Do the children and the cub look like they're having fun? *Yes.* How can you tell? (Idea: *They are all smiling.*)

**Pages 16–17.** Where are the woman and the polar bear in this illustration? (Idea: *At the ocean or a lake.*) What is the polar bear bringing the woman? *A fish.*

**Pages 18–19.** Who do you think these people are? (Ideas: *Friends; family; neighbors.* Point to the basket of fish.) Where do you think these fish came from? (Idea: *The polar bear caught them.*) What do you think the woman is saying to her neighbors?

**Pages 20–21.** These hunters look angry. What do you think they're planning to do? Where do you think the children are running? (Idea: *To tell the woman; to tell the bear.*)

**Pages 22–23.** What do you think the woman and the men are talking about? Why do you think the men all look so angry?

**Pages 24–25.** What do you think the woman is telling the polar bear? (Idea: *The hunters plan to kill him; he must leave the village.*) How do the woman and children feel in this part of the story? (Ideas: *Sad; worried; upset.*)

**Pages 26–27.** What's happening in this illustration? (Idea: *The polar bear is leaving.*) How do you think the hunters will feel when they learn the bear is gone? (Ideas: *Angry, because they didn't get to kill it; happy, because the bear has gone.*)

**Pages 28–29.** What do you think the woman is looking for? (Idea: *The polar bear.*)

**Pages 30–31.** What is happening here? (Ideas: *The polar bear has returned; the woman is running to hug it.*) Do you think this is the same polar bear? *Yes.* It certainly has grown much bigger!

**Pages 32–33.** Is this the woman's polar bear? *Yes.* How do the woman and the bear feel? (Ideas: *Happy; contented; delighted.*)

**Pages 34–35.** What is the polar bear doing in this illustration? (Idea: *Catching fish.*) What is the woman doing? (Idea: *Cutting up a seal.*) What do you think the woman will do with all this food?

**Page 36.** Where is the woman going? (Idea: *Back to her village.*) Why doesn't she take the polar bear home with her? (Idea: *She's afraid the hunters will kill it.*) Do you think the polar bear will help the woman fish again? *Yes.*

Now that we've finished our picture walk, let's talk about how Lydia Dabcovich made the illustrations for *The Polar Bear Son*. There are lots of different ways to make illustrations for a book: The artist can paint them; the artist can draw them with a pen or pencil; the artist can make them with markers, crayons, pastels, or chalk; the artist can cut out different pieces of paper and glue them together. How do you think Lydia Dabcovich made her illustrations? (Ideas: *She painted them.*)

(Show first illustration of the dog sled team.) Lydia Dabcovich used a special kind of heavy watercolors to make her paintings. She wanted you to be able to feel how thick and cold the snow was. Does this illustration make you feel cold? Tell us about how the illustration makes you feel. (Allow children time to share the feelings created by the artist.)

**Pages 28–29.** Lydia Dabcovich also wanted you to feel the big open spaces in the Arctic. Does this illustration make you think how small the woman is compared to the big open spaces around her? Tell us about it. (Allow children time to share the feelings created by the artist.)

It's your turn to ask me some questions. What would you like to know about the story? (Accept questions. If children tell about the pictures or the story instead of ask questions, prompt them to ask a question.) Ask me a where question. Ask me a how question.

### Read the Story Aloud
(Read the story to children with minimal interruptions.)

Tomorrow we will read the story again, and I will ask you some questions.

### Present Target Vocabulary
 Injured

In the story, the old woman "always looked (Kunikdjuaq) over carefully, making sure he had not been injured." That means that she made sure he had not hurt himself or had not been harmed by someone else. **Injured.** Say the word. *Injured.*

**Injured** is a describing word. It tells more about a person or animal. What kind of word is **injured?** *A describing word.*

**If you are injured, you have been hurt or have been harmed by someone else.** Say the word that means you "have been hurt or have been harmed by someone else." *Injured.*

(Correct any incorrect responses, and repeat the item at the end of the sequence.)

Let's think about some situations where a person or an animal might be injured. I'll tell about some situations. If the person or animal has been injured, say "injured." If not, don't say anything.

- Tobias scraped his knee when he fell off his bike. *Injured.*
- The cat was hurt in a fight with a raccoon. *Injured.*
- My aunt was in a car accident, but everyone was fine.
- Helicopters evacuated the people hurt in the earthquake. *Injured.*
- Yvonne went to the doctor for her yearly checkup.
- The thorn in the lion's paw was very painful. *Injured.*

What word means "have been hurt or have been harmed by someone else"? *Injured.*

## ◎ Faithful

To this day, "The Inuit tell the story of the faithful bear Kunikdjuaq and the old woman who brought him up." The bear never forgot the old woman and was always there to bring her salmon and seal. When we say the bear was faithful we mean the bear never forgot the old woman and was always there to help her. **Faithful.** Say the word. *Faithful.*

**If someone is faithful, they never forget you; you can always depend on them if you need help.** Say the word that means "never forget you; you can always depend on them if you need help." *Faithful.*

Let's think about who might be faithful to you. If I name someone who would be faithful, say "faithful." If not, don't say anything.

- Your best friend. *Faithful.*
- Your mother or father. *Faithful.*
- A stranger.
- Your dog. *Faithful.*
- The people who live on the other side of town.
- Someone who is selfish.

What word means "never forget you; you can always depend on them if you need help"? *Faithful.*

## ◎ Feast

In the story, the villagers said, Kunikdjuaq "will make a fine feast for the village." That means there would be enough meat on him that the villagers could have a great big meal and everyone could eat as much as they wanted. **Feast.** Say the word. *Feast.*

**Feast** is a naming word. It names a thing. What do we call a naming word that names a person, place, thing, or idea? *A noun.* What kind of word is **feast?** *A noun.*

**A feast is a great big meal where everyone can eat as much as they want.** Say the word that means "a great big meal where everyone can eat as much as they want." *Feast.*

Let's think about some times when people might be invited to a feast. I'll tell about a time. If you think it tells about a time when there would be a feast, say "feast." If not, don't say anything.

- Thanksgiving. *Feast.*
- October 17th.
- New Year's Day. *Feast.*
- The day before your birthday.
- When a king is crowned. *Feast.*
- When your whole family gets together. *Feast.*

What noun means "a great big meal where everyone can eat as much as they want"? *Feast.*

## ◎ Custom

In the story, "As is the custom of the Inuit, the old woman shared every good catch with the bear and the whole village." That means it was an Inuit tradition that people who had food always shared it with other people in their village. **Custom.** Say the word. *Custom.*

**Custom** is a naming word. It names an idea. What do we call a naming word that names a person, place, thing, or idea? *A noun.* What kind of word is **custom**? *A noun.*

**A custom is a tradition or way of acting among a group of people.** Say the word that means "a tradition or way of acting among a group of people." *Custom.*

Let's think about some customs of different groups of people. I'll tell about something. If you think this is a custom of the people I tell about, say "custom." If not, don't say anything.

- When the Kikuyu people of Kenya name their first child, it is named after the father's parents. The second child is named after the mother's parents. *Custom.*
- Only some of the people in our family give presents at birthdays.
- In Mexico, friends and family always come first. *Custom.*
- In America, fireworks are set off on July 4th. *Custom.*
- Some people in Italy like to have a rest in the afternoon.
- In Scotland when people get dressed up, the men wear kilts, with each clan or family having its own special tartan or design. *Custom.*

What noun means "a tradition or way of acting among a group of people"? *Custom.*

### Present Vocabulary Tally Sheet
(See Lesson 1, page 4, for instructions.)

### Assign Homework
(Homework Sheet, BLM 11a. See the Introduction for homework instructions.)

---

## DAY 2

**Preparation:** Picture Vocabulary Cards for *injured, faithful, feast, custom.*

### Read and Discuss Story

(Read story to the children. Ask the following questions at the specified points. Encourage them to use target words in their answers.)

**Page 7.** Where did this story happen? (Idea: *Way up north.*) Who was this story about? (Idea: *An old Inuit woman.*) How did the woman get food? (Ideas: *She fished and gathered seeds and berries; she depended on her neighbors.*)

**Page 9.** What did the woman think had happened to the cub's mother? (Idea: *She must have been killed.*)

**Page 10.** Where did the woman take the cub? *Home.*

**Page 12.** How did the woman think of the cub? (Idea: *As her son.*)

**Page 14.** What was the polar bear like as he grew? (Ideas: *Friendly; round; fluffy.*) What did the children in the village do with the polar bear? (Ideas: *Played; tumbled; slid on the ice.*)

**Page 16.** How did the polar bear help the old woman? (Idea: *He hunted and fished for her.*)

**Page 18.** What was the Inuit custom that the woman followed? (Idea: *She shared her food with the bear and the other people in her village.*) How did the woman feel about her son the polar bear? (Idea: *She was proud of him.*) Why was the old woman proud of the bear? (Idea: *Because he had hunted and fished well.*)

**Page 20.** Why did the hunters become angry with the polar bear? (Idea: *They were jealous because he was a better hunter than they were.*) That's right; they wanted to be able to hunt as well as the polar bear. Why did the children run to the old woman? (Idea: *To warn her of the hunters' plan to kill the polar bear.*)

**Page 23.** What did the old woman do when she learned about the hunters' plan? (Idea: *She went from house to house to beg the villagers not to kill the bear.*) What reasons did the villagers give for killing the polar bear? (Ideas: *He was getting too big and strong; he was dangerous; they could eat his meat and use his fur to stay warm.*)

**Page 24.** Why did the old woman tell the polar bear to go? (Idea: *So he wouldn't be killed.*) What did she beg the bear to do? (Ideas: *To not forget her; to remember her.*)

**Page 27.** How did the old woman and the children feel as they watched the bear leave? *Sad.*

**Page 28.** What did the woman do when she felt very lonely and hungry? (Idea: *She went far out on the ice and called for the bear.*) How do you think the bear could help the woman not feel lonely and hungry? (Ideas: *He could be someone for her to talk to; he could hunt and fish for her.*)

**Page 31.** Did the woman wait a long time for the bear to come to her? *No.*

**Page 33.** What did the bear look like when the old woman saw him? (Ideas: *Big; strong; sleek; glossy.*) When you look at the illustration you can almost feel how smooth and shiny Kunikdjuaq's fur is, can't you?

**Page 34.** What was the old woman looking for when she checked him over? (Ideas: *Injuries.*) What did the bear do to help the old woman? (Idea: *He brought her salmon and seal to eat.*)

**Page 36.** How long did the woman and the bear take care of each other? (Idea: *For many years.*)

### Review Vocabulary

(Display the Picture Vocabulary Cards. Point to each card as you say the word. Ask children to repeat each word after you.) These pictures show **injured, faithful, feast,** and **custom.**

- What noun means "a great big meal where everyone can eat as much as they want"? *Feast.*
- What noun means "a tradition or way of acting among a group of people"? *Custom.*
- What word means "hurt or harmed by someone else"? *Injured.*
- What word means "never forget you; you can always depend on them if you need help"? *Faithful.*

### Extend Vocabulary

◎━ Feast

In *The Polar Bear Son,* we learned that **feast** means "a great big meal where everyone can eat as much as they want."

Raise your hand if you can tell us a sentence that uses **feast** as a noun meaning "a great big meal where everyone can eat as much as they want." (Call on several children. If they don't use complete sentences, restate their examples as sentences. Have the class repeat the sentences.)

Here's a new way to use the word **feast.**

- Tomorrow we will **feast** on roast turkey and all the trimmings. Say the sentence.
- They **feasted** on hot dogs, corn on the cob, and ice cream. Say the sentence.
- The lions **feasted** on the body of the wildebeest. Say the sentence.

In these sentences, **feast** is an action word. Another word for an action word is a verb. What is another word for an action word? *A verb.* A verb tells what a noun does. What does a verb do? *It tells what a noun does.* What kind of word tells what a noun does? *A verb.* **In these sentences, feast is a verb that means to eat a lot of food at a large, special meal.** What verb means "eat a lot of food at a large, special meal"? *Feast.*

Raise your hand if you can tell us a sentence that uses **feast** as a verb meaning "to eat a lot of food at a large, special meal." (Call on several children. If they don't use complete sentences, restate their examples as sentences. Have the class repeat the sentences.)

### Present Expanded Target Vocabulary

◎━ Companions

In *The Polar Bear Son,* the children of the village "loved to play with (the little bear), tumbling about and sliding on the snow." Another way of saying the children and the little bear liked to play together is to say the children and the little bear were companions. **Companions.** Say the word. *Companions.*

**Companions** is a naming word. It names a group of people or animals. What do we call a naming word that names a person, place, thing, or idea? *A noun.* What kind of word is **companions?** *A noun.*

**Companions are those who spend time together enjoying each other's company.** Say the word that means "those who spend time together enjoying each other's company." *Companions.*

Let's think about people or animals that might be companions. I'll tell about a time. If the people or animals I tell about would be companions, say "companions." If not, don't say anything.

- The puppy and the little boy always played together. *Companions.*
- Shaquille and the other boys in his neighborhood liked to play basketball at the park. *Companions.*
- Hannah didn't like to play with the girls in her class.
- Ethan and the twins who lived next door loved to go to the park to play. *Companions.*
- Chantel's favorite pastime is reading.
- The three bear cubs tumbled and tussled with each other all day. *Companions.*

What noun means "those who spend time together enjoying each other's company"? *Companions.*

◎━ *Orphan*

In *The Polar Bear Son,* the woman found a polar bear cub whose mother had been killed. The cub was all alone. Another way of saying the polar bear cub had no parents is to the polar bear cub was an orphan. **Orphan.** Say the word. *Orphan.*

**Orphan** is a naming word. It names a person or an animal. What do we call a naming word that names a person, place, thing, or idea? *A noun.* What kind of word is **orphan?** *A noun.*

**An orphan is a child or a young animal whose parents have died.** Say the word that means "a child or young animal whose parents have died." *Orphan.*

I'll tell about some children or young animals. If those children or young animals are orphans, say "orphan." If not, don't say anything.

- Tyler's parents had been killed in a car accident. *Orphan.*
- The hawk had killed the chick's mother. *Orphan.*
- Alyssa lived with her mother and father and two brothers.
- Yu-Min's parents died in the war. *Orphan.*
- Kareem lived with his grandma and his mother.
- Natalie and her family lived in Baltimore, Maryland.

What noun means "a child or young animal whose parents have died"? *Orphan.*

**Preparation:** Prepare a sheet of chart paper, landscape direction, titled *The Polar Bear Son.* Underneath the title, draw 8 boxes connected by arrows.

See the Introduction for Week 11's chart.

Each child will need a copy of the Activity Sheet, BLM 11b.

## Analyze Setting–When (Literary Analysis)

Today we will learn more about how stories are made.

The setting of a story tells two things. One thing the setting tells is where the story happens. What is one thing the setting tells? *Where the story happens.* The second thing the setting tells is when the story happens. What is the second thing the setting tells? *When the story happens.*

Let's look at the pictures and talk about the story to figure out **when** *The Polar Bear Son* happened.

**Pages 6–7.** When did the story begin? (Idea: *In the <u>winter</u>.*)

**Pages 8–9.** (Read the first sentence: "One day, out on the ice, the old woman found a little white polar bear cub.") When did this part of the story happen? <u>*One day.*</u>

**Pages 12–15.** When did this part of the story happen? *When the polar bear was <u>still a cub</u>.*

**Pages 16–17.** (Show the illustration and read the text.) When did this part of the story happen? (Idea: *Spring; summer; long, dark winter; spring came again.*) We'll have to be detectives to figure out this part. If spring, summer, and long, dark winter passed, and it's spring again, how much time has passed? (Idea: *One year.*) So when did this part of the story happen? <u>*One year later.*</u> Good thinking, detectives! This part happened one year later.

**Pages 26–27.** (And read the text.) When did this part of the story happen? *<u>After</u> the <u>hunters said they would kill Kunikdjuaq</u>.*

**Pages 28–29** (And read the sentence: "From time to time, when she felt very lonely and hungry, she left her hut early in the morning and went very far out on the ice.") When did this part of the story happen? *From time to time; early morning.*

**Page 36** (And read the first sentence: "This went on for many years.") When did the end of the story happen? *For many years.*

(Point to the words as you say each time.) Winter, one day, early one morning, one year later, after the hunters said they would kill Kunikdjuaq, from time to time, early morning, for many years. (Draw a line underneath these 8 boxes.) These things all happened over many years. When did the story happen? *Over many years.* (Write the words *over many years* underneath the line.)

When is the setting of *The Polar Bear Son*? (Idea: *Over many years.*)

### Play What's My Word?

Today you will play *What's My Word?* I'll give you three clues. After I give each clue, if you are sure you know my word, you may make a guess. If you guess correctly, you will win one point. If you make a mistake, I get the point.

Let's practice. Here's my first clue. My word is a noun. Are you sure you know my word? If you are, you may make a guess. (If anyone wishes to guess, accept the guess. Award the point to either the class or the teacher.)

Here's my second clue. My word starts with the **k** sound. Are you sure you know my word? If you are, you may make a guess. (If anyone wishes to guess, accept the guess. Award the point to either the class or the teacher.)

Here's my third clue. My word names an idea. What's my word? *Custom.* (Award the point to either the class or the teacher.)

(**Note:** If a child guesses the word correctly before the last clue, give the other clues and have children decide if the answer fits those clues.)

Now you're ready to play the game. (Draw a T-chart on the board for keeping score. Children earn one point for each correct answer. If they make an error, correct them as you normally would, and record one point for yourself. Repeat missed words at the end of the game.)

- Here's my first clue. My word is a noun. Here's my second clue. My word starts with a **k** sound. Here's my third clue. My word means almost the same thing as "friends." What's my word? *Companions.*
- New word. Here's my first clue. My word is a noun. Here's my second clue. My word ends with an **n** sound. Here's my third clue. My word can be an animal or a child who has no parents. What's my word? *Orphan.*
- New word. Here's my first clue. My word starts with an **f** sound. Here's my second clue. My word can be a noun. Here's my third clue. My word can be a verb. What's my word? *Feast.*
- New word. Here's my first clue. My word is a describing word. Here's my second clue. My word tells more about a person or an animal. Here's my third clue. My word tells about someone who would never forget you; someone who would always help you if you needed help. What's my word? *Faithful.*
- New word. Here's my first clue. My word is a describing word. Here's my second clue. You would not want to be this. Here's my third clue. My word means you've been hurt. What's my word? *Injured.*

(Count the points and declare a winner.) You did a great job of playing *What's My Word?*

### Complete the Activity Sheet

(Give each child a copy of the Activity Sheet, BLM 11b. Review with children the sequence of events in *The Polar Bear Son*. Record key words and phrases on the board or on a piece of chart paper. The children will use the key words to retell the story.)

(Suggestions for Key Words: North; Inuit woman; polar bear cub; Kunikdjuaq; hunted and fished; shared; jealous; kill; away; called; came; salmon and seal; many years.)

**Preparation:** Globe or map of the world.

## Learn About Legends

Today you will learn about a special kind of folk tale called a legend. What will you learn about? *A legend.*

Folk tales, fairy tales, and legends are all stories that were once told out loud. How are folk tales, fairy tales, and legends the same? (Idea: *They are all stories that were once told out loud.*) How is a fairy tale different from a folk tale? (Idea: *Someone decided to write it down in a book a long time ago.*) A legend is a special kind of folk tale that explains how something came to be. What does a legend explain? (Idea: *How something came to be.*)

Different groups of people have different legends that explain how things around them came to be. *The Polar Bear Son* is a legend from the Inuit people. The Inuit people are the native people who live along the Arctic coasts of Siberia, Alaska, the Northwest Territories, Nunavut, Quebec, Labrador, and Greenland. (Locate these areas on the map or globe.)

Long ago, Inuit hunters believed that powerful spirits sent them the animals they depended upon and they thanked every animal they killed for allowing itself to be caught. This story explains how the Inuit people came to depend on the polar bear and why the polar bear sometimes allows the Inuit people to catch it. What does this legend explain? (Idea: *How the Inuit people came to depend on the polar bear and why the polar bear sometimes allows the Inuit people to catch it.*)

What people does *The Polar Bear Son* come from? *The Inuit.* No one knows when this legend was first told. Do we know when this legend was first told? *No.* This story was first written down by a man named Frans Boas in 1888. Who first wrote down this legend? *Frans Boas.* Lydia Dabcovich has retold the story in her own words, so she is the author of this version of the legend. Who is the author of this version of the legend? *Lydia Dabcovich.*

## Play What's My Word? (Cumulative Review)

Let's play *What's My Word?* You'll have to think really hard, because my word can be any word we've learned since we read *Suki's Kimono.*

I'll give you three clues. After I give each clue, if you are sure you know my word, you may make a guess. If you guess correctly, you will win one point. If you make a mistake, I get the point.

Let's practice. Here's my first clue. My word is a noun. Are you sure you know my word? If you are, you may make a guess. (If anyone wishes to guess, accept the guess. Award the point to either the class or the teacher.)

Here's my second clue. My word starts with the **c** sound. Are you sure you know my word? If you are, you may make a guess. (If anyone wishes to guess, accept the guess. Award the point to either the class or the teacher.)

Here's my third clue. My word means "people who spend time together enjoying each other's company." What's my word? *Companions.* (Award the point to either the class or the teacher.)

(**Note:** If a child guesses the word correctly before the last clue, give the other clues and have children decide if the answer fits those clues.)

Now you're ready to play the game. (Draw a T-chart on the board for keeping score. Children earn one point for each correct answer. If they make an error, correct them as you normally would, and record one point for yourself. Repeat missed words at the end of the game.)

- Here's my first clue. My word starts with the word part **in.** Here's my second clue. My word is a verb. Here's my third clue. My word means "tell people your name." What's my word? *Introduce.*
- New word. Here's my first clue. My word starts with the word part **in.** Here's my second clue. My word is a verb. Here's my third clue. My word means "hurt or harmed by someone or something." What's my word? *Injured.*

- New word. Here's my first clue. My word starts with a **f** sound. Here's my second clue. My word is a describing word. Here's my third clue. My word could tell about your dog if your dog never forgot you and you always depended on him if you needed help. What's my word? *Faithful.*
- New word. Here's my first clue. My word is sometimes a noun. Here's my second clue. My word is sometimes a verb. Here's my third clue. When my word is a noun it means "a big meal where you can eat as much as you want." What's my word? *Feast.*
- New word. Here's my first clue. My word starts with the word part **com.** Here's my second clue. My word is a noun. Here's my third clue. My word means "a hullabaloo." What's my word? *Commotion.*
- New word. Here's my first clue. My word is a noun. Here's my second clue. My word names an idea. Here's my third clue. My word means a "a way of acting among a group of people." What's my word? *Custom.*
- New word. Here's my first clue. My word is a noun. Here's my second clue. I wouldn't like to be this. Here's my third clue. My word means I have no parents. What's my word? *Orphan.*
- New word. Here's my first clue. My word is a noun. Here's my second clue. My word starts with a **r** sound. Here's my third clue. Your dad would need this if he wanted to know how to make a new kind of muffin. What's my word? *Recipe.*
- New word. Here's my first clue. My word ends with **e-d.** Here's my second clue. My word is a describing word. Here's my third clue. If I am this, I have made up my mind to do something and I won't let anything stop me. What's my word? *Determined.*

(Count the points and declare a winner.) You did a great job of playing *What's My Word?*

**Preparation:** Each child will need a copy of the Quiz Answer Sheet, BLM B.

## Retell Story

Today I'll show you the pictures Lydia Dabcovich made for *The Polar Bear Son.* As I show you the pictures, I'll call on one of you to tell the class that part of the story.

Tell me what happens at the **beginning** of the story. (Show the pictures on pages 6–11. Call on a child to tell what's happening.)

Tell me what happens in the **middle** of the story. (Show the pictures on pages 12–35. Call on a child to tell what's happening. Encourage use of target words when appropriate. Model use as necessary.)

Tell me what happens at the **end** of the story. (Show the pictures on page 36. Call on a child to tell what's happening.)

## Assess Vocabulary

 (Give each child a copy of the Quiz Answer Sheet, BLM B.)

Today, you're going to have a True or False quiz. Whenyou do the True or False quiz, it shows me how well you know the hard words you are learning.

If I say something that is true, circle the word **true.** What will you do if I say something that is true? *Circle the word true.*

If I say something that is false, circle the word **false.** What will you do if I say something that is false? *Circle the word false.*

Listen carefully to each item that I say. Don't let me trick you!

Item 1: If you **feasted** on blackberries, you would have eaten lots and lots of blackberries; enough for a large meal. (*True.*)

Item 2: An **injured** person might make a **decision** to see a **physician.** (*True.*)

Item 3: **Companions quarrel** all the time. (*False.*)

Item 4: It is the **custom** of many Americans to put their hand over their hearts when they sing *The Star-Spangled Banner.* (*True.*)

Item 5: If you are an **orphan,** you live with your mother and father. (*False.*)

Item 6: A person who is **forgiving** wouldn't blame people for the bad things they've done or want to get back at them. (*True.*)

Item 7: You can always depend on a **faithful companion.** (*True.*)

Item 8: Some families have a special **feast** on Thanksgiving. (*True.*)

Item 9: If you've had a **miserable** day, everything that happened to you was good. (*False.*)

Item 10: If you were **delighted,** you might have lost your **temper.** (*False.*)

You did a great job completing your quiz!

(Score children's work. A child must score 9 out of 10 to be at the mastery level. If a child does not achieve mastery, insert the missed words as additional items in the games in next week's lessons. Retest those children individually for the missed items before they take the next mastery test.)

## Extensions

### Read a Story as a Reward

 (Display copies of the folk tales and fairy tales you have read since the beginning of the program, as well as a variety of legends from different cultures. Allow children to choose which book they would like you to read to them as a reward for their hard work.)

(Read the story aloud for enjoyment with minimal interruptions.)

---

**Preparation:** Word containers for the Super Words Center. You may wish to remove some of the words from earlier lessons. Choose words that the children have mastered.

---

### Introduce the Super Words Center

(Add the new Picture Vocabulary Cards to the words from the previous weeks. Show children one of the word containers. If children need more guidance in how to work in the Super Words Center, role-play with two to three children as a demonstration.)

Let's think about how we work with our words in the Super Words Center.

This week's activity is called *What's Missing?* What's the name of this week's activity? *What's Missing?*

You will work with a partner in the Super Words Center. Whom will you work with? *A partner.*

First one partner will draw four word cards out of the container and put them on the table so both partners can see. What do you do first? (Idea: *Draw four cards out of the container and put them on the table so both partners can see.*)

Next you will take turns looking at the cards and saying the words the pictures show. What do you do next? Idea: *We take turns looking at the cards and saying the words the pictures show.*

Next partner 2 looks away while partner 1 takes one of the four cards and places it facedown on the table away from the other cards. Then partner 1 draws a new card from the container and places it on the table with the other three.

Watch while I show you what I mean. (Demonstrate this process with one student as your partner.) When you put down the new card, it's a good idea to mix the cards so they aren't in the same places any more. (Demonstrate this process as you go.)

Now partner 1 says, "What's Missing?" Partner 2 has to use his or her eyes and brain and say what old card has been taken away. After partner 2 has guessed, turn over the facedown card. If partner 2 is correct, he or she gets a point. If partner 2 is not correct, partner 1 gets the point. (Demonstrate this process as you go.)

Next partner 2 has a turn to choose four different cards and the game starts again. What happens next? (Idea: *Partner 2 has a turn to choose four different cards and the game starts again.*)

Have fun playing *What's Missing?*

**Preparation:** You will need a copy of *Dog-of-the-Sea-Waves* for each day's lesson.

You will need a copy of *The Polar Bear Son* for Day 1.

Post a copy of the Vocabulary Tally Sheet, BLM A, with this week's Picture Vocabulary Cards attached.

Each child will need one copy of the Homework Sheet, BLM 12a.

# *Dog-of-the-Sea-Waves*
author: James Rumford • illustrator: James Rumford

## Target Vocabulary

| Tier II | Tier III |
|---------|----------|
| journey | setting (when) |
| voyage | legend |
| curious | verb |
| sparkling | transparent |
| *brave | |
| *rescued | |

*Expanded Target Vocabulary Word

## DAY 1

### Introduce Book

This week's book is called *Dog-of-the-Sea-Waves.* What's the title of this week's book? *Dog-of-the-Sea-Waves.*

This book was written by James Rumford. Who's the author of *Dog-of-the-Sea-Waves*? *James Rumford.*

James Rumford also made the pictures for this book. Who is the illustrator of *Dog-of-the-Sea-Waves*? *James Rumford.* Who made the illustrations for this book? *James Rumford.*

The cover of a book usually gives us some hints of what the book is about. Let's look at the front cover of *Dog-of-the-Sea-Waves.* What do you see in the illustration? (Ideas: *A boy swimming with a seal; yellow fish; water.*)

(Assign each child a partner.) Get ready to make some predictions to your partner about this book. Use the information from the cover to help you.

(Ask the following questions, allowing sufficient time for children to share their predictions with their partners.)

- Who are the characters in this story?
- What do you think they will do?
- Where do you think the story happens?
- When do you think the story happens?
- Why do you think the boy is swimming with the seal?

- How does the seal feel about swimming with the boy?
- Do you think this story is about real people and animals? Tell why or why not.

(Call on several children to share their predictions with the class.)

### Take a Picture Walk

(Encourage children to use target words in their answers.) We're going to take a picture walk through this book. Remember that when we take a picture walk, we look at the pictures and tell what we think will happen in the story.

**Pages 4–5.** What do you see in this illustration? (Ideas: *The ocean; a volcano erupting; seals swimming; a log floating.*) Does the ocean look rough or calm in this illustration? *Rough.* Where do you think this is?

**Pages 6–7.** What is happening in this illustration? (Idea: *There is a bad storm; there is lightning; it is raining really hard.*)

**Pages 8–9.** Where do you think this part of the story takes place? (Idea: *On an island.*) Do you think it's hot or cold on this island? *Hot.* How do you know? (Ideas: *There is steam/fog coming in off the water; there are lots of plants.*)

**Pages 10–11.** Who do you think these men are? (Idea: *People that live on the island.*) What do you think they are going to do? (Ideas: *Go exploring; look for food.*)

**Pages 12–13.** What time of day is it in this part of the story? *Nighttime.* What do you think the men are looking at? (Ideas: *The moon; stars; the sky.*)

**Pages 14–15.** What has the boy found? (Idea: *A seal.*) What do you think is wrong with it?

**Pages 16–17.** What is happening here? (Idea: *The boy is swimming in the ocean with the seal.*) How do you think he feels? (Ideas: *Happy; contented.*) Where have you seen this illustration before? (Idea: *On the cover.*)

**Pages 18–19.** What is the seal doing? (Idea: *Pulling on the rope.*) What do you think will happen next? (Idea: *The man will fall into the ocean.*) That seal is a bit of a rascal, isn't he?

**Pages 20–21.** What is the seal looking at? (Idea: *The boat.*) Where do you think the boy is?

**Pages 22–23.** Where do you think the people are in this illustration? (Idea: *On another island.*)

**Pages 24–25.** (Point to the smoke.) What is this? *Smoke.* Where do you think the smoke is coming from? (Idea: *From the volcano.*) Where do you think the people are running? How do you think the people are feeling? (Idea: *Terrified.*)

**Pages 26–27.** Where are the people in this illustration? (Idea: *In the ocean.*) Is the ocean calm or rough? *Rough.*

**Pages 28–29.** What do you think is happening here? (Idea: *The boy is drowning; the seal is trying to save him.*)

**Pages 30–31.** What is happening here? (Idea: *The people are getting back on their boat.*) What do you think they are saying to the seal? (Idea: *Thank you.*) How do you think the people are feeling? (Idea: *Grateful.*)

**Pages 32–33.** Where do you think the boat is going? How do you think the seal feels? (Ideas: *Sad; lonely; miserable.*)

**Pages 34–35.** It looks like the men and the boy have returned to the island. What have they brought with them? (Ideas: *More ships; their families; animals.*) How do you think the boy and the seal feel now? (Ideas: *Happy; contented.*)

Now that we've finished our picture walk, let's talk about how James Rumford made the illustrations for *Dog-of-the-Sea-Waves*. There are lots of different ways to make illustrations for a book: the artist can paint them; the artist can draw them with a pen or pencil; the artist can make them with markers, crayons, pastels, or chalk; the artist can cut out different pieces of paper and glue them together. How do you think James Rumford made his illustrations? (Idea: *He painted them.*)

**Pages 6–7.** James Rumford used watercolors to make his paintings. In this painting, he wanted you to be able to see through the rain and the leaves in order to see what was behind them. What can you see through the rain? (Ideas: *Leaves; trees; the ocean; the mountains.*) What can you see through the leaves? (Ideas: *The bird; the trees; the rain.*)

In order to let you see through things, James Rumford used a paint that was thinner and more transparent than the paint used by Lydia Dabcovich in *The Polar Bear Son.* If something is **transparent,** you can see through it. What describing word means you can see though something? *Transparent.*

(*The Polar Bear Son:* dog sled team traveling across the snow; *Dog-of-the-Sea-Waves:* pages 6 and 7.) How was the paint James Rumford used different from the paint Lydia Dabcovich used? (Idea: *It was thinner and more transparent.*)

**Pages 8–9.** James Rumford also wanted you to feel how full of plants and animals Hawaii is. Does this illustration make you think how crowded with life the land is? Tell us about how the illustration makes you feel. (Allow children time to share the feelings created by the artist.)

(Pages 28–29 of *The Polar Bear Son;* Pages 8 and 9 of *Dog-of-the-Sea-Waves.*) How is the feeling in James Rumford's illustration different from the feeling in Lydia Dabcovich's? (Allow children time to share the different feelings created by the artists.)

It's your turn to ask me some questions. What would you like to know about the story? (Accept questions. If children tell about the story instead of ask questions, prompt them to ask a question.) Ask me a who question. Ask me a why question.

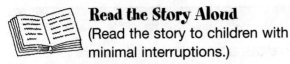 **Read the Story Aloud**
(Read the story to children with minimal interruptions.)

Tomorrow we will read the story again, and I will ask you some questions.

## Present Target Vocabulary

 Journey

In the story, the five brothers all traveled a long way to get to the islands. That means they made a journey to the islands. **Journey.** Say the word. *Journey.*

**Journey** is a noun. It names a thing. What kind of word is **journey?** *A noun.*

**A journey is a long trip to a place far away.** Say the noun that means "a long trip to a place far away." *Journey.*

**(Correct any incorrect responses, and repeat the item at the end of the sequence.)**

I'll tell about some things. If those things would be a journey, say "journey." If not, don't say anything.

- Christopher Columbus traveled across the Atlantic Ocean to reach America. *Journey.*
- The settlers traveled on foot from New York to Iowa. *Journey.*
- The dentist walked across the street to go from his home to his office.
- The children walked two blocks to school.
- The astronauts traveled all the way to moon. *Journey.*
- The men paddled their canoes the full length of the Mississippi River. *Journey.*

What noun means "a long trip to a place far away"? *Journey.*

Voyage

In the story, we found out the brothers' home "was a long ocean voyage away." That means their home was a long journey from the islands. **Voyage.** Say the word. *Voyage.*

**Voyage** is a noun. It names a thing. What kind of word is **voyage?** *A noun.*

**A voyage is a long journey by air, land, sea, or outer space.** Say the word that means "a long journey by air, land, sea, or outer space." *Voyage.*

I'll tell about some things. If those things would be a voyage, say "voyage." If not, don't say anything.

- Apollo 11 made the first landing on the moon. *Voyage.*
- Christopher Columbus traveled across the Atlantic Ocean to reach America. *Voyage.*
- We had a picnic by the lake.
- It took us two hours to drive to Delight, Arkansas.
- The two-man team traveled by hot air balloon from New York City to Paris, France. *Voyage.*
- We took a short bus trip from Brookfield Zoo to The Children's Museum.

What noun means "a long journey by air, land, sea, or outer space"? *Voyage.*

Curious

In the story, the boys were curious about whether what they saw was a cloud on the side of a mountain, or smoke. They were interested in what they saw, and they wanted to know more about it. **Curious.** Say the word. *Curious.*

**Curious** is a describing word. It tells more about a noun. What kind of word is **curious?** *A describing word.*

**If you are curious about something, you are interested in that thing, and you want to know more about it.** Say the word that means "interested in something and want to know more about it." *Curious.*

Let's think about some people. I'll tell about someone. If you think that person is curious, say "curious." If not, don't say anything.

- Jamie was interested in ants' nests, and he wanted to know more about them. *Curious.*
- Jordan and his friends wanted to know more about space, so they watched a television show about space. *Curious.*
- Fern saw a tree standing beside a stream.
- Rex had a brown Cocker Spaniel puppy.
- Everyone ran to the window to see what had happened. *Curious.*
- All of us asked about the flying squirrel and where it lived. *Curious.*

What word means "interested in something and want to know more about it"? *Curious.*

## ⊙= Sparkling

In the story, "everyone except Manu looked up at the sparkling North Star." That means the star was shining with many flashing points of light. It was glittering. **Sparkling.** Say the word. *Sparkling.*

**Sparkling** is a describing word. It tells more about a noun. What kind of word is **sparkling?** *A describing word.*

**If something is sparkling, it is shining with many flashing points of light; it is glittering.** Say the word that means "shining with many flashing points of light; glittering." *Sparkling.*

Let's think about some things that might be sparkling. I'll tell about something. If you think it is sparkling, say "sparkling." If not, don't say anything.

- We went up into the mountains to see the glittering stars. *Sparkling.*
- There was a glittering diamond on her ring. *Sparkling.*
- Dominic likes to wear plain-colored T-shirts.
- Maya likes to wear T-shirts with sequins and jewels on them. *Sparkling.*
- The fireflies were little flashing points of light in the night sky. *Sparkling.*
- It was a foggy night and we couldn't even see the streetlights.

What word means "shining with many flashing points of light; glittering"? *Sparkling.*

### Present Vocabulary Tally Sheet
(See Lesson 1, page 4, for instructions.)

### Assign Homework
(Homework Sheet, BLM 12a. See the Introduction for homework instructions.)

**Preparation:** Picture Vocabulary Cards for *journey, voyage, curious, sparkling.*

### Read and Discuss Story

(Read story to children. Ask the following questions at the specified points. Encourage them to use target words in their answers.)

**Pages 4–7.** Where does this story happen? (Idea: *In the Hawaiian Islands.*) Do you think this is a modern story or a story that happened a long time ago? (Idea: *A story that happened a long time ago.*)

**Page 8.** What lived in the forests of the Hawaiian Islands before people came? (Ideas: *Birds; insects.*)

**Page 9.** When did the first people come to the Hawaiian Islands? (Idea: *About 2,000 years ago.*)

**Page 10.** Who were the first people in the Hawaiian Islands? (Idea: *Five brothers.*) Why did the brothers come to the islands? (Idea: *To explore.*) I'll name the brothers; you tell what each one loved. Hōkū. *Loved the stars.* Nā'ale. *Loved the sea.* 'Ōpua. *Loved the clouds.* Makani. *Loved the wind.* Manu. *Loved the birds.*

**Page 12.** What were the brothers excited about? (Idea: *All the new things they were discovering.*) Was Manu excited about the new things? *No.* What did Manu want? (Ideas: *To go home; to go back to the things he was used to.*)

**Page 15.** (Read to the end of the sentence "Something familiar in this strange land.") What did Manu think he had found? *A dog.* Why was he so excited about that? (Ideas: *He had dogs at home; they were familiar to him.*)

(Read to the end of the page.) What did Manu do to help the hurt animal? (Ideas: *Cleaned the wound; built a shelter against the sun; kept its fur wet.*) Why did the brothers not want to help take care of the animal? (Ideas: *They thought it would die; they had to prepare for the voyage home.*)

**Page 16.** Why do you think Manu named the animal Dog-of-the-Sea-Waves? (Ideas: *The* animal reminded him of a dog, but it could swim among the waves in the sea.) What did Manu and Dog-of-the-Sea-Waves do together? (Ideas: *Swim; play tag in the ocean.*)

When we compare two things we tell how they are alike and how they are different. What do we do when we compare two things? *We tell how they are alike and how they are different.* How was Dog-of-the-Sea-Waves different from a dog? (Ideas: *He had no paws or ears; he didn't wag his tail; he swam in the sea.*) How was Dog-of-the-Sea-Waves similar to a dog? (Ideas: *He had whiskers; he liked to play with Manu.*)

**Page 19.** (Read to the end of the sentence, "'And sails to repair,' cried Makani.") How do you think Manu's brothers felt in this part of the story? (Ideas: *Annoyed; frustrated; angry; upset with Manu.*) Why do you think they felt this way? (Ideas: *Manu was not helping with the chores; he was only playing with Dog-of-the-Sea-Waves; he wasn't being considerate.*)

(Read to the end of the page.) What kind of trouble did Manu and Dog-of-the-Sea-Waves get into?

**Page 20.** What did Manu do during the day? (Idea: *He did chores for his brothers; he gathered berries; he fished; he got water; he twisted rope.*) Where did Manu go in the evenings? (Idea: *He went into the ocean to play with Dog-of-the-Sea-Waves.*)

**Page 21.** How long were the brothers on the island? (Idea: *For many months.*) Why do you think Dog-of-the-Sea-Waves brushed his whiskers against Manu's cheek? (Ideas: *To say goodbye; to show that he would miss Manu.*)

**Page 23.** (Read to the end of the first paragraph.) Where were the brothers in this part of the story? (Idea: *On the last island in the chain.*) Why did the brothers stop to explore this island? (Idea: *One of the brothers wanted to see if it was clouds or smoke he saw.*)

(Read to the end of the page.) Why do you think the brothers had to swim from their boat to the shore of the island? (Idea: *The water near the shore was too shallow for a boat.*) Two of the brothers noticed strange things. Then there was a jolt. What do you think happened?

**Page 24.** What happened? (Idea: *The volcano erupted.*) What did the brothers do? (Idea: *They jumped off the cliff into the sea.*)

**Page 27.** What happened to Manu? (Idea: *He was pulled under the sea.*) What did the brothers do? (Ideas: *They looked for him; shouted for him; begged the sea to be calm.*) Did the brothers find Manu? *No.* How do you think the brothers felt when they couldn't find Manu?

**Page 28.** What was Manu doing? (Idea: *Trying to get to the surface.*)

**Page 29.** Who came to help Manu? *Dog-of-the-Sea-Waves.*

**Page 30.** How did the brothers feel when they saw Dog-of-the-Sea-Waves bringing Manu to the boat? (Ideas: *Relieved; happy; thankful; grateful.*)

**Pages 32–33.** Where were the brothers heading? *Home.* Do you think they'll return to the Hawaiian Islands?

**Pages 34–35.** Who did the brothers bring back to the Hawaiian Islands? (Idea: *Their families.*) Why did they return? (Idea: *To live on the islands.*) Do you think Manu and Dog-of-the-Sea-Waves will continue to play together?

## Review Vocabulary

(Display the Picture Vocabulary Cards. Point to each card as you say the word. Ask children to repeat each word after you.) These pictures show **journey, voyage, curious,** and **sparkling.**

- What noun means "a long trip to a place far away"? *Journey.*
- What word means "shining with many flashing points of light; glittering"? *Sparkling.*
- What word means "interested in something and want to know more about it"? *Curious.*
- What noun means "a long journey by air, land, sea, or outer space"? *Voyage.*

## Extend Vocabulary

 Curious

In *Dog-of-the-Sea-Waves,* we learned that **curious** is a describing word that can be used to tell about people. When someone is curious about something it means they are "interested in something and want to know more about it."

Raise your hand if you can tell us a sentence that uses **curious** as a describing word meaning "interested in something and want to know more about it." (Call on several children. If they don't use complete sentences, restate their examples as sentences. Have the class repeat the sentences.)

Here's a new way to use the word **curious.**

- What a **curious** thing to do! Say the sentence.
- It was **curious** that Hal wouldn't speak to anyone but his cat. Say the sentence.
- It was even more **curious** that Hal's cat talked back to him. Say the sentence.

**In these sentences, curious is a describing word that means something is unusual or hard to understand.**

Tell about some other things that you would find **curious.** (Encourage children to use the following frame for their answer: "I think ____ would be curious.")

### Present Expanded Target Vocabulary
 Brave

In *Dog-of-the-Sea-Waves,* when Manu disappeared under the waves, "Makani filled his lungs with air and went to the very depths of the ocean, but there was no sign of Manu." This shows that Makani was very brave. He was willing to do something that was very hard. **Brave.** Say the word. *Brave.*

**Brave** is a describing word. It tells more about a noun. What kind of word is **brave?** *A describing word.*

**If you are brave, you are willing to do something even though it is very hard.** Say the word that means "willing to do something even though it is very hard." *Brave.*

Let's think about some times when you might be brave. If I say a time when you would be brave, say "brave." If not, don't say anything.

- Going downstairs in the dark. *Brave.*
- Playing with your favorite toy.
- Not crying or yelling when you get a bee sting. *Brave.*
- Telling your teacher the truth when you did something that you weren't supposed to do. *Brave.*

- Eating your lunch.
- Teaching your friend to play a game.

What word means "willing to do something even though it is very hard"? *Brave.*

### Rescued

In the story, Dog-of-the-Sea Waves found Manu under the water. He let Manu hold him and he took him up to the surface of the water. Dog-of-the-Sea-Waves rescued Manu. **Rescued.** Say the word. *Rescued.*

**Rescued** is an action word. Another word for an action word is a verb. What is another word for an action word? *A verb.* A verb tells what a noun does. What does a verb do? *It tells what a noun does.* What kind of word tells what a noun does? *A verb.* What kind of word is **rescued?** *A verb.*

**Rescued means got someone or something away from danger and saved them.** Say the word that means "got someone or something away from danger and saved them." *Rescued.*

I'll tell about some times. If those people or animals were in danger and you would want to save them, say "rescued." If not, don't say anything.

- Nadia's kitten was crying up in a tree. *Rescued.*
- Mick and Keith got the little girl out of the sinking boat. *Rescued.*
- Joel watched the sun setting behind the mountains.
- First, the paramedics got the old man off the roof. *Rescued.*
- Landon sat quietly in his chair and didn't say much.
- It was time to make supper.

What verb means "got someone or something away from danger and saved them"? *Rescued.*

**Preparation:** Prepare a sheet of chart paper, landscape direction, titled *Dog-of-the-Sea-Waves.* Underneath the title, draw 13 boxes connected by arrows.

See the Introduction for Week 12's chart.

Each child will need a copy of the Activity Sheet, BLM 12b.

## Analyze Setting–When (Literary Analysis)

Today we will learn more about how stories are made.

The setting of a story tells two things. One thing the setting tells is where the story happens. What is one thing the setting tells? *Where the story happens.* The second thing the setting tells is when the story happens. What is the second thing the setting tells? *When the story happens.*

Let's look at the pictures and talk about the story, to figure out **when** *Dog-of-the-Sea-Waves* happened.

**Pages 4–8.** (Show the illustrations and read the text.) This story begins "when the sun, the moon, and the stars guided birds with seeds in their bellies to these islands, when ocean waves brought driftwood teeming with life, when storms brought frightened birds in the clouds and insects on the wind."

We'll have to be detectives to figure out this part. Were there plants and animals on the Hawaiian Islands before this happened? *No.* So what words could we use to tell when the story began? (Idea: *When the plants and animals came to Hawaii.*)

**Page 9.** (Show the illustration and read the text.) When did this part of the story happen? *2,000 years ago.*

**Pages 10–11.** When did this part of the story happen? (Idea: *During the day.*)

**Pages 12–13.** When did this part of the story happen? (Idea: *At night.*)

**Pages 14–15.** (Show the illustration and read the first sentence: "The next day, as the brothers were exploring a lagoon, Manu spotted an animal lying at the water's edge.") When did this part of the story happen? *The next day.*

**Pages 16–17.** (Show the illustration and read the first sentence: "'I will call you Dog-of-the-Sea-Waves,' Manu said on the third day as he fed him fish.") When did this part of the story happen? *Three days later.*

(Read the following sentence: "At the end of the week, the two had their first swim together.") When did this part of the story happen? *At the end of the week.*

**Pages 20–21.** (Show the illustration and read the first sentence on page 21: "After many months of hard work, the boat was finally ready to leave.") When did this part of the story happen? *Many months later.*

**Pages 22–23.** When did this part of the story happen? *When they went on the last island.*

**Pages 26–29.** When did this part of the story happen? *When Manu was drowning.*

**Pages 30–31.** When did this part of the story happen? *When Manu was rescued.*

**Pages 32–33.** When did this part of the story happen? *When the brothers left.*

**Pages 34–35.** When did the story end? *When the first families came to Hawaii.*

(Point to the words as you say each time.) When plants and animals came, 2,000 years ago, during the day, at night, the next day, three days later, at the end of the week, many months later, when they went on the last island, when Manu was drowning, when Dog-of-the-Sea-Waves rescued Manu, when the brothers left, when the first families came to Hawaii. (Draw a line underneath these 13 boxes.) These things all happened about 2,000 years ago. When did the story happen? *About 2,000 years ago.* (Write the words *about 2,000 years ago* underneath the line.)

When is the setting of *Dog-of-the-Sea-Waves?* (Idea: *About 2,000 years ago.*) Is 2,000 years ago a long time ago? *Yes.* Legends usually happen long ago. When do legends usually happen? (Idea: *Long ago.*)

## Play What's My Word?

Today you will play *What's My Word?* I'll give you three clues. After I give each clue, if you are sure you know my word, you may make a guess. If you guess correctly, you will win one point. If you make a mistake, I get the point.

Let's practice. Here's my first clue. My word is a describing word. Are you sure you know my word? If you are, you may make a guess. (If anyone wishes to guess, accept the guess. Award the point to either the class or the teacher.)

Here's my second clue. There's an **s** sound in my word. Are you sure you know my word? If you are, you may make a guess. (If anyone wishes to guess, accept the guess. Award the point to either the class or the teacher.)

Here's my third clue. My word can mean "interested in something and want to know more about it." What's my word? *Curious.* (Award the point to either the class or the teacher.)

(**Note:** If a child guesses the word correctly before the last clue, give the other clues and have the children decide if the answer fits those clues.)

Now you're ready to play the game. (Draw a T-chart on the board for keeping score. Children earn one point for each correct answer. If they make an error, correct them as you normally would, and record one point for yourself. Repeat missed words at the end of the game.)

- Here's my first clue. My word is a describing word. Here's my second clue. There's an **s** sound in my word. Here's my third clue. My word means "glittering." What's my word? *Sparkling.*
- New word. Here's my first clue. There's a **v** sound in my word. Here's my second clue. My word is a describing word. Here's my third clue. My word means "not afraid to do something even though it is very hard." What's my word? *Brave.*
- New word. Here's my first clue. There's a **v** sound in my word. Here's my second clue. My

word is a noun. Here's my third clue. My word means "a long journey." What's my word? *Voyage.*

- New word. Here's my first clue. My word ends with the letters **-ed**. Here's my second clue. My word is a verb. Here's my third clue. My word means "got someone away from danger and saved him or her." What's my word? *Rescued.*
- New word. Here's my first clue. My word is a noun. Here's my second clue. My word and another word from our new words mean almost the same thing. Here's my third clue. My word means almost the same thing as **voyage.** What's my word? *Journey.*

(Count the points and declare a winner.) You did a great job of playing *What's My Word?*

## Complete the Activity Sheet

(Give each child a copy of the Activity Sheet, BLM 12b. Review with children the sequence of events in *Dog-of-the-Sea-Waves*. Record key words and phrases on the board or on a piece of chart paper. The children should use the key words to help them retell the story.)

(Suggestions for Key Words: Five brothers; Hawaii; explored; Dog-of-the-Sea-Waves; trouble; volcano; erupt; drowned; rescued; returned; families.)

---

## DAY 4

**Preparation:** Globe or map of the world.

---

## Learn About Legends

Today you will learn more about a special kind of folk tale called a legend. What will you learn about? *A legend.*

Folk tales, fairy tales, and legends are all stories that were once told out loud. How are folk tales, fairy tales, and legends the same? (Idea: *They are all stories that were once told out loud.*)

How is a fairy tale different from a folk tale? (Idea: *Someone decided to write it down in a book a long time ago.*) A legend is a special kind of folk tale that explains how something came to be. What does a legend explain? (Idea: *How something came to be.*)

Different groups of people have different legends that explain how things around them came to be. This is a legend about the Hawaiian people. The Hawaiian people live on the Hawaiian Islands. **(Locate these islands on the map or globe.)** Hawaii is the fiftieth state of the United States of America. What is the name of our state? _____. Hawaii is a state just like _____ is.

What does this legend explain? (Ideas: *How people first discovered the Hawaiian Islands; how the people came to the Hawaiian Islands; how the people came to Hawaii.*)

What people does *Dog-of-the-Sea-Waves* come from? *The Hawaiian people.*

James Rumford wrote this legend to explain how people first discovered the Hawaiian Islands and how the first families came to Hawaii. Because James Rumford wrote this story, he is the author of this legend. Who is the author of this legend? *James Rumford.*

The people of Hawaii speak a language of their own, as well as English. (Show pages 36 and 37.) Here is the story written in Hawaiian.

### Play What's My Word? (Cumulative Review)

 Let's play *What's My Word*? You'll have to think really hard, because my word can be any word we've learned since we read *Suki's Kimono.*

I'll give you three clues. After I give each clue, if you are sure you know my word, you may make a guess. If you guess correctly, you will win one point. If you make a mistake, I get the point.

Let's practice. Here's my first clue. My word ends with the letters **-ed.** Are you sure you know my word? If you are, you may make a guess. **(If anyone wishes to guess, accept the guess. Award the point to either the class or the teacher.)**

Here's my second clue. My word is a describing word. Are you sure you know my word? If you are, you may make a guess. **(If anyone wishes to guess, accept the guess. Award the point to either the class or the teacher.)**

Here's my third clue. My word means "very pleased and excited." What's my word? *Delighted.* (Award the point to either the class or the teacher.)

**(Note:** If a child guesses the word correctly before the last clue, give the other clues and have children decide if the answer fits those clues.)

Now you're ready to play the game. (Draw a T-chart on the board for keeping score. Children earn one point for each correct answer. If they make an error, correct them as you normally would, and record one point for yourself. Repeat missed words at the end of the game.)

- Here's my first clue. My word ends with the word part **-ous.** Here's my second clue. My word is a describing word. Here's my third clue. My word can mean "unusual or hard to explain." What's my word? *Curious.*

- New word. Here's my first clue. My word is a describing word. Here's my second clue. My word starts with the **m** sound. Here's my third clue. You might use my word to tell about a very grand, beautiful castle. What's my word? *Magnificent.*

- New word. Here's my first clue. My word is a describing word. Here's my second clue. My word tells more about a person. Here's my third clue. If you were this, you might rescue someone from a dangerous situation. What's my word? *Brave.*

- New word. Here's my first clue. My word ends with the word part **-ing.** Here's my second clue. My word is a describing word. Here's my third clue. My word means you are the kind of person who doesn't blame people for the bad things they've done to you. What's my word? *Forgiving.*

- New word. Here's my first clue. My word ends with the word part **-ing.** Here's my second clue. My word is a describing word. Here's my third clue. My word tells more about something that is shining with many flashing points of light. What's my word? *Sparkling.*

- New word. Here's my first clue. My word is a noun. Here's my second clue. My word begins with the sound **v.** Here's my third clue. My word is something that you could travel on a boat or ship. What's my word? *Voyage.*

- New word. Here's my first clue. My word is a verb. Here's my second clue. My word ends with the letters **-ed.** Here's my third clue. My word means "saved someone from danger." What's my word? *Rescued.*

- New word. Here's my first clue. My word is a noun. Here's my second clue. My word starts the same as the word **journal.** Here's my third clue. My word means "a long trip." What's my word? *Journey.* Do you think many people would keep a **journal** if they went on a **journey?**

- New word. Here's my first clue. My word is a describing word. Here's my second clue. My word has two different meanings. Here's my third clue. One of the meanings of my word tells more about someone who is interested in something and wants to know more about it What's my word? *Curious.*

(Count the points and declare a winner.) You did a great job of playing *What's My Word?*

---

## DAY 5

**Preparation:** Each child will need a copy of the Quiz Answer Sheet, BLM B.

---

### Retell Story

Today I'll show you the pictures James Rumford made for *Dog-of-the-Sea-Waves.* As I show you the pictures, I'll call on one of you to tell the class that part of the story.

Tell me what happens at the **beginning** of the story. (Show the pictures on pages 4–9. Call on a child to tell what's happening.)

Tell me what happens in the **middle** of the story. (Show the pictures on pages 10–33. Call on a child to tell what's happening. Encourage use of target words when appropriate. Model use as necessary.)

Tell me what happens at the **end** of the story. (Show the pictures on pages 34 and 35. Call on a child to tell what's happening.)

---

### Assess Vocabulary

 (Give each child a copy of the Quiz Answer Sheet, BLM B.)

Today you're going to have a True or False quiz. When you do the True or False quiz, it shows me how well you know the hard words you are learning.

If I say something that is true, circle the word **true.** What will you do if I say something that is true? *Circle the word true.*

If I say something that is false, circle the word **false.** What will you do if I say something that is false? *Circle the word false.*

Listen carefully to each item that I say. Don't let me trick you!

Item 1: Going on a **journey** is almost the same as going on a **voyage.** (*True.*)

Item 2: If you are a **curious** person, you want to know more about lots of **different** things. (*True.*)

Item 3: **Sparkling** is an **ingredient** in a **recipe.** (*False.*)

Item 4: A **brave** fireman might **rescue** a person from a burning building. (*True.*)

Item 5: If you spoke to me in Pig Latin instead of English, I might say "How **curious!**" (*True.*)

Item 6: If Tori is **gullible,** it's very difficult to trick her. (*False.*)

Item 7: It would be **remarkable** if you heard a dog bark. (*False.*)

Item 8: A **generous** person is selfish. (*False.*)

Item 9: If your mom **rescued** your kitten from the tree, she might have used a ladder to climb up and carry the kitten down. (*True.*)

Item 10: An astronaut might go on a **voyage** to a space station. (*True.*)

You did a great job completing your quiz!

(Score children's work. A child must score 9 out of 10 to be at the mastery level. If a child does not achieve mastery, insert the missed words as additional items in the games in next week's lessons. Retest those children individually for the missed items before they take the next mastery test.)

# Extensions

## Read a Story as a Reward

 (Display copies of the folk tales and fairy tales you have read since the beginning of the program, as well as a variety of legends from different cultures. Allow children to choose which book they would like you to read to them as a reward for their hard work.)

(Read the story aloud for enjoyment with minimal interruptions.)

> **Preparation:** Word containers for the Super Words Center. You may wish to remove some of the words from earlier lessons. Choose words that the children have mastered.

## Introduce the Super Words Center

(Add the new Picture Vocabulary Cards to the words from the previous weeks. Show children one of the word containers. If children need more guidance in how to work in the Super Words Center, role-play with two to three children as a demonstration.)

Let's review how we work with our words in the Super Words Center.

This week's activity is called *What's Missing?* What's the name of this week's activity? *What's Missing?*

You will work with a partner in the Super Words Center. Whom will you work with? *A partner.*

First one partner will draw four word cards out of the container and put them on the table so both partners can see. What do you do first? (Idea: *Draw four cards out of the container and put them on the table so both partners can see.*)

Next you will take turns looking at the cards and saying the words the pictures show. What do you do next? (Idea: *We take turns looking at the cards and saying the words the pictures show.*)

Next partner 2 looks away while partner 1 takes one of the four cards and places it facedown on the table away from the other cards. Then partner 1 draws a new card from the container and places it on the table with the other three.

Watch while I show you what I mean. (Demonstrate this process with one student as your partner.)

When you put down the new card, it's a good idea to mix the cards so they aren't in the same places any more. (Demonstrate this process as you go.)

Now partner 1 says, "What's Missing?" Partner 2 has to use his or her eyes and brain and say what old card has been taken away. After partner 2 has guessed, turn over the facedown card. If partner 2 is correct, he or she gets a point. If partner 2 is not correct, partner 1 gets the point. (Demonstrate this process as you go.)

Next partner 2 has a turn to choose four different cards and the game starts again. What happens next? (Idea: *Partner 2 has a turn to choose four different cards and the game starts again.*)

Have fun playing *What's Missing?*

**Paul Bunyan**
author: Steven Kellogg • illustrator:
Steven Kellogg

**Preparation:** You will
need a copy of *Paul Bunyan*
for each day's lesson.

You will need a copy of *The Polar Bear
Son* and *Dog-of-the-Sea-Waves* for Day 1.

Number the pages of the story to assist
you in asking comprehension questions at
appropriate points.

Post a copy of the Vocabulary Tally Sheet,
BLM A, with this week's Picture Vocabulary
Cards attached.

Each child will need one copy of the
Homework Sheet, BLM 13a.

## Target Vocabulary

| Tier II | Tier III |
|---|---|
| colossal | setting |
| interest | (where, when) |
| wilderness | legend |
| astonishing | tall tale |
| *exaggerated | |
| *unbelievable | |

*Expanded Target Vocabulary Word

- Why do you think the man is holding the
leopard cubs?
- How big do you think that man is?

(Call on several children to share their
predictions with the class.)

### DAY 1

### Introduce Book

This week's book is called *Paul
Bunyan.* What's the title of this week's
book? *Paul Bunyan.*

This book was written by Steven Kellogg. Who's
the author of *Paul Bunyan*? *Steven Kellogg.*

Steven Kellogg also made the pictures for this
book. Who's the illustrator of *Paul Bunyan*?
*Steven Kellogg.* Who made the illustrations for
this book? *Steven Kellogg.*

The cover of a book usually gives us some hints
of what the book is about. Let's look at the front
cover of *Paul Bunyan*. What do you see in the
illustration? (Ideas: *A huge man holding leopard
cubs; an eagle; an ox; mountains, a waterfall;
trees.*)

(Assign each child a partner.) Get ready to make
some predictions to your partner about this book.
Use the information from the cover to help you.

(Ask the following questions, allowing sufficient
time for children to share their predictions with
their partners.)

- Who are the characters in this story?
- What is the man holding?
- Where do you think the story happens?
When do you think the story happens?

### Take a Picture Walk

(Encourage children to use target
words in their answers.) We're going to
take a picture walk through this book.
Remember that when we take a picture walk, we
look at the pictures and tell what we think will
happen in the story.

**Page 1.** Where do you think this part of the story
happens? (Idea: *On a farm.*) Look at the boy in
the picture. Do you think he is a baby or an older
child? *A baby.* How do you know? (Idea: *It looks
like he is wearing a diaper.*) What is the baby
doing? (Idea: *Lifting a cow over his head.*) Could
a baby really lift a cow over his head? *No.* Is this
story about a real boy? *No.*

**Page 2.** What is the baby doing in this
illustration? (Idea: *Putting a tree in the wagon.*)
(Read aloud the signs on the fence.) That
means that the owners of the orchard don't
want anyone going in there. Do you think the
boy is supposed to be taking those trees? *No.*
What else makes you think the boy shouldn't be
there? (Idea: *The woman is shouting and running
toward the boy.*)

**Page 3.** When is this part of the story
happening? *Nighttime.* Why are the people

jumping out of the windows of the building? (Idea: *The boy is breaking down the tree and it is falling onto the house.*)

**Page 4.** Where is the baby's crib? *In the water.* Why do you think it's there? (Ideas: *So he can't go out and tear down trees; so he can play with the seals.*)

**Pages 5–6.** What is happening in this illustration? (Ideas: *Water is coming up onto the land; boats are smashing; houses and people are floating away.*) Does the baby look afraid? *No.* It looks like he's having lots of fun, but I don't think the other people are.

**Page 7.** Where does this part of the story happen? (Ideas: *In the woods; in the forest.*) What is the boy doing in this illustration? (Ideas: *Running with the deer; racing with the deer.*) Is he still a baby here? *No.* No, he is older now, so some time has passed.

**Page 8.** What is he doing here? (Idea: *Playing with bears.*)

**Page 9.** When does this part of the story happen? (Ideas: *In the winter; at night.*) What did the boy find in the snow? (Ideas: *A baby ox; a calf.*)
(**Note:** If children answer *an animal,* tell them that this animal is called an ox and a baby ox is called a calf.)

**Page 10.** What is the young man doing? (Idea: *Putting logs in the wagon.*) What is the ox doing? *Eating.* Wow, look how big the young man and the ox are compared to the woman!

**Page 11.** (Point to the woman who is pointing at Paul Bunyan.) Why do you think this woman is pointing at the man? (Idea: *The man is as big as the trees and so is his ox.*) How do you think the woman feels seeing the man? (Ideas: *Scared; terrified.*) How do you think the man feels about that?

**Page 12.** (Point to the cook.) What is this man doing? *Making pancakes.* (Point to the lumberjacks cutting down the tree.) What are these men doing? *Cutting down a tree.* (Point to the men carrying the logs.) What do you think the men are going to do with all these logs?

**Page 13.** What do you think the men did with all those logs? (Idea: *Built a town.*) How big is the man now? (Ideas: *Huge; gigantic; bigger than a house.*) How does the man help the lumberjacks? (Idea: *He catches the falling trees.*)

**Page 14.** (Point to the man near the rock.) Look closely; what is happening to the man? (Idea: *Something or someone is grabbing him.*)

**Pages 15–16.** What is happening here? (Idea: *Monsters are pulling the men into the rocks.*)

**Page 17.** What do you think the man and his ox have done? (Idea: *They fought off the monsters and rescued the men.*)

**Page 18.** What are the people doing in this illustration? (Idea: *Parachuting; sky diving.*) What do you think those tall buildings are?

**Pages 19–20.** What is happening in this illustration? (Ideas: *It looks like people are playing hockey; they have curious skates; others are filling a giant pitcher; others are watching the game and cheering.*)

**Page 21.** What are falling from the sky? (Idea: *Giant pancakes.*) What happened when one of the pancakes missed the stack? (Ideas: *It landed on some animals; it landed on a building.*)

**Page 22.** What is the man doing here? (Idea: *Digging rocks out of a lake.*) What is the ox pulling? (Idea: *Boats.*) What do you think is in those boats?

**Pages 23–24.** What is starting to happen while the men work? (Idea: *It is starting to snow.*) What do you think the men will do?

**Page 25.** When does this part of the story happen? (Ideas: *In the winter; at night.*) How do you think the man feels about all this snow?

**Page 26.** How is the ox feeling in this part of the story? (Ideas: *Sad; miserable.*) Why do you think the ox is so miserable? What is the little man making? (Idea: *Glasses.*) Who do you think those glasses are for?

**Pages 27–28.** How do you think the people feel about the snow finally being gone? (Ideas: *Happy; excited; delighted.*)

(Point to the barbers at the bottom of page 27.) Why do you think the men need someone to cut their hair and shave their beards? (Idea: *They were locked up in their houses for so long their hair grew long.*)

**Pages 29–30.** What have the men come across? (Idea: *A giant snake.*)

**Pages 31–32.** What do you think is wrong with the lumberjacks? (Idea: *They are hot, weak. and tired.*) It looks like the man is dragging his ax. What is it doing to the ground? (Idea: *Cutting it up.*)

**Page 33.** Where are the man and his ox in this illustration? (Idea: *On a farm.*) Are the people here afraid of this giant man and his ox? *No.* Why do you think they're not afraid of him?

**Page 34.** What are the men doing here? (Idea: *Having a snowball fight.*) Do they look cold? *No.* It seems to be pretty warm, could those really be snowballs? *No.* What do you think they might be?

**Pages 35–36.** What is the man holding over his head in this illustration? *A whale.* What did he hold over his head when he was a baby? *A cow.*

**Page 37.** What do you think the man and his ox are doing at the end of this story?

Now that we've finished our picture walk, let's talk about how Steven Kellogg made the illustrations for *Paul Bunyan*. There are lots of different ways to make illustrations for a book: the artist can paint them; the artist can draw them with a pen or pencil; the artist can make them with markers, crayons, pastels, or chalk; the artist can cut out different pieces of paper and glue them together. How do you think Steven Kellogg made his illustrations? (Ideas: *First he drew his pictures with a pencil, then he painted them, then he added lines with pen and ink.*)

**Pages 7–8.** Steven Kellogg used a pencil, watercolors, and pen and ink to make his illustrations. In his illustrations, he wanted you to be able to see the characters running and wrestling. When an artist shows his characters doing actions, we say he is showing movement. What do Steven Kellogg's illustrations show? *Movement.*

**Pages 8–9.** Steven Kellogg wanted you to find new things in his illustrations every time you look

at them. So his illustrations are quite busy. Let's look at this illustration and see what other things are happening. Tell us about some of the things that are happening. (Allow children time to share the details in the illustration.)

Steven Kellogg also likes to put things in his drawings that you might find funny. When an artist puts funny things in his illustrations we say his illustrations are humorous. Here are some of the humorous things in this illustration. (Point to the various signs and read them, including the names of the teams.) What other things in this illustration are humorous? (Allow children time to share the humor in the illustration.)

(Pages 28 and 29 of *The Polar Bear Son*; Pages 8 and 9 of *Dog-of-the-Sea-Waves*; Pages 5 and 6 of *Paul Bunyan*.) How is the feeling in Steven Kellogg's illustrations different from James Rumford's and Lydia Dabcovich's illustrations? (Ideas: *Steven Kellogg's illustrations have lots of things and people in them; they show lots of movement; they are humorous; they are funny; they make you laugh.*)

It's your turn to ask me some questions. What would you like to know about the story? (Accept questions. If children tell about the pictures or story instead of ask questions, prompt them to ask a question.) Ask me a where question. Ask me a what question.

### Read the Story Aloud
(Read the story to children with minimal interruptions.)

Tomorrow we will read the story again, and I will ask you some questions.

### Present Target Vocabulary
⊙⟜ *Colossal*

In the story, Paul built a colossal flapjack griddle. That means the flapjack griddle was extremely large. It was huge. It was enormous. **Colossal.** Say the word. *Colossal.*

**Colossal** is a describing word. It tells more about a thing. What kind of word is **colossal**? *A describing word.*

**If something is colossal, it is extremely large, huge, or enormous.** Say the word that means "extremely large, huge, or enormous." *Colossal.*

(Correct any incorrect responses, and repeat the item at the end of the sequence.)

I'll tell about some things. If those things would be colossal, say "colossal." If not, don't say anything.

- A giant. *Colossal.*
- A nightingale.
- The planet Jupiter. *Colossal.*
- Your house.
- A giant redwood tree. *Colossal.*
- An enormous castle. *Colossal.*

A colossal castle. Everyone say that. *A colossal castle.* That's a good way to remember what **colossal** means. Castles are very large, so a colossal castle would be doubly large. And both of the words start with the same sound, so it's easy to remember.

What describing word means "extremely large, huge, or enormous"? *Colossal.*

◎─ Interest

In the story, we found out that even when he was a baby Paul had an interest in the family logging business. That means Paul wanted to learn more about it. **Interest.** Say the word. *Interest.*

**Interest** is a noun. It names a thing. What kind of word is **interest?** *A noun.*

**If you show an interest in something, you have a wish to learn more about it.** Say the word that means "a wish to learn more about something." *Interest.*

I'll tell about some people and some things. If the person has an interest in learning about the thing, say "interest." If not, don't say anything. (After the children answer the positive items, add the comment in parenthesis.)

- Serena and Venus Williams had a wish to learn more about tennis. *Interest.* (And they both became famous tennis champions.)
- Ferdinand Magellan wanted to know more about sailing. *Interest.* (And he was the first person to sail around the world.)
- Daniel is bored with everything.
- Hollis Conway had a wish to learn more about high jumping. *Interest.* (And he is the only

American ever to win two Olympic medals in the high jump.)
- An elephant can be over 10 feet tall.
- Deborah Kalyn had a wish to learn more about animals. *Interest.* (And now she's a veterinarian.)

What do you have an interest in? **(Call on several children. Encourage children to use this frame for their answers: "I have an interest in _____.")** Maybe one day children will be learning about what you have done!

What noun means "a wish to learn more about something"? *Interest.*

◎─ Wilderness

In the story, Paul loved his new home in the wilderness. A wilderness can be a desert, where there is lots of sand or rocks, or a forest, where there are lots of trees and many different kinds of animals. In Paul's wilderness there were lots of trees and forest animals such as deer and grizzly bears. **Wilderness.** Say the word. *Wilderness.*

**Wilderness** is a noun. It names a place. What kind of word is **wilderness?** *A noun.*

**A wilderness is a place where no people live.** Say the word that means "a place where no people live." *Wilderness.*

I'll tell about some places. If that place is a wilderness, say "wilderness." If not, don't say anything.

- High in the mountains. *Wilderness.*
- At the North Pole. *Wilderness.*
- At a busy beach in the middle of the summer.
- In the middle of a crater on the moon. *Wilderness.*
- In the desert. *Wilderness.*
- At your house.

What noun means "a place where no people live"? *Wilderness.*

◎─ Astonishing

In the story Paul and Babe grew at an astonishing rate. That means they both grew amazingly fast. **Astonishing.** Say the word. *Astonishing.*

**Astonishing** is a describing word. It tells more about a thing. What kind of word is **astonishing?** *A describing word.*

**If something is astonishing, it is amazing and hard to believe.** Say the word that means "amazing and hard to believe." *Astonishing.*

Let's think about some things that might be astonishing. I'll tell you about something. If you think what I say is astonishing, say "astonishing." If not, don't say anything.

- If you could go in the fastest rocket on earth, it would take you nine years to get to Pluto. *Astonishing.*
- The crocodile is the only animal that sheds tears while eating. *Astonishing.*
- Most people who have pets have dogs or cats.
- A new pencil is about 10 inches long.
- A butterfly has 12,000 eyes. *Astonishing.*
- An elephant's ear can weigh as much as 110 pounds. *Astonishing.*

What describing word means "amazing and hard to believe"? *Astonishing.*

## Present Vocabulary Tally Sheet
(See Lesson 1, page 4, for instructions.)

## Assign Homework
(Homework Sheet, BLM 13a. See the Introduction for homework instructions.)

---

### DAY 2

**Preparation:** Picture Vocabulary Cards for *colossal, interest, wilderness, astonishing.*

## Read and Discuss Story

 (Read story to children. Ask the following questions at the specified points. Encourage them to use target words in their answers.)

**Page 1.** Who is this story about? *Paul Bunyan.* Where does this part of the story happen? (Idea: *Maine.*) What was special about Paul Bunyan? (Idea: *He was the largest, smartest, and strongest baby ever born in Maine.*)

**Page 2.** What was Paul's family's business? (Idea: *Logging.*) In the logging business, people cut down trees and sell the wood.

**Page 4.** What were people complaining about? (Ideas: *Paul was ripping up their trees.*) What did Paul's parents do to stop him from taking people's trees? (Idea: *They anchored his crib in the harbor.*)

**Page 5.** How did Paul's rocking cause damage? (Idea: *He was so big that rocking his crib in the water caused large waves to come up on shore, wrecking boats and people's homes.*) Why did Paul's parents decide to move to the backwoods? (Ideas: *They thought life would be more peaceful; they thought Paul would be able to stay out of trouble.*)

**Page 7.** Why did Paul like living in the backwoods? (Idea: *He could run with the deer and wrestle with the bears.*)

**Page 9.** (Read to the end of the first paragraph.) What did Paul find buried in the blue snow? (Idea: *An ox calf.*) What did Paul name the ox? *Babe.* (Read to the end of the page.) What color was Babe? (Idea: *Blue, the color of the snow.*)

**Page 10.** How do you think Paul and Babe could have helped in the family logging business?

**Page 11.** How did Paul keep his beard looking neat? (Idea: *He combed it with the top of a tree.*) Why did Paul decide to leave his family and head west? (Ideas: *Too many settlers were coming to the woods; it was getting crowded.*)

**Page 12.** What kinds of workers did Paul hire to cross the country with him? (Ideas: *Lumbermen; cooks; a blacksmith.*) A blacksmith is a person who makes and fits horseshoes and makes things out of iron. What is a blacksmith? (Ideas: *A person who makes and fits horseshoes; a person who makes things out of iron.*)

**Page 13.** What happened after Paul and his crew cleared the land? (Idea: *Pioneers moved in and set up farms and villages.*)

**Page 14.** What were Gumberoos? (Idea: *Underground ogres.*) How did Paul think he could blast the meanness out of the ogres? (Idea: *By blowing a large horn into their cave.*)

**Page 15.** Did Paul's idea work? *No.* What do you think will happen to Paul and his crew?

**Page 17.** What happened to the Gumberoos after they finally untangled themselves? (Idea: *They disappeared deep under the earth.*)

**Page 18.** How did the workers get to and from their beds? (Ideas: *They rode balloons up; they parachuted down.*) What problem came up because there were so many new workers? (Idea: *The cooks couldn't flip flapjacks [pancakes] fast enough to satisfy them.*)

**Page 19.** How did Paul solve the flapjack problem? (Idea: *He built a colossal flapjack flipper.* If children don't use the word colossal, say:) One of our new words means "extremely large, huge, or enormous." What word is that? *Colossal.* That's right; Paul's flapjack flipper was **colossal.** How did the men grease this **colossal** flapjack griddle? (Idea: *They put slabs of bacon on their feet and skated around the griddle.*) So that's what those curious-looking skates were!

**Page 21.** Where did the flapjacks normally land? (Idea: *In a neat stack beside the griddle.*)

**Page 22.** Why did Paul take a few days off from clearing the land? (Idea: *To dig out the St. Lawrence River and the Great Lakes.*) Why did Paul dig out these waterways? (Idea: *So maple syrup could be delivered for his flapjacks.*)

**Page 23.** What gave the lumbermen their energy? (Idea: *The flapjacks and syrup.*)

**Page 24.** What happened to stop the lumberjacks? (Idea: *A blizzard.*)

**Page 25.** Why did the crew have to hibernate? (Idea: *Because the blizzard lasted for several years.*)

**Page 26.** (Read to the end of the first paragraph.) What does Paul think will make Babe feel less depressed? (Idea: *A pair of sunglasses.* Read to the end of the page.) What made the treetops reappear? (Idea: *The green sunglasses made Babe think the snow was clover so he ate all the snow.*)

**Pages 27–28.** What did Paul and his friends celebrate? (Idea: *All the holidays that had been missed during the blizzard.*)

**Page 29.** What problems did the lumberjacks face as they traveled southwest? (Idea: *The blistering sun and giant Texas varmints.*) What do you think varmints are? (Ideas: *Snakes; spiders.*) That's right; varmints are any kind of animals that would bother you.

**Page 30.** What would the men rather be doing than traveling in the desert? (Ideas: *Be buried by a blizzard; be bear hugged by a Gumberoo.*) I don't think they liked the desert at all!

**Page 31.** What did the hot Arizona sun do to the flapjacks? (Idea: *It made the griddle curl up like a burned leaf and evaporated the batter.*) Without their flapjacks, how did the men feel? (Ideas: *Weak; discouraged.*)

**Page 32.** How does the story say the Grand Canyon was made? (Idea: *Paul's ax fell from his shoulder and made a trench in the earth.*)

**Page 33.** What did Paul buy to try and help his men feel better? (Idea: *A barn full of corn.*) How did he get the corn back to the desert? (Idea: *Babe pulled the entire barn.*) What happened when the sun hit the barn? (Idea: *It exploded and all the corn popped.*) How did the men feel about this? (Ideas: *Dizzy with joy; happy; excited; delighted.*)

**Page 35.** Where did Paul and his crew end up? (Ideas: *California; the Pacific Ocean.*)

**Page 37.** Where did Paul and Babe go after crossing the country? (Idea: *North to the Alaskan mountains.*)

## Review Vocabulary

(Display the Picture Vocabulary Cards. Point to each card as you say the word. Ask children to repeat each word after you.) These pictures show **colossal, interest, wilderness,** and **astonishing.**

- What word means "amazing and hard to believe"? *Astonishing.*
- What noun means "a place where no people live"? *Wilderness.*
- What word means "extremely large, huge, or enormous"? *Colossal.*
- What noun means "a wish to learn more about something"? *Interest.*

## Extend Vocabulary

◎← Interest

In *Paul Bunyan*, we learned that **interest** is a naming word that means "a wish to learn more about something."

Raise your hand if you can tell us a sentence that uses **interest** as a noun meaning "a wish to learn more about something." (Call on several children. If they don't use complete sentences, restate their examples as sentences. Have the class repeat the sentences.)

Here's a new way to use the word **interest**.

- Could I **interest** you in a trip to the lake? Say the sentence.
- Could I **interest** you in a chocolate chip cookie? Say the sentence.
- Could I **interest** your dad in a new car? Say the sentence.

In these sentences, **interest** is an action word. Another word for an action word is a verb. What is another word for an action word? *A verb.* A verb tells what a noun does. What does a verb do? *It tells what a noun does.* What kind of word tells what a noun does? *A verb.* What kind of word is **interest**? *A verb.*

**In these sentences, interest means persuade you to do something or tempt you.** What verb means "persuade you to do something or tempt you"? *Interest.*

Raise your hand if you can tell us a sentence that uses **interest** as a verb meaning "persuade you to do something or tempt you." (Call on several children. If they don't use complete sentences, restate their examples as sentences. Have the class repeat the sentences.)

### Present Expanded Target Vocabulary
◎⚞ Exaggerated

In *Paul Bunyan*, we read that Paul built enormous new bunkhouses. They were so big the men had to fly to bed in balloons and parachute down in the morning. The stories Paul told made his bunkhouses sound bigger than they really were. Paul exaggerated when he told about his bunkhouses. **Exaggerated.** Say the word. *Exaggerated.*

**Exaggerated** is an action word. Another word for an action word is a verb. What is another word for an action word? *A verb.* A verb tells what a noun does. What does a verb do? *It tells what a noun does.* What kind of word tells what a noun does? *A verb.* What kind of word is **exaggerated?** *A verb.*

**If you exaggerated, you said something was larger, more important, or more valuable than it really was.** Say the word that means "said something was larger, more important, or more valuable than it really was." *Exaggerated.*

I'll tell you about some things. If you think I have exaggerated, say "exaggerated." If not, don't say anything.

- I can run faster than a cheetah. *Exaggerated.*
- Billy can run so fast, he's invisible. *Exaggerated.*
- It's usually warm in the summer.
- Sometimes it gets so hot we can fry eggs on the sidewalk. *Exaggerated.*
- Tina had a big lunch.
- Tina ate as much as an elephant. *Exaggerated.*

What verb means "said something was larger, more important, or more valuable than it really was"? *Exaggerated.*

◎⚞ Unbelievable

In the story, Paul dragged his ax behind him, creating the Grand Canyon. I don't believe that, do you? I think that's unbelievable. **Unbelievable.** Say the word. *Unbelievable.*

**Unbelievable** is a describing word. It tells more about something. What kind of word is **unbelievable?** *A describing word.*

**Unbelievable means very hard to believe.** Say the word that means "very hard to believe." *Unbelievable.*

I'll tell you about some things. If these things are very hard to believe, say "unbelievable!" If not, don't say anything.

- Sharon said she found a ten-foot alligator in her swimming pool. *Unbelievable!*
- The moon is made of green cheese. *Unbelievable!*
- Mia can read a book in one week.
- Lee Redmond had a thumbnail that grew to be more than 30 inches long. *Unbelievable!* (This one is actually true, but also unbelievable.)
- The biggest city in the United States is New York City.

- Somewhere in the United States a baby is born every 8 seconds. *Unbelievable!* (This one is also true, and unbelievable.)

What describing word means "very hard to believe"? *Unbelievable.*

## DAY 3

**Preparation:** Prepare a sheet of chart paper, landscape direction, titled *Paul Bunyan.* Underneath the title, draw a row of 16 boxes connected by arrows.

Underneath the first row of boxes, draw a second row of 9 boxes, connected by arrows.

See the Introduction for Week 13's chart.

Map of the United States. Each child will need a copy of the Activity Sheet, BLM 13b.

## Analyze Setting–Where, When (Literary Analysis)

Today we will remember what we have learned about the setting of a story.

The setting of a story tells two things. One thing the setting tells is where the story happened. What is one thing the setting tells? *Where the story happened.* The second thing the setting tells is when the story happened. What is the second thing the setting tells? *When the story happened.*

Let's look at the pictures and talk about the story, to figure out **where** *Paul Bunyan* happens.

(Follow the procedure established in Lessons 7– 9 to identify where the story happened. Record responses in the first row of boxes.
Ideas: *Maine, harbor, wilderness, Appalachian Mountains, midwest, St. Lawrence River and Great Lakes, Great Plains, Rocky Mountains, Texas, Arizona, Grand Canyon, east, desert, California, Pacific Ocean, Alaskan mountain ranges.*)

Maine, harbor, wilderness, Appalachian Mountains, Midwest, St. Lawrence River and Great Lakes, Great Plains, Rocky Mountains,

Texas, Arizona, Grand Canyon, east, desert, California, Pacific Ocean, and Alaskan mountain ranges are all in the United States. So, if we could only use one name to tell the setting of this story, we would use the name United States. (Draw a line underneath the boxes.) Where is the setting of *Paul Bunyan? United States.* (Write *United States* underneath the line. You may wish to locate the various places that are named on a map of the United States.)

(Follow the procedure established in Lessons 10–12 to identify when the story happened. Record responses in the second row of boxes.
Ideas: *When Paul was a baby, when he was a boy, one winter, when he was seventeen, when he was a young man, the seven years of the blizzard, springtime, when he was an older man, now.*)

When Paul was a baby, when he was a boy, one winter, when he was seventeen, when he was a young man, the seven years of the blizzard, springtime, when he was an older man, and now. (Draw a line underneath these boxes.) These things all happened during Paul's lifetime. When did the story happen? *During Paul's lifetime.* (Write *during Paul's lifetime* underneath the line.)

Good work. You figured out where and when *Paul Bunyan* happened. Where did the story happen? *In the United States.* When did the story happen? *During Paul Bunyan's lifetime.*

Now it's time to play a game.

### Play What's My Word?

Today you will play *What's My Word?* I'll give you three clues. After I give each clue, if you are sure you know my word, you may make a guess. If you guess correctly, you will win one point. If you make a mistake, I get the point.

Let's practice. Here's my first clue. My word is a describing word. Are you sure you know my word? If you are, you may make a guess. (If anyone wishes to guess, accept the guess. Award the point to either the class or the teacher.)

Here's my second clue. There's the word part **-ing** at the end of my word. Are you sure you know my word? If you are, you may make a guess. (If anyone wishes to guess, accept the guess. Award the point to either the class or the teacher.)

Here's my third clue. My word means '"amazing and hard to believe." What's my word? *Astonishing.* (Award the point to either the class or the teacher.)

(**Note:** If a child guesses the word correctly before the last clue, give the other clues and have children decide if the answer fits those clues.)

Now you're ready to play the game. (Draw a T-chart on the board for keeping score. Children earn one point for each correct answer. If they make an error, correct them as you normally would, and record one point for yourself. Repeat missed words at the end of the game.)

- Here's my first clue. My word is a noun. Here's my second clue. There's an **er** sound in my word. Here's my third clue. My word means "a place where no people live." What's my word? *Wilderness.*
- New word. Here's my first clue. My word is a noun. Here's my second clue. This word has **in-** at the beginning. Here's my third clue. My word means "a wish to learn more about something." What's my word? *Interest.*
- New word. Here's my first clue. There's an **er** sound in my word. Here's my second clue. My word is a verb. Here's my third clue. My word means "said something was larger, more important, or more valuable than it really was." What's my word? *Exaggerated.*
- New word. Here's my first clue. My word is a describing word. Here's my second clue. My word has an **l** sound in the middle. Here's my third clue. My word means "extremely large, huge, or enormous." What's my word? *Colossal.*
- New word. Here's my first clue. My word is a describing word. Here's my second clue. My word starts with the word part **un-**. Here's my third clue. My word means "very hard to believe." What's my word? *Unbelievable.*

(Count the points and declare a winner.) You did a great job of playing *What's My Word?*

## Complete the Activity Sheet

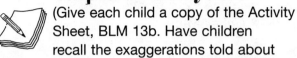

(Give each child a copy of the Activity Sheet, BLM 13b. Have children recall the exaggerations told about Paul when he was a <u>baby</u>, when he was a <u>boy</u>, when he was a <u>young man</u>, and when he was a <u>lumberman</u>. Have children recall the exaggerations about the <u>flapjack griddle</u>, the <u>bunkhouses</u>, the <u>blizzard</u>, and the <u>journey through the desert</u>. As children recall the exaggerations, write the underlined key words on the board or a sheet of chart paper. If the children have difficulty remembering these exaggerations, show the appropriate illustrations. Each student should select three exaggerations, and describe them in their own words.)

## DAY 4

### Learn About Legends

Today you will learn more about a special kind of folk tale called a legend. What will you learn about? *A legend.*

Folk tales, fairy tales, and legends are all stories that were once told out loud. How are folk tales, fairy tales, and legends the same? (Idea: *They are all stories that were once told out loud.*) A legend is a special kind of folk tale that explains how something came to be. What does a legend explain? (Idea: *How something came to be.*)

In *The Polar Bear Son,* we read a legend about the Inuit people and the polar bear. What did that legend explain? (Ideas: *How the Inuit people and the polar bear became friends; why the polar bear sometimes lets the Inuit people catch it.*)

In *Dog-of-the-Sea-Waves,* we read a legend about Hawaii. What did this legend explain? (Idea: *How people came to Hawaii.*)

Different groups of people have different legends that explain how things around them came to be. *The Polar Bear Son* comes from the Inuit people. *Dog-of-the-Sea-Waves* comes from the Hawaiian people. No one knows when these legends were first told. Do we know when these legends were first told? *No.*

*Paul Bunyan* is an American legend. It explains many different things about the United States. What are some of the things it explains? (Idea: *How the St. Lawrence River and the Great Lakes came to be; how the Grand Canyon came to be; how the forests of the midwest were cleared.*)

The legend of Paul Bunyan was first told by loggers as they sat around at night after working in the forests all day. As more and more loggers told the story of Paul Bunyan, they added more and more fantastic details to make the story more fun to tell.

After a while, people couldn't remember which things might have been true and which things were made up from the storytellers' imaginations. Because we don't know anymore which parts of the story might have been true, and which parts are made up from the storytellers' imaginations, we call this kind of legend a tall tale. What kind of legend is *Paul Bunyan*? *A tall tale.*

Even to this day, storytellers keep telling more and more tall tales about Paul Bunyan. If you ever go to Bemidji [bih-**mid**-jee], Minnesota, you will see colossal statues of Paul and Babe. Paul's statue is 18 feet high. How tall is Paul's statue? *18 feet.* The distance between Babe's horns is 14 feet. How far apart are Babe's horns? *14 feet.* (You may wish to help the children visualize the size, by measuring out these distances, or comparing them to something the children are familiar with. If you have a cement or blacktop playground, the children could use chalk to draw an outline of Paul and Babe on the playground.)

### Play What's My Word? (Cumulative Review)

Let's play *What's My Word?* You'll have to think really hard, because my word can be any word we've learned since we read *Suki's Kimono.*

I'll give you three clues. After I give each clue, if you are sure you know my word, you may make a guess. If you guess correctly, you will win one point. If you make a mistake, I get the point.

Let's practice. Here's my first clue. My word ends with the sound **n**. Are you sure you know

my word? If you are, you may make a guess. (If anyone wishes to guess, accept the guess. Award the point to either the class or the teacher.)

Here's my second clue. My word is a noun. Are you sure you know my word? If you are, you may make a guess. (If anyone wishes to guess, accept the guess. Award the point to either the class or the teacher.)

Here's my third clue. My word means "a doctor." What's my word? *Physician.* (Award the point to either the class or the teacher.)

(**Note:** If a child guesses the word correctly before the last clue, give the other clues and have children decide if the answer fits those clues.)

Now you're ready to play the game. (Draw a T-chart on the board for keeping score. Children earn one point for each correct answer. If they make an error, correct them as you normally would, and record one point for yourself. Repeat missed words at the end of the game.)

- Here's my first clue. My word can be a noun or a verb. Here's my second clue. When my word is a verb, it means "to see or be aware of something." Here's my third clue. When my word is a noun it means "a letter that is sent to a lot of people." What's my word? *Notice.*
- New word. Here's my first clue. My word can be a noun or a verb. Here's my second clue. When my word is a noun it means "a wish to learn more about something." Here's my third clue. When my word is a verb it means "persuade you to do something or tempt you." What's my word? *Interest.*
- New word. Here's my first clue. My word is a noun. Here's my second clue. There's a **v** sound in my word. Here's my third clue. My word means "prisoner." What's my word? *Captive.*
- New word. Here's my first clue. My word is a describing word. Here's my second clue. My word tells more about the size of someone or something. Here's my third clue. My word means "extremely large, huge, or enormous." What's my word? *Colossal.*

- New word. Here's my first clue. My word is a noun. Here's my second clue. My word tells about a place. Here's my third clue. My word means "a place where there are no people." What's my word? *Wilderness.*
- New word. Here's my first clue. My word is a describing word. Here's my second clue. My word means "hard to believe." Here's my third clue. My word ends with the word part **-ing.** What's my word? *Astonishing.*
- New word. Here's my first clue. My word is a describing word. Here's my second clue. My word starts with the word part **un-.** Here's my third clue. My word means "very hard to believe." What's my word? *Unbelievable.*
- New word. Here's my first clue. My word is a verb. Here's my second clue. My word ends with the letters **-ed.** Here's my third clue. My word tells what storytellers of tall tales did when they told their stories. What's my word? *Exaggerated.*
- New word. Here's my first clue. My word is a describing word. Here's my second clue. My word ends with the word part **-ous.** Here's my third clue. My word means "extremely silly or foolish." What's my word? *Ridiculous.*

(Count the points and declare a winner.) You did a great job of playing *What's My Word?*

---

### DAY 5

**Preparation:** Each child will need a copy of the Quiz Answer Sheet, BLM B.

### Retell Story

Today I'll show you the pictures Steven Kellogg made for *Paul Bunyan.* As I show you the pictures, I'll call on one of you to tell the class that part of the story.

Tell me what happens at the **beginning** of the story. (Show the pictures on pages 1–5. Call on a child to tell what's happening.)

Tell me what happens in the **middle** of the story. (Show the pictures on pages 6–36. Call on a child to tell what's happening. Encourage use of target words when appropriate. Model use as necessary.)

Tell me what happens at the **end** of the story. (Show the pictures on page 37. Call on a child to tell what's happening.)

(Show children the map at the end of the book. Help them identify where the different events took place.)

### Assess Vocabulary

 (Give each child a copy of the Quiz Answer Sheet, BLM B.)

Today, you're going to have a True or False quiz. When you do the True or False quiz, it shows me how well you know the hard words you are learning.

If I say something that is true, circle the word **true.** What will you do if I say something that is true? *Circle the word true.*

If I say something that is false, circle the word **false.** What will you do if I say something that is false? *Circle the word false.*

Listen carefully to each item that I say. Don't let me trick you!

Item 1: If a castle were extremely large, you could say it was **colossal.** (*True.*)

Item 2: If I asked you "Can I **interest** you in a trip to the park?" I would not want you to go to the park with me. (*False.*)

Item 3: If Chan told you he had a million action figures, he would have **exaggerated.** (*True.*)

Item 4: It's **unbelievable** that cows give milk. (*False.*)

Item 5: If you show an **interest** in the piano, you probably would like to take piano lessons. (*True.*)

Item 6: Much of Alaska is a **wilderness.** (*True.*)

Item 7: If something is **precious,** you would put it in the garbage. (*False.*)

Item 8: It's **astonishing** that an elephant drinks 30 gallons of water every day. (*True.*)

Item 9: If you are **reluctant** to fly in an airplane, you'd love to fly to Australia. (*False.*)

Item 10: If you are feeling **frazzled,** you are very tired and stressed out. (*True.*)

You did a great job completing your quiz!

(Score children's work. A child must score 9 out of 10 to be at the mastery level. If a child does not achieve mastery, insert the missed words as additional items in the games in next week's lessons. Retest those children individually for the missed items before they take the next mastery test.)

## Extensions

### Read a Story as a Reward

 (Display copies of the folk tales, fairy tales, and legends you have read since the beginning of the program, as well as a variety of legends and tall tales from different cultures. Allow children to choose which book they would like you to read to them as a reward for their hard work.)

(Read the story aloud for enjoyment with minimal interruptions.)

**Preparation:** Word containers for the Super Words Center. You may wish to remove some of the words from earlier lessons. Choose words that the children have mastered.

### Introduce the Super Words Center

(Add the new Picture Vocabulary Cards to the words from the previous weeks. Show children one of the word containers. If children need more guidance in how to work in the Super Words Center role-play with two to three children as a demonstration.)

*Let's review how to play the game called What's Missing?*

*Let's think about how we work with our words in the Super Words Center.*

You will work with a partner in the Super Words Center. Whom will you work with? *A partner.*

First one partner will draw four word cards out of the container and put them on the table so both partners can see. What do you do first? (Idea: *Draw four cards out of the container and put them on the table so both partners can see.*)

Next you will take turns looking at the cards and saying the words the pictures show. What do you do next? (Idea: *We take turns looking at the cards and saying the words the pictures show.*)

Next partner 2 looks away while partner 1 takes one of the four cards and places it facedown on the table away from the other cards. Then partner 1 draws a new card from the container and places it on the table with the other three.

Watch while I show you what I mean. (Demonstrate this process with one student as your partner.)

When you put down the new card, it's a good idea to mix the cards so they aren't in the same places any more. (Demonstrate this process as you go.)

Now partner 1 says, "What's Missing?" Partner 2 has to use his or her eyes and brain and say what old card has been taken away. After partner 2 has guessed, turn over the facedown card. If partner 2 is correct, he or she gets a point. If partner 2 is not correct, partner 1 gets the point. (Demonstrate this process as you go.)

Next partner 2 has a turn to choose four different cards and the game starts again. What happens next? (Idea: *Partner 2 has a turn to choose four different cards and the game starts again.*)

Have fun playing *What's Missing?*

## *Hurry and the Monarch*
author: Antoine Ó Flatharta • illustrator: Meilo So

**Preparation:** You will need a copy of *Hurry and the Monarch* for each day's lesson.

Number the pages of the story to assist you in asking comprehension questions at appropriate points.

You will need a map of North America or a globe of the world.

Post a copy of the Vocabulary Tally Sheet, BLM A, with this week's Picture Vocabulary Cards attached.

Each child will need one copy of the Homework Sheet, BLM 14a.

### Target Vocabulary

| Tier II | Tier III |
|---------|----------|
| Canada | fiction |
| Mexico | afterword |
| fascinated | main idea |
| doubt | |
| *migrate | |
| *incredible | |

*Expanded Target Vocabulary Word

- When do you think the story happens?
- Do you think this story is about real or imaginary animals? Tell why or why not.

(Call on several children to share their predictions with the class.)

---

## DAY 1

### Introduce Book

This week's book is called *Hurry and the Monarch*. What's the title of this week's book? *Hurry and the Monarch.*

This book was written by Antoine Ó Flatharta. [an-twan o fluh-tar-ta ]. Who's the author of *Hurry and the Monarch*? *Antoine Ó Flatharta.*

Meilo [my-lo]So made the pictures for this book. Who is the illustrator of *Hurry and the Monarch*? *Meilo So.* Who made the illustrations for this book? *Meilo So.*

The cover of a book usually gives us some hints of what the book is about. Let's look at the front cover of *Hurry and the Monarch*. What do you see in the illustration? (Ideas: *Many butterflies; a turtle; the butterflies are flying over the turtle.*)

(Assign each child a partner.)Get ready to make some predictions to your partner about this book. Use the information from the cover to help you.

(Ask the following questions, allowing sufficient time for children to share their predictions with their partners.)

- Who are the characters in this story?
- What do you think they will do?
- Where do you think the story happens?
- Where do you think the butterflies are going?

### Take a Picture Walk

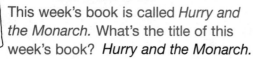(Encourage children to use target words in their answers.)We're going to take a picture walk through this book. Remember that when we take a picture walk, we look at the pictures and tell what we think will happen in the story.

**Pages 1–2.**What do you see in this first illustration? (Ideas: *A turtle and a butterfly.*)This kind of butterfly is called a monarch butterfly. How can you tell a monarch butterfly apart from other butterflies? (Idea: *It is orange and black with white spots around the edges of its wings.*) Where has the monarch butterfly landed in this illustration? (Idea: *On the turtle's back.*)

**Pages 3–4.**What do you think the monarch and the turtle are talking about?

**Page 5.**Where is the monarch sitting in this illustration? (Idea: *On the turtle's nose.*)

**Page 6.**Where do you think the monarch is flying?

**Pages 7–8.**Where is this story happening? (Idea: *In a garden.*)

**Pages 9–10.** What kind of butterflies are these? *Monarch butterflies.* Where do you think they are going?

**Page 11.** What do you think the turtle is looking at up in the sky? (Idea: *The monarchs flying.*)

**Page 12.** When do you think this part of the story happens? (Idea: *At night.*) How can you tell this part of the story happens at night? (Idea: *You can see the moon behind the monarch.*) What do you think the monarchs are doing here? (Idea: *Resting.*)

**Pages 13–14.** Where are the monarchs now? (Idea: *In the desert.*) How do you know? (Idea: *I can see cacti.*) What do you think is happening in this illustration? (Idea: *A large bird is trying to catch one of the monarchs.*)

**Pages 15–16.** Where are the monarchs now? (Idea: *In a forest.*) Do you think the monarchs have traveled a long way?

**Pages 17–18.** What do you see in this illustration? (Idea: *Many monarchs piled on the branch of a tree.*) What do you think these monarchs will do in the tree?

**Page 19.** Where is this part of the story happening? (Idea: *Back in the garden with the turtle.*) What time of year do you think it is in this illustration? (Ideas: *Spring or summer.*) What makes you think so?

**Page 20.** What do you think is happening here? (Idea: *The monarch has returned to the turtle's garden.*)

**Page 21.** What do you think the turtle is saying to the monarch?

**Page 22.** Where has the monarch landed in this illustration? (Idea: *On a curtain.*) Why do you think the monarch has landed on this curtain? (Idea: *It is covered in flowers and maybe it mistook it for a real flower.*)

**Pages 23–24.** What has caused the holes in the leaves of this plant? (Idea: *A caterpillar.*)

**Page 25.** What is this caterpillar doing? (Idea: *Eating and growing.*)

**Page 26.** The caterpillar has grown quite big. What do you think it will do now?

**Top of page 27.** What is the caterpillar doing? (Idea: *Building a cocoon.*)

**Bottom of page 27.** What is happening to the caterpillar? (Idea: *It is turning into a monarch butterfly.*)

**Page 28.** What is the monarch doing? (Idea: *Coming out of the cocoon.*) Is this the same monarch we saw earlier in the story? *No.*

**Pages 29–30.** Where do you think the monarch will go after leaving the turtle's garden?

It's your turn to ask me some questions. What would you like to know about the story? (Accept questions. If children tell about the pictures or story instead of ask questions, prompt them to ask a question.) Ask me a why question. Ask me a who question.

### Read the Story Aloud
(Read the story to children with minimal interruptions.)

Tomorrow we will read the story again, and I will ask you some questions.

### Present Target Vocabulary
◎━ *Canada*

In the story, the monarch said she broke out of her shell, grew wings, and flew away "in a place called Canada." **Canada.** Say the word. *Canada.*

**Canada** is a noun. It names a place. What kind of word is **Canada?** *A noun.*

**Canada is the country to the north of the United States.** (Point to the map of the world.) We live in the United States. (Point to the United States.) This is Canada. (Point to Canada.)

(Correct any incorrect responses, and repeat the item at the end of the sequence.)

I'll point to places on the map. If those places are in Canada, say "Canada." If those places are not in Canada, say "Absolutely not."

- (Point to Alberta.) *Canada.*
- (Point to the Pacific Ocean.) *Absolutely not.*
- (Point to the United States.) *Absolutely not.*
- (Point to Ontario.) *Canada.*
- (Point to the Yukon.) *Canada.*
- (Point to Mexico.) *Absolutely not.*

What noun names the country to the north of the United States? *Canada.*

Raise your hand if you have ever been to Canada. (Acknowledge children who raise their hands. You may wish to ask them what parts of Canada they visited, and point out those places on the map.)

 Mexico

In the story, the monarch flies "over the waters of the Rio Grande into Mexico." **Mexico.** Say the word. *Mexico.*

**Mexico** is a noun. It names a place. What kind of word is **Mexico?** *A noun.*

**Mexico is the country to the south of the United States.** (Point to the map of the world.) We live in the United States. (Point to the United States.) This is Mexico. (Point to Mexico.)

I'll point to places on the map. If those places are in Mexico, say "Mexico." If those places are not in Mexico, say "Absolutely not."

- (Point to Mexico City.) *Mexico.*
- (Point to the Atlantic Ocean.) *Absolutely not.*
- (Point to the United States.) *Absolutely not.*
- (Point to the Baja Peninsula.) *Mexico.*
- (Point to Canada.) *Absolutely not.*
- (Point to a city in Mexico.) *Mexico.*

What noun names the country to the south of the United States? *Mexico.*

Raise your hand if you have ever been to Mexico. (Acknowledge children who raise their hands. You may wish to ask them what parts of Mexico they visited, and point out those places on the map.)

 Fascinated

In the story, "the monarch seems fascinated with the old tortoise." That means the monarch was very interested in Hurry and thought about him a lot. **Fascinated.** Say the word. *Fascinated.*

**Fascinated** is a verb. It tells what happened. What kind of word is **fascinated?** *A verb.*

**If you are fascinated by something, you are very interested in that thing and you think about it a lot.** Say the word that means "interested in something and you think about it a lot." *Fascinated.*

Let's think about some people and some things that someone might be fascinated by. I'll tell about a person and a thing. If the person would be fascinated by that thing, say "fascinated." If not, don't say anything.

- A scientist looking at dinosaur bones. *Fascinated.*
- A farmer watching baby goats playing. *Fascinating.*
- An airplane pilot looking at different kinds of baking flour.
- A gardener learning a new trick to keep away garden pests. *Fascinated.*
- A bricklayer learning how to sew beautiful dresses.
- A dog walker looking at a new kind of leash that lets dogs get more exercise. *Fascinated.*

What verb means "interested in something and you think about it a lot"? *Fascinated.*

Tell me about something that fascinates you. (Call on several children. Encourage them to start their answers with the words "I am fascinated by _____ because _____.")

 Doubt

In the story, "The monarch says to Hurry, 'Maybe one day you'll break out of that shell, grow wings, and fly away.' Hurry says, 'I doubt it.'" That means Hurry doesn't think that will ever happen. **Doubt.** Say the word. *Doubt.*

**Doubt** is a verb. It tells what someone is thinking. What kind of word is **doubt?** *A verb.*

**If you doubt something you are not sure about it.** Say the verb that means "not sure about something." *Doubt.*

Let's think about some times when someone might doubt something. I'll tell you about a time. If you think someone is not sure about it, say "doubt." If not, don't say anything.

- After our second flat tire, Mom was not sure we would get home before dark. *Doubt.*
- Dad was positive he had left the car keys on the kitchen table.
- Although her grandma told Jessie a stork had brought her baby brother, Jessie wasn't sure she believed her. *Doubt.*

- Tyrell was absolutely certain he knew the right answer.
- A long time ago, people believed the world was flat.
- The teacher said the bus was coming soon to take them on their field trip, but the children weren't sure they believed her. *Doubt.*

What verb means "not sure about something"? *Doubt.*

## Present Vocabulary Tally Sheet

(See Lesson 1, page 4, for instructions.)

## Assign Homework

(Homework Sheet, BLM 14a. See the Introduction for homework instructions.)

### DAY 2

**Preparation:** Picture Vocabulary Cards for *Canada, Mexico, fascinated, doubt.*

### Read and Discuss Story

(Read story to children. Ask the following questions at the specified points. Encourage children to use target words in their answers.)

**Page 2.** Who was Hurry? (Idea: *A Texas tortoise.*) When did this part of the story happen? (Idea: *October.*) What landed on Hurry's back? *A monarch butterfly.*

**Page 3.** What question did the monarch ask Hurry? *What do you call this place?* Why do you think Hurry said, "Here we go again"?

**Page 4.** Where was the monarch? (Idea: *Wichita Falls.*) Wichita Falls is a city in the state of Texas. What state was the monarch in? *Texas.* What was wrong with Wichita Falls? (Idea: *It wasn't far enough.* Locate Wichita Falls, Texas on the map for children.)

**Page 5.** Why do you think the monarch is fascinated with Hurry?

**Page 6.** Will Hurry ever break out of his shell and grow wings? *No.* Why not? (Ideas: *Hurry is a tortoise, not a butterfly; his shell is not a cocoon.*)

**Page 7.** Where was the butterfly born? (Ideas: *In Canada; in a garden.*) Why did she leave the garden? (Ideas: *It grew cold; it was autumn; winter was coming.*) Where do you think she is going? (Idea: *Someplace warm.*)

**Page 8.** What didn't the monarch have time for? (Idea: *Time to wait for the weather to become warm again.*) Why do you think she said that? (Idea: *Butterflies don't live very long.*)

**Page 9.** How do the monarchs turn the sky orange? (Idea: *The sky looks orange because there are so many monarchs flying together.*) Which direction are the monarchs going? *South.*

**Page 11.** How is Hurry feeling? (Idea: *Sleepy.*) When winter comes, turtles go to sleep until spring. How long will Hurry sleep? (Idea: *Until spring.*)

**Page 12.** What are some places you might expect to find a butterfly resting? (Ideas: *In the grass; in a tree; on a flower.*) Where would you not expect to find a butterfly resting?

**Page 13.** What kinds of things might be dangerous to a butterfly?

**Page 14.** Where is the monarch going? (Idea: *Mexico.*)

**Page 15.** What month is it in this part of the story? *November.* What month was it when the story started? (Idea: *October.*) The monarch has been traveling for a month already. How does she feel? (Ideas: *Tired; exhausted.*)

**Page 17.** What has she found? (Idea: *The perfect place.*)

**Page 19.** What time of year is it in this part of the story? *Spring.* What has Hurry been doing since the monarch left in October? (Idea: *Sleeping.*) When Hurry wakes up, he says, "Never fails." What do you think he means? (Ideas: *The warm weather always comes back after winter; the turtle always wakes up in the spring when it gets warm.*)

**Page 20.** Where has the monarch come back to? (Idea: *Hurry's garden.*) Where is she going now? (Idea: *Back to the beginning.*) What do you think that means?

**Page 21.** What did the monarch do before she flew away? (Idea: *Laid eggs.*)

**Page 22.** What do you think happened to the butterfly? (Idea: *She died.*)

**Page 23.** Where do you think this caterpillar came from? (Idea: *From one of the eggs the monarch laid.*)

**Page 24.** Why didn't the caterpillar answer Hurry? (Idea: *It was busy eating.*)

**Page 25.** What did Hurry see the caterpillar do? (Ideas: *It grew; shed its skins; hid under a twig.*)

**Page 26.** Was Hurry able to find the caterpillar even after it hid? *Yes.*

**Page 27.** What did the monarch look like when it came out of its shell? (Idea: *Wet and wrinkled.*)

**Page 28.** What was the monarch waiting for? (Idea: *Its wings to expand and dry.*) **Expand** means "get bigger." What does **expand** mean? *Get bigger.* What word means "get bigger"? *Expand.* What do you think the monarch will do once its wings have expanded and dried?

**Page 29.** Why did Hurry say, "Here we go again"? (Idea: *That's the same thing the mother monarch had said to Hurry when she landed in his garden.*)

**Page 30.** Where do you think the monarch will go? Why do you think the mother monarch decided to lay her eggs in Hurry's garden?

### Review Vocabulary

(Display the Picture Vocabulary Cards. Point to each card as you say the word. Ask children to repeat each word after you.) These pictures show **Canada, Mexico, fascinated,** and **doubt.**

- What verb means "interested in something and you think about it a lot"? *Fascinated.*
- What verb means "not sure about something"? *Doubt.*
- What noun names the country to the north of the United States? *Canada.*
- What noun names the country to the south of the United States? *Mexico.*

### Extend Vocabulary

 Interest

In *Hurry and the Monarch*, we learned that **doubt** is a verb that means "not sure about something."

Raise your hand if you can tell us a sentence that uses **doubt** as a verb meaning "not sure about something." (Call on several children. If they don't use complete sentences, restate their examples as sentences. Have the class repeat the sentences.)

Here's a new way to use the word **doubt.**

- When it was Caleb's turn to recite his poem he was filled with **doubt.** Say the sentence.
- Sydney had her **doubts** when she started to take piano lessons, but she's getting better each day. Say the sentence.
- I was filled with **doubt** when I looked at the road map. Say the sentence.

**In these sentences, doubt is a noun that means a feeling of not being sure.** What word means "a feeling of not being sure"? *Doubt.*

Raise your hand if you can tell us a sentence that uses **doubt** as a noun meaning "a feeling of not being sure." (Call on several children. If they don't use complete sentences, restate their examples as sentences. Have the class repeat the sentences.)

### Present Expanded Target Vocabulary
◎= Migrate

In the story, the monarch flies from Canada to Mexico to spend the winter where it is warm. Another way of saying the monarch flew away to spend the winter in Mexico is to say the monarch migrated to Mexico. **Migrate.** Say the word. *Migrate.*

**Migrate** is a verb. It tells what some animals do. What kind of word is **migrate?** *A verb.*

**When birds and insects migrate, they fly away to spend the winter somewhere else.** Say the verb that means "fly away to spend the winter somewhere else." *Migrate.*

I'll tell about some animals. If that animal is migrating, say "migrate." If that animal is not migrating, don't say anything.

- The ducks flew south for the winter. *Migrate.*
- The turtle slept all winter at the bottom of the pond.
- The dragonflies flew from Canada to Mexico. *Migrate.*

- As they always did, the swallows came back to Capistrano. *Migrate.*
- The frog slept at the bottom of the pond all winter.
- The Canadian Geese flew south for the winter with their loud honking call. *Migrate.*

What verb means "fly away to spend the winter somewhere else"? *Migrate.*

◎← Incredible

In the story, the monarch flew all the way from Canada to Mexico. That's a distance of more than 2,000 miles. That's an amazing distance for a tiny insect to fly. Another way to say the migration of the monarch is amazing is to say it's incredible. **Incredible.** Say the word. *Incredible.*

**Incredible** is a describing word. It tells more about something. What kind of word is **incredible?** *A describing word.*

**If something is incredible, it is amazing or astonishing.** Say the word that means "amazing or astonishing." *Incredible.*

I'll tell you about some things. If these things are amazing or astonishing, say "incredible!" If not, don't say anything.

- Andrei Rybakov, a weightlifter from Bulgaria, can lift more than twice his own weight. *Incredible!*
- Everyone in our family likes spaghetti.
- An ostrich can run 45 miles per hour. *Incredible!*
- Dogs can have brown, white, or black fur.
- The biggest bubble ever blown with bubble gum was 23 inches across. *Incredible!*
- The Goliath Tarantula is as big as a dinner plate. *Incredible!*

What describing word means "amazing or astonishing"? *Incredible.*

**Preparation:** Prepare a sheet of chart paper titled *True or Fiction*.

Each child will need a copy of the Activity Sheet, BLM 14b, and crayons.

## Literary Analysis (Fiction)

When authors write stories, sometimes they write about things that are true and sometimes they write about things that they have made up in their imaginations. If an author writes a story about things that are made up from the author's imagination, the story is called fiction. What do you call a story that is made up from the author's imagination? *Fiction.*

Let's see if we can figure out if this story is about things that are true, or if the story is fiction. You tell me what happened in the story and I'll write it down.

**Page 1.** Do you think Hurry is a real tortoise, or a tortoise made up from Meilo So's imagination? (Idea: *Made up from Meilo So's imagination.*) What makes you think so? (Idea: *The picture doesn't look like a real tortoise.*)

**Page 4.** (Read "'Witchita Falls,' says Hurry. 'And that's my back you're standing on.'") Do you think Hurry is a real tortoise, or a tortoise made up from Antoine Ó Flatharta's imagination? (Idea: *Made up from Antoine Ó Flatharta's imagination.*) What makes you think so? (Ideas: *Real tortoises don't talk; a real tortoise wouldn't know where Witchita Falls is.*)

Most of us think Hurry is not a real tortoise, so I'll print *fiction* after his name. (Record *Hurry* on the chart and write *fiction* after his name.)

**Page 5.** Do you think the monarch is a real monarch, or a monarch made up from Meilo So's imagination? (Idea: *Made up from Meilo So's imagination.*) What makes you think so? (Idea: *The picture doesn't look like a real monarch.*)

**Page 6.** (Read "'How long have you been here?' asks the monarch.") Do you think the monarch is a real monarch, or a monarch made up from Antoine Ó Flatharta's imagination? (Idea: *Made up from Antoine Ó Flatharta's imagination.*) What makes you think so? (Idea: *Real monarchs don't talk.*)

Most of us think the monarch is not a real monarch, so I'll print *fiction* after her name.) (Record *the monarch* on the chart and write *fiction* after her name.)

**Pages 13–14.** Do you think the part of the story about monarchs flying to Mexico is true or do you think this is made up from Antoine Ó Flatharta's imagination? (Idea: *True.*) What makes you think so? (Idea: *Real monarchs do fly from Canada to Mexico when they migrate.*) Most of us think monarchs fly to Mexico. (Record *monarchs fly to Mexico* on the chart and write *true* after it.)

**Pages 27–28.** Do you think the part of the story about monarchs changing from caterpillars to butterflies is true or do you think this is made up from Antoine Ó Flatharta's imagination? (Idea: *True.*) What makes you think so? (Idea: *I've seen it happen; I've read it in a science book or on the Internet; I've seen a video or television program about it.*) Most of us think monarchs change from caterpillars to butterflies. (Record *caterpillars change to butterflies* on the chart and write *true* after it.)

(Point to the chart.) We think the part of the story about monarchs flying to Mexico is true. We think the part of the story about caterpillars changing into butterflies is true. But we think Hurry and the monarch that talks to Hurry come from Antoine Ó Flatharta's imagination.

If any part of a story is about things that are made up from the author's imagination the story is fiction. So, *Hurry and the Monarch* is what kind of story? *Fiction.* That's right; *Hurry and the Monarch* is fiction, even though the author has written some parts that are true.

We have read many other stories that are fiction. Raise your hand if you can name another story we've read that was made up from the imagination of the author. (Accept any response that names a book that is fiction.)

Collect or prepare Picture Vocabulary Cards for all of the words with dual meanings. Display them prominently in a pocket chart, on a chalkboard ledge, or in another obvious location. These words are *concentrated, special, sound, rascal, quarrel, bolted, steep, miserable, notice, calm, feast, curious, interest, doubt.*

### Play Tom Foolery

Today we will play *Tom Foolery*. I will pretend to be Tom. Tom Foolery has a reputation of trying to trick students. Tom knows that some words have more than one meaning. He will tell you one meaning that will be correct. Then he will tell you another meaning that might be correct or it might be incorrect.

If you think the meaning is correct, don't say anything. If you think the meaning is incorrect, say, "Tom Foolery!" Then Tom will have to tell the truth and tell the correct meaning. Tom is sly enough that he may include some words that do **not** have two meanings. Be careful! He's tricky!

Let's practice. If something is **incredible,** it is amazing or astonishing. **Incredible** also means something you can't eat. *Tom Foolery!* Oh, you're right. I was thinking of **inedible,** not **incredible.**

When we play *Tom Foolery*, Tom will keep score. If you catch him being tricky, you will get one point. If you don't catch him, Tom gets the point. Watch out! Tom might try to give himself extra points while you're not looking!

Now you're ready to play the game. (Draw a T-chart on the board for keeping score. Children earn one point for each correct answer. If they make an error, correct them as you normally would, and record one point for yourself. Repeat missed words at the end of the game.)

- If you are **fascinated,** you are very interested in something and think about it a lot. **Fascinated** also means hooked two things together. *Tom Foolery!* Oh, you're right. I must have been thinking of **fastened** instead of **fascinated.**
- **Migrate** is what birds do when they fly away to spend the winter somewhere else. You also call, "**Migrate!**" when someone asks you what you call the metal bars that cover your window. *Tom Foolery!* Oh, you're right. We only know the one meaning for **migrate.**
- **Canada** is the country to the north of the United States. It is also the name of a type of sneaker. *Tom Foolery!* Oh, you're right. We only know one meaning for Canada.
- **Mexico** is the country to the south of the United States. It's also the name of the company that sells combs. *Tom Foolery!* Oh, you're right. We only know one meaning for **Mexico.**
- When you have a **doubt,** you have a feeling of not being sure. A **doubt** is also a long time when no rain falls. *Tom Foolery!* Oh, you're right. I was thinking of **a drought.** Plants and animals often die during a drought.

(Count the points and declare a winner.) You did a great job of playing *Tom Foolery!*

### Complete the Activity Sheet

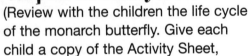

(Review with the children the life cycle of the monarch butterfly. Give each child a copy of the Activity Sheet, BLM 14b. Children will place the pictures in the sequence of the life cycle of the monarch, starting with the egg. Instruct children to color the pictures, cut them out, and paste or glue them onto the life cycle diagram, with the egg picture at the top. They will write an expository paragraph explaining the process, using key words: Key Words: egg, caterpillar, cocoon, monarch.)

### DAY 4

### Introduce Afterword

(Assign each child a partner.) Sometimes when people write a story that is fiction, they also tell about some things that are true. After they finish the story, they want to tell you some facts about the true things. This information is put in the book **after** the last **word** of the story, so it is called an **afterword.** Today I'll read the afterword that Antoine Ó Flatharta wrote for *Hurry and the Monarch,* so you can learn more about monarchs.

(Read the Afterword a paragraph at a time.)

(First paragraph.) Let's try to figure out the main idea found in this paragraph. The main idea is the reason this part was written. What is the main idea? *The reason this part was written.* When Antoine Ó Flatharta wrote these words, what do you think he wanted us to know? (Idea: *How monarchs grow from an egg and change into a caterpillar, then into a chrysalis, and then into a butterfly.*)

That's right; so the main idea found in this paragraph is monarchs grow from an egg and change into a caterpillar, then into a chrysalis, and then into a butterfly. What is the main idea found in this paragraph? *Monarchs grow from an egg and change into a caterpillar, then into a chrysalis, and then into a butterfly.*

(Second paragraph.) The main idea is the reason this part was written. What is the main idea? *The reason this part was written.* Let's try to figure out the main idea for this part. When Antoine Ó Flatharta wrote these words, what do you think he wanted us to know? (Idea: *All the monarchs born in early autumn fly to Mexico.*) That's right; so the main idea found in this part of the afterword is all the monarchs born in early autumn fly to Mexico. What is the main idea found in this paragraph? *All the monarchs born in early autumn fly to Mexico.*

(Third paragraph.) The main idea is the reason this part was written. What is the main idea? *The reason this part was written.* Let's try to figure out the main idea for this part. When Antoine Ó Flatharta wrote these words, what do you think he wanted us to know? (Idea: *The monarchs fly back to Canada in March.*) That's right; so the main idea found in this part of the afterword is the monarchs fly back to Canada in March. What is the main idea found in this paragraph? *The monarchs fly back to Canada in March.*

(Fourth paragraph.) The main idea is the reason this part was written. What is the main idea? *The reason this part was written.* Let's try to figure out the main idea for this part. When Antoine Ó Flatharta wrote these words, what do you think he wanted us to know? (Idea: *The monarchs face many dangers.*) That's right; so the main idea found in this part of the afterword is the monarchs face many dangers. What is the main idea found in this paragraph? *The monarchs face many dangers.*

(Fifth paragraph.) The main idea is the reason this part was written. What is the main idea? *The reason this part was written.* Let's try to figure out the main idea for this part. When Antoine Ó Flatharta wrote these words, what do you think he wanted us to know? (Idea: *Monarchs live for only a little while, but tortoises can live up to 100 years.*) That's right; so the main idea found in this part of the afterword is monarchs live for only a little while, but tortoises can live up to 100 years. What is the main idea found in this paragraph? *Monarchs live for only a little while, but tortoises can live up to 100 years.*

We have learned many facts about monarchs and a few facts about tortoises from this afterword. Think about the one fact that you thought was most interesting. (Pause.) Share that fact with your partner. (Pause.) Tonight, share that fact with someone at your home.

### Play Tom Foolery (Cumulative Review)

Today we will play *Tom Foolery*. I will pretend to be Tom. You know that Tom has a reputation for trying to trick students. Tom knows that some words have more than one meaning. He will tell you one meaning that will be correct. Then he will tell you another meaning that might be correct or it might be incorrect.

If you think the meaning is correct, don't say anything. If you think the meaning is incorrect, say, "Tom Foolery!" Then Tom will have to tell the truth and tell the correct meaning. Tom is sly enough that he may include some words that do <u>not</u> have two meanings. Be careful! He's tricky!

Let's practice. **Migrate** is a word that tells what insects do when they fly to warmer places for the winter. If an animal **migrates,** it can also sleep for the winter. *Tom Foolery!* Oh, you're right. I suppose I must have been thinking of **hibernate** and not **migrate.** We only know one meaning for migrate.

When we play *Tom Foolery,* Tom will keep score. If you catch him being tricky, you will get one point. If you don't catch him, Tom gets the point. Watch out! Tom might try to give himself extra points while you're not looking!

Now you're ready to play the game. (Draw a T-chart on the board for keeping score. Children earn one point for each correct answer. If they make an error, correct them as you normally would, and record one point for yourself. Repeat missed words at the end of the game.)

- A **doubt** is the feeling you have when you're not sure abut something. A **doubt** is also what you are in if you owe a lot of money. *Tom Foolery!* Oh, you are very hard to fool. When you owe a lot of money, you're in **debt,** not **doubt.**
- **Concentrated** means you thought very hard about something and didn't think about anything else. It also tells about liquids that have most of the water taken out.
- When something is **incredible,** it is amazing and astonishing. If you are **incredible,** you are visiting the town of Credible, New Mexico. *Tom Foolery!* Oh, you're right. I just made up that one.
- A **steep** mountain goes almost straight up. **Steep** is also what you do to tea.
- If you're **sound** asleep, you're hard to wake up. Anything you hear is also a **sound.**
- **Fascinated** means "very interested in something and you think about it all the time." **Fascinated** is also what you do to meat before you put it on the barbeque. *Tom Foolery!* Oh, you're right. I guess I was thinking of **marinated.** We only know one meaning for **fascinated.**
- **Mexico** is the country where monarch butterflies spend the winter. Orioles and tanagers also migrate to **Mexico.**

- **Feast** means "to eat a lot of food at a large, special meal." It also means a wild animal. *Tom Foolery!* Oh, you're right. I was thinking of **beast.** The other meaning for **feast** is "a big meal where everyone can eat as much as they want." Though if you cooked a wildebeest, it would be enough for a feast, I think.
- If you're **curious,** you want to more about things. **Curious** is also how you feel if you are really, really angry. *Tom Foolery!* Oh, you're right. I'm thinking of **furious,** not **curious.** The other meaning for **curious** is "unusual or hard to understand."

(Count the points and declare a winner.) You did a great job of playing *Tom Foolery!*

## DAY 5

:::
**Preparation:** Each child will need a copy of the Quiz Answer Sheet, BLM B.
:::

### Retell Story

Today I'll show you the pictures Meilo So made for *Hurry and the Monarch.* As I show you the pictures, I'll call on one of you to tell the class that part of the story.

Tell me what happens at the **beginning** of the story. (Show the picture on pages 1 and 2. Call on a child to tell what's happening.)

Tell me what happens in the **middle** of the story. (Show the pictures on pages 3–28. Call on a child to tell what's happening. Encourage use of target words when appropriate. Model use as necessary.)

Tell me what happens at the **end** of the story. (Show the pictures on pages 29 and 30. Call on a child to tell what's happening.)

### Assess Vocabulary

 (Give each child a copy of the Quiz Answer Sheet, BLM B.)

Today, you're going to have a True or False quiz. When you do the True or False quiz, it shows me how well you know the hard words you are learning.

If I say something that is true, circle the word **true.** What will you do if I say something that is true? *Circle the word true.*

If I say something that is false, circle the word **false.** What will you do if I say something that is false? *Circle the word false.*

Listen carefully to each item that I say. Don't let me trick you!

Item 1: **Canada** is the country to the south of the United States. (*False.*)

Item 2: **Mexico** is the country to the south of the United States. (*True.*)

Item 3: If you are **fascinated** by snakes, you think snakes are boring and uninteresting. (*False.*)

Item 4: It's **incredible** that you can walk from your kitchen to your bedroom in less than five minutes. (*False.*)

Item 5: When animals **migrate,** they sleep all winter. (*False.*)

Item 6: If you have **doubts** about someone, you are **suspicious** about them. (*True.*)

Item 7: An actor who is **ambitious** might want to win an Academy Award. (*True.*)

Item 8: A **jealous** person would be **proud** of you. (*False.*)

Item 9: A **calm** person feels **frazzled.** (*False.*)

Item 10: If I ask you if you can fly and you say "I **doubt** it," you are not sure you can fly. (*True.*)

You did a great job completing your quiz!

(Score children's work. A child must score 9 out of 10 to be at the mastery level. If a child does not achieve mastery, insert the missed words as additional items in the games in next week's lessons. Retest those children individually for the missed items before they take the next mastery test.)

## Extensions

### Read a Story as a Reward

 (Display copies of all fiction books you have read since the beginning of the program, as well as a variety of other pieces of fiction. Allow children to choose which book they would like you to read to them as a reward for their hard work.)

(Read the story aloud for enjoyment with minimal interruptions.)

---

**Preparation:** Word containers for the Super Words Center.

---

### Introduce the Super Words Center

(Add the new Picture Vocabulary Cards to the words from the previous weeks. Show children one of the word containers. If children need more guidance in how to work in the Super Words Center, role-play with two to three children as a demonstration.)

You will play a game called *What's My Word?* in the Super Words Center.

Let's think about how we work with our words in the Super Words Center.

You will work with a partner in the Super Words Center. Whom will you work with? *A partner.*

First you will draw a word out of the container. What do you do first? (Idea: *Draw a word out of the container.*) Don't show your partner the word card.

Next you will tell your partner three clues that tell about the word card. What do you do next? (Idea: *I tell my partner three clues that tell about the word card.*) After each clue, your partner can make a guess. If your partner is correct, say "yes." If your partner is not correct, say "no" and give another clue.

Let your partner make three guesses. If your partner guesses correctly on any of the guesses, your partner gets a point. If your partner does not guess correctly, tell them your word and show them the word card. Give yourself a point. Then give your partner a turn.

What do you do next? *Give my partner a turn.*

(This game need not be played for points.)

# Isabel's House of Butterflies
author: Tony Johnston • illustrator: Susan Guevara

## Preparation:
You will need a copy of the book *Isabel's House of Butterflies* for each day's lesson.

Number the pages of the story to assist you in asking the comprehension questions at the appropriate points in the story.

Post a copy of the Vocabulary Tally Sheet, BLM A, with this week's picture vocabulary cards attached.

Each child will need one copy of the homework sheet.

### DAY 1

### Introduce Book

This week's book is called *Isabel's House of Butterflies*. What's the title of this week's book? *Isabel's House of Butterflies.*

This book was written by Tony Johnston. Who's the author of *Isabel's House of Butterflies? Tony Johnston.*

Susan Guevara [**gway**-vara] made the pictures for this book. Who is the illustrator of *Isabel's House of Butterflies? Susan Guevara.* Who made the illustrations for this book? *Susan Guevara.*

The cover of a book usually gives us some hints of what the book is about. Let's look at the front cover of *Isabel's House of Butterflies*. What do you see in the illustration? (Ideas: *A little girl; a little boy; an older woman; a pig; and two dogs in a wooded area; butterflies are flying around and landing on the girl; she looks like she is dancing.*)

(Assign each child a partner.) Get ready to make some predictions to your partner about this book. Use the information from the cover to help you.

(Ask the following questions, allowing sufficient time for children to share their predictions with their partners.)

### Target Vocabulary

| Tier II | Tier III |
|---|---|
| plot | fiction |
| tourist | foreword |
| gaze | main idea |
| scarce | |
| *optimistic | |
| *imagination | |

*Expanded Target Vocabulary Word

- Who are the characters in this story?
- What do you think the children will do?
- Where do you think the story happens?
- When do you think the story happens?
- Why do you think the butterflies are on the girl?
- How do you think all those butterflies got to this place?
- Do you think this story is about real or imaginary people? Tell why or why not.

(Call on several children to share their predictions with the class.)

### Take a Picture Walk

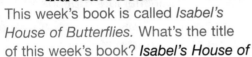(Encourage children to use target words in their answers.) We're going to take a picture walk through this book. Remember that when we take a picture walk, we look at the pictures and tell what we think will happen in the story.

**Pages 1–2.** Where does this story happen? (Idea: *In a village near the mountains.*) What do you see in the sky over the village? *Butterflies.*

**Pages 3–4.** What is the little girl doing? (Idea: *Watching the butterflies from a window.*) What do you think she is thinking about?

**Pages 5–6.** Who do you think lives in this house? (Idea: *The little girl and her family.*) Where do you think the men are leading their donkeys? (Ideas: *Back to their houses; to the market to sell the wood.*)

**Pages 7–8.** What has come to the family's home? (Idea: *Butterflies.*) Where are most of the butterflies? (Idea: *On the tree.*) In *Hurry and the Monarch*, you learned that monarch butterflies migrate to Mexico. Where do you think this family might live? (Idea: *Mexico.*) Who is in the little girl's family? (Idea: *Mother, father, baby, little brother, grandmother.*) How do you think the girl feels about the butterflies? (Ideas: *She is glad they are there; happy.*) What makes you think that?

**Pages 9–10.** What is the little girl doing here? (Idea: *Helping her mother bake.*) Do you think the little girl likes to help her mother in the kitchen? Tell why or why not.

**Pages 11–12.** How do you think this man and woman feel about the butterflies?

**Pages 13–14.** How do you think the little girl and her father feel in this illustration? (Idea: *Sad; unhappy.*) What makes you think so? Why do you think they are feeling sad and unhappy?

**Pages 15–16.** Where does this part of the story happen? (Idea: *At a market.*) A market is the place in a village where you can buy and sell things. What do we call the place in a village where you can buy and sell things? *A market.* What do you think the little girl's father is doing with their pigs at the market? (Idea: *He is going to sell them.*) Why do you think he would want to sell his pigs?

**Pages 17–18.** What time is it in this part of the story? (Idea: *Nighttime.*)

**Pages 19–20.** The little girl's father is holding a machete. A machete is a sharp blade used for cutting down small trees and tall grasses. What do we call a sharp blade used for cutting down small trees and tall grasses? *A machete.* What do you think the father is going to do with the machete? (Idea: *Cut down a tree.*) How does the family feel about this? *Sad.* Why do you think the family is sad about this?

**Pages 21–22.** How does the little girl feel in this illustration? *Sad.*

**Pages 23–24.** What is the little girl doing in this illustration? (Idea: *Sitting and watching the butterflies.*)

**Pages 25–26.** What do you think the little girl's father is about to do with his machete? (Idea: *Cut down that tree.*) What do you think the little girl is running to tell her father?

**Pages 27–28.** What is happening in this illustration? How does the little girl feel here? (Ideas: *Happy; satisfied.*) What makes you think so?

**Page 29.** How do you think the little girl is feeling here? (Ideas: *Afraid; nervous.*) What makes you think so?

It's your turn to ask me some questions. What would you like to know about the story? (Accept questions. If children tell about the pictures or the story instead of ask questions, prompt them to ask a question.) Ask me a why question. Ask me a where question.

### Read the Story Aloud
(Read the story to children with minimal interruptions.)

Tomorrow we will read the story again, and I will ask you some questions.

### Present Target Vocabulary
⊙= Plot

In the story, Isabel's father weeded a small plot of beans. That means Papa has a small piece of land where he grows beans. **Plot.** Say the word. *Plot.*

**Plot** is a noun. It names a place. What kind of word is **plot?** *A noun.*

**A plot is a small piece of land.** Say the noun that means "a small piece of land." *Plot.*

(Correct any incorrect responses, and repeat the item at the end of the sequence.)

Let's think about some things a person could grow on a small plot of land. I'll name some things. If a person could grow that thing on a small plot of land, say "plot." If not, don't say anything.

- Six tomato plants. *Plot.*
- A forest.
- A thousand corn plants.
- A herd of cattle.
- A few chickens. *Plot.*
- Three pumpkin plants. *Plot.*

What noun means "a small piece of land"? *Plot.*

## ⌖ Tourist

In the story, tourists come to see Isabel's tree. That means people who travel and visit places to enjoy themselves come to see the tree. **Tourist.** Say the word. *Tourist.*

**Tourist** is a noun. It names a person. What kind of word is **tourist?** *A noun.*

**A tourist is a person who travels and visits places to enjoy themselves.** Say the word that means "a person who travels and visits places to enjoy themselves." *Tourist.*

Let's think about some people who might be tourists. I'll tell you about some people. If they are tourists, say "tourist." If not, don't say anything.

- Tito's grandma traveled to Italy to see the sights and enjoy herself. *Tourist.*
- Julio's mother travels to France to buy things for her store
- Carlos and his family traveled to San Francisco to see the Golden Gate Bridge and Alcatraz Island. *Tourist.*
- Chase's big sister went to Chicago to go to college.
- Leah's family went hiking in the Rocky Mountains. *Tourist.*
- We never go anywhere.

What noun means "a person who travels and visits places to enjoy themselves"? *Tourist.*

If you could be a tourist, where would you like to go? (Call on several children. Encourage them to respond using the frame "If I could be a tourist I would like to go to _____ because _____.")

## ⌖ Gaze

In the story, Papa gazes at the tree full of butterflies. That means Papa looked at the tree for quite a long time before looking away. **Gaze.** Say the word. *Gaze.*

**Gaze** is a verb. It tells what someone is doing. What kind of word is **gaze?** *A verb.*

**If you gaze at something, you look at it for quite a long time before looking away.** Say the verb that means "look at something for quite a long time before looking away." *Gaze.*

Let's think about some times when someone might gaze at something. I'll tell about a time. If you think someone would gaze at something, say "gaze." If not, don't say anything.

- They looked at the gecko sunning itself on the rock for quite a long time before they looked away. *Gaze.*
- Kim took a quick peek in the oven.
- We watched the sunset until the sky turned dark. *Gaze.*
- The tourists looked at the butterfly tree for a long time before they walked away. *Gaze.*
- Anita looked off in the distance as she thought about what she had been reading. *Gaze.*
- Lou looked at the word for a second, then closed his eyes and spelled it out loud.

What verb means "look at something for quite a long time before looking away"? *Gaze.*

## ⌖ Scarce

In the story, Isabel's papa said that money was scarce. That means there was very little money. **Scarce.** Say the word. *Scarce.*

**Scarce** is a describing word. It tells more about something. What kind of word is **scarce?** *A describing word.*

**If something is scarce, there is very little of it.** Say the word that means there is "very little" of something. *Scarce.*

Let's think about some times when something might be scarce. I'll tell about a time. If you think something would be scarce, say "scarce." If not, don't say anything.

- Because there had been no rain, there were very few flowers in people's gardens. *Scarce.*
- Hundreds of geese landed on the lake.
- After the forest fire, there were very few birds left. *Scarce.*
- There were very few bugs left in the chicken pen. *Scarce.*
- There was very little fresh water on the tiny island. *Scarce.*
- Thousands of salmon went upstream to lay their eggs.

What describing word means there is "very little" of something? *Scarce.*

## Present Vocabulary Tally Sheet

(See Lesson 1, page 4, for instructions.)

## Assign Homework

(Homework Sheet, BLM 15a. See the Introduction for homework instructions.)

### DAY 2

**Preparation:** Picture Vocabulary Cards for *plot, tourist, gaze, scarce.*

### Read and Discuss Story

(**Note:** Do not read the forward on page 1 at this time. It will be read and discussed on Day 3.)

(Read story aloud to children. Ask the following questions at the specified points. Encourage children to use target words in their answers.)

**Page 3.** Who is this story about? (Idea: *An eight-year-old girl named Isabel.*) Who is telling the story? *Isabel.* That's right; in this story the author is pretending to be Isabel, so Isabel is telling the story. What does Isabel have outside her window? (Idea: *A tree.*) What does Isabel call her tree? (Ideas: *La casa de las mariposas; The House of Butterflies.*)

**Page 6.** (To the end of the first paragraph.) Where does Isabel live? (Ideas: *In Mexico; in the mountains.*) What is special about the oyamele trees? (Idea: *In autumn, butterflies come to roost there.*) What do some people in her village do to make money? (Idea: *They cut down the oyamele trees to sell the wood.*)

(Read to the end of the page.) Where do the butterflies come from? (Ideas: *The North; colder places.*) Why do the butterflies migrate to Mexico? (Idea: *To find a warmer place.*) How does Isabel's mother feel about the butterflies? (Idea: *She thinks it is a miracle that they always find their way to the House of the Butterflies.*)

**Page 7.** When do the butterflies return to Mexico? (Ideas: *In the autumn; in the fall.*) Why do Isabel and her family step on the butterflies? (Ideas: *There are so many of them, there is no place to walk; they can't help it.*) Do you think it

hurts when the butterflies step on Isabel and her family? *No.* Why does Isabel dance as if she's a butterfly? (Idea: *She is so happy the butterflies are back.*)

**Page 9.** What do Isabel and her mother make together? *Tortillas.* Why does Isabel sometimes stop patting her tortillas? (Idea: *She starts to watch the butterflies in the tree.*)

**Page 12.** What do the pigs do to the butterflies? (Idea: *Eat them.*) Why do you think tourists come to see Isabel's tree?

**Page 13.** Why does Isabel's father say this year is a tiger? (Idea: *There has been no rain; his crops are not growing.*) What do you think could happen if the beans and corn don't grow? (Ideas: *The family will have nothing to eat; they will not be able to earn any money.*)

**Page 15.** Why is Isabel's father selling the pigs in the village? (Idea: *To get money for his family.*)

**Page 17.** Why are Isabel's parents worried? (Idea: *They need money for food.*) What do you think they might have to do to get money? (Idea: *Cut down the butterfly tree and sell the wood.*)

**Page 20.** What is Isabel's father going to do? (Idea: *Cut down the butterfly tree.*) How does he feel about it? (Ideas: *Sad; it hurts his heart.*)

**Page 21.** Why is Isabel crying? (Idea: *She doesn't want her father to cut down the tree.*) Why can't he cut down another tree? (Idea: *This is the only one that belongs to him.*)

**Page 24.** What idea do you think came into Isabel's mind?

**Page 25.** What is Isabel's idea? (Idea: She *and her mother will set up a stand to make and sell butterfly-shaped tortillas to the tourists.*) Do you think her plan will work?

**Page 28.** What is Isabel looking for? *Tourists.* What does she hope the tourists will do? (Idea: *Buy many tortillas.*) What will happen if the tourists buy the tortillas? (Idea: *Isabel's family will earn money and her father won't have to cut down the tree.*)

**Page 29.** How does Isabel feel about her idea? (Ideas: *Excited; scared.*) Why would Isabel be scared? (Idea: *She might be scared that the* *tourists won't buy her tortillas and her father will still have to cut down the tree.)* What do you think will happen?

## Review Vocabulary

(Display the Picture Vocabulary Cards. Point to each card as you say the word. Ask children to repeat each word after you.) These pictures show **plot, tourist, gaze,** and **scarce.**

- What word means there is "very little of something"? *Scarce.*
- What noun means "a small piece of land"? *Plot.*
- What noun means "a person who travels and visits places to enjoy themselves"? *Tourist.*
- What verb means "look at something for quite a long time before looking away"? *Gaze.*

## Extend Vocabulary

 Plot

In *Isabel's House of Butterflies,* we learned that **plot** means "a small piece of land."

Raise your hand if you can tell us a sentence that uses **plot** as a noun meaning "a small piece of land." (Call on several children. If they don't use complete sentences, restate their examples as sentences. Have the class repeat the sentences.)

Here's a new way to use the word **plot.**

- What are you boys **plotting?** Say the sentence.
- The robbers **plotted** to steal money from the bank. Say the sentence.
- The children were **plotting** to play an April Fool's trick on their parents. Say the sentence.

**In these sentences, plot is a verb that means make secret plans to do something bad.** What verb means "make secret plans to do something bad"? *Plot.*

Raise your hand if you can tell us a sentence that uses **plot** as a verb meaning "make secret plans to do something bad." (Call on several children. If they don't use complete sentences, restate their examples as sentences. Have the class repeat the sentences.)

## Present Expanded Target Vocabulary

Optimistic

In *Isabel's House of Butterflies,* Isabel thought that if many tourists would buy her butterfly tortillas, then her family wouldn't have to cut down the butterfly tree. That way everything would turn out right. Another way of saying Isabel believed everything would turn out right is to say that Isabel was optimistic. **Optimistic.** Say the word. *Optimistic.*

**Optimistic** is a describing word. It tells more about someone. What kind of word is **optimistic?** *A describing word.*

**When someone is feeling optimistic, they believe everything will turn out right.** Say the word that means "believe everything will turn out right." *Optimistic.*

I'll tell about some people. If you think those people are feeling optimistic, say "optimistic." If not, don't say anything.

- Latoya believed she was going to get the new bicycle she wanted. *Optimistic.*
- Madison was sure it was going to rain on the day of the parade.
- Tyrone believed he would get a basketball scholarship for college. *Optimistic.*
- Carter shouted and stamped his feet.
- Trinity thought only about herself.
- Isaiah was quite sure his mom would invite his friends to stay for dinner. *Optimistic.*

What word means "believe everything will turn out right"? *Optimistic.*

Imagination

In the story, Isabel thought about butterflies. Then she thought about tortillas. Then she thought of tourists. Then she got a picture in her mind of how she might be able to save the butterfly tree. Isabel used her imagination. **Imagination.** Say the word. *Imagination.*

**Imagination** is a noun. It names a part of your mind. What kind of word is **imagination?** *A noun.*

**Your imagination is the part of your mind that lets you make pictures of things that haven't happened yet, or of things that aren't real.** Say the word that means "the part of your mind that lets you make pictures of things that haven't happened yet, or of things that aren't real." *Imagination.*

Let's think about some things that might come from someone's imagination. I'll tell about something. If you think it comes from someone's imagination, say "imagination." If not, don't say anything.

- A plan to build a new park.*Imagination.*
- A beanstalk that could grow up to the clouds. *Imagination.*
- A new kind of shoe that grows with your foot. *Imagination.*
- A cow that is black and white.
- A tree that can grow peaches.
- A bird that can fly from Canada to Mexico every winter.

What noun means "the part of your mind that lets you make pictures of things that haven't happened yet, or of things that aren't real." *Imagination.*

---

## DAY 3

Each child will need a copy of the Activity Sheet, BLM 15b and crayons.

---

### Introduce Foreword

(Assign each child a partner.) Sometimes when people write a story, they want to tell you some things before you read the story. They might want to tell you why they wrote the story. This information is put in the book **before** the first **word** of the story, so it is called a **foreword**. Today I'll read the foreword that Tony Johnston wrote for *Isabel's House of Butterflies* so you can learn why she wrote this story.

(Introductory sentence.) This sentence tells us about a real place in Mexico; the forests of Michoacán[mee-choh-wah-**kahn**] . How big is this place?*300 square miles.*

(Draw a square on the board. Move your finger around the square as you say:) These forests are very big. If you walk for 300 miles this way, 300 miles this way, 300 miles this way, and 300 miles this way, you would have walked all around the forest. If you could walk 10 miles in a day (and that's a pretty long hike) it would take you from now until _____(name the month 4 months away) to walk around these forests. Why are these forests special?(Idea: *It's where the monarchs go for the winter.*)

("With new laws ... ") The main idea is the reason this part was written. What is the main idea?*The reason this part was written.* Let's try to figure out the main idea for this part. When Tony Johnston wrote these words, what do you think she wanted us to know?(Idea: *It's hard to stop people from cutting down the trees.*) That's right; so the main idea found in this part of the foreword is it's hard to stop people from cutting down the trees. What is the main idea found in this paragraph of the foreword?*It's hard to stop people from cutting down the trees.*

("If these trees ... ") The main idea is the reason this part was written. What is the main idea? *The reason this part was written.* Let's try to figure out the main idea for this part. When Tony Johnston wrote these words, what do you think she wanted us to know?(Idea: *If people cut down the trees, the butterflies won't be here any more.*) That's right; so the main idea found in this part of the foreword is if people cut down the trees, the butterflies won't be here any more. What is the main idea found in this paragraph of the foreword?*If people cut down the trees, the butterflies won't be here any more.*

We have learned many facts about the butterflies' forests from this foreword. Think about the one fact that you thought was most interesting.(Pause.) Share that fact with your partner.(Pause.) Tonight, share that fact with someone at your home.

### Play Tom Foolery

Today we will play *Tom Foolery*. I will pretend to be Tom. Tom Foolery has a reputation of trying to trick students. Tom knows that some words have more than one meaning. He will tell you one meaning that will be correct. Then he will tell you another meaning that might be correct or it might be incorrect.

If you think the meaning is correct, don't say anything. If you think the meaning is incorrect, say, "Tom Foolery!" Then Tom will have to tell the truth and tell the correct meaning. Tom is sly enough that he may include some words that do <u>not</u> have two meanings. Be careful! He's tricky!

Let's practice. "**Calm** down" is what you would say to someone if you wanted them to become less angry, upset or excited. **Calm** down is also what you say when you want someone to walk down the stairs. *Tom Foolery!* Oh, you're right. I must have been thinking about **come** down, instead of **calm** down.

Let's do another one together. **Plot** is what someone does when they make secret plans to do something bad. **Plot** is also what someone does to pick up milk they've spilled on the table. *Tom Foolery!* Oh, you're right. I was thinking of the word **blot.** You blot up spilled milk.

When we play *Tom Foolery*, Tom will keep score. If you catch him being tricky, you will get one point. If you don't catch him, Tom gets the point. Watch out! Tom might try to give himself extra points while you're not looking!

Now you're ready to play the game. (Draw a T-chart on the board for keeping score. Children earn one point for each correct answer. If they make an error, correct them as you normally would, and record one point for yourself. Repeat missed words at the end of the game.)

- My family has a little **plot** of land that we use as a garden. We grow a few carrots, some tomatoes, some lettuce, and some onions. We often make a salad from the things we grow on our **plot.**
- When you **gaze** at the stars, you look at the stars for a long time without looking away. **Gaze** is also a kind of bandage you might put on your scraped knee. *Tom Foolery!* Oh, you're right. I must have been thinking of **gauze** instead of **gaze.**
- When your aunt is a **tourist,** she might visit the town where you live to see the sights and have some fun. A **tourist** is also an animal much like a turtle. *Tom Foolery!* Oh, you're right. I was thinking of **tortoise.** We only know the first meaning for **tourist.**
- Your **imagination** is the special part of your mind that lets you make pictures of imaginary things or of things that didn't really happen. I can use my **imagination** to make pictures of elephants the size of mice and mice the size of elephants.
- An **optimistic** person believes everything will turn out right. An **optimistic** is also a special mist you spray on your glasses. *Tom Foolery!* Oh, you're right. I just made up that one. That's why my name is Tom Foolery!

(Count the points and declare a winner.) You did a great job of playing *Tom Foolery!*

### Complete the Activity Sheet

(Reread pages 28 and 29 of *Isabel's House of Butterflies*. Ask children to close their eyes and use their imaginations to see what will happen next. Give each child a copy of the Activity Sheet, BLM 15b. The children will write a paragraph telling what happens next, and illustrate their new ending for the story.)

(**Note:** You may wish to keep these activity sheets to share on Day 5.)

**Preparation:** Prepare a sheet of chart paper titled *True or Fiction*.

## Literary Analysis (Fiction)

When authors write stories, sometimes they write about things that are true and sometimes they write about things that they have made up in their imaginations. If an author writes a story about things that are made up from the author's imagination, the story is called fiction. What do you call a story that is made up from the author's imagination? *Fiction.*

Let's see if we can figure out if this story is about things that are true, or if the story is fiction. You tell me what happened in the story and I'll write it down.

**Page 3.** Is Isabel really telling this story or is Tony Johnston pretending to be Isabel? (Idea: *Tony Johnston is pretending to be Isabel.*) What makes you think so? (Idea: *If Isabel were really telling the story, the author would be Isabel, not Tony Johnston.*)

Now we know for sure that Isabel is made up from Tony Johnston's imagination. (Record *Isabel* on the chart and write *fiction* after her name.)

**Pages 7–8.** If we know Tony Johnston is pretending to be Isabel, could this picture of Isabel's family be real or is it made up from Susan Guevara's imagination? (Idea: *This picture of Isabel's family is made up from Susan Guevara's imagination.*) What makes you think so? (Idea: *If Isabel is not real, then her family is not real.* Record *Isabel's family* on the chart and write *fiction* after those words.)

**Pages 5–6.** Do you think the part of the story about monarchs flying to Mexico is true or do you think this is made up from Tony Johnston's imagination? *True.* What makes you think so? (Ideas: *We learned that this is true in* Hurry and the Monarch; *I read about it in a science book; I saw a program about this on TV.*) Most of us think monarchs fly to Mexico. (Record *monarchs fly to Mexico* on the chart and write *true* after it.)

**Pages 7–8.** Do you think the part of the story about how monarchs gather in trees is true or do you think this is made up from Tony Johnston's imagination? (Idea: *True.*) What makes you think so? (Ideas: *I read about it in a science book; I saw it on the Internet when my mom and I looked up monarch butterflies.*) Most of us think monarchs gather in trees in Mexico. (Record *monarchs gather in trees* on the chart and write *true* after it.)

(Point to the chart.) We think the part of the story about monarchs flying to Mexico is true. We think the part of the story about monarchs gathering in trees is true. But we think Isabel and her family come from Tony Johnston's and Susan Guevara's imaginations.

If any part of a story is about things that are made up from the author's imagination, the story is fiction. So, *Isabel's House of Butterflies* is what kind of story? *Fiction.* That's right; *Isabel's House of Butterflies* is fiction, even though the author has written some parts that are true.

We have read many other stories that are fiction. Raise your hand if you can name another story we've read that was made up from the imagination of the author. (Accept any response that names a book that is fiction.)

## Play Tom Foolery (Cumulative Review)

Today we will play *Tom Foolery.* I will pretend to be Tom. You know that Tom has a reputation for trying to trick students. Tom knows that some words have more than one meaning. He will tell you one meaning that will be correct. Then he will tell you another meaning that might be correct or it might be incorrect.

If you think the meaning is correct, don't say anything. If you think the meaning is incorrect, say, "Tom Foolery!" Then Tom will have to tell the truth and tell the correct meaning. Tom is sly enough that he may include some words that do <u>not</u> have two meanings. Be careful! He's tricky!

Let's practice. **Gaze** means "to look at something for a long time before looking away." A **gaze** is also a long deep cut. *Tom Foolery!* Oh, you're right. I was thinking of **gash.** We only know one meaning for **gaze.**

Let's do another one together. **Scarce** means there's "very little of something." **Scarce** also means that someone jumps out from behind a door and yells "Boo!" *Tom Foolery!* Oh, you're right. I was thinking of **scares,** not **scarce.**

When we play *Tom Foolery*, Tom will keep score. If you catch him being tricky, you will get one point. If you don't catch him, Tom gets the point. Watch out! Tom might try to give himself extra points while you're not looking!

Now you're ready to play the game. (Draw a T-chart on the board for keeping score. Children earn one point for each correct answer. If they make an error, correct them as you normally would, and record one point for yourself. Repeat missed words at the end of the game.)

- You have a good **imagination** if you can make a picture in your mind of yourself flying an airplane. **Imagination** is also what happens if water disappears from a dish and goes into the air. *Tom Foolery!* Oh, you are very hard to fool. When water disappears from a dish and goes into the air it's **evaporation,** not **imagination.**
- A **quarrel** is "an angry argument." A **quarrel** is also a coin worth 25 cents. *Tom Foolery!* I must have been thinking of **quarter.** I'd much rather have a **quarter** than a **quarrel.** I hate quarreling!
- A **tourist** is someone who travels and visits places to enjoy themselves. **Tourist** is also a color halfway between green and blue. *Tom Foolery!* Oh, you're right. I must be thinking of **turquoise** and not **tourist.**
- **Optimistic** people always look at the good side of things. I really like optimistic people!
- A **notice** is a letter you might bring home from school telling about the spring concert. **Notice** is also green leaves you put in a salad. *Tom Foolery!* Oh, you're right. I guess I was thinking of **lettuce.** The other meaning for **notice** is "to see or be aware of." Have you **noticed** guinea pigs like **lettuce?**
- A **rascal** is someone who would lie and trick to get their own way. **Rascal** is also what Paul Bunyan did with the bears. *Tom Foolery!* Oh, you're right. I must have been thinking of

**wrestle.** A **rascal** is also "a young child who does things he or she knows are wrong."

- When birds **migrate,** they fly to a warmer place. **Migrate** is also what bears do when they sleep all winter. *Tom Foolery!* Oh, you're right. I must have been thinking of **hibernate.** It sounds like **migrate,** but it is really not the same.

(Count the points and declare a winner.) You did a great job of playing *Tom Foolery!*

---

### DAY 5

**Preparation:** Each child will need a copy of the Quiz Answer Sheet, BLM B.

**Note:** You may wish to have available the activity sheet children completed on Day 3.

## Retell Story

Today I'll show you the pictures Susan Guevara made for *Isabel's House of Butterflies.* As I show you the pictures, I'll call on one of you to tell the class that part of the story.

Tell me what happens at the **beginning** of the story. (Show the picture on pages 3 and 4. Call on a child to tell what's happening.)

Tell me what happens in the **middle** of the story. (Show the pictures on pages 5–28. Call on a child to tell what's happening. Encourage use of target words when appropriate. Model use as necessary.)

Tell me what happens at the **end** of the story. (Show the pictures on page 29. Call on a child to tell what's happening.)

(**Note:** You may wish to invite children to share the new endings they wrote for the story.)

## Assess Vocabulary

 (Give each child a copy of the Quiz Answer Sheet, BLM B.)

Today you're going to have a True or False quiz. When you do the True or False quiz, it shows me how well you know the hard words you are learning.

Listen carefully to each item that I say. Don't let me trick you!

Item 1: A **plot** can be a small piece of land. (*True.*)

Item 2: **Plot** can also mean "make secret plans to do something bad." (*True.*)

Item 3: **Optimistic** people believe everything will turn out badly. (*False.*)

Item 4: Your **imagination** is the part of your mind that lets you see things that haven't happened yet. (*True.*)

Item 5: You like to spend time with your **companions.** (*True.*)

Item 6: If you are **curious,** you aren't **interested** in finding out about new things. (*False.*)

Item 7: Firefighters, policemen, and soldiers often have to be **brave.** (*True.*)

Item 8: When Terry said his house was much, much bigger than it really was, he **exaggerated.** (*False.*)

Item 9: It's fun being a **tourist.** (*True.*)

Item 10: If trees are **scarce** in my neighborhood, there are lots and lots of trees there. (*False.*)

You did a great job completing your quiz!

(Score children's work. A child must score 9 out of 10 to be at the mastery level. If a child does not achieve mastery, insert the missed words as additional items in the games in next week's lessons. Retest those children individually for the missed items before they take the next mastery test.)

## Extensions

### Read a Story as a Reward

(Display copies of all fiction books you have read since the beginning of the program, as well as a variety of other pieces of fiction. Allow children to choose which book they would like you to read to them as a reward for their hard work.)

(Read the story aloud for enjoyment with minimal interruptions.)

---

**Preparation:** Word containers for the Super Words Center.

---

### Introduce the Super Words Center

(Add the new Picture Vocabulary Cards to the words from the previous weeks. Show children one of the word containers. If children need more guidance in how to work in the Super Words Center, role-play with two to three children as a demonstration.)

You will play a game called *What's My Word?* in the Super Words Center.

Let's think about how we work with our words in the Super Words Center.

You will work with a partner in the Super Words Center. Whom will you work with? *A partner.*

First you will draw a word out of the container. What do you do first? (Idea: *Draw a word out of the container.*) Don't show your partner the word card.

Next you will tell your partner three clues that tell about the word card. What do you do next? (Idea: *I tell my partner three clues that tell about the word card.*) After each clue, your partner can make a guess. If your partner is correct, say "yes." If your partner is not correct, say "no" and give another clue.

Let your partner make three guesses. If your partner guesses correctly on any of the guesses, your partner gets a point. If your partner does not guess correctly, tell them your word and show them the word card. Give yourself a point. Then give your partner a turn.

What do you do next? *Give my partner a turn.*

(This game need not be played for points.)

# Week 16

**Preparation:** You will need a copy of *About Birds* for each day's lesson.

Number the pages of the story to assist you in asking comprehension questions at appropriate points.

Prepare a KWL chart titled *Birds* on a sheet of chart paper.

Post a copy of the Vocabulary Tally Sheet, BLM A, with this week's Picture Vocabulary Cards attached.

Each child will need one copy of the Homework Sheet, BLM 16a.

## Target Vocabulary

| Tier II | Tier III |
|---|---|
| hatch | nonfiction |
| flock | fact |
| *skeleton | plate |
| *characteristics | afterword |
| *warm-blooded | |
| bird | |

*Expanded Target Vocabulary Word

## DAY 1

### Introduce the Series

For the next five weeks we will be reading books about different kinds of animals. We will learn about five kinds of animals: birds, mammals, reptiles, fish, and insects. What animals will we read about? (Ideas: *Birds; mammals; reptiles; fish; insects.*)

All these books are true. When an author writes books about things that are true, those books are called nonfiction books. What kinds of books are about true things? *Nonfiction books.*

### Introduce Book

This week's book is called *About Birds.* What's the title of this week's book? *About Birds.*

This book was written by Cathryn Sill. Who's the author of *About Birds? Cathryn Sill.*

John Sill made the pictures for this book. Who is the illustrator of *About Birds? John Sill.* Who made the illustrations for this book? *John Sill.*

The cover of a book usually gives us some hints of what the book is about. Let's look at the front cover of *About Birds.* What do you see in the illustration? (Ideas: *A bird; a robin; a baby bird coming out of an egg; three more eggs; a nest; a tree.*)

(Display KWL chart.) Let's think about what we **know** about birds. Raise your hand if you can tell us something you know about birds. I'll write it down under the **K. K** stands for what we **know** about birds. What does **K** stand for? *What we know about birds.* (Record all children's responses under the *K* (know) section of the chart. Do not eliminate incorrect responses. They will be addressed in later lessons during the week.)

The things we know about birds that are true are called facts. What are the true things we know about birds called? *Facts.* (Point to the *K* column on the chart.) Some of the things you have told us are facts about birds, and some of the things you have told us are not true. When we've finished reading *About Birds,* we'll come back to our chart and look at it again.

Now let's think what you **want to know** about birds. I'll write it down under the **W. W** stands for what we **want to know** about birds. What does **W** stand for? *What we want to know about birds.* (Record all children's questions under the *W* (want to know) section of the chart. If children tell about birds instead of ask questions, prompt them to ask a question.)

### Take a Picture Walk

(Encourage children to use target words in their answers.) We're going to take a picture walk through this book. When we take a picture walk through a nonfiction book, we look carefully at the pictures and tell what we see. When you look carefully at pictures, you observe those pictures. What do you do when you look carefully at pictures in a nonfiction book? *You observe those pictures.*

All of the illustrations for this book were painted by John Sill. Sometimes when a nonfiction book is published with paintings, each painting is called a plate. What are paintings for a nonfiction book sometimes called? *Plates.* The plates in a nonfiction book are usually numbered. The first plate in the book would be called Plate 1. What would we call the first plate in the book? *Plate 1.* What would we call the second plate in the book? *Plate 2.* What would we call the third plate in the book? *Plate 3.*

**Page 2.** What do you observe in Plate 1? (Idea: *A red and brown bird sitting on a branch in the snow.*)

**Page 4.** What do you observe in Plate 2? (Ideas: *The same picture that is on the cover; a bird; a robin; a baby bird coming out of an egg; three more eggs; a nest; a tree.*)

**Page 6.** What do you observe in Plate 3? (Ideas: *A little yellow and black bird on the ground; it's hard to see because it's almost the same color as the leaves and the ground; a nest; a branch; some flowers; there's a fern.*)

**Page 8.** What do you observe in Plate 4? (Ideas: *A large bird carrying a stick; an eagle carrying a stick; a nest; a dead tree; the nest is made of sticks.*)

**Page 10.** What do you observe in Plate 5? (Ideas: *Water; a lake; an ocean; a cliff; rocks; two birds; the birds are black and white; an egg; a spotted egg.*)

**Page 12.** What do you observe in Plate 6? (Ideas: *Birds flying in the shape of V's; a lake or a pond; grass; reeds; cattails; marsh; tree with no leaves; bird sitting in the tree.*)

**Page 14.** What do you observe in Plate 7? (Ideas: *A plant; leaves; a stem; flowers; honeysuckle; two birds; hummingbirds; the birds are flying; the birds are green, red, white, and brown.*)

**Page 16.** What do you observe in Plate 8? (Ideas: *Water; two birds; two ducks; one bird*

is brown with a little bit of blue; the other bird has lots of colors on it; berries; branches; the brown duck is sitting on the branch; one duck is swimming in the water.)

**Page 18.** What do you observe in Plate 9? (Ideas: *A bird running; the bird is white, black, and green; it's in the desert; there's a cactus plant with yellow flowers on it; there's a little bit of grass; not much is growing.*)

**Page 20.** What do you observe in Plate 10? (Ideas: *A whole bunch of black birds with red and yellow wings; some birds are sitting on the ground; some birds are sitting in the trees; a field; there are pieces of plants left in the field.*)

**Page 22.** What do you observe in Plate 11? (Ideas: *An owl sitting in a dead tree; it's foggy.*)

**Page 24.** What do you observe in Plate 12? (Ideas: *Five different birds; they only show the heads; there's letters by each bird; bird **a** is putting its beak in a flower; bird **b** has a seed in its mouth; bird **c** has a fish in its mouth; bird **d** has a berry in its mouth; bird **e** has an insect or a bug in its mouth.*)

**Page 26.** What do you observe in Plate 13? (Ideas: *Water; trees; three birds on tree branches; two birds are blue; one bird is brown.*)

**Page 28.** What do you observe in Plate 14? (Ideas: *A whole bunch of birds; it's all of the birds we've seen so far.*)

**Page 30.** What do you observe in Plate 15? (Ideas: *A yard; lots of birds; a house; a bird feeder; a pond.*)

### Read the Book Aloud

(Read the book to children with minimal interruptions, ending with page 29.)

Tomorrow we will read the book again, and I will ask you some questions.

### Present the Target Vocabulary
◎ Hatch

In the book, the author says, "Baby birds hatch from eggs." She is telling us that baby birds come out of eggs when they are able to live in the world. **Hatch.** Say the word. *Hatch.*

**Hatch** is a verb. It tells what something does. What kind of word is **hatch**? *A verb.*

**When an egg hatches, the animal inside the egg breaks the shell and comes out.** Say the word that means "break the shell and come out." *Hatch.*

(Correct any incorrect responses, and repeat the item at the end of the sequence.)

Let's think about eggs. I'll tell what happens to an egg. If the egg is hatching, say "hatch." If not, don't say anything.

- The baby robin broke the shell and came out of the egg. *Hatch.*
- The baby turtle broke the shell and came out of the egg. *Hatch.*
- The hen laid three eggs in her nest.
- Tiny fish came out of the eggs. *Hatch.*
- My mom broke the shell on two eggs and put them in the frying pan.
- A tiny nightingale came out of the egg. *Hatch.*

What verb means "break the shell and come out"? *Hatch.*

◎ ◄ Flock

In the book, the author says, "Birds may flock together!" She is telling us that birds sometimes gather together in a group. **Flock.** Say the word. *Flock.*

**Flock** is verb. It tells what things do. What kind of word is **flock**? *A verb.*

**When animals or people flock together, they gather or travel in a group.** Say the word that means "gather or travel in a group." *Flock.*

Let's think about some times when animals or people might flock together. I'll tell about a time. If you think the people or animals are flocking together, say "flock." If not, don't say anything.

- A hundred crows all landed in the big oak tree. *Flock.*
- Every morning at dawn, the pigeons flew away from their nests in a great crowd. *Flock.*
- One sparrow came to my bird feeder.
- Two bald eagles flew back to their nest.
- People came in crowds to the new museum on opening day. *Flock.*
- Hundreds of people went together to see the fireworks. *Flock*

What verb means "gather or travel together in a group"? *Flock.*

## Present Expanded Target Vocabulary
◎ ◄ Skeleton

Inside the bodies of birds, you will find bones. People and other animals have bones inside their bodies. Some animals, like insects, have their skeletons on the outside of their bodies. The bones that are inside our bodies are called our skeleton. **Skeleton.** Say the word. *Skeleton.*

**Skeleton** is a noun. It names something. What kind of word is **skeleton**? *A noun.*

**A skeleton is the bones that support and protect an animal.** Say the word that names "the bones that support and protect an animal." *Skeleton.*

Let's think about the word **skeleton.** I'll name some body parts. If the body part is part of the skeleton, say "skeleton." If not, don't say anything.

- Skull. *Skeleton.*
- Skin.
- Antennae.
- Ribs. *Skeleton.*
- Leg bone. *Skeleton.*
- Hair.

What noun names "the bones that support and protect an animal"? *Skeleton.*

◎ ◄ Characteristics

In *About Birds,* Cathryn and John Sill wrote about and made paintings of many different kinds of birds. When we read the words and studied the illustrations, we found out that some things were the same for all birds but made them different from other animals. We also learned that some things were the same for all bald eagles but made them different from other birds. These things are called characteristics. **Characteristics.** Say the word. *Characteristics.*

**Characteristics** is a noun. It names things. What kind of word is **characteristics**? *A noun.*

**Characteristics means the things that make a person or thing different from others.** Say the word that means "the things that make a person or thing different from others." *Characteristics.*

I'll tell about birds. If these things are characteristics of birds, say "characteristics." If not, don't say anything.

- Birds have feathers. *Characteristics.*
- Birds lay eggs. *Characteristics.*
- My favorite bird is the puffin.
- Swimming birds have webbed feet. *Characteristics.*
- Most birds fly. *Characteristics.*
- I wonder where birds go in the winter.

What noun means "the things that make a person or thing different from others"? *Characteristics.*

### Present Vocabulary Tally Sheet
(See Lesson 1, page 4, for instructions.)

### Assign Homework
(Homework Sheet, BLM 16a. See the Introduction for homework instructions.)

---

### DAY 2

**Preparation:** Picture Vocabulary Cards for *hatch, flock, skeleton, characteristics.*

### Read and Discuss Story

(Encourage children to use previously taught target words in their answers.)

**Page 1.** What fact did we learn about birds? *Birds have feathers.* Plate 1 shows a Northern Cardinal. What bird is shown in Plate 1? *A Northern Cardinal.* What color are the feathers of a Northern Cardinal? (Ideas: *Red, brown, and black.*)

**Page 3.** What fact did we learn about birds? *Baby birds hatch from eggs.* Plate 2 shows an American Robin. What bird is shown in Plate 2? *An American Robin.* How many eggs did the American Robin lay? *Three.* What color are the American Robin's eggs? (Ideas: *Blue; turquoise blue; sky blue.*)

**Page 5.** What fact did we learn about birds? *Some birds build nests on the ground.* Plate 3 shows an Ovenbird. What bird is shown in

Plate 3? *An Ovenbird.* Where does the Ovenbird lay its eggs? (Idea: *In a nest on the ground.*) What do you think the nest is made of? (Ideas: *Grass; leaves; a stick; a branch.*)

**Page 7.** What fact did we learn about birds? *Some birds build nests in very high places.* Plate 4 shows a Bald Eagle. What bird is shown in Plate 4? *A Bald Eagle.* Why do you think the Bald Eagle builds its nest in such a high place? (Ideas: *So it can see all around; animals that would eat the eggs can't get to them.*)

**Page 9.** What fact did we learn about birds? (Idea: *Some birds do not build nests at all.*) Plate 5 shows a Common Murre. What bird is shown in Plate 5? *A Common Murre.* Where does the Common Murre lay its eggs? (Idea: *On the rocks; on a cliff.*) Why would a Common Murre not build a nest? (Ideas: *There's nothing around to build the nest out of; the rocks are nice and warm in the summer.*)

**Page 11.** What fact did we learn about birds? *Birds travel in different ways.* Plate 6 shows Canada Geese. What bird is shown in Plate 6? *Canada Geese.* How do the Canada Geese travel? (Idea: *They fly in flocks; they fly in V's.*)

**Pages 13–17.** What fact did we learn about birds? (Ideas: *Most birds fly; some swim; others run.*) Plate 7 shows a Ruby-throated Hummingbird. What bird is shown in Plate 7? *A Ruby-throated Hummingbird.* How does a Ruby-throated Hummingbird travel? (Idea: *It flies.*) Plate 8 shows Wood Ducks. What birds are shown in Plate 8? *Wood Ducks.* How do Wood Ducks travel? (Idea: *They swim.*) How else might Wood Ducks travel? (Idea: *They fly.*) Plate 9 shows a Road Runner. What bird is shown in Plate 9? *A Roadrunner.* How does a Roadrunner travel? (Idea: *It runs.*) Why do you think a Roadrunner runs instead of flies? (Idea: *Its wings are very short.*)

**Pages 19–21.** What fact did we learn about birds? *Birds may flock together or live alone.* Plate 10 shows Red-winged Blackbirds. What bird is shown in Plate 10? *Red-winged Blackbirds.* How do Red-winged Blackbirds like to live? (Idea: *In groups; with other blackbirds.*) Plate 11 shows a Great Horned Owl. What bird is shown in Plate 11? *A Great Horned Owl.* How do Great Horned Owls like to live? (Idea: *Alone.*)

**Page 23.** What fact did we learn about birds? *Birds use their bills to gather food.* Plate 11 shows five different birds.

Bird **a** is a Magnificent Hummingbird. What bird is bird **a**? *A Magnificent Hummingbird.* Where do Magnificent Hummingbirds get their food? (Idea: *In flowers.*) That's right; they eat the nectar found at the bottom of the flower.

Bird **b** is an Evening Grosbeak. What bird is bird **b**? *An Evening Grosbeak.* What do Evening Grosbeaks eat? (Idea: *Seeds.*)

Bird **c** is a Great Blue Heron. What bird is bird **c**? *A Great Blue Heron.* What do Great Blue Herons eat? (Idea: *Fish.*)

Bird **d** is a Cedar Waxwing. What bird is bird **d**? *A Cedar Waxwing.* What do Cedar Waxwings eat? (Idea: *Berries.*)

Bird **e** is a Vermilion Flycatcher. What bird is bird **e**? *A Vermilion Flycatcher.* What do Vermilion Flycatchers eat? (Idea: *Flies; insects, bugs.*) Vermilion is a bright red color. Why do you think this bird is named a Vermilion Flycatcher? (Idea: *It's a bright red color.*)

**Page 25.** What fact did we learn about birds? (Ideas: *They sing to let other birds know how they feel; birds talk by singing.*) Plate 13 shows Indigo Buntings. What bird is shown in Plate 13? *Indigo Buntings.* The male, or father, bird is dark blue. What color is the male Indigo Bunting? *Dark blue.* The female, or mother, bird is brown and beige. What color is the female Indigo Bunting? *Brown and beige.* Indigo is a dark purplish blue color. Why do you think this bird is named an Indigo Bunting? (Idea: *The male is a dark purplish blue color.*)

**Page 27.** What fact did we learn about birds? *Birds come in all sizes.* Plate 14 shows some of the birds we have already learned about. I'll point to the birds; let's see if you can remember their names.

(Point to the birds and ask children to identify each one. If children cannot name the bird, tell them the name and come back to it later.) Now that you can remember these birds' names, let's

see if we can put the birds into three groups: Big birds, small birds, and medium-sized birds. Which four birds are the largest? (Ideas: *Bald Eagle, Great Blue Heron, Canada Goose, Great Horned Owl.*) Which two birds are the smallest? (Ideas: *Ruby-throated Hummingbird, Indigo Bunting.*) Which three birds are medium-sized? (Ideas: *Wood Duck, Northern Cardinal, Red-winged Blackbird.*)

**Page 29.** Cathryn Sill ended her book with an important message to us. What does she want us to remember? (Idea: *Birds are important to us.*)

(Display KWL chart.) Now that we've finished reading *About Birds,* let's look at our chart again.

(Point to the *Know* column.) As good scientists find out more about things, they sometimes change their minds about what they know is true. Let's see if we want to change our minds about any of the items on our **Know** list. (Read each item. Ask children if that item was mentioned in the book. If it was, ask if the item is true or not true. Not true items are crossed out.) We're good scientists; we know how to change our minds when we learn new facts.

(Point to the *Want to Know* column.) As good scientists find out more about things, they find answers to some of their questions, and they want to ask more questions. (Read each question. Ask children if that question was answered in the book. If it was, record the answer in the *L* (Learned) column and put a check mark in front of the question.) Are there any new questions we would like to ask about birds? (Record questions in the *W* column.) We're good scientists; we know how to use what we have learned to ask new questions.

### Review Vocabulary
(Display the Picture Vocabulary Cards. Point to each card as you say the word. Ask children to repeat each word after you.) These pictures show **hatch, flock, skeleton,** and **characteristics.**

- What word means "the things that make a person or thing different from others"? *Characteristics.*

- What word means "break the shell and come out"? *Hatch.*
- What word means "gather or travel together in a group"? *Flock.*
- What word means "the bones that support and protect an animal"? *Skeleton.*

## Extend Vocabulary

 Flock

In *About Birds,* we learned that **flock** means "gather or travel together in a group." Say the word that means "gather or travel together in a group." *Flock.*

Raise your hand if you can tell us a sentence that uses **flock** as a verb meaning "travel or gather together in a group." **(Call on several children. If they don't use complete sentences, restate their examples as sentences. Have the class repeat the sentences.)**

Here's a new way to use the word **flock.**

- A **flock** of pigeons flew over my house. Say the sentence.
- A shepherd watched over his **flock** of sheep. Say the sentence.
- The **flock** of ducks flew south for the winter. Say the sentence.

**In these sentences, flock is a noun that means a group of one kind of animal that lives, travels, or feeds together.** What word means "a group of one kind of animal that lives, travels, or feeds together"? *Flock.*

Raise your hand if you can tell us a sentence that uses **flock** as a noun meaning "a group of one kind of animal that lives, travels, or feeds together." **(Call on several children. If they don't use complete sentences, restate their examples as sentences. Have the class repeat the sentences.)**

## Present Expanded Target Vocabulary
 Warm-blooded

In *About Birds,* Cathryn and John Sill wrote about and made paintings of many different kinds of birds. We learned about many characteristics of birds. One characteristic of birds that was not in the book is that all birds are warm-blooded. **Warm-blooded.** Say the word. *Warm-blooded.*

**Warm-blooded** is a describing word. It describes a noun. What kind of word is **warm-blooded?** *A describing word.*

**Warm-blooded animals are animals whose body temperatures stay the same no matter what the temperature around them is.** Say the word that describes "animals whose body temperatures stay the same no matter what the temperature around them is." *Warm-blooded.*

I'll tell about animals. If these animals are warm-blooded, say "warm-blooded." If not, don't say anything.

- The lizard's body temperature got warmer in the hot desert sun.
- Even in the icy arctic waters, a whale's body temperature stays warm. *Warm-blooded.*
- Most humans have a body temperature of 98.6 degrees all the time. *Warm-blooded.*
- It is important to keep the water in your fish tank warm so the fishes' body temperature doesn't get too low.

What word describes "animals whose body temperatures stay the same no matter what the temperature is around them"? *Warm-blooded.*

 Bird

Scientists divide all living things into two groups: plants and animals. The animal group is divided into smaller groups. One of these groups is birds. Scientists use a scientific explanation to help people learn what a bird is. **Bird.** Say the word. *Bird.*

This is the scientific explanation of what a **bird** is. **A bird is an animal that:**
> **has a skeleton**
> **is warm-blooded**
> **lays eggs**
> **has wings**
> **is covered with feathers.**

Scientists use this information to help them decide if an animal is a bird or not. For an animal to be a bird it must have all of these characteristics. Let's be scientists and decide if a human could be a bird. **(If children answer a question incorrectly, give them the answer and explain that the characteristic is or is not a quality of that animal.)**

Does a human have a skeleton? *Yes.*

Is a human warm-blooded? *Yes.*

Does a human lay eggs? *No.*

Does a human have wings? *No.*

Is a human's body covered with feathers? *No.*

So could a human be a bird? *No.*

Good using the scientific explanation to help you make that decision.

Let's be scientists and decide if a penguin could be a bird.

Does a penguin have a skeleton? *Yes.*

Is a penguin warm-blooded? *Yes.*

Does a penguin lay eggs? *Yes.*

Does a penguin have wings? *Yes.*

Is a penguin's body covered with feathers? *Yes.*

So is a penguin a bird? *Yes.*

Good using the scientific explanation to help you make that decision.

---

## DAY 3

**Preparation:** Display KWL chart.

You may wish to photocopy the four pages of the afterword so you can show children the illustrations while you read the additional information.

---

### Introduce Afterword

Sometimes when people write a nonfiction book, after they finish the main part of the book they want to tell you more facts. This information is put in the book **after** the last **word** of the main part of the book, so it is called an **afterword.**

Today I'll read the afterword that Cathryn Sill wrote for *About Birds* so you can learn more about birds. In this afterword, Catherine Sill wrote more information to go with each plate that John Sill painted.

(Read the afterword aloud a paragraph at a time.)

### Complete KWL Chart

(Review with children the questions they still want answered from the *W* column of the KWL chart.) Let's see if Cathryn Sill answered any of our questions in the afterword of her book.

**Plate 1.** Did these facts answer any of our questions? (If the item did answer any of the remaining questions, put a check mark in front of the question, and write the answer in the *L* column next to the question. Repeat the question, and have children say the answer. If the item did not answer any of the remaining questions, ask children leading questions, such as:) What are two good things about feathers? (Ideas: *They protect the birds from the weather; they help birds fly because they are light and strong.*)

(Record the fact in the *L* column near the bottom. Do not write the fact next to any of the unanswered questions.)

(Repeat the process for the remaining plates. If there are any unanswered questions after you have read and discussed the afterword, challenge children to find the answers in the school library, on the Internet, or at home.)

### Summarize the Afterword

The afterword tells us true facts about birds. Facts are things that are true and that can be proved. For example, it is a fact that birds can fly. We can prove this fact by looking up in the sky and seeing birds flying.

When we summarize what we read we tell the most important things in our own words. I'm going to read each fact that Cathryn Sill wrote.

(Read the first fact.) My turn to summarize the fact. Feathers protect birds and help them fly. Say the fact. *Feathers protect birds and help them fly.*

(Repeat this procedure for plates 2 to 4.)

Plate 2: (Idea: *All birds hatch from eggs.*)

Plate 3: (Idea: *The ovenbird builds a nest that looks like an oven.*)

Plate 4: (Idea: *Many birds build nests high above the ground.*)

Your turn to summarize the rest of the facts. (Read each fact for plates 5 to 13 and plate 15. After you read each fact, work with the children to elicit a summative statement. Have all of the children repeat each summative fact as it is given.)

Plate 5: (Idea: *The common murre lays eggs on rocky ledges.*)

Plate 6: (Idea: *Canada geese can fly a long ways because they are strong.*)

Plate 7: (Idea: *Hummingbird wings move very, very fast.*)

Plate 8: (Idea: *The wood duck is a good swimmer and is a strong flyer.*)

Plate 9: (Idea: *Roadrunners can run very fast.*)

Plate 10: (Idea: *Red-winged blackbirds like to be together in the winter.*)

Plate 11: (Idea: *Many birds of prey live alone.*)

Plate 12: (Idea: *Birds use their bills in many different ways.*)

Plae 13: (Idea: *Birds use their voices in many different ways.*)

Plate 15: (Idea: *Birds help people in many different ways.*)

We did a great job of summarizing facts about birds.

### Play the Threesies Game

Today, you play the *Threesies* game. I'll tell you a word you learned when we read *About Birds.* After I tell you the word, you need to tell me three important things about the word. Each time you tell me something important about the word, you will win one point. If you can't tell me three things about the word, I will tell you things and I will win one point for each thing I tell you. Once three things have been said about the word, you will have a chance to win two bonus points by using the word in a good sentence. How can you win two bonus points? *By using the word in a good sentence.*

Let's practice. Here's my word. **Hatch.** Tell me one thing you know about the word **hatch.** Tell me another thing you know about **hatch.** Tell me a third thing you know about **hatch.** (Ideas:

*Hatch is a verb; hatch is something birds and some other animals do; baby birds hatch; baby turtles hatch; some fish hatch; when a bird hatches it breaks its shell and comes out of the egg.*) Now you have a chance to earn two bonus points. Raise your hand if you can use **hatch** in a good sentence.

Now you're ready to play the game. (Draw a T-chart on the board for keeping score. Children earn one point for each correct response. If they make a mistake or are unable to give an idea, give an appropriate idea and record one point for yourself. If they can use the word in a good sentence, award two points. Model a good sentence using the word if necessary, and record two points for yourself. Repeat missed words at the end of the game.)

- Your first word is **skeleton.**
- Your next word is **warm-blooded.**
- Your next word is **flock.**
- Your next word is **bird.**
- Your last word is **characteristics.**

(Tally the points and declare a winner.) You did a great job playing *Threesies!*

---

### DAY 4

**Preparation:** Photocopy and assemble the *Let's Learn About Birds* booklet.

Print the following words in two columns on the board: *watch, places, smallest, biggest, hummingbirds, feathers, humans, hair, until, babies, hatch, important.*

### Introduce the
### Let's Learn About Birds Booklet

(Point to each word as you read it.) This word is **watch.** What word? *Watch.* This word is **places.** What word? *Places.* (Repeat process for remaining words.)

Let's read these words together. First word? *Watch.* Next word? *Places.* (Repeat process for remaining words.)

Read these words by yourself. First word? *Watch.* Next word? *Places.* (Repeat process for remaining words until children can read the list accurately and confidently.)

(Use the following correction procedure if the children make an error:) This word is **important.** What word? *Important.* Yes, **important .** (Go back to the top of the list and repeat the list until the children can read it accurately and confidently.)

(Give each child a copy of the *Let's Learn About Birds* booklet.) This is your very own book about birds. The title of this book is *Let's Learn About Birds.* What's the title of the book? *Let's Learn About Birds.*

My turn to read each page of the book. You touch under each word as I read it. (Read pages 1–4.)

Let's read the book together. (Have children read chorally with you.)

(Assign each child a partner. Allow sufficient time for each child to read the first four pages of the book to his or her partner. Circulate as children read, offering praise and assistance.)

(Children should color the illustrations in their *Let's Learn About Birds* booklet. Encourage them to color the illustrations accurately.) This book is a science book. When artists color scientific illustrations, they use colors that are real. (Show children the front cover of the booklet. Point to the bird's chest.) This bird is a robin. What color should this part of the bird be? *Orange.* What color should the bird's head be? *Black.* Remember to use the real colors when you color the illustrations.

### Play the Threesies Game (Cumulative Review)

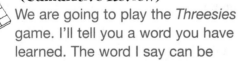 We are going to play the *Threesies* game. I'll tell you a word you have learned. The word I say can be any word you have learned since we read *Suki's Kimono,* so don't let me trick you.

After I tell you the word, you need to tell me three important things about the word. Each time you tell me something important about the word, you will win one point. If you can't tell me three things about the word, I will tell you things and I will win one point for each thing I tell you.

Once three things have been said about the word, you will have a chance to win two bonus points by using the word in a good sentence.

Now you're ready to play the game. (Draw a T-chart on the board for keeping score. Children earn one point for each correct response. If they make a mistake or are unable to give an idea, give an appropriate idea and record one point for yourself. If they can use the word in a good sentence, award two points. Model a good sentence using the word if necessary, and record two points for yourself. Repeat missed words at the end of the game.)

- Your first word is **flock.**
- Your next word is **different.**
- Your next word is **untidy.**
- Your next word is **festival.**
- Your next word is **characteristics.**
- Your next word is **bird.**
- Your next word is **warm-blooded.**
- Your next word is **hatch.**
- Your next word is **skeleton.**
- Your last word is **confident.**

(Tally the points and declare a winner.) You did a great job playing *Threesies!*

---

### DAY 5

**Preparation:** Children will need their copies of *Let's Learn About Birds.*

Prepare a piece of chart paper titled *Reading Goals.*

Each child will need a copy of the Quiz Answer Sheet, BLM B.

---

### Read the Let's Learn About Birds Booklet

(Assign each child a partner.) Today you'll read the first four pages of your book about birds to your partner. (Allow sufficient time for each child to read the first four pages of the booklet to his or her partner. Circulate as children read, offering praise and assistance.)

(Ask children to look at the back cover of their booklet about birds.) This part of the book is for people who can help you find other books to read. It tells those people about other books that are like *About Birds.* It also tells them about a place where you can find other books. Where are some places that you could go to find other books about birds? (Ideas: *To the school library; to the public library; to a bookstore.*)

(You may wish to read and discuss the information on the back cover.)

There's one more important thing on the back cover of your book. Touch the box that is at the bottom of the page. The words above the box say "My reading goal." What do the words say? *My reading goal.*

(Display the class chart titled *Reading Goals.*) A goal is something that you want to succeed at doing. What is a goal? *Something that you want to succeed at doing.* A reading goal is something that you want to succeed at doing with your reading.

I might decide that my goal is to read the book to someone with just a little bit of help. (Record goal on the chart.) I might decide that my goal is to read the book with only a few mistakes. (Record goal on the chart.)

What are some other reading goals that someone might have when they read their book? (Accept reasonable responses. Help children put their ideas into goal statements. Add to the list of goal statements. Ask children to choose a goal and copy it into the box. Children may also make up an original goal that is not on the list. If children are unable to copy the goals or to write a goal of their own, you or a helper may wish to scribe their goal statements for them before the booklets are sent home.)

## Assess Comprehension

(Ask children to turn to page 5 in their booklets.) This is what you have read in your book about birds, but with no pictures. You are going to have a little quiz to see if you can remember what you read.

(Ask children to touch under the words as they read the passage silently. Monitor to ensure that they are reading the passage. Ask them to look up at you after they have finished reading the passage. Instruct children to read and answer the questions. You may need to give additional guidance and practice if children do not know

how to fill in bubbles to indicate a correct answer.)

## Assess Vocabulary

 (Give each child a copy of the Quiz Answer Sheet, BLM B.)

Today you're going to have a True or False quiz. When you do the True or False quiz, it shows me how well you know the hard words you are learning.

If I say something that is true, circle the word **true.** What will you do if I say something that is true? *Circle the word* true.

If I say something that is false, circle the word **false.** What will you do if I say something that is false? *Circle the word* false.

Listen carefully to each item that I say. Don't let me trick you!

Item 1: If a sparrow **hatches** from an egg, it breaks the shell and comes out. (*True.*)

Item 2: A **flock** of sheep is a lamb. (*False.*)

Item 3: **Flock** can be a noun or a verb. (*True.*)

Item 4: If an animal can fly, it's a bird. (*False.*)

Item 5: My eye color and my hair color are two of my **characteristics.** (*True.*)

Item 6: You would find the **skeleton** of a human on the outside of his or her body. (*False.*)

Item 7: A **souvenir** is a celebration or a holiday. (*False.*)

Item 8: A person who has good manners could be described as a **polite** person. (*True.*)

Item 9: If an animal is **warm-blooded,** its body temperature would be lower on a cold day. (*False.*)

Item 10: A child or young animal that has lost its parents is called an **orphan.** (*True.*)

You did a great job completing your quiz!

(Score children's work. A child must score 9 out of 10 to be at the mastery level. If a child does not achieve mastery, insert the missed words as additional items in the games in next week's lessons. Retest those children individually for the missed items before they take the next mastery test.)

## Extensions

### Read Book as a Reward

(Read *About Birds* or another nonfiction book about birds to children as a reward for their hard work.)

**Preparation:** Word containers for the Super Scientists Center.

Create a 3-column chart on construction paper with the headings *nouns, verbs,* and *words that describe nouns.*

### Introduce the
### Super Scientists Center

(Place this week's Picture Vocabulary Cards in the center, removing words from previous weeks. Show children the word container and the sorting chart. If children need more guidance in how to work in the Super Scientists Center, role-play with two to three children as a demonstration.)

Let's think about how we work with our words in the Super Scientists Center.

You will work with a partner in the Super Scientists Center. Whom will you work with? *A partner.*

Scientists observe things carefully and try to find ways that things are alike. They put things that have the same characteristics together in groups. These groups are called categories. What are groups of things with the same characteristics called? *Categories.*

You are going to think about what you know about your vocabulary words and put them into categories.

First you will look at the categories I have written on this chart. What will you do first? *Look at the categories on the chart.* This week you are going to use the categories *nouns, verbs,* and *words that describe nouns.* What are your categories for this week? (Ideas: *Nouns; verbs; words that describe nouns.*)

Next you and your partner will read each word from the container. What will you and your partner do next? *Read each word.*

After you read each word, you and your partner will talk about what you know about each word and decide which category it should go in. What will you and your partner do after you read each word? (Idea: *Talk about what we know about each word and decide which category to put it in.*)

**Preparation:** You will need a copy of *About Mammals* for each day's lesson.

Number the pages of the story to assist you in asking comprehension questions at appropriate points.

Prepare a KWL chart titled *Mammals* on a sheet of chart paper.

Post a copy of the Vocabulary Tally Sheet, BLM A, with this week's Picture Vocabulary Cards attached.

Each child will need one copy of the Homework Sheet, BLM 17a.

### DAY 1

### Introduce Book

This week's book is called *About Mammals.* What's the title of this week's book? *About Mammals.*

This book is true. When an author writes books about things that are true, those books are called nonfiction books. What kinds of books are about true things? *Nonfiction books.*

This book was written by Cathryn Sill. Who's the author of *About Mammals?* *Cathryn Sill.*

John Sill made the pictures for this book. Who is the illustrator of *About Mammals?* *John Sill.* Who made the illustrations for this book? *John Sill.*

The cover of a book usually gives us some hints of what the book is about. Let's look at the front cover of *About Mammals.* What do you see in the illustration? (Ideas: *A raccoon on a log; trees; water.*)

(Display KWL chart.) Let's think about what we **know** about mammals. Raise your hand if you can tell us something you know about mammals. I'll write it down under the **K. K** stands for what we **know** about mammals. What does **K** stand for? *What we know about mammals.*

(Record <u>all</u> children's responses under the *K* (know) section of the chart. Do not eliminate

## About Mammals
author: Cathryn Sill • illustrator: John Sill

### Target Vocabulary

| Tier II | Tier III |
|---------|----------|
| both | nonfiction |
| desert | fact |
| marsh | afterword |
| protect | |
| some | |
| mammal | |

*Expanded Target Vocabulary Word

incorrect responses. They will be addressed in later lessons during the week.)

The things we know about mammals that are true are called facts. What are the true things we know about mammals called? *Facts.*

(Point to the *K* column on the chart.) Some of the things you have told us are facts about mammals, and some of the things you have told us are not true. When we've finished reading *About Mammals,* we'll come back to our chart and look at it again.

Now let's think what you **want to know** about mammals. I'll write it down under the **W. W** stands for what we **want to know** about mammals. What does **W** stand for? *What we want to know about mammals.* (Record <u>all</u> children's questions under the *W* (want to know) section of the chart. If children tell about mammals instead of ask questions, prompt them to ask a question.)

### Take a Picture Walk

(Encourage children to use target words in their answers.) We're going to take a picture walk through this book. When we take a picture walk through a nonfiction book, we look carefully at the pictures and tell what we see. When you look carefully at pictures, you observe those pictures. What do you do when you look carefully at pictures in a nonfiction book? *You observe those pictures.*

All of the illustrations for this book were painted by John Sill. Sometimes when a nonfiction book is published with paintings, each painting is

called a plate. What are paintings for a nonfiction book sometimes called? *Plates.* The plates in a nonfiction book are usually numbered. The first plate in the book would be called Plate 1. What would we call the first plate in the book? *Plate 1.* What would we call the second plate in the book? *Plate 2.* What would we call the third plate in the book? *Plate 3.*

**Page 2.** What do you observe in Plate 1? (Ideas: *The same picture from the cover; a raccoon on a log; trees; water.*)

**Page 4.** What do you observe in Plate 2? (Ideas: *Three large, hairy animals with horns standing in the snow; musk oxen.*)

**Page 6.** What do you observe in Plate 3? (Ideas: *A prickly animal on a tree branch; a porcupine.*)

**Page 8.** What do you observe in Plate 4? (Idea: *A walrus with large tusks sitting on a piece of ice in the water.*)

**Page 10.** What do you observe in Plate 5? (Ideas: *Lots of animals in the grass; one large animal close by; it is furry with a large head with horns; a baby with light brown fur is sucking on its mother; a herd of bison.*)

**Page 12.** What do you observe in Plate 6? (Ideas: *A mouse in a hole in a tree; baby mice are sucking on their mother.*)

**Page 14.** What do you observe in Plate 7? (Ideas: *A forest and mountains; two large animals are standing in the grass; elk.*)

**Page 16.** What do you observe in Plate 8? (Ideas: *Some brown and white animals with long horns running in the grass; a herd of Pronghorn Antelope.*)

**Page 18.** What do you observe in Plate 9? (Ideas: *A squirrel in a tree; there are no leaves on the branches.*)

**Page 20.** What do you observe in Plate 10? (Idea: *A whale swimming in the ocean.*)

**Page 22.** What do you observe in Plate 11? (Ideas: *Several bats flying in the sky; the bats have wings and furry bodies; it is night; they are flying over some trees.*)

**Page 24.** What do you observe in Plate 12? (Ideas: *A spotted cat carrying a rabbit in its mouth; grass; large rocks.*)

**Page 26.** What do you observe in Plate 13? (Ideas: *A small animal in a cave; it is brown and furry with long whiskers; there is grass behind it like a nest; there are some yellow flowers; dandelions; a pika.*)

**Page 28.** What do you observe in Plate 14? (Ideas: *A big black bear in the woods.*)

**Page 30.** What do you observe in Plate 15? (Ideas: *A white animal; a fox; in the snow; the animal's fur is the same color as the snow.*)

**Page 32.** What do you observe in Plate 16? (Ideas: *A big rabbit with long ears standing straight up; the desert; sand; cactus; plants.*)

**Page 34.** What do you observe in Plate 17? (Ideas: *A brown, furry animal eating some sort of plant; water; water plants; the animal's reflection in the water; a muskrat; reeds.*)

**Page 36.** What do you observe in Plate 18? (Ideas: *A man and a small child hiding behind a tall tree; lots of trees; they are looking at a deer; a squirrel climbing down a tree; a raccoon in a hole in a tree; a woodpecker making a hole in a tree.*)

### Read the Book Aloud

(Read the book to children with minimal interruptions, ending with page 35.)

Tomorrow we will read the book again, and I will ask you some questions.

### Present the Target Vocabulary
⊙— Both

In the book, the author says, "Mammals eat meat, plants, or both." She is telling us that some mammals eat meat and plants. **Both.** Say the word. *Both.*

**Both** is a describing word. It tells about things. What kind of word is **both?** *A describing word.*

**When you talk about both, you mean one thing and the other thing.** Say the word that means "one thing and the other thing." *Both.*

(Correct any incorrect responses, and repeat the item at the end of the sequence.)

Let's think about the word **both.** I'll tell about two things. If I am talking about both things, say "both." If not, don't say anything.

- Hector ate his fish but not his vegetables.
- The dog ran after the frisbee and the ball. *Both.*
- Robins and bats fly. *Both.*
- Giraffes have long necks; rhinos don't.
- For breakfast I had cereal and toast. *Both.*
- Two rabbits hopped through the grass. *Both.*

What describing word means "one thing and the other thing"? *Both.*

## ◎⟵ Desert

In the book, the author says, "They may live in cold, icy places or hot, dry deserts . . ." She is telling us that some mammals live in the desert. **Desert.** Say the word. *Desert.*

**Desert** is a noun. It names a place. What kind of word is **desert?** *A noun.*

**A desert is a dry, sandy place where few plants grow.** Say the word that means "a dry, sandy place where few plants grow." *Desert.*

Let's think about some different places. I'll tell about a place. If you think the place is a desert, say "desert." If not, don't say anything.

- Jamal went on vacation to a place with lots of trees and grass.
- Cactus grows well here with very little water. *Desert.*
- The lizard ran through the hot, dry sand. *Desert.*
- The alligator crawled through the muddy water.
- The sun beat down on the sand and it hadn't rained in months. *Desert.*
- Two squirrels chased each other through the cool shade of the trees.

What noun means "a dry, sandy place where few plants grow"? *Desert.*

## ◎⟵ Marsh

In the book, the author says, "They may live in cold, icy places or hot, dry deserts or wet marshes." **Marsh.** Say the word. *Marsh.*

**Marsh** is a noun. It names a place. What kind of word is **marsh?** *A noun.*

**A marsh is a low, wet area of land that often has a lot of grasses.** Say the word that means "a low, wet area of land that often has a lot of grasses." *Marsh.*

I'll tell you about a place. If the place is a marsh, say "marsh." If not, don't say anything.

- The frog hopped through the thick grasses around the water. *Marsh.*
- The goat climbed the rocky hills.
- An alligator crawled silently through the thick water, hiding among the grasses. *Marsh.*
- The monkeys swung through the trees.
- Whales and dolphins swim in the deep, blue water.
- Dragonflies swarm among the grasses growing out of the water. *Marsh.*

What noun means "a low, wet area of land that often has a lot of grasses"? *Marsh.*

## ◎⟵ Protect

In the book, the author says, "It is important to protect mammals where they live." **Protect.** Say the word. *Protect.*

**Protect** is a verb. It tells what something does. What kind of word is **protect?** *A verb.*

**To protect something means to keep it safe from harm.** Say the word that means "to keep something safe from harm." *Protect.*

I'll tell you about some situations. If I tell about somebody or something protecting another, say "protect." If not, don't say anything.

- I always wear my seatbelt in the car. *Protect.*
- The lion chased a rabbit.
- The mother bear chased a mountain lion away from the cave where her cubs slept. *Protect.*
- A group of people is raising money to save the rain forests. *Protect.*
- The little girl was riding her bike without her helmet.
- The mother dog growled when the man tried to touch her puppies. *Protect.*

What verb means "to keep someone or something safe from harm"? *Protect.*

### Present Vocabulary Tally Sheet
(See Lesson 1, page 4, for instructions.)

### Assign Homework
(Homework Sheet, BLM 17a. See the Introduction for homework instructions.)

**Preparation:** Picture Vocabulary Cards for *both, desert, marsh, protect.*

### Read and Discuss Story

(Encourage children to use previously taught target words in their answers.)

**Page 1.** What fact did we learn about mammals? *Mammals have hair.* Plate 1 shows a raccoon. What mammal is shown in Plate 1? *A raccoon.* What does a raccoon look like? (Ideas: *It has gray fur, rings on its tail, and a mask around its eyes.*)

**Page 3.** What fact did we learn about mammals? (Idea: *Some mammals may have thick fur.*) Plate 2 shows musk oxen. What mammal is shown in Plate 2? *Musk oxen.* What kind of places do musk oxen live in? (Idea: *Cold.*)

**Page 5.** What fact did we learn about mammals? (Idea: *Some mammals have sharp quills.*) Plate 3 shows a porcupine. What mammal is shown in Plate 3? *A porcupine.* Why do you think the porcupine has sharp quills? (Idea: *To protect itself from its enemies.*)

**Page 7.** What fact did we learn about mammals? (Idea: *Some mammals have only a few very stiff whiskers.*) Plate 4 shows a walrus. What mammal is shown in Plate 4? *A walrus.* Where does the walrus have hair? (Idea: *On its face.*)

**Page 9.** What fact did we learn about mammals? *Baby mammals drink milk from their mothers.* Plate 5 shows a bison. What mammal is shown in Plate 5? *A bison.*

**Page 11.** What fact did we learn about mammals? *Some mammals are born helpless.* Plate 6 shows white-footed mice. What mammal is shown in Plate 6? *White-footed mice.* Where did this white-footed mouse make her nest? (Idea: *In a hole in a tree.*)

**Page 13.** What fact did we learn about mammals? (Idea: *Some mammal babies can move about on their own soon after they're born.*) Plate 7 shows elk. What mammal is shown in Plate 7? *Elk.* How is a baby elk different from a baby white-footed mouse? (Idea:

*The baby elk can move around soon after it's born; the baby mouse can't.*)

**Pages 15–21.** What fact did we learn about mammals? (Idea: *Mammals move in different ways.*) Plate 8 shows pronghorns. What mammal is shown in Plate 7? *Pronghorns.* How do pronghorns travel? (Idea: *They run.*) Plate 9 shows a red squirrel. What mammal is shown in Plate 8? *A red squirrel.* How do red squirrels travel? (Idea: *They climb.*) Plate 10 shows a blue whale. What mammal is shown in Plate 10? *A blue whale.* How does a blue whale travel? (Idea: *It swims.*) Plate 11 shows a big brown bat. What mammal is shown in Plate 11? *A big brown bat.* How does a big brown bat travel? (Idea: *It flies.*)

**Pages 23–27.** What fact did we learn about mammals? (Idea: *Mammals may eat meat, plants, or both.*) Plate 12 shows a bobcat. What mammal is shown in Plate 12? *A bobcat.* What do bobcats eat? (Idea: *Meat.*) Plate 13 shows a pika. What mammal is shown in Plate 13? *A pika.* What does a pika eat? (Idea: *Plants.*) Plate 14 shows a black bear. What mammal is shown in Plate 14? *A black bear.* What do black bears eat? (Idea: *Both meat and plants.*)

**Pages 29–33.** What fact did we learn about mammals? (Idea: *Mammals live in different places.*) Plate 15 shows an arctic fox. What mammal is shown in Plate 15? *An arctic fox.* Where do arctic foxes live? (Idea: *In cold, icy places.*) Plate 16 shows a blacktail jackrabbit. What mammal is shown in Plate 16? *A blacktail jackrabbit.* Where do blacktail jackrabbits live? (Idea: *In hot, dry deserts.*) Plate 17 shows a muskrat. What mammal is shown in Plate 17? *A muskrat.* Where do muskrats live? (Idea: *In wet marshes.*)

**Page 35.** Cathryn Sill ended her book with an important message to us. What does she want us to remember? (Idea: *It is important to protect mammals where they live.*) Plate 18 shows four mammals. (Point to the humans.) Humans are mammals. What mammals are shown here? *Humans.* (Point to the raccoon in the tree.) Raccoons are mammals. What mammal is shown here? *A raccoon.* (Point to the deer.) This is a white-tailed deer. What mammal is shown here? *A white-tailed deer.* (Point to the squirrel.) This is a gray squirrel. What mammal is shown here?

*A gray squirrel.* (Point to the woodpecker.) This is a woodpecker. Is this a mammal? *No.* The woodpecker is not a mammal. What is it? *A bird.*

(Display KWL chart.) Now that we've finished reading *About Mammals,* let's look at our chart again.

(Point to the *Know* column.) As good scientists find out more about things, they sometimes change their minds about what they know is true. Let's see if we want to change our minds about any of the items on our **Know** list. (Read each item. Ask children if that item was mentioned in the book. If it was, ask if the item is true or not true. Untrue items are crossed out.) We're good scientists; we know how to change our minds when we learn new facts.

(Point to the *Want to Know* column.) As good scientists find out more about things, they find answers to some of their questions, and they want to ask more questions. (Read each question. Ask children if that question was answered in the book. If it was, record the answer in the *L* (Learned) column and put a check mark in front of the question.) Are there any new questions we would like to ask about mammals? (Record questions in the *W* column.) We're good scientists; we know how to use what we have learned to ask new questions.

## Review Vocabulary
(Display the Picture Vocabulary Cards. Point to each card as you say the word. Ask children to repeat each word after you.) These pictures show **both, desert, marsh,** and **protect.**

- What word means "a dry, sandy place where few plants grow"? *Desert.*
- What word means "one thing and the other thing"? *Both.*
- What word means "a low, wet area of land often with a lot of grasses"? *Marsh.*
- What word means "to keep someone or something safe from harm"? *Protect.*

## Extend Vocabulary
 Desert

In *About Mammals,* we learned that a **desert** is "a dry, sandy place where few plants grow." Say the word that means "a dry sandy place where few plants grow." *Desert.*

Raise your hand if you can tell us a sentence that uses **desert** as a noun meaning "a dry, sandy place where few plants grow." (Call on several children. If they don't use complete sentences, restate their examples as sentences. Have the class repeat the sentences.)

When the word **desert** is used as a verb, it is pronounced a little bit differently. Here's a new way to use the word **desert.**

- The cat **deserted** her kittens. Say the sentence.
- A sailor had to **desert** his ship. Say the sentence.
- The man **deserted** the army. Say the sentence.

**In these sentences, desert is a verb that means to leave someone or something behind even though it is your duty to stay.** What word means "to leave someone or something behind even though it is your duty to stay"? *Desert.*

Raise your hand if you can tell us a sentence that uses **desert** as a verb meaning "to leave someone or something behind even though it is your duty to stay." (Call on several children. If they don't use complete sentences, restate their examples as sentences. Have the class repeat the sentences.)

## Present Expanded Target Vocabulary
◎ ⊸ Some

In the book, the author says "Some mammals are born helpless." **Some.** Say the word. *Some.*

**Some** is a describing word. It tells more about a noun. What kind of word is **some**? *A describing word.*

**Some means an amount of something but not an exact number.** Say the word that means "an amount of something but not an exact number." *Some.*

I'll tell you about something. If I tell about an amount of that thing but not the exact number, say "some." If not, don't say anything.

- I have money in my pocket. *Some.*
- I have no money in my pocket.
- There are birds that swim. *Some.*
- There are cars that run on electricity. *Some.*

- Every fish can swim.
- Not all my children are tall. *Some.*

What describing word means "an amount of something but not an exact number"? *Some.*

⊙━ **Mammal**

Scientists divide all living things into two groups: plants and animals. The animal group is divided into smaller groups. One of these groups is mammals. Scientists use a scientific explanation to help people learn what a mammal is. **Mammal.** Say the word. *Mammal.*

This is the scientific explanation of what a **mammal** is. **A mammal is an animal that:**
> **has a skeleton**
> **is warm-blooded**
> **makes milk for its babies**
> **has hair.**

Scientists use this information to help them decide if an animal is a mammal or not. For an animal to be a mammal, it must have all of these characteristics. Let's be scientists and decide if a human could be a mammal. (If children answer a question incorrectly, give them the answer and explain that the characteristic is or is not a quality of that animal.)

Does a human have a skeleton? *Yes.*

Is a human warm-blooded? *Yes.*

Does a human make milk for its babies? *Yes.*

Does a human have hair? *Yes.*

So could a human be a mammal? *Yes.*

Good using the scientific explanation to help you make that decision.

Let's be scientists and decide if a robin could be a mammal.

Does a robin have a skeleton? *Yes.*

Is a robin warm-blooded? *Yes.*

Does a robin make milk for its babies? *No.*

Does a robin have hair? *No.*

So is a robin a mammal? *No.*

Good using the scientific explanation to help you make that decision.

What group of animals does a robin belong to? *Birds.*

**Preparation:** Display KWL chart. Photocopy the four pages of the afterword so you can show children the illustrations while you read the additional information.

## Introduce Afterword

Sometimes when people write a nonfiction book, after they finish the main part of the book they want to tell you more facts. This information is put in the book **after** the last **word** of the main part of the book, so it is called an **afterword.**

Today I'll read the afterword that Cathryn Sill wrote for *About Mammals* so you can learn more about mammals. In this afterword, Catherine Sill wrote more information to go with each plate that John Sill painted.

(Read the afterword aloud a paragraph at a time.)

## Complete KWL Chart

(Review with children the questions they still want answered from the *W* column of the KWL chart.) Let's see if Cathryn Sill answered any of our questions in the afterword of her book.

**Plate 1.** Did these facts answer any of our questions? (Some of the vocabulary used in the afterword is higher-level vocabulary and may require you to explain using simpler language. If the item did answer any of the remaining questions, put a check mark in front of the question, and write the answer in the *L* column next to the question. Repeat the question, and have children say the answer. If the item did not answer any of the remaining questions, ask children leading questions, such as:) What is a fact we learned about mammals' hair? (Idea: *It protects mammals in ways uniquely adapted for each species.*)

(Record the fact in the *L* column near the bottom. Do not write the fact next to any of the unanswered questions.)

(Repeat the process for the remaining plates. If there are any unanswered questions after you have read and discussed the afterword, challenge children to find the answers in the school library, on the Internet, or at home.)

## Summarize the Afterword

The afterword tells us true facts about mammals. Facts are things that are true and that can be proved. For example, it is a fact that baby mammals drink milk from their mothers. We can prove this fact by watching a baby mammal drink milk from its mother.

When we summarize what we read we tell the most important things in our own words. I'm going to read each fact that Cathryn Sill wrote.

(Read the first fact.) My turn to summarize the fact. Hair protects mammals. Say the fact. *Hair protects mammals.*

(Repeat this procedure for plates 2 to 4.)

Plate 2: (Idea: *Musk Oxen have hair that keeps them warm in places that are very cold.*)

Plate 3: (Idea: *Quills protect porcupines from their enemies.*)

Plate 4: (Idea: *Walruses use their whiskers to help them find food.*)

Your turn to summarize the rest of the facts.

(Read each fact for plates 5 to 18. After you read each fact, work with the children to elicit a summative statement. Have all of the children repeat each summative fact as it is given.)

Plate 5: (Ideas: *Bison are the biggest animals that live on land in North America. People almost killed all the bison.*)

Plate 6: (Idea: *White-footed Mice babies stop drinking milk from their mothers when they are about three weeks old.*)

Plate 7: (IdeaS: *Baby Elk can run very fast right after they are born. This protects them from animals that want to eat them.*)

Plate 8: (Idea: *Pronghorns are the fastest mammals in North America.*)

Plate 9: (Ideas: *Red Squirrels are rodents. Rodents have to chew lots to keep their teeth short.*)

Plate 10: (Idea: *Blue Whales are the biggest animals in the world.*)

Plate 11: (Idea: *Bats are the only mammals that fly.*)

Plate 12: (Idea: *Most of the time Bobcats hunt rabbits, squirrels, and mice.*)

Plate 13: (Ideas: *Pikas gather many things for food. They do not hibernate.*)

Plate 14: (Ideas: *Black Bears are the most common bear in North America. They eat lots of different things.*)

Plate 15: (Idea: *Artic Foxes change color to hide from their enemies and from the animals that they hunt.*)

Plate 16: (Ideas: *Blacktail Jackrabbits are not really rabbits. They are hares.*)

Plate 17: (Ideas: *Muskrats have flat tails that help them swim. They build their houses in water.*)

Plate 18: (Idea: *We must take care of our environment so that the mammals can live.*)

We did a great job of summarizing facts about mammals.

## Play the Threesies Game

Today, you are going to play the *Threesies* game. I'll tell you a word you learned when we read *About Mammals.* After I tell you the word, you need to tell me three important things about the word. Each time you tell me something important about the word, you will win one point.

If you can't tell me three things about the word, I will tell you things and I will win one point for each thing I tell you. Once three things have been said about the word, you will have a chance to win two bonus points by using the word in a good sentence. How can you win two bonus points? *By using the word in a good sentence.*

Let's practice. Here's my word. **Both.** Tell me one thing you know about the word **both.** Tell me another thing you know about **both.** Tell me a third thing you know about **both.** (Ideas: *Both is a describing word; both means one thing and another thing; some mammals eat both plants and animals.*) Now you have a chance to earn two bonus points. Raise your hand if you can use **both** in a good sentence.

Now you're ready to play the game. (Draw a T-chart on the board for keeping score. Children earn one point for each correct response. If they make a mistake or are unable to give an idea, give an appropriate idea and record one point for yourself. If they can use the word in a good sentence, award two points. Model a good sentence using the word if necessary, and record two points for yourself. Repeat missed words at the end of the game.)

- Your first word is **desert.**
- Your next word is **marsh.**
- Your next word is **protect.**
- Your next word is **mammal.**
- Your last word is **some.**

(Tally the points and declare a winner.) You did a great job playing *Threesies!*

---

## DAY 4

**Preparation:** Photocopy and assemble the *Let's Learn About Mammals* booklet.

Print the following words in two columns on the board *mammal, hair, milk, warm-blooded, questions, move, moving, climb, whales, humans, places, dry.*

---

### Introduce the
### Let's Learn About Mammals Booklet

(Point to each word as you read it.) This word is **mammal.** What word? *Mammal.* This word is **hair.** What word? *Hair.* (Repeat process for remaining words.)

Let's read these words together. First word? *Mammal.* Next word? *Hair.* (Repeat process for remaining words.)

Read these words by yourself. First word? *Mammal.* Next word? *Hair.* (Repeat process for remaining words until children can read the list accurately and confidently.)

(Use the following correction procedure if the children make an error:) This word is **move.** What word? *Move.* Yes, **move.** (Go back to the top of the list and repeat the list until children can read it accurately and confidently.)

(Give each child a copy of the *Let's Learn About Mammals* booklet.) This is your very own book about mammals. The title of this book is *Let's Learn About Mammals.* What's the title of the book? *Let's Learn About Mammals.*

My turn to read each page of the book. You touch under each word as I read it. (Read pages 1–4.)

Let's read the book together. (Have the children read chorally with you.)

(Assign each child a partner. Allow sufficient time for each child to read the first four pages of the booklet to his or her partner. Circulate as children read, offering praise and assistance.)

(Children should color the illustrations in their *Let's Learn About Mammals* booklet. Encourage them to color the illustrations accurately.) This book is a science book. When artists color scientific illustrations, they use colors that are real. (Show children the front cover of the booklet. Point to the puppy.) What color could a puppy be? (Ideas: *Brown, black, gray.* Point to the kitten.) What color could a kitten be? (Ideas: *Brown, black, gray, orange.*) Remember to use the real colors when you color the illustrations.

### Play the Threesies Game
### (Cumulative Review)

We are going to play the *Threesies* game. I'll tell you a word you have learned. The word I say can be any word you have learned since we read *Suki's Kimono,* so don't let me trick you.

After I tell you the word, you need to tell me three important things about the word. Each time you tell me something important about the word, you will win one point.

If you can't tell me three things about the word, I will tell you things and I will win one point for each thing I tell you. Once three things have been said about the word, you will have a chance to win two bonus points by using the word in a good sentence.

Now you're ready to play the game. (Draw a T-chart on the board for keeping score. Children earn one point for each correct response. If they make a mistake or are unable to give an idea, give an appropriate idea and record one point for yourself. If they can use the word in a good sentence, award two points. Model a good sentence using the word if necessary, and record two points for yourself. Repeat missed words at the end of the game.)

- Your first word is **mammal.**
- Your next word is **fascinated.**
- Your next word is **gaze.**
- Your next word is **protect.**
- Your next word is **characteristics.**
- Your next word is **both.**
- Your next word is **desert.**
- Your next word is **marsh.**
- Your next word is **warm-blooded.**
- Your last word is **custom.**

(Tally the points and declare a winner.) You did a great job playing *Threesies!*

### DAY 5

**Preparation:** Children will need their copies of *Let's Learn About Mammals.*

Class *Reading Goals* chart that was started in Week 16.

Each child will need a copy of the Quiz Answer Sheet, BLM B.

## Read the
## Let's Learn About Mammals Booklet

(Assign each child a partner.) Today you'll read the first four pages of your book about mammals to your partner. (Allow sufficient time for each child to read the first four pages of the book to his or her partner. Circulate as children read, offering praise and assistance.)

(Ask children to look at the back of their books about mammals.) This part of the book is for people who can help you find other books to read. It tells those people about other books that are like *About Mammals.* It also tells them about a place where you can find other books. Where are some places that you could go to find other books about mammals? (Ideas: *To the school library; to the public library; to a bookstore.*)

(You may wish to read and discuss the information on the back cover.)

There's one more important thing on the back cover of your book. Touch the box that is at the bottom of the page. The words above the box say "My reading goal." What do the words say? *My reading goal.*

A goal is something that you want to succeed at doing. What is a goal? *Something that you want to succeed at doing.* A reading goal is something that you want to succeed at doing with your reading.

Let's see if we can add some other reading goals to our class chart. What are some other reading goals that someone might have when they read their book? (Accept reasonable responses. Help children put their ideas into goal statements. Add to the list of goal statements. Ask children to choose a goal and copy it into the box. Children may also make up an original goal that is not on the list. If children are unable to copy the goals or to write a goal of their own, you or a helper may wish to scribe their goal statements for them before the booklets are sent home.)

### Assess Comprehension
(Ask children to turn to page 5 in their booklets.) This is what you have read in your book about mammals, but with no pictures. You are going to have a little quiz to see if you can remember what you read.

(Ask children to touch under the words as they read the passage silently. Monitor to ensure that they are reading the passage. Ask them to look up at you after they have finished reading the passage. Instruct children to read and answer the questions. You may need to give additional guidance and practice if children do not know how to fill in bubbles to indicate a correct answer.)

### Assess Vocabulary
(Give each child a copy of the Quiz Answer Sheet, BLM B.)

Today you're going to have a True or False quiz. When you do the True or False quiz, it shows me how well you know the hard words you are learning.

If I say something that is true, circle the word **true**. What will you do if I say something that is true? *Circle the word* true.

If I say something that is false, circle the word **false.** What will you do if I say something that is false? *Circle the word* false.

Listen carefully to each item that I say. Don't let me trick you!

Item 1: If you find yourself in a hot, sandy place with very few plants, you are probably in the **desert.** (*True.*)

Item 2: If someone gives you **advice,** they are telling you exactly what you must do. (*False.*)

Item 3: A group of birds flying south together is called a **flock.** (*True.*)

Item 4: If you **desert** someone or something, you stay and take care of them. (*False.*)

Item 5: If you ate only your fruit and not your vegetables, you could tell your mom you ate **both** of them. (*False.*)

Item 6: A **marsh** is a dry, sandy area where few plants grow. (*False.*)

Item 7: Wearing a bike helmet and a seatbelt are two ways to **protect** yourself from getting hurt. (*True.*)

Item 8: If there were **some** coins in the piggy bank, you wouldn't know exactly how many. (*True.*)

Item 9: A **warm-blooded** animal gets warmer when the weather is hot. (*False.*)

Item 10: People are **mammals.** (*True.*)

You did a great job completing your quiz!

(Score children's work. A child must score 9 out of 10 to be at the mastery level. If a child does not achieve mastery, insert the missed words as additional items in the games in next week's lessons. Retest those children individually for the missed items before they take the next mastery test.)

## Extensions

### Read a Book as a Reward

(Read *About Mammals* or another nonfiction book about mammals to children as a reward for their hard work.)

**Preparation:** Word containers for the Super Scientist Center.

You will need the 3-column sorting chart from Lesson 16.

You will need to make two copies of the Picture Vocabulary Card for **desert.**

 **Introduce the Super Scientists Center**

(Add this week's Picture Vocabulary Cards to the cards from Week 16. Show children the word container and the sorting chart. If children need more guidance in how to work in the Super Scientists Center, role-play with two to three children as a demonstration.)

Let's think about how we work with our words in the Super Scientists Center.

You will work with a partner in the Super Scientists Center. Whom will you work with? *A partner.*

Scientists observe things carefully and try to find ways that things are alike. They put things that have the same characteristics together in groups. These groups are called categories. What are groups of things with the same characteristics called? *Categories.*

You are going to think about what you know about your vocabulary words and put them into categories.

First you will look at the categories I have written on this chart. What will you do first? *Look at the categories on the chart.* This week you are going to use the categories *nouns, verbs,* and *words that describe nouns.* What are your categories for this week? (Ideas: *Nouns, verbs,* and *words that describe nouns.*)

Next you and your partner will read each word from the container. What will you and your partner do next? *Read each word.*

After you read each word, you and your partner will talk about what you know about each word and decide which category it should go in. What will you and your partner do after you read each word? (Idea: *Talk about what we know about each word and decide which category to put it in.*) You will find one word that has two cards. That word can be placed in two different categories depending on how it is used.

**Preparation:** You will need a copy of *About Reptiles* for each day's lesson.

Number the pages of the story to assist you in asking comprehension questions at appropriate points.

Prepare a KWL chart titled *Reptiles* on a sheet of chart paper.

Post a copy of the Vocabulary Tally Sheet, BLM A, with this week's Picture Vocabulary Cards attached.

Each child will need one copy of the Homework Sheet, BLM 18a.

## DAY 1

### Introduce Book

This week's book is called *About Reptiles*. What's the title of this week's book? *About Reptiles.*

This book is true. When an author writes books about things that are true, those books are called nonfiction books. What kinds of books are about true things? *Nonfiction books.*

This book was written by Cathryn Sill. Who's the author of *About Reptiles*? *Cathryn Sill.*

John Sill made the pictures for this book. Who is the illustrator of *About Reptiles*? *John Sill.* Who made the illustrations for this book? *John Sill.*

The cover of a book usually gives us some hints of what the book is about. Let's look at the front cover of *About Reptiles*. What do you see in the illustration? (Ideas: *A lizard on a rock; it is sunny and you can see its shadow; many large rocks; a few flowers and grasses.*)

(Display KWL chart.) Let's think about what we **know** about reptiles. Raise your hand if you can tell us something you know about reptiles. I'll write it down under the **K. K** stands for what we **know** about reptiles. What does **K** stand for? *What we know about reptiles.* (Record all children's responses under the *K* (know) section of the chart. Do not eliminate incorrect

## About Reptiles
author: Cathryn Sill • illustrator: John Sill

### Target Vocabulary

| Tier II | Tier III |
|---|---|
| hibernate | nonfiction |
| venom | fact |
| prey | plate |
| capture | afterword |
| *cold-blooded | |
| reptile | |

*Expanded Target Vocabulary Word

responses. They will be addressed in later lessons during the week.)

The things we know about reptiles that are true are called facts. What are the true things we know about reptiles called? *Facts.*

(Point to the *K* column on the chart.) Some of the things you have told us are facts about reptiles, and some of the things you have told us are not true. When we've finished reading *About Reptiles,* we'll come back to our chart and look at it again.

Now let's think what you **want to know** about reptiles. I'll write it down under the **W. W** stands for what we **want to know** about reptiles. What does **W** stand for? *What we want to know about reptiles.* (Record all children's questions under the *W* (want to know) section of the chart. If children tell about reptiles instead of ask questions, prompt them to ask a question.)

### Take a Picture Walk

(Encourage children to use target words in their answers.) We're going to take a picture walk through this book. When we take a picture walk through a nonfiction book, we look carefully at the pictures and tell what we see. When you look carefully at pictures, you observe those pictures. What do you do when you look carefully at pictures in a nonfiction book? *You observe those pictures.*

All of the illustrations for this book were painted by John Sill. Sometimes when a nonfiction book is published with paintings, each painting is

called a plate. What are paintings for a nonfiction book sometimes called? *Plates.* The plates in a nonfiction book are usually numbered. The first plate in the book would be called Plate 1. What would we call the first plate in the book? *Plate 1.* What would we call the second plate in the book? *Plate 2.* What would we call the third plate in the book? *Plate 3.*

**Page 2.** What do you observe in Plate 1? (Ideas: *A long, green snake wrapped around the branches of a tree.*)

**Page 4.** What do you observe in Plate 2? (Ideas: *A turtle walking among some plants and mushrooms.*)

**Page 6.** What do you observe in Plate 3? (Ideas: *A lizard on a rock; the lizard has spikes on its body.*)

**Page 8.** What do you observe in Plate 4? (Ideas: *A thin, long snake with stripes; tree branches; litter and leaves.*)

**Page 10.** What do you observe in Plate 5? (Ideas: *A striped lizard on a fallen tree; ferns; flowers.*)

**Page 12.** What do you observe in Plate 6? (Ideas: *A turtle swimming underwater; sea plants; fish.*)

**Page 14.** What do you observe in Plate 7? (Ideas: *The picture from the front cover; a lizard on a rock; it is sunny and you can see the lizard's shadow; rocks; some flowers and grasses.*)

**Page 16.** What do you observe in Plate 8? (Ideas: *A turtle hiding in its shell in the mud; a catfish; some trees.*)

**Page 18.** What do you observe in Plate 9? (Ideas: *A very long, thick snake with spots slithering through leaves; trees.*)

**Page 20.** What do you observe in Plate 10? (Ideas: *A turtle about to bite on a cactus; the turtle is large with a big shell.*)

**Page 22.** What do you observe in Plate 11? (Ideas: *A large snake with a diamond pattern; the snake has very long fangs; plants.*)

**Page 24.** What do you observe in Plate 12? (Ideas: *An alligator with lots of teeth; baby alligators; eggs.*)

**Page 26.** What do you observe in Plate 13? (Ideas: *A long, thin snake wrapped around itself; It has spots down the middle of its body; plants.*)

**Page 28.** What do you observe in Plate 14? (Ideas: *Lots of turtles heading toward the sea; sand; seashells.*)

**Page 30.** What do you observe in Plate 15? (Ideas: *Two small lizards; one lizard is on the sill; the other is on the flower pot; they are green.*)

### Read the Book Aloud

(Read the book to children with minimal interruptions, ending with page 29.)

Tomorrow we will read the book again, and I will ask you some questions.

### Present the Target Vocabulary

 Hibernate

In the book, the author says, "They hibernate in cold, winter weather." **Hibernate.** Say the word. *Hibernate.*

**Hibernate** is a verb. It tells an action. What kind of word is **hibernate?** *A verb.*

**When an animal hibernates, it spends the winter in a deep sleep.** Say the word that means "to spend the winter in a deep sleep." *Hibernate.*

(Correct any incorrect responses, and repeat the item at the end of the sequence.)

Let's think about the word hibernate. I'll tell about some animals. If the animals have been hibernating, say "hibernate." If not, don't say anything.

- The dog woke from a long mid-day nap.
- The bear woke in the spring after sleeping all winter and immediately went in search of food. *Hibernate.*
- A snail plugs up its shell and sleeps until spring. *Hibernate.*
- When Lonnie was sick, she stayed in bed all weekend.
- The birds flew south to spend the long, cold winter months.
- In the fall, the chipmunks stock up on food to get ready for their long sleep. *Hibernate.*

What verb means "to spend the winter in a deep sleep"? *Hibernate.*

 *Venom*

In the book, the author says, "Some reptiles use venom to capture their prey." **Venom.** Say the word. *Venom.*

**Venom** is a noun. It names a thing. What kind of word is **venom**? *A noun.*

**Venom is a poison made by some snakes, spiders, and insects.** Say the word that means "a poison made by some snakes, spiders, and insects." *Venom.*

Let's think about venom. I'll tell about some animals. If you think the animal used venom, say "venom." If not, don't say anything.

- The large snake bit the coyote and the coyote died. *Venom.*
- The cat bit the little boy.
- The spider stung its prey to kill it. *Venom.*
- The dead animal appeared to have been bitten by a snake. *Venom.*
- The lion attacked a deer in the forest.
- The spider stung the fly caught in its web and then wrapped it in silk thread to eat later. *Venom.*

What noun means "a poison made by some snakes, spiders, and insects"? *Venom.*

 *Prey*

In the book, the author tells us that some reptiles use venom to capture their prey. **Prey.** Say the word. *Prey.*

**Prey** is a noun. It names a thing. What kind of word is **prey**? *A noun.*

**Prey is an animal that is hunted by another animal for food.** Say the word that means "an animal that is hunted by another animal for food." *Prey.*

I'll tell you about some animals. If one of the animals is being hunted for food, say "prey." If not, don't say anything.

- The frog hopped after the fly. *Prey.*
- The dogs chased each other around the park.

- A lion chased after a gazelle in the grasslands of Africa. *Prey.*
- The cheetah waited silently for the animal to come out of the bushes. *Prey.*
- Two little birds flew around their nest.
- The spider approached the dragonfly that was caught in its web. *Prey.*

What noun means "an animal that is hunted by another animal for food"? *Prey.*

 *Capture*

In the book, the author tells us that some reptiles use venom to capture their prey. **Capture.** Say the word. *Capture.*

**Capture** is a verb. It tells what something does. What kind of word is **capture**? *A verb.*

**If you capture something, that means you catch it by using force.** Say the word that means "to catch something by using force." *Capture.*

I'll tell you about some situations. If I tell about somebody or something capturing another, say "capture." If not, don't say anything.

- Some spiders bite their prey to poison them. *Capture.*
- A rabbit accidentally hopped into a lion's den.
- The woman set up mousetraps in her basement. *Capture.*
- The boa constrictor squeezes its prey to death. *Capture.*
- The children caught lightning bugs in a jar. *Capture.*
- The squirrel got its paw stuck between two branches.

What verb means "to catch something by using force"? *Capture.*

### Present Vocabulary Tally Sheet
(See Lesson 1, page 4, for instructions.)

### Assign Homework
(Homework Sheet, BLM 18a. See the Introduction for homework instructions.)

**Preparation:** Picture Vocabulary
Cards for *hibernate, venom, prey, capture.*

### Read and Discuss Story

(Encourage children to use previously taught target words in their answers.)

**Page 1.** What fact did we learn about reptiles? *Reptiles have dry, scaly skin.* Plate 1 shows a Rough Green Snake. What reptile is shown in Plate 1? *A Rough Green Snake.* Where do you think a Rough Green Snake likes to live? (Idea: *Among trees and plants.*)

**Page 3.** What fact did we learn about reptiles? *Some reptiles have a hard, bony plate.* Plate 2 shows an Eastern Box Turtle. What reptile is shown in Plate 2? *An Eastern Box Turtle.*

**Pages 5–7.** What fact did we learn about reptiles? (Idea: *Some reptiles have short legs or no legs at all.*) Plate 3 shows a Texas Horned Lizard. What reptile is shown in Plate 3? *A Texas Horned Lizard.* What do you think the lizard has these horns for? (Idea: *To protect itself from its enemies.*) Plate 4 shows a Slender Glass Lizard. What reptile is shown in Plate 4? *A Slender Glass Lizard.* How do you think this lizard moves with no legs? (Ideas: *Like a snake; it slithers.*)

**Pages 9–11.** What fact did we learn about reptiles? *They move by crawling or by swimming.* Plate 5 shows a Five-lined Skink. What reptile is shown in Plate 5? *A Five-lined Skink.* Plate 6 shows a Green Turtle. What reptile is shown in Plate 6? *A Green Turtle.* What does this turtle have that makes it able to swim easily? (Idea: *Flippers.*)

**Page 13.** What fact did we learn about reptiles? *Reptiles need warm temperatures.* Plate 7 shows a Collared Lizard. What reptile is shown in Plate 7? *A Collared Lizard.*

**Page 15.** What fact did we learn about reptiles? (Idea: *Reptiles hibernate in cold winter weather.*) Plate 8 shows a Painted Turtle. What reptile is shown in Plate 7? *A Painted Turtle.* Why do Painted Turtles hibernate in the winter?

(Idea: *They are reptiles and reptiles need warm temperatures.*)

**Page 17.** What fact did we learn about reptiles? *Most reptiles are meat eaters.* Plate 9 shows a Corn Snake. What reptile is shown in Plate 8? *A Corn Snake.*

**Page 19.** What fact did we learn about reptiles? *A few eat meat and plants.* Plate 10 shows a Desert Tortoise. What reptile is shown in Plate 10? *A Desert Tortoise.*

**Page 21.** What fact did we learn about reptiles? *Some reptiles use venom to capture their prey.* Plate 11 shows an Eastern Diamondback Rattlesnake. What reptile is shown in Plate 11? *An Eastern Diamondback Rattlesnake.* How do you think this snake gets its venom into its prey? (Idea: *It bites.*)

**Page 23.** What fact did we learn about reptiles? *Baby reptiles hatch from eggs.* Plate 12 shows American Alligators. What reptile is shown in Plate 12? *American Alligators.* What other animals hatch from eggs? (Ideas: *Birds; insects.*)

**Page 25.** What fact did we learn about reptiles? (Idea: *In some reptiles, the mother carries the eggs inside her body until they are ready to hatch.*) Plate 13 shows a Common Garter Snake. What reptile is shown in Plate 13? *A Common Garter Snake.* Where are this snake's eggs? (Idea: *Inside her body.*)

**Page 27.** What fact did we learn about reptiles? (Idea: *Young reptiles care for themselves as soon as they hatch.*) Plate 14 shows Loggerhead Turtles. What reptile is shown in Plate 14? *Loggerhead Turtles.*

**Page 29.** Cathryn Sill ended her book with an important message to us. What does she want us to remember? *Reptiles are important to us.* Plate 15 shows Green Anoles. What reptile is shown in Plate 15? *Green Anoles.*

(Display KWL chart.) Now that we've finished reading *About Reptiles,* let's look at our chart again.

(Point to the *Know* column.) As good scientists find out more about things, they sometimes change their minds about what they know is true. Let's see if we want to change our minds about any of the items on our **Know** list.

(Read each item. Ask children if that item was mentioned in the book. If it was, ask if the item is true or not true. Not true items are crossed out.) We're good scientists; we know how to change our minds when we learn new facts.

(Point to the *Want to Know* column.) As good scientists find out more about things, they find answers to some of their questions, and they want to ask more questions. (Read each question. Ask children if that question was answered in the book. If it was, record the answer in the *L* (Learned) column and put a check mark in front of the question.)

Are there any new questions we would like to ask about reptiles? (Record questions in the *W* column.) We're good scientists; we know how to use what we have learned to ask new questions.

## Review Vocabulary

(Display the Picture Vocabulary Cards. Point to each card as you say the word. Ask children to repeat each word after you.) These pictures show **hibernate, venom, prey,** and **capture.**

- What word means "a poison made by some snakes, spiders, and insects"? *Venom.*
- What word means "an animal that is hunted by another animal for food"? *Prey.*
- What word means "spend the winter in a deep sleep"? *Hibernate.*
- What word means "catch something by using force"? *Capture.*

## Extend Vocabulary
 Prey

In *About Reptiles,* we learned that **prey** is "a noun meaning an animal that is hunted by another animal for food." Say the word that means "an animal that is hunted by another animal for food." *Prey.*

Raise your hand if you can tell us a sentence that uses **prey** as a noun meaning "an animal that is hunted by another animal for food." (Call on several children. If they don't use complete sentences, restate their examples as sentences. Have the class repeat the sentences.)

Here's a new way to use the word **prey.**

- Large jungle cats **prey** on other animals.

- Birds **prey** on insects and some small animals.
- Wild cats **prey** on mice and birds.

**In these sentences, prey is a verb that means to hunt and eat.** What word means "to hunt and eat"? *Prey.*

Raise your hand if you can tell us a sentence that uses **prey** as a verb meaning "to hunt and eat." (Call on several children. If they don't use complete sentences, restate their examples as sentences. Have the class repeat the sentences.)

## Present Expanded Target Vocabulary
◎= Cold-blooded

In *About Reptiles,* Cathryn and John Sill wrote about and made paintings of many different kinds of reptiles. We learned about many characteristics of reptiles. One characteristic of reptiles that was not in the book is that all reptiles are cold-blooded. **Cold-blooded.** Say the word. *Cold-blooded.*

**Cold-blooded** is a describing word. It describes nouns. What kind of word is **cold-blooded?** *A describing word.*

**Cold-blooded animals are animals whose body temperatures change to match the temperature around them.** Say the word that describes "animals whose body temperatures change to match the temperature around them." *Cold-blooded.*

I'll tell about animals. If these animals are cold-blooded, say "cold-blooded." If not, don't say anything.

- The lizard's body temperature went up in the hot desert sun. *Cold-blooded.*
- Even in the icy arctic waters, the body temperature of a walrus stays warm.
- Humans can live in many different kinds of places because their body temperature stays the same no matter what the temperature is.
- When it gets cold, fish go to the bottom of the lake to hibernate. *Cold-blooded.*
- Many reptiles hibernate in the winter because it is too cold for them. *Cold-blooded.*
- Some mammals hibernate in the winter because there is not enough food.

What word describes "animals whose body temperatures change to match the temperature around them"? *Cold-blooded.*

◎— *Reptile*

Scientists divide all living things into two groups; plants and animals. The animal group is divided into smaller groups. One of these groups is reptiles. Scientists use a scientific explanation to help people learn what a reptile is. **Reptile.** Say the word. *Reptile.*

This is the scientific explanation of what a **reptile** is. **A reptile is an animal that:**

> **has a skeleton**
> **is cold-blooded**
> **lays eggs**
> **has dry scales or hard plates on its skin.**

Scientists use this information to help them decide if an animal is a reptile or not. For an animal to be a reptile, it must have all of these characteristics. Let's be scientists and decide if a human could be a reptile.

Does a human have a skeleton? *Yes.*

Is a human cold-blooded? *No.*

Does a human lay eggs? *No.*

Is a human's skin covered in dry scales or hard plates? *No.*

So could a human be a reptile? *No.*

Good job using the scientific explanation to help you make that decision.

Let's be scientists and decide if a crocodile could be a reptile.

Does a crocodile have a skeleton? *Yes.*

Is a crocodile cold-blooded? *Yes.*

Does a crocodile lay eggs? *Yes.*

Is a crocodile's skin covered in dry scales or hard plates? *Yes.*

So is a crocodile a reptile? *Yes.*

Good job using the scientific explanation to help you make that decision.

---

### DAY 3

**Preparation:** Display KWL chart. You may wish to photocopy the four pages of the afterword so you can show children the illustrations while you read the additional information.

### Introduce Afterword

Sometimes when people write a nonfiction book, after they finish the main part of the book they want to tell you more facts. This information is put in the book **after** the last **word** of the main part of the book, so it is called an **afterword.**

Today I'll read the afterword that Cathryn Sill wrote for *About Reptiles* so you can learn more about reptiles. In this afterword, Catherine Sill wrote more information to go with each plate that John Sill painted.

(Read the afterword aloud a paragraph at a time.)

### Complete KWL Chart

(Review with children the questions they still want answered from the *W* column of the KWL chart.) Let's see if Cathryn Sill answered any of our questions in the afterword of her book.

**Plate 1.** Did these facts answer any of our questions? (If the item did answer any of the remaining questions, put a check mark in front of the question, and write the answer in the *L* column next to the question. Repeat the question, and have children say the answer. If the item did not answer any of the remaining questions, ask children leading questions, such as:) What are two ways reptiles shed their skin? (Ideas: *Bit by bit; in one long piece.* Record the fact in the *L* column near the bottom. Do not write the fact next to any of the unanswered questions.)

(Repeat the process for the remaining plates. If there are any unanswered questions after you have read and discussed the afterword, challenge children to find the answers in the school library, on the Internet, or at home.)

## Summarize the Afterword

The afterword tells us true facts about reptiles. Facts are things that are true and that can be proved. For example, it is a fact that snakes don't have legs. We can prove this fact by looking at a snake.

When we summarize what we read we tell the most important things in our own words. I'm going to read each fact that Cathryn Sill wrote.

(Read the first fact.) My turn to summarize the fact. Reptiles have dry, scaly skin. Say the fact. *Reptiles have dry, scaly skin.*

(Repeat this procedure for plates 2 to 4.)

Plate 2: (Idea: *Turtles have shells to protect them.*)

Plate 3: (Idea: *Texas horned lizards have many ways to protect themselves.*)

Plate 4: (Idea: *Slender glass lizards don't have any legs.*)

Your turn to summarize the rest of the facts.

(Read each fact for plates 5 to 15. After you read each fact, work with the children to elicit a summative statement. Have all of the children repeat each summative fact as it is given.)

Plate 5: (Idea: *Five-lined skinks live on the group in the damp woods.*)

Plate 6: (Idea: *Green turtles live in both the Atlantic and Pacific Oceans.*)

Plate 7: (Idea: *Reptiles are cold-blooded.*)

Plate 8: (Idea: *Painted turtles are the most common turtle in North America.*)

Plate 9: (Ideas: *Corn snakes are good climbers. But, most of the time you will find them on the ground or underground.*)

Plate 10: (Ideas: *Desert tortoises eat in the morning or late afternoon. They go into burrows when it gets too hot.*)

Plate 11: (Ideas: *Eastern diamondback rattlesnakes are the biggest snakes. They are the most poisonous snakes in North America.*)

Plate 12: (Idea: *American alligators are the largest reptile in North America.*)

Plate 13: (Idea: *Common garter snakes can be found almost anywhere in North America.*)

Plate 14: (Idea: *Loggerhead turtles are the most common sea turtle in North America.*)

Plate 15: (Ideas: *There are lots of green anoles in the American South. Reptiles are important because they eat rodents and insects that can hurt us.*)

We did a great job of summarizing facts about reptiles.

## Play the Threesies Game

Today you are going to play the *Threesies* game. I'll tell you a word you learned when we read *About Reptiles.* After I tell you the word, you need to tell me three important things about the word. Each time you tell me something important about the word, you will win one point.

If you can't tell me three things about the word, I will tell you things and I will win one point for each thing I tell you. Once three things have been said about the word, you will have a chance to win two bonus points by using the word in a good sentence. How can you win two bonus points? *By using the word in a good sentence.*

Let's practice. Here's my word. **Hibernate.** Tell me one thing you know about the word **hibernate.** Tell me another thing you know about **hibernate.** Tell me a third thing you know about **hibernate.** (Ideas: *Hibernate is a verb; it means to spend the winter in a deep sleep; mammals like bears and skunks hibernate because there is not enough food; some reptiles hibernate because they cannot survive the cold.*)

Now you have a chance to earn two bonus points. Raise your hand if you can use **hibernate** in a good sentence.

Now you're ready to play the game. (Draw a T-chart on the board for keeping score. Children earn one point for each correct response. If they make a mistake or are unable to give an idea, give an appropriate idea and record one point for yourself. If they can use the word in a good sentence, award two points. Model a good sentence using the word if necessary, and record two points for yourself. Repeat missed words at the end of the game.)

- Your first word is **prey.**
- Your next word is **venom.**
- Your next word is **capture.**
- Your next word is **reptile.**
- Your last word is **cold-blooded.**

(Tally the points and declare a winner.) You did a great job playing *Threesies!*

## DAY 4

**Preparation:** Photocopy and assemble the *Let's Learn About Reptiles* booklet.

Print the following words in two columns on the board: *reptiles, turtle, lizard, desert, alligator, cold-blooded, scales, crawl, hibernate, mice, people, Hawaii.*

### Introduce the
### Let's Learn About Reptiles Booklet

(Point to each word as you read it.) This word is **reptile.** What word? *Reptile.* This word is **turtle.** What word? *Turtle.* (Repeat process for remaining words.)

Let's read these words together. First word? *Reptile.* Next word? *Turtle.* (Repeat process for remaining words.)

Read these words by yourself. First word? *Reptile.* Next word? *Turtle.* (Repeat process for remaining words until children can read the list accurately and confidently.)

(Use the following correction procedure if children make an error:) This word is **crawl.** What word? *Crawl.* Yes, **crawl.** (Go back to the top of the list and repeat the list until children can read it accurately and confidently.)

(Give each child a copy of the *Let's Learn About Reptiles* booklet.) This is your very own book about reptiles. The title of this book is *Let's Learn About Reptiles.* What's the title of the book? *Let's Learn About Reptiles.*

My turn to read each page of the book. You touch under each word as I read it. (Read pages 1–4.)

Let's read the book together. (Have children read chorally with you.)

(Assign each child a partner. Allow sufficient time for each child to read the first four pages of the book to his or her partner. Circulate as children read, offering praise and assistance.)

(Children should color the illustrations in their *Let's Learn About Reptiles* booklet. Encourage them to color the illustrations accurately.) This book is a science book. When artists color scientific illustrations, they use colors that are real. (Show children the front cover of the booklet. Point to the turtle.) What color could a turtle be? (Ideas: *Light green; dark green; yellow.* Point to the squares around the edge of the shell.) What color should the inside of these squares be? (Ideas: *Reds; dark orange.*) Remember to use the real colors when you color the illustrations.

### Play the Threesies Game
### (Cumulative Review)

 We are going to play the *Threesies* game. I'll tell you a word you have learned. The word I say can be any word you have learned since we read *Suki's Kimono,* so don't let me trick you.

After I tell you the word, you need to tell me three important things about the word. Each time you tell me something important about the word, you will win one point.

If you can't tell me three things about the word, I will tell you things and I will win one point for each thing I tell you. Once three things have been said about the word, you will have a chance to win two bonus points by using the word in a good sentence.

Now you're ready to play the game. (Draw a T-chart on the board for keeping score. Children earn one point for each correct response. If they make a mistake or are unable to give an idea, give an appropriate idea and record one point for yourself. If they can use the word in a good sentence, award two points. Model a good sentence using the word if necessary, and record two points for yourself. Repeat missed words at the end of the game.)

- Your first word is **reptile.**
- Your next word is **capture.**
- Your next word is **prey.**

- Your next word is **hibernate.**
- Your next word is **jealous.**
- Your next word is **plot.**
- Your next word is **venom.**
- Your next word is **cold-blooded.**
- Your next word is **warm-blooded.**
- Your last word is **voyage.**

(Tally the points and declare a winner.) You did a great job playing *Threesies!*

## DAY 5

**Preparation:** Children will need their copies of *Let's Learn About Reptiles.*

Class *Reading Goals* chart that was started in Week 16.

Each child will need a copy of the Quiz Answer Sheet, BLM B.

### Read the
### Let's Learn About Reptiles Booklet

(Assign each child a partner.) Today you'll read the first four pages of your book about reptiles to your partner. (Allow sufficient time for each child to read the first four pages of the booklet to his or her partner. Circulate as children read, offering praise and assistance.)

(Ask children to look at the back of their booklets about reptiles.) This part of the book is for people who can help you find other books to read. It tells those people about other books that are like *About Reptiles.* It also tells them about a place where you can find other books. Where are some places that you could go to find other books about reptiles? (Ideas: *To the school library; to the public library; to a bookstore.*)

(You may wish to read and discuss the information on the back cover.)

There's one more important thing on the back cover of your book. Touch the box that is at the bottom of the page. The words above the box say "My reading goal." What do the words say? *My reading goal.*

A goal is something that you want to succeed at doing. What is a goal? *Something that you want to succeed at doing.* A reading goal is something that you want to succeed at doing with your reading.

Let's see if we can add some other reading goals to our class chart. What are some other reading goals that someone might have when they read their book? (Accept reasonable responses. Help children put their ideas into goal statements. Add to the list of goal statements. Ask children to choose a goal and copy it into the box. Children may also make up an original goal that is not on the list. If children are unable to copy the goals or to write a goal of their own, you or a helper may wish to scribe their goal statements for them before the booklets are sent home.)

### Assess Comprehension

(Ask children to turn to page 5 in their booklets.) This is what you have read in your book about reptiles, but with no pictures. You are going to have a little quiz to see if you can remember what you read.

(Ask children to touch under the words as they read the passage silently. Monitor to ensure that they are reading the passage. Ask them to look up at you after they have finished reading the passage. Instruct children to read and answer the questions. You may need to give additional guidance and practice if children do not know how to fill in bubbles to indicate a correct answer.)

### Assess Vocabulary

 (Give each child a copy of the Quiz Answer Sheet, BLM B.)

Today you're going to have a True or False quiz. When you do the True or False quiz, it shows me how well you know the hard words you are learning.

If I say something that is true, circle the word **true.** What will you do if I say something that is true? *Circle the word* true.

If I say something that is false, circle the word **false.** What will you do if I say something that is false? *Circle the word* false.

Listen carefully to each item that I say. Don't let me trick you!

Item 1: A kangaroo is a **reptile.** (*False.*)

Item 2: Some snakes use **venom** to kill their **prey.** (*True.*)

Item 3: **Prey** are animals that hunt other animals for food. (*False.*)

Item 4: A **mammal** has dry, scaly skin or hard plates. (*False.*)

Item 5: Large animals often **prey** on smaller animals to survive. (*True.*)

Item 6: Some **characteristics** of a cat are that they have four legs, a tail, pointy ears, and whiskers. (*True.*)

Item 7: Taking a two-hour nap is a form of **hibernating.** (*False.*)

Item 8: If you **capture** lightning bugs in a jar, you found them there. (*False.*)

Item 9: A **cold-blooded** animal gets warmer when the weather is hot. (*True.*)

Item 10: When birds **migrate,** they travel to a warmer place to spend the winter. (*True.*)

You did a great job completing your quiz!

(Score children's work. A child must score 9 out of 10 to be at the mastery level. If a child does not achieve mastery, insert the missed words as additional items in the games in next week's lessons. Retest those children individually for the missed items before they take the next mastery test.)

## Extensions

### Read a Book as a Reward

 (Read *About Reptiles* or another nonfiction book about reptiles to children as a reward for their hard work.)

---

**Preparation:** Word containers for the Super Scientists Center.

Create a 2-column chart on construction paper with the headings *noun (thing)* and *noun (place)*.

---

### Introduce the
### Super Scientists Center

(Add this week's Picture Vocabulary Cards to the cards from Weeks 16 and

17. Show children the word container and the sorting chart. If children need more guidance in how to work in the Super Scientists Center, role-play with two to three children as a demonstration.)

Let's think about how we work with our words in the Super Scientists Center.

You will work with a partner in the Super Scientists Center. Whom will you work with? *A partner.*

Scientists observe things carefully and try to find ways that things are alike. They put things that have the same characteristics together in groups. These groups are called categories. What are groups of things with the same characteristics called? *Categories.*

You are going to think about what you know about your vocabulary words and put them into categories.

First you will look at the categories I have written on this chart. What will you do first? *Look at the categories on the chart.* This week you are going to use the categories *nouns that are things* and *nouns that are places.* What are your categories for this week? (Ideas: *Nouns that are things; nouns that are places.*)

Next you and your partner will read each word from the container. What will you and your partner do next? *Read each word.*

After you read each word, you and your partner will talk about what you know about each word and decide which category it should go in. What will you and your partner do after you read each word? (Idea: *Talk about what we know about each word and decide which category to put it in.*) Be careful. Some words are not nouns, so they will not go on the chart. You can put those words back into the container. What do you do with words that are not nouns? *Put them back into the container.*

## About Fish

author: Cathryn Sill • illustrator: John Sill

**Preparation:** You will need a copy of *About Fish* for each day's lesson.

Number the pages of the book to assist you in asking comprehension questions at appropriate points.

Prepare a KWL chart titled *Fish* on a sheet of chart paper. `

You will need a globe of the world with the equator marked.

Post a copy of the Vocabulary Tally Sheet, BLM A, with this week's Picture Vocabulary Cards attached.

Each child will need one copy of the Homework Sheet, BLM 19a.

### Target Vocabulary

| Tier II | Tier III |
|---------|----------|
| tropical | nonfiction |
| school | fact |
| fool | plate |
| enemies | afterword |
| *species | |
| fish | |

*Expanded Target Vocabulary Word

### DAY 1

### Introduce Book

This week's book is called *About Fish.* What's the title of this week's book? *About Fish.*

This book is true. When an author writes books about things that are true, those books are called nonfiction books. What kinds of books are about true things? *Nonfiction books.*

This book was written by Cathryn Sill. Who's the author of *About Fish*? *Cathryn Sill.*

John Sill made the pictures for this book. Who's the illustrator of *About Fish*? *John Sill.* Who made the illustrations for this book? *John Sill.*

The cover of a book usually gives us some hints of what the book is about. Let's look at the front cover of *About Fish*. What do you see in the illustration? (Ideas: *A white and black fish with a yellow mouth swimming in the ocean; the fish has stripes on it and a dot near the back of its body; sea plants.*)

(Display KWL chart.) Let's think about what we **know** about fish. Raise your hand if you can tell us something you know about fish. I'll write it down under the **K. K** stands for what we **know** about fish. What does **K** stand for? *What we*

know about fish. (Record all children's responses under the *K* (know) section of the chart. Do not eliminate incorrect responses.

They will be addressed in later lessons during the week.)

The things we know about fish that are true are called facts. What are the true things we know about fish called? *Facts.*

(Point to the *K* column on the chart.) Some of the things you have told us are facts about fish, and some of the things you have told us are not true. When we've finished reading *About Fish,* we'll come back to our chart and look at it again.

Now let's think what you **want to know** about fish. I'll write it down under the **W. W** stands for what we **want to know** about fish. What does **W** stand for? *What we want to know about fish.* (Record all children's questions under the *W* (want to know) section of the chart. If children tell about fish instead of ask questions, prompt them to ask a question.)

### Take a Picture Walk

(Encourage children to use target words in their answers.) We're going to take a picture walk through this book. When we take a picture walk through a nonfiction book, we look carefully at the pictures and tell what we see. When you look carefully at pictures, you observe those pictures. What do you do when you look carefully at pictures in a nonfiction book? *You observe those pictures.*

All of the illustrations for this book were painted by John Sill. Sometimes when a nonfiction book is published with paintings, each painting is called a plate. What are paintings for a nonfiction book sometimes called? *Plates*. The plates in a nonfiction book are usually numbered. The first plate in the book would be called Plate 1. What would we call the first plate in the book? *Plate 1*. What would we call the second plate in the book? *Plate 2*. What would we call the third plate in the book? *Plate 3*.

**Page 2.** What do you observe in Plate 1? (Ideas: *A brown fish with black and red spots swimming in a river; rocks, leaves.*)

**Page 4.** What do you observe in Plate 2? (Ideas: *A long fish with white spots; it is swimming under the ice near the bottom; rocks.*)

**Page 6.** What do you observe in Plate 3? (Ideas: *A yellow and blue striped fish; coral; sea plants.*)

**Page 8.** What do you observe in Plate 4? (Ideas: *A rainbow-colored fish swimming among the rocks; a fish with lots of different colors.*)

**Page 10.** What do you observe in Plate 5? (Ideas: *Three fish; they are oval-shaped with stripes coming down from their backs; there is a black spot near their fin that looks like another eye.*)

**Page 12.** What do you observe in Plate 6? (Ideas: *Three white fish; one fish is puffed up with spines sticking out of it; another fish looks like the same kind of fish, but not puffed up; the third fish is hiding; water; barnacles on a log.*)

**Page 14.** What do you observe in Plate 7? (Ideas: *A long, skinny fish with a long nose; the fish has black spots along its body and on its fins; water plants; a group of smaller fish.*)

**Page 16.** What do you observe in Plate 8? (Ideas: *A gray fish with black spots; it looks like the fish is jumping into the waterfall; a rock.*)

**Page 18.** What do you observe in Plate 9? (Ideas: *A large fish with big eyes and mouth; it is hard to see because it blends into the bottom; rocks, sand, another little fish.*)

**Page 20.** What do you observe in Plate 10? (Ideas: *The same fish from the cover; a white fish with black stripes and a large black dot near its tail that looks like another eye; the fish has yellow on its mouth and one of its fins.*)

**Page 22.** What do you observe in Plate 11? (Ideas: *A lot of white fish swimming together; the fish have square faces; another group of fish; a water plant.*)

**Page 24.** What do you observe in Plate 12? (Ideas: *Two different pictures; a seahorse holding on to a plant with its tail; a lot of baby seahorses; a fish swimming on the bottom of a river or lake; the fish has sharp-looking spikes on its back; there is a pile of eggs under the grass; water plants.*)

**Page 26.** What do you observe in Plate 13? (Ideas: *A green fish with small fins and a big mouth; it looks like it's going after a smaller fish; there is a mossy branch in the water.*)

**Page 28.** What do you observe in Plate 14? (Ideas: *An enormous gray fish with white squares and dots on its body and fins; a scuba diver; some smaller fish.*)

**Page 30.** What do you observe in Plate 15? (Ideas: *Several fish with yellow and blue stripes; there are rows of spikes along their tails.*)

## Read the Book Aloud

(Read the book to children with minimal interruptions, ending with page 29.)

Tomorrow we will read the book again, and I will ask you some questions.

## Present the Target Vocabulary
Tropical

In the book, the author tells us that fish may be found in warm, tropical water. **Tropical.** Say the word. *Tropical.*

**Tropical** is a describing word. It tells more about a noun. What kind of word is **tropical?** *A describing word.*

**Tropical describes a place that is near the equator and very hot.** Say the word that describes a place that is "near the equator and very hot." *Tropical.* (Show children where the equator is located on the globe.)

(Correct any incorrect responses, and repeat the item at the end of the sequence.)

Let's think about the word **tropical.** I'll name some places. If the places sound tropical, say "tropical." If not, don't say anything.

- Alaska. (Point to Alaska on the globe.)
- A beautiful island with palm trees. (Point to an island near the equator.) *Tropical.*
- A snowy mountain in Colorado. (Point to Colorado.)
- A jungle. (Point to a jungle area near the equator.) *Tropical.*
- A rain forest. (Point to a rain forest area near the equator.) *Tropical.*
- The North Pole. (Point to the North Pole.)

What describing word means "near the equator and very hot"? *Tropical.*

◎⚊ School

In the book, the author says, "Many fish live together in groups called schools. **School.** Say the word. *School.*

**School** is a noun. It names a thing. What kind of word is **school?** *A noun.*

**A school is a group of fish or other sea creatures.** Say the word that means "a group of fish or other sea creatures." *School.*

Let's think about schools. I'll name some animals. If you think the animals might travel in schools, say "school." If not, don't say anything.

- Dolphins. *School.*
- Geese.
- Horses.
- Squid. *School.*
- Seahorses. *School.*
- Spiders.

What noun means "a group of fish or other sea creatures"? *School.*

◎⚊ Fool

In the book, the author tells us that some fish are marked in ways to fool their enemies. **Fool.** Say the word. *Fool.*

**Fool** is a verb. It tells what something does. What kind of word is **fool?** *A verb.*

**To fool someone or something means to trick them.** Say the word that means "to trick someone or something." *Fool.*

I'll tell you about some situations. If someone

or something is being fooled, say "fool." If not, don't say anything.

- The little boy got a balloon.
- The zebras huddled together. With their stripes, the lion couldn't tell which was which. *Fool.*
- The little girl put her quarter in her pocket and told her brother she used a trick to make it disappear. *Fool.*
- The porcupine used its quills to defend itself from the fox.
- The chameleon blended in with the leaf so the bird couldn't find it. *Fool.*
- The monkey climbed a tree to escape the rhino.

What verb means "to trick someone or something"? *Fool.*

◎⚊ Enemies

In the book, the author tells us that some fish are marked in ways to fool their enemies. **Enemies.** Say the word. *Enemies.*

**Enemies** is a noun. It names people or animals. What kind of word is **enemies?** *A noun.*

**Enemies are people or animals that want to hurt or harm each other.** Say the word that names "people or animals that want to hurt or harm each other." *Enemies.*

I'll tell you about some animals. If I tell about animals that are enemies, say "enemies." If not, don't say anything.

- Spiders and flies. *Enemies.*
- Rabbits and foxes. *Enemies.*
- Puppies and kittens.
- Snakes and mice. *Enemies.*
- Bunnies and squirrels.
- Two robins.

What noun names "people or animals that want to hurt or harm each other"? *Enemies.*

### Present Vocabulary Tally Sheet
(See Lesson 1, page 4, for instructions.)

### Assign Homework
(Homework Sheet, BLM 19a. See the Introduction for homework instructions.)

**Preparation:** Picture Vocabulary
Cards for *tropical, school, fool, enemies.*

### Read and Discuss Story
(Encourage children to use previously taught target words in their answers.)

**Page 1.** What fact did we learn about fish? *Fish live in water.* Plate 1 shows a Brown Trout. What fish is shown in Plate 1? *A Brown Trout.* What kind of water do you think this Brown Trout lives in? (Idea: *A river; freshwater.*)

**Pages 3–5.** What fact did we learn about fish? (Idea: *Fish may live in nearly freezing water or in warm, tropical water.*) Plate 2 shows an Arctic Char. What fish is shown in Plate 2? *An Arctic Char.* In what kind of water does an Arctic Char live? (Ideas: *Freezing; cold.*) Plate 3 shows a Queen Angelfish. What fish is shown in Plate 3? *A Queen Angelfish.* In what kind of water does a Queen Angelfish live? (Ideas: *Warm; tropical.*)

**Page 7.** What fact did we learn about fish? (Idea: *Fins help fish swim.*) Plate 4 shows a Rainbow Darter. What fish is shown in Plate 4? *A Rainbow Darter.*

**Page 9.** What fact did we learn about fish? (Idea: *Fish can breathe underwater because they have gills.*) Plate 5 shows a Bluegill. What fish is shown in Plate 5? *A Bluegill.*

**Page 11.** What fact did we learn about fish? *Fish protect themselves in many ways.* Plate 6 shows a Porcupine Fish. What fish is shown in Plate 6? *A Porcupine Fish.* How do you think this fish protects itself from its enemies? (Idea: *It puffs itself up so its sharp spines stick out.*)

**Page 13.** What fact did we learn about fish? (Idea: *Most fish have tough skin covered by scales.*) Plate 7 shows a Longnose Gar. What fish is shown in Plate 7? *A Longnose Gar.*

**Page 15.** What fact did we learn about fish? (Idea: *The skin of a fish is slippery.*) Plate 8 shows a Chinook Salmon. What fish is shown in Plate 7? *A Chinook Salmon.* How do you think having slippery skin helps protect fish? (Idea:

*Slippery skin would make it difficult for other animals to catch and hold on to them.*)

**Pages 17–19.** What fact did we learn about fish? (Ideas: *Fish may be colored to look like their surroundings; fish may be marked in other ways that fool their enemies.*) Plate 9 shows a Pacific Halibut. What fish is shown in Plate 9? *A Pacific Halibut.* How does looking like its surroundings help protect this fish? (Idea: *It is hard for other animals to see it.*) Plate 10 shows a Foureye Butterfly Fish. What fish is shown in Plate 10? *A Foureye Butterfly Fish.* How do you think this fish's markings help protect it? (Idea: *It looks like it has an eye on the back of its body, so other animals might think it is swimming in a different direction.*)

**Page 21.** What fact did we learn about fish? (Idea: *Many fish live together in groups called schools.*) Plate 11 shows Lookdown. What fish are shown in Plate 11? *Lookdown.*

**Page 23.** What fact did we learn about fish? (Idea: *Some fish babies are born alive and some hatch from eggs.*) Plate 12 shows Lined Seahorses and a Threespine Stickleback. What fish are shown in Plate 12? (Ideas: *Lined Seahorses; Threespine Stickleback.*)

**Page 25.** What fact did we learn about fish? (Idea: *Most fish eat meat.*) Plate 13 shows a Largemouth Bass. What fish is shown in Plate 13? *A Largemouth Bass.*

**Page 27.** What fact did we learn about fish? (Idea: *Fish keep growing as long as they live.*) Plate 14 shows a Whale Shark. What fish is shown in Plate 14? *A Whale Shark.*

**Page 29.** Cathryn Sill ended her book with an important message to us. What does she want us to remember? (Idea: *It is important to protect fish and the places that they live.*) Plate 15 shows a Yellowfin Tuna. What fish is shown in Plate 15? *A Yellowfin Tuna.*

(Display KWL chart.) Now that we've finished reading *About Fish,* let's look at our chart again.

(Point to the *Know* column.) As good scientists find out more about things, they sometimes change their minds about what they know is true. Let's see if we want to change our minds about any of the items on our **Know** list.

(Read each item. Ask children if that item was mentioned in the book. If it was, ask if the item is true or not true. Untrue items are crossed out.) We're good scientists; we know how to change our minds when we learn new facts.

(Point to the *Want to Know* column.) As good scientists find out more about things, they find answers to some of their questions, and they want to ask more questions. (Read each question. Ask children if that question was answered in the book. If it was, record the answer in the *L* (Learned) column and put a check mark in front of the question.) Are there any new questions we would like to ask about fish? (Record questions in the *W* column.) We're good scientists; we know how to use what we have learned to ask new questions.

## Review Vocabulary

(Display the Picture Vocabulary Cards. Point to each card as you say the word. Ask children to repeat each word after you.) These pictures show **tropical, school, fool,** and **enemies.**

- What noun means "people or animals that want to hurt or harm each other"? *Enemies.*
- What word means "a place near the equator that is very hot"? *Tropical.*
- What verb means "to trick someone or something"? *Fool.*
- What noun means "a group of fish or other sea creatures"? *School.*

## Extend Vocabulary

◎—◄ School

In *About Fish,* we learned that some fish live in groups called **schools.** Say the word that means "a group of fish or other sea creatures." *School.*

Raise your hand if you can tell us a sentence that uses **school** as a noun meaning "a group of fish or other sea creatures." (Call on several children. If they don't use complete sentences, restate their examples as sentences. Have the class repeat the sentences.)

Here's a new way to use the word **school.**

- Larissa went to **school** to become a dentist.
- Mya's hairdressing **school** is downtown.
- Henry goes to Lincoln Elementary **School.**

**In these sentences, school is a noun that means a place where people go to learn things.** What word means "a place where people go to learn things"? *School.*

Raise your hand if you can tell us a sentence that uses **school** as a noun meaning "a place where people go to learn things." (Call on several children. If they don't use complete sentences, restate their examples as sentences. Have the class repeat the sentences.)

## Present Expanded Target Vocabulary

◎—◄ Species

In *About Fish,* Cathryn and John Sill wrote about and made paintings of many different kinds of fish. While there are many different kinds of fish, they are all the same species. They all belong to the same group of animals we call fish. **Species.** Say the word. *Species.*

**Species** is a noun. It names something. What kind of word is **species**? *A noun.*

**A species is a group of plants or animals that all share similar characteristics.** Say the word that names "a group of plants or animals that all share similar characteristics." *Species.*

I'll tell about some animals. If these animals are all the same species, say "species." If not, don't say anything.

- Dalmatian, cocker spaniel, German shepherd. *Species.* They are all kinds of dogs, so they are the same **species.**
- Horse, cow, rabbit.
- Boy, girl, infant. *Species.* They are all humans, so they are all the same **species.**
- Tuna, bass, trout. *Species.* They are all fish, so they are all the same **species.**
- Monkey, gorilla, rattlesnake.
- Deer, buck, doe. *Species.* They are all deer, so they are all the same **species.**

What word names "a group of plants or animals that all share similar characteristics"? *Species.*

Fish

Scientists divide all living things into two groups: plants and animals. The animal group is divided into smaller groups. One of these groups is fish. Scientists use a scientific explanation to help people learn what a fish is. **Fish.** Say the word. *Fish.*

This is the scientific explanation of what a **fish** is. **A fish is an animal that:**

> **has a skeleton**
> **is cold-blooded**
> **has fins and gills**
> **lives in water.**

Scientists use this information to help them decide if an animal is a fish or not. For an animal to be a fish, it must have all of these characteristics. Let's be scientists and decide if a human could be a fish.

Does a human have a skeleton? *Yes.*

Is a human cold-blooded? *No.*

Does a human have fins and gills? *No.*

Does a human live in water? *No.*

So could a human be a fish? *No.*

Good job using the scientific explanation to help you make that decision.

Let's be scientists and decide if a shark could be a fish.

Does a shark have a skeleton? *Yes.*

Is a shark cold-blooded? *Yes.*

Does a shark have fins and gills? *Yes.*

Does a shark live in water? *Yes.*

So is a shark a fish? *Yes.*

Good job using the scientific explanation to help you make that decision.

**Preparation:** Display KWL chart. You may wish to photocopy the four pages of the afterword so you can show children the illustrations while you read the additional information.

### Introduce Afterword

Sometimes when people write a nonfiction book, after they finish the main part of the book they want to tell you more facts. This information is put in the book **after** the last **word** of the main part of the book, so it is called an **afterword**.

Today I'll read the afterword that Cathryn Sill wrote for *About Fish* so you can learn more about fish. In this afterword, Catherine Sill wrote more information to go with each plate that John Sill painted.

(Read the afterword aloud a paragraph at a time.)

### Complete KWL Chart

 (Review with children the questions they still want answered from the *W* column of the KWL chart.) Let's see if Cathryn Sill answered any of our questions in the afterword of her book.

**Plate 1.** Did these facts answer any of our questions? (If the item did answer any of the remaining questions, put a check mark in front of the question, and write the answer in the *L* column next to the question. Repeat the question, and have children say the answer. If the item did not answer any of the remaining questions, ask children leading questions, such as:) Where do fish live? (Ideas: *In almost all fresh and salt waters of the world.*) Record the fact in the *L* column near the bottom. Do not write the fact next to any of the unanswered questions.)

(Repeat the process for the remaining plates. If there are any unanswered questions after you have read and discussed the afterword, challenge children to find the answers in the school library, on the Internet, or at home.)

## Summarize the Afterword

The afterword tells us true facts about fish. Facts are things that are true and that can be proved. For example, it is a fact that fish use gills to breathe underwater. We can prove this fact by watching a fish use its gills to breathe when in the water.

When we summarize what we read we tell the most important things in our own words. I'm going to read each fact that Cathryn Sill wrote.

(Read the first fact.) My turn to summarize the fact. Fish live in fresh and salt water all over the world. Say the fact. *Fish live in fresh and salt water all over the world.*

(Repeat this procedure for plates 2 to 4.)

Plate 2: (Idea: *More fish live in warm water than in cold water.*)

Plate 3: (Ideas: *Fish that live in warm water are bright colors. Fish that live in cold water do not have so many bright colors.*)

Plate 4: (Ideas: *Fins help fish move in the water. They use them to steer, balance, and stop.*)

Your turn to summarize the rest of the facts.

(Read each fact for plates 5 to 15. After you read each fact, work with the children to elicit a summative statement. Have all of the children repeat each summative fact as it is given.)

Plate 5: (Idea: *Fish use gills for breathing rather than lungs.*)

Plate 6: (Idea: *Most fish are eaten by bigger fish.*)

Plate 7: (Ideas: *Scales protect fish. There are many different kinds of scales.*)

Plate 8: (Ideas: *Fish are covered with slime. This slime helps them move in the water.*)

Plate 9: (Ideas: *Flatfish swim on their sides on the ocean floor. They blend in with the ocean floor.*)

Plate 10: (Idea: *Some fish have markings that protect them from their enemies.*)

Plate 11: (Idea: *Fish travel in schools to keep safe.*)

Plate 12; (Ideas: *Seahorses guard their eggs and protect their babies. Not all fish guard their eggs and babies.*)

Plate 13: (Idea: *Fish eat animals and plants.*)

Plate 14: (Ideas: *A fish's scalers grow when it grows. You can tell how old a fish is by counting the rings on its scales.*)

Plate 15: (Ideas: *Fish are important to humans. They give us lots of food to eat.*)

We did a great job of summarizing facts about fish.

## Play the Threesies Game

Today you are going to play the *Threesies* game. I'll tell you a word you learned when we read *About Fish.* After I tell you the word, you need to tell me three important things about the word. Each time you tell me something important about the word, you will win one point.

If you can't tell me three things about the word, I will tell you things and I will win one point for each thing I tell you. Once three things have been said about the word, you will have a chance to win two bonus points by using the word in a good sentence. How can you win two bonus points? *By using the word in a good sentence.*

Let's practice. Here's my word. **Tropical.** Tell me one thing you know about the word **tropical.** Tell me another thing you know about **tropical.** Tell me a third thing you know about **tropical.** (Ideas: *Tropical is a describing word; it describes a place near the equator that is very hot; some fish live in warm, tropical water.*) Now you have a chance to earn two bonus points. Raise your hand if you can use **tropical** in a good sentence.

Now you're ready to play the game. (Draw a T-chart on the board for keeping score. Children earn one point for each correct response. If they make a mistake or are unable to give an idea, give an appropriate idea and record one point for yourself. If they can use the word in a good sentence, award two points. Model a good sentence using the word if necessary, and record two points for yourself. Repeat missed words at the end of the game.)

- Your first word is **fool.**
- Your next word is **species.**
- Your next word is **enemies.**

- Your next word is **fish.**
- Your last word is **school.**

(Tally the points and declare a winner.) You did a great job playing *Threesies!*

**Preparation:** Photocopy and assemble the *Let's Learn About Fish* booklet.

Print the following words in two columns on the board: *lungs, breathe, gills, enemy, enemies, spines, tough, slippery, learn, born, alive, adults.*

### Introduce the
### Let's Learn About Fish Booklet

(Point to each word as you read it.) This word is **lungs.** What word? *Lungs.* This word is **breathe.** What word? *Breathe.* (Repeat process for remaining words.)

Let's read these words together. First word? *Lungs.* Next word? *Breathe.* (Repeat process for remaining words.)

Read these words by yourself. First word? *Lungs.* Next word? *Breathe.* (Repeat process for remaining words until children can read the list accurately and confidently.)

(Use the following correction procedure if children make an error:) This word is **gills.** What word? *Gills.* Yes, **gills.** (Go back to the top of the list and repeat the list until children can read it accurately and confidently.)

(Give each child a copy of the *Let's Learn About Fish* booklet.) This is your very own book about fish. The title of this book is *Let's Learn About Fish.* What's the title of the book? *Let's Learn About Fish.*

My turn to read each page of the book. You touch under each word as I read it. (Read pages 1–4.)

Let's read the book together. (Have children read chorally with you.)

(Assign each child a partner. Allow sufficient time for each child to read the first four pages of the

book to his or her partner. Circulate as children read, offering praise and assistance.)

(Children should color the illustrations in their *Let's Learn About Fish* booklet. Encourage them to color the illustrations accurately.) This book is a science book. When artists color scientific illustrations, they use colors that are real. (Show children the front cover of the booklet. Point to the Brown Trout.) What color could a Brown Trout be? (Idea: *Brown.* Point to the dots.) What color should the dots be? (Ideas: *Red and black.*) Remember to use the real colors when you color the illustrations.

### Play the Threesies Game
### (Cumulative Review)

We are going to play the *Threesies* game. I'll tell you a word you have learned. The word I say can be any word you have learned since we read *Suki's Kimono,* so don't let me trick you.

After I tell you the word, you need to tell me three important things about the word. Each time you tell me something important about the word, you will win one point.

If you can't tell me three things about the word, I will tell you things and I will win one point for each thing I tell you. Once three things have been said about the word, you will have a chance to win two bonus points by using the word in a good sentence.

Now you're ready to play the game. (Draw a T-chart on the board for keeping score. Children earn one point for each correct response. If they make a mistake or are unable to give an idea, give an appropriate idea and record one point for yourself. If they can use the word in a good sentence, award two points. Model a good sentence using the word if necessary, and record two points for yourself. Repeat missed words at the end of the game.)

- Your first word is **fish.**
- Your next word is **fool.**
- Your next word is **physician.**
- Your next word is **tropical.**
- Your next word is **school.**
- Your next word is **mammal.**
- Your next word is **migrate.**

- Your next word is **enemies.**
- Your next word is **species.**
- Your last word is **clever.**

(Tally the points and declare a winner.) You did a great job playing *Threesies!*

---

## DAY 5

**Preparation:** Children will need their copies of *Let's Learn About Fish.*

Class *Reading Goals* chart that was started on Week 16.

Each child will need a copy of the Quiz Answer Sheet, BLM B.

### Read the Let's Learn About Fish Booklet

(Assign each child a partner.) Today you'll read the first four pages of your book about fish to your partner. (Allow sufficient time for each child to read the first four pages of the booklet to his or her partner. Circulate as children read, offering praise and assistance.)

(Ask children to look at the back of their booklets about fish.) This part of the book is for people who can help you find other books to read. It tells those people about other books that are like *About Fish.* It also tells them about a place where you can find other books. Where are some places that you could go to find other books about fish? (Ideas: *To the school library; to the public library; to a bookstore.*)

(You may wish to read and discuss the information on the back cover.)

There's one more important thing on the back cover of your book. Touch the box that is at the bottom of the page. The words above the box say "My reading goal." What do the words say? *My reading goal.*

A goal is something that you want to succeed at doing. What is a goal? *Something that you want to succeed at doing.* A reading goal is something that you want to succeed at doing with your reading.

Let's see if we can add some other reading goals to our class chart. What are some other reading goals that someone might have when they read

their book? (Accept reasonable responses. Help children put their ideas into goal statements. Add to the list of goal statements. Ask children to choose a goal and copy it into the box. Children may also make up an original goal that is not on the list. If children are unable to copy the goals or to write a goal of their own, you or a helper may wish to scribe their goal statements for them before the booklets are sent home.)

### Assess Comprehension

(Ask children to turn to page 5 in their booklets.) This is what you have read in your book about fish, but with no pictures. You are going to have a little quiz to see if you can remember what you read.

(Ask children to touch under the words as they read the passage silently. Monitor to ensure that they are reading the passage. Ask children to look up at you after they have finished reading the passage.

(Read the instructions aloud to children.) When an author contrasts two things, he or she tells how the two things are different from each other. What does an author do when he or she contrasts two things? *He or she tells how the two things are different from each other.*

(Explain to children that they will fill in the blanks to complete the comparison. Remind them to look back in the passage for the words that they need.)

### Assess Vocabulary

 (Give each child a copy of the Quiz Answer Sheet, BLM B.)

Today you're going to have a True or False quiz. When you do the True or False quiz, it shows me how well you know the hard words you are learning.

If I say something that is true, circle the word **true.** What will you do if I say something that is true? *Circle the word* true.

If I say something that is false, circle the word **false.** What will you do if I say something that is false? *Circle the word* false.

Listen carefully to each item that I say. Don't let me trick you!

Item 1: Cats, dogs, and horses are all different **species.** (*True.*)

Item 2: Something that is **colossal** is enormous. (*True.*)

Item 3: All **fish** live in the water. (*True.*)

Item 4: A **tropical** place would be good for snow-skiing. (*False.*)

Item 5: A **festival** is a time when everyone is sad and stays in their homes. (*False.*)

Item 6: **Birds** often travel in **schools.** (*False.*)

Item 7: If Mom was sure we would get home before dark, she **doubted** that we would get home before dark. (*False.*)

Item 8: **Enemies** live together happily. (*False.*)

Item 9: A **tourist** likes to go to new places. (*True.*)

Item 10: Some fish **fool** their enemies to protect themselves. (*True.*)

You did a great job completing your quiz!

(Score children's work. A child must score 9 out of 10 to be at the mastery level. If a child does not achieve mastery, insert the missed words as additional items in the games in next week's lessons. Retest those children individually for the missed items before they take the next mastery test.)

## Extensions

### Read a Book as a Reward

 (Read *About Fish* or another nonfiction book about reptiles to children as a reward for their hard work.)

---

**Preparation:** Word containers for the Super Scientists Center.

Create a 2-column chart on construction paper with the headings *verbs* and *nouns*.

---

### Introduce the
### Super Scientists Center

(Add this week's Picture Vocabulary Cards to the cards from Weeks 16–18.

Show children the word container and the sorting chart. If children need more guidance in how to work in the Super Scientists Center, role-play with two to three children as a demonstration.)

Let's think about how we work with our words in the Super Scientists Center.

You will work with a partner in the Super Scientists Center. Whom will you work with? *A partner.*

Scientists observe things carefully and try to find ways that things are alike. They put things that have the same characteristics together in groups. These groups are called categories. What are groups of things with the same characteristics called? *Categories.*

You are going to think about what you know about your vocabulary words and put them into categories.

First you will look at the categories I have written on this chart. What will you do first? *Look at the categories on the chart.* This week you are going to use the categories *verbs* and *nouns*. What are your categories for this week? (Ideas: *Verbs; nouns.*)

Next you and your partner will read each word from the container. What will you and your partner do next? *Read each word.*

After you read each word, you and your partner will talk about what you know about each word and decide which category it should go in. What will you and your partner do after you read each word? (Idea: *Talk about what we know about each word and decide which category to put it in.*)

If a card is not a noun or a verb, put it back in the container. What will you do with a picture card if the word is not a noun and not a verb? (Idea: *Put it back in the container.*)

# Week 20

**Preparation:** You will need a copy of *About Insects* for each day's lesson.

Number the pages of the book to assist you in asking comprehension questions at appropriate points.

Prepare a KWL chart titled *Insects* on a sheet of chart paper.

Post a copy of the Vocabulary Tally Sheet, BLM A, with this week's Picture Vocabulary Cards attached.

Each child will need one copy of the Homework Sheet, BLM 20a.

## DAY 1

### Introduce Book

This week's book is called *About Insects.* What's the title of this week's book? *About Insects.*

This book is true. When an author writes books about things that are true, those books are called nonfiction books. What kinds of books are about true things? *Nonfiction books.*

This book was written by Cathryn Sill. Who's the author of *About Insects? Cathryn Sill.*

John Sill made the pictures for this book. Who is the illustrator of *About Insects? John Sill.* Who made the illustrations for this book? *John Sill.*

The cover of a book usually gives us some hints of what the book is about. Let's look at the front cover of *About Insects.* What do you see in the illustration? (Ideas: *A big beetle with pincers; plants; a log that is covered with moss; some leaves.*)

(Display KWL chart.) Let's think about what we **know** about insects. Raise your hand if you can tell us something you know about insects. I'll write it down under the **K. K** stands for what we **know** about insects. What does **K** stand for? *What we know about insects.* (Record <u>all</u> children's responses under the *K* (know) section of the chart. Do not eliminate incorrect

## About Insects

author: Cathryn Sill • illustrator: John Sill

### Target Vocabulary

| Tier II | Tier III |
|---------|----------|
| waterproof | nonfiction |
| nourishment | fact |
| active | plate |
| pests | afterword |
| *predator | |
| insects | |

*Expanded Target Vocabulary Word

responses. They will be addressed in later lessons during the week.)

The things we know about insects that are true are called facts. What are the true things we know about insects called? *Facts.*

(Point to the *K* column on the chart.) Some of the things you have told us are facts about insects, and some of the things you have told us are not true. When we've finished reading *About Insects,* we'll come back to our chart and look at it again.

Now let's think what you **want to know** about insects. I'll write it down under the **W. W** stands for what we **want to know** about insects. What does **W** stand for? *What we want to know about insects.* (Record <u>all</u> children's questions under the *W* (want to know) section of the chart. If children tell about insects instead of ask questions, prompt them to ask a question.)

### Take a Picture Walk

(Encourage children to use target words in their answers.) We're going to take a picture walk through this book. When we take a picture walk through a nonfiction book, we look carefully at the pictures and tell what we see. When you look carefully at pictures, you observe those pictures. What do you do when you look carefully at pictures in a nonfiction book? *You observe those pictures.*

All of the illustrations for this book were painted by John Sill. Sometimes when a nonfiction book is published with paintings, each painting is

called a plate. What are paintings for a nonfiction book sometimes called? *Plates.* The plates in a nonfiction book are usually numbered. The first plate in the book would be called Plate 1. What would we call the first plate in the book? *Plate 1.* What would we call the second plate in the book? *Plate 2.* What would we call the third plate in the book? *Plate 3.*

**Page 2.** What do you observe in Plate 1? (Ideas: *Flowers; three small bugs on the leaves.*)

**Page 4.** What do you observe in Plate 2? (Ideas: *Black insects with red stripes and large wings; they are furry.*)

**Page 6.** What do you observe in Plate 3? (Ideas: *The same picture as on the cover; a large beetle with pincers on a fallen log.*)

**Page 8.** What do you observe in Plate 4? (Ideas: *Baby insects crawling on a branch; they are long and green.*)

**Page 10.** What do you observe in Plate 5? (Ideas: *A caterpillar on a leaf; a monarch butterfly on a flower.*)

**Page 12.** What do you observe in Plate 6? (Ideas: *Two moths on blades of grass; they have large wings and long antennae.*)

**Page 14.** What do you observe in Plate 7? (Ideas: *A horse with a fly on its face.*)

**Page 16.** What do you observe in Plate 8? (Ideas: *A grasshopper on a leaf; it has a long body, long legs, and long antennae; it is green.*)

**Page 18.** What do you observe in Plate 9? (Ideas: *Two black and white insects; they have long bodies and long wings; one is flying above the long grass; the other is standing on a piece of grass.*)

**Page 20.** What do you observe in Plate 10? (Ideas: *A long, very thin insect; it is difficult to see because it looks like a stick on the branch.*)

**Page 22.** What do you observe in Plate 11? (Ideas: *A green insect jumping from a branch; it has long legs and antennae; its wings are held against its back.*)

**Page 24.** What do you observe in Plate 12? (Ideas: *A beetle swimming on top of the water; water plants.*)

**Page 26.** What do you observe in Plate 13? (Ideas: *A stack of books with small insects crawling on them; the insects have long bodies and short legs; their tails are divided into three parts.*)

**Page 28.** What do you observe in Plate 14? (Ideas: *White flowers with three bumblebees in them; the bees are furry yellow with black stripes.*)

**Page 30.** What do you observe in Plate 15? (Ideas: *A large green and white moth on a leaf; it is night in the picture; the moth has spots on its wings; the moth is sitting on a branch with leaves.*)

**Page 32.** What do you observe in Plate 16? (Ideas: *Two brown bugs crawling around some food; they are flat but wide with long antennae.*)

**Page 34.** What do you observe in Plate 17? (Ideas: *Three ladybugs crawling on a corn plant; there are holes in the leaves as if the ladybugs have eaten them; there are little green bugs near the ladybugs; one of the ladybugs is eating one of the little green bugs.*)

**Page 36.** What do you observe in Plate 18? (Ideas: *A fish jumping out of the water after an insect; the insect has a long body and long wings; a stream with rocks; some of the rocks are covered with moss.*)

### Read the Book Aloud

(Read the book to children with minimal interruptions, ending with page 35.)

Tomorrow we will read the book again, and I will ask you some questions.

### Present the Target Vocabulary
 Waterproof

In the book, the author says "They (the insects) have a waterproof skeleton on the outside of their bodies." That means that an insect's skeleton, which is on the outside of its body, keeps the insect from getting wet. **Waterproof.** Say the word. *Waterproof.*

**Waterproof** is a describing word. It tells more about a noun. What kind of word is **waterproof?** *A describing word.*

**Something that is waterproof does not let water in.** Say the word that means "does not let water in." *Waterproof.*

(Correct any incorrect responses, and repeat the item at the end of the sequence.)

I'll tell you about something. If that thing is does not let water in, say "waterproof." If it lets water in, don't say anything.

- When it rained, the tent kept the campers dry. *Waterproof.*
- The raincoat kept Cyndi dry when she went out in the rain. *Waterproof.*
- The leaking roof let the rain come into the house.
- The shower cap kept Grandmother's hair dry. *Waterproof.*
- When the children ran through the sprinklers, they got soaked.
- The fisherman wore tall boots when he waded into the stream. *Waterproof.*

What describing means "does not let water in"? *Waterproof.*

 Nourishment

In the book, the author says, "Some insects suck animals or plants to get nourishment." **Nourishment.** Say the word. *Nourishment.*

**Nourishment** is a noun. It names a thing. What kind of word is **nourishment?** *A noun.*

**Nourishment is the food needed to keep a plant or animal strong and healthy.** Say the word that means "the food needed to keep a plant or animal strong and healthy." *Nourishment.*

Let's think about nourishment. I'll tell you about some animals. If you think the animals are getting nourishment, say "nourishment." If not, don't say anything.

- A bird eats insects. *Nourishment.*
- A dog runs.
- A mosquito bites you. *Nourishment.*
- A child eats a salad. *Nourishment.*
- A child eats candy.
- A kitten drinks its mother's milk. *Nourishment.*

What noun means "the food needed to keep a plant or animal strong and healthy"? *Nourishment.*

 Active

In the book, the author tells us that some insects are active during the day. **Active.** Say the word. *Active.*

**Active** is a describing word. It tells more about a noun. What kind of word is **active?** *A describing word.*

**Active means busy and full of energy.** Say the word that means "busy and full of energy." *Active.*

I'll tell you about some situations. If someone or something is being active, say "active." If not, don't say anything.

- The bird slept.
- The bird hunted for food. *Active.*
- The boy sat watching television.
- The boy played soccer in the park. *Active.*
- The caterpillar lay wrapped in its cocoon.
- The butterfly came out of its cocoon and flew away in search of flowers. *Active.*

What describing word means "busy and full of energy"? *Active.*

 Pests

In the book, the author tells us that some insects may be pests. **Pests.** Say the word. *Pests.*

**Pests** is a noun. It names something. What kind of word is **pests?** *A noun.*

**Pests are insects that destroy or damage plants and bite people.** Say the word that names "insects that damage plants and bite people." *Pests.*

I'll tell you about some insects. If I tell about insects that are pests, say "pests." If not, don't say anything.

- Spiders catching flies.
- Ladybugs eating aphids.
- Mosquitoes biting hikers. *Pests.*
- Moths eating leaves. *Pests.*
- Bees gathering pollen.
- Caterpillars eating leaves. *Pests.*

What noun names "insects that damage or destroy plants and bite people"? *Pests.*

## Present Vocabulary Tally Sheet

(See Lesson 1, page 4, for instructions.)

## Assign Homework

(Homework Sheet, BLM 20a. See the Introduction for homework instructions.)

**Preparation:** Picture Vocabulary Cards for *waterproof, nourishment, active, pests.*

## Read and Discuss Story

(Encourage children to use previously taught target words in their answers.)

**Pages 1–3.** What fact did we learn about insects? (Idea: *Insects have six legs and three body parts.*) Plate 1 shows Dogbane Leaf Beetles. What insects are shown in Plate 1? *Dogbane Leaf Beetles.* Do you think these beetles are helpful or pests? (Idea: *Pests.*) Why do you think that? (Idea: *They are eating the leaves of those plants.*) Plate 2 shows Cow Killers. What insects are shown in Plate 2? *Cow Killers.*

**Page 5.** What fact did we learn about insects? (Idea: *Insects have a waterproof skeleton on the outside of their bodies.*) Plate 3 shows an Elephant Stag Beetle. What insect is shown in Plate 3? *An Elephant Stag Beetle.*

**Page 7.** What fact did we learn about insects? *Young insects hatch from eggs.* Plate 4 shows Praying Mantises. What insects are shown in Plate 4? *Praying Mantises.*

**Page 9.** What fact did we learn about insects? *They go through several changes before becoming adults.* Plate 5 shows a Monarch Butterfly. What insect is shown in Plate 5? *A Monarch Butterfly.* What changes did the Monarch Butterfly go through before becoming an adult? (Idea: *It started as a caterpillar, then it wrapped itself in a cocoon and came out a butterfly.*)

**Page 11.** What fact did we learn about insects? *Antennae help insects smell and feel.* Plate 6

shows Virginia Ctenuchid [ten-u-kid] Moths. What insects are shown in Plate 6? *Virginia Ctenuchid Moths.*

**Page 13.** What fact did we learn about insects? *Some insects suck animals or plants to get nourishment.* Plate 7 shows a Black Horse Fly. What insect is shown in Plate 7? *A Black Horse Fly.*

**Page 15.** What fact did we learn about insects? *Others bite and chew their food.* Plate 8 shows a Southeastern Lubber Grasshopper. What insect is shown in Plate 7? *A Southeastern Lubber Grasshopper.* What do you think this grasshopper eats for nourishment? (Ideas: *Leaves; plants.*)

**Page 17.** What fact did we learn about insects? *Many insects fly.* Plate 9 shows White Tails. What insects are shown in Plate 9? *White Tails.*

**Page 19.** What fact did we learn about insects? *Some crawl because they have no wings.* Plate 10 shows a Giant Walkingstick. What insect is shown in Plate 10? *A Giant Walkingstick.*

**Pages 21–23.** What fact did we learn about insects? *Others jump or swim.* Plate 11 shows a Gladiator Katydid. What insect is shown in Plate 11? *A Gladiator Katydid.* Plate 12 shows a Small Whirligig Beetle. What insect is shown in Plate 12? *A Small Whirligig Beetle.*

**Page 25.** What fact did we learn about insects? *Insects live almost everywhere.* Plate 13 shows Silverfish. What insects are shown in Plate 13? *Silverfish.*

**Page 27.** What fact did we learn about insects? *Some are active during the day.* Plate 14 shows Honey Bees. What insects are shown in Plate 14? *Honey Bees.*

**Page 29.** What fact did we learn about insects? *Others are active only at night.* Plate 15 shows a Luna Moth. What insect is shown in Plate 15? *A Luna Moth.* What do you think the Luna Moth does during the day? (Idea: *Sleeps.*)

**Page 31.** What fact did we learn about insects? *Some insects may be pests.* Plate 16 shows German Cockroaches. What insects are shown in Plate 14? *German Cockroaches.*

**Page 33.** What fact did we learn about insects? (Idea: *Many insects are very helpful.*) Plate 17 shows Convergent Ladybug Beetles. What insects are shown in Plate 17? *Convergent Ladybug Beetles.*

**Page 35.** Cathryn Sill ended her book with an important message to us. What does she want us to remember? *Insects are an important part of our world.* Plate 18 shows a Mayfly. What insect is shown in Plate 18? *A Mayfly.*

(Display KWL chart.) Now that we've finished reading *About Insects,* let's look at our chart again.

(Point to the *Know* column.) As good scientists find out more about things, they sometimes change their minds about what they know is true. Let's see if we want to change our minds about any of the items on our **Know** list. (Read each item. Ask children if that item was mentioned in the book. If it was, ask if the item is true or not true. Untrue items are crossed out.) We're good scientists; we know how to change our minds when we learn new facts.

(Point to the *Want to Know* column.) As good scientists find out more about things, they find answers to some of their questions, and they want to ask more questions. (Read each question. Ask children if that question was answered in the book. If it was, record the answer in the *L* (Learned) column and put a check mark in front of the question.) Are there any new questions we would like to ask about insects? (Record questions in the *W* column.) We're good scientists; we know how to use what we have learned to ask new questions.

### Review Vocabulary
(Display the Picture Vocabulary Cards. Point to each card as you say the word. Ask children to repeat each word after you.) These pictures show **waterproof, nourishment, active,** and **pests.**

- What noun means "insects that damage or destroy plants and bite people"? *Pests.*
- What noun means "food needed to keep a plant or animal strong and healthy"? *Nourishment.*

- What describing word describes something that "does not let water in"? *Waterproof.*
- What word means "busy and full of energy"? *Active.*

### Extend Vocabulary
 **Pests**

In *About Insects,* we learned that some insects can be **pests.** Say the word that means "insects that damage plants and bite people." *Pests.*

Raise your hand if you can tell us a sentence that uses **pests** as a noun meaning "insects that damage or destroy plants and bite people." (Call on several children. If they don't use complete sentences, restate their examples as sentences. Have the class repeat the sentences.)

Here's a new way to use the word **pests.**

- When I was on the phone, my little sisters were being **pests.**
- The children were being **pests** in the grocery store.
- When the ice-cream man comes through the streets, all the children suddenly become **pests.**

**In these sentences, pests is a noun that means people who are annoying or bothering someone.** What word means "people who are annoying or bothering someone"? *Pests.*

Raise your hand if you can tell us a sentence that uses **pests** as a noun meaning "people who are annoying or bothering someone." (Call on several children. If they don't use complete sentences, restate their examples as sentences. Have the class repeat the sentences.)

### Present Expanded Target Vocabulary
**Predator**

In the last plate of the book, we see a fish jumping out of the water to catch a mayfly. The fish is a predator to the mayfly. **Predator.** Say the word. *Predator.*

**Predator** is a noun. It names something. What kind of word is **predator?** *A noun.*

**A predator is an animal that hunts other animals for food.** Say the word that names "an animal that hunts other animals for food." *Predator.*

I'll tell about some animals. If the animal I name is a predator, say "predator." If not, don't say anything.

- Renita's dog eats canned dog food.
- The lion chased the gazelle. *Predator.*
- The spider spun a web to catch flies. *Predator.*
- The beetle ate leaves from the plants.
- The snake leapt from behind the rock and bit the rabbit. *Predator.*
- The cow munched on the grass.

What word names "an animal that hunts other animals for food"? *Predator.*

 Insects

Scientists divide all living things into two groups: plants and animals. The animal group is divided into smaller groups. One of these groups is insects. Scientists use a scientific explanation to help people learn what insects are. **Insects.** Say the word. *Insects.*

This is the scientific explanation of what **insects** are. **An insect is an animal that:**

> **has a skeleton on the outslide of its body**
> **has six legs**
> **has three body parts.**

Scientists use this information to help them decide if an animal is an insect or not. For an animal to be an insect, it must have all of these characteristics. Let's be scientists and decide if a human could be an insect.

Does a human have a skeleton on the outside of its body? *No.*

Does a human have six legs? *No.*

Does a human have three body parts? *No.*

So could a human be an insect? *No.*

Good job using the scientific explanation to help you make that decision.

Let's be scientists and decide if a dragonfly could be an insect.

Does a dragonfly have a skeleton on the outside of its body? *Yes.*

Does a dragonfly have six legs? *Yes.*

Does a dragonfly have three body parts? *Yes.*

So is a dragonfly an insect? *Yes.*

Good job using the scientific explanation to help you make that decision.

**Preparation:** Display KWL chart.
You may wish to photocopy the four pages of the afterword so you can show children the illustrations while you read the additional information.

### Introduce Afterword

Sometimes when people write a nonfiction book, after they finish the main part of the book they want to tell you more facts. This information is put in the book **after** the last **word** of the main part of the book, so it's called an **afterword.**

Today I'll read the afterword that Cathryn Sill wrote for *About Insects* so you can learn more about insects. In this afterword, Catherine Sill wrote more information to go with each plate that John Sill painted.

(Read the afterword aloud a paragraph at a time.)

### Complete KWL Chart

 (Review with children the questions they still want answered from the *W* column of the KWL chart.) Let's see if Cathryn Sill answered any of our questions in the afterword of her book.

**Plate 1.** Did these facts answer any of our questions? (If the item did answer any of the remaining questions, put a check mark in front of the question, and write the answer in the *L* column next to the question. Repeat the question, and have children say the answer. If the item did not answer any of the remaining questions, ask children leading questions, such as:) How many species of insects are there in the world? (Ideas: *Over one million.*) What is the most numerous of all animals? *Insects.* (Record the fact in the *L* column near the bottom. Do not write the fact next to any of the unanswered questions.)

(Repeat the process for the remaining plates. If there are any unanswered questions after you have read and discussed the afterword, challenge children to find the answers in the school library, on the Internet, or at home.)

## Summarize the Afterword

The afterword tells us true facts about insects. Facts are things that are true and that can be proved. For example, it is a fact that insects have six legs. We can prove this fact by counting the legs on an insect.

When we summarize what we read we tell the most important things in our own words. I'm going to reead each fact that Cathryn Sill wrote.

(Read the first fact.) My turn to summarize the fact. There are more insecs than any other kind of animal. Say the fact. *There are more insects than any other kind of animal.*

(Repeat this procedure for plates 2 to 4.)

Plate 2: (Idea: *An insect's body has three parts—the head, the thorax, and the abdomen.*)

Plate 3: (Idea: *Insects have their skeletons on the outside of their bodies.*)

Plate 4: (Idea: *Some insects grow in three stages—egg, nymph, and adult.*)

Your turn to summarize the rest of the facts.

(Read each fact for plates 5 to 18. After you read each fact, work with the children to elicit a summative statement. Have all of the children repeat each summative fact as it is given.)

Plate 5: (Idea: *Some insects grow in four stages—egg, larva, pupa, and adult.*)

Plate 6: (Idea: *Insects use their antennae to smell, feel, and hear.*)

Plate 7: (Idea: *Flies use their mouths to lick up liquids.*)

Plate 8: (Idea: *Insects bite and chew food by moving their mandibles.*)

Plate 9: (Idea: *Most insects have two pairs of wings.*)

Plate 10: (Idea: *Some insects can make themselves look like plants.*)

Plate 11: (Idea: *Some insects have strong back legs to make them good jumpers.*)

Plate 12: (Idea: *Beetles that live in the water have special back legs to make them good swimmers.*)

Plate 13: (Ideas: *Insects live almost everywhere. They don't live in the ocean.*)

Plate 14: (Idea: *Bees like to live together in big nests.*)

Plate 15: (Idea: *Moths are active at night.*)

Plate 16: (Ideas: *Some insects are bad for people. They can hurt us and our food.*)

Plate 17: (Idea: *Many insects help people.*)

Plate 18: (Ideas: *Insects are important food for animals that help us. Insects help people in many ways.*)

We did a great job of summarizing facts about insects.

## Play the Threesies Game

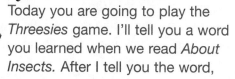

Today you are going to play the *Threesies* game. I'll tell you a word you learned when we read *About Insects.* After I tell you the word, you need to tell me three important things about the word. Each time you tell me something important about the word, you will win one point. If you can't tell me three things about the word, I will tell you things and I will win one point for each thing I tell you.

Once three things have been said about the word, you will have a chance to win two bonus points by using the word in a good sentence. How can you win two bonus points? *By using the word in a good sentence.*

Let's practice. Here's my word. **Pests.** Tell me one thing you know about the word **pests.** Tell me another thing you know about **pests.** Tell me a third thing you know about **pests.** (Ideas: *Pests is a noun; it can mean two different things; it can mean insects that damage or destroy plants; pests bite people; it can mean people who are annoying; it can mean people who bother you.*) Now you have a chance to earn two bonus points. Raise your hand if you can use **pests** in a good sentence.

Now you're ready to play the game. (Draw a T-chart on the board for keeping score. Children earn one point for each correct response. If they make a mistake or are unable to give an idea, give an appropriate idea and record one point for yourself. If they can use the word in a good sentence, award two points. Model a good sentence using the word if necessary, and record two points for yourself. Repeat missed words at the end of the game.)

- Your first word is **waterproof.**
- Your next word is **predator.**
- Your next word is **nourishment.**
- Your next word is **insects.**
- Your last word is **active.**

(Tally the points and declare a winner.) You did a great job playing *Threesies!*

---

## DAY 4

**Preparation:** Photocopy and assemble the *Let's Learn About Insects* booklet.

Print the following words in two columns on the board: *insects, dry, body, change, antennae, ways, crawl, suck, juice, chew, food, helpful.*

---

### Introduce the
### Let's Learn About Insects Booklet

(Point to each word as you read it.) This word is **insects.** What word? *Insects.* This word is **dry.** What word? *Dry.* (Repeat process for remaining words.)

Let's read these words together. First word? *Insects.* Next word? *Dry.* (Repeat process for remaining words.)

Read these words by yourself. First word? *Insects.* Next word? *Dry.* (Repeat process for remaining words until children can read the list accurately and confidently.)

(Use the following correction procedure if children make an error:) This word is **body.** What word? *Body.* Yes, **body.** (Go back to the top of the list and repeat the list until children can read it accurately and confidently.)

(Give each child a copy of the *Let's Learn About Insects* booklet.) This is your very own book about insects. The title of this book is *Let's Learn About Insects.* What's the title of the book? *Let's Learn About Insects.*

My turn to read each page of the book. You touch under each word as I read it. (Read pages 1–4.)

Let's read the book together. (Have children read chorally with you.)

(Assign each child a partner. Allow sufficient time for each child to read the first four pages of the booklet to his or her partner. Circulate as children read, offering praise and assistance.)

(Children should color the illustrations in their *Let's Learn About Insects* booklet. Encourage them to color the illustrations accurately.) This book is a science book. When artists color scientific illustrations, they use colors that are real. (Show children the front cover of the booklet. Point to the Monarch Butterfly.) What colors should a Monarch Butterfly be? (Ideas: *Orange, black, and white.* Point to the dots.) What color should the dots be? (Idea: *White.*) Remember to use the real colors when you color the illustrations.

### Play the Threesies Game
### (Cumulative Review)

 We are going to play the *Threesies* game. I'll tell you a word you have learned. The word I say can be any word you have learned since we read *Suki's Kimono,* so don't let me trick you.

After I tell you the word, you need to tell me three important things about the word. Each time you tell me something important about the word, you will win one point. If you can't tell me three things about the word, I will tell you things and I will win one point for each thing I tell you.

Once three things have been said about the word, you will have a chance to win two bonus points by using the word in a good sentence.

Now you're ready to play the game. (Draw a T-chart on the board for keeping score. Children earn one point for each correct response. If they make a mistake or are unable to give an idea, give an appropriate idea and record one point for yourself. If they can use the word in a good sentence, award two points. Model a good sentence using the word if necessary, and record two points for yourself. Repeat missed words at the end of the game.)

- Your first word is **insects.**
- Your next word is **both.**
- Your next word is **nourishment.**
- Your next word is **capture.**
- Your next word is **active.**
- Your next word is **Canada.**
- Your next word is **pests.**
- Your next word is **faithful.**
- Your next word is **predator.**
- Your last word is **waterproof.**

(Tally the points and declare a winner.) You did a great job playing *Threesies!*

---

### DAY 5

**Preparation:** Children will need their copies of *Let's Learn About Insects.*

Class *Reading Goals* chart that was started in Week 16.

Each child will need a copy of the Quiz Answer Sheet, BLM B.

---

### Read the *Let's Learn About Insects* Booklet

(Assign each child a partner.) Today you'll read the first four pages of your book about insects to your partner. (Allow sufficient time for each child to read the first four pages of the booklet to his or her partner. Circulate as children read, offering praise and assistance.)

(Ask children to look at the back of their booklets about insects.) This part of the book is for people who can help you find other books to read. It tells those people about other books that are like *About Insects*. It also tells them about a place where you can find other books. Where are some places that you could go to find other books about insects? (Ideas: *To the school library; to the public library; to a bookstore.*)

(You may wish to read and discuss the information on the back cover.)

There's one more important thing on the back cover of your book. Touch the box that is at the bottom of the page. The words above the box

say "My reading goal." What do the words say? *My reading goal.*

A goal is something that you want to succeed at doing. What is a goal? *Something that you want to succeed at doing.* A reading goal is something that you want to succeed at doing with your reading.

Let's see if we can add some other reading goals to our class chart. What are some other reading goals that someone might have when they read their book? (Accept reasonable responses. Help children put their ideas into goal statements. Add to the list of goal statements. Ask children to choose a goal and copy it into the box. Children may also make up an original goal that is not on the list. If children are unable to copy the goals or to write a goal of their own, you or a helper may wish to scribe their goal statements for them before the booklets are sent home.)

### Assess Comprehension

(Ask children to turn to page 5 in their booklets.) This is what you have read in your book about insects, but with no pictures. You are going to have a little quiz to see if you can remember what you read.

(Ask children to touch under the words as they read the passage silently. Monitor to ensure that they are reading the passage. Ask them to look up at you after they have finished reading the passage. Instruct children to read and answer the questions.)

### Assess Vocabulary

 (Give each child a copy of the Quiz Answer Sheet, BLM B.)

Today you're going to have a True or False quiz. When you do the True or False quiz, it shows me how well you know the hard words you are learning.

If I say something that is true, circle the word **true.** What will you do if I say something that is true? *Circle the word* true.

If I say something that is false, circle the word **false.** What will you do if I say something that is false? *Circle the word* false.

Listen carefully to each item that I say. Don't let me trick you!

Item 1: A **predator** eats leaves and grasses. (*False.*)

Item 2: When you are playing baseball, you are being **active.** (*True.*)

Item 3: If you are **ambitious,** you have big plans. (*True.*)

Item 4: **Insects** all have six legs and three body parts. (*True.*)

Item 5: The **desert** is a place that has lots of trees and water. (*False.*)

Item 6: A child who is constantly tugging at your sleeve whining for candy is being a **pest.** (*True.*)

Item 7: If you are wearing a **waterproof** jacket in the rain, you will get very wet. (*False.*)

Item 8: Many people **feast** during a **festival.** (*True.*)

Item 9: Fruits and vegetables are good sources of **nourishment** for children. (*True.*)

Item 10: A person who has broken his or her arm is **injured.** (*True.*)

You did a great job completing your quiz!

(Score children's work. A child must score 9 out of 10 to be at the mastery level. If a child does not achieve mastery, insert the missed words as additional items in the games in next week's lessons. Retest those children individually for the missed items before they take the next mastery test.)

## Extensions

### Read a Book as a Reward

(Read *About Insects* or another nonfiction book about insects to children as a reward for their hard work.)

---

**Preparation:** Word containers for the Super Scientists Center.

Create a 3-column chart on construction paper with the headings *nouns, words that describe nouns,* and *verb*s.

---

## Introduce the Super Scientists Center

(Add this week's Picture Vocabulary Cards to the cards from Weeks 16–19. Show children the word container and the sorting chart. If children need more guidance in how to work in the Super Scientists Center, role-play with two to three children as a demonstration.)

Let's think about how we work with our words in the Super Scientists Center.

You will work with a partner in the Super Scientists Center. Whom will you work with? *A partner.*

Scientists observe things carefully and try to find ways that things are alike. They put things that have the same characteristics together in groups. These groups are called categories. What are groups of things with the same characteristics called? *Categories.*

You are going to think about what you know about your vocabulary words and put them into categories.

First you will look at the categories I have written on this chart. What will you do first? *Look at the categories on the chart.* This week you have three categories: *nouns, words that describe nouns,* and *verbs*. What are your categories for this week? (Ideas: *Nouns; words that describe nouns; verbs*)

## Week 21

**Preparation:** You will need a copy of *I Am a Gymnast* for each day's lesson.

Number the pages of the book to assist you in asking comprehension questions at appropriate points.

Post a copy of the Vocabulary Tally Sheet, BLM A, with this week's Picture Vocabulary Cards attached.

Each child will need one copy of the Homework Sheet, BLM 21a.

# I Am a Gymnast

author: Jane Feldman • photographs: Jane Feldman

### ⌖ Target Vocabulary

| Tier II | Tier III |
|---------|----------|
| compete | nonfiction |
| routine | photograph |
| challenging | biography |
| exhausted | |
| *coordinated | |
| *dream | |

*Expanded Target Vocabulary Word

---

## DAY 1

### Introduce Series

For the next five weeks, we will be reading books that are biographies. A biography tells about the life of a real person. What does a biography tell about? *The life of a real person.* What kind of book tells about the life of a real person? *A biography.*

All these books are true. When an author writes books about things that are true, those books are called nonfiction books. What kinds of books are about true things? *Nonfiction books.*

### Introduce Book

Today's book is called *I Am a Gymnast.* What's the title of this week's book? *I Am a Gymnast.*

This book was written by Jane Feldman. Who's the author of *I Am a Gymnast*? *Jane Feldman.* Part of the story was told by McKenzie Foster, a child who is a gymnast. Who told part of the story? *McKenzie Foster.*

The pictures for this book were taken with a camera. They are called photographs. What do you call pictures taken with a camera? *Photographs.* What kind of illustrations does *I Am a Gymnast* have? *Photographs.*

The cover of a book usually gives us some hints of what the book is about. Let's look at the front cover of *I Am a Gymnast.* What do you see in the photograph? (Ideas: *A little girl standing on* the sand in a funny position; *she's wearing a red outfit; she might be at the beach.*)

### Take a Picture Walk

(Encourage children to use target words in their answers.)

We're going to take a picture walk through this book. When we take a picture walk through a nonfiction book that is a biography, we look carefully at the pictures and think about what we see.

**Page 1.** Who do you think the little girl is? (Ideas: *McKenzie Foster; a gymnast.*) Where is the little girl? (Idea: *At the beach.*) What is she doing that at the beach? (Idea: *She's practicing.*)

**Top of page 2.** Who do you think these people are? (Idea: *McKenzie's family.*)

**Bottom left of page 2.** Who do you think these people are? (Idea: *McKenzie and her sister.*)

**Bottom right of page 2.** Who do you think these people are? (Idea: *McKenzie and her brother and sister.*)

**Page 3.** Where do you think the children are? (Ideas: *In front of a school; outside.*)

**Pages 4–5.** What's happening in these photographs? (Idea: *McKenzie is practicing her gymnastics.*)

**Pages 6–7.** Where is McKenzie? (Idea: *At the gym.*) Who is she working with? (Ideas: *Her coach; her teacher.*)

**Pages 8–9.** What is McKenzie doing? (Idea: *Practicing her gymnastics.*) Who is she working with? (Ideas: *Her coach; her teacher.*)

**Pages 10–11.** What is happening in these photographs? (Ideas: *McKenzie is doing gymnastics with a whole bunch of people; McKenzie is competing.*)

**Top of page 12.** Who is McKenzie working with? (Ideas: *Her coach; her teacher.*)

**Bottom of page 12.** Who do you think this is? (Idea: *Somebody famous; McKenzie's coach or teacher.*)

**Page 13.** When do you think this photograph was taken? (Idea: *During a practice.*)

**Pages 14–15.** Why do you think McKenzie is doing these actions? (Ideas: *She's stretching; she's getting ready; she's practicing.*)

**Page 16.** What do you think is happening? (Ideas: *The mothers are getting their little girls ready; the mothers are fixing the little girls' hair; the mothers are helping their daughters.*)

**Page 17.** How do you think the little girls are feeling as they get ready to compete? (Ideas: *Nervous; excited; anxious.*)

We learned a vocabulary word in an earlier lesson that could be used to describe how the girls are feeling. What word means they "believe that everything will turn out all right"? *Optimistic.*

**Pages 18–19.** What do you think is happening? (Ideas: *The girls are in a competition; the girls are performing.*)

**Pages 20–21.** What do you think is happening in these photographs? (Idea: *The girls are performing.*)

**Page 22.** What do you think the girls are doing? (Idea: *Waiting.*) Why do you think they are waiting? (Idea: *To see if they won a prize.*) How do you think they are feeling? (Ideas: *Nervous; excited, optimistic.*)

**Page 23.** What do you think the numbers **3, 1, 2** mean? (Ideas: *Third, first, and second place.*) Why are the girls standing on the numbers? (Idea: *Because they won.*) How do you think the girls are feeling? (Ideas: *Happy; excited; proud.*)

**Pages 24–25.** Where do you think these photographs were taken? (Idea: *In a city.*) When do you think these photographs were taken? (Idea: *After the girls won a prize.*)

**Pages 26–27.** Who do you think the people are in these pictures? (Idea: *McKenzie's teammates; McKenzie's friends.*)

**Page 28–29.** Who are the people McKenzie is hugging? (Idea: *Her friends.*) Why are they hugging McKenzie? (Idea: *They are excited and amazed that she is a winner.*)

**Page 30–31.** What is happening in these photographs? (Ideas: *The girls are at a competition; the girls are doing gymnastics.*)

**Page 32.** Who do you think the girl is? (Idea: *Someone famous; a good gymnast.*)

**Page 33.** What is happening in these photographs? (Idea: *McKenzie is practicing with older girls; a strong man is holding McKenzie.*)

**Page 34.** Where is McKenzie now? (Idea: *In bed.*) When do you think this photograph was taken? (Idea: *At night.*)

**Page 35.** Who is in the photograph? (Idea: *McKenzie.*) How is she feeling? (Idea: *Proud.*)

### Read the Book Aloud
(Read the story to children with minimal interruptions.)

Tomorrow we will read the book again, and I will ask you some questions.

### Present Target Vocabulary
◎⟌ Compete

In this book, we found out that only boys compete on the rings. That means they can take part in a contest to see who is best at performing on the rings. **Compete.** Say the word. *Compete.*

**Compete** is a verb. It tells what people do. What kind of word is **compete?** *A verb.*

**If you compete, you take part in a contest or game.** Say the word that means "take part in a contest or a game." *Compete.*

(Correct any incorrect responses, and repeat the item at the end of the sequence.)

Let's think about some times when someone might compete in a contest or a game. I'll tell about a time. If you think these people are competing, say "compete." If not, don't say anything.

- Paulo plays on a soccer team. *Compete.*
- David did his kata at the karate competition. *Compete.*
- Amy likes to draw.
- We had a family picnic on July 4th.
- Melanie came first in the 100-meter race. *Compete.*
- Graham beat his grandma at checkers. *Compete.*

What verb means "to take part in a contest or a game"? *Compete.*

◎━ Routine

In the book, McKenzie says, "What makes rhythmic gymnastics fun is that the routines are choreographed, just like in dance." That means she does a series of movements in her performance. McKenzie and her coach would work together to make up a series of movements that show off what McKenzie can do. **Routine.** Say the word. *Routine.*

**Routine** is a noun. It names a thing. What kind of word is **routine?** *A noun.*

**A routine is a series of movements used in a performance.** Say the word that means "a series of movements used in a performance." *Routine.*

Let's think about some times when someone might do a routine. I'll tell about a time. If someone is doing a routine, say "routine." If not, don't say anything.

- In the rope exercise, the gymnast swung the rope over, around, and under her body. Then she tossed the rope, caught it, and swung the rope around her body two more times. *Routine.*
- When Sean dances, he lets his body move to the music.
- When she did her ribbon dance, she did a snake, a throw and catch, a figure eight, a circle, and then another snake. *Routine.*
- In the tap dance, the man did a toe-heel, toe-heel, stomp, tap, tap, clap. *Routine.*

- In my dance class, I learned the steps to do a waltz. *Routine.*
- When they play on the rings, they do something different every time.

What noun means "a series of movements used in a performance"? *Routine.*

◎━ Challenging

In the book McKenzie says, "It's very challenging to practice for six and a half hours a day." That means it is very difficult and takes lots of extra work and effort to do it. **Challenging.** Say the word. *Challenging.*

**Challenging** is a describing word. It tells more about something. What kind of word is **challenging?** *A describing word.*

**If something is challenging, it is very difficult and takes lots of extra work and effort to do it.** Say the word that means "very difficult and takes lots of extra work and effort to do." *Challenging.*

Let's think about some things that might be challenging. I'll tell about something. If you think that it would be challenging, say "challenging." If not, don't say anything.

- Climbing a very tall and steep mountain. *Challenging.*
- Running a mile very quickly. *Challenging.*
- Standing up.
- Holding your breath for more than one minute. *Challenging.*
- Saying your name.
- Counting by ones to a million. *Challenging.*

What describing word means "very difficult and takes lots of extra work and effort to do"? *Challenging.*

◎━ Exhausted

In the book, McKenzie says, "I should be exhausted, since I've been up since four o'clock in the morning." That means she should be very, very tired. **Exhausted.** Say the word. *Exhausted.*

**Exhausted** is a describing word. It tells more about someone. What kind of word is **exhausted?** *A describing word.*

**If you are exhausted, you are very, very tired.** Say the word that means "very, very tired." *Exhausted.*

Let's think about some times when someone might be exhausted. I'll tell about a time. If you think the person is feeling exhausted, say "exhausted." If not, don't say anything.

- She dug in the garden all day long. *Exhausted.*
- I watched a movie.
- We ran in a five-mile fun run. *Exhausted.*
- My mom was up all night because I had a bad fever. *Exhausted.*
- He just got up from a good night's sleep.
- Liu likes to play chess.

What describing word means "very, very tired"? *Exhausted.*

### Present Vocabulary Tally Sheet
(See Lesson 1, page 4, for instructions.)

### Assign Homework
(Homework Sheet, BLM 21a. See the Introduction for homework instructions.)

---

### DAY 2

**Preparation:** Picture Vocabulary Cards for *compete, routine, challenging, exhausted.*

---

### Read and Discuss Story

(Read story to children. Ask the following questions at the specified points. Encourage them to use target words in their answers.)

**Page 1.** What two important things did we learn about McKenzie? (Ideas: *She's almost eight; her favorite thing in the world is gymnastics.*)

**Pages 2–3.** What did we learn about McKenzie's family? (Ideas: *She has a mom and a dad, a sister and a brother; they live in New York City; her best friend is her sister, Drew; Drew, Jack, and McKenzie go the same school.*)

**Pages 4–5.** Where does McKenzie like to do gymnastics? (Ideas: *She likes to do gymnastics on the lawn in front of her apartment building; at the beach; in the gym.*)

**Page 6.** When did McKenzie start doing artistic gymnastics? (Idea: *When she was four.*) What kinds of equipment does she use when she does

artistic gymnastics? (Ideas: *The balance beam, the uneven bars; the vault; the floor.*)

**Page 7.** Why does she put chalk on her hands? (Ideas: *So her hands get a firmer grip; to keep from falling.*) Who are the adults who help her? (Ideas: *Her coach; her spotter.*)

**Pages 8–9.** What is the difference between artistic and rhythmic gymnastics? (Ideas: *In artistic gymnastics you work on an apparatus; in rhythmic gymnastics you work with an apparatus.*) What kinds of apparatus does McKenzie work with when she does rhythmic gymnastics? (Ideas: *Rope; hoop; ball; ribbon.*) Do you think rhythmic gymnastics would be hard to do? I think you'd need to be a very good athlete and be able to balance well in order to do all those things.

**Page 10.** What three things does McKenzie have to do when she's doing one of her routines? (Ideas: *Remember the steps; control her equipment; keep moving to the beat of the music.*)

**Page 11.** How do you know McKenzie is determined to be a good gymnast? (Ideas: *She practices for six and a half hours a day five days a week in the summer; she practices even when her brother and sister are enjoying the swimming pool; she doesn't mind all the hard work; she is getting stronger and stronger every day.*)

**Pages 12–13.** What did you learn about McKenzie's coach? (Ideas: *Her name is Wendy Hilliard; she was a gymnast before she was a coach; she wants all kids to have a chance to study gymnastics if they want to.*)

**Pages 14–15.** What does McKenzie do before she starts her class? (Idea: *She stretches.*) Do you think she could do splits if she didn't stretch? *No.*

**Page 16.** How old did McKenzie have to be before she could compete? (Idea: *Six years old.*)

**Page 17.** Does McKenzie mind being the smallest girl on her team? *No.*

**Pages 18–21.** How is a competition like a practice? (Idea: *McKenzie has to warm up by stretching.*) How is a competition different from a practice? (Idea: *They wear special costumes.*)

**Pages 22–23.** Why would the girls be feeling nervous and excited while they wait for the judges? (Ideas: *They aren't sure if they will win; they hope they get first place.*) How do you think they feel when their team wins? (Ideas: *Proud; excited; happy.*)

**Page 24.** What did McKenzie and her team do on National Gymnastics Day? (Ideas: *Went to Rockefeller Center; were on The Today Show on TV.*)

**Pages 25–26.** What made this day so special for McKenzie? (Ideas: *She got to meet her favorite gymnasts; she saw Ryan Weston jump higher than four stories on the trampoline; she met Nadia Comaneci and Kerri Strug; she posed for pictures with Shannon Miller, Dominique Dawes, and the Olympic coach.*)

**Pages 28–29.** What was the best part of the day for McKenzie? (Ideas: *She got to meet mentors.*) What is a mentor? (Idea: *An experienced older person who helps encourage you.*) A mentor is someone who encourages you. He or she helps you by telling you what you do well and what to do to get better at things you don't do so well. A mentor gives you confidence to keep trying. Who else have we met in this book that probably encouraged McKenzie? (Ideas: *Her coaches; her parents; her brother and sister; her teammates.*)

**Page 30.** Who are the gymnasts performing for? (Ideas: *The mentors; Bela, Shannon, and Dominique; the Olympic coach; Olympic gymnasts.*)

**Pages 32–33.** Who else performed on National Gymnastics Day? (Ideas: *Other gymnasts; Tatyana, Sasha.*)

**Page 34.** Why isn't McKenzie exhausted after her long day? (Idea: *She's too excited.*)

**Page 35.** What's McKenzie doing? (Idea: *Pretending she is standing on the Olympic podium and receiving the gold medal.*)

Do you think McKenzie will ever be an Olympic champion? Explain why or why not.

### Review Vocabulary

(Display the Picture Vocabulary Cards. Point to each card as you say the word. Ask children to repeat each word after you.) These pictures show **routine, exhausted, challenging,** and **compete.**

- What word means "very, very tired"? *Exhausted.*
- What noun means "a series of movements used in a performance"? *Routine.*
- What word means "very difficult and takes lots of extra work and effort to do"? *Challenging.*
- What verb means "take part in a contest or a game"? *Compete.*

### Extend Vocabulary
 Routine

In *I Am a Gymnast* we learned that a **routine** is "a series of movements used in a performance." Say the word that means "a series of movements used in a performance." *Routine.*

Raise your hand if you can tell us a sentence that uses **routine** as a noun meaning "a series of movements used in a performance." (Call on several children. If they don't use complete sentences, restate their examples as sentences. Have the class repeat the sentences.)

Here's a new way to use the word **routine.**

- Feeding the cat is part of my evening **routine.** Say the sentence.
- Eating a good breakfast is an important part of a healthy morning **routine.** Say the sentence.
- The children's afternoon **routine** started with time to read books. Say the sentence.

**In these sentences, routine is a noun that means a usual way or pattern of doing things.** What word means "a usual way or pattern of doing things"? *Routine.*

Raise your hand if you can tell us a sentence that uses **routine** as a noun meaning "a usual way or pattern of doing things." (Call on several children. If they don't use complete sentences, restate their examples as sentences. Have the class repeat the sentences.)

### Present Expanded Target Vocabulary
Coordinated

In the book, McKenzie had to be able to remember the steps of her routine, control the hoop and keep moving to the beat of the music, all at the same time. To do three different things all at the same time, she had to be coordinated. **Coordinated.** Say the word. *Coordinated.*

**Coordinated** is a describing word. It tells more about a person. What kind of word is **coordinated?** *A describing word.*

**Coordinated means you can make the different parts of your body all work together to do something.** Say the word that means "the different parts of your body all work together to do something." *Coordinated.*

I'll tell about some people. If these people are coordinated, say "coordinated." If not, don't say anything.

- Justin could rub his tummy and pat his head at the same time. *Coordinated.*
- Anne could jump on the trampoline and catch a ball at the same time. *Coordinated.*
- Steve fell over when he tried to stand on one foot with his arms out.
- Josh's baby brother could get his food in his spoon and move the spoon to his mouth. *Coordinated.*
- The children had trouble bouncing the basketball while running across the gym.
- When Rick played the piano, his right and left hands played different notes. *Coordinated.*

What describing word means "the different parts of your body all work together to do something"? *Coordinated.*

## ◎= Dream

In the book, McKenzie wants to one day stand on the Olympic podium and receive the gold medal. She thinks about it often and really wants it to happen. Another way of saying McKenzie often thinks about standing on the Olympic podium and winning an Olympic medal is to say winning an Olympic medal is McKenzie's dream. **Dream.** Say the word. *Dream.*

**Dream** is a noun. It names a thing. What kind of word is **dream?** *A noun.*

**A dream can be something a person thinks about often and really wants to happen.** Say the word that means "something a person thinks about often and really wants to happen." *Dream.*

Let's think about some things that might be someone's dream. I'll tell about someone. If I tell

about that person's dream, say "dream." If not, don't say anything.

- Ian often thinks about being a famous photographer who takes amazing wildlife photographs. *Dream.*
- Alex plays golf.
- Tanis really wants to be a doctor when she grows up. *Dream.*
- All the while Megan was growing up, she thought about how wonderful it would be to be a pilot. *Dream.*
- Looking out the window, Xavier saw it was a dull and rainy day.
- All through school, Jeremaine thought how great it would be if he could play professional football. *Dream.*

What noun means "something a person thinks about often and really wants to happen"? *Dream.*

---

### DAY 3

**Preparation:** Prepare a sheet of chart paper with a diagram of a tree on it, with 6 circles hanging on it, as decorations.

### Make a Celebration Tree

Today I'll show you the photographs taken for *I Am a Gymnast.* As I read about those photographs, I'll call on one of you to tell about an important event in McKenzie's life that she might choose to celebrate.

(Each time children give a response, record the underlined words in one of the ornaments on the tree.)

**Pages 10–11.** What would McKenzie celebrate in this part of her story? (Idea: *As she <u>practiced</u> she got <u>stronger</u> and stronger.*)

**Page 12.** What would McKenzie celebrate in this part of her story? (Idea: <u>*Wendy became her coach*</u>.)

**Pages 16–23.** What would McKenzie celebrate in this part of her story? (Idea: <u>*Team wins competition.*</u>)

**Pages 24–25.** What would McKenzie celebrate in this part of her story? (Idea: *They <u>perform on TV</u>.*)

**Pages 26–27.** What would McKenzie celebrate in this part of her story? (Idea: _Meets famous gymnasts._)

**Page 35.** What would McKenzie celebrate in this part of her story? (Idea: _Winning an Olympic medal._)

### Play the Super Choosing Game

Today you will play the _Super Choosing_ game. We've played a game like this before but this one is a little bit different. Let's think about the six words we have learned: **compete, routine, challenging, exhausted, coordinated,** and **dream.** (Display the Picture Vocabulary Cards.)

I will say a sentence that has two or three of the words we have learned in it. You will have to choose the correct word for that sentence. Not all of the words will be from this lesson, though. That's why it's the _Super Choosing_ game. Let's practice. (You should not show cards for the words outside of this lesson.)

• Would a person **routine** or **compete?** _Compete._

• When you do the same thing every day, is it a **routine,** a **custom,** or an **exhausted?** _Routine._

• Would it be harder to do something **clever,** something **challenging,** or something **routine?** _Something challenging._

Now you're ready to play the game. If you tell me the correct answer, you will win one point. If you can't tell me the correct answer, I get the point. (Draw a T-chart on the board for keeping score. Children earn one point for each correct answer. If they make an error, correct them as you normally would, and record one point for yourself. Repeat missed words at the end of the game.)

• When McKenzie performed at the competition, did she do a **routine,** a **journey,** or a **challenging?** _A routine._

• Would it be **routine, scarce,** or **challenging** to swim across a big lake? _Challenging._

• If you ran a 26-mile marathon, at the end would you be **coordinated, exhausted,** or **teased?** _Exhausted._

• If an ice skater can do a figure eight on one foot while holding the other foot high over her head and waving her hand, is she **grateful, fascinated,** or **coordinated?** _Coordinated._

• If you entered a diving contest, would you **compete** or be **exhausted?** _Compete._

• Ashley always wanted to be a writer. Was that her **dream,** her **quarrel,** or her **souvenir?** _Her dream._

(Count the points and declare a winner.) You did a great job of playing the _Super Choosing_ game.

---

## DAY 4

**Preparation:** Photocopy and assemble _The Biography of McKenzie Foster._

Print the following words in two columns on the board: _family, special, favorite, gym, gymnastics, beach, coach, learn, ribbon, dance, competition, stretches._

### Introduce The Biography of McKenzie Foster

(Point to each word as you read it.) This word is **family.** What word? _Family._ This word is **special.** What word? _Special._ (Repeat process for remaining words.)

Let's read these words together. First word? _Family._ Next word? _Special._ (Repeat process for remaining words.)

Read these words by yourself. First word? _Family._ Next word? _Special._ (Repeat process for remaining words.)

(Use the following correction procedure if the children make an error:) This word is **ribbon.** What word? _Ribbon._ Yes, **ribbon.** (Go back to the top of the list and repeat the list until children can read it accurately and confidently.)

(Give each child a copy of _The Biography of McKenzie Foster._ Ask children to touch under the title of the booklet.) The title of this book is _The Biography of McKenzie Foster._ What's the title of this book? _The Biography of McKenzie Foster._

Remember that a biography tells about the life of a real person. What does a biography tell about? *The life of a real person.* Is a biography fiction or nonfiction? *Nonfiction.*

(Ask children to open their books to page 1. Ask them to touch under the first set of underlined words.) These words say **McKenzie Foster.** What do these words say? *McKenzie Foster.* Yes, **McKenzie Foster.** This biography is about McKenzie Foster. Who is this biography about? *McKenzie Foster.*

(Ask children to touch under the next set of underlined words.) These words say **New York City.** What do these words say? *New York City.* Yes, **New York City.** McKenzie Foster lives near New York City. Where does McKenzie Foster live? *Near New York City.*

My turn to read each page of the book. You touch under each word as I read it. (Read pages 1–4.)

Let's read the book together. (Have children read chorally with you.)

(Assign each child a partner. Allow sufficient time for each child to read the book to his or her partner. Circulate as children read, offering praise and assistance.)

(Children should color the illustrations in their booklet. Encourage them to color the illustrations realistically.)

### Play the Super Choosing Game (Cumulative Review)

Let's play the *Super Choosing* game. I'll say a sentence that has two or three of our words in it. You will have to choose the correct word for that sentence. (Display the Picture Vocabulary Cards *compete, routine, challenging, exhausted, coordinated,* and *dream* for the three words in each sentence as you say the sentence.)

Now you're ready to play the *Super Choosing* game. (Draw a T-chart on the board for keeping score. Children earn one point for each correct answer. If they make an error, correct them as you normally would, and record one point for yourself. Repeat missed words at the end of the game.)

- If you did a series of movements in a performance, would you have done a **routine,** a **challenging,** or a **compete**? *A routine.*
- If it takes lots of extra effort and work for you to read, is reading a **routine, exhausted,** or **challenging**? *Challenging.*
- If a girl played basketball so hard that she was very, very tired, would she be **compete, exhausted,** or **routine**? *Exhausted.*
- When you're having trouble tying up your shoes even after you've tried and tried is tying shoes **coordinated** or **challenging**? *Challenging.*
- If a four-year-old could skip backwards, would he be **coordinated, exhausted,** or **routine**? *Coordinated.*
- When something happens that makes you feel very, very tired, are you feeling **exhausted** or doing a **routine**? *Feeling exhausted.*
- If I really want to be a champion figure skater and I think about it all the time, is it my **coordinated,** my **challenging,** or my **dream**? *My dream.*
- If I take part in a spelling contest, do I **compete** or **dream**? *Compete.*

Now you will have to listen very carefully, because I'm not going to show you the word cards. Think hard. I'm going to use words that you have learned in other lessons. (This part of the game includes the review words from previous lessons.)

- When you tell someone your name, do you **introduce** yourself, **notice** them, or **compete** against them? *Introduce yourself.*
- If you went on a long, long trip, would that be a **routine,** a **rescue,** or a **journey**? *Journey.*
- If you see something that is unusual or hard to understand, is it **challenging, curious,** or **routine**? *Curious.*
- If you were very, very tired after a race, would you be **sparkling, suspicious,** or **exhausted**? *Exhausted.*
- If you tried and tried to do a headstand and you just couldn't do it, would you be s**ly, coordinated,** or **frustrated**? *Frustrated.*
- If you think about something all the time and you really want to do it, is it a **dream,** a **doubt,** or an **enemy**? *A dream.*

- If you always brush your teeth just before you go to bed, is that part of your **imagination,** your **temper,** or your **routine?** *Your routine.*
- Is someone who can do gymnastics **challenging, disgusting,** or **coordinated?** *Coordinated.*
- If your home is very large and beautiful, is it **invisible, magnificent,** or **challenging?** *Magnificent.*

(Tally the points and declare a winner.) You did a great job of playing the *Super Choosing* game.

---

### DAY 5

**Preparation:** Class chart titled *Reading Goals* that was started in Week 16.

*The Biography of McKenzie Foster.*

Quiz Answer Sheet, BLM B.

---

### Read The Biography of McKenzie Foster

(Assign each child a partner.) Today you'll read the first four pages of *The Biography of McKenzie Foster* to your partner. (Allow sufficient time for each child to read the first four pages of the book to his or her partner. Circulate as children read, offering praise and assistance.)

(Ask children to look at the back of their booklets.) This part of the book is for people who can help you find other books to read. It tells those people about other books that are biographies. It also tells them about a place where you can find other biographies. Where are some places that you could go to find other biographies? (Ideas: *To the school library; to the public library; to a bookstore.*)

(You may wish to read and discuss the information on the back cover.)

There's one more important thing on the back cover of your book. Touch the box that is at the bottom of the page. The words above the box say "My reading goal." What do the words say? *My reading goal.*

What is a goal? *Something that you want to succeed at doing.* A reading goal is something that you want to succeed at doing with your reading.

Let's see if we can add some other reading goals to our class chart. What are some other reading goals that someone might have when they read their book? (Accept reasonable responses. Help children put their ideas into goal statements. Add to the list of statements on the chart. Ask children to choose a goal and copy it into the box. Children may also make up an original goal that is not on the list. If children are unable to copy the goals or to write a goal of their own, you or a helper may wish to scribe their goal statements for them before the booklets are sent home.)

### Assess Comprehension

(Ask children to turn to page 5 in their booklets.) This is what you have read in the biography about McKenzie Foster but with no pictures. You are going to have a little quiz to see if you can remember what you read.

(Ask children to touch under the words as they read the passage silently. Monitor to ensure that children are reading the passage. Ask them to look up at you after they have finished reading the passage. Instruct children to read and answer the questions.)

### Assess Vocabulary

 (Give each child a copy of the Quiz Answer Sheet, BLM B.)

Today you're going to have a True or False quiz. When you do the True or False quiz, it shows me how well you know the hard words you are learning.

If I say something that is true, circle the word **true.** What will you do if I say something that is true? *Circle the word* true.

If I say something that is false, circle the word **false.** What will you do if I say something that is false? *Circle the word* false.

Listen carefully to each item that I say. Don't let me trick you!

Item 1: If you are **exhausted,** you are very, very tired. (*True.*)

Item 2: If you were in a palace that was very large and beautiful, the palace would be **magnificent.** (*True.*)

Item 3: If something were **challenging** to do, it would be very easy to do. (*False.*)

Item 4: A dance **routine** would have a series of dance steps used in a performance. (*True.*)

Item 5: A **coordinated** person would find it very difficult to learn to skate. (*False.*)

Item 6: If you only pick up your toys once in a while, it is part of your **routine**. (*False.*)

Item 7: If you enter a music **festival** and sing you **compete** at the festival. (*True.*)

Item 8: **Dream** and **marsh** mean the same thing. (*False.*)

Item 9: If a job were **challenging,** you'd have to be **determined** to complete it. (*True.*)

Item 10: A **journey** and a **voyage** can be the same thing. (*True.*)

You did a great job completing your quiz!

(Score children's work. A child must score 9 out of 10 to be at the mastery level. If a child does not achieve mastery, insert the missed words as additional items in the games in next week's lessons. Retest those children individually for the missed items before they take the next mastery test.)

## Extensions

### Read a Book as a Reward

(Read *I Am a Gymnast* or another biography to children as a reward for their hard work. Display a number of biographies. Ask children to choose which one they would like you to read.)

### Introduce the Super Words Center (2 in 1)

(Add the new Picture Vocabulary Cards to the cards from the previous weeks. Show children one of the word containers. Role-play with two to three children as you introduce each part of the game.)

You will play a game called *2 in 1* in the Super Words Center.

Let's think about how we work with our words in the Super Words Center.

You will work with a partner in the Super Words Center. Whom will you work with? *A partner.*

First you will draw two words out of the container. What do you do first? (Idea: *Draw two words out of the container.*) Show your partner both of the words. (Demonstrate.)

Next you will say a sentence that uses both of your words. What do you do next? (Idea: *I will say a sentence that uses both of my words.*) (Demonstrate.)

If you can use both of your words in one sentence, give yourself a point. Then give your partner a turn. (Demonstrate.)

What do you do next? *Give my partner a turn.*

# Week 22

## Preparation:
You will need a copy of *Rolling Along* for each day's lesson.

Number the pages of the book to assist you in asking comprehension questions at appropriate points.

Post a copy of the Vocabulary Tally Sheet, BLM A, with this week's Picture Vocabulary Cards attached.

Each child will need one copy of the Homework Sheet, BLM 22a.

# Rolling Along
author: Jamee Riggio Heelan • illustrator: Nicola Simmonds

## Target Vocabulary

| Tier II | Tier III |
|---------|----------|
| equipment | nonfiction |
| escalator | photograph |
| elevator | biography |
| wheel | |
| *accepting | |
| *positive | |

*Expanded Target Vocabulary Word

---

## DAY 1

### Introduce Book

This week's book is called *Rolling Along.* What's the title of this week's book? *Rolling Along.*

This book was written by Jamee Riggio Heelan [jay-me rij-e-o he-lan]. Who's the author of *Rolling Along? Jamee Riggio Heelan.* But, part of the story was told by a boy named Taylor, a child who uses a wheelchair. Who told part of the story? *Taylor.*

Some of the pictures for this book were taken with a camera. They are called photographs. What do you call pictures taken with a camera? *Photographs.* What kind of illustrations does *Rolling Along* have? *Photographs.*

The cover of a book usually gives us some hints of what the book is about. Let's look at the front cover of *Rolling Along.* What do you see in the photograph? (Ideas: *A little boy sitting in a wheelchair; he is smiling.*)

*Rolling Along* is a biography. A biography tells about the life of a real person. What does a biography tell about? *The life of a real person.* What kind of book tells about the life of a real person? *A biography.*

This book is true. What kinds of books are about true things? *Nonfiction books.*

### Take a Picture Walk

(Encourage children to use target words in their answers.)

We're going to take a picture walk through this book. When we take a picture walk through a nonfiction book that is a biography, we look carefully at the pictures and think about what we see.

The pictures in this book are very interesting. Part of the picture is a photograph and part is an illustration that an artist has drawn and colored. When you look at each picture, notice which parts are photographs and which are illustrations that are drawn and colored.

**Page 1.** Who do you think the boys in this photograph are? (Ideas: *Brothers; twins; one is Taylor.*)

**Page 2.** What are the boys doing on this page? (Idea: *Coloring.*) Look closely at the picture. What parts of the picture were taken with a camera? (Idea: *The boys' faces and arms.*) What parts of the picture are illustrated? (Ideas: *Their clothes; the crayon; the book.*)

**Page 4.** How do you think the brothers feel about one another? (Ideas: *They love each other; they are friends as well as brothers.*)

**Page 5.** What do you think is happening here? (Idea: *A woman is helping Taylor stretch his leg.*)

**Page 6.** Who do you think the children are? (Ideas: *Other children who are also in* wheelchairs.) What are the children doing? (Idea: *Playing ball.*)

**Page 7.** What is Taylor doing in this picture? (Idea: *Practicing walking with a walker.*) Do you think walking with a walker is easy or difficult? Tell why.

**Page 10.** What is Taylor sitting in? (Idea: *A wheelchair.*) What do you think Taylor and this woman are talking about? (Ideas: *How to use the wheelchair; how the wheelchair will help him.*)

**Page 11.** Where do you think Taylor is? (Idea: *At school; on the playground.*) Who is he talking to? (Ideas: *His friend; someone from his class.*)

**Pages 13–14.** How is Taylor feeling in this photograph? (Ideas: *Happy; excited.*) Taylor seems excited about his gift. What is his gift? (Idea: *A wheelchair.*) Why do you think this gift is making Taylor so happy? (Idea: *It will be easier for Taylor to get around in a wheelchair rather than using his walker.*)

**Pages 15–16.** What is Taylor doing in these illustrations? (Ideas: *Practicing using his wheelchair; his brother is helping him go over a box.*)

**Page 17.** What is the problem in this illustration? (Idea: *There are stairs and Taylor can't get up them in his wheelchair.*)

**Pages 19–20.** What is Taylor's brother doing in this illustration? (Idea: *Pushing Taylor in his wheelchair up a ramp.*)

**Page 21.** What is Taylor doing here? (Idea: *Pressing a large button.*) What do you think the button does? (Idea: *Opens the door for him.*)

**Page 24.** What is Taylor doing in this illustration? (Idea: *Getting a drink from the fountain.*) How is the fountain Taylor uses different from the one his brother uses? (Idea: *It is shorter.*) Why is that fountain shorter? (Idea: *So Taylor can reach it in his wheelchair.*)

**Page 25.** What are Taylor and his brother doing in this illustration? (Ideas: *Taylor's brother is helping him stretch his leg.*)

**Pages 27–28.** What are the boys doing? (Idea: *Playing basketball.*) How is the way Taylor plays different from the way his brother plays? (Idea: *His brother is standing and Taylor is in*

his wheelchair.) Do you think playing basketball from a wheelchair would be easier or harder than playing on your feet? Why do you think so?

**Page 29.** What are the brothers doing in this illustration? (Ideas: *Going out for a ride; Taylor is in his wheelchair and his brother is riding a bike.*) Throughout this book, what parts of the illustrations have actually been photographs? (Idea: *People's faces.*)

### Read the Book Aloud
(Read the story to children with minimal interruptions.)

Tomorrow we will read the book again, and I will ask you some questions.

### Present the Target Vocabulary
⊚⫶ **Equipment**

In the book, Taylor explains that many of his friends need special equipment to help them get around. **Equipment.** Say the word. *Equipment.*

**Equipment** is a noun. It names things. What kind of word is **equipment?** *A noun.*

**Equipment is things made for a particular use.** Say the word that means "things made for a particular use." *Equipment.*

(Correct any incorrect responses, and repeat the item at the end of the sequence.)

Let's think about some times when you might use equipment. I'll tell about an activity and some equipment. If you think the equipment is used for the activity, say "equipment." If not, don't say anything.

- Ice skates and ice hockey. *Equipment.*
- Football helmet and gymnastics.
- Paintbrushes and cooking.
- Pots and pans and cooking. *Equipment.*
- Running shoes and racing. *Equipment.*
- Roller skates and basketball.

What noun names the "things made for a particular use"? *Equipment.*

⊚⫶ **Escalator**

In the book, Taylor tells us that if a building only has stairs or an escalator, he can't get to the other floors. **Escalator.** Say the word. *Escalator.*

**Escalator** is a noun. It names a thing. What kind of word is **escalator**? *A noun.*

**An escalator is a moving staircase.** Say the word that means "a moving staircase." *Escalator.*

Let's think about some places that might have escalators. I'll tell about a place. If the place would have an escalator, say "escalator." If not, don't say anything.

- A large department store. *Escalator.*
- A shopping mall. *Escalator.*
- A small, neighborhood library.
- An ice cream shop.
- A large airport. *Escalator.*
- A school.

What noun means "a moving staircase"? *Escalator.*

 Elevator

In the book, Taylor tells us that he needs to use an elevator to get to other floors of a building. **Elevator.** Say the word. *Elevator.*

**Elevator** is a noun. It names a thing. What kind of word is **elevator**? *A noun.*

**An elevator is a machine that carries people up and down between floors of buildings.** Say the word that names "a machine used for carrying people up and down between floors of buildings." *Elevator.*

Let's think about some times when an elevator might be useful. I'll tell about some situations. If you think that it would be helpful to use an elevator, say "elevator." If not, don't say anything.

- Getting to the top of a skyscraper. *Elevator.*
- Going to your bedroom on the second floor of your house.
- Getting to the basement of a department store in a wheelchair. *Elevator.*
- Pushing a cart of heavy dishes that need to go to the third floor. *Elevator.*
- Walking to the office from your classroom.

What noun names "a machine that carries people up and down between floors of buildings"? *Elevator.*

 Wheel

In the book, Taylor is able to wheel himself to the top of the ramp at his school. **Wheel.** Say the word. *Wheel.*

**Wheel** is a verb. It tells what someone does. What kind of word is **wheel**? *A verb.*

**To wheel means to push something on wheels.** Say the word that means to "push something on wheels." *Wheel.*

Let's think about some things that you might be able to wheel. I'll name some things. If you think the thing can be wheeled, say "wheel." If not, don't say anything.

- A bicycle. *Wheel.*
- The kitchen table.
- A huge truck.
- A wagon. *Wheel.*
- A wheelchair. *Wheel.*
- A house.

What verb means "to push something on wheels"? *Wheel.*

### Present Vocabulary Tally Sheet
(See Lesson 1, page 4 for instructions.)

### Assign Homework
(Homework Sheet, BLM 22a. See the Introduction for homework instructions.)

| DAY 2 |
|---|

**Preparation:** Picture Vocabulary Cards for *equipment, escalator, elevator, wheel.*

### Read and Discuss Story

 (Read story to children. Ask the following questions at the specified points. Encourage them to use target words in their answers.)

**Page 1.** What do we learn about Taylor's brother? (Ideas: *He is Taylor's twin; he is Taylor's best friend.*)

**Page 2.** What do Taylor and Tyler like to do together? (Ideas: *Eat chocolate ice cream; wrestle with each other; watch the Chicago Bulls play basketball; read about dinosaurs.*)

**Page 3.** How is Taylor different from Tyler? (Idea: *He was born with cerebral palsy.*) What does cerebral palsy do? (Idea: *It makes Tyler's brain tell his muscles to jump instead of move smoothly.*) What can Tyler do that Taylor can't? (Ideas: *Run; jump; skip; walk easily.*)

**Page 5.** What has Taylor used to help him walk? (Ideas: *Braces on his legs; a walker.*) What does Kathryn do for Taylor? (Ideas: *She stretches his muscles; helps him practice balancing and working his muscles.*)

**Page 6.** Why are some of Taylor's friends in therapy? (Ideas: *Some have never been able to get around without special equipment; some were in accidents; some can't move their arms or legs at all; they all want to get stronger.*)

**Page 8.** What was the problem with using a walker? (Idea: *Taylor moved very slowly and got tired easily.*) What things frustrated Taylor? (Ideas: *His mom would have to carry him to and from therapy; he couldn't do things by himself.*)

**Page 9.** Why do you think Taylor was so excited to try the wheelchair in therapy? (Ideas: *Using the walker was slow and tiring; his mom wouldn't have to carry him anymore; he'd be able to get around on his own.*) How did Tyler help Taylor learn to use the wheelchair? (Idea: *He pushed it for him while Taylor was getting stronger.*) What are some things Taylor had to learn to do with the wheelchair? (Ideas: *Roll the wheelchair back and forth; turn; use the brakes.*)

**Page 12.** Why did one of Taylor's school friends feel sorry for Taylor? (Ideas: *He thought that it was better for Taylor to get around on his own two feet than to ride in a wheelchair, even though it was slow.*) What reasons did Taylor give his friend for wanting to use the wheelchair? (Ideas: *He wouldn't get so tired; he wouldn't have to be carried; he would be able to move on his own.*)

**Page 13.** What surprise did Taylor get at therapy? (Idea: *His own wheelchair.*) How did Taylor feel about his new wheelchair? (Idea: *Excited.*)

**Page 15.** What kinds of things is Taylor able to do in his wheelchair? (Idea: *Turn to the right; turn to the left.*) What is he learning how to do? (Idea: *Pop a wheelie.*) Why is it important for Taylor to learn to "pop a wheelie"? (Idea: *So he can get over bumps or big cracks in the sidewalk.*)

**Page 16.** How does Tyler help Taylor learn to "pop a wheelie"? (Idea: *He lifts up the front of the chair so Taylor can practice balancing.*)

**Page 18.** What kinds of things does Taylor have to pay attention to? (Ideas: *Stairs and no ramp at the entrance of a building; heavy front doors; stairs or an escalator, but no elevator.*)

**Pages 19–23.** What changes has Taylor's school made to help people in wheelchairs? (Ideas: *They have installed a ramp around the stairs; they have put a silver button on the wall that will open the door; they put in a shorter drinking fountain; they put in a larger bathroom stall with a door that opens out.*) On page 19, Taylor tells us that the school has a ramp that **zigzags** up and around the stairs. If something **zigzags,** it moves in sharp turns from one side to the other. What verb means to "move in sharp turns from one side to the other"? *Zigzag.*

**Page 26.** What do Taylor and Tyler have to do before they can go play outside? (Idea: *Tyler helps Taylor do his leg stretches.*)

**Page 27.** What is Taylor and Tyler's favorite sport? (Idea: *Basketball.*) How does Taylor play basketball in his wheelchair? (Ideas: *He pushes and steers the chair with one hand; he dribbles with the other hand; he rolls as quickly as he can to the basket; he uses both hands to shoot.*)

**Page 29.** What does his wheelchair do for Taylor? (Ideas: *It allows him to go more places he wants to go; it allows him to do more things he wants to do.*)

### Review Vocabulary

(Display the Picture Vocabulary Cards. Point to each card as you say the word. Ask children to repeat each word after you.) These pictures show **equipment, escalator, elevator,** and **wheel.**

- What noun means "things made for a particular use"? *Equipment.*

- What noun means "a machine that carries people up and down between the floors of buildings"? *Elevator.*
- What noun means "a moving staircase"? *Escalator.*
- What verb means "to push something on wheels"? *Wheel.*

## Extend Vocabulary

◎⚊ Wheel

In *Rolling Along,* we learned that **wheel** means "to push something on wheels." Say the word that means "to push something on wheels." *Wheel.*

Raise your hand if you can tell us a sentence that uses **wheel** as a verb meaning "to push something on wheels." (Call on several children. If they don't use complete sentences, restate their examples as sentences. Have the class repeat the sentences.)

Here's a new way to use the word **wheel.**

- Mother bought a **wheel** of cheese for the party. Say the sentence.
- My dad always keeps his hands on the steering **wheel** when he drives. Say the sentence.
- I need to put a new **wheel** on my bicycle. Say the sentence.

**In these sentences, wheel is a noun that means a round object that helps a vehicle move smoothly or any object that is shaped like a wheel.** What word means "a round object that helps a vehicle move smoothly or any object that is shaped like a wheel"? *Wheel.*

Raise your hand if you can tell us a sentence that uses **wheel** as a noun meaning "a round object that helps a vehicle move smoothly or any object that is shaped like a wheel." (Call on several children. If they don't use complete sentences, restate their examples as sentences. Have the class repeat the sentences.

## Present Expanded Target Vocabulary

◎⚊ Accepting

In the book, Taylor's family and friends love him. It doesn't matter to them that he has a disability. They love him for who he is. They accept him for who he is. **Accepting.** Say the word. *Accepting.*

**Accepting** is a describing word. It tells more about a person. What kind of word is **accepting?** *A describing word.*

**Accepting means you take someone for who they are, in spite of any disabilities or problems they might have.** Say the word that means "you take someone for who they are in spite of any disabilities or problems they might have." *Accepting.*

I'll tell about some situations. If the people in the situations are being accepting, say "accepting." If not, don't say anything.

- Ethan played with Aaron and helped him get around in his wheelchair. *Accepting.*
- Marcus made fun of the boy with braces on his legs.
- The bullies teased the new girl who wore glasses and braces.
- Austin's best friend Nick has a hard time controlling his feelings, but Austin still plays with him. *Accepting.*
- The kitten was born without one leg. The children loved her even more because of it. *Accepting.*
- The child in the wheelchair was left alone in a corner of the playground while the other children ignored him.

What describing word means "you take someone for who they are, in spite of any disabilities or problems they might have"? *Accepting.*

◎⚊ Positive

In the book, Taylor does not use his disability as an excuse to not do things. He has a very positive attitude about himself. **Positive.** Say the word. *Positive.*

**Positive** is a describing word. It tells more about a person. What kind of word is **positive?** *A describing word.*

**A positive person is someone who goes through life with a good attitude.** Say the word that describes a person who "goes through life with a good attitude." *Positive.*

Let's think about some things that positive people might say. I'll tell you some things that people say. If I tell something positive, say "positive." If not, don't say anything.

- "I hate Mondays."
- "I can get this homework done. I just have to sit down and do it." *Positive.*
- "A wheelchair will be great! I'll be able to get around all by myself." *Positive.*
- "I don't want to wear glasses. Everyone will make fun of me."
- "Gee, it's raining again. That's bad. I can never go out and play when it rains."
- "Oh, look at the snow! It's so beautiful. Let's go build a snowman." *Positive.*

What word describes a person who "goes through life with a good attitude"? *Positive.*

**Preparation:** Prepare a sheet of chart paper with a tree with 9 circles hanging on it as decorations.

### Make a Celebration Tree

Today I'll show you the photographs and illustrations from *Rolling Along.* As I read about those photographs and illustrations, I'll call on different children to tell about an important event in Taylor's life that he might choose to celebrate.

(Each time children give a response, record the underlined words on one of the ornaments on the tree.)

**Pages 7–8.** What would Taylor celebrate in this part of his story? (Idea: *Kathryn taught him how to <u>use</u> a <u>walker</u>.*)

**Pages 9–10.** What would Taylor celebrate in this part of his story? (Idea: *When Kathryn let him <u>try</u> using a <u>wheelchair</u> in therapy.*)

**Pages 13–14.** What would Taylor celebrate in this part of his story? (Idea: *His <u>new wheelchair</u> had come in.*)

**Page 16.** What would Taylor celebrate in this part of his story? (Idea: *Tyler helps him <u>practice wheelies</u>.*)

**Pages 19–20.** What would Taylor celebrate in this part of his story? (Idea: *He <u>can wheel himself up to the top</u>.*)

**Page 21.** What would Taylor celebrate in this part of his story? (Idea: *He can <u>wheel himself inside</u>; he can <u>roll down the hallway</u>; he can <u>go through the rooms' doorways</u>.*)

**Pages 23–24.** What would Taylor celebrate in this part of his story? (Idea: *He can get a <u>drink of water all by himself</u> from the water fountain; he can wash his hands at the <u>lower sink</u>; he can even get in the <u>large bathroom stall</u>.*)

**Pages 27–28.** What would Taylor celebrate in this part of his story? (Ideas: *His wheelchair lets him do a lot, like <u>play all kinds of different sports</u> with Tyler; sometimes he <u>scores as many points as Tyler</u>.*)

**Page 29.** What would Taylor celebrate in this part of his story? (Idea: *His wheelchair helps him <u>go more places on his own</u> and <u>do more of the things he wants to do</u>.*)

### Play the Super Choosing Game

Today, you will play the *Super Choosing* game. We've played a game like this before but this one is a little bit different. Let's think about the six words we have learned: **equipment, escalator, elevator, wheel, accepting,** and **positive.** (Display the word cards.)

I will say a sentence that has two or three target words in it. You will have to choose the correct word for that sentence. Not all of the words will be from this lesson, though. That's why it's the *Super Choosing* game. Let's practice. (You should not show cards for the words outside of this lesson.)

- If you keep on trying and never give up, do you have **perseverance, journey,** or **ingredients?** *Perseverance.*
- If you ride on a moving staircase, are you on an **elevator,** an **escalator,** or a **routine?** *Escalator.*
- If you are in a dry, sandy place with few plants, are you in the **wilderness,** the **desert,** or a **hullabaloo?** *Desert.*

Now you're ready to play the game. If you tell me the correct answer, you will win one point. If you can't tell me the correct answer, I get the point. (Draw a T-chart on the board for keeping score. Children earn one point for each correct answer. If they make an error, correct them as you normally would, and record one point for yourself. Repeat missed words at the end of the game.)

- If you ride to the 95th floor of a building in a machine, are you in an **elevator, Mexico,** or an **escalator?** *Elevator.*
- Is a person with a good outlook on life **positive, faithful,** or **captive?** *Positive.*
- If you pushed your bike across the street, would you say you **injured** it, **schooled** it, or **wheeled** it? *Wheeled.*
- If three animals all had similar wings, bodies, and antennae, would you say they had similar **characteristics, insects,** or **companions?** *Characteristics.*
- If you took people for who they are in spite of their disabilities or problems, would you describe yourself as **fascinated, delighted,** or **accepting?** *Accepting.*
- If you had an object that was round, would you call it a **doubt,** a **wheel,** or a **pest?** *Wheel.*

(Count the points and declare a winner.) You did a great job of playing the *Super Choosing* game.

---

### DAY 4

**Preparation:** *The Biography of Taylor.*
Print the following words in two columns on the board: *basketball, dinosaurs, disability, braces, walker, wheelchair, push, own, strong, brakes, changes, fountain.*

---

### Introduce The Biography of Taylor

(Point to each word as you read it aloud.) This word is **basketball.** What word? *Basketball.* This word is **dinosaurs.** What word? *Dinosaurs.* (Repeat process for remaining words.)

Let's read these words together. First word? *Basketball.* Next word? *Dinosaurs.* (Repeat process for remaining words.)

Read these words by yourself. First word? *Basketball.* Next word? *Dinosaurs.* (Repeat process for remaining words.)

(Use the following correction procedure if children make an error:) This word is **wheelchair.**

What word? *Wheelchair.* Yes, **wheelchair.** (Go back to the top of the list and repeat the list until the children can read it accurately and confidently.)

(Give each child a copy of *The Biography of Taylor.* Ask the children to touch under the title of the booklet.) The title of this book is *The Biography of Taylor.* What's the title of this book? *The Biography of Taylor.*

Remember that a biography tells about the life of a real person. What does a biography tell about? *The life of a real person.* Is a biography fiction or nonfiction? *Nonfiction.*

(Ask children to open their booklets to page 1. Ask them to touch under the first underlined word.) This word is **Taylor.** What word? *Taylor.* Yes, **Taylor.** This biography is about Taylor. Who is this biography about? *Taylor.*

(Ask children to touch under the next underlined word.) This word is **Tyler.** What word? *Tyler.* Yes, **Tyler.** Tyler is Taylor's twin brother. Who is Tyler? *Taylor's twin brother.*

My turn to read each page of the book aloud. You touch under each word as I read it. (Read pages 1–4.)

Let's read the book together. (Have the children read the book chorally with you.)

(Assign each child a partner. Allow sufficient time for each child to read the booklet to his or her partner. Circulate as children read, offering praise and assistance.)

(Children should color the illustrations in their booklet. Encourage them to color the illustrations realistically.)

### Play the Super Choosing Game (Cumulative Review)

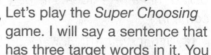 Let's play the *Super Choosing* game. I will say a sentence that has three target words in it. You will have to choose the correct word for that sentence. (Display the Picture Vocabulary Cards for *escalator, elevator, equipment, wheel, accepting,* and *positive* for the three words in each sentence as you say the sentence.)

T Now you're ready to play the *Super Choosing* game. (Draw a T-chart on the board for keeping score. Children earn one point for each correct answer. If they make an error, correct them as you normally would, and record one point for yourself. Repeat missed words at the end of the game.)

- If you rode a moving staircase to the second floor of a department store, did you ride an **escalator,** an **elevator,** or an **equipment?** *An escalator.*
- You pushed your friend in his wheelchair around the school, did you **accepting, positive,** or **wheel** her? *Wheel.*
- If your mom's office were on the 75th floor of a building, would you take an **equipment,** an **elevator,** or a **positive** to go visit her at work? *An elevator.*
- If you use special shoes when you play soccer, are the shoes part of your **wheel, elevator,** or **equipment?** *Equipment.*
- If Maria helps children with disabilities at school, is she **accepting, elevator,** or **escalator?** *Accepting.*
- If you wake up each morning thinking that it's going to be a wonderful day, are you a **positive** person, an **accepting** person, or a **wheel** person? *A positive person.*
- Is the round thing in the car that helps you turn called steering **equipment,** a steering **wheel,** or a steering **elevator?** *A steering wheel.*
- If I love all the members of my family in spite of their problems, am I **escalator, wheel,** or **accepting?** *Accepting.*

Now you will have to listen very carefully, because I'm not going to show you the word cards. Think hard. I'm going to use words that you have learned in other lessons. (This part of the game includes the review words from previous lessons.)

- If you are warm-blooded and have a skeleton inside your body are you an **insect,** a **fish,** or a **mammal?** *A mammal.*
- If you rode in a machine between floors of a building, did you ride in an **elevator,** a **dream,** or a **flock?** *An elevator.*

- If a building has moving staircases, does it have **enemies, reptiles,** or **escalators?** *Escalators.*
- If you pushed your brother in a wagon, did you **incredible** him, **active** him, or **wheel** him? *Wheel him.*
- When you bake, you use mixing bowls, spatulas, and pans. Are these baking **equipment, venoms,** or **species?** *Equipment.*
- If you are always smiling and saying nice things, are you **captured, prey,** or **positive?** *Positive.*
- Is someone who treats everyone kindly a **marsh, accepting,** or **rude?** *Accepting.*
- If you and your sister constantly beg your mother for ice cream, are you being **pests, predators,** or **polite?** *Pests.*

(Tally the points and declare a winner.) You did a great job of playing the *Super Choosing* game.

| DAY 5 |
|---|

**Preparation:** Chart titled *Reading Goals* that was started in Week 16.

*The Biography of Taylor.*

Happy Quiz Answer Sheet, BLM B.

### Read The Biography of Taylor

(Assign each child a partner.)Today, you'll read the first four pages of *The Biography of Taylor* to your partner. (Allow sufficient time for each child to read the first four pages of the booklet to his or her partner. Circulate as the children read, offering praise and assistance.)

(Ask children to look at the back of their booklet.) This part of the book is for people who can help you find other books to read. It tells those people about other books that are biographies. It also tells them about a place where you can find other biographies. Where are some places that you could go to find other biographies? (Ideas: *To the school library; to the public library; to a bookstore.*)

(You may wish to read aloud and discuss the information on the back cover.)

There's one more important thing on the back cover of your book. Touch the box that is at the bottom of the page. The words above the box say "My reading goal." What do the words say? *My reading goal.*

What is a goal? (Idea: *Something that you want to succeed at doing.*) A reading goal is something that you want to succeed at doing with your reading.

Let's see if we can add some other reading goals to our class chart. What are some other reading goals that someone might have when they read their book? (Accept reasonable responses. Help children put their ideas into goal statements. Add to the list of statements on the chart. Ask children to choose a goal and copy it into the box. Children may also make up an original goal that is not on the list. If children are unable to copy the goals or to write a goal of their own, you or a helper may wish to scribe their goal statements for them before the booklets are sent home.)

### Assess Comprehension

(Ask children to turn to page 5 in their booklet.) This is what you have read in the biography about Taylor but with no pictures. You are going to have a little quiz to see if you can remember what you read.

(Ask children to touch under the words as they read the passage about Taylor silently. Monitor to ensure that the children are reading the passage. Ask children to look up at you after they have finished reading the passage. Instruct children to read and answer the questions.)

### Assess Vocabulary

 (Give each child a copy of the Quiz Answer Sheet, BLM B.)

Today you're going to have a True or False quiz. When you do the True or False quiz, it shows me how well you know the hard words you are learning.

If I say something that is true, circle the word **true.** What will you do if I say something that is true? *Circle the word* true.

If I say something that is false, circle the word **false.** What will you do if I say something that is false? *Circle the word* false.

Listen carefully to each item that I say. Don't let me trick you!

Item 1: A square hunk of cheese is called a **wheel** of cheese. (*False.*)

Item 2: If you **compete,** you are taking part in a contest or game. (*True.*)

Item 3: An **elevator** is a moving staircase. (*False.*)

Item 4: An animal that is **active** at night sleeps at night. (*False.*)

Item 5: Many sports use special **equipment.** (*True.*)

Item 6: An **accepting** person often teases other children. (*False.*)

Item 7: A **predator** hunts **prey** for food. (*True.*)

Item 8: If you are in a wheelchair, you could use an **escalator** to get to the second floor. (*False.*)

Item 9: "I hate snow!" is not a very **positive** thing to say. (*True.*)

Item 10: A math problem that you just can't get right no matter how many times you try is **challenging** for you. (*True.*)

You did a great job completing your quiz!

(Score children's work. A child must score 9 out of 10 to be at the mastery level. If a child does not achieve mastery, insert the missed words as additional items in the games in next week's lessons. Retest those children individually for the missed items before they take the next mastery test.)

### Extensions

#### Read a Book as a Reward

(Display *Rolling Along* and a number of biographies. Ask children to choose one they would like you to read. Read the book as a reward for their hard work.)

**Preparation:** Word containers for the Super Words Center.

## Introduce the Super Words Center (2 in 1)

(Add the new Picture Vocabulary Cards to words from the previous weeks. Show children one of the word containers. Role-play with two to three children as you introduce each part of the game.)

You will play a game called *2 in 1* in the Super Words Center.

Let's think about how we work with our words in the Super Words Center.

You will work with a partner in the Super Words Center. Whom will you work with? *A partner.*

First, you will draw two words out of the container. What do you do first? (Idea: *Draw two words out of the container.*) Show your partner both of the words. (Demonstrate.)

Next you will say a sentence that uses both of your words. What do you do next? (Idea: *I will say a sentence that uses both of my words.*) (Demonstrate.)

If you can use both of your words in one sentence, give yourself a point. Then give your partner a turn. (Demonstrate.)

What do you do next? *Give my partner a turn.*

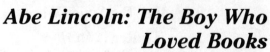

**Preparation:** You will need a copy of *Abe Lincoln: The Boy Who Loved Books* for each day's lesson.

Number the pages of the book to assist you in asking comprehension questions at appropriate points.

Post a copy of the Vocabulary Tally Sheet with this week's Picture Vocabulary Cards attached.

Each child will need one copy of the Homework Sheet, BLM 23a.

# Abe Lincoln: The Boy Who Loved Books

author: Kay Winters • illustrator: Nancy Carpenter

## 🎯 Target Vocabulary

| Tier II | Tier III |
|---|---|
| slave | nonfiction |
| grief | reproduction |
| unjust | biography |
| honest | |
| *literate | |
| *compassionate | |

*Expanded Target Vocabulary Word

## DAY 1:

### Introduce Book

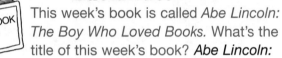

This week's book is called *Abe Lincoln: The Boy Who Loved Books.* What's the title of this week's book? *Abe Lincoln: The Boy Who Loved Books.*

This book was written by Kay Winters. Who's the author of *Abe Lincoln: The Boy Who Loved Books*? *Kay Winters.*

Nancy Carpenter made the pictures for this book. Who made the pictures for *Abe Lincoln: The Boy Who Loved Books*? *Nancy Carpenter.* Who was the illustrator for this book? *Nancy Carpenter.*

The cover of a book usually gives us some hints of what the book is about. Let's look at the front cover of *Abe Lincoln: The Boy Who Loved Books.* What do you see on this cover? (Ideas: *A boy sitting in a tree reading a book; a log cabin; a covered wagon; a man with an ax; trees; mountains.*)

*Abe Lincoln: The Boy Who Loved Books* is a biography. A biography tells about the life of a real person. What does a biography tell about? *The life of a real person.* What kind of book tells about the life of a real person? *A biography.*

This book is true. What kinds of books are about true things? *Nonfiction books.*

### Take a Picture Walk

(Encourage children to use target words in their answers.) We're going to take a picture walk through this book. When we take a picture walk through a nonfiction book that is a biography, we look carefully at the pictures and think about what we see.

Nancy Carpenter painted these pictures on canvas using oil paints. Copies of the paintings were made for this book. When a copy of a painting is made, it's called a reproduction. What do we call a copy of a painting? *A reproduction.* What is a reproduction? *A copy of a painting.*

**Pages 1–2.** What do you see in this reproduction? (Ideas: *A log cabin; tall trees; a winding road; snow.*) When does this part of the biography happen? (Idea: *In the winter.*)

**Pages 3–4.** Who do you think these people are? (Ideas: *Abe Lincoln's parents; Abe Lincoln; Abe's sister.*) When do you think Abe Lincoln lived? (Idea: *A long time ago.*) Why do you think he lived a long time ago? (Ideas: *The parents and sister are wearing old-fashioned clothes; they live in a log cabin.*)

**Pages 5–6.** When do you think this part of the biography takes place? (Ideas: *Spring; summer.* Point to the boy waving at the travelers.) Who do you think this is? (Idea: *Abe Lincoln.*)

**Page 7.** What do you think is happening here? (Idea: *Abe is in school; he is learning math; the other children are fooling around; the teacher is sleeping.*) How do you think Abe Lincoln feels about school? (Ideas: *He thinks it is important; he likes it.*) Why do you think that? (Ideas: *He is the only one trying to learn; he is showing the teacher his work.*)

**Page 8.** What is Abe doing in these pictures? (Ideas: *Practicing writing his letters with a mop and on a tree stump.*)

**Pages 9–10.** What do you think is happening in this picture? (Ideas: *Abe's father is telling a story; Abe's mother and sister are sewing; Abe is enjoying his father's story.*)

**Page 11.** What do you think is happening in these pictures? (Ideas: *The family is traveling on horseback; the family is traveling down a river with their horse.*)

**Page 12.** Where do you think the Lincolns are? (Ideas: *In the woods; at their new home.*)

**Pages 13–14.** Where is the Lincoln family in this reproduction? (Ideas: *In the woods; in a little shelter.*) When is this part of the biography happening? (Idea: *At night.*) How do you think the family feels? (Ideas: *Frightened; scared; terrified.*) Why does the family feel that way? (Ideas: *There are wild animals in the woods; they do not have a house to protect them; they are in the wilderness.*)

**Page 15.** What is happening in this picture? (Ideas: *They are building a house; they are building a log cabin.*) How is Abe helping? (Idea: *He is helping carry the logs.*)

**Page 16.** What is happening in this picture? (Idea: *Abe is climbing up to his sister's bed.*) When do you think this part of the biography is happening? (Idea: *In the winter.*) What is the problem in this part of the biography? (Idea: *The snow is coming in through the cracks in the cabin.*)

**Page 17.** What is Abe doing in this reproduction? (Idea: *He has his head down on a fallen log, his gun is next to him; maybe he's hiding; maybe he's crying.*)

**Page 18.** What is happening in this reproduction? (Idea: *Abe and his father are chopping down trees with axes.*) What is Abe doing to his tree? (Idea: *Carving the letter* A *into it.*)

**Pages 19–20.** When is this part of the biography happening? (Idea: *Winter.*) What do you think has happened? (Ideas: *Somebody died; Abe's mother died.*)

**Page 21.** Who do you think that woman is? (Ideas: *Grandmother; the new stepmother.*)

**Page 22.** What is the Lincoln family doing here? (Ideas: *Relaxing; spending quiet time together.*) What is Abe doing? (Idea: *Reading.*)

**Pages 23–24.** Where do you think the children are going in this reproduction? (Idea: *To school.*) What makes you think the children are going to school? (Idea: *They are carrying books.* Point to Abe—the tallest boy in the cap.) Do you think Abe is happy about going to school? Tell why or why not.

**Pages 25–26.** What do you see that is the same in each of these reproductions? (Idea: *In each picture, Abe either has a book or is reading a book.*) How do you think Abe feels about reading? (Ideas: *He enjoys it; he thinks it is important.*)

**Pages 27–28.** Where is Abe in this reproduction? (Ideas: *Lying on the ground; under a tree.*) What is Abe doing? (Idea: *Reading a book.*) What do you think Abe is supposed to be doing? (Ideas: *Plowing the field; working in the field.*) What do you think the other people are saying about Abe?

**Pages 29–30.** (Point to Abe on the raft.) What do you think Abe is doing in this reproduction? (Ideas: *Delivering logs; delivering firewood.*) What does Abe see from his raft? (Idea: *A slave auction; it looks like people are being sold.*)

**Pages 31–32.** Where does this part of the biography happen? (Idea: *In a little town.*) What is Abe doing here? (Idea: *Chasing after a wagon.*) Why do you think Abe is trying to catch that wagon?

**Pages 33–34.** What is Abe doing in these pictures? (Ideas: *Wrestling; fighting with another* *man.*) How did this wrestling match end? (Ideas: *Abe and the other man shook hands; they became friends.*)

**Top of page 35.** What is Abe doing in this reproduction? (Ideas: *Studying; reading.*)

**Bottom of page 35.** What do you think Abe is doing here? (Idea: *Talking to a group of people about the man on the chair.*) Abe is grown up now. What do you think he has become? (Idea: *A lawyer.*)

**Page 36.** (Point to Abe on the back of the train.) What do you think Abe is doing in this reproduction? (Ideas: *Giving a speech; trying to become President.*)

**Pages 37–38.** Where do you think Abe is in this reproduction? (Idea: *The White House; Washington, D.C.*) What has Abe become? (Idea: *President.*) What is Abe still doing? (Idea: *Reading.*)

 **Read the Book Aloud**
(Read the story to children with minimal interruptions.)

Tomorrow we will read the book again and I will ask you some questions.

## Present Target Vocabulary
 Slave

In the book, Abe is upset at seeing slaves being sold at an auction. **Slave.** Say the word. *Slave.*

**Slave** is a noun. It names a person. What kind of word is **slave?** *A noun.*

**A slave is a person who is owned by another and forced to work without pay or rights.** Say the word that means "a person who is owned by another and forced to work with no pay or rights." *Slave.*

A long time ago in the United States some people were slaves. It was a very bad thing for people to be slaves. Abraham Lincoln and many other people thought that it was wrong to keep people as slaves. They worked hard to make sure that everyone was free and that there were no more slaves in the United States.

What noun names "a person who is owned by another and forced to work without pay or rights"? *Slave.*

 Grief

In the book, when Abe's mother died, his grief was so deep, he could not speak her name. **Grief.** Say the word. *Grief.*

**Grief** is a noun. It names a feeling. What kind of word is **grief?** *A noun.*

**Grief is a deep, deep sadness.** Say the word that means a "deep, deep sadness." *Grief.*

(Correct any incorrect responses, and repeat the item at the end of the sequence.)

Let's think about some events that might cause grief. I'll tell about an event. If the event would cause grief, say "grief." If not, don't say anything.

- Your best friend has a birthday party.
- Your favorite pet runs away. *Grief.*
- A loved one dies. *Grief.*
- You lose your shoe.
- There was a very bad fire in your town. Some people were hurt and lost their homes. *Grief.*
- School is closed because of snow.

What noun means "a deep, deep sadness"? *Grief.*

 Unjust

In the book, Abe knew that it was unjust to own another person. **Unjust.** Say the word. *Unjust.*

**Unjust** is a describing word. It tells more about a noun. What kind of word is **unjust?** *A describing word.*

**If something is unjust, it is not fair or right.** Say the word that describes something that is "not fair and not right." *Unjust.*

Let's think about some situations that might be unjust. I'll tell about some situations. If you think that they are unjust, say "unjust." If not, don't say anything.

- Getting good grades because your aunt is the principal. *Unjust.*
- Getting good grades because you work hard.
- Playing quarterback on the football team because you practice hard and do well.
- Playing quarterback on the football team even though you never go to practice because your father is friends with the coach. *Unjust.*

- Owning another person and forcing them to work for no money. *Unjust.*

What describing word tells about things that are "not fair and not right"? *Unjust.*

 Honest

In the book, the people of New Salem called Abraham Lincoln "Honest Abe" because if he accidentally overcharged someone even six cents, he would give it back to them. **Honest.** Say the word. *Honest.*

**Honest** is a describing word. It tells more about a person. What kind of word is **honest**? *A describing word.*

**An honest person is always truthful and does not lie, steal, or cheat.** Say the word that describes a person who is "always truthful and does not lie, or steal, or cheat." *Honest.*

Let's think about some people and situations. I'll tell you about some things that happened. If you think the person in that situation was being honest, say "honest." If not, don't say anything.

- Graham hit the ball through Mrs. Green's kitchen window. He rang her doorbell to apologize to her. *Honest.*
- April accidentally broke her friend's game. She told her friend it was already broken when she borrowed it.
- A driver accidentally hit another car while he was pulling into the parking lot. He wrote a note with his name and phone number and left it under the car's windshield wiper. *Honest.*
- Jeremiah kept his eyes on his own paper while he took the test. *Honest.*
- Zack took a pack of gum from the grocery store without paying for it.
- I accidentally paid too much for a bottle of shampoo. The cashier caught the mistake and gave me my money back. *Honest.*

What describing word tells about a person who is "always truthful and does not lie, steal, or cheat"? *Honest.*

## Present Vocabulary Tally Sheet
(See Lesson 1, page 4, for instructions.)

## Assign Homework
(Homework Sheet, BLM 23a. See the Introduction for homework instructions.)

**DAY 2**

**Preparation:** Picture Vocabulary Cards for *slave, grief, unjust, honest.*

## Read and Discuss Story
(Read story to children. Ask the following questions at the specified points. Encourage them to use target words in their answers.)

**Page 2.** Who is this biography about? (Idea: *Abraham Lincoln.*) Where was Abraham Lincoln born? (Ideas: *In a log cabin; in the wilds of Kentucky.*)

**Page 3.** What things did Abe do in his family's cabin? (Ideas: *Said his first words; took his first steps.*) Tell us some things about the Lincoln's log cabin. (Ideas: *It had a hard dirt floor; it had a little window; it had a wood-burning fireplace; the door had leather hinges.*)

**Page 5.** What happened when Abe was two? (Idea: *His family moved to Knob Creek.*) Who did Abe meet and talk to as he grew older? (Ideas: *Travelers; peddlers; pioneers; traders; slaves.*) What happened to Abe as he talked to these travelers (Ideas: *He learned that the world was wider than his own; his ideas stretched; his questions rose; his dreams were stirred.*) What do you think the words "his ideas stretched" mean? (Ideas: *He thought about bigger things; he thought about more important things.*)

When we read *I Am a Gymnast,* we learned dreams could be things a person thinks about often and really wants to have happen. What do you think the words "his dreams were stirred" mean? (Ideas: *He started to believe all people should be free; he started to think of a country where everyone would have a chance to live a good life.*)

**Page 7.** What did Abe learn at school? (Ideas: *To count to ten; to write his letters.*)

**Page 8.** Where did Abe practice writing his letters? (Ideas: *In school; at home; in dust; in snow; on logs of wood.*)

**Page 9.** Had Abe's parents gone to school? (Idea: *No.*) What would the Lincoln family do in the evenings? (Ideas: *Mother would tell Bible stories; Father spun yarns, told jokes, made them laugh.*) It says in the story that Abe's father "spun yarns." That means he told stories about things that had happened, but he exaggerated a lot.

**Page 11.** What happened when Abe was seven? (Idea: *The family moved again.*) How far away did they move? (Idea: *100 miles away.*) How did the family get to Indiana? (Idea: *They walked and rode horses.*)

**Page 12.** What did the Lincoln family have to do to get to the land they claimed? (Ideas: *Go across the Ohio River on a makeshift ferry; hack a trail through the trees and vines.*)

**Page 13.** Why was there no cabin for the Lincolns to live in? (Ideas: *They were in the wilderness; nobody else had ever lived there before.*) How did the family protect itself from the wild animals? (Idea: *They kept a fire going.*) What kinds of animals were in the forest? (Ideas: *Bears; wolves; panthers.*)

**Page 16.** How did the family get a home? (Idea: *Other settlers came and helped them build a house.*) What did Abe like to do in his cabin? (Idea: *Climb up to his sleeping place.*) What problem did the cabin have? (Idea: *Snow and wind blew through the cracks.*)

**Page 17.** How did Abe feel about shooting the turkey? (Ideas: *Sad; upset.*)

**Page 18.** What did Abe do when he was eight? (Ideas: *Helped his father clear the land; helped his father cut down trees; learned to swing an ax.*) What was Abe's dream? (Ideas: *To go back to school; to learn from books.*)

**Page 19.** What happened when Abe was nine? (Idea: *His mother died.*)

**Page 21.** Who did Abe's father bring home? (Ideas: *A new wife; a new mother for Sarah and Abe; a new family.*)

**Page 22.** What did this new wife have that excited Abe? (Idea: *Books.*)

**Page 23.** Where did the new wife send the children? (Idea: *Back to school.*) What did Abe learn to do in school? (Ideas: *Add; subtract.*) What did he love to do most of all? (Ideas: *Read; win spelling bees; spin yarns; tell tales.*)

**Page 25.** What did Abe do when school was out? (Ideas: *Worked for farmers; split rails; dug wells; chopped trees.*) What did Abe really want to do? (Idea: *Learn.*)

**Page 26.** Why did Abe have to pull stalks of corn for his friend's family? (Ideas: *He borrowed a book from the friend; rain leaked on it and ruined it; he had to earn the money to replace the ruined book.*)

**Page 27.** How did Abe reward himself for plowing a row? (Idea: *At the end of each row, he would read a page from his book.*) What did people think of Abe? (Idea: *He was lazy.*)

**Page 28.** What was Abe's dream? (Idea: *To learn from books.*)

**Page 29.** What did Abe do when he was nineteen? (Ideas: *Poled a flatboat down the river; left home; saw people and places beyond the backwoods; saw slaves being sold at an auction.*)

**Page 30.** How did Abe feel about the act of selling slaves? (Idea: *He thought it was unjust.*)

**Page 31.** Where did Abe settle? (Idea: *New Salem, Illinois.*) What did Abe do in New Salem? (Idea: *Ran the general store.*) Why did the people of New Salem call him "Honest Abe"? (Idea: *He once walked miles to return six cents to a customer he overcharged.*)

**Pages 33–34.** Why did Abe have to wrestle Jack Armstrong? (Idea: *To prove his worth.*) The storeowner and the people of New Salem wanted Abe to prove he was a good man by showing his strength rather than how smart he was. What happened when Jack saw Abe's strength? (Ideas: *He shook his hand; they became friends.*)

**Page 35.** Why did Abe become a lawyer? (Ideas: *He saw that words could jail or free a man; he found that words could change the way people thought.*) What do you think is the highest office in the land? (Idea: *President.*) What did Abe think he could do as a politician? (Ideas: *Make the wrong things right.*)

**Page 37.** What happened to Abe Lincoln? (Idea: *He became the sixteenth President of the United States.*) What helped Abe become President? (Ideas: *He knew the power of words; he used words well.*)

## Review Vocabulary

(Display the Picture Vocabulary Cards. Point to each card as you say the word. Ask children to repeat each word after you.) These pictures show **slave, grief, unjust,** and **honest.**

- What word means "not fair and not right"? *Unjust.*
- What noun means "a deep, deep sadness"? *Grief.*
- What word means "always truthful and never lies, steals, or cheats"? *Honest.*
- What noun means "a person owned by another and forced to work without pay or rights"? *Slave.*

## Extend Vocabulary

◎ ᐊ Slave

In *Abe Lincoln: The Boy Who Loved Books,* we learned that a **slave** is "a person owned by another and forced to work without pay or rights." Say the word that means "a person owned by another and forced to work without pay or rights." *Slave.*

Raise your hand if you can tell us a sentence that uses **slave** as a noun meaning "a person owned by another and forced to work without pay or rights." (Call on several children. If they don't use complete sentences, restate their examples as sentences. Have the class repeat the sentences.)

Here's a new way to use the word **slave.**

- Mother **slaved** all day over a hot stove preparing the holiday meal. Say the sentence.
- Alex **slaves** away at his job six days a week. Say the sentence.
- Melissa **slaved** over her science project for hours. Say the sentence.

**In these sentences, slave is a verb that means to work very hard.** What word means "to work very hard"? *Slave.*

Raise your hand if you can tell us a sentence that uses **slave** as a verb meaning "to work very hard." (Call on several children. If they don't use complete sentences, restate their examples as sentences. Have the class repeat the sentences.)

## Present Expanded Target Vocabulary

◎ ᐊ Literate

In the book, Abe learned to read and write. He became literate. **Literate.** Say the word. *Literate.*

**Literate** is a describing word. It tells more about a person. What kind of word is **literate?** *A describing word.*

**Literate means you are able to read and write.** Say the word that means that you are "able to read and write." *Literate.*

I'll tell about some people. If the person I tell about is literate, say "literate." If not, don't say anything.

- My 2-year-old sister cannot read yet.
- My great grandfather never went to school. He never learned to read and write.
- My father can read and write in three different languages. *Literate.*
- Liam read a book and then wrote a report about it. *Literate.*
- The first graders have all learned how to read and write. *Literate.*
- Many children in other countries don't go to school. They never learn how to read and write.

What describing word means that you are "able to read and write"? *Literate.*

◎ ᐊ Compassionate

In the book, Abe became very upset when he killed the turkey and when he saw people being sold like tools. He felt sorry for them. **Compassionate.** Say the word. *Compassionate.*

**Compassionate** is a describing word. It tells more about people. What kind of word is **compassionate?** *A describing word.*

**A compassionate person is someone who feels sorry for another's suffering and wants to help.** Say the word that describes a person who "feels sorry for another's suffering and wants to help." *Compassionate.*

Let's think about some things that compassionate people might say. I'll tell you some things that people say. If I tell something compassionate, say "compassionate." If not, don't say anything.

- "I hope you are feeling better today." *Compassionate.*
- "I know it must be hard to lose your cat. Is there anything I can do to help?" *Compassionate.*
- "Ha ha! You fell off the swing."
- "I really don't care if you don't feel well, sit down and do your work."
- "I'm so sorry you feel sad today." *Compassionate.*
- "I wish there was a way to help. I think I'll donate money to help those people." *Compassionate.*

What word describes a person who "feels sorry for another's suffering and wants to help"? *Compassionate.*

---

### DAY 3

**Preparation:** Prepare a sheet of chart paper with a diagram of a tree on it, with 7 circles hanging on it as decorations. Record the underlined words in the ornaments on the tree.

### Make a Celebration Tree

Today I'll show you the reproductions of the oil paintings done for *Abe Lincoln: The Boy Who Loved Books.* As I read about those reproductions, I'll call on one of you to tell about an important event in Abe Lincoln's life that he might choose to celebrate.

**Pages 3–4.** What would Abe celebrate in this part of his life? (Idea: *Abe said his first words; took his first steps.*)

**Page 7.** What would Abe celebrate in this part of his life? (Idea: *He worked with numbers; shaped his letters.*)

**Page 16.** What would Abe celebrate in this part of his life? (Idea: *Now Abe and Sarah had a loft to call their own.*)

**Page 18.** What would Abe celebrate in this part of his life? (Idea: *He learned to swing an ax and fell the trees.*)

**Page 22.** What would Abe celebrate in this part of his life? (Idea: *She let Abe read when chores were done.*)

**Page 23.** What would Abe celebrate in this part of his life? (Idea: *He learned to add and subtract.*)

**Pages 37–38.** What would Abe celebrate in this part of his life? (*Idea: Elected our sixteenth President.*)

### Introduce Author's Note

Sometimes when people write a biography, they know more about the person than they can fit in the story. The author wants you to have this information as well.

The author gives you this information in note form rather than in story form. This part of a book is called the Author's Note. What do we call the part of a biography where the author shares his or her notes about the person? *The author's note.*

The Author's Note can come before or after the story itself. Today, I'll read the Author's Note that Kay Winters wrote for *Abe Lincoln: The Boy Who Loved Books* so you can learn more about Abe Lincoln. In this Author's Note, Kay Winters wrote more information about the life of Abraham Lincoln.

Let's see if Kay Winters included any events Abe could have celebrated in the Author's Note section of her book.

(Read the Author's Note one paragraph at a time. At the end of each paragraph, ask:) Is there anything we can add to our Celebration Tree? (Add an ornament for each new celebration children suggest, such as *married Mary Todd; had four boys.*)

### Play the Super Choosing Game

Today you will play the *Super Choosing* game. We've played a game like this before but this one is a little bit different. Let's think about the six words we have learned: **slave, grief, honest, unjust, literate,** and **compassionate.** (Display the Picture Vocabulary Cards.)

I will say a sentence that has two or three of the words we have learned in it. Your job is to choose the correct word for that sentence. Sometimes the answer will be hard. You have to choose the <u>best</u> answer. Not all of the words will be from this lesson, though. That's why it's called the *Super Choosing* game. Let's practice. (Do not show cards for the words outside of this lesson.)

- If you feel sorry for a person and want to help them, are you **compassionate, accepting,** or **exhausted?** *Compassionate.*
- If you are very, very sad, do you have a **temper** or **grief?** *Grief.*
- Are you a **positive** person or an **honest** person if you are always truthful? *An honest person.*

Now you're ready to play the game. If you tell me the correct answer, you will win one point. If you can't tell me the correct answer, I get the point. (Draw a T-chart on the board for keeping score. Children earn one point for each correct answer. If they make an error, correct them as you normally would, and record one point for yourself. Repeat missed words at the end of the game.)

- If you work very hard at something, do you **prey** on it, **slave** at it, or **notice** it? *Slave at it.*
- If you perform the same moves in order every time you dance, are you performing a **routine,** a **compete,** or an **unjust?** *A routine.*
- If a person knows how to read and write, are they a **slave, honest,** or **literate?** *Literate.*
- People who are owned by others and forced to work without pay or rights are called **capture, slaves,** or **birds?** *Slaves.*
- Something that is not fair and not right is **incredible** or **unjust?** *Unjust.*

- A person who has made up their mind about something and won't let anything stop them is **determined, unbelievable,** or **compassionate?** *Determined.*

(Count the points and declare a winner.) You did a great job of playing the *Super Choosing* game.

---

### DAY 4

**Preparation:** Photocopy and assemble *The Biography of Abe Lincoln.*

Print the following words in two columns on the board: *penny, coin, presidents, sure, bear, stove, young, stacked, learn, died, later, brought.*

---

### Introduce The Biography of Abe Lincoln

(Point to each word as you read it.) This word is **penny.** What word? *Penny.* This word is **coin.** What word? *Coin.* (Repeat process for remaining words.)

Let's read these words together. First word? *Penny.* Next word? *Coin.* (Repeat process for remaining words.)

Read these words by yourself. First word? *Penny.* Next word? *Coin.* (Repeat process for remaining words.)

(Use the following correction procedure if the children make an error:) This word is **learn.** What word? *Learn.* Yes, **learn.** (Go back to the top of the list and repeat the list until children can read it accurately and confidently.)

(Give each child a copy of *The Biography of Abe Lincoln.* Ask them to touch under the title of the booklet.) The title of this book is *The Biography of Abe Lincoln.* What's the title of this book? *The Biography of Abe Lincoln.*

Remember that a biography tells about the life of a real person. What does a biography tell about? *The life of a real person.* Is a biography fiction or nonfiction? *Nonfiction.*

(Ask children to open their books to page 1. Ask them to touch under the first underlined words.) These words are **Abe Lincoln.** What words? *Abe Lincoln.* Yes, **Abe Lincoln.** This biography is about Abe Lincoln. Who is this biography about? *Abe Lincoln.*

(Ask children to touch under the next underlined words.) These words are **United States.** What words? *United States.* Yes, **United States.**

My turn to read each page of the book. You touch under each word as I read it. (Read pages 1–4.)

Let's read the book together. (Have children read chorally with you.)

(Assign each child a partner. Allow sufficient time for each child to read the book to his or her partner. Circulate as children read, offering praise and assistance.)

(Children should color the illustrations in their booklet. Encourage them to color the illustrations realistically.)

## Play the Super Choosing Game (Cumulative Review)

Let's play the *Super Choosing* game. I'll say a sentence that has three of our words in it. Your job is to choose the correct word for that sentence.
(Display the Picture Vocabulary Cards *slave, grief, unjust, honest, literate,* and *compassionate* for the three words in each sentence as you say the sentence.)

Now you're ready to play the *Super Choosing game.* (Draw a T-chart on the board for keeping score. Children earn one point for each correct answer. If they make an error, correct them as you normally would, and record one point for yourself. Repeat missed words at the end of the game.)

- If you were owned by another person and forced to work with no pay or rights, would you be **compassionate,** a **slave,** or **honest?** *A slave.*
- If you told your neighbor that it was your baseball that broke her window, would you be **compassionate,** a **slave,** or **honest?** *Honest.*
- If someone close to you were in a car accident, would you feel **grief, unjust,** or **literate?** *Grief.*

- A person who is able to read the newspaper and write a letter to the editor is probably **compassionate, literate,** or **unjust?** *Literate.*
- Tanner is the quarterback because his dad is the coach. He doesn't even go to practice. Is that **unjust, honest,** or **slave?** *Unjust.*
- You worked from 8 in the morning until 5 in the evening building your science fair project. Did you **slave** over it, **honest** about it, or **literate** it? *Slave over it.*
- If you donate your old toys to charity because you want to help children who don't have the things you have, are you **honest, unjust,** or **compassionate?** *Compassionate.*

Now you will have to listen very carefully, because I'm not going to show you the word cards. This is very hard because I'm going to use words that you have learned in earlier lessons. (This part of the game includes the review words from previous lessons.)

- If you work very hard on something, do you **quarrel** with it, **slave** over it, or **wheel** it? *Slave over it.*
- If there is very little of something, is it **precious, hibernating,** or **scarce?** *Scarce.*
- If you are deeply sad, do you have **grief,** a **fool,** or some **equipment?** *Grief.*
- Is a person who is forced to work for someone called **Mexico,** a **slave,** or a **plot?** *A slave.*
- If something is not fair and not right, is it a **fish, nourishment,** or **unjust?** *Unjust.*
- If you do the same things each morning before school, is that a **routine,** a **custom,** or a **commotion?** *A routine.*
- Is a person who always tells you the truth being a **school, honest,** or **active?** *Honest.*
- If you know how to read and write, are you an **escalator, literate,** or a **gaze?** *Literate.*

(Tally the points and declare a winner.) You did a great job of playing the *Super Choosing game.*

**Preparation:** Class chart titled *Reading Goals* that was started in Week 16.

*The Biography of Abe Lincoln.*

Quiz Answer Sheet, BLM B.

## Read The Biography of Abe Lincoln

(Assign each child a partner.) Today, you'll read the first four pages of *The Biography of Abe Lincoln* to your partner. (Allow sufficient time for each child to read the first four pages of the booklet to his or her partner. Circulate as children read, offering praise and assistance.)

(Ask children to look at the back of their booklets.) This part of the book is for people who can help you find other books to read. It tells those people about other books that are biographies. It also tells them about a place where you can find other biographies. Where are some places that you could go to find other biographies? (Ideas: *To the school library; to the public library; to a bookstore.*)

(You may wish to read and discuss the information on the back cover.)

There's one more important thing on the back cover of your book. Touch the box that is at the bottom of the page. The words above the box say "My reading goal." What do the words say? *My reading goal.*

What is a goal? *Something that you want to succeed at doing.* A reading goal is something that you want to succeed at doing with your reading.

Let's see if we can add some other reading goals to our class chart. What are some other reading goals that someone might have when they read their book? (Accept reasonable responses. Help children put their ideas into goal statements. Add to the list of statements on the chart. Ask them to choose a goal and copy it into the box. Children may also make up an original goal that is not on the list. If children are unable to copy the goals or to write a goal of their own, you or a helper may wish to scribe their goal statements for them before the booklets are sent home.)

## Assess Comprehension

(Ask children to turn to page 5 in their booklets.) This is what you have read in the biography about Abe Lincoln but with no pictures. You are going to have a little quiz to see if you can remember what you read.

(Ask children to touch under the words as they read the passage silently. Monitor to ensure that children are reading the passage. Ask them to look up at you after they have finished reading the passage. Instruct children to read and answer the questions.)

## Assess Vocabulary

 (Give each child a copy of the Quiz Answer Sheet, BLM B.)

Today you're going to have a True or False quiz. When you do the True or False quiz, it shows me how well you know the hard words you are learning.

If I say something that is true, circle the word **true.** What will you do if I say something that is true? *Circle the word* true.

If I say something that is false, circle the word **false.** What will you do if I say something that is false? *Circle the word* false.

Listen carefully to each item that I say. Don't let me trick you!

Item 1: A **literate** person is unable to read and write. (*False.*)

Item 2: If you are **exhausted,** you should probably go to bed. (*True.*)

Item 3: Getting a well-paying job because you have worked hard and gone to school is **unjust.** (*False.*)

Item 4: An **honest** person would always pay for items at a store. (*True.*)

Item 5: Some birds and insects **migrate** to warmer places in the winter. (*True.*)

Item 6: A **slave** is paid well for the work he or she does. (*False.*)

Item 7: A person who **slaves** at their job is lazy. (*False.*)

Item 8: Climbing a mountain would be more **challenging** than climbing a staircase. (*True.*)

Item 9: If a loved one dies, you will feel **grief.** (*True.*)

Item 10: A person who laughs when you fall down is very **compassionate.** (*False.*)

You did a great job completing your quiz!

(Score children's work. A child must score 9 out of 10 to be at the mastery level. If a child does not achieve mastery, insert the missed words as additional items in the games in next week's lessons. Retest those children individually for the missed items before they take the next mastery test.)

## Extensions

### Read a Book as a Reward

(Read *Abe Lincoln: The Boy Who Loved Books* or another biography about a president of the United States to children as a reward for their hard work. Display a number of biographies about presidents. Ask children to choose which one they would like you to read.)

---

**Preparation:** Word containers for the Super Words Center.

---

### Introduce the Super Words Center (2 in 1)

(Add the new Picture Vocabulary Cards to the words from the previous weeks. Show children one of the word containers. Role-play with two to three children as you introduce each part of the game.)

Let's review how to play the game called *2 in 1* in the Super Words Center.

Let's think about how we work with our words in the Super Words Center.

You will work with a partner in the Super Words Center. Whom will you work with? *A partner.*

First you will draw two words out of the container. What do you do first? (Idea: *Draw two words out of the container.*) Show your partner both of the words. (Demonstrate.)

Next you will say a sentence that uses both of your words. What do you do next? (Idea: *I will say a sentence that uses both of my words.* Demonstrate.)

If you can use both of your words in one sentence, give yourself a point. Then give your partner a turn. (Demonstrate.)

What do you do next? *Give my partner a turn.*

*MR. LINCOLN'S WHISKERS*

## Mr. Lincoln's Whiskers
author: Karen Winnick • illustrator: Karen Winnick

**Preparation:** You will need a copy of *Mr. Lincoln's Whiskers* for each day's lesson.

Number the pages of the book to assist you in asking comprehension questions at appropriate points.

Post a copy of the Vocabulary Tally Sheet, BLM A, with this week's Picture Vocabulary Cards attached.

Each child will need one copy of the Homework Sheet, BLM 24a.

### Target Vocabulary

| Tier II | Tier III |
|---|---|
| suggestion | nonfiction |
| election | reproduction |
| vote | biography |
| opinion | |
| *thoughtful | |
| *courteous | |

*Expanded Target Vocabulary Word

---

## DAY 1

### Introduce Book

This week's book is called *Mr. Lincoln's Whiskers.* What's the title of this week's book? *Mr. Lincoln's Whiskers.*

This book was written by Karen Winnick. Who's the author of *Mr. Lincoln's Whiskers*? *Karen Winnick.*

Karen Winnick also made the pictures for this book. Who is the illustrator of *Mr. Lincoln's Whiskers*? *Karen Winnick.* Who made the illustrations for this book? *Karen Winnick.*

The cover of a book usually gives us some hints of what the book is about. Let's look at the front cover of *Mr. Lincoln's Whiskers.* What do you see in the illustration? (Ideas: *A young girl with curls and a blue dress; she is sitting in a chair looking at a picture of Abraham Lincoln; it is night.*)

*Mr. Lincoln's Whiskers* is a biography. A biography tells about the life of a real person. What does a biography tell about? *The life of a real person.* What kind of book tells about the life of a real person? *A biography.*

This book is true. What kinds of books are about true things? *Nonfiction books.*

### Take a Picture Walk

(Encourage children to use target words in their answers.) We're going to take a picture walk through this book. When we take a picture walk through a nonfiction book that is a biography, we look carefully at the pictures and think about what we see.

Karen Winnick painted these pictures using oil paints. Copies of the paintings were made for this book. When a copy of a painting is made, it is called a reproduction. What do we call a copy of a painting? *A reproduction.* What is a reproduction? *A copy of a painting.*

**Pages 1–2.** What do you see in this reproduction? (Ideas: *A young girl running out of the house to meet her father; a horse-drawn carriage.*) When does this the biography happen? (Idea: *A long time ago.*)

**Page 3.** Who do you think these people are? (Idea: *The girl's family.*)

**Page 4.** What is the young girl looking at? (Ideas: *A picture of Abraham Lincoln.*) Who do you think gave her the picture? (Ideas: *Her father; a relative; a friend.*)

**Page 5.** What do you think is happening here? (Idea: *The family is having a special dinner.*)

**Page 6.** Where do you think the girl is going? (Idea: *To bed.*) What is she taking with her? (Idea: *The picture of Abraham Lincoln.*) Do you think she's happy about leaving the dinner table? (Idea: *No.*) Tell why or why not.

**Pages 7–8.** When does this part of the biography happen? (Idea: *At night.*)

**Page 9.** What is the girl doing in this reproduction? (Ideas: *Writing; writing a letter.*) Who do you think she is writing to? (Idea: *Abraham Lincoln.*)

**Page 10.** What is the girl holding? (Ideas: *A letter; the letter she wrote.*)

**Page 11.** What is happening in this reproduction? (Idea: *The girl is sleeping.*) What do you think this is, tucked under her pillow? (Idea: *The letter to Abraham Lincoln.*)

**Page 12.** Where do you think the girl is going? (Ideas: *To mail the letter; to school.*)

**Page 13.** Where is the girl in this reproduction? (Ideas: *At the post office; mailing the letter.*)

**Page 14.** Where is the girl in this reproduction? (Idea: *Coming out of the post office.*) How is she feeling? (Idea: *Sad.*) Why do you think she feels sad?

**Page 15.** Where are all these people? (Idea: *At the post office.*) Why do you think they are there? (Idea: *To get their mail.*)

**Page 16.** What does the man have for the girl? (Idea: *A letter.*) Who do you think the letter is from? (Idea: *Abraham Lincoln.*)

**Page 17.** Where do you think the girl is going? (Idea: *Home.*) What is she doing as she is running? (Idea: *Reading the letter.*) How do you think she feels about receiving the letter? (Ideas: *Happy; excited.*)

**Page 18.** Who is waiting for the girl when she gets home? (Idea: *Her family.*)

**Page 19.** What is the girl doing in this reproduction? (Idea: *Reading the letter to her family.*)

**Page 20.** What is the girl holding here? (Idea: *A letter.*)

**Page 21.** How do you think the girl's family feels about her letter? (Ideas: *Happy; excited; surprised.*)

**Page 22.** What is the girl looking at in this reproduction? (Ideas: *Her family going out.*) What do you think she is thinking?

**Page 23.** What is happening in this reproduction? (Ideas: *The girl and her father are*

hugging; people outside are cheering.*) What do you think all the excitement is about?

**Page 24.** What is the girl's father doing in this reproduction? (Idea: *Reading the paper.*) How do you think the girl feels about what her father has read to her? (Ideas: *Excited; surprised; amazed; astonished.*)

**Pages 25–26.** Where are all these people? (Idea: *At a train station.*) What are many of the people holding? (Idea: *American flags.*) Who do you think they have come to see? (Ideas: *The President; Abraham Lincoln.*)

**Page 27.** Who are the people all looking at? (Idea: *The girl.*) Why do you think they are looking at her?

**Page 28.** Where do you think the girl is going? (Ideas: *Closer to the train; to meet Abraham Lincoln.*)

**Page 29.** What is Abraham Lincoln showing the girl? (Idea: *His beard.*) Why do you think he is showing her his beard? (Idea: *She wrote him a letter about growing a beard.*)

**Page 30.** What is happening in this reproduction? (Idea: *The girl is getting a hug from Abraham Lincoln.*) How do you think she feels? (Ideas: *Happy; excited; amazed; astonished.*)

**Page 31.** These pictures were taken with a camera. What do we call pictures that were taken with a camera? (Idea: *Photographs.*) What are these photographs of? (Idea: *Letters.*)

### Read the Book Aloud

The back cover of this book gives us a summary of what the book is about. There is an interesting fact here. (Read the paragraph on the back cover to the class.) What interesting fact did you learn about Abraham Lincoln from this paragraph? (Idea: *He was the first President to wear a beard.*) Is this going to be a biography about Abraham Lincoln? *No.* Who is this biography about? (Ideas: *An eleven year-old girl; Grace Bedell; the girl who told Abraham Lincoln to grow a beard.*)

(Read the story to children with minimal interruptions.)

Tomorrow we will read the book again, and I will ask you some questions.

## Present Target Vocabulary

 **Suggestion**

In the book, Grace made a suggestion that Abraham Lincoln grow whiskers. **Suggestion.** Say the word. *Suggestion.*

**Suggestion** is a noun. It names a thing. What kind of word is **suggestion?** *A noun.*

**A suggestion is an idea or plan for someone to think about.** Say the word that means "an idea or plan for someone to think about." *Suggestion.*

(Correct any incorrect responses, and repeat the item at the end of the sequence.)

Let's think about some things people might say. I'll say something someone said. If you think the person gave a suggestion, say "suggestion." If not, don't say anything.

- I think you should cut your hair; you would look much nicer. *Suggestion.*
- You must clean up this room before dinner.
- Children should never be allowed to stay up past 8:00 in the evening.
- You would probably feel better if you went to bed early tonight. *Suggestion.*
- I think you should serve roast beef and salad for dinner. *Suggestion.*
- Don't you dare eat that cake before supper!

What noun names "an idea or plan for someone to think about"? *Suggestion.*

 **Election**

In the book, Abraham Lincoln was staying in Springfield, Illinois during the election. **Election.** Say the word. *Election.*

**Election** is a noun. It names a thing. What kind of word is **election?** *A noun.*

**An election is the process of choosing someone for a public office like president by voting.** Say the word that means "the process of choosing someone for a public office like president by voting." *Election.*

Let's think about some situations. I'll tell about a person in a situation. If the person got into the situation because people voted, say "election." If not, don't say anything.

- The king died and his son became the new king.
- More than half of the children chose Chris Williams for class president. *Election.*
- Mr. Daney wanted to be mayor again and the people voted for him. *Election.*
- The woman started her own company and became its president.
- The school hired a new principal.
- In November, people will vote for a new president. *Election.*

What noun means "the process of choosing someone for a public office by voting"? *Election.*

**Vote**

In the book, Grace tells her brother that if she could, she would vote for Abraham Lincoln. **Vote.** Say the word. *Vote.*

**Vote** is a verb. It names an action. What kind of word is **vote?** *A verb.*

**To vote means to make a choice in an election.** Say the word that means "to make a choice in an election." *Vote.*

Let's think about some situations in which you might vote. I'll tell about some situations. If you think that you would vote, say "vote." If not, don't say anything.

- Mrs. Thompson is giving a math test today.
- We can have a pizza party or a game day. *Vote.*
- Which of the three singers is your favorite? *Vote.*
- You need to eat your dinner, take a bath, and go to bed.
- The school is raising money to buy new playground equipment. You can either sell wrapping paper or do a walk-a-thon. *Vote.*

What verb means "to make a choice in an election"? *Vote.*

**Opinion**

In the book, when Levant said that Mr. Lincoln looked like a rail-splitter, Grace told him, "That's your opinion." **Opinion.** Say the word. *Opinion.*

**Opinion** is a noun. It names an idea. What kind of word is **opinion?** *A noun.*

**An opinion is what a person thinks or believes about something or someone.** Say the word that means "what a person thinks or believes about something or someone." *Opinion.*

Let's think about some ideas. I'll tell you about some ideas that people have. If you think the idea is an opinion, say "opinion." If not, don't say anything.

- Two plus three equals five.
- I think that green is the prettiest color. *Opinion.*
- I think that cats are better pets than dogs. *Opinion.*
- All fish live in the water.
- All mammals are warm-blooded.
- I think that insects are cool. *Opinion.*

What noun means "what a person thinks or believes about something or someone"? *Opinion.*

### Present Vocabulary Tally Sheet
(See Lesson 1, page 4, for instructions.)

### Assign Homework
(Homework Sheet, BLM 24a. See the Introduction for homework instructions.)

---

## DAY 2

**Preparation:** Picture Vocabulary Cards for *suggestion, election, vote, opinion.*

### Read and Discuss Story
(Read story to children. Ask the following questions at the specified points. Encourage them to use target words in their answers.)

**Page 2.** Who was Grace hoping her father had seen at the fair? (Idea: *Abraham Lincoln.*) Where was Mr. Lincoln? (Idea: *In Springfield, Illinois.*) Where does this biography happen? (Idea: *New York.*)

**Page 3.** What did Papa bring his children from the fair? (Idea: *Presents.*)

**Page 4.** What was Grace's present? (Idea: *A poster of Abraham Lincoln.*) What did Grace think about the way Mr. Lincoln looked in the poster? (Ideas: *He looked kind; his face was sad.*)

**Page 5.** What did Grace and her brothers discuss at dinner? (Ideas: *Abraham Lincoln; Lincoln's ideas about slavery; what would happen if he were elected President.*)

**Page 6.** Why did Levant say that it's a good thing girls couldn't vote? (Idea: *He didn't think Lincoln should be President.*) Why did Grace get upset and leave the table? (Ideas: *She thought Abe Lincoln should be President; her brother Levant disagreed with her; she was mad because she didn't get to vote.*)

**Page 7.** What did Grace do in her room? (Idea: *Looked at the poster of Lincoln.*) What gave Grace the idea that Lincoln looked less sad? (Idea: *The shadow from the moonlight covered part of his face like whiskers.*) What do you think Grace's idea was? (Ideas: *That Abraham Lincoln should grow whiskers; he should grow a beard.*)

**Page 9.** What did Grace decide to do? (Idea: *Write a letter.*)

**Letter on page 10.** What reasons did Grace give Mr. Lincoln for growing whiskers? (Ideas: *He would look better because his face was so thin; all the ladies liked whiskers.*) What would Grace do if she were a man? (Idea: *Vote for Lincoln.*) What did Grace promise to do? (Idea: *Try to get everyone she could to vote for him.*)

**Page 11.** Where was Grace going to send the letter? (Idea: *To Springfield, Illinois.*)

**Page 12.** What did Grace hurry to do before school? (Idea: *Mail the letter.*) Why did she think Levant would laugh at her if he knew she had written the letter? (Ideas: *She was just a little girl; he didn't think Lincoln should be President.*) What suggestion did Grace make to Mr. Lincoln? (Idea: *That he should grow whiskers.*)

**Page 13.** Where did Grace take her letter? (Idea: *To the post office.*) Why didn't Mr. Mann think Abraham Lincoln would write back to Grace? (Idea: *He was a very busy man.*)

**Page 14.** When Grace went back to the post office a few days later, was there a letter from

Mr. Lincoln? *No.* Did she give up waiting? *No.* How do you know she didn't give up? (Idea: *She went back the next day and the day after that.*)

**Page 15.** How many days had it been since Grace sent the letter to Mr. Lincoln? *Seven.* Who met Grace at the post office? (Idea: *A crowd of people.*)

**Page 16.** What had arrived at the post office for Grace? *A letter from Mr. Lincoln.* How did Grace feel about receiving a letter from Abraham Lincoln? (Ideas: *Excited; happy; amazed; astonished.*)

**Page 17.** Why didn't Grace tell the little boy what was written in the letter? (Idea: *She was already rushing home.*)

**Page 18.** Did Grace's family know she had written to Mr. Lincoln? *No.* What did they want to know? (Ideas: *What she said; where she sent it; what Lincoln's letter said.*)

**Pages 19–20.** Why did Abraham Lincoln tell Grace that he had no daughters, only three sons? (Idea: *Grace had asked him if he had daughters.*) Has Mr. Lincoln ever worn whiskers? *No.*

**Page 21.** What did Levant make a face about? (Idea: *Because Grace wrote to Mr. Lincoln about growing whiskers.*) What did Grace's parents think about the letter? (Idea: *They were surprised; they thought she should be proud.*)

**Page 22.** What were Papa and Grace's brothers voting for? (Idea: *President of the United States.*) Who did Grace think should be the next President? *Abraham Lincoln.*

**Page 23.** Who was winning the election? *Abraham Lincoln.* Who do you think Grace's father voted for? (Idea: *Abraham Lincoln.*)

**Page 24.** Who was going to be coming to Grace's town? *Abraham Lincoln.*

Where was Mr. Lincoln going when he stopped in Westfield? *To Washington, D.C.* What did Levant think about the letter Grace wrote to Mr. Lincoln? (Idea: *It was foolish.*)

**Page 25.** Where is Grace? *At the train station.* Why was Grace at the train station? (Idea: *She was hoping to see Abraham Lincoln.*)

**Page 26.** What can Grace see? (Ideas: *Nothing; people's hats and bonnets.*) What can she hear? (Ideas: *Cheering; clapping.*)

**Page 27.** Why are people turning around? (Idea: *They are looking for Grace.*)

**Page 28.** Why is Mr. Mann bringing Grace to the front of the platform? (Idea: *To meet Abraham Lincoln.*) What do you think the people are whispering?

**Page 29.** What improvement had Grace advised Mr. Lincoln to make? (Idea: *Growing a beard.*)

**Page 30.** Why do you think Abraham Lincoln wanted to meet Grace? (Ideas: *He had taken her suggestion and won the election; he wanted to meet the girl who had written him the letter.*)

### Review Vocabulary

(Display the Picture Vocabulary Cards. Point to each card as you say the word. Ask children to repeat each word after you.) These pictures show **suggestion, election, vote,** and **opinion.**

- What noun means "what a person thinks or believes about something or someone"? *Opinion.*
- What verb means "to make a choice in an election"? *Vote.*
- What noun means "an idea or plan for someone to think about"? *Suggestion.*
- What noun means "the process of choosing someone for office by voting"? *Election.*

### Extend Vocabulary

 ≈ *Vote*

In *Mr. Lincoln's Whiskers,* we learned that to **vote** is "to make a choice in an election." Say the word that means "to make a choice in an election." *Vote.*

Raise your hand if you can tell us a sentence that uses **vote** as a verb meaning "to make a choice in an election." (Call on several children. If they don't use complete sentences, restate their examples as sentences. Have the class repeat the sentences.)

Here's a new way to use the word **vote.**

- The teacher asked for a **vote** of raised hands for children who wanted to go outside. Say the sentence.

- The neighbors took a **vote** to see which day would be best for the block party. Say the sentence.
- The student council took a **vote** to find out if students wanted a dance in the fall or in the spring. Say the sentence.

**In these sentences, vote is a noun that means a choice made by a group.** What word means "a choice made by a group"? *Vote.*

Raise your hand if you can tell us a sentence that uses **vote** as a noun meaning "a choice made by a group." (Call on several children. If they don't use complete sentences, restate their examples as sentences. Have the class repeat the sentences.)

### Present Expanded Target Vocabulary
 Thoughtful

In the book, Grace thought about what could help Mr. Lincoln win the election. She wrote a letter to him that considered his feelings and needs. She wrote him a thoughtful letter. **Thoughtful.** Say the word. *Thoughtful.*

**Thoughtful** is a describing word. It tells more about a person. What kind of word is **thoughtful**? *A describing word.*

**Thoughtful describes a person who considers the feelings and needs of others.** Say the word that means that you "consider the feelings and needs of others." *Thoughtful.*

I'll tell about some people. If the person I tell about is thoughtful, say "thoughtful." If not, don't say anything.

- Amy brought flowers to her sick aunt. *Thoughtful.*
- Miranda walked past the crying girl without saying a word.
- Grace wrote a kind letter to Mr. Lincoln, making a suggestion that could help him become President. *Thoughtful.*
- Levant made fun of his sister's letter.
- Josiah very carefully chose the words for his letter so he wouldn't hurt his friend's feelings. *Thoughtful.*

What describing word means that you "consider people's feelings and needs"? *Thoughtful.*

⊙═ *Courteous*

In the book, Grace wrote a letter to Mr. Lincoln that used courteous language. **Courteous.** Say the word. *Courteous.*

**Courteous** is a describing word. It tells more about people. What kind of word is **courteous**? *A describing word.*

**If you are courteous, you do things in a polite manner.** Say the word that describes a person who "does things in a polite manner." *Courteous.*

Let's think about some things that courteous people might say. I'll tell you some things that people say. If I tell something courteous, say "courteous." If not, don't say anything.

- "Thank you." *Courteous.*
- "Yuck! I'm not eating that!"
- "I'm not helping clean up the classroom."
- "Excuse me, please. May I sit here?" *Courteous.*
- "Pardon me?" *Courteous.*
- "Move over."

What word describes a person who "does things in a polite manner"? *Courteous.*

---

### DAY 3

**Preparation:** Prepare a sheet of chart paper with a diagram of a tree on it, with 7 circles hanging on it, as decorations. Record the underlined words in the ornaments on the tree.

### Make a Celebration Tree

Today I'll show you the reproductions of the oil paintings done for *Mr. Lincoln's Whiskers.* As I read about those reproductions, I'll call on one of you to tell about an important event in Grace Bedell's life that she might choose to celebrate.

**Page 4.** What would Grace celebrate in this part of her life? (Idea: *Receiving a poster of Mr. Lincoln.*)

**Page 16.** What would Grace celebrate in this part of her life? (Idea: *A letter came from Mr. Lincoln.*)

**Page 23.** What would Grace celebrate in this part of her life? (Idea: *The telegraph says Mr. Lincoln is winning.*)

**Page 24.** What would Grace celebrate in this part of her life? (Idea: *His train will stop for wood and water right here in Westfield.*)

**Page 29.** What would Grace celebrate in this part of her life? (Idea: *She got to meet Abraham Lincoln; Mr. Lincoln took her suggestion and grew whiskers.*)

### Play the Super Choosing Game

 Today you will play the *Super Choosing* game. We've played a game like this before but this one is a little bit different. Let's think about the six words we have learned: **suggestion, election, vote, opinion, thoughtful,** and **courteous.** (Display the Picture Vocabulary Cards.)

I'll say a sentence that has two or three of the words we have learned in it. Your job to choose the correct word for that sentence. Not all of the words will be from this lesson, though. That's why it's the *Super Choosing* game. Let's practice. (You should not show cards for the words outside of this lesson.)

- If you do things in a polite manner, are you being **courteous, literate,** or an **orphan?** *Courteous.*
- If many people choose you to become President, have you won a **routine,** an **elevator,** or an **election?** *An election.*
- If two animals want to hurt or harm each other, are they **pests, enemies,** or **reptiles?** *Enemies.*

Now you're ready to play the game. If you tell me the correct answer, you will win one point. If you can't tell me the correct answer, I get the point. (Draw a T-chart on the board for keeping score. Children earn one point for each correct answer. If they make an error, correct them as you normally would, and record one point for yourself. Repeat missed words at the end of the game.)

- If your teacher asks you to raise your hand to choose an activity, is she taking a **voyage** or a **vote?** *A vote.*

- If you believe anything anybody tells you, are you **compassionate, unbelievable,** or **gullible?** *Gullible.*
- If you are allowed to make a choice in an election, are you able to **prey, vote,** or **gaze?** *Vote.*
- Ideas and beliefs people have about someone or something are their **opinions** or their **slaves?** *Opinions.*
- Is someone who considers other people's feelings and needs **thoughtful, honest,** or **unjust?** *Thoughtful.*
- When you give someone an idea to think about, are you making a **vote,** an **opinion,** or a **suggestion?** *A suggestion.*

(Count the points and declare a winner.) You did a great job of playing the *Super Choosing* game.

---

## DAY 4

**Preparation:** Photocopy and assemble *The Biography of Grace Bedell.*

Print the following words in two columns on the board: *imagine, writing, wrote, eleven, brought, poster, thought, shadow, beard, idea, knew, surprise.*

### Introduce: The Biography of Grace Bedell

(Point to each word as you read it.) This word is **imagine.** What word? *Imagine.* This word is **writing.** What word? *Writing.* (Repeat process for remaining words.)

Let's read these words together. First word? *Imagine.* Next word? *Writing.* (Repeat process for remaining words.)

Read these words by yourself. First word? *Imagine.* Next word? *Writing.* (Repeat process for remaining words.)

(Use the following correction procedure if children make an error:) This word is **beard.** What word? *Beard.* Yes, **beard.** (Go back to the top of the list and repeat the list until children can read it accurately and confidently.)

(Give each child a copy of *The Biography of Grace Bedell.* Ask children to touch under the title of the booklet.) The title of this book is *The*

*Biography of Grace Bedell.* What's the title of this book? *The Biography of Grace Bedell.*

Remember that a biography tells about the life of a real person. What does a biography tell about? *The life of a real person.* Is a biography fiction or nonfiction? *Nonfiction.*

(Ask children to open their booklets to page 1. Ask them to touch under the first underlined words.) These words are **Grace Bedell.** What words? *Grace Bedell.* Yes, **Grace Bedell.** This biography is about Grace Bedell. Who is this biography about? *Grace Bedell.*

My turn to read each page of the book. You touch under each word as I read it. (Read pages 1–4.)

Let's read the book together. (Have children read chorally with you.)

(Assign each child a partner. Allow sufficient time for each child to read the booklet to his or her partner. Circulate as children read, offering praise and assistance.)

(Children should color the illustrations in their booklet. Encourage them to color the illustrations realistically.)

### Play the Super Choosing Game (Cumulative Review)

Let's play the *Super Choosing* game. I'll say a sentence that has three of our words in it. You will have to choose the correct word for that sentence. (Display the Picture Vocabulary Cards for *suggestion, election, vote, opinion, thoughtful,* and *courteous* for the three words in each sentence as you say the sentence.)

Now you're ready to play the *Super Choosing* game. (Draw a T-chart on the board for keeping score. Children earn one point for each correct answer. If they make an error, correct them as you normally would, and record one point for yourself. Repeat missed words at the end of the game.)

- If you mentioned to your teacher that it might be helpful to write the schedule on the board,

would you be making a **vote,** a **suggestion,** or an **opinion?** *A suggestion.*

- If you saw that your friend was sad and you tried to cheer her up, would you be **thoughtful, polite,** or **election?** *Thoughtful.*

- If all the students in school voted for a class president, would they be holding a **suggestion,** an **election,** or a **thoughtful?** *An election.*

- If you circle your favorite school lunch and place the paper in a box with other students' papers, are you taking part in a **thoughtful,** a **vote,** or an **opinion?** *A vote.*

- If you are allowed to state your choice for Teacher of the Year, are you being allowed to **opinion, suggestion,** or **vote?** *Vote.*

- Are the ideas you have about somebody your **suggestions, votes,** or **opinions?** *Opinions.*

Now you will have to listen very carefully, because I'm not going to show you the word cards. (This part of the game includes the review words from previous lessons.)

- If you take people for who they are, are you **polite, compassionate,** or **accepting?** *Accepting.*

- If you raise your hand to choose an activity, are you **voting, hatching,** or a **species?** *Voting.*

- If people vote for the President of the United States, are they having a **wheel,** an **election,** or an **opinion?** *Election.*

- Giving your sister an idea about how to wear her hair is a **suggestion, coordinated,** or a **sparkling?** *A suggestion.*

- A person who makes fun of someone else is not very **unjust, brave,** or **thoughtful?** *Thoughtful.*

- Would climbing a mountain be **tropical, venom,** or **challenging?** *Challenging.*

- Your ideas and beliefs about someone or something are your **opinions, nourishment,** or **predator?** *Opinions.*

- When you say "please" and "thank you," are you being a **rascal, courteous,** or **rude?** *Courteous.*

(Tally the points and declare a winner.) You did a great job of playing the *Super Choosing* game.

**Preparation:** Class chart titled *Reading Goals* that was started in Week 16.

*The Biography of Grace Bedell.*

Quiz Answer Sheet, BLM B.

## Read The Biography of Grace Bedell

(Assign each child a partner.) Today you'll read the first four pages of *The Biography of Grace Bedell* to your partner. (Allow sufficient time for each child to read the first four pages of the booklet to his or her partner. Circulate as children read, offering praise and assistance.)

(Ask children to look at the back of their booklets.) This part of the book is for people who can help you find other books to read. It tells those people about other books that are biographies. It also tells them about a place where you can find other biographies. Where are some places that you could go to find other biographies? (Ideas: *To the school library; to the public library; to a bookstore.*)

(You may wish to read and discuss the information on the back cover.)

There's one more important thing on the back cover of your book. Touch the box that is at the bottom of the page. The words above the box say "My reading goal." What do the words say? *My reading goal.*

What is a goal? *Something that you want to succeed at doing.* A reading goal is something that you want to succeed at doing with your reading.

Let's see if we can add some other reading goals to our class chart. What are some other reading goals that someone might have when they read their book? (Accept reasonable responses. Help children put their ideas into goal statements. Add to the list of statements on the chart. Ask them to choose a goal and copy it into the box. Children may also make up an original goal that is not on the list. If children are unable to copy the goals or to write a goal of their own, you or a helper may wish to scribe their goal statements for them before the booklets are sent home.)

## Assess Comprehension

(Ask children to turn to page 5 in their booklets.) This is what you have read in the biography about Grace Bedell but with no pictures. You are going to have a little quiz to see if you can remember what you read.

(Ask children to touch under the words as they read the passage silently. Monitor to ensure that children are reading the passage. Ask them to look up at you after they have finished reading the passage. Instruct children to read and answer the questions.)

## Assess Vocabulary

 (Give each child a copy of the Quiz Answer Sheet, BLM B.)

Today you're going to have a True or False quiz. When you do the True or False quiz, it shows me how well you know the hard words you are learning.

If I say something that is true, circle the word **true.** What will you do if I say something that is true? *Circle the word* true.

If I say something that is false, circle the word **false.** What will you do if I say something that is false? *Circle the word* false.

Listen carefully to each item that I say. Don't let me trick you!

Item 1: An **opinion** is a fact that everybody agrees on. (*False.*)

Item 2: An **honest** person would never steal something. (*True.*)

Item 3: When people go out and **vote** for someone to become President, they are having an **election.** (*True.*)

Item 4: If you go on vacation to a **tropical** place, be sure to pack a heavy coat, hat, and gloves because it will be cold. (*False.*)

Item 5: The **courteous** thing to say if you want to get past somebody is, "Move it!" (*False.*)

Item 6: When you are sick, you might go to a **physician.** (*True.*)

Item 7: Telling somebody what they must do is a **suggestion.** (*False.*)

Item 8: A **thoughtful** person will ask you how you are feeling after you've been sick. (*True.*)

Item 9: When a teacher asks students to raise their hands to choose an activity, she is taking a **vote**. (*True.*)

Item 10: When the man said he caught a fish as big as a house, he **exaggerated.** (*True.*)

You did a great job completing your quiz!

(Score children's work. A child must score 9 out of 10 to be at the mastery level. If a child does not achieve mastery, insert the missed words as additional items in the games in next week's lessons. Retest those children individually for the missed items before they take the next mastery test.)

## Extensions

### Read a Book as a Reward

(Read *Mr. Lincoln's Whiskers* or another biography about a brave woman or girl to children as a reward for their hard work. Display a number of biographies about brave women or girls. Ask children to choose which one they would like you to read.)

---

**Preparation:** Word containers for the Super Words Center.

---

## Introduce the Super Words Center (2 in 1)

(Add the new Picture Vocabulary Cards to the words from the previous weeks. Show children one of the word containers. Role-play with two to three children as you introduce each part of the game.)

Let's review how to play the game called *2 in 1* in the Super Words Center. Let's think about how we work with our words in the Super Words Center.

You will work with a partner in the Super Words Center. Whom will you work with? *A partner.*

First you will draw two words out of the container. What do you do first? (Idea: *Draw two words out of the container.*) Show your partner both of the words. (Demonstrate.)

Next you will say a sentence that uses both of your words. What do you do next? (Idea: *I will say a sentence that uses both of my words.* Demonstrate.)

If you can use both of your words in one sentence, give yourself a point. Then give your partner a turn. (Demonstrate.)

What do you do next? *Give my partner a turn.*

### Wilma Unlimited
author: Kathleen Krull • illustrator: David Diaz

**Preparation:** You will need a copy of *Wilma Unlimited* for each day's lesson.

Number the pages of the book to assist you in asking comprehension questions at appropriate points.

Post a copy of the Vocabulary Tally Sheet, BLM A, with this week's Picture Vocabulary Cards attached.

Each child will need one copy of the Homework Sheet, BLM 25a.

### Target Vocabulary

| Tier II | Tier III |
|---------|----------|
| paralyzed | nonfiction |
| concentrating | biography |
| gathering | photographs |
| victory | |
| *overcame | |
| *heroic | |

*Expanded Target Vocabulary Word

## DAY 1

### Introduce Book

This week's book is called *Wilma Unlimited.* What's the title of this week's book? *Wilma Unlimited.*

This book was written by Kathleen Krull. Who's the author of *Wilma Unlimited? Kathleen Krull.*

David Diaz made the pictures for this book. Who is the illustrator of *Wilma Unlimited? David Diaz.* Who made the illustrations for this book? *David Diaz.*

The cover of a book usually gives us some hints of what the book is about. Let's look at the front cover of *Wilma Unlimited.* What do you see in the illustration? (Ideas: *A woman running; it looks like she's crossing the finish line in a race; a race track.*)

*Wilma Unlimited* is a biography. A biography tells about the life of a real person. What does a biography tell about? *The life of a real person.* What kind of book tells about the life of a real person? *A biography.*

This book is true. What kinds of books are about true things? *Nonfiction books.*

### Take a Picture Walk

(Encourage children to use target words in their answers.) We're going to take a picture walk through this book. When we take a picture walk through a nonfiction book that is a biography, we look carefully at the pictures and think about what we see.

David Diaz painted the pictures for this book. The backgrounds on each page were done with a camera. When pictures are taken with a camera, they are called photographs. What do we call pictures taken with a camera? *Photographs.*

David Diaz and Cecilia Zieba-Diaz put together and photographed the background pictures. (As you discuss each illustration, look also at the background photograph. Ask children what might have been used in the photograph.)

**Page 2.** What do you see in this illustration? (Ideas: *A mother holding a baby; a birthday cake; family gathered around; it's the baby's first birthday.*)

**Page 4.** Who do you think this girl is? (Idea: *Wilma.*) What is Wilma doing in this illustration? (Idea: *Jumping out of a wagon.*)

**Page 6.** What is happening in this illustration? (Ideas: *Wilma is sick; a doctor is looking at Wilma.*)

**Page 8.** What do you see in this illustration? (Idea: *People riding on a bus.*)

**Page 10.** What is Wilma looking at in this illustration? (Idea: *Kids outside.*) Where do you think those kids are going? (Idea: *To school.*) How do you think Wilma feels in this illustration? (Idea: *Sad; different than the other children; frustrated; jealous; miserable.*)

**Page 12.** What is Wilma doing in this illustration? (Idea: *Watching kids play basketball*.)

(Point to the brace on Wilma's leg.) Wilma has a brace on her leg. Why do you think she has that? (Idea: *To help her walk; she injured her leg*.)

**Page 14.** What do you see in this illustration? (Ideas: *Wilma adjusting her brace; a book and a purse; people going into a building*.) How do you know that's Wilma? (Idea: *Because of the leg brace*.)

**Pages 15–16.** Where is Wilma in this illustration? (Idea: *At church*.) What do you think the two boys in the back are saying? How do you think that makes Wilma feel?

**Page 18.** What is Wilma doing in this illustration? (Idea: *Walking up an aisle*.) How do you think Wilma is feeling here? (Idea: *Proud*.) Wilma looks like she's feeling proud of herself. Why do you think she is feeling proud? (Idea: *She is able to walk on her own*.)

**Page 20.** What do you think Wilma is doing in this illustration? (Idea: *Packing her brace in a box*.)

**Page 22.** What is Wilma doing in this illustration? (Idea: *Playing basketball*.)

**Page 24.** What do you think is happening in this illustration? (Idea: *The man is watching Wilma play basketball*.)

**Page 26.** What is Wilma doing in this illustration? (Idea: *Tying her shoe*.) What do you think Wilma is about to do? (Idea: *Run in a race; compete in a race*.)

**Page 28.** What is Wilma doing in this illustration? (Ideas: *Running in a race; winning a race; crossing the finish line*.)

**Page 30.** What is happening in this illustration? (Idea: *Wilma is racing*.)

**Pages 31–32.** What kind of race do you think these people are running? (Ideas: *A relay race; a race where they pass a baton or stick to the next runner*.) Who looks like they are winning? (Ideas: *The blue team; Wilma's team*.)

**Page 34.** What is Wilma doing in this illustration? (Ideas: *Finishing the race; crossing the finish line; winning the race*.)

**Page 36.** What is happening here? (Idea: *Wilma is showing her medal*.) Why does Wilma have a medal around her neck? (Idea: *She won the races*.)

### Read the Book Aloud
(Read the book to children with minimal interruptions.)

Tomorrow we will read the book again, and I will ask you some questions.

### Present Target Vocabulary
 Paralyzed

In the book, the doctors helped Wilma do exercises to make her paralyzed leg stronger. **Paralyzed.** Say the word. *Paralyzed.*

**Paralyzed** is a describing word. It tells more about a thing. What kind of word is **paralyzed**? *A describing word.*

**If someone or something is paralyzed, it is unable to move.** Say the word that means "unable to move." *Paralyzed.*

(Correct any incorrect responses, and repeat the item at the end of the sequence.)

Let's think about some things that would be paralyzed. I'll tell about some things. If you think the thing is paralyzed, say "paralyzed." If not, don't say anything.

- After the wasp stung the insect, the insect was unable to move. *Paralyzed.*
- The boy rode his bike down the hill.
- After her car accident, the woman was no longer able to move her legs. *Paralyzed.*
- The bird got hit by a car and could no longer move its right wing. *Paralyzed.*
- The snake's venom caused the mongoose to be unable to move. *Paralyzed.*
- I am not strong enough to move this desk by myself.

What word describes something or someone that is "unable to move"? *Paralyzed.*

## ⊙← Concentrating

In the book, when Wilma decided to try walking without her brace, she took her mind off her knees by concentrating on her breath. **Concentrating.** Say the word. *Concentrating.*

**Concentrating** is a verb. It tells an action. What kind of word is **concentrating?** *A verb.*

**Concentrating means focusing attention on something.** Say the word that means "focusing attention on something." *Concentrating.*

Let's think about some situations. I'll tell about a person in a situation. If the person is concentrating, say "concentrating." If not, don't say anything.

- Janinne had the TV and radio on while she did her homework.
- Moira was so focused on her book that she didn't hear her parents come home. *Concentrating.*
- Abel focused on dribbling the soccer ball and making a goal. He didn't even see the other players. *Concentrating.*
- Suzanne watched a bird fly by as her teacher taught a math lesson.
- Michael was learning to tie his shoes. He focused on getting the loops just right. *Concentrating.*
- During the math test, Sally was daydreaming about her next swimming class.

What verb means "focusing attention on something"? *Concentrating.*

## ⊙← Gathering

In the book, whispers rippled throughout the gathering as Wilma walked without her brace. **Gathering.** Say the word. *Gathering.*

**Gathering** is a noun. It names a thing. What kind of word is **gathering?** *A noun.*

**A gathering is a group of people who have come together for a purpose.** Say the word that means "a group of people who have come together for a purpose." *Gathering.*

Let's think about some situations in which people might come together for a purpose. I'll tell about some situations. If you think that it is

a gathering, say "gathering." If not, don't say anything.

- There were over a hundred people at the wedding. *Gathering.*
- Dr. Stephens rode the train to work every day.
- A large group of people stood together in front of the building holding signs. *Gathering.*
- One of my friends went on a hike.
- People from all over the country came to Times Square in New York City to celebrate New Year's Eve. *Gathering.*

What noun means "a group of people that come together for a purpose"? *Gathering.*

## ⊙← Victory

In the book, Wilma led her high school basketball team to one victory after another. **Victory.** Say the word. *Victory.*

**Victory** is a noun. It names a thing. What kind of word is **victory?** *A noun.*

**A victory is a win in a game or contest.** Say the word that means "a win in a game or contest." *Victory.*

Let's think about some situations. I'll tell you about some things that happened. If you think it was a victory, say "victory." If not, don't say anything.

- The young boy won the state spelling contest. *Victory.*
- The runner won the race. *Victory.*
- The teacher gave Jake a sticker for helping pass out the milk.
- Ann Marie's soccer team lost its last three games.
- The football team has not lost any games this season. *Victory.*
- The two boys tied in the race.

What noun means "a win in a game or contest"? *Victory.*

### Present Vocabulary Tally Sheet
(See Lesson 1, page 4, for instructions.)

### Assign Homework
(Homework Sheet, BLM 25a. See the Introduction for homework instructions.)

**Preparation:** You will need the Picture Vocabulary Cards for *paralyzed, concentrating, gathering, victory.*

### Read and Discuss Story

(Read story to children. Ask the following questions at the specified points. Encourage them to use target words in their answers.)

**Page 1.** Why didn't people expect Wilma to have a first birthday? (Ideas: *She was so small; she weighed just over 4 pounds at birth.*) What did Wilma have that most babies didn't have? (Ideas: *Nineteen brothers and sisters to watch over her; a mother who knew home remedies; a father who worked several jobs.*)

**Page 3.** What did Wilma do instead of walking? (Ideas: *Ran; jumped.*) Why did Wilma worry people? (Idea: *She was small and sickly.*) Why didn't Wilma see a doctor when she was sick? (Ideas: *Doctors were a luxury; they were expensive; only one doctor would treat black people.*)

**Page 5.** What happened to Wilma just before she turned five? (Idea: *She got sicker than ever.*) What happened to Wilma's left leg during that sickness? (Ideas: *It turned inward; she couldn't move it.*) Why did children with polio either die or become crippled in those days? (Idea: *There was no cure.*)

**Page 7.** How did Wilma get around? (Idea: *She hopped on one foot.*) What did Wilma and her mother do twice a week? (Ideas: *Took a bus to Nashville; went to a hospital; saw doctors.*) What did the doctors and nurses do to help Wilma's leg become stronger? (Idea: *They helped her do exercises.*) Wilma practiced her exercises at home even when they hurt. What does that tell you about Wilma? (Ideas: *She is strong; she is determined; she has perseverance.*)

**Page 9.** What hurt Wilma the most? (Idea: *She wasn't allowed to go to school because she couldn't walk.*) What decision did Wilma make? (Idea: *To fight back somehow.*)

**Page 11.** What did Wilma do to get her leg stronger? (Idea: *Worked hard at her exercises.*) What did the doctors give Wilma that allowed her to go to school? (Idea: *A heavy steel brace for her leg.*) Why wasn't school a happy place for Wilma? (Ideas: *Her classmates made fun of her brace; she couldn't play with the other children; the other children teased her.*) What did Wilma do to fight the sadness? (Idea: *She did more leg exercises.*)

**Page 13.** Where was Wilma's favorite place in the world? (Idea: *Church.*) What was the bravest thing Wilma had ever done? (Idea: *She took off her brace and tried to walk on her own.*) How did Wilma take her mind off her shaking knees? (Idea: *By concentrating on her breath.*)

**Page 17.** What were people staring at in church? (Ideas: *Wilma; Wilma walking down the aisle without her brace.*) How did Wilma feel when she made it to the front of the church? (Ideas: *Triumphant; amazed; astonished; happy; proud.*) In the book, it says that Wilma was triumphant. If a person is triumphant, they are very happy because they have won a victory. What word means that Wilma was very happy that she had won a victory? *Triumphant.*

**Page 19.** When was Wilma able to take her brace off for good? (Idea: *When she was 12 years old.*) What did Wilma and her mother do with the brace? (Idea: *They packed it in a box and sent it back to the hospital.*)

**Page 21.** What sport was Wilma excited to play? (Idea: *Basketball.*) If Wilma had never played basketball before, how did she know all the rules and all the moves? (Idea: *She used to watch the other children play.*) How do you know Wilma was a good basketball player? (Idea: *She led her team to the state championships.*) Did Wilma's team win the state championships? *No.*

**Page 23.** Why did Wilma slump on the bench after the game? (Ideas: *She was upset that her team lost; she wasn't used to losing.*) Who saw Wilma play at the state championships? (Idea: *A college coach.*) What did the coach want Wilma to do? (Idea: *Run on his track team.*) What was special about Wilma going to college? (Idea: *She was the first in her family to go.*)

**Page 25.** Why did Wilma go to Rome, Italy in 1960? (Idea: *To run in the Olympics.*) Why would the Olympics be especially difficult for Wilma? (Ideas: *Just walking in Rome's heat was difficult; athletes from other countries had run faster races than she had; women weren't thought to be good runners; the Olympics would be shown on television and one hundred million people would be watching; Wilma had twisted her ankle.*) Do you think Wilma will give up? *No.* What vocabulary word did we learn in an earlier lesson that would describe how Wilma felt about the Olympics? *Optimistic.*

**Page 27.** What happened once it was Wilma's turn to race? (Idea: *She forgot her pain, the heat, and her fear.*) Who won the 100-meter dash? (Idea: *Wilma Rudolph.*) What did Wilma get for winning the race? (Idea: *A gold medal.*)

**Page 29.** What helped Wilma forget the rain that was falling as she started the 200-meter dash? (Idea: *The crowd was chanting her name.*) How did Wilma do in the 200-meter dash? (Ideas: *She won; she got another gold medal.*) Why was Wilma nervous about the 400-meter relay? (Ideas: *Her team was facing the toughest competition; she was the one who had to cross the finish line.*)

**Page 33.** How was Wilma's team doing before the baton got to her? (Idea: *They were winning.*) What happened when the third runner passed the baton to Wilma? (Idea: *She nearly dropped it.*) What did Wilma do so she could win the race? (Idea: *She concentrated.*) How did Wilma do in this race? (Ideas: *She won; she won another gold medal.*)

**Page 35.** How many gold medals did Wilma Rudolph win in Rome? *Three.*

### Review Vocabulary

(Display the Picture Vocabulary Cards. Point to each card as you say the word. Ask children to repeat each word after you.) These pictures show **paralyzed, concentrating, gathering,** and **victory.**

- What verb means "focusing attention on something"? *Concentrating.*
- What describing word means "unable to move"? *Paralyzed.*

- What noun means "a group of people who have come together for a purpose"? *Gathering.*
- What noun means "a win in a game or contest"? *Victory.*

### Extend Vocabulary

 = Gathering

In *Wilma Unlimited,* we learned that a **gathering** is "a group of people who have come together for a purpose." Say the word that means "a group of people who have come together for a purpose." *Gathering.*

Raise your hand if you can tell us a sentence that uses **gathering** as a noun meaning "a group of people who have come together for a purpose." (Call on several children. If they don't use complete sentences, restate their examples as sentences. Have the class repeat the sentences.)

Here's a new way to use the word **gathering.**

- The teacher began **gathering** up the materials from the art project. Say the sentence.
- The squirrels were **gathering** nuts for the winter. Say the sentence.
- The two boys began **gathering** their clothes to be washed. Say the sentence.

**In these sentences, gathering is a verb that means picking up things and putting them together in a pile so you can use them later.** What word means "picking up things and putting them together in a pile so you can use them later"? *Gathering.*

Raise your hand if you can tell us a sentence that uses **gathering** as a verb meaning "picking up things and putting them together in a pile so you can use them later." (Call on several children. If they don't use complete sentences, restate their examples as sentences. Have the class repeat the sentences.)

### Present Expanded Target Vocabulary
= Overcame

In the book, Wilma overcame her paralysis to become the fastest woman in the world. **Overcame.** Say the word. *Overcame.*

**Overcame** is a verb. It tells an action. What kind of word is **overcame**? *A verb.*

**Overcame means won against or got past a problem.** Say the word that means "won against or got past a problem." *Overcame.*

I'll tell about some people. If the person I tell about overcame a problem, say "overcame." If not, don't say anything.

- Peyton couldn't find her shoe.
- After working for many years to make her paralyzed arm stronger, the young woman was able to play tennis. *Overcame.*
- Despite going blind when she was 18, Jennifer went on to college and became a teacher. *Overcame.*
- Even though he was deaf, Beethoven became one of the most famous composers in the world. *Overcame.*
- When she broke her leg, Megan just sat and pouted.

What verb means "won against or got past a problem"? *Overcame.*

◎◄ Heroic

Wilma Rudolph did many brave things and became a hero for other people. She was heroic. **Heroic.** Say the word. *Heroic.*

**Heroic** is a describing word. It tells more about people. What kind of word is **heroic**? *A describing word.*

**If you are heroic, you do brave things and act as a role model for others.** Say the word that describes a person who "does brave things and acts as a role model for others." *Heroic.*

Let's think about some things that people might do. I'll tell you some things that people do. If I tell something heroic, say "heroic." If not, don't say anything.

- Seeing a speeding car, the man pushed a small child to safety. *Heroic.*
- The young girl stood from her wheelchair and walked for the first time in three years. *Heroic.*
- The little boy ate all of his broccoli.
- The elderly couple took in several children who had no families. *Heroic.*

- The firefighter climbed to the top of the building, went in a window, and came out of the smoke and flames with a small baby. *Heroic.*
- Will shared his toys with his baby brother.

What word describes a person who "does brave things and acts as a role model for others"? *Heroic.*

## DAY 3

**Preparation:** Prepare a sheet of chart paper with a diagram of a tree on it, with 8 circles hanging on it as decorations. Record the underlined words in the ornaments on the tree.

### Make a Celebration Tree

Today I'll show you the illustrations done for *Wilma Unlimited.* As I read about those illustrations, I'll call on one of you to tell about an important event in Wilma Rudolph's life that she might choose to celebrate.

**Page 4.** What would Wilma celebrate in this part of her story? (Idea: *Wilma would <u>celebrate</u> her <u>first</u> <u>birthday</u>.*)

**Page 18.** What would Wilma celebrate in this part of her story? (Idea: *She was <u>walking</u>.*)

**Page 20.** What would Wilma celebrate in this part of her story? (Idea: *They <u>wrapped up</u> the hated <u>brace</u> in a box and <u>mailed</u> it <u>back to the hospital</u>.*)

**Page 22.** What would Wilma celebrate in this part of her story? (Idea: *She took the team all the way to the Tennessee <u>state championships</u>.*)

**Page 24.** What would Wilma celebrate in this part of her story? (Idea: *She was the first member of her family to <u>go to college</u>.*)

**Page 28.** What would Wilma celebrate in this part of her story? (Idea: *She won an Olympic <u>gold medal</u> for the <u>100-meter dash</u>.*)

**Page 30.** What would Wilma celebrate in this part of her story? (Idea: *She won an Olympic <u>gold medal</u> for the <u>200-meter dash</u>.*)

**Page 34.** What would Wilma celebrate in this part of her story? (Idea: *She won an Olympic gold medal* for the *400-meter relay*.)

### Present Author's Note

Sometimes when people write a biography, they learn more about the person than they can fit in the story. The author wants you to have this information as well.

The author gives you this information in note form rather than in story form. This part of a book is called the Author's Note. What do we call the part of a biography where the author shares his or her notes about the person? *The Author's Note.*

The Author's Note can come before or after the main part of the book. Today I'll read the Author's Note that Kathleen Krull wrote for *Wilma Unlimited* so you can learn more about Wilma Rudolph. In this Author's Note, Kathleen Krull wrote more information about the life of Wilma Rudolph.

Let's see if Kathleen Krull included any events Wilma could have celebrated in the Author's Note section of her book.

(Read the Author's Note one paragraph at a time. At the end of each paragraph, ask:) Is there anything we can add to our Celebration Tree? (Add an ornament for each new celebration children suggest, such as: *first American woman to win three gold medals in one Olympics; became a second-grade teacher.*)

### Play the Super Choosing Game

Today you will play the *Super Choosing* game. We've played a game like this before but this one is a little bit different. Let's think about the six words we have learned: **paralyzed, concentrating, gathering, victory, overcame,** and **heroic.** (Display the Picture Vocabulary Cards.)

I will say a sentence that has two or three of the words we have learned in it. You will have to choose the correct word for that sentence. Not all of the words will be from this lesson, though.

That's why it's the *Super Choosing* game. Let's practice. (You should not show cards for the words outside of this lesson.)

- If you are unable to move your leg, is it **captive, heroic,** or **paralyzed?** *Paralyzed.*
- Is a group of people who come together for a purpose called a **grief** or a **gathering?** *A gathering.*
- Are the things that make a person or thing different from others called **customs, heroic,** or **characteristics?** *Characteristics.*

T Now you're ready to play the game. If you tell me the correct answer, you will win one point. If you can't tell me the correct answer, I get the point. (Draw a T-chart on the board for keeping score. Children earn one point for each correct answer. If they make an error, correct them as you normally would, and record one point for yourself. Repeat missed words at the end of the game.)

- If you worked really hard to learn to read even though you have a learning disability, did you **compete** with the disability or **overcome** it? *Overcome it.*
- If you strongly believe in yourself and the things that you can do, are you **determined, disgusting,** or **confident?** *Confident.*
- If you put a bunch of things in a pile to use later, are you **forgiving** them or **gathering** them? *Gathering them.*
- If you are focusing very hard on completing a task, are you **concentrating, thoughtful,** or **challenging?** *Concentrating.*
- If someone does something brave, have they been **cold-blooded, heroic,** or **captured?** *Heroic.*
- If you win a game or contest, do you have a **slave,** a **victory,** or a **dream?** *A victory.*

(Count the points and declare a winner.) You did a great job of playing the *Super Choosing* game.

**Preparation:** Photocopy and assemble *The Biography of Wilma Rudolph.*

Print the following words in two columns on the board: *Sunday, church, amazed, amazing, coach, college, Olympics, won, races, medals, fastest, world.*

### Introduce The Biography of Wilma Rudolph

(Point to each word as you read it.) This word is **Sunday.** What word? *Sunday.* This word is **church.** What word? *Church.* (Repeat process for remaining words.)

Let's read these words together. First word? *Sunday.* Next word? *Church.* (Repeat process for remaining words.)

Read these words by yourself. First word? *Sunday.* Next word? *Church.* (Repeat process for remaining words.)

(Use the following correction procedure if children make an error:) This word is **won.** What word? *Won.* Yes, **won.** (Go back to the top of the list and repeat the list until children can read it accurately and confidently.)

(Give each child a copy of *The Biography of Wilma Rudolph.* Ask children to touch under the title of the booklet.) The title of this book is *The Biography of Wilma Rudolph.* What's the title of this book? *The Biography of Wilma Rudolph.*

Remember that a biography tells about the life of a real person. What does a biography tell about? *The life of a real person.* Is a biography fiction or nonfiction? *Nonfiction.*

(Ask children to open their booklets to page 1. Ask them to touch under the first underlined words.) These words are **Wilma Rudolph.** What words? *Wilma Rudolph.* Yes, **Wilma Rudolph.** This biography is about Wilma Rudolph. Who is this biography about? *Wilma Rudolph.*

My turn to read each page of the book. You touch under each word as I read it. (Read pages 1–4.)

Let's read the book together. (Have children read chorally with you.)

(Assign each child a partner. Allow sufficient time for each child to read the booklet to his or her partner. Circulate as children read, offering praise and assistance.)

(Children should color the illustrations in their booklet. Encourage them to color the illustrations realistically.)

### Play the Super Choosing Game (Cumulative Review)

 Let's play the *Super Choosing* game. I will say a sentence that has two or three of our words in it. You will have to choose the correct word for that sentence. (Display the Picture Vocabulary Cards for *paralyzed, concentrating, gathering, victory, overcame,* and *heroic* for the three words in each sentence as you say the sentence.)

Now you're ready to play the *Super Choosing* game. (Draw a T-chart on the board for keeping score. Children earn one point for each correct answer. If they make an error, correct them as you normally would, and record one point for yourself. Repeat missed words at the end of the game.)

- Wilma was unable to move her left leg. Was she **overcome, paralyzed,** or **victory?** *Paralyzed.*
- If a group of people got together to vote in an election, would they be called a **gathering,** a **victory,** or a **concentrating?** *A gathering.*
- If you overcame a disability to compete in the Olympics, would that be a **victory,** a **gathering,** or **paralyzed?** *A victory.*
- If you had a problem and were able to beat it, would you say you **paralyzed** it, **overcame** it, or were **concentrating?** *Overcame it.*
- If you picked up all of your toys and put them in the toy box to play with later, would you be **gathering** them, **concentrating** them, or **overcoming** them? *Gathering them.*
- If you are really focusing on getting your work done, are you **gathering, concentrating,** or **paralyzed?** *Concentrating.*
- If someone is a role model because they do brave things, are they **paralyzed, concentrating,** or **heroic?** *Heroic.*

Now you will have to listen very carefully, because I'm not going to show you the word cards. (This part of the game includes the review words from previous lessons.)

- Are firefighters **waterproof, pests,** or **heroic?** *Heroic.*
- If something is very hard to believe, is it **suspicious, unbelievable,** or a **fool?** *Unbelievable.*
- Are fruits and vegetables a good source of **ingredients, wilderness,** or **nourishment?** *Nourishment.*
- When you focus all of your attention on something, are you **concentrating, colossal,** or in **Canada?** *Concentrating.*
- A group of people has come together to talk about the books they like to read, are they a **suggestion,** a **gathering,** or a **predator?** *A gathering.*
- Would an **accepting** person or a **frazzled** person be likely to take people for who they are? *An accepting person.*
- Amber is able to do a cartwheel into a forward flip on the balance beam. Is she **exhausted, coordinated,** or **paralyzed?** *Coordinated.*
- The puppy's parents have died. Is it a **prey,** an **orphan,** or a **bird?** *An orphan.*

(Tally the points and declare a winner.) You did a great job of playing the *Super Choosing* game.

---

## DAY 5

**Preparation:** Class chart titled *Reading Goals* that was started in Week 16.

*The Biography of Wilma Rudolph.*

Quiz Answer Sheet, BLM B.

### Read The Biography of Wilma Rudolph

(Assign each child a partner.) Today you'll read the first four pages of *The Biography of Wilma Rudolph* to your partner. (Allow sufficient time for each child to read the first four pages of the booklet to his or her partner. Circulate as children read, offering praise and assistance.)

(Ask children to look at the back of their booklets.) This part of the book is for people who can help you find other books to read. It tells those people about other books that are biographies. It also tells them about a place where you can find other biographies. Where are some places that you could go to find other biographies? (Ideas: *To the school library; to the public library; to a bookstore.*)

(You may wish to read and discuss the information on the back cover.)

There's one more important thing on the back cover of your book. Touch the box that is at the bottom of the page. The words above the box say "My reading goal." What do the words say? *My reading goal.*

What is a goal? *Something that you want to succeed at doing.* A reading goal is something that you want to succeed at doing with your reading.

Let's see if we can add some other reading goals to our class chart. What are some other reading goals that someone might have when they read their book? (Accept reasonable responses. Help children put their ideas into goal statements. Add to the list of statements on the chart. Ask them to choose a goal and copy it into the box. Children may also make up an original goal that is not on the list. If children are unable to copy the goals or to write a goal of their own, you or a helper may wish to scribe their goal statements for them before the booklets are sent home.)

### Assess Comprehension

(Ask children to turn to page 5 in their booklets.) This is what you have read in the biography about Wilma Rudolph but with no pictures. You are going to have a little quiz to see if you can remember what you read.

(Ask children to touch under the words as they read the passage silently. Monitor to ensure that children are reading the passage. Ask them to look up at you after they have finished reading the passage. Instruct children to read and answer the questions.)

## Assess Vocabulary

 (Give each child a copy of the Quiz Answer Sheet, BLM B.)

Today you're going to have a True or False quiz. When you do the True or False quiz it shows me how well you know the hard words you are learning.

If I say something that is true, circle the word **true.** What will you do if I say something that is true? *Circle the word* true.

If I say something that is false, circle the word **false.** What will you do if I say something that is false? *Circle the word* false.

Listen carefully to each item that I say. Don't let me trick you!

Item 1: A **heroic** person is brave and a good role model. (*True.*)

Item 2: Something that is **unjust** is fair. (*False.*)

Item 3: The Tigers beat the Colts 17 to 12. The Colts got the **victory.** (*False.*)

Item 4: If you daydream during science class, it means that you are **concentrating** on what the teacher is saying. (*False.*)

Item 5: Seatbelts and bike helmets are made to **protect** you. (*True.*)

Item 6: A person who had a disability and never left their room because of it **overcame** it. (*False.*)

Item 7: **Fish** are **cold-blooded** animals that live in the water. (*True.*)

Item 8: An animal that is unable to move after being stung by a poisonous **reptile** is **paralyzed.** (*True.*)

Item 9: A family who gets together to celebrate a birthday is having a **gathering.** (*True.*)

Item 10: If you collect all of your library books and put them in a pile by the door, you are **gathering** them. (*True.*)

You did a great job completing your quiz!

(Score children's work. A child must score 9 out of 10 to be at the mastery level. If a child does not achieve mastery, insert the missed words as additional items in the games in next week's lessons. Retest those children individually for the missed items before they take the next mastery test.)

## Extensions

### Read a Book as a Reward

(Read *Wilma Unlimited* or another biography about an athlete to children as a reward for their hard work. Display a number of biographies about athletes. Ask children to choose which one they would like you to read.)

---

**Preparation:** Word containers for the Super Words Center.

---

### Introduce the Super Words Center (2 in 1)

 (Add the new Picture Vocabulary Cards to the words from the previous weeks. Show children one of the word containers. Role-play with two to three children as you introduce each part of the game.)

Let's review how to play the game called *2 in 1* in the Super Words Center.

Let's think about how we work with our words in the Super Words Center.

You will work with a partner in the Super Words Center. Whom will you work with? *A partner.*

First you will draw two words out of the container. What do you do first? (Idea: *Draw two words out of the container.*) Show your partner both of the words. (Demonstrate.)

Next you will say a sentence that uses both of your words. What do you do next? (Idea: *I will say a sentence that uses both of my words.* Demonstrate.)

If you can use both of your words in one sentence, give yourself a point. Then give your partner a turn. (Demonstrate.)

What do you do next? *Give my partner a turn.*

## Week 26

**Preparation:** You will need a copy of *One Duck Stuck* for each day's lesson.

Number the pages of the book to assist you in asking comprehension questions at appropriate points.

Post a copy of the Vocabulary Tally Sheet, BLM A, with this week's Picture Vocabulary Cards attached.

Each child will need one copy of the Homework Sheet, BLM 26a.

### DAY 1

### Introduce Series

For the next five weeks we will be reading books that are written as poems or that include poems. Poems are pieces of writing that rhyme or have a certain rhythm. What do poems have? (Ideas: *Rhyming words; certain rhythms.*) What kind of writing has rhyme or rhythm? *A poem.*

### Introduce Book

This week's book is called *One Duck Stuck.* What's the title of this week's book? *One Duck Stuck.* What do you notice about the words in the title *One Duck Stuck*? (Idea: *Duck and stuck rhyme.*) What kind of writing uses rhyming words? *Poems.* Today's book is a poem that uses rhyming words.

There are many different kinds of poems. Today's book is a counting poem. What kind of poem is today's book? *A counting poem.*

This book was written by Phyllis Root. Who's the author of *One Duck Stuck*? *Phyllis Root.*

Jane Chapman made the pictures for this book. Who is the illustrator of *One Duck Stuck*? *Jane Chapman.* Who made the illustrations for this book? *Jane Chapman.*

The cover of a book usually gives us some hints of what the book is about. Let's look at the front cover of *One Duck Stuck.* What do you see in the illustration? (Idea: *A duck stuck in the mud.*)

### One Duck Stuck
author: Phyllis Root • illustrator: Jane Chapman

#### Target Vocabulary

| Tier II | Tier III |
|---------|----------|
| slimy | counting poem |
| muck | rhyme |
| wakes | |
| plod | |
| *cooperate | |
| *eventually | |

*Expanded Target Vocabulary Word

(Assign each child a partner.) Get ready to make some predictions to your partner about this book. Use the information from the cover to help you.

(Ask the following questions, allowing sufficient time for children to share their predictions with their partners.)

- Who do you think this poem is about?
- Where do you think the poem happens?
- When do you think the poem happens?
- How do you think the duck got stuck in the mud?
- How do you think the duck will get out of the mud?

(Call on several children to share their predictions with the class.)

### Take a Picture Walk

(Encourage children to use target words in their answers.) We're going to take a picture walk through this book. Remember that when we take a picture walk, we look at the pictures and tell what we think will happen in the story.

**Pages 1–2.** Where does this story happen? (Idea: *Near a pond or lake.*) What has happened to this duck? (Idea: *Its foot has sunk into the mud; it has gotten stuck in the mud.*)

**Pages 3–4.** Who has come to help the duck? (Idea: *Two fish.*) What are they doing to the duck? (Idea: *Splashing it.*) Do you think that splashing the duck will help it get unstuck? *No.*

**Pages 5–6.** Who has come to help the duck? (Idea: *Three moose.*) How do you think the moose will try to help the duck?

**Pages 7–8.** Who has come to help the duck? (Idea: *Four crickets; four insects.*) How do you think the crickets will try to help the duck? (Idea: *Pull him out.*)

**Pages 9–10.** Who has come to help the duck? (Idea: *Five frogs.*) How do you think the frogs will try to help the duck?

**Pages 11–12.** Who has come to help the duck? (Idea: *Six skunks.*) How do you think the skunks will try to help the duck?

**Pages 13–14.** Who has come to help the duck? (Idea: *Seven snails.*) How do you think the snails will try to help the duck?

**Pages 15–16.** Who has come to help the duck? (Idea: *Eight possums.*) How do you think the possums will try to help the duck?

**Pages 17–18.** Who has come to help the duck? (Idea: *Nine snakes.*) How do you think the snakes will try to help the duck?

**Pages 19–20.** Who has come to help the duck? (Idea: *Ten dragonflies.*) How do you think the dragonflies will try to help the duck?

**Pages 21–22.** What are all the animals doing? (Idea: *Looking at the duck.*) Will looking at the duck help it get unstuck? *No.* What do you think the animals will do to get the duck out of the mud? (Ideas: *Cooperate; work together.*)

**Pages 23–24.** How have the animals tried to help the duck? (Point to each illustration one by one.) (Ideas: *The fish splashed; the moose ate; the crickets jumped on the duck; the frogs hopped around the duck; the skunks threw sticks at the duck; the snails crawled on the duck; the possums put flowers on the duck; the snakes slithered around the duck; the dragonflies flew around the duck.*)

**Pages 25–26.** What is happening in this illustration? (Ideas: *The animals are working together to get the duck out; the animals are making a chain to pull the duck out; the duck is grabbing a stick with its foot.*)

**Pages 27–28.** What is happening in this illustration? (Idea: *The duck pulled its foot free.*) How does the duck get free from the mud? (Idea: *It stepped on a stick with one foot and pulled its other foot free.*)

**Pages 29–30.** What did the duck do once it was free of the mud? (Idea: *It flew away.*) How do you think the duck felt? (Ideas: *Happy; contented; calm; delighted; exhausted; grateful.*)

**Page 31.** Where do you think the duck will go now?

**Page 33.** Are all the animals happy at the end of this poem? *No.* What happens to the moose? (Idea: *It gets stuck in the mud.*)

It's your turn to ask me some questions. What would you like to know about the poem? (Accept questions. If children tell about the pictures or the story instead of ask questions, prompt them to ask a question.) Ask me a why question. Ask me a where question.

### Read the Poem Aloud
(Read the poem to children with minimal interruptions.)

Tomorrow we will read the poem again, and I will ask you some questions.

### Present Target Vocabulary

Slimy

In the poem, the duck was down by the sleepy, slimy marsh. **Slimy.** Say the word. *Slimy.*

**Slimy** is a describing word. It tells about what something feels like. What kind of word is **slimy?** *A describing word.*

**If something feels slimy, it feels wet, soft, and slippery.** Say the word that means "wet, soft, and slippery." *Slimy.*

(Correct any incorrect responses, and repeat the item at the end of the sequence.)

Let's think about some things that could be slimy. I'll tell about some things. If these things might feel slimy, say "slimy." If not, don't say anything.

- A bowl of spaghetti. *Slimy.*
- A fish. *Slimy.*
- Chalk.

- A slice of bread.
- A snail's trail. *Slimy.*
- A worm in the mud. *Slimy.*

What describing word means "wet, soft, and slippery"? *Slimy.*

###  Muck

In the poem, the duck got stuck in the muck. **Muck.** Say the word. *Muck.*

**Muck** is a noun. It names a thing. What kind of word is **muck?** *A noun.*

**Muck is anything that is dirty, wet, sticky, or slimy.** Say the word that means "something that is dirty, wet, sticky, or slimy." *Muck.*

Let's think about some things that could be called muck. I'll tell about a thing. If it could be called muck, say "muck." If not, don't say anything.

- After playing by the river, Josiah had wet, slimy stuff all over his face. *Muck.*
- While walking in the woods after a rainstorm, Alia stepped in something that pulled her shoe right off her foot. *Muck.*
- Aaron filled the kitchen sink with warm water and soap.
- Charlie had to take his shoes off before getting in the car after picking apples because he had been in the wet, slimy mud. *Muck.*
- Kellie swept the hay and oats from the floor of the horse's stall.
- After finger painting, Jerome's hands were full of wet, sticky paint. *Muck.*

What noun means "anything that is dirty, wet, sticky, or slimy"? *Muck.*

###  Wakes

In the poem, the snakes left little wakes as they slithered to the duck. That means the snakes left little waves as they moved through the water. **Wakes.** Say the word. *Wakes.*

**Wakes** is a noun. It names a thing. What kind of word is **wakes?** *A noun.*

**Wakes are the waves that are left behind when something moves through water.** Say the word that means "the waves that are left behind when something moves through water." *Wake.*

Let's think about some times when something might leave a wake. I'll name some things. If the things leave a wake, say "wake." If not, don't say anything.

- Oleg walked through the door of the classroom.
- The small boat sped through the water. *Wake.*
- The green water snake slithered through the water. *Wake.*
- The hurricane made large waves as it move through the water. *Wake.*
- Su Li pulled a brush through her hair.
- The dog ran through the grass.

What noun means "the waves that are left behind when something moves through water"? *Wake.*

### Plod

In the poem, the moose plodded to the duck. **Plod.** Say the word. *Plod.*

**Plod** is a verb. It tells an action. What kind of word is **plod?** *A verb.*

**Plod means walk in a slow and heavy way.** Say the word that means "walk in a slow and heavy way." *Plod.*

Let's think about some ways that people and animals move. I'll tell about a person or an animal. If the person or animal would be walking slowly and heavily, say "plod." If not, don't say anything.

- Dustin knew he was going to get in trouble when he got home, so he was walking slowly and heavily. *Plod.*
- The gazelle ran lightly through the forest.
- The ground shook as the hippo slowly made its way to the edge of the water. *Plod.*
- The heavy elephant slowly walked down the path at the zoo. *Plod.*
- Four crickets jumped quickly through the air.
- The giant hog made its way slowly towards the barn after the rest of the animals. *Plod.*

What verb means "walk in a slow and heavy way"? *Plod.*

### Present Vocabulary Tally Sheet
(See Lesson 1, page 4, for instructions)

## Assign Homework

(Homework Sheet, BLM 26a. See the Introduction for homework instructions.)

**Preparation:** Picture Vocabulary Cards for *slimy, muck, wake, plod*.

### Read and Discuss Poem

(Read the poem to children. Ask the following questions at the specified points. Encourage them to use target words in their answers.)

Now I'm going to read *One Duck Stuck*. When I finish each part, I'll ask you some questions.

**Page 1.** Who is this poem about? (Idea: *One duck.*) How many ducks are in this poem? *One.* What happened to the duck? (Idea: *It got stuck in the muck.*)

(Write *duck* on the board. Underline *uck*.) When words have the same ending sound, we say they rhyme. What do we say words do when they have the same ending sound? *Rhyme.* What sound do you hear at the end of duck? *Uck.* What other words on this page end with the **uck** sound? (Ideas: *Stuck; muck.*) What other words do you know that rhyme with **duck?** (Ideas: *Luck; truck; puck.*)

**Page 2.** What did the duck ask? *Help! Help! Who can help?*

**Page 3.** Who came to help the duck? *Two fish.* What did the fish do to help? *They swam to the duck.*

(Write *fish* on the board. Underline *ish*.) What sound do you hear at the end of fish? *Ish.* What other words on this page end with the **ish** sound? (Ideas: *Swish; splish.*) What other words do you know that rhyme with **fish?** (Ideas: *Wish; dish.*)

**Page 4.** What did the duck ask? *Help! Help! Who can help?*

**Page 5.** Who came to help the duck? *Three moose.* What did the moose do to help? (Idea: *They plodded to the duck.*)

(Write *moose* on the board. Underline *oose*.) What sound do you hear at the end of **moose?** *Oose.* What other word on this page ends with the **oose** sound? *Spruce.* What other words do you know that rhyme with **moose?** (Ideas: *Loose; goose.*)

**Page 6.** What did the duck ask? *Help! Help! Who can help?*

**Page 7.** Who came to help the duck? *Four crickets.* What did the crickets do to help? (Idea: *Leapt to the duck.*)

(Write *crickets* on the board. Underline *ickets*.) What sound do you hear at the end of **crickets?** *Ickets.* What other word on this page ends with the **ickets** sound? *Thickets.* What other words do you know that rhyme with **crickets?** (Idea: *Tickets.*)

**Page 8.** What did the duck ask? *Help! Help! Who can help?*

**Page 9.** Who came to help the duck? *Five frogs.* What did the frogs do to help? (Idea: *They jumped to the duck.*)

(Write *frogs* on the board. Underline *ogs*.) What sound do you hear at the end of **frogs?** *Ogs.* What other word on this page ends with the **ogs** sound? *Logs.* What other words do you know that rhyme with **frogs?** (Ideas: *Dogs; bogs; hogs.*)

**Page 10.** What did the duck ask? *Help! Help! Who can help?*

**Page 11.** Who came to help the duck? *Six Skunks.* What did the skunks do to help? (Idea: *Crawled to the duck.*)

(Write *skunks* on the board. Underline *unks*.) What sound do you hear at the end of **skunks?** *Unks.* What other word on this page ends with the **unks** sound? *Trunks.* What other words do you know that rhyme with **skunks?** (Ideas: *Bunks; monks, chunks.*)

**Page 12.** What did the duck ask? *Help! Help! Who can help?*

**Page 13.** Who came to help the duck? *Seven snails.* What did the snails do to help? (Idea: *Slid to the duck.*)

(Write *snails* on the board. Underline *ails*.) What sound do you hear at the end of **snails?** *Ails.* What other word on this page ends with the **ails** sound? *Trails.* What other words do you know that rhyme with **snails?** (Ideas: *Nails; tails; pails; fails; bales; whales; hails.*)

**Page 14.** What did the duck ask? *Help! Help! Who can help?*

**Page 15.** Who came to help the duck? *Eight possums.* What did the possums do to help? (Idea: *Crawled to the duck.*)

(Write *possums* on the board. Underline *ossums*.) What sound do you hear at the end of **possums?** *Ossums.* What other word on this page ends with the **ossums** sound? (Idea: *Blossoms.*)

**Page 16.** What did the duck ask? *Help! Help! Who can help?*

**Page 17.** Who came to help the duck? *Nine snakes.* What did the snakes do to help? (Idea: *Slithered to the duck.*)

(Write *snakes* on the board. Underline *akes*.) What sound do you hear at the end of **snakes?** *Akes.* What other word on this page ends with the **akes** sound? *Wakes.* What other words do you know that rhyme with **snakes?** (Ideas: *Bakes; stakes; makes; fakes; lakes.*)

**Page 18.** What did the duck ask? *Help! Help! Who can help?*

**Page 19.** Who came to help the duck? *Ten dragonflies.* What did the dragonflies do to help? (Idea: *Whirred to the duck.*)

(Write *dragonflies* on the board. Underline *ies*.) What sound do you hear at the end of **dragonflies?** *Ies.* What other word on this page ends with the **ies** sound? *Skies.* What other words do you know that rhyme with **dragonflies?** (Ideas: *Cries; highs, pies.*)

**Page 20.** What did the duck ask? *Help! Help! Who can help?*

*One Duck Stuck* is a counting poem. Why do you think *One Duck Stuck* is called a counting poem? (Idea: *As the poem goes along, it counts animals from one to ten.*)

**Page 21.** Who is going to help the duck? (Idea: *All of the animals.*)

**Pages 23–24.** What are these words describing? (Idea: *The sound each animal made when it came to help the duck.*) These words sound like the sounds they describe. Can you think of any other words that sound like the sounds they describe? (Ideas: *Whir; whoosh; whoo-whoo; buzz.*)

**Page 25.** What did the animals do? (Idea: *They all worked together to help the duck get out of the muck.*)

**Page 28.** What do you think **spluck** is? (Idea: *The sound the duck's foot made when it came out of the mud.*) What words from the poem does **spluck** rhyme with? (Ideas: *Duck, stuck, muck.* Add *spluck* to the list of words under *duck.*)

**Page 29.** To whom is the duck saying "Thanks"? (Idea: *All of the animals that helped it get out of the muck.*)

### Review Vocabulary

(Display the Picture Vocabulary Cards. Point to each card as you say the word. Ask children to repeat each word after you.) These pictures show **slimy, muck, wake,** and **plod.**

- What verb means "walk in a slow and heavy way"? *Plod.*
- What noun names "anything that is dirty, wet, sticky, or slimy"? *Muck.*
- What word means "wet, soft, and slippery"? *Slimy.*
- What noun means "the waves that are left behind when something moves through water"? *Wake.*

### Extend Vocabulary

 Wake

In *One Duck Stuck,* we learned that a **wake** is "the waves that are left behind when something moves through water." Say the noun that means "the waves that are left behind when something moves through water." *Wake.*

Raise your hand if you can tell us a sentence that uses **wake** as a noun meaning "the waves that are left behind when something moves through water." (Call on several children. If they don't use complete sentences, restate their examples as sentences. Have the class repeat the sentences.)

Here's a new way to use the word **wake**.

- Tomorrow I will **wake** up at 6:00 in the morning. Say the sentence.
- Mother tried to **wake** me, but I was sound asleep. Say the sentence.
- During the school year, I have to **wake** up early. Say the sentence.

**In these sentences, wake is a verb that means to come out of sleep.** Raise your hand if you can tell us a sentence that uses **wake** as a verb meaning "to come out of sleep." (Call on several children. If they don't use complete sentences, restate their examples as sentences. Have the class repeat the sentences.)

### Present Expanded Target Vocabulary
 Cooperate

In the poem, all of the animals had to work together to help the duck. They had to cooperate. **Cooperate.** Say the word. *Cooperate.*

**Cooperate** is a verb. It tells an action. What kind of word is **cooperate?** *A verb.*

**Cooperate means work together.** Say the word that means "work together." *Cooperate.*

I'll tell about some people. If those people are cooperating, say "cooperate." If not, don't say anything.

- Regina and Tamara argued over the toy.
- Grandma and I baked cookies together. *Cooperate.*
- The first graders worked as a team to clean up the playground. *Cooperate.*
- Thelma did her math homework while her brother watched a movie.
- While Dad made dinner, my sister and I set the table. *Cooperate.*
- We didn't get our work done because two students didn't do their part.

What verb means "work together"? *Cooperate.*

 Eventually

In the poem, it took some time, but the duck eventually got unstuck from the muck. **Eventually.** Say the word. *Eventually.*

**Eventually** is a describing word. It tells more about when something happened. What kind of word is **eventually?** *A describing word.*

**Eventually means finally or at last.** Say the word that means "finally or at last." *Eventually.*

I'll tell about some events. If the events eventually happened, say "eventually." If not, don't say anything.

- Camden tried and tried and finally learned how to tie his shoes. *Eventually.*
- I never did get to see that movie.
- Unfortunately, the soccer game was cancelled because of rain.
- Samantha finally read an entire chapter book on her own. *Eventually.*
- Carter practiced every day and finally made the state baseball team. *Eventually.*

What describing word means "finally or at last"? *Eventually.*

### DAY 3

**Preparation:** Activity Sheet, BLM 26b and crayons.

### Play Poetic Definitions

 Today you'll play a game called Poetic Definitions. I'll say a little poem that describes the meaning of one of our vocabulary words. If you can tell me the word that the poem is using, you will win one point. If you can't tell me, I get the point. Let's think about the six words we have learned: **slimy, muck, wake, plod, cooperate,** and **eventually.** (Display the Picture Vocabulary Cards.)

Let's practice. The snake went slither thither through the water. I can see right there where he did pass. What vocabulary word names what the snake left? *Wake.*

Now you're ready to play the game. (Draw a T-chart on the board for keeping score. Children earn one point for each correct answer. If they make an error, correct them as you normally would, and record one point for yourself. Repeat missed words at the end of the game.)

- I didn't mean to step in goo, but oh me, oh my, it's on my shoe! What vocabulary word describes what I stepped in? *Muck.*
- The snail's trail was slippery and wet. He thought to himself, "I'll get there yet!" What vocabulary word describes the snail's trail? *Slimy.*
- Clomp, clomp. Heavy stomp. Walk so slow as I chomp. What vocabulary word describes the way the animal is walking? *Plod.*
- Working together 1, 2, 3. Working together you and me. What vocabulary word describes what you and I are doing? *Cooperating.*
- Someday I'll do it! If I work hard and think well. Someday I'll do it! Only time will tell. What vocabulary word describes when something will happen? *Eventually.*
- Sleep is over! Time to rise! Open up those sleepy eyes! What vocabulary word describes what it's time to do? *Wake.*

(Count the points, and declare a winner.) You did a great job of playing Poetic Definitions.

### Complete the Activity Sheet

Today I'll show you the pictures Jane Chapman made for *One Duck Stuck.* As I show you the pictures, I'll call on one of you to remind the class about how many animals helped the duck.

(Revisit each page of the poem, having children tell how many of each animal helped the duck. Record each number and kind of animal in list form on the board.)

Today we are going to make a bar graph to show the animals that helped the duck in our poem get unstuck. When we make a bar graph, we color in one box for each animal we count

(Distribute copies of BLM 26b children. Draw the class's attention to the column of animals on the left of the page.) Touch under the first picture. What animal is that? *Fish.* How many fish helped

the duck? *Two.* Two fish helped the duck, so I am going to color in two boxes on the fish's line. (Demonstrate coloring in the first two boxes next to the picture of the fish.) Your turn. Pick a color and color in two boxes to show the two fish that helped the duck.

(Repeat this process for each animal on the graph. Have children use a different color for each bar of the graph. If they have difficulty remembering the number of animals, revisit the page in the book.)

Touch under the first word of the sentence at the bottom of the page. We are going to read this sentence together. When you get to the blank, say "blank." Get ready. (Signal.) *I counted blank boxes all together.*

Count all of the boxes you colored. Write the number in the blank. (Give children time to count the boxes and record the number.) Let's read the sentence together. *I counted 54 boxes all together.*

---

### DAY 4

**Preparation:** Prepare a sheet of chart paper with the letters *D, U, C, K, S* written vertically down the left-hand side of the paper.

---

### Guided Writing–Acrostic Poem

For the next five weeks, we are going to be reading books that are poems or that include poems. At the end of the five weeks, we are going to have a poetry contest. For the poetry contest, you will each write your own poem. I am going to teach you how to write four different kinds of poems. Today we will write our first poem.

The poem we will write today is called an acrostic poem. What kind of poem will we write today? *An acrostic poem.*

The first thing we do when we write an acrostic poem is decide what to write about. What is the first thing we do when we write an acrostic poem? *Decide what to write about.*

Today we are going to write an acrostic poem about ducks. What will today's acrostic poem be about? *Ducks.*

The next thing we do when we write an acrostic poem is write the word down the side of the paper. What is the next thing we do when we write an acrostic poem? *Write the word down the side of the paper.* (Show chart paper with *DUCKS* written vertically.) These letters spell **ducks.** What do these letters spell? *Ducks.*

The next thing we do is think of a word or a sentence about ducks for each letter of the word. What is the next thing we do? (Idea: *Think of a word or sentence for each letter of the word* ducks.)

What is a word or a sentence about ducks that starts with the letter **D?** (Accept reasonable responses. Write an appropriate word or phrase next to the *D.* Repeat the process for the remaining letters in *DUCKS.*)

(Sample acrostic for DUCKS:
　　　Diving in the water.
　　　Under a blue sky.
　　　Calling to other ducks.
　　　Kicking and splashing.
　　　Swimming with webbed feet.)

(Read the completed poem aloud.) We did a great job of writing an acrostic poem about ducks. Tomorrow you will write your own acrostic poem.

### Play Poetic Definitions (Cumulative Review)

Let's play the game Poetic Definitions. I'll say a little poem that describes the meaning of one of our vocabulary words. If you can tell me the word that the poem is using, you will win one point. If you can't tell me, I get the point. Let's think about the six words we have learned: **slimy, muck, wake, plod, cooperate,** and **eventually.** (Display the Picture Vocabulary Cards.)

Let's practice. The snail's trail was slippery and wet. He thought to himself, "I'll get there yet!"

What vocabulary word describes the snail's trail? *Slimy.*

T　Now you're ready to play the game. (Draw a T-chart on the board for keeping score. Children earn one point for each correct answer. If they make an error, correct them as you normally would, and record one point for yourself. Repeat missed words at the end of the game.)

- I didn't mean to step on you, but oh me, oh my, it's wet and slimy and on my shoe! What vocabulary word describes what I stepped in? *Muck.*
- Jack and Jill went to the store to buy some milk and bread. Jack saw gum and wanted some, and so bought that instead. What vocabulary word describes what Jack and Jill are? *Customers.*
- Oh my. I cannot keep a deep sleep. I must get up. What vocabulary word names what I have to do? *Wake.*
- Clomp, clomp. Slowly I stomp. Walk so slowly I hardly move. What vocabulary word describes the way the animal is walking? *Plod.*
- Wings and feathers. Laying eggs. Walking around on two little legs. What vocabulary word is being described in this poem? *Bird.*
- Working together 1, 2, 3. Then we can be free. What vocabulary word describes what you and I are doing? *Cooperate.*
- Someday I'll do it! Someday it will fit. Someday I'll have a baseball mitt. Only time will tell. What vocabulary word describes when something will happen? *Eventually.*
- Oh, sleep. Such a wonderful thing. Wake me up when it is spring. What vocabulary word is the poem describing? *Hibernate.*
- Now is not the time to sleep. An alarm is going beep, beep, beep. What vocabulary word describes what it's time to do? *Wake.*

(Count the points and declare a winner.) You did a great job of playing Poetic Definitions.

**Preparation:** Quiz Answer Sheet, BLM B.

## Assess Vocabulary

 (Give each child a copy of the Quiz Answer Sheet, BLM B.)

Today you're going to have a True or False quiz. When you do the True or False quiz, it shows me how well you know the hard words you are learning.

If I say something that is true, circle the word **true.** What will you do if I say something that is true? *Circle the word* true.

If I say something that is false, circle the word **false.** What will you do if I say something that is false? *Circle the word* false.

Listen carefully to each item that I say. Don't let me trick you!

Item 1: Something that is **slimy** is very dry and smooth. (*False.*)

Item 2: If you believe everything will turn out okay, you are **optimistic.** (*True.*)

Item 3: Mud and finger paints can be described as **muck.** (*True.*)

Item 4: The **wake** of a boat is the path it leaves as it passes through the water. (*True.*)

Item 5: If you have been **injured,** someone has hurt you. (*True.*)

Item 6: To run fast is to **plod.** (*False.*)

Item 7: When you go to bed at night, you **wake.** (*False.*)

Item 8: If you and your friends work together to complete a job, you **cooperate.** (*True.*)

Item 9: If you dance a different way every time you hear music, you are doing a **routine.** (*False.*)

Item 10: Something that will happen sooner or later will happen **eventually.** (*True.*)

You did a great job completing your quiz!

(Score children's work. A child must score 9 out of 10 to be at the mastery level. If a child does not achieve mastery, insert the missed words as additional items in the games in next week's lessons. Retest those children individually for the missed items before they take the next mastery test.)

**Preparation:** Prepare a sheet of chart paper with the letters of your name written vertically down the left-hand side of the paper.

## Independent Writing—Acrostic Poem

Yesterday you learned how to write an acrostic poem. What kind of poem did you learn to write yesterday? *An acrostic poem.*

The first thing we do when we write an acrostic poem is decide what to write about. What is the first thing we do when we write an acrostic poem? *Decide what to write about.*

Today you are going to write your own acrostic poem about yourself. What will today's acrostic poem be about? *Ourselves.*

The next thing we do when we write an acrostic poem is write the word down the side of the paper. What is the next thing we do when we write an acrostic poem? *Write the word down the side of the paper.* (Show chart paper with your name written vertically.) These letters spell my name, *[your name].* What do these letters spell? (Idea: *Your name.*)

The next thing I do is think of a word or a sentence about myself for each letter of my name. What is the next thing I do? (Idea: *Think of a word or sentence for each letter of my name.*)

(Quickly demonstrate filling in the lines for your acrostic. Sample acrostic for MARIA:

> Many smiles
> Always happy
> Really quiet
> Is smart
> Able to do anything.)

(Read the completed poem aloud.) Now it's your turn to write an acrostic about yourself. First, write the letters of your name down the left side of your paper. (Allow children time to do this.) Next you will fill in words or sentences that tell about you. If you need help, raise your hand.

(Allow children time to work on their acrostic poems. Circulate around the room, providing encouragement and assistance if needed. Allow children to share their completed poems.)

## Extensions

### Read a Poem as a Reward

(Read *One Duck Stuck* or another book that is written as a poem to children as a reward for their hard work. Display a number of books of poetry. Ask children to choose which one they would like you to read.)

---

**Preparation:** Word containers for the Super Words Center.

---

### Introduce the Super Words Center

(Remove the words from previous lessons from the word containers. Place in the container the new Picture Vocabulary Cards from Week 26 plus the following words from previous lessons: *overcame, victory, gathering, vote, slave, unjust, wheel, dream.* Show children the word container. If children need more guidance in how to work in the Super Words Center, role-play with two to three children as a demonstration.

(**Note:** You may wish to leave the word *muck* out of the game cards or to caution children about using rhyming words that are polite.)

You will play a game called *Rhyme Time* in the Super Words Center.

Let's think about how we work with our words in the Super Words Center.

You will work with a partner in the Super Words Center. Whom will you work with? *A partner.*

First you will draw a word out of the container. What do you do first? (Idea: *Draw a word out of the container.*) Show your partner the word card.

Next you will tell your partner the word that the card shows. What do you do next? (Idea: *I tell my partner the word that the card shows.*)

If you say the correct word, you get a point. What do you do if you say the correct word? *Get a point.*

Next you will say a word that rhymes with the word on the word card. What will you do next? *Say a word that rhymes with the word on the word card.*

If you can say a word that rhymes with the word on the card, you get another point. What do you do if you can say a word that rhymes with the word on the card? *Get another point.*

After you have said the word and said a word that rhymes, give your partner a turn. What do you do next? *Give my partner a turn.*

## To Market, To Market
author: Anne Miranda • illustrator: Janet Stevens

**Preparation:** You will need a copy of *To Market, To Market* for each day's lesson.

Number the pages of the book to assist you in asking comprehension questions at appropriate points.

Post a copy of the Vocabulary Tally Sheet, BLM A, with this week's Picture Vocabulary Cards attached.

Each child will need one copy of the Homework Sheet, BLM 28a.

### Target Vocabulary

| Tier II | Tier III |
|---|---|
| market | nursery rhyme |
| stubborn | rhyme |
| cranky | |
| disgrace | |
| *humorous | |
| *chaos | |

*Expanded Target Vocabulary Word

### DAY 1

#### Introduce Book

This week's book is called *To Market, To Market.* What's the title of this week's book? *To Market, To Market.*

There are many different kinds of poems. *One Duck Stuck* was a counting poem. What kind of poem was *One Duck Stuck*? (Idea: *A counting poem.*)

This week's book is a nursery rhyme. What kind of poem is today's book? *A nursery rhyme.* A nursery is a room where babies or young children sleep or play. What is a nursery? (Idea: *A room where babies or young children sleep or play.*)

You know about words that rhyme. Tell me a word that rhymes with **hat.** (Ideas: *Mat, cat.*)

Rhymes are also a kind of short poem. Poems that have rhymes often have words that rhyme at the end of each line. What are rhymes? (Idea: *Poems that have words that rhyme at the end of each line.*)

A nursery rhyme is a short poem told to babies or young children. What do you call a short poem told to babies or young children? *A nursery rhyme.*

This book was written by Anne Miranda. Who's the author of *To Market, To Market*? *Anne Miranda.*

Janet Stevens made the pictures for this book. Who is the illustrator of *To Market, To Market*? *Janet Stevens.* Who made the illustrations for this book? *Janet Stevens.*

The cover of a book usually gives us some hints of what the book is about. Let's look at the front cover of *To Market, To Market.* What do you see in the illustration? (Ideas: *A woman at a grocery store or market; she has a duck on her head.*)

This book has an illustration on the back cover as well. (Show the back cover.) What do you see in this illustration? (Ideas: *A pig; grocery store shelves; a can of food.*)

(Assign each child a partner.) Get ready to make some predictions to your partner about this book. Use the information from the covers to help you.

(Ask the following questions, allowing sufficient time for children to share their predictions with their partners.)

- Who do you think this nursery rhyme is about?
- Where do you think the nursery rhyme happens?
- Why do you think the woman is at the market with a duck on her head?
- Why do you think there is a pig at the market?

(Call on several children to share their predictions with the class.)

## Take a Picture Walk

(Encourage children to use target words in their answers.) We're going to take a picture walk through this book. Remember that when we take a picture walk, we look at the pictures and tell what we think will happen in the story.

**Page 1.** Where does this nursery rhyme happen? (Idea: *At a market; at a grocery store.*) How do you know this nursery rhyme happens at a market? (Ideas: *You can see the wheels of the shopping cart in the picture at the top of the page; the woman is pushing a grocery cart.*) What is the woman buying at the market? (Idea: *A pig.*)

**Page 2.** Where has the woman brought the pig? (Ideas: *Home; to her house.*)

**Page 3.** What did the woman buy at the market in this illustration? (Ideas: *A hen; a chicken.*)

**Page 4.** Where has the woman brought the hen? (Ideas: *Home; to her house.*) What has happened in this illustration? (Idea: *Things have been pulled out of the refrigerator.*) Who do you think made this mess? *The pig.*

**Page 5.** What did the woman buy at the market in this illustration? *A goose.*

**Page 6.** Where has the woman brought the goose? (Ideas: *Home; to her house.*) What has happened in this illustration? (Idea: *Things have been knocked over.*) Who do you think made this mess? (Ideas: *The hen; the pig.*)

**Page 7.** What did the woman buy at the market in this illustration? (Ideas: *A fish; a trout.*)

**Page 8.** Where has the woman brought the fish? (Ideas: *Home; to her house.*) What has happened in this illustration? (Idea: *Things have been pulled out of the refrigerator.*) Who do you think made this mess? (Ideas: *The goose; the hen; the pig.*) What is the woman trying to do? (Idea: *Catch the goose.*)

**Page 9.** What did the woman buy at the market in this illustration? (Ideas: *A lamb; a sheep.*)

**Page 10.** Where has the woman brought the lamb? (Idea: *Home; to her house.*) What has happened in this illustration? (Ideas: *The goose is in the sink; the pig is eating food from the refrigerator; the fish has gotten out of the bucket; the hen is in the freezer.*) Who do you think made this mess? (Ideas: *The pig; the hen; the goose.*)

**Page 11.** What did the woman buy at the market in this illustration? *A cow.*

**Page 12.** Where has the woman brought the cow? (Ideas: *Home; to her house.*) What has happened in this illustration? (Ideas: *The animals are making a mess; they are into everything.*) Who do you think made this mess? (Ideas: *The pig; the goose; the hen; the lamb; the fish.*)

**Page 13.** What did the woman buy at the market in this illustration? *A duck.*

**Page 14.** Where has the woman brought the duck? (Ideas: *Home; to her house.*) What animal is missing from this illustration? *The cow.* Who do you think made this mess? (Ideas: *The pig; the goose; the hen; the fish; the cow.*)

**Page 15.** What did the woman buy at the market in this illustration? *A goat.*

**Page 16.** Where has the woman brought the goat? (Idea: *Home; to her house.*) What has happened in this illustration? (Idea: *The animals have wrecked the woman's house.*)

**Pages 17–18.** What is the woman doing in this illustration? (Idea: *Yelling at the animals.*)

(Point to each animal.) What is this animal doing? (Ideas: *Pig: sitting on the counter eating spaghetti out of a pot; hen: sitting on the dish washer; goose: in the dish washer; fish: jumping out of its bucket; lamb: hanging over the door of the freezer; cow: coming in from outside; duck: sitting on woman's head; goat: eating the rug.*)

**Page 19.** What is the pig doing? (Idea: *Eating out of a pot.*) Where is the lamb? (Idea: *In the bed.*) Where is the cow? (Idea: *On the couch.*)

**Page 20.** What is the duck doing? (Idea: *Sitting on the woman's head.*)

**Page 21.** Where is the hen? (Idea: *In a cabinet.*) Where is the goose? (Idea: *In the cabinet.*)

**Page 22.** What is the goat doing? (Idea: *Eating the woman's shoe.*)

**Pages 23–24.** How do you think the woman is feeling in this illustration? (Ideas: *Frustrated; angry; upset; frazzled; miserable; horrible.*)

Where is the woman's other shoe? (Idea: *The goat took it.*)

**Page 25.** What is happening in this illustration? (Idea: *All of the animals are taking the woman back to the market.*)

**Pages 26–29.** What is the woman doing in these illustrations? (Idea: *Buying fruits and vegetables.*)

**Page 30.** Where do you think the woman is taking her groceries? (Ideas: *Home; to her house.*)

**Page 31.** What is the woman making with all of her vegetables? (Idea: *Soup.*)

**Page 32.** What do you think will happen next in the story? (Idea: *The woman and the animals will eat the soup.*)

**Page 33.** What has happened in this illustration? (Idea: *The woman has fallen asleep on the floor with all the animals around and on top of her.*)

It's your turn to ask me some questions. What would you like to know about the nursery rhyme? (Accept questions. If children tell about the pictures or the story instead of ask questions, prompt them to ask a question:) Ask me a why question. Ask me a where question.

 **Read the Nursery Rhyme Aloud** (Read the nursery rhyme to children with minimal interruptions.)

Tomorrow we will read the nursery rhyme again, and I will ask you some questions.

## Present Target Vocabulary
 Market

In the nursery rhyme, the woman went to the market to buy different animals. **Market.** Say the word. *Market.*

**Market** is a noun. It names a place. What kind of word is **market?** *A noun.*

**A market is a place where people buy food and other things.** Say the word that means "a place where people buy food and other things." *Market.*

(Correct any incorrect responses, and repeat the item at the end of the sequence.)

Let's think about some situations. I'll tell about some people. If these people are in a market, say "market." If not, don't say anything.

- The woman went shopping for food. *Market.*
- The little boy picked out a toy from the toy shelf to buy. *Market.*
- The dog ran along the beach.
- Six birds flew down and sat on the bench.
- The man stopped to get dog food on his way home from work. *Market.*
- The children learned to read.

What noun means "a place where people go to buy food and other things"? *Market.*

⊙ Stubborn

In the nursery rhyme, the woman bought a stubborn goat at the market. **Stubborn.** Say the word. *Stubborn.*

**Stubborn** is a describing word. It tells more about a noun. What kind of word is **stubborn?** *A describing word.*

**Stubborn means not willing to do something.** Say the word that means "not willing to do something." *Stubborn.*

Let's think about some people and animals that could be stubborn. I'll tell about a person or animal. If the person or animal is being stubborn, say "stubborn." If not, don't say anything.

- Jack happily put on his coat and hat.
- Jakiel refused to eat his green beans. *Stubborn.*
- The dog would not go to the tub for its bath. *Stubborn.*
- The first graders did their reading quietly.
- Martin held on to the doorframe and would not go into his bedroom. *Stubborn.*
- Julio waited patiently for his mother to get off the phone.

What describing word means "not willing to do something"? *Stubborn.*

⊙ Cranky

In the nursery rhyme, the woman was hungry and cranky. **Cranky.** Say the word. *Cranky.*

**Cranky** is a describing word. It tells more about someone's feelings. What kind of word is **cranky?** *A describing word.*

**Cranky means grouchy or in a bad mood.**
Say the word that means "grouchy or in a bad mood." *Cranky.*

Let's think about some times when someone might be cranky. I'll name a situation. If the situation would make someone cranky, say "cranky." If not, don't say anything.

- Waiting in a long, slow line at the market. *Cranky.*
- Getting a gift from you grandmother.
- Having someone tell you that you are clever.
- Not getting what you want at the store. *Cranky.*
- Having to wake up in the middle of the night. *Cranky.*
- Getting a shot at the doctor's office. *Cranky.*

What describing word means "grouchy or in a bad mood"? *Cranky.*

◎◁ Disgrace

In the nursery rhyme, the woman called herself a shopping disgrace. **Disgrace.** Say the word. *Disgrace.*

**Disgrace** is a noun. It names a thing. What kind of word is **disgrace?** *A noun.*

**A disgrace is a shameful thing.** Say the word that means "a shameful thing." *Disgrace.*

Let's think about some ways that people could be a disgrace. I'll tell about a person. If the person is a disgrace, say "disgrace." If not, don't say anything.

- The little boy down the street is always rude to people. *Disgrace.*
- The woman bought silly things at the market that made her house a mess. *Disgrace.*
- The little girl got a perfect score on her spelling test.
- The children bullied a smaller child. *Disgrace.*
- The neighbor helped get the little girl's cat down from the tree.
- The second grader lied to his teacher about taking another student's toy. *Disgrace.*

What noun means "a shameful thing"? *Disgrace.*

### Present Vocabulary Tally Sheet
(See Lesson 1, page 4, for instructions)

## Assign Homework
(Homework Sheet, BLM 27a. See the Introduction for homework instructions.)

---

### DAY 2

**Preparation:** Picture Vocabulary Cards for *market, stubborn, cranky, disgrace.*

---

### Read and Discuss Nursery Rhyme

(Read the nursery rhyme to children. Ask the following questions at the specified points. Encourage them to use target words in their answers.)

Now I'm going to read *To Market, To Market.* When I finish each part, I'll ask you some questions.

**Pages 1–2.** Why did the woman go to the market? *To buy a fat pig.*

(Write *pig* on the board. Underline *ig.*) When words have the same ending sound, we say they rhyme. What do we say words do when they have the same ending sound? *Rhyme.* What sound do you hear at the end of **pig?** *Ig.* What other word on these pages ends with the **ig** sound? *Jig.* What other words do you know that rhyme with **pig?** (Ideas: *Fig; dig; big.*)

**Pages 3–4.** Why did the woman go to the market? *To buy a red hen.*

(Write *hen* on the board. Underline *en.*) What sound do you hear at the end of **hen?** *En.* What other word on these pages ends with the **en** sound? *Pen.* What other words do you know that rhyme with **hen?** (Ideas: *When; Jen; Ken.*)

**Pages 5–6.** Why did the woman go to the market? *To buy a plump goose.*

(Write *goose* on the board. Underline *oose.*) What sound do you hear at the end of **goose?** *Oose.* What other word on these pages ends with the **oose** sound? *Loose.* What other words do you know that rhyme with **goose?** (Ideas: *Juice; spruce, moose.*)

**Pages 7–8.** Why did the woman go to the market? *To buy a live trout.*

(Write *trout* on the board. Underline *out.*) What sound do you hear at the end of **trout?** *Out.* What other word on these pages ends with the **out** sound? *Out.* What other words do you know that rhyme with **trout?** (Ideas: *Pout; shout.*)

**Pages 9–10.** Why did the woman go to the market? *To buy a spring lamb.*

(Write *lamb* on the board. Underline *amb.*) What sound do you hear at the end of **lamb?** *Am.* What other word on these pages ends with the **am** sound? *Swam.* What other words do you know that rhyme with **lamb?** (Ideas: *Am; ham; ma'am; Sam.*)

**Pages 11–12.** Why did the woman go to the market? *To buy a milking cow.*

(Write *cow* on the board. Underline *ow.*) What sound do you hear at the end of **cow?** *Ow.* What other word on these pages ends with the **ow** sound? *Now.* What other words do you know that rhyme with **cow?** (Ideas: *Bow; how.*)

**Pages 13–14.** Why did the woman go to the market? *To buy a white duck.*

(Write *duck* on the board. Underline *uck.*) What sound do you hear at the end of **duck?** *Uck.* What other word on these pages ends with the **uck** sound? *Luck.* What other words do you know that rhyme with **duck?** (Ideas: *Muck; truck; stuck.*)

**Pages 15–16.** Why did the woman go to the market? *To buy a stubborn goat.*

(Write *goat* on the board. Underline *oat.*) What sound do you hear at the end of **goat?** *Oat.* What other word on these pages ends with the **oat** sound? *Coat.* What other words do you know that rhyme with **goat?** (Ideas: *Boat; float; note.*)

**Pages 17–18.** Why did the woman shout at the animals? (Idea: *Because they made a mess in her house.*) Why did the woman call herself a shopping disgrace? (Idea: *She bought all the animals and they were not good purchases.*)

(Write *disgrace* on the board. Underline *ace.*) What sound do you hear at the end of **disgrace?** *Ace.* What other word on these

pages ends with the **ace** sound? *Place.* What other words do you know that rhyme with **disgrace?** (Ideas: *Face; case; trace.*)

**Pages 19–20.** Where are the animals in this part of the nursery rhyme? (Ideas: *In the kitchen; on the bed; on the couch; on her head.*)

(Write *bed* on the board. Underline *ed.*) What sound do you hear at the end of **bed?** *Ed.* What other word on these pages ends with the **ed** sound? *Head.* What other words do you know that rhyme with **bed?** (Ideas: *Red; said; led.*)

**Pages 21–22.** What are the animals doing in this part of the nursery rhyme? (Ideas: *Sitting in the cabinets; eating her shoe.*)

(Write *too* on the board. Underline *oo.*) What sound do you hear at the end of **too?** *Oo.* What other word on these pages ends with the **oo** sound? *Shoe.* What other words do you know that rhyme with **too?** (Ideas: *Boo; blue; flew.*)

**Pages 23–24.** What's wrong with the woman? (Idea: *She's hungry and cranky.*) Why do you think the woman is cranky? (Ideas: *The animals have messed up her house; she's hungry.*)

(Write *zoo* on the board. Underline *oo.*) What sound do you hear at the end of **zoo?** *Oo.* What other word on these pages ends with the **oo** sound? *Do.* What other words do you know that rhyme with **zoo?** (Ideas: *Two; who; new.*)

**Pages 25–26.** Where did the animals take the woman? *To the market.* What kinds of things is the woman buying this time? (Ideas: *Potatoes; celery; beets; tomatoes; vegetables.*) What words rhyme on these pages? (Ideas: *Potatoes; tomatoes.*)

**Pages 27–28.** What else did the woman buy? (Ideas: *Pea pods; peppers; garlic; spice.*)

**Pages 29–30.** What else did the woman buy? (Ideas: *Cabbage; brown rice; okra; onions; carrots.*) Where did the woman and her animals go after buying all these vegetables? *Home.*

**Pages 31–32.** What did the woman make for lunch? *Hot soup.*

Let's read these last few pages again and listen for words that rhyme. (Reread pages 27–32 aloud.) What words on these pages rhyme? (Ideas: *Spice and rice; bunch and lunch.*)

(Write *rice* on the board. Underline *ice.*) What sound do you hear at the end of *rice? Ice.* What other word on these pages ends with the **ice** sound? *Spice.* What other words do you know that rhyme with **spice?** (Ideas: *Twice; nice; mice.*)

(Write *bunch* on the board. Underline *unch.*) What sound do you hear at the end of **bunch?** *Unch.* What other word on these pages ends with the **unch** sound? *Lunch.* What other words do you know that rhyme with **bunch?** (Ideas: *Crunch; munch; hunch, lunch.*)

## Review Vocabulary

(Display the Picture Vocabulary Cards. Point to each card as you say the word. Ask children to repeat each word after you.) These pictures show **market, stubborn, cranky,** and **disgrace.**

- What noun means "something shameful"? *Disgrace.*
- What noun names "a place where people go to buy food and other goods"? *Market.*
- What word means "unwilling to do something"? *Stubborn.*
- What word means "grouchy or in a bad mood"? *Cranky.*

## Extend Vocabulary
◎= Market

In *To Market, To Market* we learned that a **market** is "a place where people go to buy food and other goods." Say the noun that means "a place where people go to buy food and other goods." *Market.*

Raise your hand if you can tell us a sentence that uses **market** as a noun meaning "a place where people go to buy food and other goods." (Call on several children. If they don't use complete sentences, restate their examples as sentences. Have the class repeat the sentences.)

Here's a new way to use the word **market.**

- Mother **markets** every Saturday. Say the sentence.
- I really need to **market;** we have no food. Say the sentence.
- When you **market,** will you buy me some graham crackers? Say the sentence.

**In these sentences, market is a verb that means to go shopping in a market or store.** Raise your hand if you can tell us a sentence that uses **market** as a verb meaning "to go shopping in a market or store." (Call on several children. If they don't use complete sentences, restate their examples as sentences. Have the class repeat the sentences.)

## Present Expanded Target Vocabulary
◎= Humorous

This was a humorous nursery rhyme. It made us laugh. **Humorous.** Say the word. *Humorous.*

**Humorous** is a describing word. It tells more about a person or thing. What kind of word is **humorous?** *A describing word.*

**Humorous means funny or amusing.** Say the word that means "funny or amusing." *Humorous.*

I'll tell about some people or situations. If those people or situations are humorous, say "humorous." If not, don't say anything.

- Albie told a funny joke. *Humorous.*
- The clown made balloon animals and pretended they were real. *Humorous.*
- The teacher taught the class a thoughtful lesson.
- Julio fell off the swing and cut his knee.
- Ralphie imitated the talking cat on TV. *Humorous.*
- The children couldn't stop giggling about the movie they had watched. *Humorous.*

What word means "funny or amusing"? *Humorous.*

◎= Chaos

By the end of the nursery rhyme, the woman's house was a mess; it was in chaos. **Chaos.** Say the word. *Chaos.*

**Chaos** is a noun. It names an idea. What kind of word is **chaos?** *A noun.*

**Chaos means complete confusion or disorder.** Say the word that means "complete confusion or disorder." *Chaos.*

I'll tell about some situations. If the situations seem like they are in chaos, say "chaos." If not, don't say anything.

- Three dogs tore around the living room. A cat climbed the curtains. Two birds chirped away loudly. I couldn't even think. *Chaos.*
- Alex couldn't find anything in his desk. Pencils were everywhere. Papers were not in folders. His pencil box had spilled. *Chaos.*
- Mrs. Ellis keeps her classroom very neat. Coats are always hung up. Children know where to go and what to do. It is very calm.
- During the first fire drill, children ran wildly down the halls. Children screamed. Teachers called children's names. Everyone was confused. *Chaos.*
- Joseph's bedroom is very tidy and clean.

What noun means "complete confusion or disorder"? *Chaos.*

---

## DAY 3

**Preparation:** Activity Sheet, BLM 27b, a pencil, and crayons. Print the words from BLM 27b on a piece of chart paper.

### Play Poetic Definitions

Today you'll play Poetic Definitions. I'll say a little poem that uses the meaning of one of our vocabulary words. If you can tell me the word that the poem is describing, you will win one point. If you can't tell me, I get the point. Let's think about the six words we have learned: **market, stubborn, cranky, disgrace, humorous,** and **chaos.** (Display the Picture Vocabulary Cards.)

Let's practice. Places to go and people to see. I went here to buy milk and tea. Which vocabulary word tells where I went? *Market.*

Now you're ready to play the game. (Draw a T-chart on the board for keeping score. Children earn one point for each correct answer. If they make an error, correct them as you normally would, and record one point for yourself. Repeat missed words at the end of the game.)

- I won't do it. I refuse. You can't make me wear those shoes! What vocabulary word is being described in this poem? *Stubborn.*

- Socks on the floor. Shoes in the bed. To look at this room hurts my head! Books all over. Clothes lie around. I can't even see the ground! What vocabulary word is being described in this poem? *Chaos.*
- It was a shameful thing he did. To make such a terrible mess. He's just a dog; don't you know? He doesn't know better, I guess. What vocabulary word is being described in the first line of this poem? *Disgrace.*
- I don't want to, I don't care. I'm not happy anywhere! What vocabulary word describes how I am feeling? *Cranky.*
- Oh my gosh! It's just so funny! That dog is hopping like a bunny! What vocabulary word describes this situation? *Humorous.*
- Peanut butter, jelly, veggies, and meat. Mom went to the store, so now we can eat! What vocabulary word tells what Mom did? *Market.*

(Count the points and declare a winner.) You did a great job of playing Poetic Definitions.

### Write a Class Poem

Today we are going to write our own rhyming poem in the style of *To Market, To Market.*

(Point to the writing form on the chart paper.)

My turn to read the poem. When I come to a line, I will say "blank." Follow along as I read. (Read the poem through once.)

Let's read the poem together. You read the words as I point to them. When we come to a line, say "blank." (Read the poem through once as a class.)

Your turn to read the poem by yourselves. You read the words as I point to them. When we come to a line, say "blank." (Touch under each word as the children read.)

Now we are going to fill in the blanks of this poem. I am going to read the first line again. Follow along as I read. (Read aloud the first line of the poem.) What word could we write in the blank? (Idea: *Dinosaur.* Print the word on the line. Read the completed line aloud to the class.)

(Touch under the first word in the second line of the poem.) Follow along as I read the second line of our poem. (Read the second line.)

Tell me how we can end this line so it rhymes with **dinosaur.** (Call on several children, accepting reasonable responses. Write one response on the line. Ideas: *Liggity linosaur; rippety roar.* Read the second line aloud.)

(Repeat the steps for the last two lines of the poem.) Now we have a class poem. Let's read our poem together. (Point to each word as you read the poem as a class.)

You did a great job writing a class poem. Now you are going to write your own version of *To Market, To Market.*

(Distribute a copy of BLM 27b to each child. Encourage children to come up with their own ideas for completing the poem. Have them illustrate their poems after writing them.)

## DAY 4

### Guided Writing–Two-Word Poem

At the end of this poetry unit, we are going to have a poetry contest. For the poetry contest, you will each write your own poem. I am going to teach you how to write four different kinds of poems. Last week you wrote an acrostic poem. Today we will write our second poem.

The poem we will write today is called a two-word poem. What kind of poem will we write today? *A two-word poem.*

The first thing we do when we write a two-word poem is decide what to write about. What is the first thing we do when we write a two-word poem? *Decide what to write about.*

Today we are going to write a two-word poem about best friends. What will today's two-word poem be about? *Best friends.*

The next thing we do when we write a two-word poem is write the title of our poem. What is the next thing we do when we write a two-word poem? *Write the title.*

A two-word poem has a two-word title. How many words are in the title of a two-word poem? *Two.* We are writing a poem about best friends. What do you think the title of our two-word poem should be? (Idea: *Best Friends.* Write *Best Friends* at the top of a piece of chart paper.)

The next thing we do is think of two words that finish the phrase "Best friends ...." What is the next thing we do? (Idea: *Think of two words to finish the phrase "Best friends ....")*

My turn. Best friends take walks. (Write *take walks* on the first line beneath the title.)

Your turn. What are two words that tell about best friends? Start your poem with **Best friends.** (Ideas: *Give hugs; play games; help out; share food; sleep over.*)

(Repeat the steps, reading each new line after adding it.)

(Read the completed poem aloud.) You did a great job of writing a two-word poem about best friends. Tomorrow you will write your own two-word poem.

### Play Poetic Definitions (Cumulative Review)

Let's play Poetic Definitions. I'll say a little poem that uses the meaning of one of our vocabulary words. If you can tell me the word that the poem is using, you will win one point. If you can't tell me, I get the point. Let's think about the six words we have learned: **market, stubborn, cranky, disgrace, humorous,** and **chaos.** (Display the Picture Vocabulary Cards.)

Let's practice. Places to go and people to see. I went here to buy milk and tea. Which vocabulary word tells where I went? *Market.*

Now you're ready to play the game. (Draw a T-chart on the board for keeping score. Children earn one point for each correct answer. If they make an error, correct them as you normally would, and record one point for yourself. Repeat missed words at the end of the game.)

- Sleep is over! Time to rise! Open up those sleepy eyes! What vocabulary word describes what it's time to do? *Wake.*
- Dark clouds of gray fill the sky. There is no sun to see. The rain falls down on my head. It's dark, and cold, and gloomy. What vocabulary word describes this day? *Miserable.*
- I won't do it. I refuse. You can't make me eat these horrible peas! If I do, I will sneeze. What

vocabulary word is being used in this poem? *Stubborn.*

- I don't want to, I won't play. I'm not happy today! What vocabulary word describes how I am feeling? *Cranky.*
- Up in the sky! What could it be? Twelve geese flying in the shape of a V. What vocabulary word describes the group of geese? *Flock.*
- It was a shameful thing she did. She told a lie. Her mother does know, she should not get to go. What vocabulary word can be used in the first line of this poem? *Disgrace.*
- Oh my gosh! It's just so funny! That bear is covered with honey! What vocabulary word describes this situation? *Humorous.*
- Look at my house. Tess has made a mess. This is bad. It makes me sad. Things all over. Now I'm mad. What vocabulary word describes this situation? *Chaos.*
- We are sweet and have to eat. Dad needs to appear here. What vocabulary word tells where Dad needs to appear? *Market.*
- I wish I had a doll like hers. I wish I had her clothes. I wish I had my hair like hers. In pigtails with little bows. What vocabulary word describes how I'm feeling? *Jealous.*

(Count the points and declare a winner.) You did a great job of playing Poetic Definitions.

---

## DAY 5

> **Preparation:** Quiz Answer Sheet, BLM B.
> Each child will need a copy of BLM 27c.

### Assess Vocabulary

 (Give each child a copy of the Quiz Answer Sheet, BLM B.)

Today you're going to have a True or False quiz. When you do the True or False quiz, it shows me how well you know the hard words you are learning.

If I say something that is true, circle the word **true.** What will you do if I say something that is true? *Circle the word* true.

If I say something that is false, circle the word **false.** What will you do if I say something that is false? *Circle the word* false.

Listen carefully to each item that I say. Don't let me trick you!

Item 1: If you are always willing to do things, you are a **stubborn** child. (*False.*)

Item 2: A house full of animals that should be on a farm can quickly turn into **chaos.** (*True.*)

Item 3: If you **wheel** your bike across the street, you get off and push it across. (*True.*)

Item 4: A person who is in a bad mood is **cranky.** (*True.*)

Item 5: If someone goes to the store to buy food, you can say they are **marketing.** (*True.*)

Item 6: A **market** is a place where people go to play games and ride roller coasters. (*False.*)

Item 7: Someone who is **clever** takes a long time to understand new things. (*False.*)

Item 8: You might be a **disgrace** if you often do shameful things. (*True.*)

Item 9: Jokes are meant to be **humorous,** not mean. (*True.*)

Item 10: A man who **rescues** a small child is **heroic.** (*True.*)

You did a great job completing your quiz!

(Score children's work. A child must score 9 out of 10 to be at mastery level. If a child does not achieve mastery, insert the missed words as additional items in the games in next week's lessons. Retest those children individually for the missed items before they take the next mastery test.)

> **Preparation:** Display the chart paper with the poem *Best Friends* from yesterday's lesson.

### Independent Writing—Two-Word Poem

Yesterday you learned how to write a two-word poem. What kind of poem did you learn to write yesterday? *A two-word poem.*

The first thing we do when we write a two-word poem is decide what to write about. What is the first thing we do when we write a two-word poem? *Decide what to write about.*

Today you are going to write your own two-word poem about best friends. What will today's two-word poem be about? *Best friends.*

The next thing we do when we write a two-word poem is write the title of the poem at the top of our paper. What is the next thing we do when we write a two-word poem? *Write the title of the poem at the top of the paper.*

(Display chart paper with the *Best Friends* poem. Point to the title.) The title of your poem will be **Best Friends**. What will the title of your poem be? *Best Friends.*

You're going to write a draft of your poem before you write the final copy. What will you write before the final copy? *A draft.* You will write your draft on notebook paper. What will you write your draft on? *Notebook paper.* (Distribute notebook paper to each student.)

Touch the top line of your paper. You will write the title of your poem on the top line. What will you write on the top line? *The title.* (Allow sufficient time for children to write their titles on the line.)

Next you will write word pairs for each line of your poem. Your poem will have ten lines. How many lines will your poem have? *Ten.* How many word pairs will you write for your poem? *Ten.* You may make up your own word pairs or use word pairs from the poem we wrote yesterday.

(Show BLM 27c.) After you write your draft, check your poem. Then I will give you paper to use for writing your final copy.

You will copy your poem onto this paper neatly. You will write only two words on each line. How many words will you write on each line? *Two.*

Then you will draw one illustration for each line of your poem. How many illustrations will you draw for each line of your poem? *One.* How many lines will your poem have? *Ten.* So how many illustrations will you do? *Ten.* You will draw ten illustrations. There are ten boxes. Draw one illustration in each box.

(Allow children time to work on their two-word poems. Circulate around the room, providing encouragement and assistance if needed. Allow children to share their completed poems.)

## Extensions

### Read a Poem as a Reward

(Read *To Market, To Market* or another book that is written as a nursery rhyme to children as a reward for their hard work. Display a number of books of nursery rhymes. Ask children to choose which one they would like you to read.)

---

**Preparation:** Word containers for the Super Words Center.

---

### Introduce the Super Words Center

(Remove the words from previous lessons from the word containers. Place the Picture Vocabulary Cards from Weeks 26 and 27 in the containers. Show children the word container. If children need more guidance in how to work in the Super Word Center, role-play with two to three children as a demonstration.

(**Note:** You may wish to leave the word *muck* out of the game cards or to caution children about using rhyming words that are polite.)

You will play a game called *Rhyme Time* in the Super Words Center.

Let's think about how we work with our words in the Super Words Center.

You will work with a partner in the Super Words Center. Whom will you work with? *A partner.*

First you will draw a word out of the container. What do you do first? (Idea: *Draw a word out of the container.*) Show your partner the word card.

Next you will tell your partner the word that the card shows. What do you do next? (Idea: *I tell my partner the word that the card shows.*)

If you say the correct word, you get a point. What do you do if you say the correct word? *Get a point.*

Next you will say a word that rhymes with the word on the word card. What will you do next? *Say a word that rhymes with the word on the word card.*

If you can say a word that rhymes with the word on the card, you get another point. What do you do if you can say a word that rhymes with the word on the card? *Get another point.*

After you have said the word and said a word that rhymes, give your partner a turn. What do you do next? *Give my partner a turn.*

# When Cats Go Wrong
author: Norm Hacking • illustrator: Cynthia Nugent

## Preparation:
You will need a copy of *When Cats Go Wrong* for each day's lesson.

Number the pages of the book to assist you in asking comprehension questions at appropriate points. Start with page 1 on the page opposite the copyright page.

Post a copy of the Vocabulary Tally Sheet, BLM A, with this week's Picture Vocabulary Cards attached.

Each child will need one copy of the Homework Sheet, BLM 28a.

## DAY 1

### Introduce Book

This week's book is called *When Cats Go Wrong*. What's the title of this week's book? *When Cats Go Wrong.*

There are many different kinds of poems. *One Duck Stuck* was a counting poem. What kind of poem was *One Duck Stuck*? *A counting poem. To Market, To Market* was a nursery rhyme. What kind of poem was *To Market, to Market*? *A nursery rhyme.* Today's book is a song. What kind of poem is today's book? *A song.* A song uses rhythm. Rhythm is a regular beat. What is rhythm? *A regular beat.* (Demonstrate keeping a regular beat by tapping or clapping a simple rhythm.)

This book was written by Norm Hacking. Who's the author of *When Cats Go Wrong*? *Norm Hacking.*

Cynthia Nugent made the pictures for this book. Who is the illustrator of *When Cats Go Wrong*? *Cynthia Nugent.* Who made the illustrations for this book? *Cynthia Nugent.*

The cover of a book usually gives us some hints of what the book is about. Let's look at the front cover of *When Cats Go Wrong*. What do you see in the illustration? (Ideas: *A boy playing an accordion and singing; a black cat dancing.*)

### Target Vocabulary

| Tier II | Tier III |
|---|---|
| admit | rhythm |
| mournful | verse |
| amuse | |
| ornaments | |
| *warning | |
| * mischievous | |

*Expanded Target Vocabulary Word

(Assign each child a partner.) Get ready to make some predictions to your partner about this book. Use the information from the covers to help you.

(Ask the following questions, allowing sufficient time for children to share their predictions with their partners.)

- Who do you think this song is about?
- What do you think the boy is singing about?
- Do you think this song is about a real cat or an imaginary cat?

(Call on several children to share their predictions with the class.)

### Take a Picture Walk

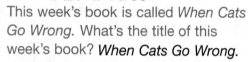

(Encourage children to use target words in their answers.) We're going to take a picture walk through this book. Remember that when we take a picture walk we look at the pictures and tell what we think will happen in the story.

**Pages 2–3.** What is happening in these illustrations? (Ideas: *The boy is buying books at a bookstore; the boy is at an accordion lesson; the boy is getting his hair cut; the boy is at the dentist; the boy is riding his bike.*)

**Page 4.** What feeling do you think is being shown on this page? (Ideas: *Worry; concern.*)

**Page 5.** Where do you think the boy is running? (Ideas: *Home, to his house.*)

**Page 6.** Why does the boy look upset? (Idea: *The fish is gone from its bowl.*) What do you think has happened to the fish? (Idea: *The cat got it.*)

**Pages 8–9.** What is the cat doing in this illustration? (Idea: *Jumping from the bookshelf to the top of the china cabinet.*) What is the boy worried about here? (Idea: *The cat will break all the dishes/vases.*) Is this cat well behaved or naughty? *Naughty.*

**Page 10.** What is happening in this illustration? (Ideas: *The boy is playing his accordion and singing; the cat is dancing.*) What do you think the boy is singing about? (Idea: *His naughty cat.*)

**Page 12.** What is the cat doing in this illustration? (Ideas: *Swinging from the chandelier.*) Why does the boy look upset? (Idea: *The cat has destroyed the room; the cat has torn up the chair cushions; everything is in chaos.*)

**Pages 14–15.** What is happening in this illustration? (Ideas: *The cat is chasing a ball of yarn; the cat is knocking over a table; the boy is angry.*) How do you think the bird in that cage feels about the cat? (Ideas: *Scared; frightened; afraid; terrified.*)

**Page 16.** What is happening in this illustration? (Ideas: *The boy is playing his accordion and singing; the cat is dancing.*) What do you think the boy is singing about? (Idea: *His naughty cat.*)

**Pages 18–19.** What is the cat doing in this illustration? (Idea: *Trying to get the bird.*) What is the boy doing? (Idea: *Trying to get the cat down from the birdcage.*) Where do you think the bird has gone? (Idea: *It has flown away to hide.*)

**Page 20.** What is happening in this illustration? (Idea: *The boy's shoe fell off while he was walking.*)

**Page 21.** What did the boy find under his bed? *The cat.* What do you think the cat is playing with? (Ideas: *A string; the boy's shoelace.*)

**Pages 22–23.** What is happening in this illustration? (Idea: *The boy is trying to get the cat off the curtains.*)

**Page 24.** What is happening in this illustration? (Ideas: *The boy is pulling a piece of string for the cat; the cat is playing with a mouse; the boy and the cat are playing together.*)

**Page 25.** How do you think the cat and the boy feel about each other? (Idea: *They love each other.*)

**Page 26.** What is happening in this illustration? (Ideas: *The boy is singing; the cat is trying to take things off the table.*) (Point to the statue of the couple dancing.) This statue shows a couple dancing. They are doing a dance called the tango. What kind of dance is the couple doing? *The tango.*

**Pages 28–29.** What is happening in this illustration? (Idea: *The boy and his mother are lying together; the cat is lying with them.*) Do you think the mother and the little boy love the cat even though it's naughty sometimes? *Yes.*

It's your turn to ask me some questions. What would you like to know about the song? (Accept questions. If children tell about the pictures or the story instead of ask questions, prompt them to ask a question.) Ask me a why question. Ask me a where question.

### Read the Song Aloud
(Read the song to children with minimal interruptions. If available, play the CD of Norm Hacking singing the song he wrote. If using the CD, tell children:)

This song was written in the style of a tango. What style of music was this song written in? *A tango.* A tango is a serious, emotional form of music. The author chose this serious form of tango to make his funny story even more humorous. (Show the illustrations as the song plays.)

Tomorrow I will read the song again, and I will ask you some questions.

### Present Target Vocabulary
◎ Admit

In the song, the author says that he must admit he worries. **Admit.** Say the word. *Admit.*

**Admit** is a verb. It tells an action. What kind of word is **admit?** *A verb.*

**Admit means tell the truth even though you may not really want to.** Say the word that means "to tell the truth even though you may not really want to." *Admit.*

(Correct any incorrect responses, and repeat the item at the end of the sequence.)

Let's think about some things people might say. I'll tell some things people said. If these people are admitting something, say "admit." If not, don't say anything.

- I'm sorry, Mom, I broke the vase. *Admit.*
- It wasn't me!
- Nathan did it.
- I am afraid of the dark. *Admit.*
- I didn't give my broccoli to the dog. I don't know how he got it.
- Yes, I pushed all my toys under the bed instead of putting them away. *Admit.*

What verb means "to tell the truth even though you may not really want to"? *Admit.*

◎ Mournful

The author calls his song "mournful." **Mournful.** Say the word. *Mournful.*

**Mournful** is a describing word. It tells more about a noun. What kind of word is **mournful?** *A describing word.*

**Mournful means filled with grief or sadness.** Say the word that means "filled with grief or sadness." *Mournful.*

Let's think about some situations. I'll tell about a situation. If the situation calls for a mournful song, say "mournful." If not, don't say anything.

- Mary's best friend is moving far away. *Mournful.*
- Josiah is marching in a holiday parade.
- On the last day of school, we had a pizza party.
- Jamal's grandfather passed away. *Mournful.*
- A car hit the dog that Lisa had her whole life. *Mournful.*
- Vanessa won the spelling bee.

What describing word means "filled with grief or sadness"? *Mournful.*

◎ Amuse

In the song, the boy's shoelace is just another cat toy to amuse his pet. **Amuse.** Say the word. *Amuse.*

**Amuse** is a verb. It names an action. What kind of word is **amuse?** *A verb.*

**Amuse means to entertain someone or hold their interest.** Say the word that means "to entertain someone or hold their interest." *Amuse.*

Let's think about some things that might amuse a naughty cat. I'll name some things. If the thing would amuse a naughty cat, say "amuse." If not, don't say anything.

- A ball of yarn. *Amuse.*
- A big dog.
- An empty room.
- A bag of cat toys. *Amuse.*
- A goldfish in an open bowl. *Amuse.*
- A bird in a cage. *Amuse.*

What verb means "to entertain or hold someone's attention"? *Amuse.*

◎ Ornaments

In the song, the author asked if broken ornaments used to be on a shelf." **Ornaments.** Say the word. *Ornaments.*

**Ornaments** is a noun. It names things. What kind of word is **ornaments?** *A noun.*

**Ornaments are decorations that are added to make something more beautiful to look at.** Say the word that means "decorations that are added to make something more beautiful to look at." *Ornaments.*

Let's think about some ways that people might make something more beautiful to look at. I'll tell about some things. If the things are ornaments, say "ornaments." If not, don't say anything.

- Mother washed the windows.
- Mrs. Nash put three beautiful statues above the fireplace. *Ornaments.*
- April hung crystals from thread along the window. *Ornaments.*
- The boys tracked mud through the house.
- Rose put beautiful flowers and clips in her hair for the wedding. *Ornaments.*
- Sheila cleaned up her bedroom.

What noun means "decorations that are added to make something more beautiful to look at"? *Ornaments.*

What kind of song did the boy write? (Ideas: *A mournful song; a sad song.*) Why is his song mournful? (Idea: *Because it makes him sad that his cat is so naughty.*) What words rhyme in this verse? (Ideas: *Pretty and kitty; song and wrong.*)

**Page 13.** What has the cat done to the couch? (Ideas: *Ripped it; torn it apart; pulled out the stuffing.*) What has the cat done to the litter box? (Idea: *Emptied all the gravel out and thrown it around the room.*) What words rhyme in this verse? (Idea: *Out and about.*)

**Page 15.** What makes the boy grouchy and cranky? (Idea: *Everything's in disarray.*) What words rhyme in this verse? (Idea: *Mutter and butter.*)

**Page 17.** This verse appeared earlier in the song. When a verse repeats throughout a song, we call it a refrain. What do we call a verse that repeats throughout a song? *A refrain.* What are some things the cat has done that might make the boy feel like singing a mournful song? (Ideas: *Taken the goldfish from the bowl; knocked the ornaments off the shelves; ripped the couch; thrown the kitty litter around; gotten cat hair on the tablecloth; licked the butter.*)

**Page 19.** What kind of animal is Budgie? (Ideas: *A bird; a parakeet.*) Who do you think is traumatizing the bird? *The cat.* What words rhyme in this verse? (Idea: *Floor and door.*)

**Page 20.** What are some things the cat has done in this verse? (Ideas: *Clawed the lampshade; left paw prints on the mirror; taken the boy's shoelace.*) What words rhyme in this verse? (Idea: *Mirror and clearer.*)

**Page 22.** What is just another cat toy to amuse the boy's little pet? (Idea: *His shoelace.*) What does the cat like to do to the nice lace curtains? (Idea: *Shred them.*) Are there any rhyming words in this verse? *No.*

**Page 25.** What other toys does the cat like to play with? (Idea: *A ball of twine; a catnip mouse.*) What words rhyme in this verse? (Idea: *Spool and drool.*)

**Page 27.** Here's that repeating verse again. What do we call a verse that repeats throughout a song? *A refrain.* What has happened in

---

## Present Vocabulary Tally Sheet
(See Lesson 1, page 4, for instructions)

## Assign Homework
(Homework Sheet, BLM 28a. See the Introduction for homework instructions.)

---

### DAY 2

**Preparation:** Picture Vocabulary Cards for *admit, mournful, amuse, ornaments.*

---

### Read and Discuss Song

 (Read the song to children. Ask the following questions at the specified points. Encourage them to use target words in their answers.)

Now I'm going to read *When Cats Go Wrong.* Each part of a song or poem is called a verse. What do we call one part of a song or poem? *A verse.* A verse is a group of sentences that go together in a song or poem. What is a verse? *A group of sentences that go together in a song or poem.* A verse is made up of several lines. When I finish reading each verse, I'll ask you some questions.

**Pages 2–3.** What happens when the boy leaves the house? (Idea: *He worries.*) What are the rhyming words in this verse? (Idea: *Worry and hurry.*)

**Pages 4–5.** What makes the boy worry? (Idea: *The thought of what a cat might do when left home alone.*) What is the boy afraid of? (Idea: *What he might find when he gets home.*) Are there any rhyming words in this verse? *No.*

**Page 7.** What is the boy looking for in this verse? (Ideas: *The goldfish; his mother's balls of wool.*) Are there any rhyming words in this verse? *No.*

**Pages 8–9.** What happened to the ornaments? (Idea: *The cat knocked them off the shelf and they broke.*) Why do you think the boy is feeling sorry for himself? What words rhyme in this verse? (Idea: *Shelf and myself.*)

**Page 11.** Why isn't life with a naughty kitty very pretty? (Idea: *The cat makes a mess out of*

---

the last few verses that would make the boy want to sing a mournful song? (Ideas: *The cat has traumatized the bird; it has clawed the lampshade; it has left paw prints on the mirror; it has taken the boy's shoelace; it has shredded the lace curtains.*)

### Review Vocabulary

(Display the Picture Vocabulary Cards. Point to each card as you say the word. Ask children to repeat each word after you.) These pictures show **admit, mournful, amuse,** and **ornaments.**

- What word means "filled with grief"? *Mournful.*
- What verb means "tell the truth even though you may not want to"? *Admit.*
- What noun names "decorations that are added to make something more beautiful"? *Ornaments.*
- What verb means "entertain someone or hold their interest"? *Amuse.*

### Extend Vocabulary

 Admit

In *When Cats Go Wrong,* we learned that **admit** means "to tell the truth even though you may not want to." Say the verb that means "to tell the truth even though you may not want to." *Admit.*

Raise your hand if you can tell us a sentence that uses **admit** as a verb meaning "to tell the truth even though you may not want to." (Call on several children. If they don't use complete sentences, restate their examples as sentences. Have the class repeat the sentences.)

Here's a new way to use the word **admit.**

- You will not be **admitted** into the movie unless you are at least 13 years old. Say the sentence.
- The principal **admitted** the tardy students into the school. Say the sentence.
- Will you **admit** him into the party? Say the sentence.

**In these sentences, admit is a verb that means to let in.** Raise your hand if you can tell us a sentence that uses **admit** as a verb meaning "to let in." (Call on several children. If they don't use complete sentences, restate their examples as sentences. Have the class repeat the sentences.)

### Present Expanded Target Vocabulary

Warning

This song is a warning to people about what naughty cats can do to a house. **Warning.** Say the word. *Warning.*

**Warning** is a noun. It names a thing. What kind of word is **warning?** *A noun.*

**A warning is something that tells that something bad could happen.** Say the word that means "something that tells that something bad could happen." *Warning.*

I'll tell about some things people say. If those people are giving a warning, say "warning." If not, don't say anything.

- Watch out for the hole! *Warning.*
- A mean dog lives in that house. *Warning.*
- Be careful! This is a busy street. *Warning.*
- My cat had kittens.
- Don't go in the pool if there's no lifeguard. *Warning.*
- I rode my bike safely down the street.

What word means "something that tells that something bad could happen"? *Warning.*

Mischievous

The cat in this song is very mischievous. **Mischievous.** Say the word. *Mischievous.*

**Mischievous** is a describing word. It tells more about a person or animal. What kind of word is **mischievous?** *A describing word.*

**Mischievous means troublesome or annoying.** Say the word that means "troublesome or annoying." *Mischievous.*

I'll tell about some things a cat might do. If the cat is being mischievous, say "mischievous." If not, don't say anything.

- Sleeping in the sun.
- Climbing the curtains. *Mischievous.*
- Swatting at the bird. *Mischievous.*
- Eating.
- Sneaking up on the dog. *Mischievous.*

What word means "troublesome or annoying"? *Mischievous.*

**Preparation:** Activity Sheet, BLM 28b, a pencil, and crayons. Print the words from BLM 28b on a piece of chart paper.

### Play Poetic Definitions

Today you'll play Poetic Definitions. I'll say a little poem that uses the meaning of one of our vocabulary words. If you can tell me the word that the poem is describing, you will win one point. If you can't tell me, I get the point. Let's think about the six words we have learned: **admit, mournful, amuse, ornaments, warning,** and **mischievous.** (Display the Picture Vocabulary Cards.)

Let's practice. It's just so sad, I cannot lie. It's so sad, I want to cry. What vocabulary word describes how I am feeling? *Mournful.*

Now you're ready to play the game. (Draw a T-chart on the board for keeping score. Children earn one point for each correct answer. If they make an error, correct them as you normally would, and record one point for yourself. Repeat missed words at the end of the game.)

- I don't want to say it, but I guess I should. I really wasn't being good. Which vocabulary word is being described in this poem? *Admit.*
- Does it make you laugh? Does it make you smile? Does it hold your attention all the while? What vocabulary word is described in this poem? *Amuse.*
- Come in! Come in! Oh, can't you see? We are having a big party! What vocabulary word is being described in this poem? *Admit.*
- Stay out! Beware! Don't go in there! What vocabulary word is being described in this poem? *Warning.*
- He pulled the dog's tail, ripped a book, dumped the flour. And I've only been watching him for half an hour! What vocabulary word describes the little boy? *Mischievous.*
- The statues up on the shelf, the art up on the wall. They make the room feel just like home, not like a classroom at all. What

vocabulary word describes the statues and art? *Ornaments.*

(Count the points and declare a winner.) You did a great job of playing Poetic Definitions.

### Complete the Activity Sheet

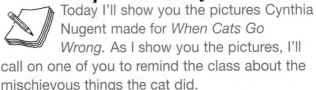

Today I'll show you the pictures Cynthia Nugent made for *When Cats Go Wrong.* As I show you the pictures, I'll call on one of you to remind the class about the mischievous things the cat did.

(Revisit each page of the book, having children tell the things that the cat did.)

Today you are going to help the boy from the song put things in his house back together.

(Distribute copies of BLM 28b to children.) Touch the first picture in the first column. What is this? *A goldfish.* (Repeat for each picture in the left-hand column.)

Touch the first picture in the second column. What is this? *A birdcage.* (Repeat for each picture in the right-hand column.)

You will draw a line from the picture in the first column to a picture it goes with in the second column. When you are done, write a sentence at the bottom of the page that tells about one mischievous thing the cat did in the song.

## DAY 4

**Preparation:** Copy the diamante writing frame (BLM 28c) onto a piece of chart paper.

### Guided Writing-Diamante Poem

At the end of this poetry unit, we are going to have a poetry contest. For the poetry contest, you will each write your own poem. You are going to learn how to write four different kinds of poems. So far you have written an acrostic poem and a two-word poem. Today we will write our third kind of poem. (Display the writing frame on the chart paper.)

The poem we will write today is called a diamante poem. What kind of poem will we write today? *A diamante poem.* When a diamante poem is finished, it is in the shape of a diamond. What shape is a diamante poem when it is finished? *A diamond.*

The first thing we do when we write a diamante poem is decide what to write about. What is the first thing we do when we write a diamante poem? *Decide what to write about.*

An opposite is a word whose meaning is completely different from that of another word. What is an opposite? *A word whose meaning is completely different from that of another word.* **Hot** and **cold** are opposites. **Big** and **little** are opposites.

In a diamante poem, we write about two opposite things. What do we write about in a diamante poem? *Two opposite things.* Today we are going to write a diamante about summer and winter. What will today's diamante poem be about? *Summer and winter.*

The next thing we do when we write a diamante poem is write the title of our poem. What is the next thing we do when we write a diamante poem? *Write the title.*

The title of a diamante poem contains the names of the two things we are writing about. We are writing a poem about summer and winter. What do you think the title of our diamante poem should be? *Summer and Winter.* (Write *Summer and Winter* on the top line of the writing frame.)

We are writing about summer and winter. The first line of a diamante poem is the name of the first thing we are writing about. What should I write in the first line of our poem? *Summer.*

(Write *Summer* on the first line beneath the title.) The last line of a diamante poem is the name of the second thing we are writing about. What should I write in the last line of our poem? *Winter.* (Write *Winter* on the last line of the frame.)

Each line of a diamante poem uses a certain kind of word. The second line of a diamante poem must have two describing words that tell more about the first word of the poem. What are some describing words that tell more about summer? (Accept appropriate responses. Choose two words and write them on the lines.)

The third line of a diamante poem must have three verbs that end in **-ing**. The verbs must be about the first word of the poem. What are some things that you do in the summer? (Accept reasonable responses. Choose three words and write them on the lines.)

The fourth line of a diamante poem must have four nouns. The first two nouns go with the first word of the poem. What are some nouns that go with summer? (Accept reasonable responses. Choose two words and write them on the first two lines of Line 4.) The second two nouns go with the last word of the poem. What are some nouns that go with winter? (Accept reasonable responses. Choose two words and write them on the second two lines of Line 4.)

The fifth line of a diamante poem must have three verbs that end in **-ing**. The verbs must be about the last word of the poem. What are some things that you do in the winter? (Accept reasonable responses. Choose three words and write them on the lines.)

The sixth line of a diamante poem must have two describing words that tell more about the last word of the poem. What are some describing words that tell more about winter? (Accept reasonable responses. Choose two words and write them on the lines.)

The last line of the poem names the final word from our title. What is the last word in our poem? *Winter.*

(Read the completed poem aloud.) We did a great job of writing a diamante poem about summer and winter. Tomorrow you will write your own diamante poem.

(Sample diamante poem about summer and winter:

Summer,

hot,      humid,

swimming, biking, running,

pool,   bike,   sled,   ice rink

skating, skiing, sledding,

cold,    snowy,

Winter)

## Play Poetic Definitions (Cumulative Review)

Let's play Poetic Definitions. I'll say a little poem that uses the meaning of one of our vocabulary words. If you can tell me the word that the poem is describing, you will win one point. If you can't tell me, I get the point. Let's think about the six words we have learned: **admit, mournful, amuse, ornaments, warning,** and **mischievous.** (Display the Picture Vocabulary cards.)

Let's practice. Does it make you laugh? Is this all a joke? Does the sentence that is spoken make a smile? What vocabulary word is described in this poem? *Amuse.*

Now you're ready to play the game. (Draw a T-chart on the board for keeping score. Children earn one point for each correct answer. If they make an error, correct them as you normally would, and record one point for yourself. Repeat missed words at the end of the game.)

- I'm not feeling so swell. I think that I'm not well. I'm in a mood and want no food. What vocabulary word describes how I am feeling? *Cranky.*
- Beware! Don't you dare go in there! What vocabulary word is being described in this poem? *Warning.*
- It's just so sad. This is very bad. What vocabulary word describes how I am feeling? *Mournful.*
- These are the best of all. Put them on the wall. Cool and nifty. Make this place pretty. What vocabulary word describes what will make this place pretty? *Ornaments.*
- Come in! Come in! We want you in. Bring your smile and a grin. What vocabulary word is being described in this poem? *Admit.*
- What is that? Who are you? I really need to know. Why? When? Where? Are you going there? When do I get to go? What vocabulary word describes the person asking these questions? *Curious.*
- That girl with a curl has been a pest. She has yet to be the best. She is clever and ever in

trouble. What vocabulary word describes the girl? *Mischievous.*
- I don't want to say this, but I guess I should. That ball did nearly your window miss. Which vocabulary word is being described in this poem? *Admit.*
- By gosh! I think that I need to wash. That muck is yuck. It's wet, soft, and slippery. What vocabulary word is being described in this poem? *Slimy.*

(Count the points and declare a winner.) You did a great job of playing Poetic Definitions.

---

## DAY 5

**Preparation:** Quiz Answer Sheet, BLM B.

Each child will need a copy of BLM 28c.

---

### Assess Vocabulary

 (Give each child a copy of the Quiz Answer Sheet, BLM B.)

Today you're going to have a True or False quiz. When you do the True or False quiz, it shows me how well you know the hard words you are learning.

If I say something that is true, circle the word **true.** What will you do if I say something that is true? *Circle the word* true.

If I say something that is false, circle the word **false.** What will you do if I say something that is false? *Circle the word* false.

Listen carefully to each item that I say. Don't let me trick you!

Item 1: If your little brother is teasing the bird and spreading his toys all around the house, he is being **mischievous.** (*True.*)

Item 2: If you **admit** something, you describe what a beautiful sunset looks like. (*False.*)

Item 3: If you travel to the country north of the United States, you will be in **Mexico.** (*False.*)

Item 4: If you hear a **warning** on the radio that a dangerous tornado is coming, you should stay inside. (*True.*)

Item 5: If a ticket says, "**Admit** one person," that means one person is allowed in. (*True.*)

Item 6: If your teacher gives the class three choices, and you are asked to raise your hand for the one you want, your teacher is letting you **vote.** (*True.*)

Item 7: **Ornaments** make things less pretty. (*False.*)

Item 8: A **mournful** song is very upbeat and happy. (*False.*)

Item 9: The waves left by a water snake swimming through the water is called its **wake.** (*True.*)

Item 10: If something holds your attention and entertains you, it **amuses** you. (*True.*)

You did a great job completing your quiz!

(Score children's work. A child must score 9 out of 10 to be at mastery level. If a child does not achieve mastery, insert the missed words as additional items in the games in next week's lessons. Retest those children individually for the missed items before they take the next mastery test.)

---

**Preparation:** Display the chart paper with the poem *Summer and Winter* from yesterday's lesson. Make two copies of the writing frame for each student.

---

### Independent Writing—Diamante Poem

Yesterday you learned how to write a diamante poem. What kind of poem did you learn to write yesterday? *A diamante poem.*

The first thing we do when we write a diamante poem is decide what to write about. What is the first thing we do when we write a diamante poem? *Decide what to write about.*

Today you are going to write your own diamante poem about dogs and cats. What will today's diamante poem be about? *Dogs and cats.*

(Distribute one writing frame to each student.) This is a writing frame. It will help you remember what kinds of words to use in your diamante poem.

Touch the line above the diamante poem frame. You will write the title of your poem on the top line. What will you write on the top line? *The title.* Today's diamante poem is going to be about dogs and cats. What do you think the title of your poem will be? *Dogs and Cats.* Write **Dogs and Cats** on the line. (Allow time for children to write the title.)

Touch the top line inside the frame. You will write the first word of your title on this line. What will you write on this line? *The first word of my title.* What is the first word of your title? *Dogs.* Write **dogs** on the first line. (Allow children time to write the first line of their poem.)

Touch the next two lines inside the frame. You will write two words that describe dogs on these lines. What will you write on these lines? *Two words that describe dogs.* (Allow children time to write the second line of their poems. Encourage children to use inventive spelling if they don't know how to spell a word.)

(Repeat the process for each line of the poem, following these guidelines:
    Line 3: Three *-ing* verbs about dogs
    Line 4: Two nouns about dogs, two nouns about cats
    Line 5: Three *-ing* verbs about cats
    Line 6: Two adjectives about cats
    Line 7: *Cats.*)

Now that you have finished writing your draft, you need to check your poem. Make sure you have a word on every line and that that you have spelled your words correctly. (Assist children as needed in editing their poems. Write the correct spelling of words on the board. The class can be asked if they know how to spell a word. Call on an individual to assist with the spelling.)

You will copy your poem onto a new writing frame. Use your neatest printing. When you are finished, you may illustrate your poem.

(Allow children time to copy their diamante poems onto a new frame. Circulate around the room, providing encouragement and assistance if needed. Allow children to share their completed poems.)

## Extensions

### Read a Song as a Reward

 (Read *When Cats Go Wrong* or another book that is written as a poem or song to children as a reward for their hard work. Display a number of books of poetry or songs. Ask children to choose which one they would like you to read.)

---

**Preparation:** Word containers for the Super Words Center.

---

### Introduce the Super Words Center

(Remove the words from previous lessons from the word containers. Place the Picture Vocabulary Cards from Weeks 26–28 in the containers. Show children the word container. If children need more guidance in how to work in the Super Words Center, role-play with two to three children as a demonstration. (**Note:** You may wish to leave the word *muck* out of the game cards or to caution children about using rhyming words that are polite.)

You will play a game called *Rhyme Time* in the Super Words Center.

Let's think about how we work with our words in the Super Words Center.

You will work with a partner in the Super Words Center. Whom will you work with? *A partner.*

First you will draw a word out of the container. What do you do first? (Idea: *Draw a word out of the container.*) Show your partner the word card.

Next you will tell your partner the word that the card shows. What do you do next? *Tell my partner the word that the card shows.*

If you say the correct word, you get a point. What do you get if you say the correct word? *A point.*

Next you will say a word that rhymes with the word on the word card. What will you do next? *Say a word that rhymes.*

If you can say a word that rhymes with the word on the card, you get another point. What do you get if you can say a word that rhymes with the word on the card? *Another point.*

After you have said the word and said a word that rhymes, give your partner a turn. What do you do next? *Give my partner a turn.*

## Preparation:
You will need a copy of the book *Stopping by Woods on a Snowy Evening* for each day's lesson.

Number the pages of the poem to assist you in asking the comprehension questions at the appropriate points.

Post a copy of the Vocabulary Tally Sheet, BLM A, with this week's Picture Vocabulary Cards attached.

Each child will need one copy of the Homework Sheet, BLM 29a.

## DAY 1:

### Introduce Book

This week's book is called *Stopping by Woods on a Snowy Evening.* What's the title of this week's book? *Stopping by Woods on a Snowy Evening.*

There are many different kinds of poems. What kind of poem was *One Duck Stuck*? *A counting poem. To Market, To Market* was a nursery rhyme. What kind of poem was *To Market, To Market*? *A nursery rhyme. When Cats Go Wrong* was a song. What kind of poem was *When Cats Go Wrong*? *A song.* Today's poem has a rhyming pattern. What kind of pattern does today's poem have? *A rhyming pattern.*

This book was written by Robert Frost. Who's the author of *Stopping by Woods on a Snowy Evening*? *Robert Frost.*

Susan Jeffers made the pictures for this book. Who is the illustrator of *Stopping by Woods on a Snowy Evening*? *Susan Jeffers.* Who made the illustrations for this book? *Susan Jeffers.*

The cover of a book usually gives us some hints of what the book is about. Let's look at the front cover of *Stopping by Woods on a Snowy Evening.* What do you see in the illustration on this cover? (Ideas: *A man riding in a horse-drawn sleigh through the woods; snow; large trees.*)

## Stopping by Woods on a Snowy Evening
author: Robert Frost • illustrator: Susan Jeffers

### Target Vocabulary

| Tier II | Tier III |
|---|---|
| queer | verse |
| mistake | rhyming pattern |
| promises | narrator |
| woods | |
| *pleasure | |
| *peaceful | |

*Expanded Target Vocabulary Word

(Assign each child a partner.) Get ready to make some predictions to your partner about this poem. Use the information from the cover to help you.

(Ask the following questions, allowing sufficient time for children to share their predictions with their partners.)

- Who do you think this poem is about?
- Why do you think the man is in the woods in the snow?
- What do you think the man will do in the woods?
- Where do you think the man is going?
- When do you think this poem happens?

(Call on several children to share their predictions with the class.)

### Take a Picture Walk

(Encourage children to use target words in their answers.) We're going to take a picture walk through this book. Remember that when we take a picture walk, we look at the pictures and tell what we think will happen.

**Pages 1–2.** What do you see in this illustration? (Ideas: *A man in a horse-drawn sleigh riding through the woods; lots of trees; lots of snow.*) What season of the year is it in this poem? *Winter.*

**Pages 3–4.** What do you see in this illustration? (Ideas: *A town; houses; snow; trees.*)

**Pages 5–6.** What do you see in this illustration? (Ideas: *The man on his sleigh with his horse; lots of trees; an owl.*)

**Pages 7–8.** What is the man doing in this illustration? (Ideas: *Making a snow angel; playing in the snow.*) What animals do you see in this illustration? (Ideas: *Owl; birds; squirrel; rabbits; fox.*) What are the animals doing here? (Idea: *Running or flying from the man.*) Why do you think the animals are leaving? (Ideas: *The man has scared them; they are not used to people being in the woods in the winter.*)

**Pages 9–10.** What are the man and the horse looking at in this illustration? (Idea: *The snow angel the man made.*)

**Pages 11–12.** What is happening in this illustration? (Ideas: *The man is taking something from his sleigh; an animal is looking at the man and his horse.*)

**Pages 13–14.** What has the man taken from his sleigh? (Idea: *A large pile of sticks.*) Why do you think the man has brought a pile of sticks into the woods? (Idea: *For the animals.*) What do you think the animals are going to do with the sticks?

**Pages 15–16.** What do you see in this illustration? (Idea: *The man is looking into the woods.*) What do you think the man sees?

**Pages 17–18.** How do you think the man is feeling in this illustration? (Ideas: *Happy; like he has helped the animals; contented; considerate; compassionate; delighted; generous; thoughtful.*)

**Pages 19–20.** What is the man doing in this illustration? (Idea: *Covering his horse with a blanket.*) What else do you see in this illustration? (Ideas: *Deer; two squirrels; a rabbit.*)

**Pages 21–22.** What is happening in this illustration? (Ideas: *The man has returned home; his wife is hugging him; children are feeding the horse; a girl is running with a sled and a dog; it is snowing.*)

**Pages 23–24.** What animals do you see in this illustration? (Ideas: *Deer; birds; squirrels; rabbits.*) What are the animals doing? (Idea: *Watching the man leave the woods.*)

**Pages 25–26.** What is happening in this illustration? (Idea: *The man is riding home; there is a big snowstorm.*)

It's your turn to ask me some questions. What would you like to know about the poem? (Accept questions. If children tell about the pictures or the poem instead of ask questions, prompt them to ask a question.) Ask me a why question. Ask me a where question.

### Read the Poem Aloud
(Read the poem to children with minimal interruptions.)

Tomorrow we will read the poem again, and I will ask you some questions.

### Present Target Vocabulary
 Queer

The poem says, "The little horse must think it queer to stop without a farmhouse near." **Queer.** Say the word. *Queer.*

**Queer** is a describing word. It tells more about a noun. What kind of word is **queer?** *A describing word.*

**Queer means odd or strange.** Say the word that means "odd or strange." *Queer.*

(Correct any incorrect responses, and repeat the item at the end of the sequence.)

Let's think about some things. I'll tell about some things. If these things are queer, say "queer." If not, don't say anything.

- A car painted to look like a dog. *Queer.*
- A red fire truck.
- A house with a big, yellow smiley face painted on the roof. *Queer.*
- A child reading a book.
- A child reading a book upside down. *Queer.*
- A horse wearing a shirt and tie. *Queer.*

What word means "odd or strange"? *Queer.*

Mistake

In the poem, the horse wonders if they have stopped in the snowy woods by mistake. **Mistake.** Say the word. *Mistake.*

**Mistake** is a noun. It names a thing. What kind of word is **mistake?** *A noun.*

**A mistake is a thought or action that is not correct.** Say the word that means "a thought or action that is not correct." *Mistake.*

Let's think about some thoughts and actions. I'll tell about a thought or action. If the thought or action is a mistake, say "mistake." If not, don't say anything.

- Jane thought that 2 + 2 equaled 5. *Mistake.*
- Lamar went into the girls' bathroom instead of the boys'. *Mistake.*
- Eva counted, "1, 2, 3, 4, 5."
- Sydney put her empty glass in the refrigerator and the milk in the sink. *Mistake.*
- Eric got all the answers correct on the math test.
- Jillian woke up on Saturday morning and started getting ready for school. *Mistake.*

What noun means "a thought or action that is not correct"? *Mistake.*

 *Promise*

In the poem, the man has promises to keep. **Promise.** Say the word. *Promise.*

**Promise** is a noun. It names a thing. What kind of word is **promise?** *A noun.*

**A promise is something you say that will happen for sure.** Say the word that means "something you say that will happen for sure." *Promise.*

Let's think about some things that people might say. I'll give some statements. If the statement is a promise, say "promise." If not, don't say anything.

- We will go to the park for sure this weekend. *Promise.*
- Mr. Rose bought a new car.
- The lights are still on.
- For sure, I will take you to the carnival this week. *Promise.*
- You will surely earn an A if you do all the work correctly. *Promise.*
- The doorbell rang.

What noun means "something you say that will happen for sure"? *Promise.*

 Woods

In the poem, the man thinks he knows whose woods these are. **Woods.** Say the word. *Woods.*

**Woods** is a noun. It names a place. What kind of word is **woods?** *A noun.*

**Woods is a place with many trees.** Say the word that means "a place with many trees." *Woods.*

Let's think about some places. I'll tell about some places. If the places are woods, say "woods." If not, don't say anything.

- The family walked among the hundreds of trees. *Woods.*
- My house has six trees in the yard.
- The deer and squirrels ran among the many trees. *Woods.*
- There was barely room to walk between the many trees. *Woods.*
- We planted a tree for Arbor Day.
- The few trees that are along the side of the road are very pretty.

What noun means "a place with many trees"? *Woods.*

### Present Vocabulary Tally Sheet
(See Lesson 1, page 4, for instructions)

### Assign Homework
(Homework Sheet, BLM 29a. See the Introduction for homework instructions.)

---

**DAY 2**

**Preparation:** Picture Vocabulary Cards for *queer, mistake, promise, woods.*

---

### Read and Discuss Poem

 (Read the poem to children. Ask the following questions at the specified points. Encourage them to use target words in their answers.)

I'm going to read *Stopping by Woods on a Snowy Evening.* Each part of a song or poem is called a verse. What do we call one part of a song or poem? *A verse.* A verse is a group of sentences that go together in a song or poem. What is a verse? *A group of sentences that go together in a song or poem.*

A verse is made up of several lines. In this poem, each verse is four lines long. How long is each verse of this poem? *Four lines.* When I finish reading each verse, I'll ask you some questions.

In this poem, someone is telling a story. A person who tells a story is called a narrator. What do we call a person who tells a story? *A narrator.*

**Pages 1–5.** This is the first verse of the poem. Now I will read each line separately.

**Page 1.** Does the narrator know whose woods these are? *Yes.*

**Page 4.** Does the owner of the woods live there? *No.* Where does the owner live? *In the village.*

**Page 5.** Why is the narrator stopping in the woods? (Idea: *To watch the snow.*)

**Pages 9–12.** This is the second verse of the poem. Now I will read each line.

**Page 9.** What does the narrator think his horse finds queer? (Idea: *Stopping where there's no farmhouse.*)

**Page 12.** Where has the narrator stopped? (Idea: *Between the woods and a frozen lake.*) What time of day is it? (Idea: *Evening.*)

**Pages 14–18.** This is the third verse of the poem. Now I will read each line separately.

**Page 14.** Who is the narrator talking about here? (Idea: *The little horse.*) What mistake would the horse think had been made? (Idea: *They stopped in the wrong place.*)

**Pages 15–18.** What sounds does the narrator hear in the woods? (Ideas: *Wind; snow falling.*)

**Pages 20–25.** This is the fourth verse of the poem. Now I will read each line separately.

**Page 20.** How does the narrator describe the woods? (Ideas: *Lovely; dark; deep.*) Do you think the narrator likes being there? *Yes.*

**Page 22.** Why can't the narrator stay in the woods? *He has promises to keep.* What kinds of promises do you think the narrator has to keep?

**Page 24.** Why else can't the narrator stay in the woods? *He has miles to go.* Where do you think the narrator has to go?

**Page 25.** What has Robert Frost done differently at the end of this poem? (Idea: *He repeated the same line twice.*) Why do you think Robert Frost repeated the line "And miles to go before I sleep"? (Ideas: *To show that the narrator is very busy; to show that he really doesn't have the time to spend watching the snow, but it was so special he had to make the time.*)

### Review Vocabulary

(Display the Picture Vocabulary Cards. Point to each card as you say the word. Ask children to repeat each word after you.) These pictures show **queer, mistake, promise,** and **woods.**

- What noun means "a place with many trees"? *Woods.*
- What noun means "a thought or action that is not correct"? *Mistake.*
- What word means "odd or strange"? *Queer.*
- What noun means "something you say that will happen for sure"? *Promise.*

### Extend Vocabulary

 Promise

In *Stopping by Woods on a Snowy Evening,* we learned that a **promise** is "something you say that will happen for sure." Say the noun that means "something you say that will happen for sure." *Promise.*

Raise your hand if you can tell us a sentence that uses **promise** as a noun meaning "something you say that will happen for sure." (Call on several children. If they don't use complete sentences, restate their examples as sentences. Have the class repeat the sentences.)

Here's a new way to use the word **promise.**

- I **promise** you we'll go clothes shopping this weekend. Say the sentence.
- I **promise** I'll be good! Say the sentence.
- Do you **promise** to take the trash out before dinner? Say the sentence.

**In these sentences, promise is a verb that means to give your word that you will do something.** Raise your hand if you can tell us a sentence that uses **promise** as a verb meaning

"to give your word that you will do something."
(Call on several children. If they don't use complete sentences, restate their examples as sentences. Have the class repeat the sentences.)

### Present Expanded Target Vocabulary
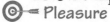 Pleasure

In the poem, the narrator found pleasure in watching the woods fill up with snow. **Pleasure.** Say the word. *Pleasure.*

**Pleasure is a noun. It names a feeling. What kind of word is pleasure?** *A noun.*

**Pleasure is a feeling of happiness, delight, or joy.** Say the word that means "a feeling of happiness, delight, or joy." *Pleasure.*

I'll tell about some people in situations. If the people are finding pleasure in the situation, say "pleasure." If not, don't say anything.

- Scott began to cry after his brother hit him.
- Jana smiled as she watched the snow fall on the grass. *Pleasure.*
- Singing in the choir makes Jameka happy. *Pleasure.*
- Travis hated taking math tests.
- Aaron's favorite thing to do is curl up in a comfy chair with a good book. *Pleasure.*
- Anson's mouth was sore after getting cavities filled at the dentist.

What word means "a feeling of happiness, delight, or joy"? *Pleasure.*

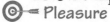 Peaceful

This poem gives a peaceful description of the snow falling in the woods. **Peaceful.** Say the word. *Peaceful.*

**Peaceful is a describing word. It tells more about a noun. What kind of word is peaceful?** *A describing word.*

**Peaceful means quiet and calm.** Say the word that means "quiet and calm." *Peaceful.*

I'll describe some places. If the places are peaceful, say "peaceful." If not, don't say anything.

- A grassy field on a bright summer day. *Peaceful.*
- The school cafeteria at lunchtime.

- An empty beach on a calm, warm day. *Peaceful.*
- A football stadium during a big game.
- Your bedroom at night when you are sleeping. *Peaceful.*

What word means "quiet and calm"? *Peaceful.*

---

### DAY 3

**Preparation:** Activity Sheet, BLM 29b.

---

### Play Poetic Definitions

Today you'll play Poetic Definitions. I'll say a little poem that uses the meaning of one of our vocabulary words. If you can tell me the word that the poem is describing, you will win one point. If you can't tell me, I get the point. Let's think about the six words we have learned: **queer, mistake, promises, woods, pleasure,** and **peaceful.** (Display the Picture Vocabulary Cards.)

Let's practice. A statement that says we'll do it for sure today. A statement that says for sure we'll go out and play. What kind of statement is it? *A promise.*

Now you're ready to play the game. (Draw a T-chart on the board for keeping score. Children earn one point for each correct answer. If they make an error, correct them as you normally would, and record one point for yourself. Repeat missed words at the end of the game.)

- I have to say, while at play, a mistake I did make. Which vocabulary word is being described in this poem? *Admit.*
- A purple cow. A bright green bear. Strange things are everywhere. What word describes these animals? *Queer.*
- Rabbits and squirrels, birds and deer. Through all these trees, no words do I hear. Where am I? *In the woods.*
- A sailboat floats upon the sea. Blue sky above, blue water under me. Up and down on the water, slow and sweet. What kind of scene is described in this poem? *Peaceful.*

- Two plus two is five. Three plus three is seven. And I do believe, that five plus five is eleven. What vocabulary word can be used to describe this person's thoughts? *Mistake.*
- Mom said, "For sure we'll go to the store. We'll buy you some new pants. And maybe something more." What did Mom do? *Promise.*
- I curl up in a cozy, comfy chair. There are no sounds anywhere. I take out my book, my special friend. I read and read until the end. What is reading for me? *A pleasure.*

(Count the points and declare a winner.) You did a great job of playing Poetic Definitions.

### Complete the Activity Sheet

 Today we are going to look for the rhyming pattern Robert Frost used in *Stopping By Woods on a Snowy Evening.* In a rhyming pattern, the last word of each line rhymes with the last word of a different line.

(Distribute copies of BLM 29b to children.) Touch under the first word of the poem. My turn to read. Touch under each word as I read it. (Read the first line of the poem.) What is the last word in the line? *Know.* (Write *know* on the board.)

The first part of the pattern is going to rhyme with **know.** What will the first part of the pattern rhyme with? *Know.* We call the first part of the pattern **A.** What do we call the first part of the pattern? *A.* Write a capital **A** on the line next to the first line of the poem.

Touch under the first word of the second line. My turn to read. Touch under each word as I read it. (Read the second line of the poem.) What is the last word in the line? *Though.* Does **though** rhyme with **know?** *Yes.* (Write *though* on the board under *know.*) So **though** is part of the **A** pattern. What pattern is **though** a part of? *The A pattern.* Write **A** on the line next to the second line of the poem.

Touch under the first word of the third line. My turn to read. Touch under each word as I read it. (Read the third line of the poem.) What is the last word in the line? *Here.* Does **here** rhyme with **know?** *No.* (Write *here* on the board next to *know.*) So **here** is the beginning of a new

pattern. We'll call this new pattern **B.** What do we call the new pattern? *B.* What pattern is **here** a part of? *The B pattern.* Write **B** on the line next to the third line of the poem.

Touch under the first word of the fourth line. My turn to read. Touch under each word as I read it. (Read the fourth line of the poem.) What is the last word in the line? *Snow.* Does **snow** rhyme with **know** or **here?** *Know.* (Write *snow* on the board beneath *know.*) So **snow** is part of the **A** pattern. What pattern is **snow** a part of? *The A pattern.* Write **A** on the line next to the fourth line of the poem.

(Continue with the other three verses of the poem. The final pattern will be AABA BBCB CCDC DDDD.)

Let's read the whole pattern together. *AABA BBCB CCDC DDDD.* What do you notice about the last verse of the poem? (Idea: *All of the lines end with the same pattern sound, "eep."*)

---

### DAY 4

**Preparation:** You will need a piece of blank chart paper.

---

### Guided Writing–Concrete Poem

At the end of this poetry unit, we are going to have a poetry contest. For the poetry contest, you will each write your own poem. I am going to teach you how to write four different kinds of poems. So far you have written an acrostic poem, a two-word poem, and a diamante poem. Today we will write our fourth kind of poem. (Display the writing frame you copied onto the chart paper.)

The poem we will write today is called a concrete poem. What kind of poem will we write today? *A concrete poem.* When poets write concrete poems, they make their poems in the shape of objects they want to write about like a cloud, a tree, or a mountain.

The first thing we do when we write a concrete poem is decide what to write about. What is the first thing we do when we write a concrete poem? *Decide what to write about.*

Today we are going to write a concrete poem about clouds. What will today's concrete poem be about? *Clouds.* The title of our poem will be **Clouds.** What will the title of our poem be? *Clouds.* (Write *Clouds* at the top of the chart paper.)

The next thing we do when we write a concrete poem is draw the outline of the object. What is the next thing we do when we write a concrete poem? *Draw the outline.* (Quickly sketch the outline of a cloud on the sheet of chart paper.)

Poetry is about choosing good words. Not all poems have to rhyme. In a concrete poem, poets choose words that give the reader good images of the object. The next thing a poet does is think of good words to describe the object. What is the next thing a poet does? (Idea: *Think of good words to describe the object.*)

Let's think of some words that describe clouds. (Write *clouds* at the top of the chalkboard and underline it.) Think about how clouds might look, feel, smell, and sound. Think about what clouds do. (Write children's ideas on the board under *clouds.*)

(Once you have a sufficient list of words, say:)

After poets brainstorm good words to describe the object, they write the words around the outline. Where do poets write the words in a concrete poem? *Around the outline.* Our concrete poem is going to start and end with the word **clouds.** How will our concrete poem start and end? *With the word clouds.* (Choose words from the list and write them around the outside of the cloud outline.) Now the poem is in the shape of a cloud.

(Read the completed poem aloud.) We did a great job of writing a concrete poem about clouds. Tomorrow you will write your own concrete poem.

(Sample concrete poem about clouds: clouds–pillowy–dark–light–heavy–rolling–rumbling–thundering–spinning–turning–rising–falling–whooshing–sighing–crashing–booming–tingling–feathery–wispy–cotton candy–fluffy–clouds.)

## Play Poetic Definitions (Cumulative Review)

Let's play Poetic Definitions. I'll say a little poem that uses the meaning of one of our vocabulary words. If you can tell me the word that the poem is describing, you will win one point. If you can't tell me, I get the point. Let's think about the six words we have learned: **queer, mistake, promises, woods, pleasure,** and **peaceful.** (Display the Picture Vocabulary Cards.)

Let's practice. Grass that is not green. A kind man who is mean. Silly ladies in long underwear. Strange things are everywhere. What word describes this scene? *Queer.*

Now you're ready to play the game. (Draw a T-chart on the board for keeping score. Children earn one point for each correct answer. If they make an error, correct them as you normally would, and record one point for yourself. Repeat missed words at the end of the game.)

- I'm sure that **cow** is spelled w-o-c and **wow** is spelled the same way as **now.** What vocabulary word can be used to describe this person's thoughts? *Mistake.*
- I like my life the way it is. I wouldn't change a thing. I am satisfied with how I am. I wouldn't change a thing. What vocabulary word tells how I feel about my life? *Contented.*
- I will say that this is a good day. For sure I tell you, we'll go out to play. What kind of statement is it? *A promise.*
- I open the door and say "thank you" more. I say "please" with ease. What kind of person does the poem describe? *A courteous person.*
- There are trees everywhere. No matter where I look they are there. Where am I? *In the woods.*
- Galloping through the woods on my horse. Trotting across the field. No greater joy can life yield. What is the rider feeling? *Pleasure.*
- The sweet baby is sound asleep. The kitten is curled up with the dog not making a peep. What kind of scene is described in this poem? *Peaceful.*

- Here they come off the ship. What can they see? They ask us to give a tip. They walk so fast to see it all. Who does this poem describe? *Tourists.*
- I will do my best for you. It will be the best I can do. You will know for sure. What did I do? *Promise.*

(Count the points and declare a winner.) You did a great job of playing Poetic Definitions.

## DAY 5

### Assess Vocabulary

 (Give each child a copy of the Quiz Answer Sheet, BLM B.)

Today you're going to have a True or False quiz. When you do the True or False quiz, it shows me how well you know the hard words you are learning.

If I say something that is true, circle the word **true.** What will you do if I say something that is true? *Circle the word* true.

If I say something that is false, circle the word **false.** What will you do if I say something that is false? *Circle the word* false.

Listen carefully to each item that I say. Don't let me trick you!

Item 1: If you are in a nice, quiet, calm place, you are probably feeling **peaceful.** (*True.*)

Item 2: Something that you hate doing is a **pleasure.** (*False.*)

Item 3: If you travel to the country north of the United States, you will be in **Canada.** (*True.*)

Item 4: A place with very few trees is called the **woods.** (*False.*)

Item 5: If a person tells you they will for sure do something, they **promise** you they will do it. (*True.*)

Item 6: If you are thinking very hard about only one thing, you are **concentrating.** (*True.*)

Item 7: If you make a statement that you are for sure going to do something, you are making a **promise.** (*True.*)

Item 8: Giving a correct answer is called a **mistake.** (*False.*)

Item 9: A blue bird, a brown dog, and a white cat are all **queer** animals. (*False.*)

Item 10: Fruits and vegetables are good sources of **nourishment.** (*True.*)

You did a great job completing your quiz!

(Score children's work. A child must score 9 out of 10 to be at mastery level. If a child does not achieve mastery, insert the missed words as additional items in the games in next week's lessons. Retest those children individually for the missed items before they take the next mastery test.)

### Independent Writing–Concrete Poem

Yesterday you learned how to write a concrete poem. What kind of poem did you learn to write yesterday? *A concrete poem.*

The first thing we do when we write a concrete poem is decide what to write about. What is the first thing we do when we write a concrete poem? *Decide what to write about.*

Today you are going to write your own concrete poem about trees. What will today's concrete poem be about? *Trees.*

The first thing you need to do is brainstorm words that describe trees. (Write *Trees* at the top of the board.) Think about how trees might look, feel, sound, and smell. Think about what trees do. (Write children's ideas on the board under the heading *Trees.*)

(Distribute a writing frame to each student.) Now you will write your concrete poem. You will write your poem around the outside outline of this tree. Where will you write your poem? (Idea: *Around the outside outline of the tree.*) You may use words from the board, or you may use your own words. Put a dash like this (demonstrate making a dash on the board) between each word. What will you put between each word? *A dash.* You will start and end your poem with the word **trees.** How will you start and end your poem? *With the word trees.*

(Allow children time to write their concrete poems. Circulate around the room, providing encouragement and assistance if needed. Offer an opportunity for children to share their completed poems.)

## Extensions

### Read a Poem as a Reward

(Read *Stopping by Woods on a Snowy Evening* or another poem that was written by Robert Frost to children as a reward for their hard work. Display a collection of Robert Frost poems. Read out the titles of a number of his poems. Ask children to choose which ones they would like you to read.)

---

**Preparation:** Word containers for the Super Words Center.

---

### Introduce the Super Words Center

(Remove the words from previous lessons from the word containers. Place the Picture Vocabulary Cards from Weeks 26–29 in the containers. Show children the word container. If children need more guidance in how to work in the Super Words Center, role-play with two to three children as a demonstration.)

**(Note:** You may wish to leave the word *muck* out of the game cards or to caution children about using rhyming words that are polite.)

You will play a game called *Rhyme Time* in the Super Words Center.

Let's think about how we work with our words in the Super Words Center.

You will work with a partner in the Super Words Center. Whom will you work with? *A partner.*

First you will draw a word out of the container. What do you do first? (Idea: *Draw a word out of the container.*) Show your partner the word card.

Next you will tell your partner the word that the card shows. What do you do next? *Tell my partner the word that the card shows.*

If you say the correct word, you get a point. What do you get if you say the correct word? *A point.*

Next you will say a word that rhymes with the word on the word card. What will you do next? *Say a word that rhymes.*

If you can say a word that rhymes with the word on the card, you get another point. What do you get if you can say a word that rhymes with the word on the card? *Another point.*

After you have said the word and said a word that rhymes, give your partner a turn. What do you do next? *Give my partner a turn.*

**Preparation:** You will need a copy of *A Cake for Herbie* for each day's lesson.

Number the pages of the story to assist you in asking comprehension questions at appropriate points.

Post a copy of the Vocabulary Tally Sheet, BLM A, with this week's Picture Vocabulary Cards attached.

Each child will need one copy of the Homework Sheet, BLM 30a.

## *A Cake for Herbie*
author: Petra Mathers • illustrator: Petra Mathers

### ⊚ Target Vocabulary

| Tier II | Tier III |
| --- | --- |
| contest | alphabet poem |
| grumpy | alliteration |
| endless | rhyme |
| sweaty | |
| *disappointed | |
| *creative | |

*Expanded Target Vocabulary Word

---

### DAY 1

### Introduce Book

This week's book is called *A Cake for Herbie*. What's the title of this week's book? *A Cake for Herbie.*

There are many different kinds of poems. What kind of poem was *One Duck Stuck*? *A counting poem.* What kind of poem was *To Market, To Market*? *A nursery rhyme.* When *Cats Go Wrong* was a song. What kind of poem was *When Cats Go Wrong*? *A song. Stopping by Woods on a Snowy Evening* used a rhyming pattern. What kind of pattern does *Stopping by Woods on a Snowy Evening* have? *A rhyming pattern.*

This week's book is a story about a poet who writes an alphabet poem. What kind of poem is in today's book? *An alphabet poem.* In an alphabet poem, each line starts with the next letter of the alphabet. What does each line in an alphabet poem start with? (Idea: *The next letter of the alphabet.*)

This book was written by Petra Mathers. Who's the author of *A Cake for Herbie*? *Petra Mathers.* Look at Petra Mathers's name on the cover of this book. Do you notice anything unusual about it? (Idea: *It has no capital letters*.) Sometimes an artist will write his or her name differently in order to catch the reader's attention.

Petra Mathers also made the pictures for this book. Who is the illustrator of *A Cake for Herbie*? *Petra Mathers.* Who made the illustrations for this book? *Petra Mathers.*

The cover of a book usually gives us some hints of what the book is about. Let's look at the front cover of *A Cake for Herbie*. What do you see in the illustration on this cover? (Ideas: *A duck on a stage; a large cake; the duck is reading something on a piece of paper; there are birds in the audience.*)

(Assign each child a partner.) Get ready to make some predictions to your partner about this book. Use the information from the covers to help you.

(Ask the following questions, allowing sufficient time for children to share their predictions with their partners.)

- Who do you think this story is about?
- Do you think this story is about real animals or imaginary ones?
- What do you think the duck is doing up on stage?
- Why do you think it is doing that?

(Call on several children to share their predictions with the class.)

### Take a Picture Walk

(Encourage children to use target words in their answers.) We're going to take a picture walk through this book. Remember that when we take a picture walk, we look at the pictures and tell what we think will happen in the story.

**Page 1.** What do you see in this illustration? (Ideas: *A bridge; a river; a town; a ship; trees.*)

**Page 2.** What is this picture of? (Ideas: *A poster; a notice.* Read the poster aloud.) What is this poster for? (Idea: *A poetry contest.*) What does the winner of the poetry contest get? *A cake.*

**Page 3.** Point to the first illustration.) Where are the birds coming from? (Idea: *The market; a store.* Point to the second illustration.) What is Herbie carrying? (Idea: *A bag of groceries.*)

**Page 4.** How are the birds getting home? (Idea: *On a scooter.*)

**Page 5.** Point to the first illustration.) What is Herbie doing in this illustration? (Idea: *Writing.*) What do you think Herbie is writing? (Idea: *A poem for the contest.* Point to the second illustration.) Now what is Herbie doing? (Idea: *Cooking something.*) What is on Herbie's head? (Idea: *An ice pack.*) Why do you think Herbie has an ice pack on his head?

**Page 6.** Who lives in this house? *Herbie.* What is Herbie doing? (Ideas: *Watching the sunrise; watching the water.*)

**Page 7.** Who is Herbie talking to here? (Ideas: *His friend; another bird.*) What is the other bird doing? (Idea: *Working in the garden.*)

**Page 8.** What is happening in the first illustration on this page? (Ideas: *Herbie is on stage; he is tied up and his beak is also tied up; the prize cake is flying away.*) What is Herbie doing in the second illustration? (Idea: *Sleeping.*) Do you think Herbie was really tied up on stage with a cake flying by? Tell why you think so. (Idea: *No, it was a dream.*)

**Page 9.** What is happening in these illustrations? (Ideas: *Herbie's friend is sick; Herbie is visiting her.*)

**Page 10.** What is Herbie doing in these illustrations? (Ideas: *He is going to the theater where the poetry contest is being held.*)

**Page 11.** What is happening in this illustration? (Idea: *A bird is on a stage saying a poem.*)

**Page 12.** What is Herbie doing in this part of the story? (Idea: *He is on a stage reading his poem for the contest.*)

**Page 13.** Do you think the birds in the audience liked Herbie's poem? *No.*

**Page 14.** What is happening in this illustration? (Ideas: *Herbie is leaving the stage; he is leaving the theater; it is raining on him.*)

**Page 15.** Where is Herbie in this part of the story? (Ideas: *In an alley; behind a restaurant.*) The sign on the dumpster and on the wall both say "Ship's Inn." What do you think the Ship's Inn is? (Idea: *A restaurant.*) Who do you think this other animal is? (Ideas: *A cook at the restaurant; a worker at the restaurant.*)

**Page 16.** Where does this part of the story happen? (Idea: *In a crowded restaurant.*)

**Page 17.** What is happening in these illustrations? (Ideas: *A cat is giving Herbie some spaghetti; a bird is carrying a plate of food.*)

**Page 18.** What is happening in these illustrations? (Ideas: *The bird is giving the plate of food to a rabbit; another bird is mixing something in a bowl.*)

**Page 19.** What is happening in these illustrations? (Ideas: *Herbie is taking his hat off and saying something to the bird with the bowl; dogs are carrying cakes and desserts.*)

**Page 20.** What is happening in this illustration? (Ideas: *Herbie is sitting at a table with some other animals; they are eating cake.*) What do you think Herbie is telling the animals? (Idea: *His poem.*)

**Page 21.** What is happening in this illustration? (Ideas: *Someone gave Herbie a big cake; Herbie is thinking of something.*) The word in this think bubble is Lottie. Who do you think Lottie is? (Idea: *Herbie's friend.*) Why do you think Herbie is thinking of Lottie? (Idea: *Because she is home sick.*)

**Page 22.** What is happening in these illustrations? (Ideas: *Herbie is leaving the restaurant; one of the dogs is bringing his cake; Herbie is driving his car.*) Where do you think Herbie is driving? (Idea: *To Lottie's house.*)

**Page 23.** Where is Herbie in this part of the story? (Idea: *At Lottie's house.*) What time of day is it in this part of the story? (Idea: *Night.*) Why do you think Herbie went to Lottie's house at nighttime? (Idea: *To tell her about his evening.*)

**Page 24.** What do you think Herbie and Lottie are talking about? (Ideas: *The poetry contest; the Ship's Inn; the animals he met in the restaurant.*)

It's your turn to ask me some questions. What would you like to know about the story? (Accept questions. If children tell about the pictures or the story instead of ask questions, prompt them to ask a question.) Ask me a why question. Ask me a where question.

### Read the Story Aloud
(Read the story to children with minimal interruptions.)

Tomorrow we will read the story again, and I will ask you some questions.

## Present Target Vocabulary
 Contest

In the story, Herbie enters a poetry contest. **Contest.** Say the word. *Contest.*

**Contest** is a noun. It names a thing. What kind of word is **contest?** *A noun.*

**A contest is a competition to win something.** Say the word that means "a competition to win something." *Contest.*

(Correct any incorrect responses, and repeat the item at the end of the sequence.)

Let's think about some events. I'll tell about some things people are doing. If these people are in a contest, say "contest." If not, don't say anything.

- Jan took a spelling test.
- Abel and Giovanni raced for first place. *Contest.*
- Norm hoped to win the blue ribbon for the blueberry pie he baked. *Contest.*
- Erica and Michael played tag.
- The cleanest classroom wins the award at the end of the week. *Contest.*
- The children danced to hip-hop music in the talent show and won second place. *Contest.*

What noun means "a competition to win something"? *Contest.*

 Grumpy

In the story, the chef was grumpy because his custard was lumpy. **Grumpy.** Say the word. *Grumpy.*

**Grumpy** is a describing word. It tells about a feeling. What kind of word is **grumpy?** *A describing word.*

**Grumpy means grouchy or in a bad mood.** Say the word that means "grouchy or in a bad mood." *Grumpy.* You learned another word that means "grouchy or in a bad mood." What word was it? *Cranky.* Yes, **cranky** and **grumpy** both mean "grouchy or in a bad mood."

Let's think about some situations. I'll tell about a situation. If the situation would make a person grumpy, say "grumpy." If not, don't say anything.

- You worked for hours building a model airplane and the glue didn't hold. As soon as you picked up the model, it fell apart. *Grumpy.*
- You made all As on your report card.
- You thought you understood the math lesson, but failed the quiz. *Grumpy.*
- The cookies you baked burned. *Grumpy.*
- Your mother was very happy that you picked her favorite flowers for her.
- You get a very special present from your grandmother for no reason at all.

What describing word means "grouchy or in a bad mood"? *Grumpy.*

Endless

In the story, when Herbie was trying to get back to Lottie, the road seemed endless. **Endless.** Say the word. *Endless.*

**Endless** is a describing word. It tells more about a noun. What kind of word is **endless?** *A describing word.*

**Endless means having no end.** Say the word that means "having no end." *Endless.*

Let's think about some things that might seem endless. I'll tell about some situations. If the situation could seem endless, say "endless." If not, don't say anything.

- A fun game.
- The night before going to a huge amusement park. *Endless.*

- The last hour of school on a beautiful Friday afternoon when you have plans to go over to your best friend's house to play until dinnertime. *Endless.*
- An interesting book.
- Sitting in time-out. *Endless.*
- Playing a fun game with your family.

What describing word means "having no end"? *Endless.*

 Sweaty

In the story, one of the waitresses introduced herself as "sweaty Betty." **Sweaty.** Say the word. *Sweaty.*

**Sweaty** is a describing word. It tells more about a person. What kind of word is **sweaty?** *A describing word.*

**Sweaty means covered with moisture because you are hot or nervous.** Say the word that means "covered with moisture because you are hot or nervous." *Sweaty.*

Let's think about some activities. I'll tell about some things people are doing. If the things would make a person sweaty, say "sweaty." If not, don't say anything.

- Jamel ran three miles. *Sweaty.*
- Angela sat in the air-conditioned classroom.
- Suki spent all afternoon sitting in the hot sun. *Sweaty.*
- Alex was very nervous about going to the dentist. *Sweaty.*
- Simone walked slowly through the cool woods.
- Austin took a nice long nap in the cool shade of a tree.

What word means "covered with moisture because you are hot or nervous"? *Sweaty.*

### Present Vocabulary Tally Sheet
(See Lesson 1, page 4, for instructions)

### Assign Homework
(Homework Sheet, BLM 30a. See the Introduction for homework instructions.)

**Preparation:** Picture Vocabulary Cards for *contest, grumpy, endless, sweaty.*

### Read and Discuss Story

 (Read the story to children. Ask the following questions at the specified points. Encourage them to use target words in their answers.)

Now I'm going to read *A Cake for Herbie.* When I finish reading each part, I'll ask you some questions.

**Page 1.** Who are the characters in this story? (Idea: *Lottie and Herbie.*) What do Lottie and Herbie do each week? (Idea: *Go shopping for groceries in town.*)

**Page 2.** What did Herbie see at Hawkie's Market? (Idea: *A poster for a poetry contest.*)

**Page 3.** Why did Herbie decide to enter the poetry contest? (Idea: *He wanted to win the cake.*) Does Herbie think he can write a poem? *Yes.*

**Page 4.** What was Lottie saying she thought she heard? (Idea: *The cookies shouting, "Open up, let us out!"*) Did Lottie really hear the cookies shout? (Idea: *No, Herbie was making up a poem.*) What kind of poem did Herbie decide to write? (Idea: *An alphabet poem.*)

An alphabet poem is a poem that has a line or verse for each letter of the alphabet. What kind of poem has a line or verse for each letter of the alphabet? *An alphabet poem.*

**Page 5.** How many days did Herbie have to write his poem? *Three.* What happened when Herbie was thinking? (Idea: *His head got hot.*) Look at the picture. What did Herbie do to cool his head? (Idea: *He put an ice pack on it.*) What did the cold do to Herbie? (Idea: *It made him hungry.*)

**Page 6.** What did Herbie eat? (Idea: *A big bowl of chocolate pudding.*) Did that help Herbie get to work writing his poem? *Yes.* How long did Herbie write? (Ideas: *All night; until dawn; until the next morning.*)

**Page 7.** How far into the alphabet did Herbie get? (Idea: *To the letter K.*) What was wrong with Herbie's verse for the letter **K**? (Idea: *Caramel custard starts with C, not K.*)

Herbie is using something called alliteration in his poem. Say the word alliteration. *Alliteration.* Alliteration is using the same beginning sound for each word in a group of words. What do we call using the same beginning sound in each word in a group of words? *Alliteration.* What words in Herbie's poem use alliteration? (Idea: *Caramel custard.*)

**Page 8.** What happened to Herbie the night before the contest? (Idea: *He had a bad dream.*) What made Herbie feel better about the contest? (Idea: *He knew that Lottie would be there.*)

**Page 9.** What happened to Lottie the night before the contest? (Idea: *She got sick.*) What advice did Lottie give to Herbie? (Idea: *Think of the cake and take a deep breath.*)

**Page 10.** Why do Herbie's knees feel like Jell-O®? (Idea: *He is nervous about the contest.*)

**Page 11.** Who is saying this poem? (Idea: *The bird on the stage.*) What is the bird's poem about? (Idea: *Knowing a gnome.*) What do you think Herbie thinks about this bird's poem?

**Page 12.** Herbie thinks that he is going to win the contest. What vocabulary word have you learned that would describe how he is feeling? *Optimistic.* What is the title of Herbie's poem? *From Herbie's Kitchen A to Z.* What food is the first verse of Herbie's poem about? *Artichokes.* Does Herbie use any alliteration in the first verse? *Yes.* What words? <u>Art</u>ie and <u>art</u>ichokes.

What is the second verse of Herbie's poem about? *The Belly Beast.* Does Herbie use any alliteration in the second verse? *Yes.* What words? <u>Belly Beast.</u> Are there any rhyming words in the second verse? *Yes.* What words? *Beast and least.*

**Page 13.** What is the third verse of Herbie's poem about? *Cookies.* Does the audience like Herbie's poem? *No.*

**Page 14.** How did Herbie feel when the audience started yelling at him? (Ideas: *Sad; upset; embarrassed; frustrated; miserable.*) What

was Herbie looking for when he left the theater? (Idea: *A place to hide.*)

**Page 15.** Who did Herbie run into? (Idea: *A cook from the Ship's Inn.*) Was the cook nice to Herbie? *Yes.*

**Page 16.** Where did the cook say he found Herbie? *Sitting on the curbie.* Is curbie a real word? *No.* Why did the cook say "curbie" instead of "curb"? (Idea: *So it would rhyme with Herbie.*)

**Page 17.** Who did Herbie meet next? *Betty.* What words in this paragraph rhyme? *Sweaty, Betty, and spaghetti.* Why do you think Herbie felt better at the Ship's Inn? (Idea: *The animals there liked making rhymes.*)

**Page 18.** What are some rhyming words on this page? *Griddle and middle; grumpy and lumpy.* What are some words that use alliteration on this page? *Caramel custard.*

**Page 19.** Where did Herbie get the idea for saying "At least there's no mustard in your caramel custard"? (Idea: *He had used a similar line in his poem.*) What are some rhyming words on this page? (Ideas: *Mustard and custard; Gus and us.*)

**Page 20.** What did they want Herbie to tell them? *Another line from his poem.*

**Page 21.** Everyone shouted "Bravo!" How did they feel about Herbie's poem? (Idea: *They liked it.*) What did Herbie get for his poem? *A cake.* Who did Herbie want to tell? *Lottie.*

**Page 22.** How was Herbie feeling after his evening with his new friends? (Ideas: *Excited; happy; more confident; delighted; grateful; proud.*) Why did the road to Lottie's house seem endless to Herbie? (Idea: *He was excited about telling her about his night.*)

**Page 23.** Was Lottie excited to hear about Herbie's night? *Yes.* What do you think Herbie will tell Lottie? (Ideas: *That the audience at the poetry contest didn't like his poem; that he met new friends at the Ship's Inn; that his new friends loved his poem and gave him a cake.*)

## Review Vocabulary

(Display the Picture Vocabulary Cards. Point to each card as you say the word. Ask children to repeat each word after you.) These pictures show **contest, grumpy, endless,** and **sweaty.**

- What word means "grouchy or in a bad mood"? *Grumpy.*
- What noun means "a competition to win something"? *Contest.*
- What word means "covered with moisture from being hot or nervous"? *Sweaty.*
- What word means "having no end"? *Endless.*

## Extend Vocabulary

### ⊚⊶ Contest

In *A Cake for Herbie,* we learned that a **contest** is "a competition to win something." Say the noun that means "a competition to win something." *Contest.*

Raise your hand if you can tell us a sentence that uses **contest** as a noun meaning "a competition to win something." (Call on several children. If they don't use complete sentences, restate their examples as sentences. Have the class repeat the sentences.)

Here's a new way to use the word **contest.** When you use **contest** this way, it is pronounced **con-TEST.**

- James said he would **contest** the judge's decision. Say the sentence.
- The man went to court to **contest** the speeding ticket. Say the sentence.
- The children **contested** the teacher's decision to stay inside for recess. Say the sentence.

**In these sentences, contest is a verb that means to fight or argue for something.** Raise your hand if you can tell us a sentence that uses **contest** as a verb meaning "to fight or argue for something." (Call on several children. If they don't use complete sentences, restate their examples as sentences. Have the class repeat the sentences.)

### Present Expanded Target Vocabulary
### ⊚⊶ Disappointed

In this story, Herbie was disappointed because the audience at the poetry contest did not

like his poem. **Disappointed.** Say the word. *Disappointed.*

**Disappointed** is a describing word. It tells more about how a person is feeling. What kind of word is **disappointed**? *A describing word.*

**Disappointed means feeling let down because you failed to do something.** Say the word that means "feeling let down because you failed to do something." *Disappointed.*

I'll tell about some situations. If the people in these situations are disappointed, say "disappointed." If not, don't say anything.

- Andrea did well on her spelling test.
- Leela missed the free throw. *Disappointed.*
- Jacob did not pass his math test and had to take it again *Disappointed.*
- Raymond scored a goal in his soccer game.
- The man did not get a raise at work. *Disappointed.*
- The cat had kittens.

What word means "feeling let down because you failed to do something"? *Disappointed.*

### ⊚⊶ Creative

Herbie liked to make up rhymes and poems. He was very creative. **Creative.** Say the word. *Creative.*

**Creative** is a describing word. It tells more about a person. What kind of word is **creative**? *A describing word.*

**Creative means able to make or do something with imagination.** Say the word that means "able to make or do something with imagination." *Creative.*

I'll tell about some things people do. If the people are doing something creative, say "creative." If not, don't say anything.

- Follow a recipe.
- Make up a new recipe for cookies. *Creative.*
- Write a poem. *Creative.*
- Read a book.
- Paint a picture. *Creative.*

What word means "able to make or do something with imagination"? *Creative.*

**Preparation:** Activity Sheet,
BLM 30b.

## Play Poetic Definitions

Today you'll play Poetic Definitions. I'll say a little poem that uses the meaning of one of our vocabulary words. If you can tell me the word that the poem is using, you will win one point. If you can't tell me, I get the point. Let's think about the six words we have learned: **contest, grumpy, endless, sweaty, disappointed,** and **creative.** (Display the Picture Vocabulary Cards.)

Let's practice. I ran a race. I ran so fast. I ran like the wind. But he ran right past! What vocabulary word is described in this poem? *Contest.*

Now you're ready to play the game. (Draw a T-chart on the board for keeping score. Children earn one point for each correct answer. If they make an error, correct them as you normally would, and record one point for yourself. Repeat missed words at the end of the game.)

- I don't think this grade is right. I think it's wrong. I studied hard. I studied long. I studied half the night. What vocabulary word can be used to describe what this student is doing about his grade? *Contesting.*
- I'm cranky. I'm tired. I'm in a bad mood. I'm crabby. I'm grouchy. I don't want to be good. What vocabulary word is described by this poem? *Grumpy.*
- This night is so long. I want it to be day. I can't wait until tomorrow, when I can go out and play. What vocabulary word can be used to describe the night? *Endless.*
- I ran so far. I ran so fast. I ran up the hill and back at last. What vocabulary word describes how this person is probably feeling now? *Sweaty.*
- I thought I could. I thought I should. Make that final goal. I feel so bad. I feel so sad. I didn't make the goal. What vocabulary word describes how this soccer player is feeling? *Disappointed.*

- First I take the paint and rub it all around. Then I sprinkle glitter. Some gets on the ground. I take a couple of buttons and glue them on for eyes. Then my picture's done. What is it? A surprise! What vocabulary word is described in this poem? *Creative.*

(Count the points and declare a winner.) You did a great job of playing Poetic Definitions.

## Complete the Activity Sheet

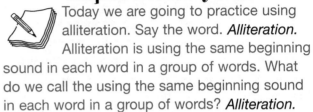

Today we are going to practice using alliteration. Say the word. *Alliteration.* Alliteration is using the same beginning sound in each word in a group of words. What do we call the using the same beginning sound in each word in a group of words? *Alliteration.*

A sample of alliteration is: Suzie sells salmon at the store. Say that sentence. *Suzie sells salmon at the store.* What sound is repeated in the sentence? *Ssss.*

(Distribute copies of BLM 30b to children.) Today you are going to think of words that start with the same sound to describe a thing.

Touch Item 1. My turn to read. Cool, calico cat. Your turn to read the words. *Cool, calico cat.* What sound is repeated at the beginning of each of these words? *C.*

Touch each word as we read it. The next word is bird. What word? *Bird.* (Repeat for each word in the list.)

Touch item 2. What word do we need to describe in item 2? *Bird.* What sound do you hear at the beginning of bird? *B.* Can you think of any words that begin with the **b** sound and that could describe a bird? (List children's responses on the board. Ideas: *Beautiful; blue; brilliant; bobbing; bad; brown; black.*) Copy two words that start with the **b** sound onto the lines for item 2.

(Repeat the process for the remaining items.)

You did a great job of using alliteration.

**Preparation:** Post class poems that were written in previous weeks.

## Poetry Review

This is the last week of our poetry unit. We are going to have a poetry contest tomorrow. For the poetry contest, you will each write your own poem. You have learned how to write four different kinds of poems. You have learned to write a two-word poem, an acrostic poem, a diamante poem, and a concrete poem. (Point to each kind of class poem. For each poem ask:) What kind of poem is this?

(Point to the acrostic poem.) The first kind of poem we wrote was an acrostic poem. In an acrostic poem, you use the letters of a word to start each line. What kind of poem uses a letter of the word to start each line? *An acrostic poem.* Let's read our acrostic poem together. (Read the poem with children.)

(Point to the two-word poem.) The second kind of poem we wrote was a two-word poem. In a two-word poem, each line contains two words that describe the subject of the poem. What kind of poem uses two words on each line to describe the subject of the poem? *A two-word poem.* Let's read our two-word poem together. (Read the poem with children.)

(Point to the diamante poem.) The third kind of poem we wrote was a diamante poem. In a diamante poem, you use certain kinds of words for each line of the poem. The poem ends up in the shape of a diamond when it is finished. What kind of poem uses certain kinds of words in each line and ends up in the shape of a diamond? *A diamante poem.* Let's read our diamante poem together. (Read the poem with children.)

(Point to the concrete poem.) The fourth kind of poem we wrote was a concrete poem. In a concrete poem, you write your words around the outside outline of a shape. What kind of poem has words written around the outside outline of a shape? *A concrete poem.* Let's read our concrete poem together. (Read the poem with children.)

Tomorrow you will write your own poem. Your poem can be an acrostic, a two-word poem, a diamante poem, or a concrete poem. I will give you ideas about what to write about or you may choose your own subject.

## Play Poetic Definitions (Cumulative Review)

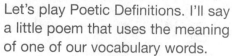

Let's play Poetic Definitions. I'll say a little poem that uses the meaning of one of our vocabulary words. If you can tell me the word that the poem is describing, you will win one point. If you can't tell me, I get the point. Let's think about the six words we have learned: **contest, grumpy, endless, sweaty, disappointed,** and **creative.** (Display the Picture Vocbulary Cards.)

Let's practice. I would like to say. That I do not think this is the way. You know that I am right. So let's not have a fight. What vocabulary word is being described in this poem? *Contest.*

☐ Now you're ready to play the game. (Draw a T-chart on the board for keeping score. Children earn one point for each correct answer. If they make an error, correct them as you normally would, and record one point for yourself. Repeat missed words at the end of the game.)

- I want a prize. It's no surprise. I want to win. Then I will grin. What vocabulary word is described in this poem? *Contest.*
- This road is bumpy. This bed is lumpy. It's making me mad. I'm feeling bad. What vocabulary word is described by this poem? *Grumpy.*
- I love this book. It makes me chuckle. It's all it took to make me laugh. What vocabulary word describes this book? *Humorous.*
- I cannot stand this wait. It's getting late. The day goes on and on. I must get out to play. What vocabulary word can be used to describe the day? *Endless.*
- This is horrible. I feel so terrible. I thought I got a win. Now, I have not. What vocabulary word describes how this person is feeling? *Disappointed.*
- This song is too long. Rick will write a new song that is not so long. It will be the one

for having fun. What vocabulary word is described in this poem? *Creative.*

- The snail's trail was slippery and wet. He thought to himself, "I'll get there yet!" What vocabulary word describes the snail's trail? *Slimy.*
- I give you this advice. If you are far too active, you will get his moisture on you yet. What vocabulary word describes how this person is probably feeling now? *Sweaty.*
- I told you once before. This room would get a very low score. Things all over is not very clever. Such a mess will help you never! What vocabulary word would describe this room? *Chaos.*

(Count the points, and declare a winner.) You did a great job of playing Poetic Definitions.

---

## DAY 5

**Preparation:** Quiz Answer Sheet, BLM B.

Make copies of the poetry frames for children to choose from for the poetry contest.

### Assess Vocabulary

 (Give each child a copy of the Quiz Answer Sheet, BLM B.)

Today you're going to have a True or False quiz. When you do the True or False quiz, it shows me how well you know the hard words you are learning.

If I say something that is true, circle the word **true.** What will you do if I say something that is true? *Circle the word* true.

If I say something that is false, circle the word **false.** What will you do if I say something that is false? *Circle the word* false.

Listen carefully to each item that I say. Don't let me trick you!

Item 1: If you **compete** against someone to see who is the best speller, you are having a spelling **contest.** (*True.*)

Item 2: A person who can make up really good poems is not at all **creative.** (*False.*)

Item 3: If you argue with your sister, you are having a **quarrel.** (*True.*)

Item 4: **Grumpy** and **cranky** both mean happy and in a good mood. (*False.*)

Item 5: When you are excited about doing something, the time you have to wait might seem **endless.** (*True.*)

Item 6: A person who wins a very long race has had a **victory.** (*True.*)

Item 7: If you argue with your mother about your bedtime, you are **contesting** your bedtime. (*True.*)

Item 8: Winning the soccer game would probably make you feel **disappointed.** (*False.*)

Item 9: If you are hot or nervous, you might get **sweaty.** (*True.*)

Item 10: A place you go to buy food and other things is called a **market.** (*True.*)

You did a great job completing your quiz!

(Score children's work. A child must score 9 out of 10 to be at mastery level. If a child does not achieve mastery, insert the missed words as additional items in the games in next week's lessons. Retest those children individually for the missed items before they take the next mastery test.)

**Preparation:** Display the four kinds of poems written in weeks 26–29.

### Independent Writing–Poetry Contest

Yesterday we reviewed the four kinds of poems we have written during our poetry unit. Let's name them again. (Point to each poem in turn and say:) What kind of poem is this?

Today you are going to write a poem for the poetry contest. You can write any kind of poem that you have learned about.

(Under the class acrostic poem, write *friend's name.*) If you choose to write an acrostic poem, you can write about one of your friends. What can you write an acrostic poem about? *A friend.* Write their name down the side of your paper and write one line for each letter of their name.

You can choose to write about something else if you wish.

(Under the class two-word poem, write *My pet*.) If you choose to write a two-word poem, you can write about your pet or a pet that you would like to have. What can you write a two-word poem about? (Ideas: *My pet or a pet that I would like to have.*) Write two words on each line about your pet or the pet that you would like to have. You will write ten pairs of words and then draw ten pictures. How many pairs of words and pictures will you make? *Ten.* You can choose to write about something else if you wish.

(Under the class diamante poem, write *Night and Day*.) If you choose to write a diamante poem, you can write about night and day. What can you write a diamante poem about? *Night and day.* You need to read to see what kinds of words go on each line. You can choose to write about something else if you wish.

(Under the class concrete poem, write *Flowers*.) If you choose to write a concrete poem, you can write about flowers. What can you write a concrete poem about? *Flowers.* A concrete poem does not have to rhyme. You can choose to write about something else if you wish.

(Allow children time to write and edit a draft of their poems on a poetry frame. Circulate among children, offering support as needed.)

(When children finish the editing process, give them a fresh frame on which to copy their poem. Have children share their poems with the class.)

You did a great job writing poems for the poetry contest. You are all winners! (You may wish to make up an award certificate for each child as he or she presents his or her poem to the class.)

## Extensions

### Read a Story as a Reward

(Read *A Cake for Herbie* or another poetry book. Display a number of books of poetry. Ask children to choose which one they would like you to read.)

### Introduce the Super Words Center

(Remove the words from previous lessons from the word containers. Place the Picture Vocabulary Cards from Weeks 26–30 in the containers. Show children the word container. If children need more guidance in how to work in the Super Words Center, role-play with two to three children as a demonstration.)

(**Note:** You may wish to leave the word *muck* out of the game cards or to caution children about using rhyming words that are polite.)

You will play a game called *Rhyme Time* in the Super Words Center.

Let's think about how we work with our words in the Super Words Center.

You will work with a partner in the Super Words Center. Whom will you work with? *A partner.*

First you will draw a word out of the container. What do you do first? (Idea: *Draw a word out of the container.*) Show your partner the word card.

Next you will tell your partner the word that the card shows. What do you do next? *Tell my partner the word that the card shows.*

If you say the correct word, you get a point. What do you get if you say the correct word? *A point.*

Next you will say a word that rhymes with the word on the word card. What will you do next? *Say a word that rhymes.*

If you can say a word that rhymes with the word on the card, you get another point. What do you get if you can say a word that rhymes with the word on the card? *Another point.*

After you have said the word and said a word that rhymes, give your partner a turn. What do you do next? *Give my partner a turn.*

Appendices

# Appendices

# Vocabulary Tally Sheet

| Picture Vocabulary Card | Weekly Tally | Picture Vocabulary Card | Weekly Tally |
|---|---|---|---|
| Picture Vocabulary Card | Weekly Tally | Picture Vocabulary Card | Weekly Tally |
| Picture Vocabulary Card | Weekly Tally | Picture Vocabulary Card | Weekly Tally |

# Quiz Answer Sheet

Name: _____ Date: _____

Week: _____ Score: _____

## Mastery Achieved:

1. True        False

2. True        False

3. True        False

4. True        False

5. True        False

6. True        False

7. True        False

8. True        False

9. True        False

10. True        False

## Sharing What You've Learned at School

**Note:** Children are not expected to be able to read the words. They are for your information.

**DAY 1:** (Cut the Picture Vocabulary Cards apart. Place the picture cards for *festival, souvenir, concentrated,* and *introduce* in a container or small plastic bag.) (Show the child each picture card.) **What word does the picture show?** (Idea: *The picture shows a child holding a souvenir.*)

**Tell me what you know about this word.** (You may wish to share what you know about the word with the child as well.)

**DAY 2:** (Add in 2 new words, *confident* and *different.* Repeat procedure from Day 1.) **Tell me anything more that you know about this word.**

**DAY 3:** *Choosing* Game (Round One)
**Let's play the *Choosing* game that you learned at school. I'll say sentences with two of the words you know in them. You have to choose the correct word for the sentence. If you choose correctly, you will win one point. If you don't choose correctly, I get the point.**

- If you mixed water with the can of orange juice, was the orange juice **concentrated** or a **souvenir?** *Concentrated.*
- If you went to a special party and ate great Japanese food, listened to the Japanese drums, and watched the ladies do a Bon dance, were you at a **souvenir** or a **festival?** *A festival.*
- When you first meet someone, do you **festival** or **introduce** yourself? *Introduce.*
- If you thought only about doing a somersault, would you have **concentrated** or **introduced?** *Concentrated.*
- When you tell someone your name, do you **introduce** yourself or **concentrate?** *Introduce.*
- If you bought something small to help you remember your trip to New York City, did you buy a **souvenir** or a **festival?** *A souvenir.*

(If the child is enjoying this game, you may wish to add additional examples.)

**DAY 4:** *Choosing* Game (Round Two)
(Add the last two words, *confident* and *different,* to the bag or container. Repeat procedure from Day 3.)

The boys were _____ to her.

Suki _____ for the class.

_____ wanted to wear her _____ .

Suki _____ all the way home.

Suki made a new _____ .

Everyone _____ for Suki.

ingredients

recipe

special

customers

decision

proud

## Sharing What You've Learned at School

**Note:** Children are not expected to be able to read the words. They are for your information.

**DAY 1:** (Cut the Picture Vocabulary Cards apart. Place the picture cards for *ingredients, recipe, special,* and *customers* in a container or small plastic bag.) (Show the child each picture card.) **What word does the picture show?** (Idea: *The picture shows customers at a checkout.*)
**Tell me what you know about this word.** (You may wish to share what you know about the word with the child as well.)

**DAY 2:** (Add in 2 new words, *decision* and *proud.* Repeat procedure from Day 1.) **Tell me anything more that you know about this word.**

**DAY 3:** *Choosing* **Game (Round One)**
Let's play the *Choosing* game that you learned at school. I'll say sentences with two of the words you know in them. You have to choose the correct word for the sentence. If you choose correctly, you will win one point. If you don't choose correctly, I get the point.

- If you went to the store and the price of bananas was less than it was yesterday, are the bananas **proud** or on **special?** *On special.*
- Is the first day of school a **special** day or a **customer?** *Special.*
- If your mom asks you to go to the corner store to buy milk, are you an **ingredient** or a **customer?** *A customer.*
- If you read the instructions to make Swedish flatbread, did you read the **recipe** or the **customers?** *The recipe.*
- If you wore your best shoes to school, did you wear your **special** shoes or your **proud** shoes? *Special.*
- If you need onions, ground beef, an egg, and breadcrumbs to make a meatloaf, are those items the **recipes** or the **ingredients?** *The ingredients.*

(If the child is enjoying this game, you may wish to add additional examples.)

**DAY 4:** *Choosing* **Game (Round Two)**
(Add the last two words, *decision* and *proud,* to the bag or container. Repeat procedure from Day 3.)

Maybe I'll bring _____
_____.

Maybe I'll bring _____
_____.

Maybe I'll bring _____
_____.

Pablo asked, "What should I bring to _____.

I know, I'll bring _____
_____.

Maybe I'll bring _____
_____.

complained

untidy

sound

amazed

uncooperative

disgusting

## Sharing What You've Learned at School

**Note:** Children are not expected to be able to read the words. They are for your information.

**DAY 1:** (Cut the Picture Vocabulary Cards apart. Place the picture cards for *complained, untidy, sound,* and *amazed* in a container or small plastic bag.)
(Show the child each picture card.) **What word does the picture show?** (Idea: *The picture shows someone who is amazed.*)
**Tell me what you know about this word.** (You may wish to share what you know about the word with the child as well.)

**DAY 2:** (Add in 2 new words, *uncooperative* and *disgusting.* Repeat procedure from Day 1.) **Tell me anything more that you know about this word.**

**DAY 3:** *Choosing* Game (Round One)
**Let's play the *Choosing* game that you learned at school. I'll say sentences with two of the words you know in them. You have to choose the correct word for the sentence. If you choose correctly, you will win one point. If you don't choose correctly, I get the point.**

- **If your printing is messy and hard to read, is it untidy or sound?** *Untidy.*
- **If you went to the doctor and told her you were unhappy about your sore arm, would you have complained or amazed?** *Complained.*
- **If your puppy was lying on the mat sleeping and he didn't wake up when you called him, would he be untidy or sound asleep?** *Sound asleep.*
- **If your room looked like Christopher's, would your room be sound or untidy?** *Untidy.*
- **If you heard the rain on the roof, would you have heard a sound or an untidy?** *A sound.*
- **If you saw an ant that could jump ten times its body length, would you be sound asleep or amazed?** *Amazed.*

(If the child is enjoying this game, you may wish to add additional examples.)

**DAY 4:** *Choosing* Game (Round Two)
(Add the last two words, *uncooperative* and *disgusting,* to the bag or container. Repeat procedure from Day 3.)

_____
thought they might die.

_____ said he
would get his people to help.

Christopher decided to
_____.

The cockroaches spelled
_____.

Christopher would not
_____.

The last cockroach went away
when _____.

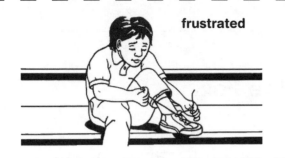

frustrated

rascal

horrible

sly

terrified

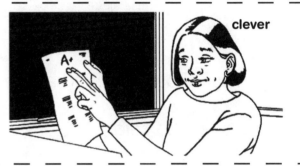

clever

## Sharing What You've Learned at School

**Note:** Children are not expected to be able to read the words. They are for your information.

**DAY 1:** (Cut the Picture Vocabulary Cards apart. Place the picture cards for *sly, rascal, terrified,* and *horrible* in a container or small plastic bag.)
(Show the child each picture card.) **What word does the picture show?** (Idea: *The picture shows someone who is terrified.*)
**Tell me what you know about this word.** (You may wish to share what you know about the word with the child as well.)

**DAY 2:** (Add in 2 new words, *clever* and *frustrated.* Repeat procedure from Day 1.) **Tell me anything more that you know about this word.**

**DAY 3:** *Whoopsy!* **(Round One)**
**Let's play the** *Whoopsy!* **game that you learned at school. I'll say sentences using words you learned. If the word doesn't fit in the sentence, say "Whoopsy!" Then I'll ask you to say a sentence where the word fits. If you can do it, you get a point. If you can't do it, I get the point. If the word I use fits the sentence, don't say anything.**

- **Angelina was terrified by...the beautiful, sunny day.** *Whoopsy!* **Say the beginning of the sentence again.** *Angelina was terrified by.* **Can you finish the sentence?** (Idea: *Angelina was terrified by the thunder and lightning.*)
- **It was horrible when...all my friends could come to my party.** *Whoopsy!* **Say the beginning of the sentence again.** *It was horrible when.* **Can you finish the sentence?** (Idea: *It was horrible when none of my friends could come to my party.*)
- **You are a rascal if...you lie and trick to get your own way.**
- **The wolf was sly when...he couldn't think of a way to trick the three little pigs.** *Whoopsy!* **Say the beginning of the sentence again.** *The wolf was sly when.* **Can you finish the sentence?** (Idea: *The wolf was sly when he thought of a way to trick the three little pigs.*)

(If the child is enjoying this game, you may wish to add additional examples.)

**DAY 4:** *Whoopsy!* **(Round Two)**
(Add the last two words, *clever* and *frustrated,* to the bag or container. Repeat procedure from Day 3.)

Name _____

# Flossie & the Fox

Flossie had lots of fun tricking the fox. Tell what other animals she said the fox was like.

When Flossie touched the fox's fur she said _____ .

When Flossie looked at the fox's pointed nose, she said

_____ .

When Flossie looked at the fox's yellow eyes and sharp

claws, she said _____

_____ .

When Flossie looked at the fox's bushy tail, she said

_____ .

When the fox said he had sharp teeth and could run very

fast, Flossie said _____ .

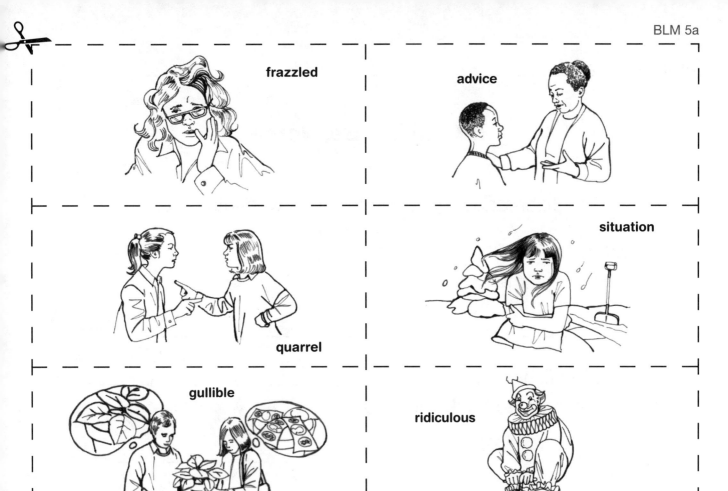

**frazzled**

**advice**

**quarrel**

**situation**

**gullible**

**ridiculous**

## Sharing What You've Learned at School

**Note:** Children are not expected to be able to read the words. They are for your information.

**DAY 1:** (Cut the Picture Vocabulary Cards apart. Place the picture cards for *frazzled, advice, quarrel,* and *situation* in a container or small plastic bag.) (Show the child each picture card.) **What word does the picture show?** (Idea: *The picture shows someone who is frazzled.*)
**Tell me what you know about this word.**

**DAY 2:** (Add in 2 new words, *gullible* and *ridiculous.* Repeat procedure from Day 1.) **Tell me anything more that you know about this word.**

**DAY 3:** *Whoopsy!* (Round One)
**Let's play the *Whoopsy!* game that you learned at school. I'll say sentences using words you learned. If the word doesn't fit in the sentence, say "Whoopsy!" Then I'll ask you to say a sentence where the word fits. If you can do it, you get a point. If you can't do it, I get the point. If the word I use fits the sentence, don't say anything.**

• **Leah and Tomas quarreled when...they agreed to do the dishes together.** *Whoopsy!* **Say the beginning of the sentence again.** *Leah and Tomas quarreled when.* **Can you finish the sentence?** (Idea: *Leah and Toby quarreled when they couldn't*

decide who would wash and who would dry the dishes.)

• **It was a good situation when...Grandpa lost his car keys.** *Whoopsy!* **Say the beginning of the sentence again.** *It was a good situation when.* **Can you finish the sentence?** (Idea: *It was a good situation when Grandpa found his car keys.*)

• **There was a big quarrel when...everyone wanted to play the same game.** *Whoopsy!* **Say the beginning of the sentence again.** *There was a big quarrel when.* **Can you finish the sentence?** (Idea: *There was a big quarrel when everyone wanted to play a different game.*)

• **I was frazzled when...everything was quiet and calm.** *Whoopsy!* **Say the beginning of the sentence again.** *I was frazzled when.* **Can you finish the sentence?** (Idea: *I was frazzled when everything was noisy and confused.*)

• **I followed my mom's advice when...I didn't do what she suggested.** *Whoopsy!* **Say the beginning of the sentence again.** *I followed my mom's advice when.* **Can you finish the sentence?** (Idea: *I followed my mom's advice when I did what she suggested.*)

**DAY 4:** *Whoopsy!* (Round Two)
(Add the last two words, *gullible* and *ridiculous,* to the bag or container. Repeat procedure from Day 3.)

*Appendix*  **9**

Name _____

# It Couldn't Be Worse!

The fishmonger gave the farmer's wife lots of advice.

First, he said _____ .
When she came back she said

_____ .

Next, the fishmonger said _____ .
When she came back she said

_____ .

Next, he said _____ .
When she came back she said

_____ .

Next, the fishmonger said _____ .
When she came back she said

_____ .

Next, the fishmonger said _____ .
When she came back she said

_____ .

Finally, the fishmonger said _____ .
When the farmer's wife came back she said

_____ .

rude

tease

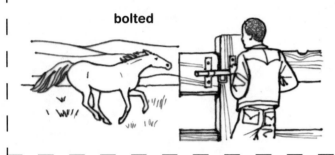

bolted

perseverance

reluctant

braggart

## Sharing What You've Learned at School

**Note:** Children are not expected to be able to read the words. They are for your information.

**DAY 1:** (Cut the Picture Vocabulary Cards apart. Place the picture cards for *rude, tease, bolted,* and *perseverance* in a container or small plastic bag.) (Show the child each picture card.) **What word does the picture show?** (Idea: *The picture shows someone who is rude.*)
**Tell me what you know about this word.**

**DAY 2:** (Add in 2 new words, *reluctant* and *braggart.* Repeat procedure from Day 1.) **Tell me anything more that you know about this word.**

**DAY 3:** *Whoopsy!* **(Round One)**
**Let's play the *Whoopsy!* game that you learned at school. I'll say sentences using words you learned. If the word doesn't fit in the sentence, say "Whoopsy!" Then I'll ask you to say a sentence where the word fits. If you can do it, you get a point. If you can't do it, I get the point. If the word I use fits the sentence, don't say anything.**

- **People tease you when...they say nice things to you.** *Whoopsy!* **Say the beginning of the sentence.** *People tease you when.* **Can you finish the sentence?** (Idea: *People tease you when they say mean things to you.*)

- **The dog bolted after the cat when...it never moved from the porch.** *Whoopsy!* **Say the beginning of the sentence.** *The dog bolted after the cat when.* **Can you finish the sentence?** Idea: *The dog bolted after the cat when it chased the cat off the porch.*

- **My sister bolted the door when...she left the door unlocked.** *Whoopsy!* **Say the beginning of the sentence.** *My sister bolted the door when.* **Can you finish the sentence?** (Idea: *My sister bolted the door when she put on the lock.*)

- **Teresa showed perseverance when...she gave up after she got one wrong answer.** *Whoopsy!* **Say the beginning of the sentence.** *Teresa showed perseverance when.* **Can you finish the sentence?** (Idea: *Teresa showed perseverance when she refused to give up.*)

- **The clerk in the store was rude when...she asked if she could help us.** *Whoopsy!* **Say the beginning of the sentence.** *The clerk in the store was rude when.* **Can you finish the sentence?** (Idea: *The clerk in the store was rude when she talked to her friends instead of helping us.*)

**DAY 4:** *Whoopsy!* **(Round Two)**
(Add the last two words, *reluctant* and *braggart,* to the bag or container. Repeat procedure from Day 3.)

Name _____

# The Tortoise and the Hare

Tortoise                                          Hare

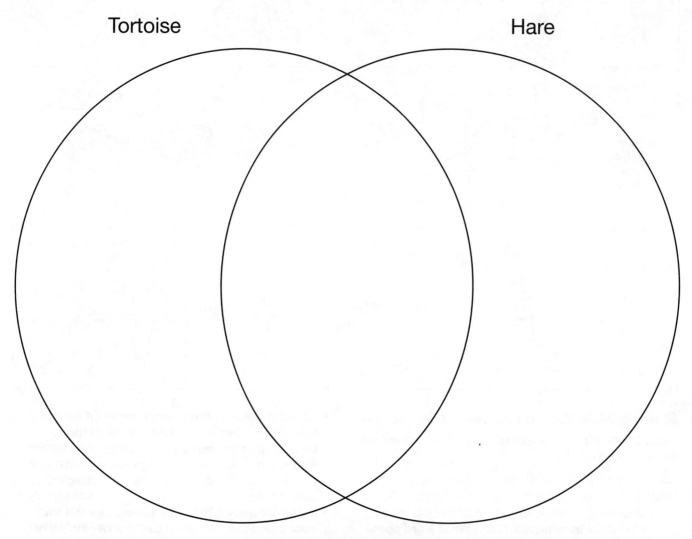

## Word Bank

| friendly | animal | went in a race | stopped to visit Bear |
|---|---|---|---|
| rude | reluctant | learned a lesson | trained for the race |
| talked | flashy | did things slowly | lost the race |
| quiet | braggart | did things quickly | won the race |

perseverance

suspicious

invisible

steep

determined

contented

## Sharing What You've Learned at School

**Note:** Children are not expected to be able to read the words. They are for your information.

**DAY 1:** (Cut the Picture Vocabulary Cards apart. Place the picture cards for *hullabaloo, suspicious, invisible,* and *steep* in a container or small plastic bag.) (Show the child each picture card.) **What word does the picture show?** (Idea: *The picture shows a hullabaloo.*) **Tell me what you know about this word.**

**DAY 2:** (Add in 2 new words, *determined* and *contented*. Repeat procedure from Day 1.) **Tell me anything more that you know about this word.**

**DAY 3:** *Whoopsy!* **(Round One)**
**Let's play the *Whoopsy!* Game that you learned at school. I'll say sentences using words you learned. If the word doesn't fit in the sentence, say "Whoopsy!" Then I'll ask you to say a sentence where the word fits. If you can do it, you get a point. If you can't do it, I get the point. If the word I use fits the sentence, don't say anything.**

- **Gabriel was suspicious when...his best friend talked to him after school.** *Whoopsy!* **Say the beginning of the sentence.** *Gabriel was suspicious when.* **Can you finish the sentence?** (Idea: *Gabriel was suspicious when a stranger talked to him after school.*)

- **When we climbed the steep hill...we had lots of energy left.** *Whoopsy!* **Say the beginning of the sentence.** *When we climbed the steep hill.* **Can you finish the sentence?** (Idea: *When we climbed the steep hill we were tired and out of breath.*)

- **I steeped the tea when...I put the teabag in the cupboard.** *Whoopsy!* **Say the beginning of the sentence.** *I steeped the tea when.* **Can you finish the sentence?** (Idea: *I steeped the tea when I put the teabag in the boiling water.*)

- **There was a hullabaloo in the gym when... everyone was standing still listening to the teacher.** *Whoopsy!* **Say the beginning of the sentence.** *There was a hullabaloo in the gym when.* **Can you finish the sentence?** (Idea: *There was a hullabaloo in the gym when the children were shouting and running around.*)

- **Air is invisible because...you can see it.** *Whoopsy!* **Say the beginning of the sentence.** *Air is invisible because.* **Can you finish the sentence?** (Idea: *Air is invisible because you can't see it.*)

(If the child is enjoying this game, you may wish to add additional examples.)

**DAY 4:** *Whoopsy!* **(Round Two)**
(Add the last two words, *determined* and *contented,* to the bag or container. Repeat procedure from Day 3.)

*Appendix* **13**

Name _____

# The Three Little Javelinas

Third Little Javelina                                        Coyote

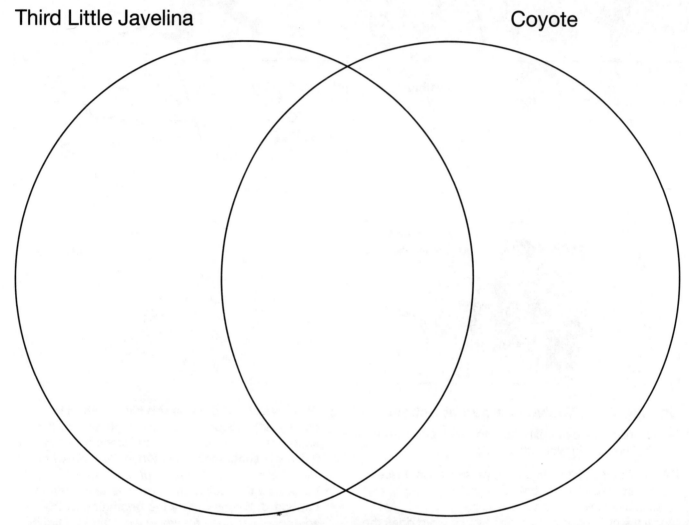

## Word Bank

| neckerchief | animal | used tricks | has two brothers |
|---|---|---|---|
| determined | boy (male) | got burned | lived happily ever after |
| clever | sly | lived in the desert | built an adobe house |
| polite | girl (female) | howls at night | has a sun umbrella |

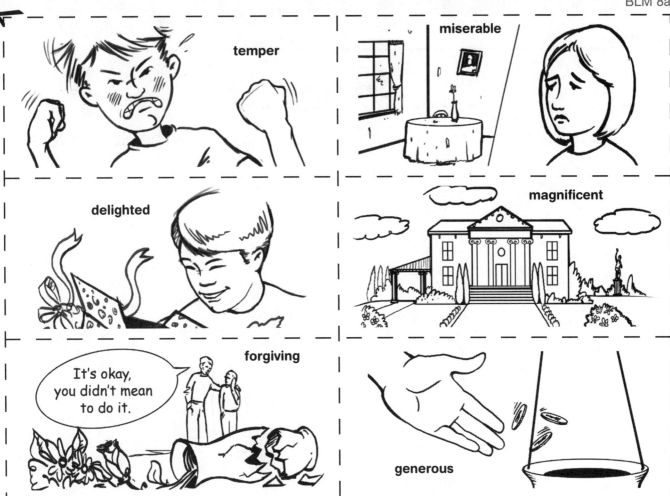

## Sharing What You've Learned at School

**Note:** The children are not expected to be able to read the words. They are for your information.

**DAY 1:** (Cut the Picture Vocabulary Cards apart. Place the picture cards for *temper, miserable, delighted* and *magnificent* in a container or small plastic bag.) (Show the child each picture card.) **What word does the picture show?** (Idea: *The picture shows someone who is delighted.*)
**Tell me what you know about this word.**

**DAY 2:** (Add in 2 new words, *forgiving* and *generous.* Repeat procedure from Day 1.) **Tell me anything more that you know about this word.**

**DAY 3:** *Chew the Fat* (Round One)
**Let's play the *Chew the Fat* game that you learned at school. I'll say sentences with your vocabulary words in them. If I use the word correctly, say "Well done!" If I use the word incorrectly, say "Chew the fat." Then I'll ask you to finish the sentence so that it makes sense.**

- **I know Wyatt has a bad temper because . . . he is always calm and contented.** *Chew the fat.* **I know Wyatt has a bad temper because. How can we finish the sentence so it makes sense?** (Idea: *He gets irritated and angry very quickly.*) **Let's say the sentence together.** *I know Wyatt has a bad temper because he gets irritated and angry very quickly.*

- **It was a miserable day because . . . the sun was shining and the air was warm.** *Chew the fat.* **It was a miserable day because. How can we finish the sentence so it makes sense?** (Idea: *It was dark and cold.*) **Let's say the sentence together.** *It was a miserable day because it was dark and cold.*

- **Annette's mom felt miserable because . . . she was healthy and full of energy.** *Chew the fat.* **Annette's mom felt miserable because. How can we finish the sentence so it makes sense?** (Ideas: *She was sick.*) **Let's say the sentence together.** *Annette's mom felt miserable because she was sick.*

- **Rick was delighted because . . . everyone enjoyed his poem.** *Well done!*

- **Her clothes were magnificent because . . . they were plain and ordinary.** *Chew the fat.* **Her clothes were magnificent because. How can we finish the sentence so it makes sense?** (Idea: *They were very beautiful to look at.*) **Let's say the sentence together.** *Her clothes were magnificent because they were very beautiful to look at.*

**DAY 4:** *Chew the Fat* (Round Two)
(Add the last two words, *forgiving* and *generous,* to the bag or container. Repeat procedure from Day 3.)

Name _____

# Cinderella

Cinderella                       The Stepsisters

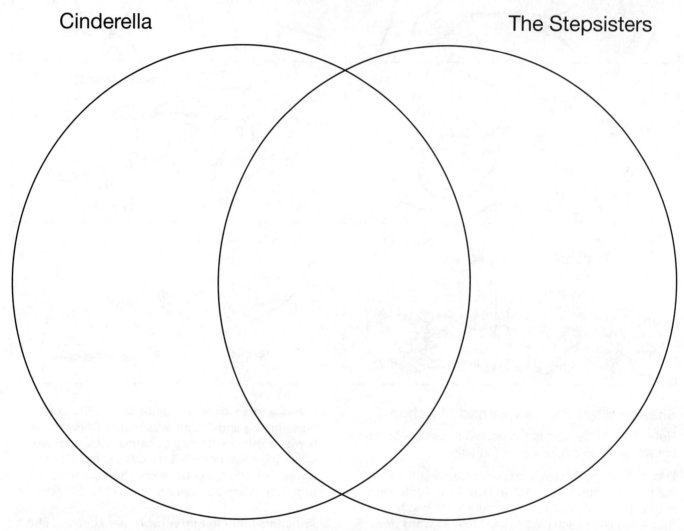

## Word Bank

| good | got married | went to the ball | had a fairy godmother |
|------|-------------|------------------|------------------------|
| mean | selfish | begged forgiveness | lived at the palace |
| rude | beautiful | married the prince | made fun of someone |
| sweet | girl | sat in the cinders | had a beautiful gown |

remarkable

precious

notice

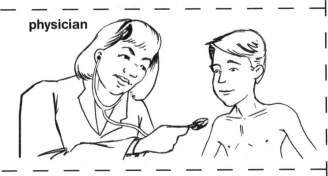

physician

grateful

captive

## Sharing What You've Learned at School

**Note:** The children are not expected to be able to read the words. They are for your information.

**DAY 1:** (Cut the Picture Vocabulary Cards apart. Place the picture cards for *remarkable, precious, notice,* and *physician* in a container or small plastic bag.) (Show the child each picture card.) **What word does the picture show?** (Idea: *The picture shows a physician.*)
**Tell me what you know about this word.**

**DAY 2:** (Add in 2 new words, *grateful* and *captive.* Repeat procedure from Day 1.) **Tell me anything more that you know about this word.**

**DAY 3:** *Chew the Fat* (Round One)
**Let's play the *Chew the Fat* game that you learned at school. I'll say sentences with your vocabulary words in them. If I use the word correctly, say "Well done!" If I use the word incorrectly, say "Chew the fat." Then I'll ask you to finish the sentence so that it makes sense.**

- **Although Lisa is blind, she is remarkable because . . . she can't read.** *Chew the fat.* **Although Lisa is blind, she is remarkable because. How can we finish the sentence so it makes sense?** (Idea: *She can read with her fingers.*)

Let's say the sentence together. *Although Lisa is blind, she is remarkable because she can read with her fingers.*
- **Lorinda noticed the black clouds when . . . she didn't see them.** *Chew the fat.* **Lorinda noticed the black clouds when. How can we finish the sentence so it makes sense?** (Idea: *She saw them coming closer.*) **Let's say the sentence together.** *Lorinda noticed the black clouds when she saw them coming closer.*
- **Jackson's model of a Spitfire airplane was precious because . . . it was the first one he'd ever made.** *Well done!*
- **Enrique brought home a notice when . . . he gave the letter to his dad.** *Well done!*
- **Derrick's mom is a physician because . . . she sells things in a store.** *Chew the fat.* **Derrick's mom is a physician because. How can we finish the sentence so it makes sense?** (Ideas: *She helps sick people get well.*) **Let's say the sentence together.** *Derrick's mom is a physician because she helps sick people get well.*

(If the child is enjoying this game, you may wish to add additional examples.)

**DAY 4:** *Chew the Fat* (Round Two)
(Add the last two words, *grateful* and *captive,* to the bag or container. Repeat procedure from Day 3.)

*Appendix* **17**

Name _____

# The King of Morocco's Palace

The king's palace was the most beautiful in the world.

It was made of _____ .

It had, _____ .

Inside, _____ .

In the king's bedroom _____ .

The king's gardens _____ .

The trees _____ .

The flowers _____ .

Everyone _____ .

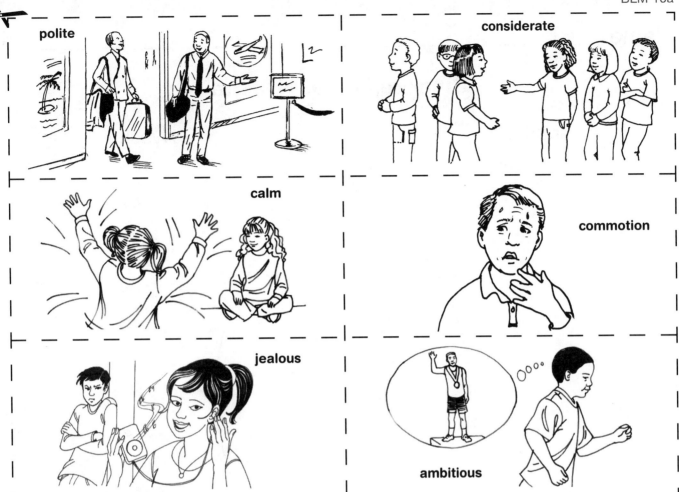

polite

considerate

calm

commotion

jealous

ambitious

## Sharing What You've Learned at School

**Note:** The children are not expected to be able to read the words. They are for your information.

**DAY 1:** (Cut the Picture Vocabulary Cards apart. Place the picture cards for *polite, considerate, calm,* and *commotion* in a container or small plastic bag.) (Show the child each picture card.) **What word does the picture show?** (Idea: *The picture shows someone who is polite.*)
**Tell me what you know about this word.**

**DAY 2:** (Add in 2 new words, *jealous* and *ambitious.* Repeat procedure from Day 1.) **Tell me anything more that you know about this word.**

**DAY 3:** *Chew the Fat* (Round One)
**Let's play the *Chew the Fat* game that you learned at school. I'll say sentences with your vocabulary words in them. If I use the word correctly, say "Well done!" If I use the word incorrectly, say "Chew the fat." Then I'll ask you to finish the sentence so that it makes sense.**

- **There was a commotion when . . . the dog was asleep in its dog house.** *Chew the fat.* **There was a commotion when. How can we finish the sentence so it makes sense?** (Idea: *The dog chased the cat around the back yard.*) **Let's say the sentence together.** *There was a commotion when the dog chased the cat around the back yard.*

- **Mason was polite when . . . he didn't write his uncle a thank you letter for his birthday gift.** *Chew the fat.* **Mason was polite when. How can we finish the sentence so it makes sense?** (Idea: *He wrote his uncle a thank you letter for his birthday gift.*) **Let's say the sentence together.** *Mason was polite when he wrote his uncle a thank you letter for his birthday gift.*

- **Eva was considerate when . . . she used her quiet voice in the library.** *Well done!*

- **The lake is calm when . . . the wind is blowing really hard.** *Chew the fat.* **The lake is calm when. How can we finish the sentence so it makes sense?** (Idea: *There is no wind.*) **Let's say the sentence together.** *The lake is calm when there is no wind.*

- **Marilyn told us to calm down when . . . we were quietly watching TV.** *Chew the fat.* **Marilyn told us to calm down. How can we finish the sentence so it makes sense?** (Idea: *When we were making too much noise.*) **Let's say the sentence together.** *Marilyn told us to calm down when we were making too much noise.*

**DAY 4:** *Chew the Fat* (Round Two)
(Add the last two words, *jealous* and *ambitious,* to the bag or container. Repeat procedure from Day 3.)

Name _____

# Cinderella and Nyasha

Cinderella

Nyasha

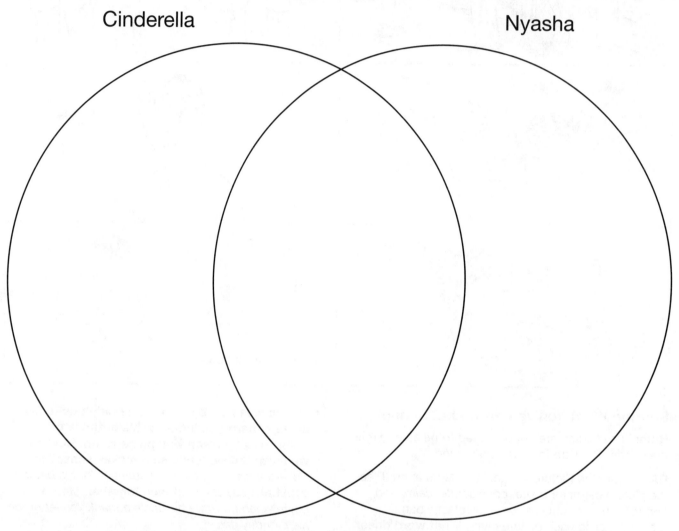

## Word Bank

| | | |
|---|---|---|
| treated badly | good | had a fairy godmother |
| kind | rode in a coach | lived at the palace |
| polite | married the prince | married the king |
| worked in the garden | worked in the house | had a beautiful gown |
| brave | lived in Africa | talked to snakes |
| beautiful | had one sister | had two stepsisters |
| got married | went to the balls | sweet |

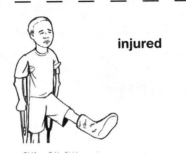

injured

faithful

feast

custom

companions

orphan

## Sharing What You've Learned at School

**Note:** The children are not expected to be able to read the words. They are for your information.

**DAY 1:** (Cut the Picture Vocabulary Cards apart. Place the picture cards for *injured, faithful, feast,* and *custom* in a container or small plastic bag.)
(Show the child each picture card.) **What word does the picture show?** (Idea: *The picture shows someone who is injured.*)
**Tell me what you know about this word.** (You may wish to share what you know about the word with the child as well.)

**DAY 2:** (Add in 2 new words, *companions* and *orphan.* Repeat procedure from Day 1.) **Tell me anything more that you know about this word.**

**DAY 3:** *What's My Word?* (Round One)
**I'll give you three clues. After I give each clue, if you are sure you know my word, you may make a guess. If you guess correctly, you will win one point. If you make a mistake, I get the point.**

- **Here's my first clue. My word is a noun. Here's my second clue. My word starts with a "c" sound. Here's my third clue. My word names an idea that tells about a tradition among a group of people. What's my word?** *Custom.*

- **New word. Here's my first clue. My word starts with a "f" sound. Here's my second clue. My word can be a noun. Here's my third clue. My word can be a verb. What's my word?** *Feast.*
- **New word. Here's my first clue. My word is a describing word. Here's my second clue. You would not want to be this. Here's my third clue. My word means you've been hurt. What's my word?** *Injured.*
- **New word. Here's my first clue. My word is a describing word. Here's my second clue. My word tells more about a person or an animal. Here's my third clue. My word tells about someone who would never forget you; someone who would always help you if you needed help. What's my word?** *Faithful.*

(If the child is enjoying this game, you may wish to add additional examples.)

**DAY 4:** *What's My Word?* (Round Two)
(Add the last two words, *companions* and *orphan,* to the bag or container. Repeat procedure from Day 3.)

Name _____

# The Polar Bear Son

_____

_____

_____

_____

_____

_____

_____

_____

_____

_____

_____

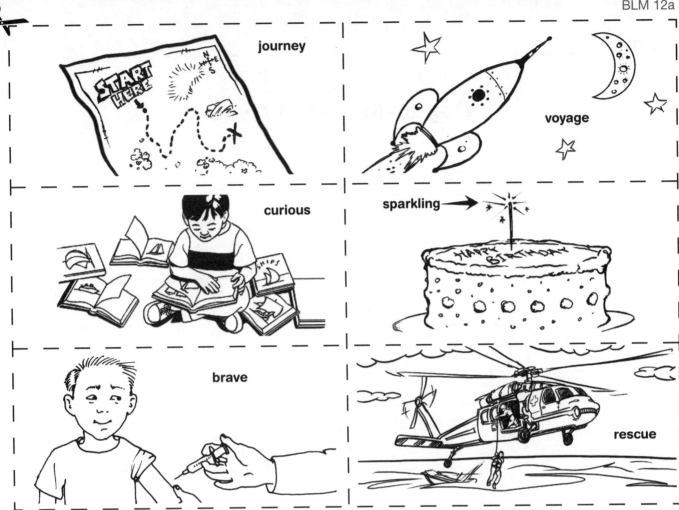

journey

voyage

curious

sparkling

brave

rescue

## Sharing What You've Learned at School

**Note:** The children are not expected to be able to read the words. They are for your information.

**DAY 1:** Cut the Picture Vocabulary Cards apart. Place the picture cards for *journey, voyage, curious,* and *sparkling* in a container or small plastic bag.
Show child each picture card. **What word does the picture show?** (Idea: *The picture shows a rocket ship going on a space voyage.*)
**Tell me what you know about this word.** You may wish to share what you know about the word with child as well.

**DAY 2:** (Add in 2 new words, *brave* and *rescued.* Repeat procedure from Day 1.) **Tell me anything more that you know about this word.**

**DAY 3:** *What's My Word?* **(Round One)**
I'll give you three clues. After I give each clue, if you are sure you know my word you may make a guess. If you guess correctly, you will win one point. If you make a mistake, I get the point.

- **Here's my first clue. My word is a describing word. Here's my second clue. There's an "s" sound in my word. Here's my third clue. My word means glittering. What's my word?** *Sparkling.*

- **New word. Here's my first clue. There's a "v" sound in my word. Here's my second clue. My word is a noun. Here's my third clue. My word means a long journey. What's my word?** *Voyage.*
- **New word. Here's my first clue. My word is a noun. Here's my second clue. My word and another word from our new words mean almost the same thing. Here's my third clue. My word means almost the same thing as voyage. What's my word?** *Journey.*
- **New word. Here's my first clue. My word is a describing word. Here's my second clue. There's an "s" sound in my word. Here's my third clue. My word can mean interested in something and want to know more about it. What's my word?** *Curious.*

(If child is enjoying this game, you may wish to add additional examples.)

**DAY 4:** *What's My Word?* **(Round Two)**
(Add the last two words, *brave* and *rescued,* to the bag or container. Repeat procedure from Day 3.)

Name _____

# Dog-of-the-Sea-Waves

colossal

interest

wilderness

astonishing

exaggerated

unbelievable

## Sharing What You've Learned at School

**Note:** The children are not expected to be able to read the words. They are for your information.

**DAY 1:** (Cut the Picture Vocabulary Cards apart. Place the picture cards for *colossal, interest, wilderness,* and *astonishing* in a container or small plastic bag.) (Show the child each picture card.) **What word does the picture show?** (Idea: *The picture shows the wilderness.*)
**Tell me what you know about this word.** (You may wish to share what you know about the word with the child as well.)

**DAY 2:** (Add in 2 new words, *exaggerated* and *unbelievable.* Repeat procedure from Day 1.) **Tell me anything more that you know about this word.**

**DAY 3:** *What's My Word?* (Round One)
**I'll give you three clues. After I give each clue, if you are sure you know my word, you may make a guess. If you guess correctly, you will win one point. If you make a mistake, I get the point.**

- **Here's my first clue. My word is a noun. Here's my second clue. There's an "er" sound in my word. Here's my third clue. My word means "a place where no people live." What's my word?** *Wilderness.*

- **New word. Here's my first clue. My word is a describing word. Here's my second clue. My word has an "l" sound in the middle. Here's my third clue. My word means "extremely large, huge, or enormous." What's my word?** *Colossal.*

- **New word. Here's my first clue. My word is a verb. Here's my second clue. My word starts with the word part "in-." Here's my third clue. My word means "persuade you to do something or tempt you." What's my word?** *Interest.*

- **New word. Here's my first clue. My word is a describing word. Here's my second clue. There's the word part "-ing" at the end of my word. Here's my third clue. My word means "amazing and hard to believe." What's my word?** *Astonishing.*

(If the child is enjoying this game, you may wish to add additional examples.)

**DAY 4:** *What's My Word?* (Round Two)
(Add the last two words, *exaggerated* and *unbelievable,* to the bag or container. Repeat procedure from day 3.)

Name _____

# Paul Bunyan

_____

_____

_____

_____

_____

_____

_____

_____

_____

_____

_____

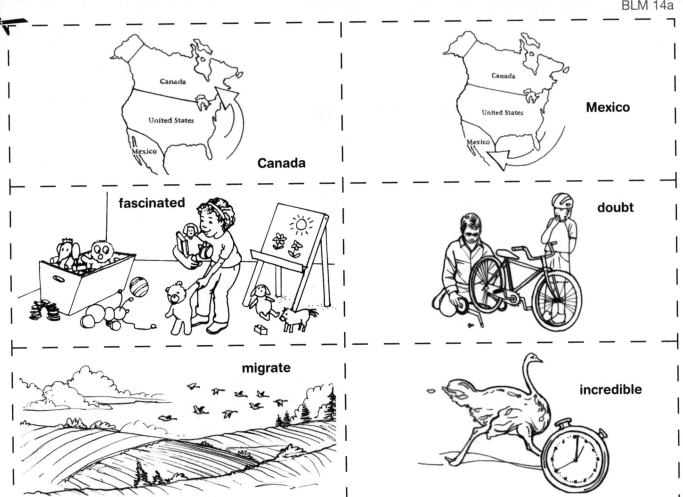

fascinated

doubt

Canada

Mexico

migrate

incredible

## Sharing What You've Learned at School

**Note:** The children are not expected to be able to read the words. They are for your information.

**DAY 1:** (Cut the Picture Vocabulary Cards apart. Place the picture cards for *Canada, Mexico, fascinated,* and *doubt* in a container or small plastic bag.)
(Show the child each picture card.) **What word does the picture show?** (Idea: *The picture shows Canada.*) **Tell me what you know about this word.** (You may wish to share what you know about the word with the child as well.)

**DAY 2:** (Add in 2 new words, *migrate* and *incredible.* Repeat procedure from Day 1.) **Tell me anything more that you know about this word.**

**DAY 3:** *Tom Foolery* **(Round One)**
Let's play the *Tom Foolery* game that you learned at school. I'll tell you what a word means. Then I'll tell you another meaning for that word. If I tell something that's not correct, say "Tom Foolery!" If I say something correct, don't say anything. If you say *Tom Foolery!* and you're right, you get a point. If you're wrong, I get the point.

- If you are **fascinated,** you are very interested in something and think about it a lot. **Fascinated** also means "hooked two things together." *Tom Foolery!* Oh, you're right. I must have been thinking of **fastened** instead of **fascinated.**
- **Canada** is the country to the north of the United States. Canadians live in **Canada.**
- **Mexico** is the country to the south of the United States. It's also the name of the company that sells combs. *Tom Foolery!* Oh, you're right. You only know one meaning for **Mexico.**
- When you have a **doubt,** you have a feeling of not being sure. A **doubt** is also a long time when no rain falls. *Tom Foolery!* Oh, you're right. I was thinking of a **drought.** Plants and animals often die during a **drought.**

(If the child is enjoying this game, you may wish to add additional examples.)

**DAY 4:** *Tom Foolery* **(Round Two)**
(Add the last two words, *migrate* and *incredible,* to the bag or container. Repeat procedure from Day 3.)

Name _____

# Monarch Butterflies

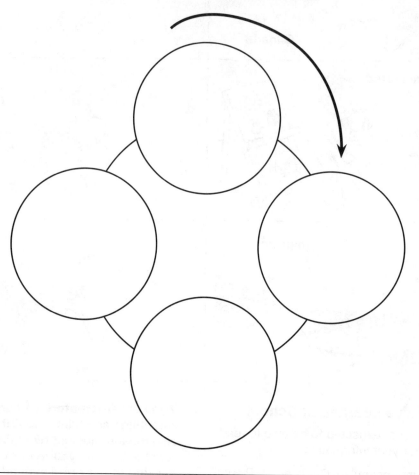

_____
_____
_____
_____
_____

plot

tourist

gaze

scarce

imagination

optimistic

## Sharing What You've Learned at School

**Note:** The children are not expected to be able to read the words. They are for your information.

**DAY 1:** (Cut the Picture Vocabulary Cards apart. Place the picture cards for *plot, tourist, gaze,* and *scarce* in a container or small plastic bag.)
(Show the child each picture card.) **What word does the picture show?** (Idea: *The picture shows something that is scarce.*)
**Tell me what you know about this word.** (You may wish to share what you know about the word with the child as well.)

**DAY 2:** (Add in 2 new words, *optimistic* and *imagination*. Repeat procedure from Day 1.) **Tell me anything more that you know about this word.**

**DAY 3:** *Tom Foolery* **(Round One)**
**Let's play the *Tom Foolery* game that you learned at school. I'll tell you what a word means. Then I'll tell you another meaning for that word. If I tell something that's not correct, sing "Tom Foolery!" If I say something correct, don't say anything. If you say *Tom Foolery!* and you're right, you get a point. If you're wrong, I get the point.**

- **Plot** is what someone does when they make secret plans to do something bad. **Plot** is also

what someone does to pick up milk they've spilled on the table *Tom Foolery!* **Oh, you're right. I was thinking of the word blot. You blot up spilled milk.**
- **When you gaze at the stars, you look at the stars for a long time without looking away. Gaze is also a kind of bandage you might put on your scraped knee.** *Tom Foolery!* **Oh, you're right. I must have been thinking of gauze instead of gaze.**
- **When your aunt is a tourist, she might visit the town where you live to see the sights and have some fun. A tourist is also an animal much like a turtle.** *Tom Foolery!* **Oh, you're right. I was thinking of tortoise. We only know the first meaning for tourist.**
- **Scarce means there's very little of something. Scarce also means that someone jumps out from behind a door and yells "Boo!"** *Tom Foolery!* **Oh, you're right. I was thinking of scares, not scarce.**

(If the child is enjoying this game, you may wish to add additional examples.)

**DAY 4:** *Tom Foolery* **(Round Two)**
(Add the last two words, *optimistic* and *imagination,* to the bag or container. Repeat procedure from Day 3.)

Name _____

# Isabel's House of Butterflies

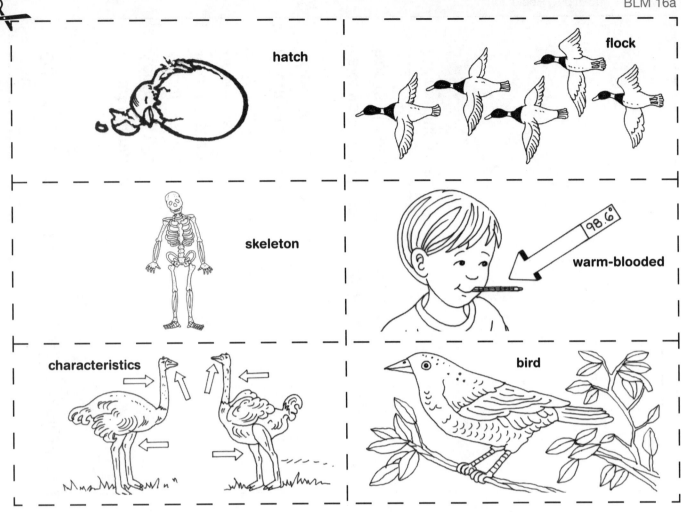

hatch

flock

skeleton

warm-blooded

98.6°

characteristics

bird

## Sharing What You've Learned at School

**Note:** The children are not expected to be able to read the words. They are for your information.

**DAY 1:** (Cut the Picture Vocabulary Cards apart. Place the cards for *hatch, flock, skeleton,* and *characteristics* in a container or small plastic bag.)
(Show the child each picture card.) **What word does the picture show?** (Idea: *The picture shows a bird hatching out of an egg.*)
**Tell me what you know about this word.** (You may wish to share what you know about the word with thechild as well.)

**DAY 2:** (Add in 2 new words, *warm-blooded* and *bird.* Repeat procedure from Day 1.) **Tell me anything more that you know about this word.**

**DAY 3:** *Threesies* **Game (Round One)**
**Let's play the *Threesies* game that you learned at school. I'll tell you a word you learned when you listened to *About Birds*. After I tell you the word, you need to tell me three important things about the word. Each time you tell me something important about the word, you will win one point. If you can't tell me three things about the word, I will tell you things and I will win one point for each thing I tell you. Once three things have been** said about the word, you will have a chance to win two bonus points by using the word in a good sentence.

- **Your first word is skeleton.**
- **Your next word is characteristics.**
- **Your next word is flock.**
- **Your next word is hatch.**

(If the child is enjoying this game, you may wish to add additional examples.)

**DAY 4:** *Threesies* **Game (Round Two)**
(Add the last two words, *characteristics* and *bird,* to the bag or container. Repeat procedure from Day 3.)

Other titles in the ABOUT series your child might enjoy:

About Mammals
About Reptiles
About Amphibians
About Insects
About Fish
About Arachnids
About Crustaceans
About Mollusks

Take your child to the public library to find more books about the different kinds of birds.

My reading goal:

7

**Let's Learn About Birds**

1

If you look around outside, you will find birds. You can spot birds in the park or in the woods. When you look up in the sky, you may see birds flying. If you look on the ground you might see bird tracks. The next time you go outside, see if you can spot a bird.

1. What would you find inside a bird?
   ○ feathers
   ○ bones
   ○ legs

2. One way that birds help humans is …
   ○ they eat bugs.
   ○ they sing.
   ○ they fly.

3. This book is mostly about …
   ○ cows.
   ○ eagles.
   ○ birds.

4. Two best places to spot birds are …
   ○ the pet store and the forest.
   ○ inside the school.
   ○ at the park and in the woods.

5. A bird's home is called a …
   ○ next.
   ○ nest.
   ○ net.

6

The homes of birds are called nests. Some birds make their nests on the ground. Others nest in trees. Some birds pile sticks to make nests. Others get grass, hair, and mud to make nests. Mother bird lay eggs in the nest. She and father bird sit on the eggs until the babies are ready to hatch.

3

Farmers like birds because they eat lots of bugs. Birds also keep our yards free of bugs. When you eat chicken you are eating a bird. Some birds eat rats and mice that are pests. Birds are important to our lives.

4

If you look around outside, you will find birds.
You can spot birds in the park or in the woods.
When you look up in the sky, you may see birds
flying. If you look on the ground you might see
bird tracks. The next time you go outside, see if
you can spot a bird.

Birds come in many colors and sizes. The
smallest birds are hummingbirds. Some of the
biggest birds are eagles. Every bird has feathers
and two legs. You will find bones inside a bird.
Birds move in many ways. Most birds fly. Some
birds swim. Some birds are runners.

The homes of birds are called nests. Some birds
make their nests on the ground. Others nest in
trees. Some birds pile sticks to make nests. Others
get grass, hair, and mud to make nests. Mother
bird lays eggs in the nest. She and father bird sit on
the eggs until the babies are ready to hatch.

Farmers like birds because they eat lots of
bugs. Birds also keep our yards free of bugs.
When you eat chicken you are eating a bird.
Some birds eat rats and mice that are pests.
Birds are important to our lives.

5

Birds come in many colors and sizes. The
smallest birds are hummingbirds. Some of the
biggest birds are eagles. Every bird has feathers
and two legs. You will find bones inside a bird.
Birds move in many ways. Most birds fly. Some
birds swim. Some birds are runners.

2

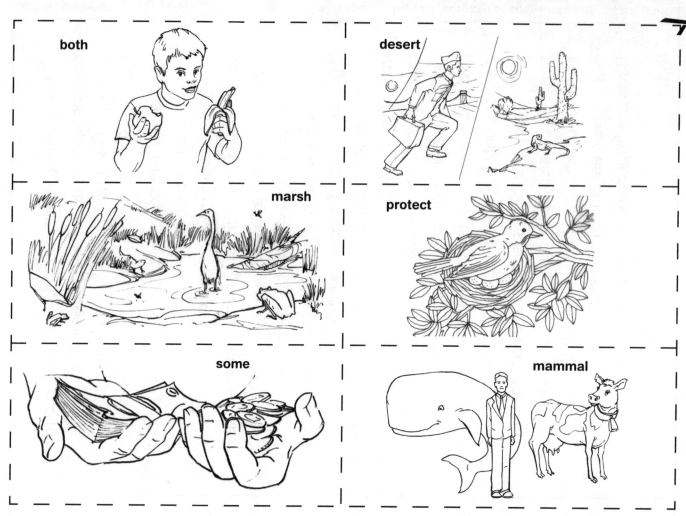

## Sharing What You've Learned at School

**Note:** The children are not expected to be able to read the words. They are for your information.

**DAY 1:** (Cut the Picture Vocabulary Cards apart. Place the cards for *both, desert, marsh,* and *protect* in a container or small plastic bag.)
(Show the child each picture card.) **What word does the picture show?** (Idea: *The picture shows a boy eating both a banana and an apple.*)
**Tell me what you know about this word.** (You may wish to share what you know about the word with the child as well.)

**DAY 2:** (Add in 2 new words, *some* and *mammal.* Repeat procedure from Day 1.) **Tell me anything more that you know about this word.**

**DAY 3:** *Threesies* Game (Round One)
**Let's play the *Threesies* game that you learned at school. I'll tell you a word you learned when you listened to *About Mammals*. After I tell you the word, you need to tell me three important things about the word. Each time you tell me something important about the word, you will win one point. If you can't tell me three things about the word, I will tell you things and I will win one point for each thing I tell you. Once three things have been**

said about the word, you will have a chance to win two bonus points by using the word in a good sentence.

- **Your first word is both.**
- **Your next word is desert.**
- **Your next word is protect.**
- **Your next word is marsh.**

(If the child is enjoying this game, you may wish to add additional examples.)

**DAY 4:** *Threesies* Game (Round Two)
(Add the last two words, *some* and *mammal,* to the bag or container. Repeat procedure from Day 3.)

Other titles in the ABOUT series your child might enjoy:

About Birds
About Reptiles
About Amphibians
About Insects
About Fish
About Arachnids
About Crustaceans
About Mollusks

Take your child to the public library to find more books about the different kinds of mammals.

My reading goal:

7

**Let's Learn About Mammals**

1

Did you know that you are a mammal?
Mammals have hair. Do you have hair? Mammals
drink milk from their mothers. Can human babies
drink milk from their mothers? Mammals are
warm-blooded. Are you warm-blooded? Did you
answer yes to all of those questions? Then you
are a mammal.

1. A whale is a mammal that ...
   - ○ is very small
   - ○ lives on land
   - ○ swims

2. Which thing does not tell about mammals?
   - ○ Mammals have hair.
   - ○ All mammals live on land.
   - ○ Mammals drink milk from their mothers.

3. You would read this book if you wanted to learn about ...
   - ○ mammals.
   - ○ snakes.
   - ○ birds.

4. How do mammals move?
   - ○ They all drive cars.
   - ○ They walk, run, swim, and climb.
   - ○ They only walk or run.

5. Are humans mammals?
   - ○ yes
   - ○ no
   - ○ maybe

6

3

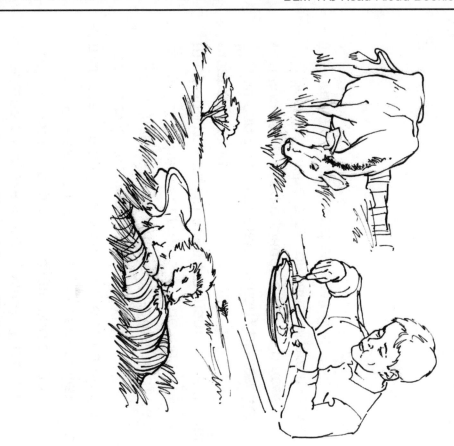

Mammals eat many things. Some mammals eat meat. Others eat plants. Some mammals eat meat and plants. Humans are mammals that eat meat and plants.

You can find mammals in many places. You can find them in cold places and hot places. You find them where it is dry and where it is wet.

4

(Note to teacher: These pages should photocopy onto the backside of pages 3 and 4.)

5

Did you know that you are a mammal? Mammals have hair. Do you have hair? Mammals drink milk from their mothers. Can human babies drink milk from their mothers? Mammals are warm-blooded. Are you warm-blooded? Did you answer yes to all of those questions? Then you are a mammal.

Mammals move in many ways. They walk and run. Some mammals climb and some swim. Whales are mammals that swim. Bats are mammals that fly. Can you name a mammal for each way of moving?

Mammals eat many things. Some mammals eat meat. Others eat plants. Some mammals eat meat and plants. Humans are mammals that eat meat and plants.

You can find mammals in many places. You can find them in cold places and hot places. You find them where it is dry and where it is wet. Mammals can be found everywhere.

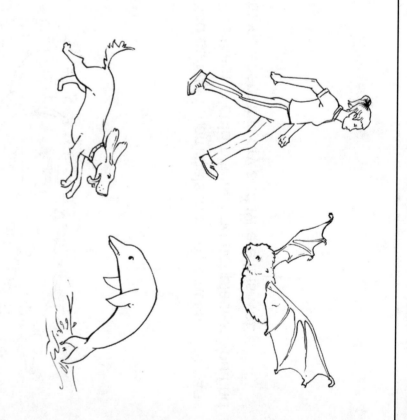

Mammals move in many ways. They walk and run. Some mammals climb and some swim. Whales are mammals that swim. Bats are mammals that fly. Can you name a mammal for each way of moving?

2

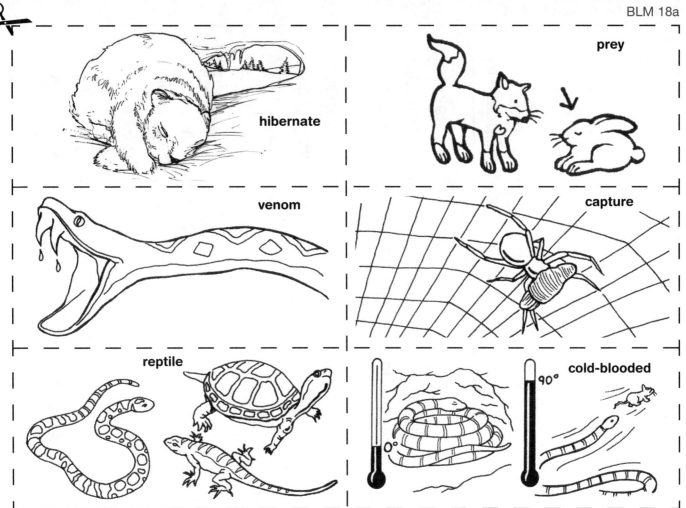

hibernate

prey

venom

capture

reptile

cold-blooded

90°

## Sharing What You've Learned at School

**Note:** The children are not expected to be able to read the words. They are for your information.

**DAY 1:** (Cut the Picture Vocabulary Cards apart. Place the cards for *hibernate, prey, capture,* and *venom* in a container or small plastic bag.)
(Show the child each picture card.) **What word does the picture show?** (Idea: *The picture shows a bear hibernating in its den.*)
**Tell me what you know about this word.** (You may wish to share what you know about the word with the child as well.)

**DAY 2:** (Add in 2 new words, *cold-blooded* and *reptile.* Repeat procedure from Day 1.) **Tell me anything more that you know about this word.**

**DAY 3:** *Threesies* **Game (Round One)**
**Let's play the** *Threesies* **game that you learned at school. I'll tell you a word you learned when you listened to** *About Reptiles.* **After I tell you the word, you need to tell me three important things about the word. Each time you tell me something important about the word, you will win one point. If you can't tell me three things about the word, I will tell you things and I will win one point for each thing I tell you. Once three things have been**

said about the word, you will have a chance to win two bonus points by using the word in a good sentence.

- **Your first word is hibernate.**
- **Your next word is venom.**
- **Your next word is capture.**
- **Your next word is prey.**

(If the child is enjoying this game, you may wish to add additional examples.)

**DAY 4:** *Threesies* **Game (Round Two)**
(Add the last two words, *cold-blooded* and *reptile,* to the bag or container. Repeat procedure from Day 3.)

Other titles in the ABOUT series your child might enjoy:

About Birds
About Mammals
About Amphibians
About Insects
About Fish
About Arachnids
About Crustaceans
About Mollusks

My reading goal:

Take your child to the public library to find more books about the different kinds of reptiles.

7

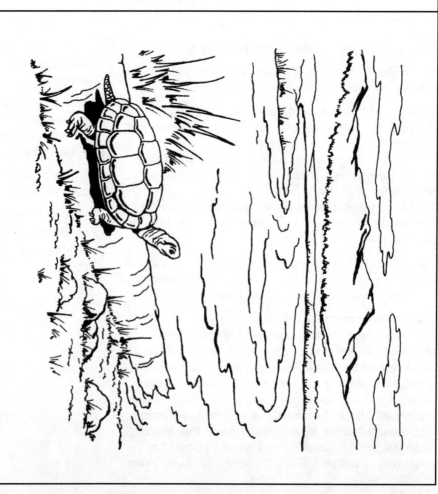

**Let's Learn About Reptiles**

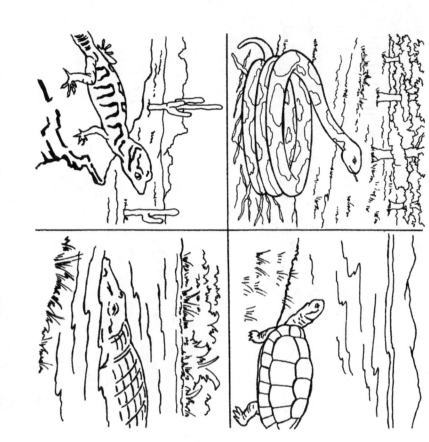

Reptiles can be found in many places. You can see a snake in the woods. At the lake, a turtle can be sitting in the sun. A lizard can be found in the desert. An alligator can be found in the swamp.

1

1. This book is mostly about …
   - ◯ mammals.
   - ◯ birds.
   - ◯ reptiles.

2. One way that reptiles help humans is …
   - ◯ they eat bugs and mice.
   - ◯ they make nests.
   - ◯ they are good to eat.

3. Which fact does not tell about reptiles?
   - ◯ Reptiles have scales.
   - ◯ Reptiles are cold-blooded.
   - ◯ Reptiles are warm-blooded.

4. Which reptile would you find in the desert?
   - ◯ a snake.
   - ◯ a turtle.
   - ◯ an alligator.

5. When it is cold, reptiles …
   - ◯ play outside.
   - ◯ hibernate.
   - ◯ run fast.

6

Reptiles move in many ways. Some reptiles crawl. Other reptiles swim. Some move fast and some move slowly. When it is cold reptiles hibernate. They sleep and sleep until spring.

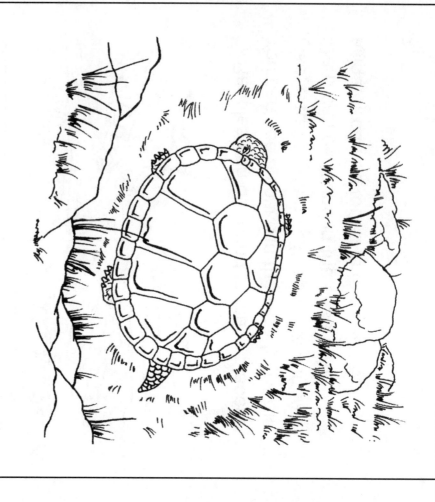

3

Farmers love reptiles. They eat bugs and mice that eat the crops. In Hawaii lizards keep houses free of bugs. Turtles help keep ponds free of bugs that bite. Reptiles are important to us.

4

Reptiles can be found in many places. You can see a snake in the woods. At the lake a turtle can be sitting in the sun. A lizard can be found in the desert. An alligator can be found in the swamp.

Reptiles are cold-blooded. They are cold when it is cold outside. When it is warm, they are warm. Reptiles have scales on their skin. Some reptiles have hard shells like turtles. Some reptiles have short legs. Others have no legs at all like snakes.

Reptiles move in many ways. Some reptiles crawl. Other reptiles swim. Some move fast and some move slowly. When it is cold reptiles hibernate. They sleep and sleep until spring.

Farmers love reptiles. They eat bugs and mice that eat the crops. In Hawaii lizards keep houses free of bugs. Turtles help keep ponds free of bugs that bite. Reptiles are important to us.

5

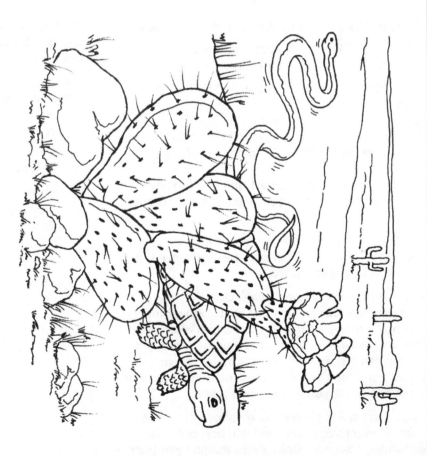

Reptiles are cold-blooded. They are cold when it is cold outside. When it is warm, they are warm. Reptiles have scales on their skin. Some reptiles have hard shells like turtles. Some reptiles have short legs. Others have no legs at all like snakes.

2

tropical

school

fool

enemies

fish

species

## Sharing What You've Learned at School

**Note:** The children are not expected to be able to read the words. They are for your information.

**DAY 1:** (Cut the Picture Vocabulary Cards apart. Place the cards for *tropical, school, fool,* and *enemies* in a container or small plastic bag.)
(Show the child each picture card.) **What word does the picture show?** (Idea: *The picture shows a tropical island.*)
**Tell me what you know about this word.** (You may wish to share what you know about the word with the child as well.)

**DAY 2:** (Add in 2 new words, *species* and *fish.* Repeat procedure from Day 1.) **Tell me anything more that you know about this word.**

**DAY 3:** *Threesies* **Game (Round One)**
**Let's play the *Threesies* game that you learned at school. I'll tell you a word you learned when you listened *About Fish.* After I tell you the word, you need to tell me three important things about the word. Each time you tell me something important about the word, you will win one point.**

**If you can't tell me three things about the word, I will tell you things and I will win one point for each thing I tell you. Once three things have been**

said about the word, you will have a chance to win two bonus points by using the word in a good sentence.

- **Your first word is enemies.**
- **Your next word is school.**
- **Your next word is fool.**
- **Your next word is tropical.**

(If the child is enjoying this game, you may wish to add additional examples.)

**DAY 4:** *Threesies* **Game (Round Two)**
(Add the last two words, *species* and *fish,* to the bag or container. Repeat procedure from Day 3.)

Other titles in the ABOUT series your child might enjoy:

*About Birds*
*About Mammals*
*About Amphibians*
*About Insects*
*About Reptiles*
*About Arachnids*
*About Crustaceans*
*About Mollusks*

Take your child to the public library to find more books about the different kinds of fish.

My reading goal:

7

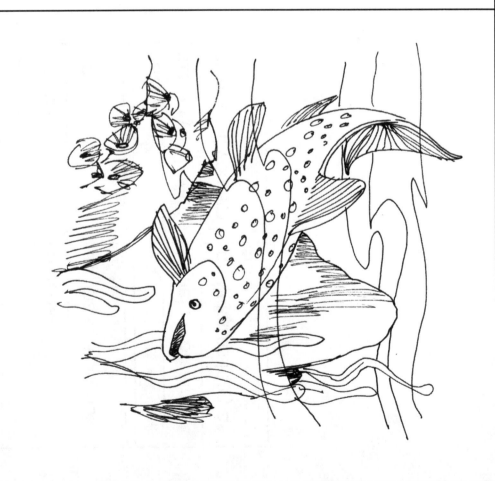

**Let's Learn About Fish**

1

You live on land. Fish live in the water. You have arms and legs to help you move about. Fish have a tail and fins to help them swim. Fish have scales on their skin. Do you?

The book *Let's Learn About Fish* compares you to a fish. Fill in the chart to compare you to a fish.

| You | A Fish |
| --- | --- |
| You | A Fish |
| live on _____. | lives in _____. |
| are _____ blooded. | is _____ blooded. |
| go to school to _____. | swims in a school to be _____. |
| have _____ to help you breathe. | has _____ to help it breathe. |
| grow until you are _____. | grow for as long as they _____. |

6

Fish have enemies. If you eat fish you are one of their enemies. Fish have many things that save them from being eaten. Some have spines to save them. Most fish have tough skin and some are slippery. Some fish fool their enemies.

3

You go to school to learn. Fish swim in schools to be safe. A human baby is born alive. Some fish babies are born alive and others hatch from eggs. Both humans and fish eat plants and meat. Humans grow until they are adults. Fish grow for as long as they live.

4

(Note to teacher: These pages should photocopy onto the backside of pages 3 and 4.)

5

You live on land. Fish live in the water. You have arms and legs to help you move about. Fish have a tail and fins to help them swim. Fish have scales on their skin. Do you?

You are warm-blooded. Your body is warm even if it is cold. Fish are cold-blooded. They are cold when it is cold. When it is warm, they are warm. Lungs help you breathe. Fish have gills to help them breathe.

Fish have enemies. If you eat fish you are one of their enemies. Fish have many things that save them from being eaten. Some fish have spines to save them. Most have tough skin and some are slippery. Some fool their enemies.

You go to school to learn. Fish swim in schools to be safe. A human baby is born alive. Some fish babies are born alive and others hatch from eggs. Both humans and fish eat plants and meat. Humans grow until they are adults. Fish grow for as long as they live.

You are warm-blooded. Your body is warm even if it is cold. Fish are cold-blooded. They are cold when it is cold. When it is warm, they are warm. Lungs help you breathe. Fish have gills to help them breathe.

2

waterproof

pests

active

nourishment

insects

predator

## Sharing What You've Learned at School

**Note:** The children are not expected to be able to read the words. They are for your information.

**DAY 1:** (Cut the Picture Vocabulary Cards apart. Place the cards for *waterproof, nourishment, pests,* and *active* in a container or small plastic bag.)
(Show the child each picture card.) **What word does the picture show?** (Idea: *The picture shows a child being a pest.*)
**Tell me what you know about this word.** (You may wish to share what you know about the word with the child as well.)

**DAY 2:** (Add in 2 new words, *predator* and *insects.* Repeat procedure from Day 1.) **Tell me anything more that you know about this word.**

**DAY 3:** *Threesies* Game (Round One)
**Let's play the *Threesies* game that you learned at school. I'll tell you a word you learned when you listened to *About Insects*. After I tell you the word, you need to tell me three important things about the word. Each time you tell me something important about the word, you will win one point. If you can't tell me three things about the word, I will tell you things and I will win one point for each thing I tell you. Once three things have been**

**said about the word, you will have a chance to win two bonus points by using the word in a good sentence.**

- **Your first word is active.**
- **Your next word is pests.**
- **Your next word is nourishment.**
- **Your next word is waterproof.**

(If the child is enjoying this game, you may wish to add additional examples.)

**DAY 4:** *Threesies* Game (Round Two)
(Add the last two words, *predator* and *insects,* to the bag or container. Repeat procedure from Day 3.)

Other titles in the ABOUT series your child might enjoy:

About Birds
About Mammals
About Amphibians
About Fish
About Reptiles
About Arachnids
About Crustaceans
About Mollusks

My reading goal:

Take your child to the public library to find more books about the different kinds of insects.

7

**Let's Learn About Insects**

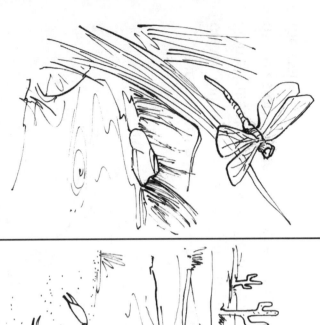

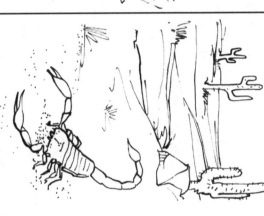

1

Did you know that insects live almost everywhere? Insects can be found where it is hot or warm. Insects can be found where it is wet or dry. If you look, you may find insects in your school or home. You will find insects in your yard.

1. If you saw an animal with six legs it might be …
   ○ an insect.
   ○ a mammal.
   ○ a fish.

2. This book is mostly about …
   ○ rats.
   ○ spiders.
   ○ insects.

3. Which fact tells about insects?
   ○ An insect has a skeleton inside its body.
   ○ An insect has a skeleton outside its body.
   ○ An insect does not have a skeleton.

4. Where would you not find an insect?
   ○ where it is warm
   ○ where it is cold
   ○ where it is hot

5. An insect has …
   ○ six legs and three body parts.
   ○ eight legs and two body parts.
   ○ antennae and two legs.

6

3

Insects move in many ways. Some insects crawl. Other insects fly. Some jump and hop. Some insects can swim. Some insects like to move about in the day. Others move about in the dark.

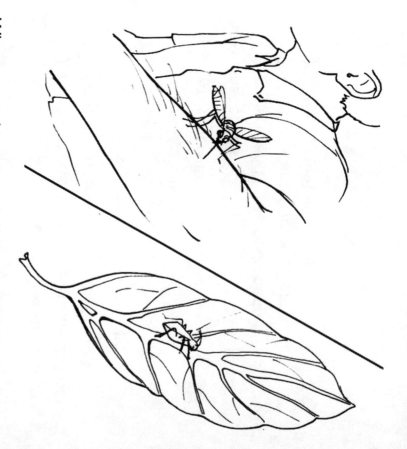

When some insects eat, they suck blood from animals or juice from plants. Some insects eat plants. Insects can be pests. Some insects like to get into our food. Some help by eating other insects that are pests.

4

5

Did you know that insects live almost everywhere? Insects can be found where it is hot or warm. Insects can be found where it is wet or dry. If you look, you may find insects in your school or home. You will find insects in your yard.

Insects are small animals with six legs and three body parts. An insect has its skeleton on the outside of its body. Antennae help insects smell and feel things. Insects hatch from eggs. Some insects change many times before they become adults.

Insects move in many ways. Some insects crawl. Other insects fly. Some jump and hop. Some insects can swim. Some insects like to move about in the day. Others move about in the dark.

When some insects eat, they suck blood from animals or juice from plants. Some insects eat plants. Some help by eating other insects that are pests.

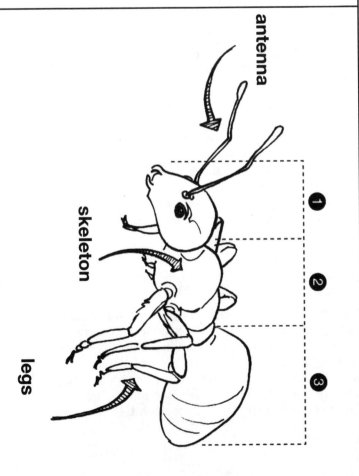

antenna

skeleton

legs

① ② ③

Insects are small animals with six legs and three body parts. An insect has its skeleton on the outside of its body. Antennae help insects smell and feel things. Insects hatch from eggs. Some insects change many times before they become adults.

2

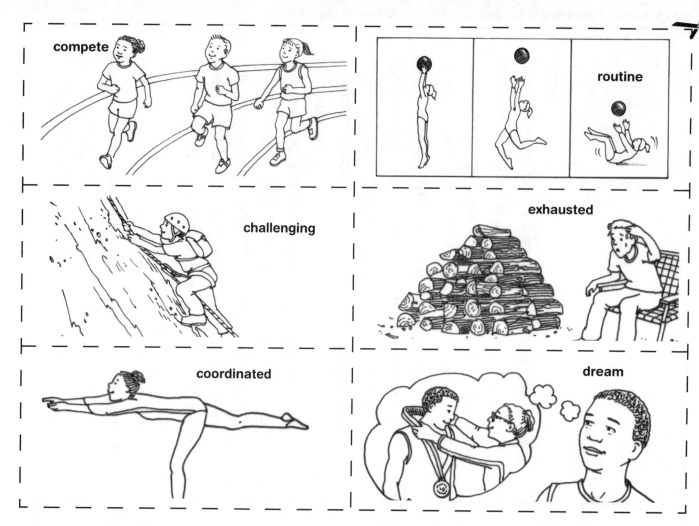

## Sharing What You've Learned at School

**Note:** The children are not expected to be able to read the words. They are for your information.

**DAY 1:** (Cut the Picture Vocabulary Cards apart. Place the cards for *compete, routine, challenging,* and *exhausted* in a container or small plastic bag.) (Show the child each picture card.) **What word does the picture show?** (Idea: *The picture shows kids competing in a race.*)
**Tell me what you know about this word.** (You may wish to share what you know about the word with the child as well.)

**DAY 2:** (Add in 2 new words, *coordinated* and *dream.* Repeat procedure from Day 1.) **Tell me anything more that you know about this word.**

**DAY 3: The *Super Choosing* Game (Round One)**
Let's play the *Super Choosing* game that you learned at school. I'll say sentences with two or three of the words you know in them. You have to choose the correct word for the sentence. If you choose correctly, you will win one point. If you don't choose correctly, I get the point.

- **When McKenzie performed at the competition, did she do a routine or a challenging?** *A routine.*
- **Would it be routine, frustrated, or challenging to swim across a big lake?** *Challenging.*
- **If it was your job to take out the garbage every evening, would that be a rescue, a routine, or competing?** *A routine.*
- **Would you be exhausted or challenging if you were very, very tired?** *Exhausted.*
- **If you entered a diving contest, would you compete, whine, or be exhausted?** *Compete.*
- **Would a person routine or compete?** *Compete.*
- **When you do the same thing every day, is it challenging, a routine, or exhausted?** *Routine.*
- **Would it be harder to do something challenging or something routine?** *Something challenging.*

If your child is enjoying this game, you may wish to add additional examples.

**DAY 4: The *Super Choosing* Game (Round Two)**
(Add the last two words, *coordinated* and *dream,* to the bag or container. Repeat procedure from Day 3.)

Other biographies your child might enjoy:

*Chico* by Sandra Day O'Connor

*Johnny Appleseed* by Jane Kurtz

*A Weed is a Flower* by Aliki

*Ben Franklin and His First Kite* by Stephen Krensky

*Firetalking* by Patricia Polacco

*Pioneer Girl* by William Anderson

*The Artist* by John Bianchi

*Satchmo's Blues* by Alan Schroeder

Take your child to the public library to find more biographies that you and your child can enjoy together.

My reading goal:

7

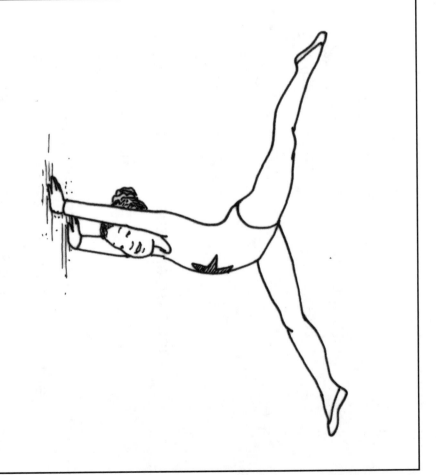

# The Biography of McKenzie Foster

7

1

Meet *McKenzie Foster*. She is a girl about your age. She has a mom, a dad, a sister, and a brother. She lives near New York City. McKenzie has something that is special about her. She is a gymnast.

1. McKenzie lives …
   ○ on a farm.
   ○ in a town.
   ○ near New York City.

2. This biography is about …
   ○ Wendy Hillard.
   ○ McKenzie Foster.
   ○ how to do gymnastics.

3. What thing is not used by McKenzie?
   ○ A set of rings.
   ○ A hoop.
   ○ A ribbon.

4. Who helps McKenzie learn about gymnastics?
   ○ Her mother.
   ○ Her father.
   ○ Her coach.

5. What is special about McKenzie?
   ○ She has a sister and a brother.
   ○ She is a gymnast.
   ○ She is a girl.

6

McKenzie has a coach to help her and her team learn what to do. McKenzie works hard with her coach each day. She has to work with a rope, a hoop, a ball, and a ribbon. What she does is like a dance.

3

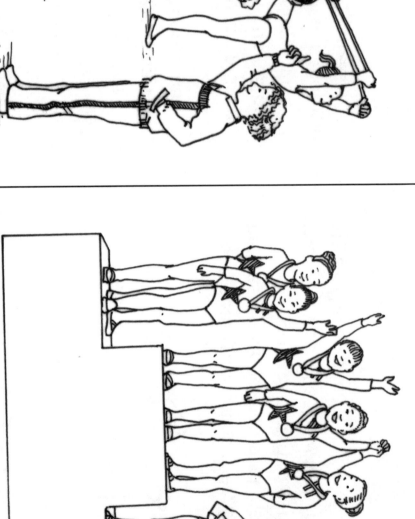

At the competition, McKenzie must get ready. She stretches to warm up her body. McKenzie and her team perform. It is good. They sit and wait to hear if they win. They do!

4

5

Meet *McKenzie Foster*. She is a girl about your age. She has a mom, a dad, a sister, and a brother. She lives near *New York City*. McKenzie has something that is special about her. She is a gymnast.

She does gymnastics everywhere—on the grass, near her home, at the beach, and at the gym. She started gymnastics when she was little. Now that she is older, she can be on a team.

McKenzie has a coach to help her and her team learn what to do. McKenzie works hard with her coach each day. She has to work with a rope, a hoop, a ball, and a ribbon.

At the competition, McKenzie must get ready. She stretches to warm up her body. McKenzie and her team perform. It is good. They sit and wait to hear if they win. They do!

She does gymnastics everywhere—on the grass, near her home, at the beach, and at the gym. She started gymnastics when she was little. Now that she is older, she can be on a team.

2

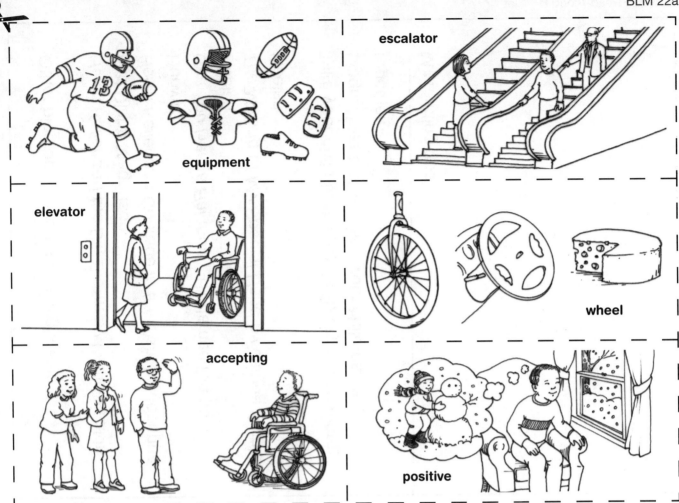

equipment

escalator

elevator

wheel

accepting

positive

## Sharing What You've Learned at School

**Note:** The children are not expected to be able to read the words. They are for your information.

**DAY 1:** (Cut the Picture Vocabulary Cards apart. Place the picture cards for *equipment, escalator, elevator,* and *wheel* in a container or small plastic bag.) (Show the child each picture vocabulary card.) **What word does the picture show?** (Idea: *The picture shows a football player with all of his equipment.*) **Tell me what you know about this word.** (You may wish to share what you know about the word with your child as well.)

**DAY 2:** (Add in 2 new words, *accepting* and *positive.* Repeat procedure from Day 1.) **Tell me anything more that you know about this word.**

**DAY 3: The *Super Choosing* Game (Round One)** Let's play the *Super Choosing* game that you learned at school. I'll say sentences with three target words in them. You have to choose the correct word for the sentence. If you choose correctly, you will win one point. If you don't choose correctly, I get the point.

- Would you ride to the second floor in an **escalator,** an **elevator,** or **equipment** if you used a wheelchair? *An elevator.*
- Would you use special **equipment,** wheels, or **elevators** to play hockey? *Special equipment.*
- If your bike had a flat tire, would you have to fix the **elevator,** the **wheel,** or the **escalator?** *The wheel.*
- Instead of stairs, which would be faster, a **wheel,** an **escalator,** or **equipment?** *An escalator.*
- A round hunk of cheese could be called an **elevator, equipment,** or a **wheel?** *A wheel.*

(If the child is enjoying this game, you may wish to add additional examples.)

**DAY 4: The *Super Choosing* Game (Round Two)** (Add the last two words, *accepting* and *positive,* to the bag or container. Repeat procedure from Day 3.)

Other biographies your child might enjoy:

*Helen Keller and the Big Storm* by Patricia Lakin and Diana Magnuson

*Helen Keller and Courage in the Dark* by Johanna Hurwitz

*Can You Hear a Rainbow?* By Jamee Riggio Heelan

*The Making of My Special Hand* by Jamee Riggio Heelan

Take your child to the public library to find more biographies that you and your child can enjoy together.

My reading goal:

7

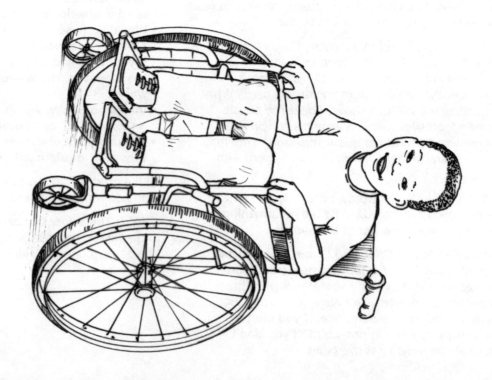

## The Biography of Taylor

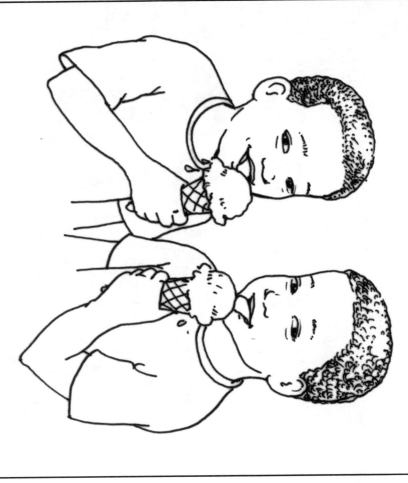

Meet *Taylor*. He has a twin brother named *Tyler*. Taylor likes ice cream and basketball and reading about dinosaurs. Taylor has something that is special about him. He has a disability. He cannot run, jump, skip, or walk, but he still gets around.

1

special water fountain. He can wash his hands in the special sink. Best of all, Taylor can play basketball!

1. This biography is about . . .
   ○ Tyler.
   ○ how to make a wheelchair work.
   ○ Taylor.

2. Which things does Taylor like?
   ○ Ice cream, books, and cars
   ○ Dinosaurs, basketball, and ice cream
   ○ Basketball, cats, and dogs

3. What thing did the school not do to help Taylor?
   ○ made him a special lunch
   ○ put a special button by the door
   ○ made him a special sink

4. What does Taylor have on his wheelchair to make it stop?
   ○ wheels
   ○ bars
   ○ brakes

6

Now, Taylor is happy. He can move faster in the wheelchair. He can get around on his own and not get so tired. Taylor's friends are happy for him.

3

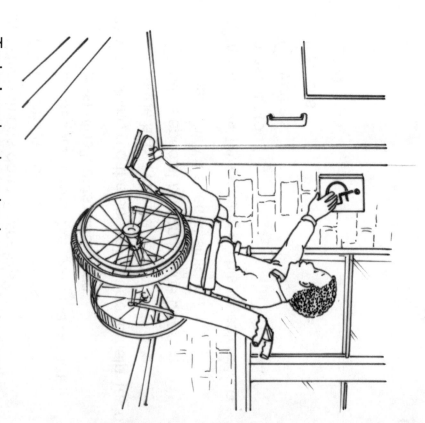

Taylor's school made changes to help him get around in his wheelchair. The school now has a ramp and a special button to open the door. He can get a drink from the special water fountain and wash his hands in the special sink. Best of all, Taylor can play basketball!

4

(Note to teacher: These pages should photocopy onto the backside of pages 3 and 4.)

BLM 22b Read-Aloud Booklet

Meet *Taylor*. He has a twin brother named *Tyler*. Taylor likes ice cream and basketball and reading about dinosaurs. Taylor has something that is special about him. He has a disability. He cannot run, jump, skip, or walk, but he still gets around.

At first Taylor had braces on his legs and he used a walker. This was too slow, so he got a wheelchair. At first, it was hard for Taylor to move the wheelchair on his own. He worked to make his arms strong and learned how to roll, turn, and stop the wheelchair. He had to learn to use the brakes to stop the wheelchair.

Now, Taylor is happy. He can move faster in the wheelchair. He can get around on his own and not get so tired. Taylor's friends are happy for him.

Taylor's school made changes to help him get around in his wheelchair. The school now has a ramp and a special button to open the door. He can get a drink from the special water fountain and wash his hands in the special sink. Best of all, Taylor can play basketball!

5

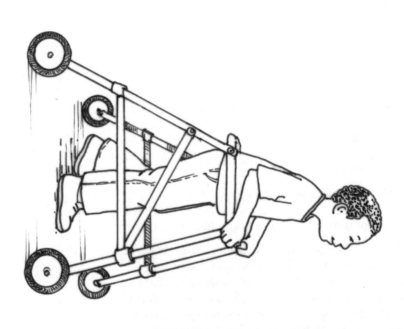

At first Taylor had braces on his legs and he used a walker. This was too slow, so he got a wheelchair. At first, it was hard for Taylor to move the wheelchair on his own. He worked to make his arms strong and learned how to roll, turn, and stop the wheelchair. He had to learn to use the brakes to stop the wheelchair.

2

## Sharing What You've Learned at School

**Note:** The children are not expected to be able to read the words. They are for your information.

**DAY 1:** (Cut the Picture Vocabulary Cards apart. Place the picture cards for *slave, grief, unjust,* and *honest* in a container or small plastic bag.)
(Show the child each picture card.) **What word does the picture show?** (Idea: *The picture shows slaves working in a field and a student slaving over his project.*)
**Tell me what you know about this word.** (You may wish to share what you know about the word with the child as well.)

**DAY 2:** (Add in 2 new words, *literate* and *compassionate.* Repeat procedure from Day 1.) **Tell me anything more that you know about this word.**

**DAY 3: The *Super Choosing Game* (Round One)**
**Let's play the Super *Choosing* game that you learned at school. I'll say sentences with three of the words you know in them. You have to choose the correct word for the sentence. If you choose correctly, you will win one point. If you don't choose correctly, I get the point.**

- **Would you feel grief, honest,  or slave if your dog ran away?** *Grief.*
- **If you work very hard on making dinner, do you unjust, slave,  or honest over it?** *Slave.*
- **If someone always told the truth, would they be honest, unjust,  or a slave?** *Honest.*
- **If something is not fair, is it honest, grief,  or unjust?** *Unjust.*
- **A person who is owned by another is called an unjust,  a slave,  or a grief?** *A slave.*

(If the child is enjoying this game, you may wish to add additional examples.)

**DAY 4: The *Super Choosing* Game (Round Two)**
(Add the last two words, *literate* and *compassionate,* to the bag or container. Repeat procedure from Day 3.)

Other biographies your child might enjoy:

*George Washington and the General's Dog* by Frank Murphy

*Abe Lincoln and the Muddy Pig* by Stephen Krensky

*Abe Lincoln's Hat* by Martha Brenner

*Lewis and Clark: A Prairie Dog for the President* by Shirley Raye Redmond

*So You Want to Be President* by Judith St. George

Take your child to the public library to find more biographies about presidents that you and your child can enjoy together.

My reading goal:

7

## The Biography of Abe Lincoln

1

The next time you have a penny, look at who is on the coin. It is *Abe Lincoln*. He was one of the best presidents of the *United States*. He worked hard to make sure that all people were free.

1. This biography is about ... .
   - ○ Abe Lincoln's mother.
   - ○ Abe Lincoln.
   - ○ Able Lincoln's father.

2. Where did Abe live?
   - ○ In a town.
   - ○ At a lake.
   - ○ In the woods.

3. What did Abe want to do most of all?
   - ○ learn
   - ○ chop down trees
   - ○ work on the farm

4. Abe lived...
   - ○ now.
   - ○ a long time ago.
   - ○ today.

5. Abe was one of the best ...
   - ○ farmers.
   - ○ fathers.
   - ○ presidents.

6

Abe had to work hard when he was young. He only got to go to school for a year. Then he had to work hard on the farm. He cut and stacked wood. Abe and his dad cut down trees to make a new cabin. Abe worked and worked. The thing he wanted most of all was to learn.

3

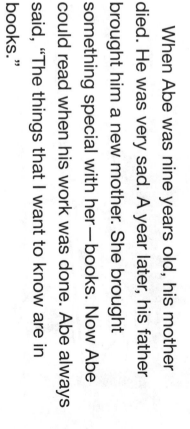

When Abe was nine years old, his mother died. He was very sad. A year later, his father brought him a new mother. She brought something special with her—books. Now Abe could read when his work was done. Abe always said, "The things that I want to know are in books."

4

(Note to teacher: These pages should photocopy onto the backside of pages 3 and 4.)

The next time you have a penny, look at who is on the coin. It is *Abe Lincoln*. He was one of the best presidents of the *United States*. He worked hard to make sure that all people were free.

When Abe was a little boy, he lived in the woods. He didn't have a bed like you. His bed was made from cornhusks. His covers were bear skins. His small house was made from logs with a hard dirt floor. His house didn't have a stove. His mom cooked food over a fire.

Abe had to work hard when he was young. He only got to go to school for a year. Then he had to work hard on the farm. He cut and stacked wood. The thing he wanted most of all was to learn.

When Abe was nine years old, his mother died. He was very sad. A year later, his father brought him a new mother. She brought something special with her—books. Now Abe could read when his work was done. Abe always said, "The things that I want to know are in books."

5

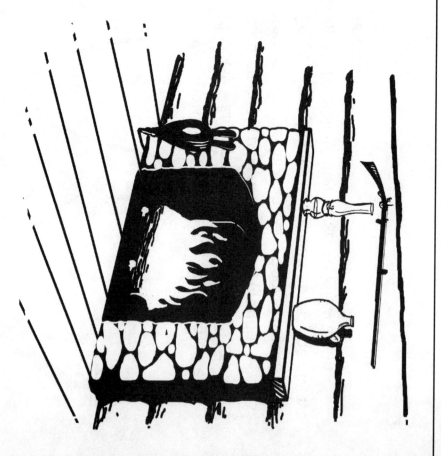

When Abe was a little boy, he lived in the woods. He didn't have a bed like you. His bed was made from cornhusks. His covers were bear skins. His small house was made from logs with a hard dirt floor. His house didn't have a stove. His mom cooked food over a fire.

2

election

vote

opinion

thoughtful

courteous

suggestion

## Sharing What You've Learned at School

**Note:** The children are not expected to be able to read the words. They are for your information.

**DAY 1:** (Cut the Picture Vocabulary Cards apart. Place the picture cards for *suggestion, election, vote,* and *opinion* in a container or small plastic bag.) (Show the child each picture card.) **What word does the picture show?** (Idea: *The picture shows a girl making a suggestion that the other girl change her hair.*)
**Tell me what you know about this word.** (You may wish to share what you know about the word with the child as well.)

**DAY 2:** (Add in 2 new words, *thoughtful* and *courteous.* Repeat procedure from Day 1.) **Tell me anything more that you know about this word.**

**DAY 3: The *Super Choosing* Game (Round One)**
Let's play the *Super Choosing* game that you learned at school. I'll say sentences with three of the words you know in them. You have to choose the correct word for the sentence. If you choose correctly, you will win one point. If you don't choose correctly, I get the point.

- **Would you go to an opinion, a vote, or an election** to vote for the President? *An election.*
- **When you want to choose a reward for the class, do you suggestion, vote, or election?** *Vote.*
- **If you think someone's skirt is pretty, is that your opinion, suggestion, or vote?** *Opinion.*
- **If you give someone an idea about how to solve a problem, did you give a vote, an election, or a suggestion?** *A suggestion.*
- **If you want to know what the class's favorite movie is, could you take a vote, an election, or a suggestion?** *A vote.*

(If the child is enjoying this game, you may wish to add additional examples.)

**DAY 4: The *Super Choosing* Game (Round Two)**
(Add the last two words, *thoughtful* and *polite,* to the bag or container. Repeat procedure from Day 3.)

Other biographies your child might enjoy:

*Minty* by Alan Schroeder

*Amelia Earhart More than a Flier* by Patricia Lakin

*A Lesson for Martin Luther King Jr.* by Denise Lewis Patrick

*A Picture Book of Florence Nightingale* by David A. Adler

*Bessie Coleman Daring to Fly* by Sally M. Walker

Take your child to the public library to find more biographies that you and your child can enjoy together.

My reading goal:

7

**The Biography Grace Bedell**

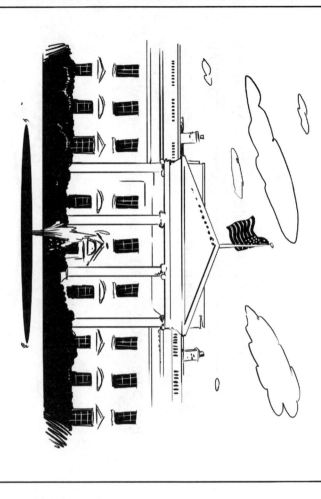

Can you imagine writing a letter to the President of the United States? Grace Bedell wrote a letter to Abe Lincoln. She was only eleven years old.

1

1. This biography is mostly about …
   - ◯ Grace Bedell.
   - ◯ Abe Lincoln.
   - ◯ The President of the United States.

2. Which word would best tells about Grace?
   - ◯ Small.
   - ◯ Lived on a farm.
   - ◯ Kind.

3. What two things did Grace do?
   - ◯ She wrote a letter and ate lunch.
   - ◯ She wrote a letter and mailed it.
   - ◯ She wrote a letter and made a picture.

4. Who gave Grace a poster for a gift?
   - ◯ Her brother.
   - ◯ Her father.
   - ◯ Her mother.

5. What did Abe Lincoln do when he met Grace?
   - ◯ He gave her a kiss.
   - ◯ He gave her a gift.
   - ◯ He shook her hand.

6

3

Now Grace knew what to do. She would write Mr. Lincoln a letter. She would tell him that he would look better if he had a beard and then more people would vote for him. She said that she would vote for him if she were a man.

One day Grace got a big surprise in the mail. Mr. Lincoln answered Grace's letter. A month later she got an even bigger surprise. Mr. Lincoln came to her town. He asked to see Grace. Imagine her surprise. Mr. Lincoln now had a beard. He gave Grace a kiss. His whiskers tickled her cheek.

4

Can you imagine writing a letter to the President of the United States? *Grace Bedell* wrote a letter to Abe Lincoln. She was only eleven years old.

Grace's dad brought her a poster of Abe for a gift. Grace thought Abe looked like a kind man. She liked his face. She thought he looked sad. The moon made a shadow on the poster. The shadow made it look like Abe had a beard. Grace had an idea! Mr. Lincoln would not look so sad if he had a beard.

Now Grace knew what to do. She would write Mr. Lincoln a letter. She would tell him that he would look better if he had a beard and then more people would vote for him. She said that she would vote for him if she were a man.

One day Grace got a big surprise in the mail. Mr. Lincoln answered Grace's letter. A month later she got an even bigger surprise. Mr. Lincoln came to her town. He asked to see Grace. Imagine her surprise. Mr. Lincoln now had a beard. He gave Grace a kiss. His whiskers tickled her cheek.

5

Grace's dad brought her a poster of Abe for a gift. Grace thought Abe looked like a kind man. She liked his face. She thought he looked sad. The moon made a shadow on the poster. The shadow made it look like Abe had a beard. Grace had an idea! Mr. Lincoln would not look so sad if he had a beard.

2

paralyzed

concentrating

gathering

victory

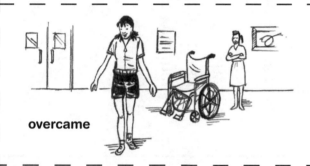

overcame

heroic

## Sharing What You've Learned at School

**Note:** The children are not expected to be able to read the words. They are for your information.

**DAY 1:** (Cut the Picture Vocabulary Cards apart. Place the picture cards for *paralyzed, concentrating, gathering,* and *victory* in a container or small plastic bag.)
(Show the child each picture card.) **What word does the picture show?** (Idea: *The picture shows a person who is concentrating.*)
**Tell me what you know about this word.** (You may wish to share what you know about the word with the child as well.)

**DAY 2:** (Add in 2 new words, *overcame* and *heroic.* Repeat procedure from Day 1.) **Tell me anything more that you know about this word.**

**DAY 3: The *Super Choosing* Game (Round One)**
**Let's play the *Super Choosing* game that you learned at school. I'll say sentences with three of the words you know in them. You have to choose the correct word for the sentence. If you choose correctly, you will win one point. If you don't choose correctly, I get the point.**

- **If you were unable to move your arms or legs, would you be concentrating, gathering, or paralyzed?** *Paralyzed.*
- **If your classmates got together at the park for a game of soccer, would it be a concentrating, a gathering, or a victory?** *A gathering.*
- **If your team won the state championship, would it be paralyzed, concentrating, or a victory?** *A victory.*
- **If you picked up all of your dirty clothes and put them in a basket to be washed, would you be gathering them, concentrating them, or paralyzed?** *Gathering them.*
- **If you were really focused on the television program you were watching, would you be concentrating, paralyzed, or gathering?** *Concentrating.*

(If the child is enjoying this game, you may wish to add additional examples.)

**DAY 4: The *Super Choosing* Game (Round Two)**
(Add the last two words, *overcame* and *heroic,* to the bag or container. Repeat procedure from Day 3.)

Other biographies your child might enjoy:

*Babe Ruth and the Ice Cream Mess* by Dan Gutman and Elaine Garvin

*A Picture Book of Jesse Owens* by David A. Adler

*Salt in His Shoes* by Deloris Jordan

*Roberto Clemente: Baseball Hall of Famer* by Maritza Romero

*Jackie Robinson (A Rookie Biography)* by Carol Greene

Take your child to the public library to find more biographies about sports heroes that you and your child can enjoy together.

My reading goal:

7

**The Biography of Wilma Rudolph**

1

*Wilma Rudolph was special. When she was born, she was very small. No one thought she would live. She was often sick. The most special about Wilma was that she always ran.*

1. This biography is about …
   ○ the Olympics.
   ○ many runners.
   ○ Wilma Rudolph.

2. Who helped Wilma go to college?
   ○ A basketball coach.
   ○ Her friends.
   ○ Her mother.

3. How many gold medals did Wilma win?
   ○ one
   ○ two
   ○ three

4. Where did Wilma show everybody that she could walk?
   ○ At the race.
   ○ At church.
   ○ At home.

5. Which word on page 1 means the same things as little?
   ○ Special.
   ○ Small.
   ○ Most.

6

One Sunday, Wilma took off the leg brace. She walked into church. Everyone was amazed! Years later, Wilma played basketball. A coach watched her play. He was amazed at how fast she could run. He helped Wilma go to college.

3

Wilma could run so fast that she went to the Olympics. She ran better than everyone else and won all of the races. She won three gold medals. Now the sick little girl was the fastest woman in the world.

4

5

*Wilma Rudolph was special. When she was born, she was very small. No one thought she would live. She was often sick. The most special about Wilma was that she always ran.*

When Wilma was five, she got very sick. Her leg would not work. She was told that she would never walk again. She was very sad but worked to make her leg strong. Wilma got a leg brace that helped her walk and she went back to school.

One Sunday, Wilma took off the leg brace. She walked into church. Everyone was amazed! Years later, Wilma played basketball. A coach watched her play. He was amazed at how fast she could run. He helped Wilma go to college.

Wilma could run so fast that she went to the Olympics. She ran better than everyone else and won all of the races. She won three gold medals. Now the sick little girl was the fastest woman in the world.

When Wilma was five, she got very sick. Her leg would not work. She was told that she would never walk again. She was very sad but worked to make her leg strong. Wilma got a leg brace that helped her walk and she went back to school.

2

slimy

muck

wake

plod

cooperate

eventually

## Sharing What You've Learned at School

**Note:** The children are not expected to be able to read the words. They are for your information.

**DAY 1:** (Cut the Picture Vocabulary Cards apart. Place the picture cards for *slimy, muck, plod,* and *wake* in a container or small plastic bag.)
(Show the child each picture card.) **What word does the picture show?** (Idea: *The picture shows someone stepping in muck.*)
**Tell me what you know about this word.** (You may wish to share what you know about the word with the child as well.)

**DAY 2:** (Add in 2 new words, *cooperate* and *eventually.* Repeat procedure from Day 1.) **Tell me anything more that you know about this word.**

**DAY 3:** *Poetic Definitions* (Round One)
**Let's play *Poetic Definitions* that you learned at school. I'll read you a short poem. If you can tell me the vocabulary word described in the poem, you will win one point. If you can't tell me, I get the point.**

- **The snail's trail was slippery and wet. He thought to himself, "I'll get there yet!" What vocabulary word describes the snail's trail?** *Slimy.*
- **Clomp, clomp. Heavy stomp. Walk so slow as I chomp. What vocabulary word describes the way the animal is walking?** *Plod.*
- **Sleep is over! Time to rise! Open up those sleepy eyes! What vocabulary word describes what it's time to do?** *Wake.*
- **The snake went "slither" thither through the water. I can see right there where he did pass. What vocabulary word names what the snake left?** *Wake.*
- **I didn't mean to step in goo, but oh me, oh my, it's on my shoe! What vocabulary word describes what I stepped in?** *Muck.*

(If the child is enjoying this game, you may wish to add additional examples.)

**DAY 4:** *Poetic Definitions* (Round Two)
(Add the last two words, *cooperate* and *eventually,* to the bag or container. Repeat procedure from Day 3.)

**Name** _____

# Who Unglued the Stuck Duck?

I counted _____ boxes altogether.

market

stubborn

cranky

disgrace

humorous

chaos

## Sharing What You've Learned at School

**Note:** The children are not expected to be able to read the words. They are for your information.

**DAY 1:** (Cut the Picture Vocabulary Cards apart. Place the picture cards for *market, stubborn, cranky,* and *disgrace* in a container or small plastic bag.) (Show the child each picture card.) **What word does the picture show?** (Idea: *The picture shows a child being stubborn.*)
**Tell me what you know about this word.** (You may wish to share what you know about the word with the child as well.)

**DAY 2:** (Add in 2 new words, *humorous* and *chaos.* Repeat procedure from Day 1.) **Tell me anything more that you know about this word.**

**DAY 3:** *Poetic Definitions* (Round One)
**Let's play *Poetic Definitions* that you learned at school. I'll read you a short poem. If you can tell me the vocabulary word described in the poem, you will win one point. If you can't tell me, I get the point.**

• **Places to go and people to see. I went here to buy milk and tea. Which vocabulary word tells where I went?** *Market.*
• **I won't do it. I refuse. You can't make me wear shoes! What vocabulary word is being described in this poem?** *Stubborn.*
• **I don't want to, I don't care. I'm not happy anywhere! What vocabulary word describes how I am feeling?** *Cranky.*
• **It was a shameful thing he did. To make such a terrible mess. He's just a dog; don't you know? He doesn't know better, I guess. What vocabulary word is described in the first line of this poem?** *Disgrace.*
• **Peanut butter, jelly, veggies, and meat. Mom went to the store, so now we can eat! What vocabulary word tells what Mom did?** *Market.*

(If the child is enjoying this game, you may wish to add additional examples.)

**DAY 4:** *Poetic Definitions* (Round Two)
(Add the last two words, *humorous* and *chaos,* to the bag or container. Repeat procedure from Day 3.)

# Two-Word Poem

_____

_____

_____

_____

_____

_____

_____

_____

_____

admit

mournful

amuse

ornaments

mischievous

BEWARE
OF
DOG

warning

## Sharing What You've Learned at School

**Note:** The children are not expected to be able to read the words. They are for your information.

**DAY 1:** (Cut the Picture Vocabulary Cards apart. Place the picture cards for *admit, mournful, amuse,* and *ornaments* in a container or small plastic bag.) (Show the child each picture card.) **What word does the picture show?** (Idea: *The picture shows a person singing a mournful song.*)
**Tell me what you know about this word.** (You may wish to share what you know about the word with the child as well.)

**DAY 2:** (Add in 2 new words, *warning* and *mischievous.* Repeat procedure from Day 1.) **Tell me anything more that you know about this word.**

**DAY 3:** *Poetic Definitions* (Round One)
**Let's play *Poetic Definitions* that you learned at school. I'll read you a short poem. If you can tell me the vocabulary word described in the poem, you will win one point. If you can't tell me, I get the point.**

- **I don't want to say it, but I guess I should. I really wasn't being good. Which vocabulary word is being described in this poem?** *Admit.*
- **Come in! Come in! Oh, can't you see? We are having a big party! What vocabulary word is being described in this poem?** *Admit.*
- **It's just so sad, I cannot lie. It's so sad, I want to cry. What vocabulary word describes how I am feeling?** *Mournful.*
- **Does it make you laugh? Does it make you smile? Does it hold your attention all the while? What vocabulary word is being described in this poem?** *Amuse.*
- **The statues up upon the shelf, the art upon the wall, they make the room feel like home, not like a classroom at all. What vocabulary word describes the statues and art?** *Ornaments.*

(If the child is enjoying this game, you may wish to add additional examples.)

**DAY 4:** *Poetic Definitions* (Round Two)
(Add the last two words, *warning* and *mischievous,* to the bag or container. Repeat procedure from Day 3.)

Name _____

# *That Mischievous Cat!*

That mischievous cat has made a mess of the boy's house. Help him put things back where they belong.

Write a sentence telling one thing the mischievous cat did in the song.

Name _____

_____

_____ ,

_____ , _____ ,

_____ , _____ , _____ ,

_____ , _____ , _____ , _____ —

_____ , _____ , _____ ,

_____ , _____ ,

_____

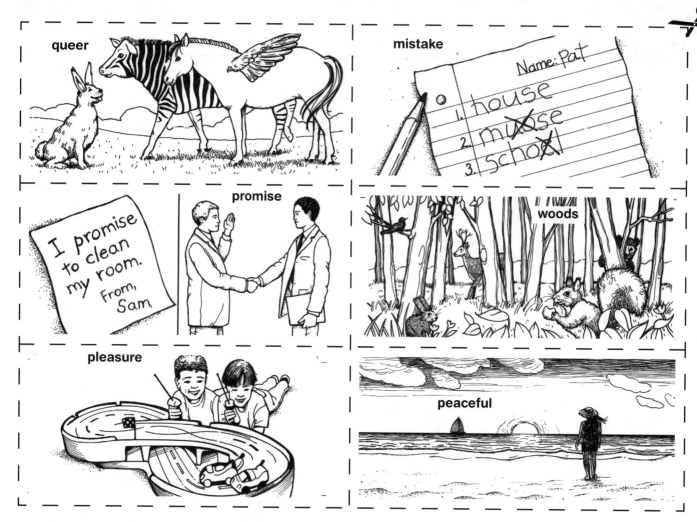

## Sharing What You've Learned at School

**Note:** The children are not expected to be able to read the words. They are for your information.

**DAY 1:** (Cut the Picture Vocabulary Cards apart. Place the picture cards for *queer, mistake, promise,* and *woods* in a container or small plastic bag.)
(Show the child each picture card.) **What word does the picture show?** (Idea: *The picture shows some queer animals.*)
**Tell me what you know about this word.** (You may wish to share what you know about the word with the child as well.)

**DAY 2:** (Add in 2 new words, *pleasure* and *peaceful.* Repeat procedure from Day 1.) **Tell me anything more that you know about this word.**

**DAY 3:** *Poetic Definitions* **(Round One)**
**Let's play** *Poetic Definitions* **that you learned at school. I'll read you a short poem. If you can tell me the vocabulary word described in the poem, you will win one point. If you can't tell me, I get the point.**

- **A purple cow. A bright green bear. Strange things are everywhere. What word describes these animals?** *Queer.*
- **Two plus two is five. Three plus three is seven. And I do believe, that five plus five is eleven. What vocabulary word can be used to describe this person's thoughts?** *Mistake.*
- **A statement that says we'll do it today for sure. A statement that says for sure we'll go out and play. What kind of statement is it?** *A promise.*
- **Mom said, "For sure, we'll go to the store. We'll buy you some new pants. And maybe something more." What did Mom do?** *Promise.*
- **Rabbits and squirrels, birds and deer. Through all these trees, no words do I hear. Where am I?** *Woods.*

(If the child is enjoying this game, you may wish to add more items.)

**DAY 4:** *Poetic Definitions* **(Round Two)**
(Add the last two words, *pleasure* and *peaceful,* to the bag or container. Repeat procedure from Day 3.)

Name _____

# Stopping by Woods on a Snowy Evening

**Show the pattern Robert Frost used in his poem.**

Whose woods these are I think I know         \_\_\_\_

His house is in the village, though,         \_\_\_\_

He will not see me stopping here         \_\_\_\_

I watch his woods fill up with snow.         \_\_\_\_

My little horse must think it queer         \_\_\_\_

To stop without a farmhouse near         \_\_\_\_

Between the woods and frozen lake         \_\_\_\_

The darkest evening of the year.         \_\_\_\_

He gives his harness bells a shake         \_\_\_\_

To ask if there is some mistake         \_\_\_\_

The only other sound's the sweep         \_\_\_\_

Of easy wind and downy flake.         \_\_\_\_

The woods are lovely, dark and deep         \_\_\_\_

But I have promises to keep         \_\_\_\_

And miles to go before I sleep         \_\_\_\_

And miles to go before I sleep.         \_\_\_\_

**Name** _____

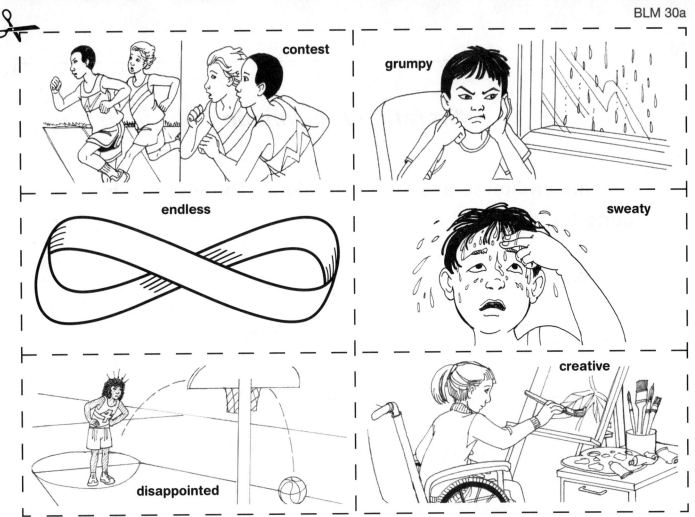

contest

grumpy

endless

sweaty

disappointed

creative

## Sharing What You've Learned at School

**Note:** The children are not expected to be able to read the words. They are for your information.

**DAY 1:** (Cut the Picture Vocabulary Cards apart. Place the picture cards for *contest, grumpy, endless,* and *sweaty* in a container or small plastic bag.) (Show the child each picture card.) **What word does the picture show?** (Idea: *The picture shows two children having a running contest.*) **Tell me what you know about this word.** (You may wish to share what you know about the word with the child as well.)

**DAY 2:** (Add in 2 new words, *disappointed* and *creative.* Repeat procedure from Day 1.) **Tell me anything more that you know about this word.**

**DAY 3:** *Poetic Definitions* **(Round One)**
**Let's play** *Poetic Definitions* **that you learned at school. I'll read you a short poem. If you can tell me the vocabulary word described in the poem, you will win one point. If you can't tell me, I get the point.**

- **I ran a race. I ran so fast. I ran like the wind. But he ran right past! What vocabulary word is described in this poem?** *Contest.*

- **I don't think this grade is fair. I think it's wrong. I studied hard. I studied long. I studied half the night. What vocabulary word can be used to describe what this student is doing about his grade?** *Contesting.*

- **I'm cranky. I'm tired. I'm in a bad mood. I'm crabby. I'm grouchy. I don't want to be good. What vocabulary word is described by this poem?** *Grumpy.*

- **This night is so long. I want it to be day. I can't wait until tomorrow, when I can go out and play. What vocabulary word can be used to describe the night?** *Endless.*

- **I ran so far. I ran so fast. I ran up the hill and back at last. What vocabulary word describes how this person is probably feeling now?** *Sweaty.*

(If the child is enjoying this game, you may wish to add additional examples.)

**DAY 4:** *Poetic Definitions* **(Round Two)**
(Add the last two words, *disappointed* and *creative,* to the bag or container. Repeat procedure from Day 3.)

Name _____

## *Alliteration Afficionado*

**Use alliteration to describe each thing. The first one is done for you.**

1. cool, calico cat

2. _____, _____ bird

3. _____, _____ cookies

4. _____, _____ sister

5. _____, _____ brother

6. _____, _____ dog

7. _____, _____ duck

8. _____, _____ pencil

9. _____, _____ day

10. _____, _____ summer

# CONGRATULATIONS!!!!

**To** _____

## A Poet with Style and Grace!!
## You take the cake!

_____          _____

*Date*                              *Teacher*

Name _____

# Two-Word Poem

_____
_____
_____
_____

_____
_____
_____
_____

Name _____

# Concrete Poem

Name _____

# Diamante Poem

_____,
First word

_____, _____,
describe first word

_____, _____, _____,
-ing words about first word

_____, _____, _____, _____–
2 nouns about first word        2 nouns about last word

_____, _____, _____,
3 –ing words about last word

_____, _____,
describe last word

_____
last word